PRAIRIE STATE COLLEGE LEARNING CENTER
T3-BXA-530

SOCIAL PROBLEMS

SOCIAL PROBLEMS

Ronald W. Maris
University of South Carolina

The Dorsey Press
Chicago, Illinois 60604

Acquisitions editor: *Paul E. O'Connell*
Project editor: *Gladys True*
Production manager: *Stephen K. Emry*
Designer: *Stuart Paterson*
Artist: *Alice B. Thiede*
Part opener photo: *Joe Viesti*
Compositor: *Graphic World Inc.*
Typeface: *10/12 Century Old Style*
Printer: *R. R. Donnelley & Sons Company*

ISBN 0-256-03178-9
Library of Congress Catalog Card No. 87–72742

Printed in the United States of America

1 2 3 4 5 6 7 8 9 0 DO 5 4 3 2 1 0 9 8

To Amanda and Gabriella and to a world in which they
and other children can thrive.

PREFACE

Many students enrolling in a social problems course are at least vaguely interested in social change. How can our society be more fair? Does social inequality need to be reduced? Is it possible to make our world a little bit better place to live in? These are some of the central questions underlying a book like the one before you. Hopefully, many of you also either are or will become fascinated by social behavior and social structure. While our individual actions may make sense to us, social interaction can result in some curious collective problems. I think of the obvious irony of individuals paying into a federal social security system that may not even be there when they reach retirement age and need to draw from it.

This textbook makes a great deal of fuss about theory. It is even somewhat unique in this regard. We believe that one key to confronting America's social problems is to have a citizenry that can think critically about social issues and use its sociological imagination. Our theoretical approach here is unabashedly comprehensive. All of the major theoretical perspectives in sociology (namely, conflict theory, functionalism and neofunctionalism, structuralism, symbolic interactionism, deviance theory, exchange theory, and sociobiology) have something important to tell us about social problems. It is still premature to claim that one theory is better than another or that sociological theories can be integrated into a more general theory of social problems. In fact, in the interest of theoretical comprehensiveness for the first time we will apply exchange theory and recent structural sociology to the study of social problems.

Accordingly, our approach to social problems is different in that we start by "thinking small" (especially in Chapters 4 through 9). Thus, we can consider the social behaviors and problems of real-life individuals interacting in relatively small face-to-face groups. We believe that the values, rewards, meanings, structures, and so on of small groups of socially interacting individuals are highly relevant to the creation and resolution of most social problems. The biology and social psychology of social problems needs to be considered as well. Of course, thinking small has its limits (as our macrosociology colleagues will quickly remind us)! Thus, from the very beginning of our book we complement subinstitutional or small-group theories with institutional-level theories (particularly in Chapters 10 through 15). No understanding of social problems is complete without both theoretical approaches.

The above is not meant to slight the importance of research and data in the study of social problems. Actually this book is probably somewhat more in the objective condition tradition than the subjective interpretation tradition. With French sociologist Émile Durkheim we emphasize "social facts." Social problems are not just whimsical social constructions. There is a social world out there to be described, measured, counted, probed, and provoked. In the vein of George Homans's exchange theory and B. F. Skinner's behaviorism we have an abiding interest in actual human behaviors (as opposed to attitudes). Some of the important social facts that need to be attended to concern what we call nonproblematic society. For example, to understand sickness requires examining health; that is, social problems need to be contrasted with the ordinary routine workings of society that are usually not considered problematic.

Although I shall strive to be objective, comprehensive, and fair, my values obviously still affect the choice of problem topics and their treatment. Thus, these values need to be brought out in the open. First, I am a generalist. For example, I believe that the study of social problems should not be reduced to one theoretical perspective. I also believe that social problems need not have *only* social explanations. Therefore, if biology, history, economics, the arts, psychology, and so on will help our understanding, then (within limits) they will be incorporated. Second, I am a little right of center and conservative. Social behaviors must be understood before we try to change them. Although some social problems clearly require resolutions, others may not be as problematic as they seem at first blush. Certainly some social problems are highly resistant to permanent resolution. Third, microsociology will be taken as far as possible. Social institutions ultimately must have a payoff to some real individuals or they will eventually wither and perhaps even die. Conversely, apparently problematic social behaviors that do persist (e.g., prostitution or alcoholic use) are to some degree socially useful. Fourth, I champion quantitative sociology, research, and data. Although social "facts" can be erroneous, subjective, indicative of power or social inequality, and so on, some facts must be taken into account. One should be empirical, careful, and thorough in the investigation of social problems.

A word about the selection of particular social problems in this book is in order. Some social problems simply cannot be ignored. They appear in all social problems textbooks and almost demand our attention. These problems include—at least—ageism, sexism, racism, mental and physical disorders, drug and alcohol abuse, social inequality, and crime and violence. Other social problems, which are newer and more discretionary, shall be examined here. They include terrorism, nuclear war, the environment, family violence, social stress, the political economy, and the new American family.

These substantive topics are organized into an expanded introduction (Part I) consisting of three chapters on the sociology of social problems, theoretical perspectives, and empirical methods and data; a second part (II) (Chapters 4 through 9) on subinstitutionally related social problems; and finally (Part III) a six-chapter set of institutional or macrosocial problems. Each chapter begins with an overview of a social problem from the major theoretical perspectives. Next there is a "vivid case" or example of the chapter's specific social problem(s) in a panel. The introduction to each chapter consists of a topical lead-in, listing of salient issues, key definitions, prevalence of the problem, and a brief natural history. Each social problem section is subdivided into three parts: stating the problem, analyzing the problem (from some or all of the seven theoretical perspectives), and resolving the problem. Finally, each chapter concludes with a summary, notes for elaboration of chapter points, a glossary of terms, and six annotated further readings. At the end of the book the student will find an extensive bibliography, as well as name and subject indexes.

This is a student-centered textbook. We have tried hard to make it readable and relevant to college students. There are an abundance of examples to help make abstract ideas clearer. Instead of being dull and dry, the topics are presented with humor and cartoons, where appropriate. There are panels of brief research reports, current news releases, competing viewpoints, pertinent historical data, and so on. Numerous figures, tables, pictures, and graphs appear throughout the book. Of course, I trust the book reflects the twenty-five years I have been teaching social problems courses to undergraduates and my deep interest in and respect for college students.

There is also an accompanying manual to assist both students and instructors. This manual contains test items (multiple-choice, true-false, fill-in-the-blank, short and extended essay questions—all with a key to correct answers for self-paced study), discussion questions and class exercises, suggested class activities, lecture ideas, chapter outlines, relevant film lists, and of course, the glossaries and bibliography referred to earlier (in the text itself).

This book has been five years in writing and production. Many key people have sustained and assisted me during these years. First and foremost have been my wife, Beth, and Dorsey Press's Consulting Editor, Charles M. Bonjean. Both in their own ways have believed in me when I needed it and yet helped me get the best out of myself. Dorsey's Senior Editor Paul E. O'Connell has been a man of his word. He has been fair, critical when need be, and has always insisted on uncomprising standards of excellence. I am indebted to several anonymous reviewers of this book; they should be able to see the fruit of their criticisms in this final product. While I honestly did not always welcome their unflinching candor, having survived it the book and I are better for it. I also wish to thank the following nonanonymous reviewers: Scott J. South (University of New York at Albany), Anthony Orum (University of Illinois, Chicago), and James D. Orcutt (Florida State University). Since I did not always take their advice, they are not responsible for this final product. Of course, my students and colleagues at the University of South Carolina have been pestered over the years for data and ideas. My longtime friend Eui-Hang (Ken) Shin has been especially patient and dependable. John V. Skvoretz, Bruce H. Mayhew, Lynn Smith-Lovin, James A. McRae, Patrick D. Nolan, Jimy M. Sanders, Charles W. Tucker, Beth W. Ghiloni, Miriam Lee, Nancy Vigander-Winfrey, Clare Morris, and Darla Ladkau assisted in various capacities in the manuscript preparation.

Please, tell us what you like and dislike about the book. Future generations of students will benefit from your advice. This has been a long and sometimes exhausting project. I would like to think I have earned a few parting horatory thoughts. It saddens me to see that so much social inequity and injustice remains in America. Yet there is a great resiliency in both societies and individuals. There will always be social risks and problems; nothing is free. A major social and personal goal is to live well, not just live long. Perhaps in the last analysis the best that societies and individuals can hope for is to use themselves and their resources wisely—and to have the social opportunity to do just that.

Ronald W. Maris

CONTENTS

CHAPTER 11
Economic Inequality *409*

CHAPTER 12
Family and Marital Relations *449*

LIST OF FIGURES

LIST OF TABLES

LIST OF PANELS

P·A·R·T
I
The Sociology of Social Problems

C·H·A·P·T·E·R

1

Introduction to the Study of Social Problems

Social problems are general patterns of human behavior or social conditions that are perceived to be threats to society by significant numbers of the population, powerful groups, or charismatic individuals and that could be resolved or remedied.

One of the major stumbling blocks to understanding and controlling social problems is the absence of a general theory of both problematic and routine human behavior and social conditions. Usually, social problems textbooks present a smorgasbord of isolated problems with highly segmented explanations.

This text attempts to move toward a more general understanding of social problems based in exchange theory; the enduring social structures generated from human exchanges; conflict over the social distribution of power, status, and property; the symbolic or subjective meanings of human interaction; the objective (functional) consequences of general patterns of social behaviors; social pressures to deviate from norms; and biology-sociobiology.

Pick up almost any major newspaper and think about its headlines:

> "1980 Census Finds Sharp Decline in Size of American Households"
> "Saudis Offer to Lift Oil Price if Others in OPEC Cut Theirs"
> "Strike by Miners Hits South Africa"
> "Highway Deaths Rise as Small Automobiles and Speeding Increase"
> "Two Polish Officials of Giereck Period Commit Suicide"
> "Air in New York Called Cleaner But Pollution's Extent Unknown"
> "U.S. Issues Ban on Sulfites Use"

What strikes you about these news reports? For one thing the mass media tend to report *only* problems. There is almost no mention of "normal" everyday routines of ordinary people. The accounts of social life in the papers read like a script from "Dallas" or "As the World Turns." Social problems make up a large part of our collective thinking. The newspapers, television, informal conversation, movies, and books seem almost obsessed with the problems of society. This preoccupation with problems is not hard to understand. Social problems tend to be inherently interesting while normal everyday behaviors are not particularly newsworthy. This is especially true if people tend to be bored and trivialized by mechanized and routine jobs and relationships. Bizarre, eccentric, unusual events tend to provide dramatic relief or escape from the humdrum existence of everyday life. Then too there is probably a common fear that if some major social problems are not resolved, sooner or later society itself may not survive. While these concerns may be exaggerated (Can you think of a society that in fact "died?"), it does seem reasonable that failure to deal with some social problems (such as economic shifts, war, nuclear controls, virulent diseases, and so on) may eventually result in drastic changes in at least the quality of life.[1]

Another reaction you may have had to the newspaper headlines was to wonder how social life is possible with all these problems. Thomas Hobbes (1588–1679) argued in *Leviathan* (1651) that people's natural condition was to be selfish individualistic animals constantly at war with one another. According to Hobbes people's principal motive for entering into social contracts was their fear of a violent death in natural (nonsocial) life situations. Sometimes social problems can be thought of as collective sacrifices of life for the sake of social growth and development. Suppose someone came to you and said: "You may have this marvelous new invention that will revolutionize transportation, but you must sacrifice 45,800 American lives each year." In fact that was the human price paid in 1984 in the United States for having cars.

Still another thought you may have had about the headlines was why some other social issues were *not* considered problems. Not too long ago many people in the United States were busy building bomb shelters preparing themselves for "the nuclear holocaust." *On the Beach* was a popular movie depicting the end of the world due to radioactive poisoning.[2] Now we seldom read or hear much about the nuclear holocaust (although we did see ABC's celebrated

Drawing by Lorenz; © 1983 *The New Yorker* Magazine, Inc.

nuclear war program "The Day After" on December 20, 1983). Is the problem any less real now? Probably not. In fact, based on the sheer prevalence of nuclear weapons and nuclear power plants, the risk is probably greater now than before. Beneath this issue is the question of whether social problems are based on objective facts or on subjective conditions. For example, can some powerful individual or group stamp out marijuana use or abortion if they simply *believe* these are major social problems?[3]

Perhaps one of the most important questions about the headlines for our purposes in this textbook is whether diverse social problems concerning oil prices, census counts, terrorism, highway deaths, suicide, pollution, the economy, and so on have anything in common. That is, is it possible to arrive at a more general understanding of all social problems? Or must we explain each individual social problem on its own unique terms? We will argue here that social problems can be explained by principles of human face-to-face exchange; by the enduring social structures generated from human interaction; by conflict over the social distribution of power, status, and property; by the symbolic or subjective meanings of human interaction; by the more objective functional consequences of general patterns of social behaviors; by social pressures to deviate from norms; and by sociobiological factors.

This is not to claim that social problems can be explained only by these seven theoretical perspectives. "Social problems" are not one thing and should not be expected to have one cause or one explanation. While we strive for a general understanding of social problems, we must use extreme care to avoid prematurely reducing our considerations to *any* one theoretical perspective. There are in fact many diverse (sometimes overlapping) theoretical perspectives in sociology, each of which probably contributes something relatively unique to our understanding and resolution of social problems. Although we shall emphasize the theoretical perspectives of exchange, structural sociology, and sociobiology somewhat, this is mainly because they are fairly new and underdeveloped perspectives in the study of social problems; not because they are better explanations than others. In the analysis of specific substantive social problems that will be presented later, the seven theoretical perspectives will be selectively used. However, this somewhat arbitrary emphasis on some theories and the occasional neglect of others is not meant to detract from our objective of a general theory of social problems using several different perspectives. The diversity of what we call "social problems" means that we must keep our theoretical options open.

Finally, can the social problems mentioned in the headlines be solved? To say something is a "problem" suggests that it has a *solution* or *resolution.* For example, highway deaths in the United States went down when the national speed limit was lowered to fifty-five miles per hour. Thus, we could reasonably conclude that highway fatalities were somehow related to speeding. Since many social problems persist over long periods of time, perhaps the best we can hope for is a partial *re*solution. The recurring nature of social problems reminds us that they are seldom easily or finally solved. Realizing that the problems in which we are interested are *social,* we might suspect that their resolutions would also be collective. However, before there can be any hope of resolving our questions it is necessary to be much clearer about how social problems will be defined.

• Definition of "Social Problems" and Its Implications

It might seem to most of us that we already know what social problems are. Why bother to define them? To begin with, one of our major objectives is to develop a more general theoretical understanding of social problems. An essential ingredient of any theoretically adequate statement is precise definitions that allow for accurate measurement and ultimately for support or falsifications of its theoretical propositions.[4] Furthermore, as we have already seen, people do not always agree on what social problems are. Is homosexuality among consenting adults a social problem? The 1986 U.S. Supreme Court decision on sodomy implies it is. How about the equal rights amendment (ERA) and the situations it addresses, or prayers in public schools? What is the difference between a *personal* trouble and a *social* problem?[5] In what way do facts or objective conditions determine what gets counted as a social problem? And if they do, how many people must agree that some social condition constitutes a social problem before that condition comes to be accepted as a social problem? It begins to become apparent that considerable confusion surrounds the concept of a social problem, some of which can be dispelled by a careful definition.

Social problems can be defined as general patterns of human behavior or social conditions that are perceived to be threats to society by significant numbers of the population, powerful groups, or charismatic individuals and that could be resolved or remedied.[6] At least four major implications of our definition need to be examined separately and more carefully.

First, social problems are general patterns of human behavior or social conditions. The focus here will be on *patterns* of human behavior; that is, on social structure, how structure emerges from actual face-to-face exchange, and how some social structures come to be considered social problems. Unlike most social problems texts, we will often consider the normal, routine, nonproblematic aspects of society along with the problematic, for social problems cannot be understood apart from the generation and operation of the whole of society (in much the same way that physical illnesses cannot be understood without considering what it means to be physically healthy). That which is a problem can be thought of as a threat to social norms. Thus, normative behavior and routine expectations themselves must be examined.

Social problems tend to be general or widespread, not isolated, provincial, or individual. Although the interaction of only two individuals is social (especially if the two are very powerful individuals), for the most part we tend to emphasize those conditions or behaviors that involve large numbers of society.[7] Generally, the rarer a behavior pattern or social condition, the less likely it will ever come to be considered a social problem. For example, some individuals—or even entire families—are hyperallergenic (unusually sensitive to natural substances like molds, grasses, certain foods, dust, pollen, animal hair, and so forth). Occasionally we will read of an unfortunate child (most people with severe allergies do not survive to adulthood) who lives in an antiseptic plastic bubble and is allergic to almost everything the rest of us tolerate fairly well. Yet Congress appropriates little or no money to study allergic conditions, no public outcry for cures arises, no associations to champion the cause tend to appear, and so forth. On the other hand, cancer is regarded as a major social problem. There is a federal agency with an annual budget of about a billion dollars, an American Cancer Society, frequent coverage in the mass media about cancer, and much more. One reason for this difference between cancer and allergies is that 443,000 people die each year (1983 figures) in the United States alone from malignant neoplasms, whereas only 5,000 to 10,000 die from allergic reactions.

Second, social problems are perceived to be threats to society. More precisely, social problems are socially defined threats to basic human values, societal norms, institutional routines, the social order in general, sometimes to special vested interests, and in extreme cases, to the continued existence of society itself.[8] Thus, it is essential in any text on social problems to discover the relevant values, norms, laws, and social expectations. Furthermore, we must know how basic or fundamental these social expectations are.

For example, you can think of widespread general behavior patterns that are not threatening to society (although you might be surprised to learn how regulated all behavior is). William Graham Summer (1840–1910) called our evolving popular habits and traditions "folkways" (1960). Folkways that were thought essential to the welfare of society, and thus more basic, were designated "mores." Whether you wear a tie in public (a folkway) might seem trivial, whereas strangling another person with your tie (a more) is clearly serious business! Yet some restaurants and clubs will not seat or serve customers without ties. On the other hand, if most manual laborers wore ties to work, they would be considered strange and would be subjected to ridicule.

Some children have such severe allergies that they are forced to spend their lives in antiseptic bubbles. Yet the small number of such allergies works against them ever being defined as social problems. (AP/Wide World Photos)

A threat implies that some behavior pattern or social structure is held undesirable. That is, there is an irreducible element of subjectivity in what gets perceived and defined as a social problem. Some sociologists (for example, Spector and Kitsuse, 1977; cf. Schneider, 1985) go so far to reduce social problems to the "claims-making activities" of those who would define social problems, virtually ignoring objective conditions or at least arguing that "the facts" have a very complex and subtle relationship to social problems. It follows that social problems change as perceived threats wax and wane, that social problems have natural histories. However, it is our position that these changes are neither whimsical nor entirely subjective. The facts are relevant to what is perceived as a threat and to what gets defined as a social problem. More will be said about this later in the chapter.

Third, social problems must be called to our attention by significant numbers of the population, powerful groups, or charismatic individuals. Generally, large numbers of the population must agree that certain behaviors or conditions constitute social problems. It is not sufficient for a few isolated individuals to be convinced that exercise will kill you or that studying causes cancer, even

"I realize, of course, that we're not a threat, but just once it would be nice to be perceived as a threat."

Drawing by Lorenz; © 1981 *The New Yorker* Magazine, Inc.

if they are right! It is important to realize that charismatic leaders like Adolf Hitler or the Reverend Jim Jones of Guyana were not isolated individuals.[9] On the contrary, they were individuals with a large number of followers over whom they exercised powerful psychological and physical controls.

Critics of the importance of numbers in defining social problems may ask cynically: "How many people must agree before some behavior or condition is defined as a social problem? Two, two hundred, twenty thousand?"[10] The fact that an exact number cannot be given does not invalidate our point. Generally, the more poeple who agree that something is a social problem, the more likely it is to emerge as a social problem. Conversely, the fewer people who agree that some behavior or condition is a social problem, the less likely that behavior or condition is to ever appear in our news headlines, have voluntary associations formed to combat it, have money appropriated to study and prevent it, or even to be known about.

As a case in point the National Rifle Association (NRA) has more members and is better organized than those who oppose gun control legislation (recall the failed handgun control crusade in 1986 of Sarah Brady, wife of U.S. Press Secretary James Brady). Thus (although there are other factors involved), on the grounds of numbers alone, gun control has not emerged as a major social problem in the United States. Interestingly, even after being shot himself by a "Saturday night special," U.S. President Ronald Reagan still opposes hand gun control legislation and believes that he was spared by divine (not governmental or policy) intervention.[11]

Finally, most social problems can be resolved or remedied. As we have seen already, to argue that something is a social problem usually implies that at least in principle it has a solution or resolution. This textbook will devote a major section in each substantive chapter to issues of social control or the prevention of the social problem under discussion. Most texts on social problems are far better at analysis than they are at resolution. In part this is because many academics are content to stop with understanding something. Only recently has there been a renewed interest among behavioral scientists in the applications of basic knowledge to the social control of social problems (see Freeman, Dynes, Rossi, and Whyte, 1983). One might speculate that some social scientists consider applied sociology more like social work than scientific sociology. Traditionally, all science has been divided into at least pure and applied branches. Many scholars still feel that social engineering or social change should be kept separate from the advancement of basic knowledge about social behaviors.

Another, perhaps more salient, reason why sociologists have not done much to resolve social problems is that often the required knowledge is simply missing. Solutions to major social problems tend to be complex and difficult to come by. It is remarkable how little we still know and how limited some of our understanding is. Just to take one example, prostitution has been around for thousands of years. Many naive attempts to eliminate prostitution have failed. So-called functional sociologists (see below) like Robert K. Merton (1910–) argue that prostitution as a social institution actually meets basic human needs and that any attempt to eradicate or control prostitution without substituting an acceptable "functional alternative" is doomed to failure (1957:52ff.; 1975).

Social problems usually have social solutions through collective action. If, for example, we agree with Karl Marx (1818–83) that most social problems have their roots in differences in the distribution of wealth, power, and prestige in a population (1848), then it would seem to follow that solving social problems requires a radical reordering of the structure of social classes and a redistribution of wealth. Or consider that many social problems in adult life (like drug abuse, violence, promiscuity, alcoholism, and more) probably have their beginnings in common pathological family and child-rearing situations. Such problems may be resolved only by primary prevention (Caplan, 1964) of the original social conditions associated with the later social problems.

Of course, social problems always have some nonsocial elements. Biological, genetic, chromosomal, bacteriological, viral, and similar nonsocial conditions often have profound social consequences. It is not always clear when a problem is social and when it is not.[12] In some cases of agitated violent behavior, mental patients have their frontal brain lobes surgically severed (Wallace, King, and

Sanders, 1981). That is, the solution to common asocial behavior is strictly nonsocial, here surgical. Even less esoteric biological differences like age, sex, and race may have major implications for social behavior and social problems (of course, age, sex, and race also have social components). Many sociologists tend to minimize biological differences and their role in social problems. They tend to see all important differences as social. We shall have to return to this important issue and examine it in context and detail. For now, suffice it to say that we believe that nonsocial differences among people are real and major. Not all social problems have purely social origins or resolutions.

Resolutions to social problems can be either specific or general. Since we tend to conceive of social problems as a product of the total society and do not isolate pathological conditions from more "normal" conditions, as you might expect we will favor general common solutions to social problems rather than ad hoc, isolated problem-specific solutions.

Finally, most social problems are not permanently resolved. Russian-born sociologist Pitirim Sorokin (1889–1968) argued that basic cultural types (common values fluctuating between emphasis on ideas and the senses) were cyclical (1937–41). For example, contemporary American society is largely sensational and physical, as was the culture of the later stages of the Roman empire. Culture in the Middle Ages in Western Europe was largely ascetic and otherworldly. Obviously, as basic values or societal norms evolve and change, new social problems will emerge and previous resolutions to old social problems can become inadequate.

One of the absolutely basic issues raised by our definition of social problems is how objective the conditions defining social problems really are. Are social problems facts that anyone can plainly see and would agree must be dealt with? Or are social problems much more subjective than we might think, more socially constructed, products of special interest groups? In the next section of Chapter 1 the objective versus the subjective conditions of social problems are considered more carefully.

• Subjective versus Objective Conditions of Social Problems

Almost all of contemporary textbooks agree with our definition of social problems. These include books by Eitzen (1986:5), Henslin and Light (1983:5), and DeFleur (1986:4). These texts in turn have theoretical roots in two seminal articles by Fuller and Myers (1941a and b) in which a social problem is defined as: "a condition which is defined by a considerable number of persons as a deviation from some norm, which they cherish" (1941b:320). Perhaps the theoretical father of us all in the objective condition tradition is Robert K. Merton (1910–), whose early paper, "Social Structure and Anomie" (1938), did much to encourage a focus on the objective conditions of social structure in understanding deviant behavior. Actually French sociologist Emile Durkheim

(1858–1917) is commonly regarded as the first major social scientist to consider social facts as "things" and was the person who did most to legitimate the study of anomie, social structure, and functional analysis.[13]

The conceptualization of social problems that differs most from the objective condition view is developed elegantly and thoroughly by Spector and Kitsuse (1977), although this view of social problems too has historical antecedents in the important work of German sociologist Max Weber (1864–1920)[14] and the American sociologists George H. Mead (1863–1931), Herbert Blumer (1900–), Howard S. Becker (1928–) and Peter L. Berger and T. Luckman (1966). If Fuller and Myer can loosely be thought of as emphasizing objective conditions, the primary alternative viewpoint, exemplified by Spector and Kitsuse's work (1977), can be thought of as subjective (cf. Schneider, 1985). Spector and Kitsuse define social problems as "the activities of individuals or groups making assertations of grievances and claims with respect to some putative conditions" (1977:75). The subjectivists claim that objective conditions at best have a vague, complex, and even tenuous relationship with what gets labeled as a social problem. At worst, they claim, focusing on objective conditions distracts us from the proper investigation of individuals who actively claim that something is a social problem and respond as if it were a problem. These activities attempt to label, construct, and define social reality and what is a social problem—often without much regard for prevailing norms or objective conditions in a society.

Much of the early work on the subjective meanings of social behavior was done by Max Weber (1922). Weber maintained that observational or empirical understanding is very different from motivational or subjective understanding. For example, empirical understanding of religion and economics could be achieved by discovering the rates of participation of Protestants, Catholics, and Jews in business—such as Weber undertook in his book *The Protestant Ethic and the Spirit of Capitalism* (1904). On the other hand, subjective understanding focuses on the discovery of meaning. Social behavior exists only when the individual's conduct is meaningfully related to that of others. That is, the subjective intention of action is an indispensable criterion for determining social situations.

Sociologists like George Mead (1934) and Herbert Blumer (1969) developed the subjective perspective still further. For example, Mead maintained that while people are born with bodies, they must acquire a social self. Men and women become aware of themselves only when, and if, they are able to see themselves as others do. One gets outside himself by taking the attitudes of others toward him. It follows that the self is not physically given, but socially constructed in human interaction, through action and reaction.[15] Nevertheless, the self is more than the organized set of attitudes of others toward internalized (what Mead called the "me"). There is also a part of the self that is future oriented, impulsive, uncertain, and free—that Mead called the "I." The "I" can be thought of as the individual's response to the attitudes of others. Thus, not only is the self socially constructed, it is also innovative and partially undetermined.

Herbert Blumer (1969), widely regarded as the founder of a school of thought known as symbolic interaction followed Mead on the faculty of the University of Chicago. Like Mead, Blumer's work emphasized the social or subjective construction of reality.[16] Blumer made three main claims. First, people act toward things on the basis of the meanings that things have for them (i.e., meanings are always somewhat subjective). Unlike the Greek philosopher (Plato 437–347 B.C.?), or the German philosopher, I. Kant (1724–1804), Blumer did not believe that things in themselves had any essential meanings. Second, meanings are derived from social interaction. That is, people impart meaning to objects through social interaction (actual face-to-face exchange). Third, meanings are handled in and modified by an interpretative process used by persons.[17] Actors must indicate what has meaning to them and transform meanings in light of specific social situations (1969:50ff.). Unlike "objectivists," symbolic interactionists contend that society consists in action, not in static products of prior action like social structure. Social interaction is between actors, not between factors (such as age, sex, race, and so on) imputed to actors. An object is anything that can be indicated or referred to. Objects are social creations; they are not just "out there." Objects are not like the Durkheimian external and constraining "social facts," to be discussed below (Durkheim, 1895). Since language is clearly an important vehicle for conveying meaning, conducting interaction, interpreting behavior, and so on, most subjectivists are more interested in language than are objectivists.

Obviously the proponents of the subjective or "social" conditions of social problems perspective offer a major alternative definition of social problems that complements the objective condition definition. Accordingly, we must take pains to be fair to the subjective condition perspective, to understand it, and to use it when it makes sense. In fact, we hold that the subjective conditions approach ought to be integrated with the objective approach. What better way to understand the subjectivists' approach than to present a few celebrated examples of the way they see social problems?

Let's begin by considering the effects of an unprescribed illegal drug, marijuana, and how marijuana use may have come to be seen as a social problem. Now it may seem that drugs like marijuana have little to do with social meanings, interpretative processes, definitions of the situation, and the like. After all, doesn't a drug have an objective effect based on physiological (chemical) changes directly produced by the drug? Whatever subjective meanings individuals may or may not add, it would seem clear that marijuana itself causes you to "get high" and that these physical and psychological changes can be measured.

But does it? Howard S. Becker, a professional musician turned sociologist, in an influential paper in the *American Journal of Sociology* (1953) claims that marijuana use is a "function of the individual's conception of marijuana and of the uses to which it can be put, and that this conception *develops* (italics ours) as the individual's experience with the drug [and other drug users] increases" (1953:42).[18] Becker argues that to define yourself as someone who uses marijuana for pleasure, you must learn to produce real effects, learn to associate effects with drug use, and learn to enjoy the drug effects. Such learning experiences necessitate interaction with other marijuana users who have themselves learned to use marijuana for pleasure. Let's examine Becker's three points more closely.

First, getting high on marijuana does not follow automatically from smoking. There's a "right" and a wrong way to smoke marijuana. If the proper techniques are not learned, then the effects may not be produced. One of Becker's respondents described the procedure (remember, folks, this paper was written over thirty-five years ago).

> Take in a lot of air, you know I don't know how to describe it, you don't smoke it like a cigarette, you draw in a lot of air and get it deep down in your system and then keep it there, keep it there as long as you can. (1953:47)

Second, not only does one have to produce effects, one also has to learn to perceive the effects and to associate them with marijuana. One of the study informants cites the case of a marijuana user who failed to perceive the effects.

> As a matter of fact, I've seen a guy who was high out of his mind and didn't know it. [How can that be, man?] Well it's pretty strange, I'll grant you that, but I've seen it. This guy got on with me, claiming that he'd never got high, one of those guys, and he got completely stoned. And he kept insisting that he wasn't high. So I had to prove to him that he was. (1953:49)

This example raises the question of what the symptoms are of being high that help you perceive the high. Many marijuana smokers report feelings of intense hunger (especially for sweets); others report that their sense of time is distorted. Now you may not associate hunger or a changed perception of time with marijuana use. Other people may have to teach you to associate these symptoms with being high and marijuana use. If you drink alcohol while smoking, it may not be possible for you to separate the effects of marijuana from whiskey, beer, or wine.

Third, in much the same way that you have to learn to enjoy drinking scotch straight, smoking a pipe, eating raw oysters, eating ginger, or even making love, Becker claims that the pleasurable effects of smoking marijuana must be learned. Marijuana users often report feeling dizzy, thirsty, having their scalps tingle, misjudging time and distance, having rapid heartbeats, and experiencing numbness in their hands and feet. In rare instances they report feeling like they are losing their minds. Clearly, such effects are not intrinsically pleasurable. When the effects are produced and perceived, some marijuana users just become sick.

> It started taking effect, and I didn't know what was happening, you know, what it was, and I was very sick. I walked around the room, walking around

Sociologists stressing the subjective conditions of social problems do not accept that objective facts ever completely or unambiguously determine a situation. Using marijuana for pleasure is a result of social interactions and learning, not just a simple chemical reaction to the physical properties of the drug. (Charles Gatewood/Stock, Boston)

> the room trying to get off, you know; it just scared me at first, you know. I wasn't used to that kind of feeling. (1953:53)

In sum, Becker argues that one who uses marijuana for pleasure must go through a learning process involving interaction with other users. Drug effects, especially those perceived as pleasurable, do *not* happen automatically as the result of physiological changes or some predisposition in individuals.

A second example of the subjective conditions approach to the study of social problems is Jack D. Douglas's work on the social meanings of suicide (1967; cf. Jacobs, 1982). Again, as with marijuana use, it might seem at first as if suicide were clear-cut and objective. People kill themselves; this act must be recorded on death certificates and then filed with a department of vital statistics. These official statistics collected from coroners, physicians, and police reports contain important facts about suicide that are available to any responsible investigator. Usually, suicide rates are computed and statistically analyzed. Completely straightforward, right? Well, not really, says Douglas.

To begin with, whose definition of suicide is being used to classify suicides (and what is the definition)? Some medical examiners will only record a death as a suicide if a suicide note is left. But only 15 percent to 25 percent of all suicides even leave notes.[19] Thus, immediately a large source of error is introduced. There may be as many different "official" statistics as there are officials (Datel and Johnson, 1979; cf. Pescosolido and Mendelsohn, 1986).

Suicide has many meanings. There are different types of suicides and it is not difficult to imagine an official misclassifying accidental or homicidal deaths as suicides. According to Douglas one of the biggest differences in the meanings of suicide is that between the individual who killed him- or herself and the third-party observer who classifies the death. Douglas contends that we must try "to determine the meanings [of suicide] to the people actually involved [the situated meanings]; the meanings to the labeled rather than the labelers, rather than taking as definitions the unknown but assumed definitions of unseen officials" (1967:163–231). Contrary to Durkheim (whom we shall discuss shortly), Douglas argues that there is a need to consider the internal meanings of the external associations of suicide and abstract social characteristics like anomie or egoism. That is, Douglas is making a plea for what Weber called *verstehen* (subjective understanding). Douglas's methodology shows affinity for what sociologist Harold Garfinkel (1967) has dubbed "ethnomethodology"; that is, uncovering the unstated, implicit, common sense perceptions held and acted on by participants in a situation (cf. Turner, 1986: Ch. 19).

For the reasons just given, Douglas does not believe that the official statistics of suicide are reliable or valid. Any so-called objective study of suicide (like Durkheim's) based on vital statistics is, in fact, highly biased and garbled. What passes for scientific sociology, says Douglas, is based on confusion of meanings and unknown errors, all analyzed with powerful statistical procedures that assume falsely that definitions and classifications of suicide are not problematic.

Of course, implicit throughout our examination of both the subjective and objective conditions controversy is what may be called the problem of bias. Before proceeding to an elaboration of the objective conditions of social phenomena, a few words are in order about bias. All of us have values, preferences, vested interests, and so on that make it difficult for us to be impartial and fair. We have already seen that definitions of social problems vary, that theoretical approaches to the study of social problems differ widely, and that there is no consensus on what counts as "data." Even what topic gets included or left out of this text as a social problem is somewhat subjective. The point is for you the reader to be aware of possible biases. *Bias* is not a bad word. It is not synonymous with *error, irrational, dogmatic,* and the like. Nevertheless, you the student should learn to read critically, to realize that just because something is in print doesn't make it true, that most of what you read is an argument, not a fact of nature, and that bias is always there, usually disguised as fact. Be on guard, have a healthy skepticism without degenerating into cynicism. Having pronounced this caveat, let us learn more about the objective conditions of social problems.

Probably the most influential sociologist in the objective condition approach to the study of social problems has been the French sociologist Emile Durkheim (1858–1917). Along with Auguste Comte (1798–1857), Durkheim is usually thought of as the founding father of sociology and particularly of the empirical study of social problems using vital statistics. Perhaps Durkheim's most famous work in this vein is *Suicide* (1897). Here Durkheim conducted an early form of multivariate analysis (see Chapter 3) on suicide death records mainly from Western Europe. Durkheim argues that individualistic explanations of suicide cannot explain the social suicide rate. The Social transcends individuals. Social facts are external to and constraining of individuals (1895). It is proper to think of a social fact as a thing, as something "out there" with a life of its own. Although the Social is never completely captured in material or visible forms, often it comes close. For example, there are codes of law, statements of religious dogma, monuments, buildings exemplifying types of architecture and basic values, rules of etiquette, and statistical regularities (like suicide rates).

One of Durkheim's favorite examples of the Social is what he calls the "collective conscience," a representation that is the totality of beliefs and sentiments common to citizens of the same society. It is the totality of social likenesses (1893:79, 80–81, 396). The Social orders life, makes it possible. For example, the collective conscience manifests itself in what Durkheim terms "repressive law" (as in the Ten Commandments of the Judeo-Christian Bible) and prompts "mechanical solidarity" (see Turner, 1986:Ch.2).

Without the Social all kinds of problems arise. As a case in point, Durkheim claims that when social norms fail (anomie) or meaningful social involvements are minimal (egoism), then the suicide rate (and other manifestations of social pathology) rises. As he says himself, "Suicide varies inversely with the degree of integration of the social groups of which the individual forms a part" (1897:209). Whereas suicide may seem among the least social or most private of all acts, according to Durkheim suicide too is social.

Finally, note that if social facts are *things,* then one is not free to make any interpretation or definition of the situation one wishes. As even sociologists like Garfinkel (1929–) and Goffman (1922–83) acknowledge, the Social can rise up and "bite you" if it is provoked. Social facts are out there, they are not just whimsical willy-nilly constructions of individuals for special interactive purposes. Note too that things can be counted. Social facts and the conditions for social problems have an irreducible obdurate character (Blumer, 1969; cf. Turner, 1986:Ch. 15).

Thinking of social facts as things that can be counted leads nicely into our second example of the importance of objective conditions. Viennese born sociologist Peter M. Blau is a structuralist who, like George Simmel (1858–1918), emphasizes the crucial importance of sheer numbers in human society (1977; cf. Blau and Merton, 1981). For example, Blau contends that the rate of intergroup associations of a smaller group must exceed that of a larger group (1977:21). Consider race relations. Most whites do not have black friends or spouses, in part because there are fewer blacks with whom to interact. If we assume that there are roughly ten whites in the United States for every black person, then the predicted frequency of whites associating with other whites is 82 percent ($.10^2 + .90^2$). Blau argues that such quantitative factors explain, for example, racial intermarriage far better than, say, a racial group's values. Of course, proximity or closeness also plays a major role in determining social associations. If you have a neighbor who is a different race than you, you are more likely to associate with him or her even though his or her values may be very different from your own. We shall have much more to say about Blau's structural sociology later (especially in Chapter 2). Finally, it would seem that the conditions for social problems cannot be solely subjective, interpretative, symbolic, or definitional since increases in the prevalence or incidence of social conditions often have consequences regardless of what people think or feel about those conditions. Furthermore, increases in rates of social conditions make it easier for people to perceive these conditions as threats to society. After all, the conditions are more visible. These are two somewhat different points.

The first amounts to saying that the rates of some social conditions can be so high or increase to such a point that the interpretation of definitions people give to them are almost irrelevant. Global nuclear warfare might be a good example of such a condition. If the entire human race were wiped off the face of the earth, that would surely be a "threat to society!"

The second point is more interesting. It says in effect that perceived threats to society are in part a function of the rate of the social condition in question. According to the *Statistical Abstract of the United States, 1986* (page 3ff.), the total divorced persons (per 1,000 married persons) was 35 in 1960, but 121 in 1984. That is, the number of divorced persons in 1984 was 3.5 times higher than it was in 1960. On the basis of these relatively objective conditions alone, it is much more likely that the American people considered divorce a social problem in 1984 than in 1960.

Clearly our own definition of social problems includes both subjective and objective components. So the real question is not which perspective is correct, but rather how do the two components interact to determine what gets defined as social problems? This is turn requires close examination of what we call the "natural histories" of social problems. That is, in the actual development of widely acknowledged social problems, how did subjective and objective conditions jointly determine the evolution of a problem? What this means is that we cannot say in advance how subjective or objective a particular social problem is. All we can say for certain at this point is that our "bias," if you will, leans toward the objective conditions perspective. This does not mean that we hold that how social conditions get labeled, defined, interpreted, and so on is unimportant. Far from it! It does mean that we believe that perception of threats to society does not usually proceed haphazardly or capriciously apart from generally acknowledged objective societal conditions. Furthermore, we believe these conditions can be counted, measured, analyzed statistically, predicted, and otherwise manipulated quantitatively. Such quantitative procedures are useful in studying social problems. They need not "miss the point" as some subjectivist critics complain.

• Nonproblematic Society

We have seen already that newspaper, television, radio, and magazines tend to exaggerate the problems of society. If you used the mass media for a guide, you would be forced to conclude that there is far more abnormality, pathology, and deviance in society than there in fact is. Much, if not most, of our collective existence is nonproblematic and routine. It is precisely the nonproblematic aspects of society that need to be understood before the concept of a "social problem" makes much sense. If we concede that a social problem is some condition (never mind for a moment if it is objective or subjective) that is a "threat to society," then we still need to know what is meant by *society*. Thus, we must define concepts like interaction, activity, sentiment, role, norm, value, culture, class, status, power, and institution—at the very least. Also, we must realize that many of the readers of this text have never had another sociology course. Until we understand something about the routine structure and process of normal society, it is difficult to speak intelligibly about society "going wrong" or "having problems."

Actually there are two distinct questions to be kept straight here. First, we want to know how normal, routine, ordinary society is defined. What are the key concepts in our understanding of "society"? How does social structure evolve? What are the basic principles of social behavior? A second and somewhat different issue is, are social problems normal or healthy? As we shall see shortly, a number of sociologists have claimed that crime (Durkheim, 1895) or deviant behavior is a normal integral part of any healthy society (Erikson, 1966).

Perhaps the fundamental issue in this section is from what do problematic behaviors or conditions depart? To argue that social conditions are abnormal, pathological, deviant, or problematic implies that we know something about the workings of normal, healthy, routine, nonproblematic society. More precisely, the concept of a "problem" makes sense only in the context of fairly specific theoretical assumptions about social behavior. For example, if you saw society through the eyes of a conflict theorist, Marxist, or neo-Marxist (Currie and Skolnick, 1985; Collins, 1975; Dahrendorf, 1959), then concentration of wealth, power, and prestige in the hands of elites would be a problem, and socialism, broadly construed, would be a solution. On the other hand, if you were a functionalist (see Merton, 1957; Merton and Nisbet, 1976), then any unanticipated consequence of social behaviors that contributed to the maladjustment or maladaptation of a particular social system could be considered "problematic" and making previously latent dysfunctions manifest could be a solution (see glossary at the end of Chapters 1 and 2). Finally, if you saw society as sociologist George C. Homans does (1974:59ff.), then any small group that was "imbalanced"[20] could be problematic, and balancing the social group would be the solution (cf. Turner, 1986; Part III). What is problematic then is defined by our understanding and assumptions about the workings of nonproblematic society. Let's begin by defining some core concepts in the nonproblematic understanding of society championed primarily, but not exclusively, by George C. Homans (1974, 1950). In so doing, we do not intend to restrict ourselves now or later on in the text to an exchange theory perspective. Finally, we shall take up the related issue of whether social problems themselves are normal.

Activity, Sentiment, and Interaction Activities are what people do (for example, give help, seek approval, walk, sit, talk, play, smoke, drink, eat, sleep, make love, read sociology books, and so on). Any exchange between two or more people is an activity (Homans, 1974:21; 1950:34–35). Commonly we speak of the frequency, efficiency, or degree of similarity of activities. Deprivation and satiation determine the rate of activity. Obviously, here we are talking primarily about activity in face-to-face exchanges in relatively small groups. This is a good place to start, but does not mean that we must stop with the acts that Homans calls "subinstitutional" settings (1974:Ch. 16). Later we shall have to expand the concept of activity to more complex organizations where most human acts are not face-to-face, are more complex, have longer chains (or "spans") of action, are more impersonal, use more generalized reinforcers (like money and status), and so on. It will be necessary to introduce (in Chapter 10) the idea of corporate actors (Coleman, 1974), in which large social units function as individuals do in smaller groups. We will also have to use other sociological perspectives in addition to exchange theory to explain adequately more macro- or institutional-level social problems. Of course, the concept of social action is more complicated than simple behavior (for example, see Mead, 1934:6), but for starters this definition will do.

Sentiments are the signs of the attitudes or feelings a person has for another (such as anger, fear, liking, or social approval). Since sentiments are a special class of activities, they should be observable. Sentiments vary in intensity and in the number of people holding them (Homans, 1974:40; 1950:37ff.). One of the major complications with most theories of nonproblematic society is that they act as if people did not feel. Any truly complete understanding of society must take into account that humans have feelings in addition to minds and bodies. Vilfredo Pareto (1848–1923) and Talcott Parsons (1902–1979) both realized the importance of sentiments in society. Pareto referred to the constant element in nonlogical theories as "residues" (see Parsons, 1937:Ch. 7). Residues are not sentiments themselves, but rather are linguistic manifestations of sentiments. Parsons acknowledges that action can be expressive (have no goal except action itself) and that each actor must identify objects relevant to his or her interests (cf. Coleman, 1974). More specifically, Parsons argues that we "cathect" or attach ourselves to gratifying objects (1951:5). Motivations are not merely cognitive or evaluative.

For Homans when an activity or sentiment is emitted and rewarded (or punished), then social interaction is said to have occurred. To illustrate how activities, sentiments, and interaction might be related, we can imagine that if someone does a person a service (for example, acts as a best friend or a psychotherapist), then the person is apt both to like the other person (a sentiment) and to interact with him or her often. Homans feels that activities, sentiments, and interaction are so basic to human social behavior that he calls them "elements" (1950:33–40; 1974:2–3). Other sociologists point to properties of emergence, contingency, and meaning in social interaction.

For example, Durkheim (1924:25–26) claims that although society may be the product of human interaction (he calls it "association"), in the process of interaction transcendent social facts emerge. For Durkheim the essence of the social is not "subinstitutional" (see Chapter 10), but rather is institutional. The Social for Durkheim is thought to be exterior to and constraining of individual interaction. Parsons too shares Durkheim's idea of the emergence properties of social interaction and goes on to stress the contingencies involved in interaction. In a rudimentary social situation involving any two people (call them ego and alter), the meaning of interaction is rooted in many "ifs" and "alternative meanings" based at least in the double contingency of one's (ego's) actions and reactions and other's (alter's) actions and reactions (Parsons, 1951:10–11, 36 ff.; cf. Turner, 1986, Ch. 3). Finally, Max Weber insists that social interaction exists only when an individual's conduct is meaningfully oriented toward that of another or others (1925:Vol. I, Part 1; cf. Parsons, 1937:529–639). This is in part a plea for subjective understanding (i.e., for *verstehen*) and in part to rule out prayer, relations to inanimate objects, and a common response to an external stimulus (such as all of us raising umbrellas when it rains) from the concept of social interaction.

Norm, Value, and Culture So far we have dealt with observables, with activities, sentiments, and interaction. This was intentional because we wish to ground our understanding of social problems in actual behaviors, in the basic

For exchange theorists when an activity is emitted and rewarded (or punished), then social interaction is said to have occurred. Principles of human social behavior are often derived from animal experiments concerning reinforcement, punishment, satiation, and deprivation. (AP/Wide World Photos)

principles of face-to-face interaction in nonproblematic society. Much of previous social problems theory has erred in getting too far removed from observables and in losing the individual in social abstractions. Some of my structuralist sociology colleagues brag that they teach introductory sociology without ever mentioning people. As another case in point, functional theorists (described later on) started out studying norms (see Homans, 1964:809), clusters of norms called roles, and clusters of roles called institutions. The functionalists were primarily interested in roles, not in acting individuals. Functionalists seldom, if ever, thought to ask why there should be any roles or norms at all.

Exchange theorists argue that social norms arise from general patterns of social behaviors that individuals have found rewarding and valuable.

Still, it is true that our theory takes ideas, not merely observables, into account. Social problems have been defined as "threats to society." What is usually threatened is not actual behavior, but rather social expectations embodied in norms, values, and culture. Both norms and values are often defined as "shared standards of desirable behavior" (Wilson, 1983). One difference is that norms often refer to specific expectations in given circumstances, whereas values often refer to more diffuse ideas about what is right or proper. Some feel that values are so diffuse as to be unconscious assumptions members of society make (Homans, 1974:25 ff.; 1950:127).

A working definition of a norm is "an idea in the minds of the members of a group, an idea that can be put in the form of a statement specifying what the members or other [people] should do, ought to do, are expected to do, under given circumstances" (Homans, 1974:2; 1950:123). Norms vary in intensity or degree of seriousness. We have seen already that Sumner differentiated folkways from mores. Obviously, some common expectations can be fairly trivial (such as what to wear or say on a particular occasion), while others are extremely serious (for example, norms concerning aggression or incest). It is tempting to say that all serious norms tend to become law and nonconformity is formally punished. Yet we all realize that even the law is differentiated into misdemeanors and felonies (see Chapter 15). Sometimes very fundamental norms are part of religious codes with "only" moral, not civil or criminal, sanctions. A good example of such norms would be the Ten Commandments of Deuteronomy in the Judeo-Christian Bible. However, it is true that some of the Ten Commandments are also civil or criminal laws (murder).

One interesting trait of norms, regardless of their degree of seriousness, is that most people tend to follow them almost automatically (Milgram, 1963; Berkowitz, 1975:Ch. 11).[21] Of course, it is of paramount importance to this book if most people conform to most norms. We shall discover if this general tendency to conform is in fact true, and if so, why (see Zimbardo, 1970). Much of what follows will be concerned with the relationship of actual behavior to various social norms. We have reason to suspect that people tend to be more alike in the norms they espouse than in their actual behaviors (Homans, 1974:127–30 and 299–302; 1950:126). Also, the more frequently people interact, the more likely they are to become similar in the norms they hold.

For Homans values are the degree of reward of an action (1974:25). Why certain patterns of human behavior or action get repeated and tend to evolve into recurring social structure is clearly related to what people find valuable. In Chapter 2 of this text, where we elaborate our seven theoretical perspectives, we shall have much more to say about the basic propositions that exchange theorists claim account for human behavior, and especially about what Homans calls the "value proposition." Some values are general, tend to be shared widely, and do not lead easily to satiation. For example, it is hard for most people to get enough money or social approval. On the other hand, whereas food or sex may be very rewarding when you are in a state of deprivation, you can fairly quickly get enough of them for the time being (I know some of you find this hard to believe). However, most of us never have enough money or praise (cf. Maslow, 1954; 1963). Sociologist Robin Williams has written a classic book on some of the common values in American society (1951:389–442; cf. the *General Social Survey* of the University of Chicago, Davis, 1980). Acording to Williams these values include (among others) secular occupational achievement, work and activity, material comfort, and what he calls the "Puritan ethic." Other values are extremely particularistic. That is, what men and women find rewarding can vary greatly (see Homans, 1974:27). Thus, while almost everyone does what is of value to them, we often do not agree on what is rewarding. One person's pleasure may be another's pain.

Culture includes values and norms, but is also a much broader concept. For example, Harris argues that a culture "is the total socially-acquired life-way or life-style of a particular group of people" (1971:136; 1977; Campbell, 1985). Another way of putting it is that culture concerns all of the shared products of social activity, values, and much more. In a classic "omnibus" definition of culture, Edward Tylor calls culture "that complex whole which includes knowledge, belief, art, morals, law, custom, and any other capabilities and habits acquired by man as a member of society" (1871:1).

Role, Status, Class, and Power This next group of concepts concerning aspects of nonproblematic society fit together somewhat loosely. Usually the concept of status-role is considered as two dimensions of one concept. Originally sociologist Ralph Linton defined status as the social position and role as the expectations associated with the positions, the dynamic aspect of status, if you will (1936; cf., Turner, 1986:16). Likewise class, status, and power are usually thought to be the three major determinants of social stratification (Lenski, 1984). That is, wealth, prestige, and power are combined either objectively (see Reiss, 1961; Powers, 1982) or subjectively (as in Warner et al., 1949) to form layers of society that are ranked in various categories like upper-, middle-, lower-class, white-collar versus blue-collar workers, capitalists versus proletariats, rich versus poor, the propertied versus the propertyless, and so forth. Usually occupation and income are held to be major factors in determining social position (Powers, 1982). The number of strata in a society is somewhat arbitrary. The U.S. Census Bureau lists eleven major occupational groups; Warner's studies of social class in America finds six major social classes; Marx claims there are only two.

Social roles can be thought of as a special kind of norm. More precisely, a role is a norm that states the expected relationship of a person in a certain position to others with whom he or she comes into contact (Homans, 1974:334–336; 1950:124). Clearly there are exceptions associated with all social positions in a society. Think of those norms for fathers, physicians, secretaries, best friends, lovers, elected officials, preschool children, and so on. Each of these broad roles has certain rights, privileges, duties, and obligations related to it.

For example, a father or mother commands certain respect and authority in a family, but is also expected to provide economically and emotionally for his or her family. Clearly a person and a role are different. The same role can be filled by many different people. Sometimes people do not "live up" to their role expectations. A flagrant example of this failure is the parent who has sexual relations with his or her own children (cf., *New York Times,* June 15, 1981:B9). Also, one person plays many different roles and often these various role expectations (the role set) are in conflict. This conflict can cause stress and anxiety for the individual who has to resolve it, and disorganization for the society.

Status can be defined simply as the rank of a person in a group (Homans, 1974:Ch. 9). The fundamental dimensions of status are those along which men and women can be ranked according to what they give to others and what they get from them (Homans, 1974:198). For example, occupations can be thought of as what we give and income as what we get. Randall Collins says much the same thing when he claims the crucial factor in any society is where one stands when orders are given (1975). For example, a high-status person gives many orders and takes very few. Like roles, which can be in conflict, statuses can be congruent or incongruent. Sometimes status incongruency produces ranking dilemmas. For example, on the North-Hatt Occupational Prestige Scale (Hodge, Trieman, and Rossi, 1966), college professors rank very near the top in spite of their relatively low incomes (which may only demonstrate that class and status are different); and policemen rank about in the middle of the status hierarchy even though they carry guns (which may mean status and power are different).

Max Weber made some of the early distinctions among status, class, and power (1925, Part III, Ch. 4:631–640). Weber claimed that status groups, unlike social classes, are normally communities. Status for Weber is determined by lifestyle. A social class, on the other hand, exists when a number of people have in common a specific [economic] component of their life chances. Property is particularly crucial in determining social class. Of course, Karl Marx also believed that class was determined primarily by economic factors. For Marx and Engels a social class was "any aggregate of persons who perform the same function in the organization of production" (1848). There were two main social classes, a ruling class (which owned and controlled the means of production), and an oppressed class (which owned little and was exploited by the ruling class). Interestingly, George Homans does not even list the word *class* in the indexes of his two primary books, being content instead to confine himself to observations on status and power.

Weber defines power as "the chance of a man or a number of men to realize their will in a communal action even against the resistance of others who are participating in the action" (1925, Part III, Ch. 4). Homans, on the other hand, defines power in terms of differences in people's ability to reward others and to thereby make them change their behavior (see Chapter 10). For example, if my reward in a given exchange is less than yours and you change your behavior, then I have power over you. This phenomenon is related to the "principle of least interest" (see Waller and Hill, 1951:191; Molm, 1985). That is, the person who is able to dictate the conditions of association is the one whose interest in the continuation of the affair is least. It is important for our purposes to realize that the bases for least interest and power can result from differences in money, physical strength, intellectual ability, attractiveness, age, sex, love, fear, and many more—as well as from social position. Note that power also has roots in what we might call biological inequality as well as in social inequality. Finally, with authority, the ability to control others lies outside any actual exchange, whereas with power control derives from the exchange itself. One of the keys to keeping power is to not have to reveal the basis for it, to not have your power tested (like the gun fighter who does not have to "draw" or the presence of nuclear weapons without nuclear war).

Institution and Subinstitution We have seen already that an institution can be thought of as a cluster of roles. As such, an institution is an example par excellence of a Durkheimian social fact. A more elaborate definition of *institution* that suits our purposes is this one by Gusfield: "An institution is a societally prescribed system of more or less differentiated behavior by means of which recurrent human problems are resolved" (1963:484). What this means is that normal routine societal systems, among other things, function to resolve common problems. More accurately, institutions meet social needs before they become problematic. It is easy to think of several major social institutions in just this way. For example, the family addresses the need to regulate reproduction and to socialize the young; medicine deals with sickness and injury; science with understanding and controlling nature; the economy with the production and distribution of goods and services; and so forth.

An interesting thought you may have had is if institutions resolve recurrent human problems, then why do we even have social problems? It may be that many institutions are just not working well. After all, social, moral, economic, and technological changes may help make prior institutional resolutions inappropriate or irrelevant. What is rewarding and valuable to society may change dramatically. That is, behavior patterns may have shifted but general expectations stayed about the same. The expectations may be out of synch with contemporary behavior. Formal organizations often change very slowly (Aldrich, 1979).

Another possibility is that norms, roles, and social institutions never prescribe human behavior completely. If so, this is a very good reason for our textbook to focus somewhat more on what Homans calls "subinstitutional" behavior (1974:Ch. 16). Subinstitutional behavior concerns establishing the principles of actual face-to-face interaction of individuals (see Chapter 10). As Homans writes in another place, "If a serious effort is made to construct theories that will even begin to explain social phenomena, it turns out their general propositions are not about the equilibrium of societies but about the behavior of men" (1964:818). Just what these general propositions may be will be discussed in Chapter 2, where we develop our theoretical perspectives.

The Bank Wiring Observation Room After so much sustained abstraction in defining basic concepts of nonproblematic society, it would be wise to give you a concrete example of a small group and to use it to illustrate our newly acquired concepts. From 1927 to 1932 an extensive research project was conducted at the Western Electric Company's Hawthorne Works in Chicago (Roethlisberger and Dickson, 1939; cf. Homans, 1950; 1974:200ff.).[22] The primary purpose of this research was to inform management of the sources of employee satisfaction or dissatisfaction at work. The group chosen for study was a section from a department that assembled switches for telephone equipment. In particular, this group wired banks of terminals (hence the name Bank Wiring Observation Room). Fourteen men were taken from the department and isolated in a room by themselves: nine wiremen, three soldermen, and two inspectors (See Figure 1.1).

A bank was a piece of plastic about one and one-half inches high and four inches long with 100 to 200 terminals. A finished equipment was ten or eleven of these banks long and two or three banks—about 3,000 to 3,300 connections in each. A wiremen (W) connected the terminals of the banks together with wire. A solderman (S) soldered the connections in place and the inspector (I) tested the work of both the wireman and the solderman. One solderman could solder the connections for about three wiremen.

When two completed equipments were finished (about 6,000 to 6,600 connections), the men thought they had done enough for the day, whether they were tired or not and even if it was relatively early in the workday. Another way of putting it was that two completed equipments were the norm for the group. Workers who did more were considered ratebusters, those who did less, chiselers. If you did too much or too little work, you were subject to social controls by the groups. For example, Mueller (W_2) wired about 7,404 connections a day (activity) in spite of the 6,000 to 6,600 connections norm. Mueller was a ratebuster (they nicknamed him Cyclone). Although he belonged to clique A, a dotted circle was drawn around his position to indicate that Mueller was unsociable and a loner. Mueller seldom talked or helped others.

Taylor (W_3), on the other hand, was the best liked workman in the group. He was on friendly terms with everyone else. Interestingly, his work output came closest to realizing the group's norms. Homans observes that leaders are in some way the least free group members in that the higher one's status, the more one must conform to the group's norms (1974:269–296; 1950:149).

Winowski (W_1), Meuller (W_2), Taylor (W_3), Donovan (W_4), Allen (I_1), and Steinhardt (S_1) tended to form a subgroup or clique (A), as did Krupa (W_6), Hasulak (W_7), Oberleitner (W_8), Green (W_9) and Cermak (S_4)—that is clique B. Mazmanian (I_3), Capek (W_5) and Matchek (S_2) were excluded from both cliques. How did these cliques emerge? Actually there is a theorem known as the structure theorem (Kemeny and Snell, 1962:100 ff; cf. Norman and Roberts, 1972:Ch. 14) that predicts clique formation. A thorough discussion of this theorem requires that we introduce some concepts that are too advanced for this text. Thus, it will have to suffice to observe differences between cliques A and B on concepts already defined. To begin with, cliques A and B did

FIGURE 1.1 The Bank Wiring Observation Room

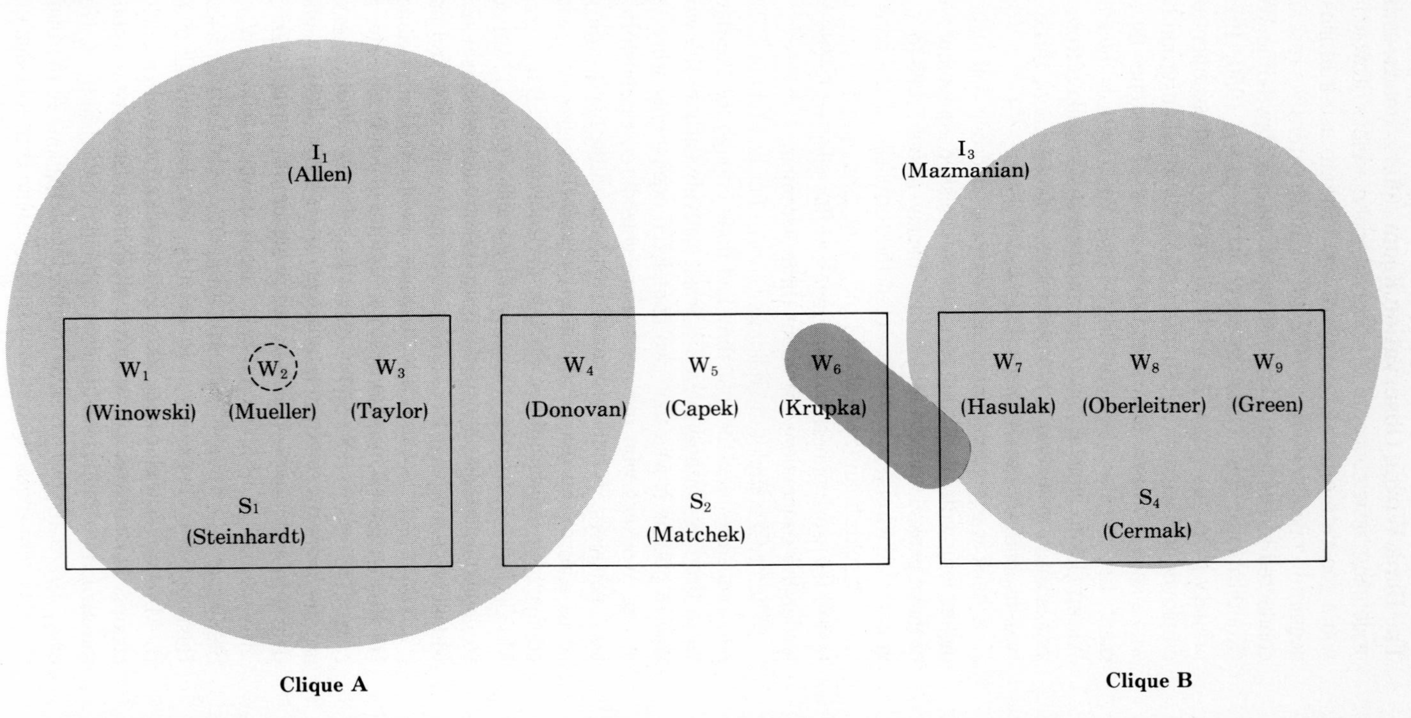

Source: From *The Human Group* by George C. Homans, copyright 1950 by Harcourt Brace Jovanovich, Inc.; renewed 1978 by George C. Homans. Reprinted by permission of the publisher.

different types of activities. Clique A wired connectors (6,600 connections) while clique B wired selectors (6,000 connections). More importantly, Hasulak, Oberleitner, and Green had the lowest output of the whole group, but they tended to report more connections than they had actually made. They tended not to take their work very seriously. Clique B was a lower social rank than clique A. Finally, clique B received more interaction than it initiated.

Clique A had high output, was more serious about its work, was closer to output norms than clique B, initiated more interaction, and had higher social rank. Both cliques interacted more with clique members than with nonclique members and had more similar values among members. Of those workers excluded from both cliques, Mazmanian (I_3) was the oldest worker, the most educated, and the least liked (sentiment). Capek (W_5) was also strongly disliked, was contemptuous of others, and rarely smiled. Matchek (S_2) had a speech defect and was excluded largely for that reason alone.

Based on our observations of the Bank Wiring Observation Room we can derive the following tentative general propositions about the principles of nonproblematic small-group behavior:

1. The higher the social rank (status) of an individual or subgroup, the closer the individual or subgroup will come in all activities to realizing the norms of the group as a whole.
2. The higher a person's social rank, the larger the number of persons for whom he initiates interaction.
3. The more people interact with one another, the more they will come to like one another, and the more similar they will become.
4. The more people who like one another, the more group activities will conform to a norm.
5. The more valuable to other people a person's activities are, the more that person will be esteemed by the group.

Of course, we could derive more generalizations (and in Chapter 2 we will). The point here is to begin to see how all (not just problematic) social behavior can be explained from one's theoretical perspectives. These few general propositions can be thought of as a sample of some general research results, as hypothetical propositions borne out by some data. In the next chapter we shall be much more precise about theoretical perspectives and their uses. Of course, the exchange theory perspective will not suffice to explain all social problems. Rather, the purpose here has been to illustrate some general sociological concepts as one (but not the only one) backdrop against which our later consideration of social problems might make some sense. For now, we conclude this section with the second major issue in nonproblematic society, which is whether social problems are normal.

Are Social Problems Normal? In a way it is a mistake to characterize routine everyday society as nonproblematic. For one thing putting it this way seems to imply that social problems are unhealthy or abnormal, that in a perfected social order there would not be any social problems. Or the phrase "nonproblematic society" may be taken to mean that social problems are somehow separate from social conditions that are not problematic. No less a social thinker than Emile Durkheim has argued that in fact a certain crime rate is normal. To begin with, there has never been and can never be any society without crime (1895, Chapter III, 67ff.). Durkheim implies that there are optimal rates of all kinds of deviant behavior such that if the assault or suicide rates (for example) fall too much this decline itself can be an indicator of some serious problem in society at large. Paradoxically, the reduction of some specific "social problems" may imply the malfunctioning of society itself. Crime rates can be a barometer of social illness in a very curious sense—namely, if they are far too low, something is wrong rather than right!

Much of Durkheim's argument is logical, not empirical. If social facts (like the collective conscience) are external and constraining, then there cannot be a society in which any given individuals conform to the collective conscience exactly. No single individual embodies all of the collective representations of a society. Thus, some deviance is required. This is particularly true in modern urban-industrial societies organized on the principle of what Durkheim calls organic solidarity (1893). In such societies a high division of labor and population heterogeneity form the basis of social cooperation (actually, functional interdependency). Too much social likeness and too little deviance could signal a regressive social development characteristic of so-called primitive societies.

One of the better-known contemporary champions of Durkheim's position is Erik Erikson's son Kai (1966). Erikson writes about the social determinants of witchcraft in seventeenth-century Boston. When the pilgrims arrived in Salem, Massachusetts, they found a normative as well as a physical wilderness (1966:157). People often were not sure what was expected of them, especially since many migrants rejected important norms of their countries of origin. In this setting deviants helped define normalcy. That is, the normal was what wasn't deviant. Accordingly, deviants were needed for normal society to function.

A second major point Erikson makes is very different from Durkheim's position. Erikson argues that deviance is not an objective condition, but is instead a property conferred by labelers (a "public reaction," if you will). For example, a few young girls in 1692–93 were primarily responsible for branding (stigmatizing) women they did not like as witches. Erikson argues that the amount of deviant behavior tends to be constant in a population over time, even when convictions for various deviant acts increase (1966:174). Thus, the amount of the reaction, not the amount of the deviance, changes. Deviance is often structurally determined. As a case in point the rate of craziness can be "increased" by simply adding more psychiatric hospital beds. Again, declaring more holidays can increase the rate of violent acting out in a population.

Durkheim's contention that crime is normal would seem to extend to the argument that problems are inseparable from social growth, change, devel-

French sociologist Emile Durkheim was one of the pioneers in the objective condition approach to the study of social problems like suicide. Durkheim argued that a certain rate of crime or deviance in a society is normal. (The Bettmann Archive)

opment, evolution, and the like. It would follow that any dynamic or rapidly changing society (even change for the "good") must have problems. Paradoxically, to not have problems would be pathological. In this regard it is instructive to think of utopias such as Aldous Huxley's *Brave New World* (1939). This brave new world minimized many social problems, but at the expense of individuality, creativity, and freedom.

Finally, if the social conditions that are perceived to be a threat to society change or differ (in perception) among major groups, then the same conditions may be either normal or problematic. Erikson comments that one and the same action can make one a saint or sinner, a war hero or a psychopathic murderer (1966:5). Obviously, if the same conditions can be either problematic or nonproblematic, then the line between social normalcy and social pathology is fine indeed.

• Organization and Objectives

This book has fifteen chapters on major American social problems, because most university or college terms are about fifteen weeks long—give or take a week. Instructors may have to supplement (or delete from) this text to make everything come out right. Obviously, the problems presented represent a synthesis of consensus on important topics as seen by leading social scientists and those problems that are of special interest to me. This text contains many relatively new social problems topics such as terrorism, stress, dying, family violence, suicide, nuclear war, and the like. Of course, the heart of the book consists of recurring human social problems that just about everyone would agree are important and deserving of inclusion (such as aging, gender roles, racial discrimination, mental illness, poverty, the urban transformation, crime, and so on).

Part I of this book (Chapters 1–3) is an introduction to the study of social problems. Any uniqueness this particular text may have, however, does not reside in its choice of social problems, but rather in its theoretical approach to the study of social problems. A major objective is to attempt a more systemic integrated general theoretical thrust than is usually presented in social problems textbooks. The reader will be introduced to three relatively new theoretical perspectives—those of exchange theory, structuralism, and sociobiology/biology. Of course, it is our position that social problems probably cannot and should not be reduced to one, two, or even three theoretical perspectives at this time. Social problems are too rich and diversified and the science of social problems is too infantile for any such reductionism. Accordingly, we will also make generous reference to conflict, functional, symbolic interaction, and deviance theoretical perspectives in what follows. In Chapter 2 we will elaborate our theoretical perspectives. In Chapter 3 we will introduce the data and research methods necessary to begin to test our theoretical perspectives of social problems.

Part II (Chapters 4–9) focuses on what we call subinstitutional problems. Although there will be a subinstitutional emphasis in these chapters this is not to imply that aging, gender roles, racial discrimination, and so on are not in part institutional problems. Of course they are. Here we consider various aspects of age and aging, sex and gender roles, race, physical and mental health, and drug and alcohol use. This grouping is somewhat arbitrary. Although not a strict rule, there will be some tendency in the six chapters of Part II to emphasize face-to-face social exchanges, small-group social structure, and the influence of biology on problematic social relations. As the book progresses we shall tend to go from small face-to-face social situations to larger, more complex, formally organized, and indirect social relations. There will also be a corresponding shift of emphasis on theoretical perspectives, from micro-level explanations, such as exchange theory, to structuralism, conflict theory, and other more macro-level explanations in the later chapters of the text (especially in Chapters 10 through 15). Hence, Part III is labeled "Institutional and Macro-System Problems." It includes six chapters (Chapters 10–15) on power, economy, the family, population, energy and environmental issues, violence, crime, and war.

The twelve "substantive" chapters of the text (Chapters 4 through 15) will all have the same format. Each chapter will begin with a highly general overview

TABLE 1.1 Major Objectives of the Text

1. To begin to develop a sociology of social problems that will aim for an integrated, general theory based on exchange theory, structural sociology, conflict theory, symbolic interactionism, functionalism, deviance theory, and sociobiological/biological theory.
2. To introduce the student to the minimum necessary data and methods needed to begin to construct theories and test hypotheses about social problems.
3. To cover most major contemporary social problems; to update coverage of classical social problems; and to include some important new social problems.
4. To understand the sociological perspective of social problems as opposed to those of other major disciplines.
5. To present all materials in as lively and engaging a reading style as possible.

of the social problems from the theoretical perspectives. This will be followed by a vivid case (in a boxed panel) highlighting a limited aspect of the problem in an individual or otherwise concrete manner. Each problem will then be concisely stated and defined, with an emphasis on key issues for the chapter. We shall also detail objective conditions, subjective perceptions, and a brief history of the social problem. The "stating the problem" section will be done both generally (at the start of each chapter) and specifically (for each particular subproblem considered in a chapter).

For each major social problem considered in a chapter, there will be a section analyzing the problem that will discuss the prevalence of the problem, relevant data and methods, and consider the role of the major theoretical perspectives in understanding and explaining the problem(s). The analysis parts of each chapter will tend to be long sections since it is here that a major effort will be made to develop our somewhat novel theoretical approaches to the study of social problems.

Finally, each section on particular social problems will conclude with a resolution (or resolutions) of the problem. Here control and prevention issues will be examined, as will the impact of social movements and collective action. Each chapter will be summarized, a glossary of key terms provided, and a short list of annotated further readings provided.

Throughout the text there will be panel inserts on actual cases or instances of the social problem being examined, and ample use of pictures and cartoons. It is imperative that we present social problems to you in as lively and engaging a manner as possible. We want you to enjoy our book and the subject of social problems. There is no reason at all why the study of social problems should be dull.

• Summary

We in the United States are a problem oriented society. This is understandable. If social problems are not resolved, then the quality of life or even life itself can be threatened. Social problems may also function to distract us from our own private troubles or provide dramatic relief from mechanical routinized work and dull personal lives. Social problems are general patterns of behavior or social conditions that are perceived to be threats to society by significant numbers of the population, powerful groups, or charismatic individuals and that could be resolved or remedied. This definition calls attention to the patterns of human behavior or of social conditions, to the generality of social problems, to why some behaviors or conditions and not others are seen to be threats, to how many people feel that behaviors or social conditions are threatening, and, finally, to the fact that to call something a problem implies that it can be resolved.

In contrast to our own definition of social problems, which favors somewhat the view that objective conditions or Durkheimian social facts "out there" play a major part in determining what gets counted as social problems, others hold a more subjective view. For example, Spector and Kitsuse see social problems as claims-making activities of groups or individuals relative to alleged conditions. That is, the actual social conditions are not as crucial as the effectiveness of the claims that some behaviors or conditions are problematic. Examples of marijuana smoking and suicide were considered.

The context for understanding social problems has to be not just problems or pathology but the generation, operation, and maintenance of all recurring social behaviors and conditions—what we have referred to as nonproblematic or routine society. Problems only make sense in the context of norms or "normal" society. Basic concepts in nonproblematic society were defined. These included the core sociological notions of activity, sentiment, interaction, norm, value, culture, role, status, class, power, institution, and subinstitution. An illustration of these concepts in Homans's Bank Wiring Room study was given. Social problems themselves may be normal in that some rates of deviant behavior seem irreducible beyond a certain level or optimum prevalence. Also, social problems can help to define what is nonproblematic or conforming, as in Erikson's study of witchcraft.

Although we shall emphasize the relatively new application of exchange theory, structuralism, and sociobiology/biology to the study of social problems, it is important for the student to be aware that there are other, equally cogent theoretical viewpoints. In Chapter 2 some of these complementary theories of social problems (i.e., conflict theory, symbolic interaction and labeling theory, functionalism, and deviance theory) will be reviewed, along with the uses of theory for social problems in general and a modest elaboration of exchange theory and structuralism in particular.

• Notes

1. A survey by the Chicago Title Insurance Company (October 1985) revealed that the median price of a single-family dwelling unit in the United States rose to an all-time high of $89,400 (in 1984). New home sales dropped 14 percent in April of 1981. It is now estimated that over 97 percent of the American population cannot afford to purchase a new (first) home. The average monthly payment (1984) for the current average home price at $89,400 was $868. Mortgage payments averaged 30 percent of the owner's total income. As is true already in much of Western Europe, it appears as if traditional single-family dwellings may become virtually extinct in the United States in the not-too-distant future.

2. *On the Beach,* 1959, United Artists, Stanley Kramer, director. Based on the novel by Nevil Shute.

3. See the role of what Becker (1963) calls moral entrepreneurs. For example, the active involvement of federal narcotics Commissioner H. J. Anslinger in pointing out the evils of marijuana usage (Becker, 1953:142) culminating in the Harrison Marijuana Tax Act of 1937.

4. For a general statement on the place of definitions in theories, see Turner, 1986: Ch. 1.

5. C. W. Mills (1959) distinguishes between a "personal trouble" and a "public issue" (cf. Horowitz, 1983). He argues that many personal troubles must be seen as part of larger social issues to be resolved. That is, in many cases the real problem is social, not individual.

6. For alternative definitions of social problems see Eitzen, 1986:5; Henslin and Light, 1983:5; DeFleur, 1986:4.

7. A discussion of the importance of numbers in social behavior is provided by Blau, 1977: Chapter 2; Blau and Merton, 1981; cf. Simmel, 1902.

8. Not too long ago there was the very real possiblity of New York City's financial problems resulting in municipal bankruptcy (see Auletta, 1980). Imagine what would happen if New York City were insolvent. Essential services would stop, people would be forced to move in search of other jobs, general disorder would prevail, and so on. Such a catastrophic event seems unthinkable. But it could happen.

9. See McRandle's book on Hitler, *The Track of the Wolf* (1965) and Klineman et al., *The Cult That Died* (1980).

10. As Spector and Kitsuse do (1977:74).

11. See Barbara Walters Special, June 3, 1981, on CBS television.

12. One has to be careful not to let professional investments or biases distort one's perception of the world. Just because I was trained as a sociologist does not keep me from seeing that some problems have very little to do with sociology. For example, psychoanalysts often end up trying to assist their patients in seeing that they may be able to change themselves, but not their parents, and certainly not society!

13. See Emile Durkheim's *Division of Labor in Society* (1893), *The Rules of Sociological Method* (1895), and *Suicide* (1897).

14. Max Weber, *Wirtschaft and Gesellschaft* (1925), Chapter One. Cf. Talcott Parsons, *The Structure of Social Action* (1937), pp. 579–639.

15. Berger and Luckmann, 1966; Cf. Turner, 1986:Part IV.

16. The word *subjective* is often used interchangeably with *social* in the literature. Of course, the Social can be considered objective too (as in Durkheim, 1895).

17. Compare W. I. Thomas's similar concept of "definition of the situation" (1918–1920); cf. Wilson, 1983:Ch. 8.

18. See Sutherland's concept of "differential association" (1937).

19. Maris, 1981.

20. A "balanced" situation is a situation in which the relations among the entities fit together harmoniously; there is no stress toward change (Heider, 1967:201–202; Turner, 1986:289–295).

21. The argument is in part circular in that norms are defined as what people routinely do.

22. Our account of the bank-wiring observation room draws heavily from Homans, 1950, 1974.

• Glossary

Activity. What people do. Any exchange between two or more people is an activity.

Conflict Theory. The general view that competing interests and differential distribution of wealth, power, and prestige are basic aspects of human society—perhaps more basic than cooperation and order.

Culture. The total socially acquired lifeway or lifestyle of a particular group of people.

Deviance. Departure from social norms that is usually felt to be negative and is often sanctioned or punished by society.

Exchange Theory. The view that enduring social structures result from actual human exchanges in relatively small groups that are rewarding and valuable.

Functional Analysis. The practice of interpreting data by establishing consequences for larger structures in which the data are implicated.

Institution. A societally prescribed system of more or less differentiated behavior by means of which recurrent human problems are resolved.

Interaction. What occurs when an activity or sentiment is emitted and rewarded (or punished).

Nonproblematic Society. The routine structure and process of normal society.

Nonsocial Conditions. Biological, genetic, chromosomal, bacteriological, viral, and similar conditions.

Norm. An idea in the minds of the members of a group that can be put in the form of a statement that specifies what the members or other people should do, ought to do, or are expected to do under given circumstances.

Objective Condition. A "thing" (something "out there") with a life of its own. External to and constraining of individuals. Can be counted or otherwise measured. Somewhat independent of perception.

Personal Trouble. Something that is problematic for an individual but is not necessarily a public issue or a social problem.

Power. Differences in people's ability to reward other people and thereby to make them change their behavior.

Role. A norm that states the expected relationship of a person in a certain position to others with whom he or she comes into contact.

Sentiment. The sign of the attitude or feeling a person has for another person.

Social Problem. A general pattern of human behavior or social condition that is perceived to be a threat to society by significant numbers of the population, powerful groups, or charismatic individuals and that could be resolved or remedied.

Social Needs. The basic traits all societies must have to survive. These are often thought to include social differentiation, socialization, integration, regulation of affect, and equilibrium; as well as more physical needs such as food, reproduction, and shelter.

Sociobiology. A biologically based explanation of social behavior. Individuals act to maximize survival of their gene pool. Each person is concerned with increasing his or her own biological fitness.

Status. The rank of a person in a group.

Structuralism. The view that society can be conceptualized in terms of different social positions, the numbers of their incumbents, and the implications of differentiation among positions for social relations.

Subinstitution. The principles of actual face-to-face interaction of individuals. Elementary social behavior as distinguished from social institutions.

Subjective Condition. A claim, perception, definition, social construction, interpretation, or label about a putative condition.

Symbolic Interaction. The view that people act toward things and other people on the basis of the meanings they have for them. These meanings are derived from social interaction. Meanings are handled in and modified by interpretative processes.

• Further Reading

Blau, Peter M. *Inequality and Heterogeneity.* New York: The Free Press, 1977. A fairly technical statement on the importance of size, numbers, and human differentiation by one of the leading proponents of structural sociology. See also Blau and Merton, eds. *Continuities in Structural Inquiry.* Beverly Hills: Sage Publications, 1981.

Bryjak, George J. and Michael P. Soroka. *Sociology: The Biological Factor.* Palo Alto, CA: Peek Publications, 1985. A good introduction to the biological component in sociology, with special attention to social problems of crime and war.

Homans, George C. *Social Behavior: Its Elementary Forms.* New York: Harcourt Brace Jovanovich, 1974. A theoretical monograph using secondary data from small-group experiments and field research studies to develop and illustrate the basic exchange principles of face-to-face interaction that generate enduring social structures.

Rubington, Earl and Martin S. Weinberg. *The Study of Social Problems: Five Perspectives.* New York: Oxford University Press, 1971. Examines five different perspectives on social problems: those of symbolic interaction (labeling), deviance, value conflict, social disorganization, and social pathology. This book remains a fine introduction to basic theoretical perspectives used to understand social problems.

Skolnick, Jerome H. and Elliott Currie, eds. *Crisis in American Institutions.* Boston: Little, Brown, 1985. A fascinating and captivating collection of satirical and journalistic essays in the conflict theory tradition detailing in purple prose how the system, power, and those with privilege dump on the little guys.

Social Problems. The official journal of the Society for the Study of Social Problems (ISSN 0037-7791). Contains useful theoretical and empirical articles on various aspects of specific social problems. Published five times each year. Most recent business address is Journals Department, University of California Press, 2120 Berkeley Way, Berkeley, California 94720.

Spector, Malcolm and John I. Kitsuse. *Constructing Social Problems.* Menlo Park, CA: The Benjamin/Cummings Co., 1977 (Reprinted, 1987). A truly thoughtful original work seeking to establish a sociology of social problems on the foundations of symbolic interactionism. Social problems are seen as products of claims-making activities about putative conditions. You may have to get this book from your library, not the bookstore. Cf. Joseph W. Schneider, "Social Problems Theory: The Constructionist View." In Ralph H. Turner, ed. *Annual Review of Sociology, Volume II.* Palo Alto: Annual Reviews, Inc., 1985:209–230.

C·H·A·P·T·E·R

2

Theoretical Perspectives on Social Problems

A general understanding of theoretical perspectives is required before we can hope to resolve social problems. The exchange, structural, and sociobiological-biological approaches are relatively recent theoretical perspectives and usually have not been applied to the study of social problems. The more common traditional theoretical perspectives on social problems are conflict theory, functional analysis, symbolic interactionism and labeling, and deviance theories.

The primary claim of the exchange perspective is that social problems tend to arise out of actual human exchanges that are not rewarding, not valuable, nor consistent with social expectations, and that tend to generate social imbalance and social inequality. Once inequality and heterogeneity are present, they have profound implications for social interaction. Many social problems are purely structural in that they result from differences in size, number, and proximity of groups, rather than from the values or culture of groups. A reformulated definition of social problems based on structural and exchange theoretical perspectives is offered.

Conflict theorists believe that everyone in a society pursues their own best line of advantage according to their resources. Social problems arise when small groups of elites corner the scarce resources of society and ensure that their own interests will be realized, often at the expense of the interests of minority groups. The symbolic interactionist perspective sees social meanings as emerging in active processes of interpretation. Social problems can result simply from defining certain conditions or labeling certain behaviors problematic. The functionalist perspective holds that when social needs are met, that society tends toward equilibrium and is relatively problem-free. However, unintended and unanticipated consequences, or latent dysfunctions, of social patterns can disrupt the integration and equilibrium of society, giving rise to social problems.

Our theoretical perspectives are tremendously important for understanding social problems. Theoretical perspectives play a major part in how we see the world. Our definitions of social problems clearly allow for differing perceptions of what is threatening to or problematic for society. But beyond the perception of threat is the issue of what social conditions or patterns of behavior even get attended to. Obviously, we cannot be concerned about everything all the time. Whatever else it is, a theory is a way of seeing the world. Perhaps more importantly, every way of seeing is also a way of *not* seeing. Kenneth Burke (1935) once commented on the irony of the "trained incapacity" of chickens who were called to slaughter by the same bell that had called them to be fed in the past. John Dewey claimed that sometimes our commitment to a particular occupation's skills and values can be so great as to make us almost "psychotic" to other work styles or views (1922). Sociologist Pitirim Sorokin once wrote that water is probably the last thing a fish notices.

Often our theoretical perspectives are influenced by our position in society. Alas, few sociologists are wealthy or powerful people. Thus, in a sense many of the social reforms we advocate cost us personally very little. An interesting historical note is the close tie of sociology with Judeo-Christian religion. A surprisingly large number of early American sociologists, like Talcott Parsons, were sons of Protestant ministers. Emile Durkheim himself studied to be a rabbi before founding French sociology. Early American sociology at the University of Chicago was largely a response to a multitude of practical urban problems in the city of Chicago. Given this background it is not surprising that a large segment of American sociology and American sociologists are dedicated to social reform and social welfare.

To illustrate how one's theoretical perspective can color both social facts and whether they are regarded as problematic, consider tax laws in the United States (Brandon, Rowe, and Stanton, 1982). The fact is that the very wealthy pay taxes at about the rate as that imposed on people far less well off.[1] Before 1987 federal income tax should have amounted to 14 percent of the first $500 earned, to 70 percent on income over $100,000 a year (these rates were changed in 1986). Yet the "effective" (actual) rate of taxes on those making $100,000 to $500,000 a year was about 25 percent, after deductions and tax loopholes (Brandon et al., 1982). Starting in 1987 those making over $90,000 a year paid taxes at a rate of 38.5 percent. Eventually there will be just two

PANEL 2.1

What Are Sociological Theories?

Most of us think of theorizing as quite divorced from the business of gathering facts. It seems to require an abstractness of thought remote from the practical activity of empirical research. But theory building is not a separate activity within sociology. Without theory, the empirical researcher would find it impossible to decide what to observe, how to observe it, or what to make of the observations. . . .

A statement is not a theory unless it offers an explanation of facts. A theory must specify the conditions under which some things happen rather than others. There are many statements in sociology that look like theories but fail to qualify because they offer no explanation. Some are empirical generalizations, merely summarizing existing knowledge. The statement "members of higher income groups belong to more social clubs" is an empirical generalization because it is derived from existing knowledge rather than from a general law or principle. The more abstract principle could do what an empirical generalization cannot do. It could predict that the poor (who have few resources) would join fewer social clubs. The theory, unlike the empirical generalization, enables us to imagine new facts.

Source: John Wilson, *Social Theory,* 1983:1–2. Reprinted by permission of Prentice-Hall, Inc., Englewood Cliffs, NJ.

tax rates—15 and 28 percent (and fewer deductions). However, the suspicion is that the wealthy will still not pay a fair share of taxes on their income. With U.S. social security taxes all income above a certain amount ($42,000 in 1986) is completely tax free. Thus, some people pay social security tax on all of their salary income, while others pay social security tax on only a small fraction of their income.

Depending on your theoretical perspective these same "facts" may be seen as problematic or nonproblematic. Many people tend to see all differential advantages of wealth, power, prestige, and property as bad, evil, unfair, and oppressive of various minorities. Thus, social reforms are called for to resolve this social problem. On the other hand, those who have great wealth, power, and prestige may see the same facts as proof of the natural superiority of wealthy elites (a kind of social Darwinism in which only the economically fit survive and prosper; see Gilder, 1981), as stimulating the national economy by providing incentives and necessary profit margins for big businesses, or as just rewards for rugged individual entrepreneurs and just punishment for less meritorious ordinary citizens who just want to "get by and get along." In other words, the tax breaks for the wealthy and powerful are not viewed as a social problem. This group may even contest the purported "facts" of taxation. After all, do the wealthy not have other risks, do they not contribute part of their profits to charitable organizations, do they not provide jobs, do they not run the risk of business failure, do they not need funds for economic development and growth? Whatever side you take in this spirited debate, the key point is that your theoretical perspective does a lot to determine what is or is not counted as a social problem. Given the changes in federal tax law after 1986, obviously many people felt that the wealthy should not have so many tax "loophole" advantages.

• The Uses of Theory in Social Problems

Of course, the place to begin is with some kind of understanding about what theory is. What follows is somewhat abstract. Stick with it; it is important material. In ordinary language theory is usually distinguished from practice. Thus, one basic meaning of theory is to contemplate or think about something as opposed to doing something.[2] If one's contemplation involves a systematic statement of principles, then it is proper to speak of a theory rather than a hypothesis. Much of what passes for theory in social science is no more than predicted hypothetical relationships sometimes encompassing only two variables. Sociologists like C. Wright Mills, in his classical book *The Sociological Imagination* (1959; cf. Horowitz, 1983), have been correctly critical of calling such hypotheses theory. Mills refers to hypothesis testing as "the statistical ritual," implying that mechanical research procedures are being substituted for imaginative creative thinking. For the most part he is right. Many sociologists are not taught to think broadly about their subjects, but rather to apply "cookbook" statistical techniques to isolated propositions derived all too often from data the sociologists themselves have not even collected (the euphemism for this procedure is "secondary analysis").

For our purposes it will be useful to differentiate among what we shall call metatheory, deductive or axiomatic theory, embryonic theory, and statistical explanation. Metatheories are orienting propositions—broad variables, concepts, typologies, or perspectives—that could be constructed into theories. As such, metatheories sensitize the reader to relevant conceptual groupings. However, metatheories in and of themselves do not explain anything. Consider this statement made by Karl Marx and F. Engels (1848): "Accumulation of wealth at one end of the pole is, therefore, at the same time accumulation of agony, toil, slavery, ignorance, brutality, mental degradation, at the opposite pole." Such metatheoretical propositions are not readily testable or systematic. This is not to argue that conflict sociology need be metatheoretical. For example, Randall Collins has attempted to construct an explicit theory of social stratification in which conflict forms the cornerstone (1975). The main point here is that theories of social problems should not stop with metatheory.

Traditionally, the strictest concept of theory has been reserved for a set of laws and definitions that are deductively or logically interrelated. For example, there is the model Werkmeister offers for constructing systematic deductive theory (1959; cf. Freese, 1980). Werkmeister's connotation of theory is sometimes referred to as axiomatic theory.[3] Euclidean geometry is constructed on this model. In sociology the work of George Homans (1974), Peter Blau (1977, 1981), and Randall Collins (1975), and others closely approximates deductive theory.[4] All theorems need not be empirical, but to falsify theories, at least some theorems must be empirical. Obviously, theories can be valid or logically consistent without being true.[5] Although more have been fielded lately, we do not see many axiomatic theories in the behavioral sciences or the study of social problems because it is rare that laws of human behavior are discovered. However, if one is willing to accept lawlike propositions as axioms, then we can at least sketch out explanations that approach deductive theories—"embryonic theories," as Hempel has tagged them (cf. Maris, 1970, 1971, 1981:Ch. 11).

We are primarily concerned with taking the first step in formulating theories of social problems patterned after Werkmeister's conception of explanation (See Figure 2.1 and Emerson, 1972:Chs. 3 and 4; Chadwick-Jones, 1976:218 ff.). However, given the magnitude of that undertaking, the infancy of any science of social problems, and the introductory nature of this text, we will settle for Hempel's embryonic theories (1959), or what Clarence Schrag has similarly named explanation sketches (1967). The main difference between explanation sketches and systematic deductive theory is that the first are less abstract, formal, and comprehensive. In Schrag's words, explanation sketches "aim primarily at organizing selected research findings and suggesting further avenues of inquiry" (Schrag, 1967:244). To construct a partial theoretical sketch we must list major research results (confirmed hypotheses), consider these research results as theorem candidates, construct a few very general propositions (axioms or postulates) and definitions of key terms, and suggest how the major research of theorems might be derived logically from the axioms and definitions of key terms (cf. Turner, 1986:Chs. 11 and 20).

For our purposes a final meaning of *explanation* is that of statistical explanation (see Chapter 3). Statistical explanations of data usually are not theories. Rather, they allow one to test theories. For example, multivariate analyses (procedures for systematically examining the effects of many independent variables on a dependent variable) allow the researcher to see whether a posited relationship actually exists at a statistically significant level while controlling for the influences of other variables. In short, statistics help us sharpen, refine, and specify a theory.

It follows from this brief consideration of types of theory that we shall try to be as systematic and formal as we reasonably can be in theorizing about social problems. At the same time we want to avoid being mechanical and unimaginative or losing you by employing ideas that are too advanced. Theories of social problems that hope to be useful in the sense of being predictive must take some pains to make clear assumptions and definitions, to assert some truly general and imaginative propositions from which particular empirical regularities can be deduced, to get the facts right, to be sensitive to measurement problems and sources of error, and to relate specific research results to general principles of human behavior.

Since social problems are seen by many to threaten basic values or to thwart common social expectations (i.e., norms), their discussion usually generates a great deal of emotion. Under such adverse affectual conditions it is hard for one to be reasonable. Another way of saying the same thing is that it is difficult to be "theoretical" about most social problems in the sense of dispassionately stating assumptions, making clear definitions, and determining if observed patterns (more precisely, propositions relating to observed patterns) can be logically inferred from assumptions and definitions.

The examination of social problems, especially in the news media or by people "on the street," can become clouded by such deep-running feelings. It follows that genuine understanding tends to be missing for most social problems. It would take only a moment to convince yourself of this. For example, the incest taboo is virtually universal. The very thought of sexual relations with one's own children is repugnant to most people. Yet this strong affect makes it difficult to think impartially about incest. Have you ever wondered why incest is so strongly tabooed? For one thing mother-son or father-daughter sexual relationships tend to disrupt the organization of the family as an institution. Almost no mothers or fathers could compete physically or sexually with their adolescent daughters or sons. One result of even entertaining such competition could be familial anarchy with attendant problems of role and status confusion and failure to integrate and link outside families together through marriage. Of course, there are many other problems related to incest that we have not even mentioned.[6]

Like affect, basic values can also be "atheoretical" in that one's assumptions can hinder being able to see facts clearly and objectively. The recent debate of the creationists and the evolutionists over the origin of mankind and which version to teach in schools is a good case in point (Asimov, 1982). Grossly oversimplifying, if man was created in God's image, then it is difficult to accept the premise that we evolved from apes.[7] In listening to such debates over human origins it becomes apparent that theological versus natural science value differences almost preclude any theoretical consensus. Since basic assumptions of religion and natural science are so general, the theories constructed from them cannot be falsified. The real differences are in the working assumptions or basic values of those disagreeing.

Of course, special interests can also cloud understanding and resolving of social problems. Ask yourself whether you would be more likely to believe studies of the relationship of health and cigarette smoking done by the Philip Morris tobacco company or the United States Surgeon General's office. In a celebrated case the Ford Motor Company decided that the fact that the gas tanks on their Pinto automobiles could burst into flames upon a rear-end collision of over five miles per hour was not a problem (Dowie, 1985). The costs of repairing the gas tanks was more ($137 million) than the legal costs for settling fire damages ($49.5 million). Incidentally, Ford figured in 1972 that a human life was worth $200,000. (See Chapter 10 for a more detailed discussion.)

Finally, many studies of social problems are atheoretical in that they are

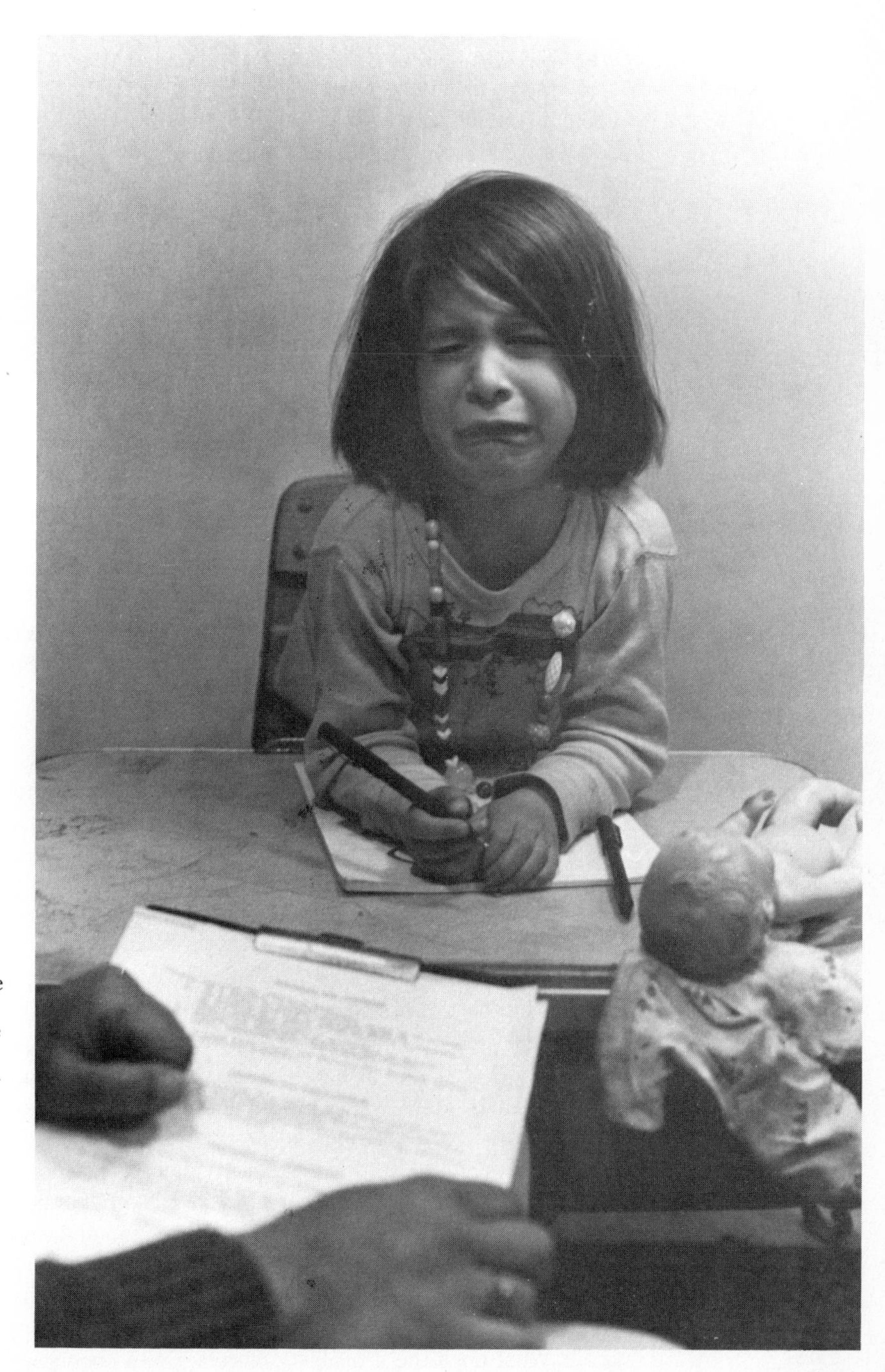

It is difficult to formulate clear unbiased theories of social problems, since many social behaviors arouse deep-seated feelings or threaten basic social values. The strong affect surrounding incest makes it difficult to consider this problem impartially. Here a young girl is interviewed by a psychologist about parental sexual abuse. (Michael Weisbrot/Stock, Boston)

naively epidemiological. It is not enough to simply report rates of the phenomena being examined. Descriptive statistics on the level of percentage differences or rate comparisons really do not help very much. For example, it is common to discuss race relations by saying things like "In 1985 the black unemployment rate was 15.6 percent versus a white rate of 6.6," or "In between 1960 and 1984 the median income of black families remained at 55 percent of white median family income," and so on. The important theoretical issues of why these differences exist or how they relate to other factors or how they derive from some general propositions of social behavior are usually never explained. Even assuming that such facts are stated subtly and carefully, they themselves call for explanation.

Another use of theory is to focus our thinking about social problems and to integrate seemingly disparate patterns of human behavior. How well our theories of social problems focus and integrate patterns of human behavior or social conditions depends in part on the level of generality of the theories. We have seen already that what is called theory ranges from low-level hypotheses about two variables to extremely abstract formal theories about all human behavior or society in general. As a rule most social problems theories have been either special theories for special problems or have had nothing to say about what we call nonproblematic society.

This is understandable in an age of specialization where precise predictions about limited (especially pathological) events are emphasized. Imagine that you had a ruptured appendix. Would you turn to a medical philosopher practicing holistic healing or a surgeon who did "nothing" but appendectomies every morning? The answer is obvious. It is also misleading. To strive for general theories of social problems does not preclude technical resolution of very limited issues. Getting back to our hot appendix example, perhaps a better long-term resolution of most intestinal disorders would include changing social conditions that induce stress, promote infection, or poor diets. That is, primary prevention may be a better answer. Of course, we would still need surgeons and technicians for acute disorders.

Two of the main reasons we do not have general theories of social problems is that arbitrary professional boundaries have discouraged interdisciplinary work and special social problems are thought to require ad hoc, after-the-fact, usually technical resolutions. If someone kills another person, usually only police, prison officials, and lawyers are involved. The resolution is usually to arrest, try, and convict the offender, incarcerate him or her, and in some rare cases to execute the murderer. The general conditions promoting murder go virtually unexamined or are even unknown. Why are other types of professionals not involved? Where are the biologists, chemists, philosophers, psychologists, sociologists, engineers, and so on when murder is committed? What about the role of poverty, deprivation, and distributive injustice (to be discussed below) in murder? Why is violence portrayed positively in the media or even portrayed at all? What does the availability of guns do to encourage murder? What proportions of homicides are committed under the influence of alcohol or drugs? How does homicide relate to mental disorder, suicide, family background, religion, economic deprivation, race, education, and so forth? Without answers to some of these questions (and others) one suspects that very little change in current patterns of violence will be seen.

Our statements of exchange and structural theories of social problems will try to be general and modestly systematic, not an unintegrated conglomerate of ad hoc hypotheses about special problems of mental illness, violence, environment, gender roles, minority group relations, aging, and so on. Although based in empirical reality as best we can determine it and emphasizing objective conditions, our theory is still somewhat biased. That is, we will emphasize exchange, structural, and biological theories. However, these theories are clearly not the only general theories. Indeed we shall insist on including several complementary alternative theoretical perspectives of social problems in the next sections of this chapter and use them generously to explain substantive social problems later on.

Part of the usefulness of our general theories requires that we purposely overstate or exaggerate them somewhat. Robert Bierstedt referred to such exaggeration as theoretical bias (1974:319–320). We do not wish to be misunderstood here. We are concerned that most social problems theories are not very broadly conceived and tend to stop with rather tentative confirmation of low-level hypotheses. In emphasizing general theories of human exchange, social structure and biology-sociobiology, we are well aware that we have theoretical biases just as much as conflict theory, symbolic interaction or labeling theory, functional analysis, or deviance perspectives do. Our theoretical perspectives need to be tempered and supplemented by these other complementary theoretical perspectives (that is by conflict theory, symbolic interactionism, and functionalism).

A major use of the more formal statement of theoretical perspectives is that it allows for falsification of the perspectives.[8] Using a model for construction of formal theories like that depicted in Werkmeister (See Figure 2.1) enables one to predict what should follow from the various theories' definitions and assumptions. If at least some of the theorems or inferences of theories of social problems have empirical referents, and if the theorems are inconsistent with empirical reality, this may suggest that our theory is not very useful (of course, we hope this will not be the case); that it fails to account for the "facts." This is a tremendous advantage over less systematic theories in which one is hard-pressed to know what evidence would disconfirm the theory.[9] We contend that one should be as empirical as possible in attempting to construct theories of social problems. Questions of data, measurement, and methods are part and parcel of theory. One way data can enter our theories is that theorems can be tested. If a compendium of research results on important social problems exists, then, if properly stated, these results should be derivable from our theories.

Finally, theoretical perspectives have a critical relationship with problem solving. One's theories indicate scope, what the relevant variables are, and what can be ignored. For example, if schizophrenia turns out to be primarily genetically or biochemically determined, then a purely social theory of mental

FIGURE 2.1 A Model for Constructing Formal Theory

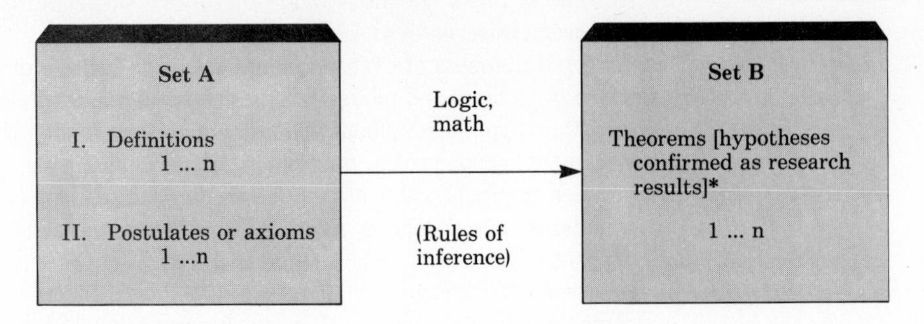

*Parenthetical elaboration is ours.

*Parenthetical elaboration is ours.

Source: W. H. Werkmeister, "Theory Construction and the Problem of Objectivity," 1959. Copyright © 1959 by W. H. Werkmeister. Reprinted by permission of Harper & Row, Publishers, Inc.; cf., Lee Freese, "Formal Theorizing," 1980.

illness (such as labeling theory) will largely miss the mark. Or again, if social problems emerge from the routine workings of normal society, then resolving only social pathology does not solve the problems. More systematic theories of all social conditions suggest not only how society works but also how it can go wrong and what adjustments are required to correct social problems.

As a case in point, exchange theory includes the concept of balance (Heider, 1967; Chadwick-Jones, 1976:Ch. 11). An interpersonal theory of balance claims that most enduring social configurations are balanced. A balanced situation is one in which relations among entities fit together harmoniously. Imbalanced social sets are assumed to be stressful; costs tend to exceed rewards. Following the lead of balance theory we might postulate that all problematic social conditions or human behaviors tend to be imbalanced. We then could attempt to draw graphs of specific problematic social conditions or human behaviors—say, those related to racial or sexual relations. If such a graph could be produced, then one should be able to see where and how balance might be achieved and, presumably, how the social problem would be resolved. Also, exchange theory would suggest that social problems tend to be alleviated by encouraging those groups or individuals with conflicts or negative attitudes toward one another to interact. Under most conditions continued social interaction leads to increased liking. For example, one might conceive of busing to achieve integration as grounded in this assumption.

Major Theoretical Perspectives on Social Problems

How have social scientists writing about social problems sought to conceptualize and explain "general patterns of human behavior of social conditions"? Table

2.1 attempts to summarize the main theoretical perspectives on social problems.[10] We find the primary theories of social problems to be exchange, structuralism, conflict, symbolic interaction and labeling, functionalism, deviance, and biology (including sociobiology).[11] Of course, it would be easy to quibble with this classification, since the boundaries among sociological theories overlap somewhat. For example, structuralism used to be considered part of functionalism, rather than an independent theory or part of exchange theory (Wilson, 1983:73ff.; Poloma, 1979:Ch. 2). Deviance theory also overlaps with functionalism (Merton, 1957; Higgins and Butler, 1982:163–165). Other social problems texts list theories of "social pathology," "social disorganization," or "value conflict" (Julian and Kornblum, 1986). Most of these theories of other social problems textbooks are subsumed under one or more of our seven categories. Many social problems texts do not refer to biology or sociobiology at all. In the pages that follow we will elaborate the basic assumptions, sources of social problems, problem resolutions, and primary weaknesses of each of the seven major theoretical perspectives contained in Table 2.1. Since the exchange and structural perspectives have not been applied much to social problems before and are of some special interest to us, we will elaborate their assumptions a little more than those of the other theoretical perspectives. This section will be more dry than the chapters that follow, but bear with us. It will be important to our later arguments and to your understanding of social problems.

• The Exchange Perspective

The exchange theoretical perspective has several advantages over other perspectives on social problems. To begin with, it is a theory of how all social structure is built up and maintained, not merely a special theory of problematic behaviors or conditions. Second, the exchange perspective emphasizes actual face-to-face interaction and the principles governing it. This will allow us to consider the social behavior of real people, rather than merely abstract patterns or formal organization of society. As such, our approach should have a chance of being interesting and attention holding. Of course, there are also dangers here of our being too folksy, being misled by common sense, or of failing to generalize from particulars.

The exchange perspective assumes that enduring social structures (sometimes referred to as institutions) result from actual exchanges in relatively small groups (the so-called subinstitutional level—see Chapter 10) that are rewarding and valuable. Stable social structures tend to be those that are balanced and harmonious. There is little stress in them. In general, interaction patterns persist if the rewards of individuals participating exceed their costs. Another way of putting it is that in recurring patterns of social behavior, all parties tend to be profiting. The more people interact with one another, unless that interaction is coercive or across statuses, the more similar they tend to become and the more they tend to express mutual sentiments of liking. Let us go into a little more detail about the assumptions of the exchange perspective.

Of all the random social groups that are possible, most do not exist at all or are extremely transitory. Those social structures that do persist are surprisingly few, routine, and predictable. According to sociologist George Homans (1974:Ch. 2), five general statements or propositions determine which social conditions, patterns of human behavior, or social configurations will develop into "enduring social structures" and which will become problematic (not all social problems are transitory). Normal society (including norms, roles, and institutions) is shaped by differential reward, value, satiation-deprivation, expectations related to rewards, and a few derived concepts (such as balance).

The Success Proposition Homan's first proposition concerns why some human acts get repeated and others do not (see Panel 2.2). The first proposition implies that if someone is doing a voluntary (nonreflex) act and receives something like food, money, praise, sexual gratification, or the like for it, then the person will (other things being equal) be likely to repeat that act. Moreover, the probability that a particular act will be repeated varies directly with the frequency of its being rewarded (e.g., the more an action is rewarded, the more likely it will be repeated). These repeated acts in society give rise to enduring social structures, which, after all, is what we are primarily interested in.

TABLE 2.1 Major Theoretical Perspectives on Social Problems

	Assumptions about Society	**Sources of Social Problems**	**Resolutions to Social Problems**	**Weaknesses of Viewpoint**
Exchange	Enduring social structures result from actual exchanges that are rewarding and valuable. Stable social structures are balanced and harmonious.	Institutional patterns cease to be subinstitutionally meaningful, rewarding, valuable. Actual social exchanges are unprofitable or imbalanced.	Keep people interacting with one another. Reduce imbalanced sets.	Psychological reductionism may not be able to account for institutional patterns well.
Structuralism	Population distributions are central, as are the size and proximity of groups.	Differential inequality, heterogeneity, and size of groups.	Increase population's heterogeneity, proximity, and penetrating differentiation.	More concerned with "enduring" social structure than with principles of social deviance or change.
Conflict	Everyone pursues their best line of advantage according to their values and resources. Society is in tension and conflict. Violence is always a potential resource for resolving conflicts.	Small groups of elites corner the scarce resources of society and ensure that their own interests will be realized. Inequality and injustice can lead to protest, even revolution by the disenfranchised.	Oppressed groups unite with a few dissenting elites in social movements to overthrow ruling elites. Revolutions may be required. Redistribute wealth, power, and prestige in society.	Tends to reduce all social issues to economics and the narrow political world view of Marx. Ignores real biological differences of people. Has naive view of how stratification emerges.

TABLE 2.1 *(concluded)*

	Assumptions about Society	Sources of Social Problems	Resolutions to Social Problems	Weaknesses of Viewpoint
Symbolic Interaction and Labeling	Social order turns on people having shared meanings. Social meanings emerge in active processes of interpretation. Subjective conditions are basic.	Defining certain conditions or labeling certain behaviors problematic. Fads, fashions, and "moral entrepreneurs" determine what is considered a problem. Public reaction to initial deviation can cause real problems.	Change definitions of problematic conditions or behaviors. Beware of public reactions. Reduce profits in labeling some behaviors as problematic.	Underestimates role of objective conditions in shaping social problems. Not all interaction is symbolic. Most behavior is governed by routines.
Functionalism	When social needs are met society tends toward equilibrium. Various parts of the social system must be integrated in order for whole of society to be stable.	Unintended and unanticipated consequences ("latent dysfunctions") of social patterns disrupt the integration and equilibrium of society. Social needs not being met by social institutions.	Must concentrate on bringing the entire social system into equilibrium by reducing dysfunctional consequences. Be aware of all consequences of social patterns.	What are the "needs" of society? Tends to be too conservative a view of society. Not really a special theory of society.
Deviance	Social norms produce conformity and social order. Institutional means for realizing social expectations must be commensurate with social goals.	Nonconformity to norms based in learning deviant behavior or in disenchantment from aspiring to expectations or norms that are in fact socially blocked. Sometimes norms themselves are in conflict.	Reduce opportunities for deviant socialization. State norms clearly and consistently. Be certain norms are learned. Sanction violators and reward conformers.	Many social problems do not involve deviant behavior at all. Norms never govern all behaviors.
Biology/Sociobiology	Individuals act to maximize survival of their gene pool. Basic biological differences are often reflected in and determining of social organization.	Questions arise about who is "fit" to survive. Criminal types are genetically given. Chemical imbalances or physical differences in population give rise to social behaviors, aggression.	Minimize biological faults. Incarcerate or eliminate those who are considered undesirable. Fund research for natural sciences.	Cannot account for altruism. Biological defects have no clear relation to social problems. Not clear that there is a criminal type. Used to argue for genocide and racism.

Suppose you are walking across campus on a bright sunny day and you are inspired to say to an attractive man, "How are you, isn't it a great day!" Assume further (this is my story, I can assume what I want) that he replies something like, "What a pleasant person, you want to go out to dinner tonight?" If this happens to you repeatedly, you might soon become a very friendly person. Conversely, if every young man you said, "Hi, how are you," to spits in your face, before long you'd mind your own business.

The Stimulus Proposition The second proposition of the exchange perspective is very similar to the first in that it refers to past successes where acts have been rewarded. If some situation is similar to a past situation in

Harvard sociologist George C. Homans applied the psychology of B. F. Skinner and classical economics to the study of social behavior. Homans's social exchange theory emphasizes actual face-to-face interaction in small groups and the principles governing it. (Harvard University News Office)

which action was rewarded, then that similar situation can stimulate one to act. This claim is pretty straightforward. We will not bother to illustrate it.

The Value Proposition Having claimed in the first proposition that activity is related to reward, it is now necessary to qualify the degree of reward. Value is the degree of reward. Positive values are referred to as rewards and negative values as punishments. There are two main classes of rewards, those that are intrinsic and those that allow one to avoid punishment. In general, exchange theorists maintain that punishment is an inefficient means of getting a person to act, since punishment is likely to produce anger.

Recently a student athlete came into one of my classes just ten minutes

PANEL 2.2

Five Basic Propositions of the Exchange Theoretical Perspective

The Success Proposition
A1.* For all actions taken by persons, the more often a particular action of a person is rewarded, the more likely the person is to perform that action (1974:16).

The Stimulus Proposition
A2. If in the past the occurrence of a particular stimulus, or set of stimuli, has been the occasion on which a person's action has been rewarded, then the more similar the present stimuli are to the past ones, the more likely the person is to perform the action, or some similar action, now (1974:22–23).

The Value Proposition
A3. The more valuable to a person is the result of his/her action, the more likely s/he is to perform the action (1974:15).

The Deprivation-Satiation Proposition
A4. The more often in the recent past a person has received a particular reward, the less valuable any further unit of that reward becomes for him/her (1974:29).

The Aggression-Approval Propositions
A5. *a.* When a person's action does not receive the reward s/he expected, or receives punishment s/he did not expect, s/he will be angry; s/he becomes more likely to perform aggressive behavior, and the results of such behavior become more valuable to him/her (1974:37).
A5. *b.* When a person's action receives the reward s/he expected, especially a greater reward than s/he expected, or does not receive punishment s/he expected, s/he will be pleased; s/he becomes more likely to perform approving behavior, and the results of such behavior become more valuable to him/her (1974:39).

*"A" stands for axiom.
Source: From *Social Behavior: Its Elementary Forms* by George C. Homans, copyright © 1974 by Harcourt Brace Jovanovich, Inc. Reprinted by permission of the publisher.

before class was over, had to borrow a pencil and paper, and then took no notes. One might reasonably conclude that getting good grades or even an education was not as valuable to some good athletes. After all they can probably get much of what they want from life on their athletic skills alone.

Notice that the value proposition sidesteps the issue of what is valuable. All it says is that if some result of acting is valuable, then one is more likely to act. We still have to determine what is valuable to particular individuals or groups. Clearly punishment could be rewarding to a masochist, but not to most other people. Some critics have also argued that the value proposition is a tautology (i.e., is circular), since the only measure of value is the frequency with which activity is performed. That is, the critics claim there is no independent measure of value.

Since values can be learned, they also tend to be varied. If all values were genetically or biologically determined, then the problem of what is valuable would be much simpler. Values would be broadly determined by food, sex, shelter, sleep, and the like, and would be widely shared. In fact men and women find some of the damnest things valuable—although this point should not be exaggerated. Many social values are highly generalized. Money and social approval are rewarding to large numbers of people and have the interesting trait of not being easily satiating. No matter how much money or esteem you have, you can always use more. The same is not true for rewards like food or sex (I realize you may not believe this).

The Deprivation-Satiation Proposition Rewards are not always effective in producing action. The fourth general proposition of the exchange perspective specifies the conditions under which rewards may become ineffective. Rewards satiate differentially. Specific (or intrinsic) rewards satiate a man or a woman relatively sooner than generalized reinforcers. Included here would be rewards like food, sex, sleep, and the like. Clearly, if you are very hungry or thirsty (short of starving), you will be likely to eat and drink, given an opportunity. Moreover, under the condition of being extremely hungry, you are more likely to eat than, say, make love (trust me). This is so even if you have been deprived of sex for as long as you have been deprived of food. However, once you have eaten your fill, sex may then become a powerful reward. One sated reward renders other alternative rewards relatively more potent. All this implies a hierarchy of rewards, although the exchange perspective never makes this explicit.[12] Perhaps this is because exchange theorists want to avoid the bugaboo of claiming there are basic social needs.[13]

The Aggression-Approval Propositions Finally, any theory about actual human behavior should reflect that people feel as well as think. Much of routine face-to-face behavior is emotional. Thus, the exchange perspective speaks of sentiments as well as of activities (Homans, 1962). Anger and aggression can both have profound social consequences. One of the quickest ways to get removed from free society (hospitalized, imprisoned, and so on) is to be harmful to yourself or others. Clearly, any social problems book is going to have to take aggressive behavior very seriously, if for no other reason than the fact that patterned aggressive behavior is seen by most commentators as posing a threat to society. You only need think of war, homicide, terrorism, rape, suicide, and the like to convince yourself of this.

Imagine that you are getting an A in this course (think big) and that you study hard and consistently for the final exam, only to receive a final grade of C. Very likely you are going to be very angry and demand to see your final exam. It is hard to believe that your performance could have fallen that much. You thought you deserved a better grade, you had every reason to expect a better grade.

Note that expectations are a crucial factor in both aggression and approval. As we shall see later, frustrated expectations and perceived distributive injustice—not actual deprivation of rewards (i.e., proposition A5 in Panel 2.2) are related to the development of many social problems. For example, black median income has risen considerably in the last several years, but so have black expectations for a middle-class lifestyle. This accounts (in part) for why inner-city riots occurred while black lifestyles were actually improving. Of course, the discrepancy between black and white average incomes did not help either. How we actually use these five general propositions to explain, predict, and control problematic social behaviors and conditions will only become apparent as we actually discuss particular social problems.

The Concept of Balance The five general propositions of exchange theory just elaborated refer to the principles of singular exchanges in interpersonal situations. Balance theory (Heider, 1967; Chadwick-Jones, 1976:264ff.) is concerned with multiple, not singular, exchanges. To oversimplify, balance theory asks what happens when the interpersonal exchange of one person and another person is generalized from selves to issues, to other people, or to other exchanges. As Homans claims, "Balance theory is concerned with the mutual influence of *two or more different kinds* (italics ours) of exchange on the relationships between persons" (1974:64). Do these new exchanges reinforce or strain old relationships?

If multiple exchanges tend to reinforce singular exchanges, then the prior relationship tends to be stabilized or balanced. Balanced multiple exchanges are likely to be harmonious, consistent, without tension or conflict. Partly because of these traits, balanced multiple exchanges tend to get repeated; they are "social-structure generating." On the other hand, if multiple exchanges are predominantly imbalanced, then interaction may cease and relationships tend to be discontinued or otherwise changed. Repeated multiple exchanges tend to lead to liking, similarity, and common unit relations among actors.[14] Repeated multiple exchanges tend to generate balanced social structures that in turn tend to become enshrined in norms. In this special case, what is becomes what ought to be. One of the great advantages of the exchange perspective is that it demonstrates one way social norms come into and stay in existence (see Homans, 1974).

The sources of social problems from an exchange perspective viewpoint are that institutional patterns for various reasons cease to be subinstitutionally meaningful, rewarding, or valuable. Sometimes with social change actual social exchanges may become unprofitable or imbalanced. At other times powerful groups or individuals may force unprofitable social exchange arrangements upon subordinates. In general, social problems can arise when large numbers of individuals are investing more into society or into particular social arrangements than they are getting back (distributive injustice). A case in point is that until recently many married couples paid more taxes than if they were simply living together and paying taxes as single persons. That is, from a taxation standpoint, being married was less profitable than being single.

From the exchange perspective many social problems can be resolved simply by keeping people interacting with one another, since interaction under most

"No question about it, Louise—we've been married too long."

conditions promotes liking and similarity. One can imagine that this issue was part of the earlier federal decision to mandate school busing of black students to predominantly white schools and vice versa. Clearly, making social returns more equal to social investments (distributive justice) should help resolve social problems.

The exchange perspective has been criticized for being a form of psychological reductionism that is not able to explain institutional patterns well (Wilson, 1983:32ff.; Heath, 1976). Indeed, in Chapters 10 through 15 we shall find exchange principles less useful in explaining more macro-level, institutional social problems, and we will need to emphasize the conflict, functional, and structural theoretical perspectives more. Another weakness, as we have seen, is that the value proposition may be circular. To say that "people do what is valuable and what is valuable is what people do" seems to beg the question of value. Homans is not particularly concerned with how people come to value certain things or activities and not others. Finally, the exchange perspective has been criticized for being more concerned with enduring social structures than with principles of social deviance or social change. It is accused of being a conservative theory unable to adequately suggest resolutions to social problems.

• The Structuralism Perspective

The structural perspective as presented by Viennese-born sociologist Peter Blau is not especially concerned with how enduring social structures emerge,[15] but rather with what the implications of social structures are for human social interaction once certain structures are given (Blau, 1977; cf. Wilson, 1983:Ch. 4). The assumptions of Blau's version of structural sociology are formal, impersonal, and macrolevel (cf. Turner, 1986:Ch. 12; McPherson and Smith-Lovin, 1986). The focus of structural sociology is on "structures of differentiated positions and their influences on the relations of human beings" (Blau, 1977:4). Whereas the exchange perspective's building blocks or elements were activities, sentiments, and interaction, those of structural sociology are different social positions, the numbers of their incumbents, and the implications of differentiation among positions for social relations. Social structure can be defined as "a multidimensional space of different social positions among which a population is distributed" (Blau, 1977:4). One may say that the exchange perspective is microsociological, while the structural perspective is macrosociological. We shall have more to say about the relationship of the exchange and structural perspectives after we have elaborated structuralism.

Structural sociology has its roots in the seminal writings of Georg Simmel (1858–1918).[16] Simmel was among the first sociologists to argue for the importance of sheer numbers for human interaction. One difference from Blau's structuralism is that Simmel concentrated on formal properties of small groups while Blau is more interested in the consequences of size, proximity, and differentiated positions for entire societies. Many students may also realize that structuralism in sociology has historical ties with the British anthropologists Radcliffe-Brown (1881–1955; 1952) and Levi-Strauss (1908–; 1963) and the functionalist perspective to be discussed later. While both structural-functionalism and Blau's structural sociology are concerned with the objective consequences (functions, if you will) of formal properties of social systems, Blau is determined to extricate himself from issues of system needs, societal survival, and so forth (Spencer, 1904), as well as to detach himself from Parsons' (1951) focus upon the interrelationships of social institutions (Turner, 1986:Ch. 3). Furthermore, while Levi-Strauss contended that structures were only models of empirical social realities, Blau holds that social structure is observable and measurable.[17]

The Importance of Size and Number in the Structural Perspective

Structural theorists tend to assume the importance of size of groups and number of incumbents of social positions for social relations (Blau, 1977:19ff.), usually completely apart from considerations of culture, values, or psychological factors. For example, Simmel noted that all two-person groups (dyads), unlike larger groups, need the death or removal of only one member to dissolve the entire group (Turner, 1986:122–142). Or again, Durkheim (1893:262) argued that as the "volume" and "density" of societies increased, labor is increasingly divided into more and more specialized occupational groups. One main result is that society is integrated on a principle of mutual interdependence or organic solidarity (cf. penetrating differentiation; Blau, 1977:160ff.).[18] Even the exchange perspective contends that as groups get large, dissimilarity and disliking tend to increase and with them the probability of clique formation and hierarchical ranking. Face-to-face interaction is not as prevalent in institutional contexts as it is in small groups (Homans, 1974:Ch. 16).

To illustrate the structuralist's position on the importance of size and number as sources of social problems, let us consider the example of black-white relations in the United States. The relative deprivation of American blacks vis-à-vis American whites has been well documented (see Chapter 6). Most social problems theorists assume that the plight of black minorities results primarily from long-standing oppression and systematic discrimination. While prejudice toward and discrimination against black Americans no doubt are a real part of the problem, it is interesting that structuralists claim to be able to explain black-white relations largely on the basis of reference to size and number alone. There is really little need, they claim, to refer to prejudice (or values for that matter) at all, and discrimination is at most a secondary consideration.[19] A basic claim of the structural perspective is that "the rate of intergroup associations (here across race categories) of the smaller group (blacks) must exceed that of the larger (whites)" (Blau, 1977:21). Most whites do not have black friends, spouses, or whatever because there are fewer blacks with whom to interact—not because whites are prejudiced and discriminate against blacks. If there were no discrimination, then it would be predicted that all blacks would eventually have white friends, but most whites would still not have black friends. Proximity and mobility are also claimed to affect social interaction. Based on proximity in general, in-group associations are more prevalent than out-group associations. Social mobility, on the other hand, promotes intergroup associations.

The Concept of Heterogeneity We have seen that the criteria implicit in social distinctions, like age, race, education, and so on, can be subdivided into nominal *parameters* (Blau's term). *Heterogeneity* refers to nominal differences among groups that are inherently unranked. Included here would be variables like sex, religion, and race, among others. Heterogeneity is concerned with how horizontal differentiation affects social relations and can be defined as "the chance expectation that two randomly chosen persons do not belong to the same group" (Blau, 1977:78). Put positively, heterogeneity is the probability that two randomly chosen individuals belong to different groups.[20]

The structuralism theoretical perspective concentrates on the importance of size and number for social interaction. Racial problems may result from the relatively small number of blacks in the United States available for whites to interact with, not from prejudiced attitudes. (Norman Hurst/Stock, Boston)

Heterogeneity is at a maximum for a given number of groups when the population is evenly divided among them. For example, if a population is split evenly on some variable (say, sex), then heterogeneity is at a maximum. Of course, if there are more than two groups and the population is evenly distributed among them, then heterogeneity is higher. In general, the larger the number of groups, the smaller the proportion of the population that belongs to one or a few groups, the greater the heterogeneity (Blau, 1977:77).

The Concept of Inequality Sometimes we observe problematic general patterns of human behavior that cannot be readily explained by the concept of heterogeneity. For example, the sex ratio of males to females in the United States is roughly equal.[21] We know that if the ratio of males and females in a population is fifty-fifty, then the expected rate of out-group associations (that is, heterogeneity) is also 50 percent. Thus, out-group sexual associations are expected to be much more likely than, say, black-white, or aged-nonaged associations in the United States. We might expect that inequality is more likely than heterogeneity to be at the root of sexual social problems. Unlike heterogeneity, inequality refers to the distribution of people or a status dimension (Blau, 1977:45). You will recall that status refers to differences (vertical differentiation) in the ranks of social positions or persons. Thus, inequality designates social positions varying by graduation, such as power, prestige, income, education, and so forth.

Status differences themselves have profound influences on human interaction or social association. Although we spoke briefly of the concepts of status, class, and stratification in Chapter 1, we have had relatively little to say about the shape of status distributions. Unlike racial or sexual groups, status groupings have no natural boundaries. Whether we posit status divisions in white-collar and blue-collar, middle or lower classes, Warner et al.'s six prestige classes (1949), or whatever is somewhat arbitrary. Structuralists (Blau, 1977:48) tend to assume that status distributions take the shape of a truncated diamond. That is, there are very few elites, a great number of lower-middle classes, and a lot of lower-class occupational groups (but not quite as many as the lower middle class).

Two striking traits of such distributions is that the upper status group tends to be very small and is a great social distance from the lower status group. For example, if we define *elites* as the upper 1 percent of a population's status distribution, then some important consequences for social interaction follow. For one, most people never interact with elites (Blau, 1977:47). This follows from what we said earlier about size and number. Upper-status people have more extensive contacts with lower-status people than vice versa in part because a smaller group always has more extensive out-group associations. They have to. If there are millions of lower-status people and "only" thousands of elites, obviously based on numbers alone most lower-status individuals will have no elites with whom to associate. Any person can have only so many friends and associates. There just are not enough elites to go around, if you will.

Upper-lower status contacts are further limited by social distance. People tend not to interact across great social distances. Lack of proximity has much to do with this. If you routinely do not come into contact with someone, you will never even have the opportunity to associate with them. Furthermore, given the shape of the status distribution, the probability of interacting one status group down is greater than interacting one status group up (Blau, 1977:51)—except for the very lowest status group, of course. The reason for this is obvious. There are fewer people above you with whom to interact.

Structurally, social problems could be resolved by increasing a population's or social group's heterogeneity, proximity, and penetrating differentiation (Blau, 1977). In effect, what this claim amounts to is that many social problems could be reduced simply by increasing our structural interdependency upon one another (cf. Durkheim's concept of organic solidarity, 1893). Like the exchange perspective, structuralism has been criticized for being more concerned with enduring social structures than with principles of social deviance or social change. Unlike exchange theory, structuralism leaves out consideration of people; their values, expectations, and motives. It is better able to describe how social facts or patterns are than how they were produced. Many sociologists are put off by structuralism's increasingly formal, abstract, and mathematical traits (Wilson, 1983:58ff.).

The Relationship of the Exchange and Structural Theoretical Perspectives: The Definition of Social Problems Reformulated Here we need to pause in our review of theoretical perspectives on social problems and ask how the exchange and structural theoretical perspectives are related to each other and how our definition of social problems might be modified to take the exchange and structural perspectives into account. This consideration is not meant to detract from the relevance or importance of the remaining theoretical perspectives. It should be clear that while the exchange and structural perspectives are both axiomatic and quantitative theories and both are concerned with the consequences of social structure for human social interaction, there are also some important differences. For one, structuralism tends to take social structure for granted. It is not very concerned with how social structure is generated. Exchange theory, on the other hand, is explicitly interested in the principles of face-to-face human behavior that result in enduring social structures. For another, the exchange perspective focuses on actual small-group behaviors and conditions (the micro level), while structuralism tends to concentrate upon expected patterns of association in very large groups of people or total societies (the macro level). Finally, the exchange perspective admits values, culture, sentiments or feelings, expectations, and motives as appropriate variables in the theory's propositions, but structuralism tends to emphasize size, number, inequality, and heterogeneity and to conceive of values, sentiments, and so on as irrelevant (epiphenomena) to the theory of human behavior.

Blau summarizes some of these primary differences between the exchange and structural perspectives as follows:

> Microsociological studies of interpersonal relations and small groups focus on the influences of social processes on the emergent differences in and positions, whereas macrosociological studies of established social positions in societies focus on influences the structures of these positions exert on processes of associations. (1977:4)

Given these differences in theoretical perspective it is argued that exchange and structural theories complement one another and that both are required for a complete explanation of social problems (as indeed are the other theoretical perspectives that follow). Actually Blau's early work attempted to integrate the exchange and structural perspectives (1964). The integrated theoretical perspective was aptly dubbed exchange-structuralism (Turner, 1986:Ch. 12). However, in later works (1975, 1977, 1981) Blau largely abandoned exchange-structuralism and concentrated on the structural perspective. Thus, while the exchange and structural perspectives overlap some, we will tend to treat them as if they were two distinct theoretical perspectives.

Of course, now that the exchange and structural perspectives have been elaborated, this elaboration has implications for our definition of social problems. It would be possible to reformulate the definition of social problems given in Chapter 1 in the language of the exchange and structural perspective (or the other five perspectives, for that matter). These reformulations are presented in Table 2.2. The reformulated definitions are an advance because they (1) specify the types of human behavior and social conditions more exactly, (2) help define what is meant by threat to society, (3) focus our attention on social interaction and the consequences of interaction, and (4) begin to indicate how social problems might be resolved or remedied. These reformulated definitions will be incorporated into the organizational plan of this textbook mentioned in Chapter 1. More precisely, we shall examine various aspects of human behavior and social conditions under the substantive chapters' subheading "Stating the Problem." Under the subheading "Analyzing the Problem," we shall routinely examine relevant rewards, values, issues of balance, anger, inequality, heterogeneity, and so forth. It is proper to think of the reformulated definitions

TABLE 2.2 Reformulation of Definition of Social Problems in the Language of the Exchange and Structural Perspectives

<table>
<tr><th>Original Definition</th><th>Exchange Reformulation</th><th>Structural Reformulation</th></tr>
<tr><td>Social problems are created by general patterns of human behavior or social conditions—</td><td>Social problems are created by general patterns of face-to-face human behavior or social conditions—</td><td>Social problems are created by general distributions of the population into differentiated social positions—</td></tr>
<tr><td rowspan="2">that are perceived as threats to society—</td><td>that tend to be unrewarding, not valuable, anger producing (unjust), or imbalanced and tend to result in inequality—</td><td>that tend to display inequality and modest heterogeneity—</td></tr>
<tr><td colspan="2">and, as such, are restrictive of social interaction—*</td></tr>
<tr><td>by significant numbers of the population, powerful groups, or charismatic individuals—</td><td>for significant numbers of the population, powerful groups, or charismatic individuals—</td><td>for significant numbers of the population—</td></tr>
<tr><td rowspan="2">and that could be resolved or remedied.</td><td>and that could be resolved by making human behavior or social conditions more rewarding, changing values, balancing interaction, or distributing rewards more justly—</td><td>and that could be resolved by reducing inequality and increasing penetrating differentiation or extreme heterogeneity—</td></tr>
<tr><td colspan="2">and thus, promoting social interaction.</td></tr>
</table>

*Social interaction and social problems actually have a complex relationship. It can be argued that restricting social interaction sometimes discourages social problems, since conflicts are minimized. Even the exchange perspective acknowledges that coercive social interaction or interaction across broadly disparate social statuses is not conducive to liking, similarity; in short, it does not reduce social problems.

of social problems as elaborations and specifications of the original definition. They are not contradictory with the original definition, nor are they intended to replace it. For general purposes, we shall continue to use the original definition of social problems.

The Conflict Perspective Conflict theorists Marx (1848), Dahrendorf (1959), Coser (1967), Collins (1975), and Skolnick and Currie (1985) all see individuals pursuing their best line of advantage according to their resources compared with those of competitors. Competing interests and differential distribution of wealth, power, and prestige are more real than cooperation. According to Karl Marx, since the capitalists control the means of production (e.g., factories, machinery, property, and so on), the oppressed working social classes really lack the power or resources within the present social order to pursue their own interests effectively. A social revolution, such as the Russian revolution of 1917, is needed to reconstitute society and to make equality and justice possible (not all conflict theorists believe that revolution is needed). In all nonsocialist economies the workers have been oppressed. For example, in capitalist economies the "surplus value" that the workers produce by their labor goes largely into the pockets of the owners of industry. Profits tend not to get redistributed among the workers. Thus, the poor get poorer and more miserable, even though there is industrial and technological development. Given these fundamental inequalities between capitalists and workers, society is always in tension and conflict. Likewise, violence is always a potential resource for resolving social conflicts.[22]

Social problems arise because over time small groups of elites manage to monopolize the scarce resources of society and thereby ensure that their own interests will be realized at the expense of the interests and welfare of the nonelites. All special social problems (such as poverty, mental illness, poor physical health, sexual deviance, discrimination, family problems, environmental issues, and so on) stem from the disenfranchisement of the proletariat (worker) from their deserved share of societal wealth, power, and prestige. Thus, the central social problem is the oppression of nonelites (especially of minorities like women, American blacks, certain ethnic groups, and so on) who lack the resources and power of the elites. This inequality and injustice eventually lead to protest, and even revolution, as the disenfranchised workers attempt to "throw off their shackles."

More specifically, oppressed groups unite with a few dissenting elites in revolutionary movements to overthrow ruling elites and institutional arrangements that serve only the elites' interests. Revolutions of one sort or another are often required to wrest power from rulers. Without revolution, usually no real changes occur. The wealth, power, and prestige in a society must be redistributed. No one is going to give up their privileges or property voluntarily. Usually the elites pass their accumulated advantages on to their own children, even if their offspring are not especially fit or the most deserving.

Critics of conflict theory note that it tends to reduce all social issues to economic conflict and, more precisely, to the narrow politico-economical world views of Karl Marx and the neo-Marxists. Is it true that all struggles are class struggles? Marx tends to treat all differences as social, in his special macroeconomic sense. He ignores real biological differences among people. It could be argued that some people would never be gifted, talented, successful, and so on) even if they had all the social and economic opportunities possible. Some contend that many social differences (not all) emerge from original biological differences in intelligence, strength, beauty, and so forth. Of course, a highly stratified society can discourage the full discovery of talent and promise. For example, in the United States for years now blacks have never ever had the chance for the quality of life many whites consider their birthright, regardless of their talents and skills (Becnel, 1979; Edelman, 1985). It should also be noted that Marx is not particularly interested in the kind of face-to-face exchanges that the exchange perspective concentrates on or in principles of subinstitutional behavior.[23]

The Symbolic Interaction and Labeling Perspective This perspective assumes that subjective conditions are more basic than objective conditions (Spector and Kitsuse, 1977; Wilson, 1983:Ch. 8; Schneider, 1985). Our earlier comments in Chapter 1 on subjective conditions are also relevant here. Social order depends on people having shared meanings (Blumer, 1969). Social meanings emerge in active processes of interpretation of what is happening in a particular interaction situation. As W. I. Thomas (1863–1947) claimed: "If men define situations as real, then they are real in their consequences" (1923:42). Social interaction is symbolic (Mead, 1934); it has special meanings imparted by the unique actors in a particular exchange.

Social problems are constructed by defining certain conditions or labeling certain behaviors (stigmatization, Goffman, 1963) as problematic, sometimes completely apart from the "facts" or objective conditions. Fads, fashions, and "moral entrepreneurs" often determine what is considered a social problem. One remembers Senator Joseph McCarthy's zealous concern with communism in America or H. J. Anslinger's (United States Federal Commissioner of Narcotics in the mid-1930s) seeming obsession with the evils of marijuana usage (Becker, 1953:142–144). As Lemert (1967) has noted, public reaction to initial relatively harmless deviations can sometimes lead to more serious incorrigible social problems (secondary deviance; cf. McAuliffe in Gove, 1975). For example, often the experience of being arrested (especially if one is convicted) can be crucial in determining a criminal or deviant career. As a case in point, a transitory drug problem by a young man can become more permanent once the behavior is labeled drug abuse. Again, a young woman may casually perform sex for money, be arrested, and be labeled a prostitute for life. Here the contingency of arrest and conviction is often a critical factor in determining whether a particular behavior will be transitory or more inveterate. Ironically, the response, rather than the initial deviance, may be seen as causing the problem.

To resolve social problems, symbolic interactionists and labeling theorists

Drawing by CEM; © 1961 *The New Yorker* Magazine, Inc.

would remind us to beware of public reactions to initial deviance. As a rule, do not create the very problems you feel ought to be resolved. If social problems are definitional, then we must change definitions of problematic conditions or behaviors previously labeled problems, rather than change what people do. One factor in this change of meaning is to reduce profits in labeling some behaviors and not others problematic. Is there any great advantage to sticking adolescents with the label of drug abuser or sexual deviant? In fact, the secondary deviance concept would suggest that society would be better off if it looked the other way for many transitory relatively harmless acts of deviance that almost all adolescents commit.

The symbolic interaction and labeling perspective is weak in that it underestimates the role of objective conditions in shaping social problems. After all, usually rules, laws, or norms are broken, something is done, before labels are applied or meanings given. Usually labels are not applied unless one is a fairly chronic offender. Some labels can be helpful too. For example, treatment or other positive responses often depend on identifying some behavior or condition as a problem first. Not all interaction is symbolic in that every human exchange must be negotiated every time. Most behavior is governed by mutually understood routines (See Scheff's concept of residual norms, 1966; 1975). Thus, the social rules, rather than overzealous moralists or sadistic individuals, create problems. Most people know what will happen if they do something, especially if they do it repeatedly. It may not be fair to say that such individuals were innocent victims of overly enthusiastic and premature public reactions. Crusading policemen or lawyers are usually not able on their own to "spoil" the lives of otherwise normal citizens.

The Functionalist Perspective A function is assumed to be an observed objective consequence that contributes to the adjustment or adaptation of society or of some social unit (Merton, 1957; 1975; Blau and Merton, 1981). If the consequence is maladaptive or maladjustive, then it is sometimes referred to as a dysfunction. Sociologists have been especially interested in dysfunctions that are latent; that is, in unanticipated or unintended disruptive consequences. Social consequences are usually carefully distinguished from individual dispositions, motives, or intentions. Functional analysis is "the practice of interpreting data by establishing *consequences* [italics ours] for larger structures in which the data are implicated" (Wilson, 1983:Ch. 5). Functionalism got an early start in the work of British anthropologist A. R. Radcliffe-Brown (1881–1955) and B. Malinowski (1844–1942), building on the work of French sociologist Emile Durkheim on primitive Australian religion (1912). Just as an individual has needs (to eat, sleep, and so on), Radcliffe-Brown assumed that social institutions functioned to meet the needs of the social organism (1952). Malinowski argued that all human beings have needs for food, reproduction, shelter, and so on. On the social level, magic, for example, meets the need for action when knowledge is insufficient. Religion is concerned with meeting needs related to major crises in human life, such as birth, puberty, marriage, and death (Malinowski, 1962). If social needs are met, then society tends toward equilibrium. The various parts of social systems must be integrated for the whole of society to be stable (Boudon, 1980). Functionalists believe generally that all recurring social activities have the function of maintaining society.

From the functionalists' viewpoint, social problems arise especially when unintended and unanticipated consequences (latent dysfunctions) of social patterns disrupt the integration and equilibrium of society. For example, one of the problems with prohibition (of alcohol consumption and distribution) in the United States was that no functional alternative for alcohol was provided. Since alcohol had been meeting many social needs (for tension reduction, socializing, business, and so on), it was naive to think that all the institutionalized behaviors surrounding alcohol could be simply legislated away. The result was understandable. There was disorganization, resistance, criminal activity, and finally, repeal of the Eighteenth Amendment (Gusfield, 1963). Generally, when social needs are not met by social institutions, social problems tend to develop. Social systems can become disorganized or be sent into disequilibrium by very rapid social change (cf. Durkheim's concept of anomie).

Have you ever wondered why prostitution has persisted for so long even though our legal codes criminalize it, our churches preach against it, and the general population for the most part disapproves of the practice? Functional theorists have argued that prostitution has and is still meeting important social needs. As with the prohibition movement, any attempt to eliminate prostitution without providing a functional alternate to meet the social need will be doomed to failure. Some of the social needs that prostitutes meet could include providing sex for those persons that are unattractive for various reasons, offering sexual experiences that many spouses will not (e.g., fellatio), making sexual activities available to men in remote areas away from their families (such as war zones, construction sites, conventions, and so on), allowing for sexual variety that is not possible in any finite marital relationship, and so on. Interestingly, as more permissive values toward pre- and extramarital sex and more structural opportunities (e.g., more women in the labor force) for male-female interaction have developed, there has been a sharp decline in the proportion of the American population who have ever paid for sexual relations with a prostitute.

To resolve social problems, functionalists contend that we must concentrate on bringing the entire society into equilibrium by reducing dysfunctional consequences and increasing social integration. Since society is seen as a system, changes in any one social unit tend to have consequences for all other system units. This means that piecemeal solutions of particular social problems usually do not work. What is needed is a total society that is harmonious, integrated, and meets all basic needs, not just healthy or problem-free individuals. As a first step we must assess the primary consequences of all major social patterns, insofar as this is feasible.

Functionalism has had as many critics as it has had champions. Some have argued that functionalism is not a special theory (Davis, 1959); that it simply does what any good explanation does (Poloma, 1979:Ch. 2). Others have pointed out that societies do not have any clear and consistent needs, since society is not a living organism. Furthermore, unlike individuals, it is difficult to imagine society not surviving, if certain needs were not met. Still others complain that functionalism has too conservative an image of society. It encourages us to think about stability, equilibrium, routines, institutions, and so on, rather than about social change, growth, deviance, individuals, and the like. Recently, sociologists have tried to resurrect functional analysis by claiming that it can be dynamic, methodologically rigorous, and not ideologically tainted (Faia, 1986; Alexander, 1983).

The Deviance Perspective As we have seen, most sociologists, including Durkheim and Homans, have been impressed with the ability of social norms to control the behavior of people. Most norms tend to be followed almost automatically (Zimbardo, 1970). If properly internalized and not inconsistent with each other, social norms can produce conformity and social order. Of course, the institutional means for realizing specific social expectations must be available and commensurate with social goals. Starting at least with Merton's famous paper on anomie (1938) or normlessness (and perhaps with Durkheim's *Suicide* in 1897), sociologists have sought to determine the conditions under which people would deviate from social norms, especially on a scale large enough to generate social problems (Higgins and Butler, 1982). These studies of anomie have been extended to cover topics like delinquency, mental disorder, alcoholism, and drug addiction (Clinard, 1964).

One view of deviance leading to social problems is that while a society generally internalizes common norms, the institutionalized means (social structure) for realizing these norms is not available to all. This disjunction of cultural goals and social means can lead to deviant behavior on a large scale and, eventually, to anomie. Merton claims deviants "innovate" when their opportunities to achieve widely valued cultural ends are blocked (1957; 1975). That is, norms tend to be deviated from when the social ends or goals are highly valued but the social means are not open to all. In this case deviant behavior and social problems are produced by structural strains. The norms may be clear and commonly agreed to but the means to achieving these social goals are unevenly distributed. For example, if a society expected almost everyone to go to college but did not provide equal early educational opportunities for some people (especially, for women, blacks, and other minorities), then one should not be surprised by widespread cheating on examinations, buying of term papers, sexual favors or money being provided in return for grades, and so on.

In other cases certain segments of the population actually learn not to conform to norms (Sutherland and Cressey, 1978; Akers et al., 1978; Akers, 1985). An early book on professional thieves by Sutherland (1937) emphasizes that deviant behavior is learned through differential association. You will remember that Becker argued much the same thing about marijuana use (Chapter 1). In some ways deviance can become highly systematized and organized. In this case deviance is not merely random criminal individuals avoiding social norms for various reasons, but virtually a contraculture with its own (often different) norms and highly integrated subcultures. Finally, social problems can arise when norms themselves are vague, mutually contradictory, or otherwise attenuated. Obviously, if norms are not clear, are impossible to follow, or impossible to follow without violating other important norms, then deviant behavior can be socially produced regardless of the goodness of individual intentions.

Resolutions to deviance turn on norms being stated clearly and consistently. Families and schools must be sure that certain very crucial or basic norms are learned early and reinforced often. A system of formal and informal sanctions for norm violators must be in place and norm conformers must be rewarded. It is not sufficient merely to punish norm violators. Of course, if we wish to avoid deviance we must be sure that all important norms can be followed by most people. Finally, opportunities for deviant socialization and deviant subcultures must be reduced.

Probably the most telling criticism of the deviant viewpoint is that many major social problems do not involve deviant behavior at all. We have already noted that most people follow most important norms most of the time, and yet there are still social problems. Although every pattern of human behavior probably deviates from some norm of some group, it is not difficult to think of problematic social conditions that have little to do with deviance or norm violating. For example, how is aging breaking a norm? Clearly, people who grow old are not breaking any law. Even the general conditions surrounding the current problems in the world economy do not clearly and singly derive from a few greedy individuals or countries pursuing their own advantages. Among other things there are limited world resources (most conspicuously of oil) in spite of production, distribution, and consumption norms. A major criticism of the deviance perspective is that it assumes norms are more central than they perhaps are. For one thing norms never govern all behaviors.

The Biological Perspective What loosely may be called the biological perspective maintains that basic biological differences are reflected in and determining of social problems. Not all human differences, of course, are social and not all social problems have purely social origins. The fact that human beings are male and female, young and old, sick and healthy, and so forth reflects more than social expectations, roles, and norms related to these social categories. Lombroso (1836–1909) argued for a biological theory of criminal behavior (cf. Mednick and Christiansen, 1977; Bryjak and Soroka, 1985). He felt that criminals were animalistic throwbacks and were born criminals. He comments about his insights while examining Villela, a master Italian criminal.

> At the sight of that skull, I seemed to see all of a sudden, lighting up as a vast plain under a flaming sky, the problem of the nature of the criminal—an atavistic being who reproduces in his person the ferocious instincts of primitive humanity and the inferior animals. Thus, were explained the enormous jaws, high cheekbones, prominent superciliary arches . . . found in criminals, savages, and apes, insensibility to pain, extremely acute sight, tattooing, excessive idleness, love of orgies, and the irresistible craving for evil for its own sake, the desire not only to extinguish life in the victim, but to mutilate the corpse, tear its flesh, and drink its blood. (Lombroso, in Cohen, 1966:50)

However, Lombroso made a fundamental methodological mistake (not to mention overdramatizing his point!). He measured the skulls and bodies of only criminals. Later research (Goring, 1913) found no physiological differences between criminals and noncriminals. It is true that work on body types of delinquents by Sheldon (1949) and Gleuck (1956) found that more delinquents than nondelinquents were what Sheldon called mesomorphs. Mesomorphs tended to be energetic, hyperactive, impulsive people. There is also evidence that some male violent sex offenders (Richard Speck, who murdered and raped seven nurses in 1966 was falsely thought to be an XYY) have an extra Y chromosome. The XYY male is often very tall, impulsive, and delinquent at an early age. A problem here is that very few males have XYY chromosome

The biological perspective of Cesare Lombroso saw criminals as physically different from noncriminals—as similar to prehistoric men. Criminals were thought driven by their primitive animal aggressive instincts—not by social forces. (Courtesy, Field Museum of Natural History)

abnormalities, far fewer than the deviant populations the chromosome abnormality theory seeks to explain.

More recently, biology has entered into sociology in the form of "sociobiology" (Wilson, 1975; see criticisms by Sahlins, 1976, and Quadagno, 1979, 1980).[24] Very generally, sociobiologists claim that individuals act to maximize survival of their gene pool. As such sociobiology is an application of Darwinian laws of natural selection to social behavior. The reproduction of individuals is designed to maximize the number of their successful offspring. People are concerned with increasing their own "fitness" and the survival of their kin (de Catanzaro, 1981). Altruism is difficult for sociobiologists to account for.

Social problems tend to arise from the biological viewpoint because criminal or deviant characters or types are genetically given. Chemical imbalances, hormonal abnormalities, or other physiological differences in populations give rise to asocial behaviors and aggression. From the sociobiological standpoint questions can arise as to who is "fit" to survive and whether society should protect "weaklings" and "freaks."

To resolve social problems, the biological viewpoint would recommend preventing or minimizing biological faults and "imperfections." The biological perspective tends to support funding of basic research in the natural sciences and adopting a medical model for understanding social problems. It is interesting to think of United States President Reagan's social and economic programs in the 1980s as biologically based. They tend to assume, in spite of all arguments to the contrary, that some people are better and more deserving than others. For example, many poor people (largely blacks) had their welfare benefits reduced and were told to "get a job." Research was cut off or reduced for the social sciences, but actually increased for some of the natural sciences.

The biological perspective is weak in that biological defects or biological uniqueness often have no clear, proven, or singular relationships to social problems. Even if biological differences can be shown to be associated with certain social problems, it still is not clear that the biological traits caused the social problems. It certainly is not proven that there is a "criminal" type, certainly not in the proportions of the criminal behaviors the type seeks to account for. For example, only a small fraction of murderers have XYY chromosomal configurations, brain damage, endocrinological imbalances, or whatever. Perhaps most damning, the biological perspective has often been used to provide an excuse for genocide and racism. One naturally thinks of Adolf Hitler and the Third Reich's near extermination of European Jews in the early 1940s, or the racial persecution of American blacks by the Ku Klux Klan. Sociobiology has also been criticized for assuming that human behavior represents maximized fitness, for being unable to account for altruism, and for trying to reduce culture to nature.

• Summary

In the present chapter we reviewed seven major theoretical perspectives on social problems and discussed the general uses of theory in the study of social problems. Three relatively new theoretical perspectives in which we have a special interest and that have not been applied much earlier in sociology's attempt to understand social problems are exchange theory, structuralism, and biology-sociobiology.

From the exchange and structural perspectives, social problems are seen to arise out of actual human social interactions that are not rewarding, not valuable, or consistent with social expectations, and that tend to generate social imbalance and, ultimately, social inequality. Once inequality and heterogeneity are present, they have profound implications for social interaction. Many social problems are purely structural that they result from differences in size, number, and proximity of groups, rather than from the values or culture of groups. Several important concepts of the theoretical perspectives of exchange and structure were presented. These included the five basic propositions of exchange theory, the concept of interpersonal balance, distributive justice, and the concepts of size, number, heterogeneity, and inequality. All of these concepts will become valuable tools when we attempt to resolve substantive social problems later on.

An attempt was also made to relate the exchange and structural perspectives. The exchange perspective is concerned more with the principles of face-to-face actual human interaction that determine enduring social structures (i.e., is a micro-level analysis); while the structural perspective assumes differentiated social positions across which populations are variously distributed and is interested primarily in the consequences, not the emergence, of these social structures (i.e., is a macro-level analysis). The definition of social problems given in Chapter 1 was reformulated in the language of the exchange and structural perspectives.

Four other complementary theoretical perspectives were also reviewed in relation to their basic assumptions about society, perceived sources of social problems, resolutions to social problems, and their theoretical weaknesses. All seven perspectives will be used selectively in analyzing substantive social problems in following chapters. Conflict theorists believe that everyone in a society pursues their own best line of advantage according to their resources. Social problems arise when small groups of elites corner the scarce resources of society and ensure that their own interests will be realized, often at the expense of the interests of minority groups. The symbolic interactionist perspective sees social meanings as emerging in active processes of interpretation. Social problems can result simply from defining certain conditions or labeling certain behaviors problematic. The functionalist perspective holds that when social needs are met, society tends toward equilibrium and is relatively problem-free. However, unintended or unanticipated consequences or latent dysfunctions of social patterns can disrupt the integration and equilibrium of society, giving rise to social problems. The biology-sociobiology and deviance theoretical perspectives were also elaborated above, but they are not as central to our arguments and analysis in Chapters 4 through 15 as exchange theory, structuralism, conflict theory, symbolic interactionism, and functionalism.

Since our theoretical perspectives take social facts and objective reality seriously, it will be necessary in Chapter 3 to consider empirical and methodological aspects of social problems. Chapter 3 will be particularly concerned with the role of data in developing, constructing, and revising theories of social problems. We shall also need to review the basic research methods used in gathering and analyzing data relevant to the study of social problems.

• Notes

1. This was an issue in President Reagan's tax reforms. Critics complained that only those individuals making $50,000 or more a year really benefited from the tax reductions. See *The New York Times,* August 2, 1981, and June 19, 1986 ("Senate Reject Tax Amendment to Benefit Middle-Income People").

2. The implication is that theorists don't really do anything and the suspicion is that they cannot do anything.

3. Cf. McNall, 1979:Part III; Poloma, 1979:Chs. 1 and 9; Wilson, 1983:Chs. 1–3; Turner, 1982:Ch. 1 and Part III.

4. Cf. Blau, 1977. Although exchange theory approaches deductive theory, serious logical problems still exist. See my paper in the *American Sociological Review,* 1970, and replies in the *ASR,* August 1971.

5. In fact, only propositions are true or false; arguments never are.

6. Especially those related to possible long-term biological or genetic defects resulting from inbreeding.

7. A related problem arose when Copernicus first discovered that the sun, not the earth, was the center of our universe. A heliocentric astronomy seemed to make man and earth less important and thus had theological implications.

8. Axiomatic or formal theory in and of itself does not have to have any relationship with empirical reality. See Freese, 1980.

9. This also indicates another departure of our theoretical perspective from that of Bierstedt. Bierstedt (1974) extols theories that cannot be falsified. We argue that theoretical exaggeration need not and should not exclude falsification.

10. Compare Eitzen, 1986; Henslin and Light, 1983; and DeFleur, 1986.

11. For representative examples of exchange theory see Cook, 1987; Homans, 1974; Blau, 1964; Chadwick-Jones, 1976; Gergen et al., 1980; Cook, Emerson et al. 1981; Molm, 1985; for structuralism see Blau, 1975, 1977; for functionalism see Merton, 1957, 1975; Blau and Merton, 1981; Demerath and Peterson, 1967; Faia, 1986; Alexander, 1983; for conflict theory see Collins, 1975, and, of course, Marx, 1848; for deviance see Merton, 1957; Becker, 1963; Higgins and Butler, 1982; Akers, 1985; for symbolic interaction see Blumer, 1969, and Spector and Kitsuse, 1977; Schneider, 1985; finally, for sociobiology see Wilson, 1975; de Catanzaro, 1981; and Bryjak and Soroka, 1985.

12. Indeed Homans never even mentions sex as a reward. This is curious for a theory supposedly founded in subinstitutional behavior.

13. See Turner, 1986:Ch. 2 for some of the problems functionalism got into trying to specify social needs.

14. Unit relations refers to conditions like ownership. Balance implies, for example, that if you and I like each other and I own, say, a Datsun 300 ZX car, that you will be more likely to own a Datsun too (or at least a car).

15. However, see Blau's earlier work (1964), where exchange and the social-psychological foundations of social structure were examined. Curiously, Blau seems to have discarded his early exchange theory work from his later structural sociology (1975, 1977, 1981).

16. See, especially Simmel, 1908.

17. For other writings on structuralism see Mayhew, 1976 and 1980; South et al., 1982; and Molotch and Boden, 1985.

18. Mayhew and Levinger predict that the expected time per social contact decrease with increasing size of place and number of social contacts (1976).

19. Discrimination is an intervening variable specifying the relationship between size, number, and intergroup relations.

20. As can be seen by considering the computational formula, heterogeneity is an indicator of the expected frequency of outgroup associations:

$$H = 1 - \Sigma Pi^2$$

where Pi^2 = the expected frequency of ingroup associations and 1 is all associations. Pi equals the fraction of the population in each group.

21. Actually, males outnumber females at conception (the sex ratio is about 120), birth (106), and in early life (104–102). But by about ages 20–24, females begin to outnumber males (97). By ages 65 and over, the sex ratio is about 82.

22. More on Marx's political economy is in Turner, 1986:Part III.

23. Wilson, 1983:Ch. 11.

24. Other important works are *Bioscience,* Volume 26, No. 3 (March, 1976):182–190; the *New York Times Magazine* (October 12, 1975); *The New York Review of Books* (Allen et al., 1975); *Time* magazine, March 19, 1976; de Catanzaro, 1981; McNall, 1979:Part VII; and Bryjak and Soroka, 1985.

• Glossary

Aggression Proposition. When a person's action does not receive the reward s/he expected, or receives punishment s/he did not expect, s/he will be angry; s/he becomes more likely to perform aggressive behavior, and the results of such behavior become more valuable to him/her.

Approval Proposition. When a person's action receives rewards s/he expected, especially a greater reward than s/he expected, or does not receive punishment s/he expected, s/he will be pleased; s/he becomes more likely to perform approving behavior, and the results of such behavior become more valuable to him/her.

Axiom. A primitive statement in a theory that is assumed to be universally true or lawlike. Such statements are sometimes referred to as postulates.

Balance. A situation in which the relations among entities fit together harmoniously, there is no stress toward change. A positive product of all the signs of all relationships in a cycle of a graph. Imbalance is a negative product of the signs.

Definition. A statement that attempts to clarify the meanings of symbols.

Deprivation-Satiation Proposition. Refers to a situation in which an individual or group considers their comparative rewards just, consistent with their needs or expectations.

Exchange-Structuralism. A crude, but convenient, way of referring to the complementary theoretical perspectives of exchange and structuralism, which are in fact separate and distinct theoretical perspectives.

Explanation Sketch. Aims primarily at organizing selected research findings and supporting further inquiries. Not as formal or comprehensive as systematic theory.

Heterogeneity. The chance expectation that two randomly chosen individuals belong to different groups.

Hypothesis. A usually fairly limited and specific statement about a future event, or an event the outcome of which is unknown at the time of the prediction, set forth in such a way that it can be rejected.

Inequality. Designates social positions varying by graduation, such as power, prestige, social class, income, or education.

Law. A proposition of universal conditional form that must be confirmed by the relevant information available.

Lawlike Proposition. A proposition that has the attributes of a law, except that it might be false.

Metatheory. An orienting proposition or propositions that could be constructed into a theory or theories.

Proposition. A declarative statement made up of a subject, copula, and predicate; it can be true or false.

Proximity. Refers to closeness; usually physical propinquity affecting social associations.

Reward. Anything that reinforces repeating of a particular act or behavior. Money and status are general rewards.

Social Facts. Objective conditions that are external to and constraining of the subjective aspects of social relations.

Social Structure. A multidimensional space of different social positions among which a population is distributed.

Stimulus Proposition. If in the past the occurrence of a particular stimulus, or set of stimuli, has been the occasion on which a person's action has been rewarded, then the more similar the present stimuli are to the past ones, the more likely the person is to perform the action, or some similar act, now.

Success Proposition. For all actions taken by persons, the more often a particular action of a person is rewarded, the more likely the person is to perform that action.

Theory. A set of laws and definitions that are deductively interrelated. Propositions generated from the laws and definitions are called theorems. At least some of the theorems must have empirical referrents (be falsifiable), if a theory is to be testable.

Value. The degree of reward.

Value Proposition. The more valuable to a person is the result of his/her action, the more likely s/he is to perform the action.

• Further Reading

Blau, Peter M. and Robert K. Merton, eds. *Continuities in Structural Inquiry.* Beverly Hills: Sage, 1981. An edited volume by two of the founders of structural sociology. Twelve chapters on Levi-Strauss, Marxist structuralism, economic interdependence, rank differentiation, undesired consequences, and so on.

Ekeh, Peter P. *Social Exchange Theory: The Two Traditions.* Cambridge, MA: Harvard University Press, 1974. Discusses differences between French social scientist C. Levi-Strauss's collectivistic tradition of social exchange and the more individualistic approach of Homans growing out of the British utilitarianism of Radcliffe-Brown and Malinowski. Criticizes Homans for unnecessarily combining micro-economics of exchange (developed later by Blau) and the behavioral psychology of exchange (developed later by Emerson). Cf. Cook, 1987.

McNall, Scott G., ed. *Theoretical Perspectives in Sociology.* New York: St. Martin's Press, 1979. This edited volume has several papers on sociological theory usually not found in theory texts. Included are sections on biosocial approaches, a world-systems perspective (Wallerstein), contemporary Marxist theory, a women's perspective in sociology, a discussion of Homan's postulates, behavioral sociology, dialectics, environmental sociology, and the sociology of emotions.

Riley, Norbert, ed. *Sociological Theory* published by the American Sociological Association, 1722 N Street NW, Washington, DC. This is a biannual journal dedicated to current topics in sociological theory. First published as hardback book in 1983 and 1984 (Randall Collins, editor).

Turner, Jonathan H. *The Structure of Sociological Theory.* Chicago, IL: The Dorsey Press, 1986. A thorough and readable review of major theoretical perspectives in sociology. See particularly the chapter on "Sociological Theorizing" (Chapter 1) and the chapters on exchange theorizing (10 through 13). Note that Turner also uses the concept of exchange structuralism (Chapter 12), but restricts it to the early work of Peter M. Blau. Some of the early work of Blau (*Exchange and Power in Social Life,* 1964) was very similar to that of Homans.

Wilson, John. *Social Theory.* Englewood Cliffs, NJ: Prentice-Hall, 1983. An up-to-date review of exchange theory, structural sociology, functional analysis, symbolic interactionism, and conflict theory (historical materialism). While this smallish paperback is not about social problems, it is a good introduction to most of the major theoretical perspectives in sociology.

C·H·A·P·T·E·R

3

Methodological and Empirical Aspects of Social Problems

Since most theoretical perspectives of social problems are based on facts and claim to be objective, the research methods by which empirical data are produced, as well as how these empirical considerations relate to our definition of social problems, are examined. It is important to try to know if human behaviors are general patterns or individual idiosyncracies, what social conditions really are as opposed to what they are thought to be, if some social conditions are actually a threat to society or in fact are relatively innocuous, whether a lot or only a few people (and which people) see social conditions as problematic, and how specific social changes resolving social problems could be made.

Research methods and data analysis have been conspicuously absent from most social problems textbooks. This is not merely because authors and publishers want to keep their texts simple. Rather, it is probably also the result of theoretical emphases on the subjective aspects of social problems.[1] For example, if you argue that mental illness is a "myth" or that society and hospitals "manufacture" mental illness (Szasz, 1961, 1985; Maris, 1986), then you will not be especially enamored with attempts to determine the "true" prevalence or incidence of schizophrenia, depression, and so forth. This is because you will see the critical factor in who gets labeled emotionally ill to be the subjective

PANEL 3.1

The Foundations of Social Science

Science is sometimes characterized as logico-empirical. This ugly term carries an important message: the two pillars of science are (1) logic or rationality, and (2) observation. A scientific understanding of the world must make sense and correspond with what we observe. Both of these elements are essential to science.

As a gross generalization, scientific theory deals with the logical aspect of science, and research deals with the observational aspect. A scientific theory describes the logical relationships that appear to exist among parts of the world, and research offers means for seeing whether those relationships actually exist in the real world. Though too simplistic, perhaps, this statement provides a useful jumping-off point for the examination of theory and research.

Social scientific theory has to do with what is, not with what should be. I point that out at the start, since social theory for many centuries has combined these two orientations. Social philosophers mixed liberally their observations of what happened around them, their speculations as to why, and their ideas about how things ought to be. Although modern social scientists may do the same from time to time, it is important to realize that social science has to do with how things are and why.

Source: Earl Babbie, *The Practice of Social Research,* Wadsworth, Inc., 1986:16–17.

reaction of society or powerful individuals. Many sociologists see mental illness not as an objective (certainly not organic) condition, but rather as "behavior that exceeds the tolerance of others" (Cockerham, 1981:100ff.; Eitzen, 1986: 456) and are quick to contend that there are probably more crazy people outside of hospitals than in them (Goffman, 1961). Clearly, subjective approaches to the study of social problems are a legitimate enterprise, one that we shall use and attempt to explain.

However, since the present textbook also emphasizes objective conditions; measuring, counting, and the like are more critical for us. Indeed, the general question in Chapter 3 is how do methods and data enter into the construction, elaboration, and resolution of social problems? More specifically, we shall ask what is the nature of the propositions that comprise the theoretical perspectives we just considered in Chapter 2? For example, what conditions must be satisfied before we accept propositions as true (or false)? What rules are needed to be able to make particular inferences from more general propositions? How is the truth of a proposition different from the validity or persuasiveness of an argument? How do confirmed research hypotheses enter into our theories of social problems? How does one go about sorting out bias, value, sentiment, and perceived threats from impartiality, reason, value-neutrality, and "social facts" (as Durkheim, 1895, used to call them)?

These and other questions suggest that we discuss briefly informal and formal fallacies. Informal fallacies refer to such traits as the ambiguity or irrelevancy of many ordinary language arguments. For example, fundamental ambiguities are contained in all of the following statements:

> "Clean and Decent Dancing Every Night Except Sunday"
> "Good steaks are rare these days, so you shouldn't
> order yours well done."
> "Save soap and waste paper."
> "Some dogs have fuzzy ears. My dog has fuzzy ears.
> Therefore, my dog is *some* dog!"[2]

Formal fallacies, on the other hand, concern violations of rules of inference stipulated for an argument to be considered valid.

To be savvy about the objective aspects of social problems we must also at least be familiar with tables and how to read them, rates of various social conditions and human behavior, and measures of central tendency (like the mean) and dispersion. We should also know when a sample is adequate or inadequate, how one states a hypothetical proposition for testing, under what conditions to accept or reject a hypothesis, and what it means to correlate variables, test hypotheses, and explain variation in dependent variables. Finally, we shall need to consider four basic methodological approaches to gathering data and studying social problems: those involving official documents, individual cases, surveys, and experiments. We begin with a discussion of the place of logical methods and data in developing the seven theoretical perspectives of social problems elaborated in the last chapter.

• The Roles of Logic and Data in Developing Social Problems Theories

Although we have talked generally about theoretical perspectives on social problems in the first two chapters, we have yet to get down to the nitty-gritty of how one would actually construct or test a theory. More specifically, we have not really thoroughly examined methods of theory construction, or what correspondence theories may have with the "real (empirical) world." For example, how would we ever know if our theories of social problems did *not* explain what they purported to? In a theory all statements are propositions. Propositions are the elements of any theory and have the important trait of being either true or false, although we may not be able to determine the truth or falsity of some propositions. Arguments, made up of logically connected propositions, are usually not considered true or false, but rather valid or invalid, useful or useless, powerful or weak, and so on.

Some propositions, like Homans's five axioms of exchange theory (stated in Panel 2.2) are highly general and abstract, may not even be directly testable, or may be assumed always to be true (i.e., to be "laws"—see Glossary). Other propositions are more specific and concrete and have clearer (operational) definitions that allow for more precise measurement. Such propositions can be particular hypotheses taken as "confirmed" or as "research results." In more formal social theories, such as those of exchange theory (Homans, 1974) or structuralism (Blau, 1977), confirmed hypothetical propositions are not said to be "explained" until they become theorems, that is, not until they are logically inferred from more general propositions (such as Homans's five axioms mentioned in Chapter 2).

In a classic study of gang behaviors in a Boston slum sociologist William F. Whyte (1943) found some rather curious research results. One of the thirteen boys in the street corner gang, Alec, was an excellent bowler—when he did not bowl with the gang. However, in general, Alec's social status was among the very lowest of all the gang members. When Alec bowled with everyone else on Saturday night he simply could not bowl the same high scores he achieved when he bowled alone earlier in the week. In fact, the ranking of the thirteen boys determined by their bowling scores was almost exactly the same as their social ranking in the gang. Why should this be, expecially since Alec could bowl very well in other circumstances? To explain this research result we need to refer to more general statements like those axioms we considered in Panel 2.2. For example, the exchange perspective tells us that a general tendency exists in all social groups for there to be congruence or similarity between ranks on all dimensions of social status (Homans 1974:264). When the whole gang bowled together the other boys harassed Alec until his bowling performance dropped to a level consistent with his general social status in the gang. Notice that research result (i.e., a similarity between the two ranks of bowling scores and gang membership status) was explained by relating it to a more general proposition about social status congruence.

Definitions in a theory facilitate inferences and expand the scope and clarify the meaning of one's theory.[3] Of special interest to us are operational definitions, which define by reference to the outcomes of specific measurements (Turner, 1986:3–4). The relevant definitions of our theoretical perspectives will be found in the chapter glossaries of this text. For example, we have already attempted definitions of such terms as *social structure, norm, status, interaction, role, power, value, reward, heterogeneity, inequality,* and *social problems*.

Rules of inference are standard forms of valid arguments that, if the propositions making up its premises are true, ensure that conclusions properly derived from the argument forms will also be true. That is, in a valid argument, if the premises are true, then the conclusion must be true. For example, one simple rule of inference says that if A implies B and B implies C, then A implies C (it's called a hypothetical syllogism). In Chapter 14 we point out that profit motives require cheap energy, cheap energy usually means using coal (rather than oil or electrical energy), burning coal produces sulfur dioxide and nitrous oxides, which in turn make acid rain. Using the hypothetical syllogism rule, it follows logically that profit motives produce acid rain (which may not have been obvious to start with). However, it is important to note that a valid argument may have all false propositions, since logical validity has nothing to do with the empirical world. False premises may still produce a true conclusion, since the truth of an argument's conclusion does not ensure the truth of its premises. Arguments or theories are not true or false, although their propositions may be. A social theory may have little to do with the empirical world in that it is "only" logically consistent or coherent as a logical or mathematical system of propositions (Freese, 1980; cf. Wilson, 1983:5).

However, in our textbook we are not especially interested in this sense of theory, since we seek to explain observable social conditions or patterns of human behavior that are claimed to be social problems. Thus, one might say that our theoretical perspectives on social problems assume a correspondence theory of truth. That is, we are concerned primarily with general propositions that predict and explain (i.e., correspond well with) observed regularities of social behaviors or structures that are considered problematic. Of course, we have seen already that empirical testing of theories is a slippery business. Minimally we must endeavor not to try to explain conditions or behaviors that are not clear or regular enough to even require an explanation,[4] to formulate lawlike propositions that have a high probability of in fact being laws and are capable of falsification,[5] and not to make any glaring logical errors in relating laws to research results.

Let's take another example of explaining research results through generalizations or lawlike propositions in the study of social problems. Emile Durkheim was an early French functional sociologist who studied suicide rates and tried to explain them (1897). He started out hypothesizing a large number of hypothetical relationships. For example, he theorized that Protestants would have higher suicide rates than Catholics, that old people would have higher rates than young people, that the suicide rates of the divorced and single would exceed those of the married, that married people who also had children would have lower suicide rates than people who were married but had no children, that elite soldiers and highly educated persons would have higher suicide rates than enlisted men or the less educated, and so on. He first established that these hypothesized relationships were sufficiently frequent to require an explanation. By examining death certificates and other social data he conninced himself that these relationships actually were "social facts" (as he called them).

But Durkheim did not stop here. He said: "These being the facts, what is their explanation?" That is, he asked himself if there were any axioms, social laws, or higher-level generalizations from which *all* of his particular research results could be logically deduced or inferred. He concluded that all of his research results on suicide rates could be inferred from the proposition that "suicide rates varied negatively with the degree of social integration." That is, the less social regulation or involvement of a group, the higher its suicide rate. Protestants, older people, divorcées, educated people, elite soldiers, the child-

Sociologist Emile Durkheim generalized from the obvious social isolation of an individual suicide to empirical traits of most suicides collectively. Suicide rates vary negatively or inversely with social integration.
(George Malare/Stock, Boston)

less, and so on were all from social groups or social situations that were relatively socially deregulated (Durkheim called them anomic) or socially isolated (he called these egoistic). Part of the beauty of Durkheim's generalization about suicide rates and social integration was that other relationships (i.e., theorems) could be derived from it. For example, other things being equal, people who live alone ought to have higher suicide rates than people who have large families.

Theorems are derived, yet often highly abstract and general, propositions of a theory. Theorems may have empirical (real world) referrents or they may be purely formal. Since theorems (once derived from assumptions or axioms and definitions) can be used for further inferences, theorems practically are not terribly different from laws or axioms. For example, in Blau's structural theory, unlike Homans's exchange theory, the really important general propositions are derived theorems. Consider that propositions like, "The rate of intergroup associations of the smaller group must exceed that of the larger" (Blau, 1977:21), are theorems, not assumptions.

Logically, then, constructing a theory of anything involves working with axioms and definitions to generate theorems. All the propositions in a formal theory are interrelated. One way of thinking of theory is as a system of related arguments. It must be admitted that ordinary language is often so rich and vague that the formal propositions of one's theory fail to capture all the ordinary language meanings. Theory construction is much more complex than we can ever hope to demonstrate here.[6]

So much for our brief consideration of the logical methods of social theory construction and their relations to data in general. It must be remembered that this textbook is not about any old data concerning any old subjects. Rather, we try to focus on certain kinds of data relevant to social problems. More precisely our definition of social problems (see especially Table 2.2) specifies the data to which we should attend. First, we will watch what people actually do (activities, behaviors, interactions), in addition to what they claim to or believe they do. Second, whenever possible we shall determine what people do in relatively small face-to-face groups and sometimes conceive of larger social units (e.g., countries, corporations, races, sexes, ages, and so on) as if they were individual actors (see Chapter 10). Of course, as our analysis deals more with social problems in large groups, the principles of small-group behaviors will be less use to us and we shall need to rely more on the perspectives of structuralism, functionalism, and conflict theory.

Third, we will focus on social interaction, not just action. After all, this is a *social* problems textbook. Fourth, we shall investigate the larger structural configurations of social interaction. Data indicating social inequality, conflict, and social heterogeneity will be especially pertinent. Fifth, we want to know how widespread are the interaction patterns and population distributions we study. How many people do something, value something, are in such-and-such social positions, and so on? Finally, we need to measure the actual values and sentiments of relevant groups and individuals. As an applied sociology text

By permission of Johnny Hart and Creators Syndicate

concerned with the resolution of human social problems and social change, we cannot afford to be indifferent to actual human values.

This last point is worth elaborating. Our definition of social problems (Chapter 2) speaks of general patterns of human behavior or social conditions "that are perceived to be threats to society." This phrase raises the general question of the methodological implications of affect, sentiment, perception, felt threats, and other presumably subjective components in social problems theories that we argue are (on the whole) objective. Part of the answer to this question is provided in the reformulated definitions of perceived threats (Table 2.2). That is, in addition to the subjective concept of perceived threats, we shall be interested in human values and rewards, distributive injustice, structural imbalance, inequality, and heterogeneity. All of these concepts have fairly objective measures.

Perhaps the most problematic of these concepts is that of value. What is rewarding and how rewarding it is (i.e., its value) can vary considerably among human populations. Functionalists try to avoid some of this variation by speaking of basic societal "needs" or of universal "functional imperatives" (Parsons, 1951:167ff.; Turner, 1986:19–120). Human rewards can be very concrete (e.g., food, drink, shelter, sleep, sex, and so on) or more abstract (e.g., social status, money, esteem, reproduction, adaptability, and so on; Maslow, 1954; cf. Mussen et al., 1977:173ff.). How valuable even biologically based rewards are can vary considerably across sexes, ages, races, and social classes. Yet for all this complexity and variability it does make sense to speak of general common values. For example, the exchange perspective contends that almost everyone finds money and social status generally reinforcing (Homans, 1974). Williams has claimed in a similar vein that secular occupational success is of prime importance to most Americans (1951; cf. Durkheim, 1893).

Even more relevant to our point, theoretically we can determine in a given population roughly what is and what is not valuable and how valuable it is. For example, exchange theorists suggest that whatever people do a lot of, how much energy they expend to get something, and so on is a good indicator of their values.[7] Although measurement of values presents us with some thorny problems, we need not capitulate and surrender to undue subjectivism in the face of these problems.

• Empirical Methods in Developing Social Problems Theories

Generally speaking, one must decide theoretical issues before the facts even become relevant. After all, we cannot examine all facts. As we shall see shortly, one's theoretical model also specifies what we mean by error and allows us to measure it. The primary questions in this section are: in studying social problems what are the facts, which facts does one attend to, how confident are we that something actually is a fact, how do we arrive at the facts, and how do we select and interpret facts?

Let's take a concrete example from the social problems of crime to start to answer these questions. Suppose we wished to establish the truth (or falsity) of the following simple crime argument:

"If the enforcement of laws is strict, then crime will diminish."

Of course, a theory sketch of anything requires that we examine the truth of *several* propositions and that we categorize these propositions as axioms, definitions, theorems, and so on—as just discussed in the previous logic of the social science section (see Figure 2.1). Forget about this for the moment and let us examine the single proposition concerning law enforcement and crime prevalence.

To begin with, how do we measure law enforcement and crime prevalence? What procedures does one use for obtaining relevant empirical data? For example, do we collect our own data (some sociologists in the symbolic interaction camp argue that we "produce" data; i.e., it is not just lying around to be collected) or shall we use data already compiled by official agencies like local police departments or the Federal Bureau of Investigation? How will we decide if the data we use are any good; how much we can trust the data? How shall we organize and present the data? After all, sources such as the FBI's *Uniform Crime Reports* probably will not give us the exact tables we need. When we construct a table, how do we read it and summarize its information? Which techniques are appropriate to test the relationship between law enforcement and crime prevalence? These and other important issues will now be considered.

Major crimes are usually divided into violent crimes (murder and nonnegligent manslaughter, forcible rape, robbery, and aggravated assault) and property crimes (burglary, larceny, and auto theft).[8] One simple answer to our question about law enforcement and crime prevalence could be derived by finding out the arrest rates for the seven major crimes and comparing the prevalence rates of crimes over time, controlling for arrest rates. That is, those major crimes with the highest arrest rates (i.e., one operational definition of *enforcement*) ought to diminish more. It turns out that the strictest enforcement as measured by arrest rates is for murder. About 75 percent of all murders known about are cleared by arrest (*Uniform Crime Reports,* July, 1986:153). The lowest arrest rate for major crimes is for auto theft. Only 15 percent of auto offenses are cleared by arrest. The above proposition of the crime argument might lead us to believe that the murder rate would diminish over time and the auto theft rate would not diminish over time (or would diminish less than the murder rate).

To examine these predictions (when properly formulated, sociologists call them *hypotheses*) and elaborate some fundamental concepts of empirical methods we must have some *data.* To get started let us refer to the data presented in Table 3.1, the number of homicides and auto thefts in the United States by offenses known and arrests made in 1960, 1980, and 1984. We will use the data in Table 3.1 to illustrate measurement issues, sampling issues, descriptive statistics, hypothesis testing, the concept of correlation, and statistical inference. Obviously, in a beginning social problems course we can only introduce you, in a very elementary way, to social statistics and research methods in the few pages that follow.[9]

Measurement Issues How do we know when some proposition is true? To be honest, most of the time we really do not know. Remember that for centuries most people believed that the earth was flat or that the earth (not the sun) was at the center of our solar system. Nevertheless, certain basic methods can help us be more confident that our theoretical propositions have a high probability of being true. We will discuss some of these methods in relation to the data presented in Table 3.1 shortly. Note that most sociological propositions are not laws. That is, few social generalizations are invariably true.

In Chapter 6 we are going to discuss the proposition that "black athletes are naturally superior to white athletes." Superficially there would seem to be

TABLE 3.1 Number of Homicides and Auto Thefts in the United States by Offenses Known and Arrests Made, 1960, 1980, and 1984

	Offenses Known			Arrests Made		
Offense	**1960**	**1980**	**1984**	**1960**	**1980**	**1984**
Homicide	9,050	23,044	18,692	6,307	20,040	13,832
Auto theft	326,400	1,114,651	1,032,165	54,202	138,300	154,825
United States population	179,323,175	224,349,264	236,681,000	179,323,175	225,349,264	236,681,000

Source: Adapted from *Uniform Crime Reports for the United States,* 1980, 1984. Washington, DC: U.S. Government Printing Office, 1980, 1984.

much evidence supporting this hypothesis. For example, although American blacks comprise about 11 to 12 percent of our population, they are in a vast majority in professional football, basketball, and baseball. In the late 1980s most top college basketball teams in the United States were predominantly black. Still the success of the black athlete in the United States may be because other social opportunities for black advancement have been blocked. Perhaps blacks are only superior to whites in athletics in a country with a social history of slavery and racism? Furthermore, how do we account for the considerable variation in athletic ability among blacks themselves? Unlike physics, the scientific study of social problems probably could not (ethically or practically) design a convincing experiment that would provide a definite answer to the question of the superiority of the black athlete.

The most we may be able to hope is that a proposition is likely to be true under certain given circumstances or assumptions. Even here a statement with a high probability of being true also has a certain probability of being false, an error term. We need to be sensitive to how statements about social problems might come to be in error. For example, a proposition might be false because a person's or group's values bias their perceptions, because their measurements are imprecise or crude, because the data they considered are not representative of the population they wish to describe, and so on. It is customary in statistics to speak of "Types I and II" errors (Mansfield, 1986:305, 310-325; Blalock, 1979:112ff.). A Type I error is made when we reject a true hypothesis, while Type II error is made when we accept a false hypothesis.

It is also traditional to distinguish between the reliability and validity of empirical measurements (Babbie, 1986:109–113). If a procedure or instrument is *reliable,* then it produces consistent results. Suppose we administered an IQ test to people that were in fact all highly intelligent, but the test indicated some were dull and others bright. Such a test would be unreliable. Empirical validity should not be confused with logical validity. Empirical validity of a procedure or instrument refers to the truth of the results. Thus, *validity* means actually measuring what you intend to measure (Macionis, 1987:33). Obviously, we could have consistent results that were false. For example, we could make repeated measurements with an eleven-inch ruler, thinking it to be twelve inches. Using the IQ test example, tests that show black ghetto children to have low IQs often are invalid because the test items are really measuring culture rather than intelligence. With the issue at hand it is common to ask about the reliability and validity of crime statistics and other "official" statistics. For example, how do we know that all 16,000 or so policing agencies that report crimes in the United States to the FBI use the same criteria for deciding what criminal offense has been committed or that a higher number of offenses known in a certain area is not just a reflection of better police action?

Variables, like major criminal offenses, form scales. For our purposes the most important types of scales are nominal, ordinal, and interval scales. When we merely classify categories but make no assumptions about the relationships among categories, as with the seven major crimes just described, it is proper to speak of a nominal scale. When a scale is ordered on a greater or less-than principle, without being able to say anything about the magnitude of the differences among categories, then we have an ordinal scale. Most gross classifications of socioeconomic status are ordinal scales. Thus, we speak of upper, middle, or lower classes.

Finally, when we rank categories or elements and specify exact distances among them, then we have an interval scale. A thermometer is a good example of an instrument using an interval scale. Assumptions about scales are important in determining the appropriateness of certain kinds of statistical tests of hypothesis. Of course, standard scales are also used to measure behaviors or conditions such as social class, social participation, intelligence, political attitudes, social interaction, social distance, personality, organizational structure, and much more (Babbie, 1986:377–381).

Although we shall illustrate four basic methodological approaches used in studying social problems below, it is important to emphasize here that how some behaviors or conditions are measured can vary considerably in directness or indirectness, obtrusiveness or unobtrusiveness, often with profound implications for the truthfulness of the results. In much of human behavior that is considered problematic or deviant, it may be necessary to use unobtrusive measurements (Babbie, 1986:Ch. 11). A good example of an unobtrusive measurement would be to simply notice to which stations people left their car radio dials tuned. Without asking anyone anything you could get some idea of people's values, whether they listened to music or news, whether they liked country, classical, or rock music, and so on. Of course, such unobtrusive measures might also produce large unknown errors as well. The very act of conspicuously asking about or even attempting to naturalistically observe certain behaviors (such as homosexuality, drug use, white collar crime, and so on) may distort or bias the findings. This is especially the case with criminal behaviors. Obviously many criminal behaviors are never detected or reported, since such behaviors are socially disapproved or can be punished. Thus, in studying social problems, the investigator may have to be ingenious in devising ways to measure and observe human behaviors or social conditions without being intrusive. Often serious ethical problems will be involved. The student of social problems always needs to weigh the advantages of knowing something against the disadvantages of violating an individual's or group's right to privacy.

Sampling Issues If it were practical, obviously we would consider *all* cases relevant to a truth claim made in a proposition. For example, the data in Table 3.1 represent all murder and auto theft offenses known to over 16,000 law enforcement agencies. That is, the offenses known are not samples, but rather all the cases that are known about (the universe). However, if behavioral scientists cannot get all cases, and usually they cannot, then they usually try to get a large sample selected in a special way. Perhaps the most common sampling procedure is the simple random sampling (Mansfield, 1986:217–253). In such a sample each individual and each combination of individuals must have

The crime argument contends that if law enforcement is strict, then crime will diminish. By using proper social research methods empirical data can be produced to test the crime argument. (Rick Smolan/Stock, Boston)

an equal chance of being selected. Of course simple random sampling assumes that a list of that which is to be sampled (for example, of murders or auto thefts) can be drawn up. Each item on the list is numbered. Then, using a table of random numbers, the investigator selects items from the list (after a random start) until the desired number of cases has been obtained. One has to decide whether items will be replaced on the list once they have been chosen. The distinct advantage of random samples is that every individual has a known probability of being selected. Other common sample procedures are called systematic (e.g., one could pick every tenth item on the list), stratified (e.g., taking samples within social classes), or clustered (e.g., taking samples from several census tracts).

In addition to using the correct procedures for selecting cases, one must pay attention to the sample size. Obviously, if we picked only a few cases (even using random sampling), then the sample might be biased, or not representative of that which we wished to study. This bias can be present even in large samples. For example, Hite studied over 3,000 females in her research on sexual behavior and attitudes (1976). But—and this is important—she sent out over 100,000 questionnaires. That is, she had only a 3 percent response rate. There is no way of knowing if her 3,000 respondents were representative of all American females, since the sample was not properly drawn.

However, if repeated simple random samples are drawn from a normal population, then the sampling distribution will be normal. Generally, if we use correct sampling procedures, as the sample gets large we tend to have a representative sample of that which we wish to investigate. How large is large enough depends on one's research objectives and other considerations. For example, if you need to subdivide your sample to look at the effects of other factors (say age, sex, race, marital status, and so on), you will need a larger original sample. Crudely, most studies of social problems are based on a few hundred to a few thousand cases.

An important point to make here is that much of the data for the study of social problems tends to be generated from nonprobability samples. For example, the *Uniform Crime Reports,* from which Table 3.1 was derived, are not based on a probability sample. Many criminal offenses are never reported to the police (see Chapter 15). Some community law enforcement agencies are more efficient than others. Other communities may not even have law enforcement agencies. Obviously, we have no way of knowing if most newspaper accounts are representative samples. Typically one quotes some "man-in-the-street" or a local "expert." Studies done by many physicians or psychologists based on patients they have treated are also nonprobability samples. In fact, most studies based on "treated" populations (criminals, state hospital patients, schoolchildren, and so forth) are potentially biased and error cannot be specified. Usually research is a secondary concern among treated clinical populations. Finally, most statistical inferences assume random sampling. If our samples are not random, then most statistical testing or inferences we may wish to do are inappropriate.

Descriptive Statistics Ignoring for present purposes that the data in Table 3.1 are not a probability sample, we still need to ask how we can read, describe, and summarize the table. It should be apparent that in the form of raw data Table 3.1 does not permit us readily to know if strict enforcement of laws deters crime. Furthermore, it is important in our study of social problems to know how to read a table, construct other tables from the original data, correct for population changes, and so on. Our social problems textbook will contain many tables for us to analyze data in support of our theoretical claims. To begin with here, the frequencies in Table 3.1 need to be converted to percentages and rates. For example, using arrests as an indicator of enforcement, we might want to see how strictly homicide and auto theft offenses were enforced in 1960 and 1980 (for simplicity we shall ignore the 1984 data for the most part). To determine this we can simply divide the number of arrests by the number of offenses for each year (e.g., 6,307 ÷ 9,050 = 70 percent for 1960, and so on). The results are presented in Table 3.2.

Enforcement in 1960 (here arrests) is much stricter for homicides (70 percent) than for auto thefts (17 percent). This enforcement differential is even greater in 1980, being 87 percent and 12 percent, respectively (in 1984 it is 74 percent and 15 percent). But what about the prevalence of the two offenses over time? The first proposition in the crime argument would lead us to predict that the rate of homicide should diminish between 1960 and 1980, while auto theft rates should not change much or even go up some. To test our prediction we must convert the frequencies in Table 3.1 into rates that correct for the number of people in a population. To do this we simply divide the offenses known by the population and multiply the result by some fixed standard number (here 100,000). Thus, the homicide rate for 1960 is:

$$\frac{9{,}050}{179{,}323{,}175} \times 100{,}000 = 5.1.$$

Rates are an important descriptive tool in the study of social problems because frequencies could go up or down just because there were more or less people in a society. When we calculate the rates for all categories, Table 3.3 is the result.

Now, comparing Tables 3.2 and 3.3 what can we conclude about the first

TABLE 3.2 Percentage of Offenses Resulting in Arrests for Homicide and Auto Theft in the United States: 1960, 1980, and 1984

	1960	1980	1984
Homicide	70%	87%	74%
Auto theft	17	12	15

Source: Table 3.1, above.

TABLE 3.3

Homicide and Auto Theft Rates in the United States, 1960, 1980 and 1984 (per 100,000 population)

	1960	1980	1984
Homicide	5.1	10.2	7.9
Auto theft	182	494	436

Source: Table 3.1, above.

proposition in the crime argument? While it is true that *overall* homicide rates are lower than auto theft rates, their stricter enforcement in 1980 was associated with an *increased* rate (although the homicide rate decreased some in 1984)—not the predicted decreased rate. In short, it does not seem that stricter enforcement of laws, at least as indicated by percentage of arrests for these two types of crime, has very much influence on crime prevalence over time. In fact, other studies (see Chapter 15) reveal that all of the seven crime categories on the crime index have shown dramatic increases over the last twenty years in spite of differential enforcement (at least until the early 1980s). Thus, we may want to tentatively conclude that the crime argument proposition is false. The student should be aware that truth and falsity are usually very difficult to determine in the study of social problems. We always need to remind ourselves not to be dogmatic, moralistic, or overconfident of our own pet theoretical perspectives or empirical claims about social problems. Most often the results of social research are inconclusive and further investigation and research are usually necessary.

Before we move on to discuss measures of central tendency and dispersion a few more words need to be said about population bases. First, when population bases are very small, percentages and rates can be misleading. For example, at one time 33 percent of Johns Hopkins University coeds were married to their professors. That is, in the days before coeducation at Hopkins there were three female students and one married a professor. Second, by itself, a percentage is meaningless. Robins reports that 50 percent of suicides were either depressed or alcoholic (1981). We need to know what percent of nonsuicides in a comparable group (such as white, middle-aged men) are depressed or drink too much. In another instance a newspaper headline blares: "Adolescent suicide rates up 200 percent in twenty years." What the headline does not tell us is that suicide is so rare among the very young that a slight absolute increase (one that perhaps could happen by chance) can make a dramatic-sounding percentage gain. Finally, you must be sensitive to changes in the base on which percentages are computed.

The other primary descriptive statistics you will encounter in this textbook are measures of central tendency and dispersion, such as the mean, median, mode, and standard deviation. Although we cannot really illustrate these concepts well with the data from Table 3.1, consider the data in Table 3.4. One

TABLE 3.4 Murder and Nonnegligent Manslaughter in the United States, 1970–1984

Years	Number of Offenses
1970	16,000
1971	17,780
1972	18,670
1973	19,640
1974	20,710
1975	20,510
1976	18,780
1977	19,120
1978	19,560
1979	21,460
1980	23,040
1981	22,520
1982	21,010
1983	19,308
1984	18,692

Source: *Uniform Crime Reports,* July 28, 1985:41.

common way of summarizing such data is to average them. For example, to compute the mean number of homicide from 1970 to 1984 simply add the column in Table 3.4 and divide by 15. Thus,

$$\frac{296,800}{15} = 19,786.$$

When there are a few extreme cases (the distribution is said to be skewed), the median is usually a better measure of central tendency than the mean. The median is that score that has exactly one-half the remaining scores above and below it. By ordering the homicide offenses in Table 3.4 from low to high, you can see that the median score is 19,560. It can also be seen that the distribution in Table 3.4 is slightly skewed; that is, the median is below the mean. The final measure of central tendency, for our purposes, is the mode. The mode is simply the most common score. Since no scores occur more than once in Table 3.4, it has no mode.

It is also useful to note how much dispersion or variance there is around the central tendency (for example, around the mean) of a distribution. One easy way of gauging dispersion is simply to present the range of the scores. In Table 3.4 the range is from 16,000 to 23,040 homicides. However, a more useful measure of dispersion is the standard deviation. Given a normal distribution about 68 percent of the cases fall within one standard deviation on either side of the mean. The standard deviation is computed by taking each individual score, subtracting the mean, squaring the result, adding the squared numbers, dividing by the number of cases, and taking the square root of the result. Doing this for Table 3.4 we discover that the standard deviation is 1,758. That is, just over two-thirds of the homicide scores fall between the mean (19,786) and plus or minus one standard deviation from the mean (1,758), or between 18,028 and 21,544.

Hypothesis Testing Traditionally, if behavioral scientists wish to test propositions like

> If the enforcement of laws is strict,
> then crime will diminish,

they tend to state them as hypotheses and then use routine statistical procedures to help them decide whether the hypotheses are true and what the probability of truth is, given certain assumptions. Of course, we have already done this for the above proposition using percentages, rates, and just plain common sense. However, sometimes we cannot simply "eyeball" data and expect everything to be self-evident. Minimally, to test a hypothesis we must

1. Make certain assumptions.
2. Obtain a sampling distribution.
3. Select a significance level.
4. Compute a test statistic.
5. Make a decision.

To explain these steps in hypothesis testing and to give, perhaps, a more adequate test of the proposition about law enforcement and crime rates, we need a more elaborate set of data—one in which enforcement and crime rates vary more. Such a data set is provided in Table 3.5 (for 1960 to 1980 only).

Table 3.5 presents arrest rates (i.e., enforcement) and homicide rates (crime) for twenty-one years in the United States. The hypothesis here is that as arrest rates go up, homicide rates will go down. Another way of saying the same thing is that we expect law enforcement and crime rates to have a negative association (called the research hypothesis or H_1). Ordinarily, we state a hypothesis by assuming no relationship (called the null hypothesis or H_0). If the test statistic in fact reveals a relationship (of sufficient strength), then we can reject the null hypothesis. Of course, given that there is some relationship, we still need to determine if the relationship is positive or negative. We may decide to reject both H_0 and H_1. Most tests of hypotheses also make assumptions about sampling (e.g., is the sample random?) and scales (here, are the scales of the two variables at least ordinal?).

If our assumptions are correct, then we can generate an expected distribution of possible outcomes, each with a known probability. This distribution is called a sampling distribution. Sampling distributions are mathematical con-

TABLE 3.5

Number of Homicide* Offenses, Arrests, Arrest Rates, and Homicide Rate in the United States, 1960 through 1980

Year	Offense	Arrest	(X) Arrest Rate	(Y) Homicide Rate
1960	9,050	6,307	.70	5.0
1961	8,680	5,847	.67	4.7
1962	8,480	6,089	.72	4.6
1963	8,580	6,129	.71	4.5
1964	9,300	6,412	.69	4.9
1965	9,900	7,348	.74	5.1
1966	10,970	7,826	.71	5.6
1967	12,160	9,145	.75	6.1
1968	13,720	10,394	.76	6.9
1969	14,890	11,509	.77	7.3
1970	15,890	12,836	.81	7.9
1971	17,670	14,549	.82	8.6
1972	18,550	15,049	.81	9.0
1973	19,510	14,399	.72	9.4
1974	20,710	13,818	.67	9.8
1975	20,510	16,485	.81	9.6
1976	18,780	14,113	.75	8.8
1977	19,120	17,163	.90	8.8
1978	19,560	18,755	.96	9.0
1979	21,460	18,264	.85	9.7
1980	23,044	20,040	.87	10.2
			$\bar{X}$ = .77	$\bar{X}$ = 7.4

*Homicide means murder and nonnegligent manslaughter.
Source: Derived from *Crime in the United States,* 1960–1980.

structions based on our assumptions. For example, a sampling distribution for the expected probabilities of getting heads in flipping a coin one to ten times is given in Table 3.6. Testing hypotheses involves comparing test results with expected outcomes given in sampling distributions. To illustrate, if crime and law enforcement are in fact totally unrelated, then we would expect a zero association. If our test association departs enough from zero, then we can reject the null hypothesis. If the association is positive,. then we can also reject the research hypothesis.

When we say "if our association departs enough from zero, then we can reject H_0," we are implying that we must choose a significance level to test a hypothesis. For example, how many heads in the ten flips of a coin would we get in a test before we concluded, say, that the coin was weighted (i.e., that

TABLE 3.6 Sampling Distribution for 0 to 10 Heads in a Very Large Number of Flips of a Coin

Number of Heads	Probabilities
0	.001
1	.010
2	.044
3	.117
4	.205
5	.246
6	.205
7	.117
8	.044
9	.010
10	.001
	1.000

Source: Hubert M. Blalock, Jr., *Social Statistics,* 1979:154.

someone was cheating)? If we got zero or ten heads in ten flips, the chance expectation would be one in a thousand. If our hypothesis were that the coin was honest, ten heads in ten trials might lead us to reject our hypothesis. By convention, depending on particulars, most social scientists use .05, .01, and .001 as significance levels. Any results as rare or rarer than 95, 99 percent, or 999 per thousand could be considered in a critical region. A test result in the critical region could be rejected. Under such conditions there are very small probabilities of rejecting a true null hypothesis (making a Type I error). Thus, for our coin example with a critical region of .05, 0–2 or 8–10 heads in ten trials would lead to our rejecting the null hypothesis.

Of course, there are many test statistics for hypotheses depending on sampling procedures, sample sizes, how the data are grouped, and so on (see Anderson and Sclove, 1978:Ch. 12). Presentation and calculation of most test statistics involve procedures too advanced for this introductory social problems textbook (cf. Babbie, 1986:58ff.; Davis, 1971). Essentially what such test statistics tell us is the strength of associations of two or more variables (like law enforcement and crime rates). If every instance of more law enforcement resulted in lower crime rates, we would have a perfect association (i.e., 1.0). Crudely, that is, every time laws were enforced, crime rates were less and every time laws were not enforced crime rates went up. Under certain assumptions, if an association or correlation between two variables is sufficiently strong, social scientists tend to conclude their relationship is not explained by chance alone. For example, we might assume that law enforcement in some way actually influences crime rates.

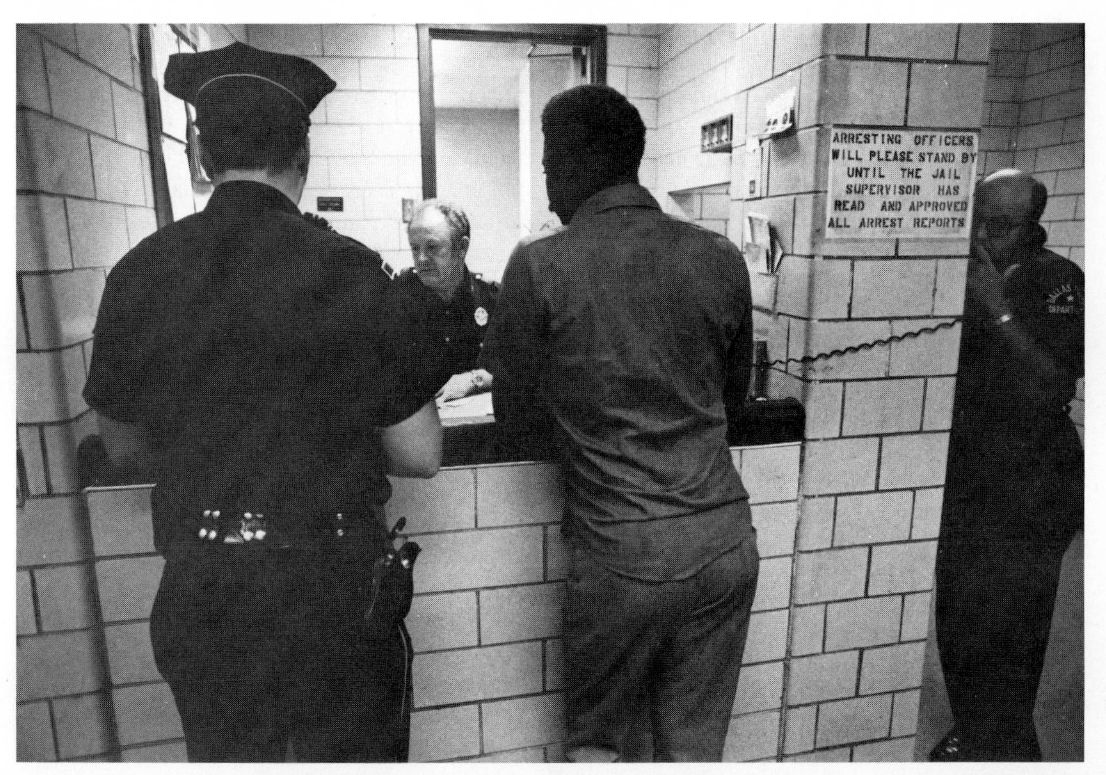

By examining arrest rates for homicide and homicide rates over time, we can get an idea if strict law enforcement reduces crime rates. However, a correlation of arrest and homicide rates does not prove a causal relationship. (Carl Wolinsky/Stock, Boston)

Causal Inference Of course, we must stress that correlation is not causation. Just because two variables, such as strictness of law enforcement and crime rates, may be highly correlated does not prove that one causes the other; nor does it say which one causes the other, if there should be a causal relationship. It is possible that the wind velocity in Chicago is strongly associated with the birthrate in India (that is, there is a spurious relationship). In the relationship between arrest rates and homicide rates, even with consistently high positive associations, theoretical interpretations concerning possible causal relations are still required. For example, do high arrest rates cause high rates of homicide (by encouraging discovery of their true prevalence), or do high homicide rates and the great number of homicides encourage more arrests? Thus, in the present chapter we have come full circle. That is, we return once more to theory and the theoretical perspectives discussed in Chapter 2. Theory is the primary determinant of causal models and meaningful statistics.

We make causal assumptions based on everything that is known about the phenomena we are studying—including previous studies and hunches. For example, Palmer found in his homicide research that age, sex, frustration, and socioeconomic status were important factors in determining homicidal aggression (1960; cf. Conklin, 1986:27, 275). Using Palmer's study we might construct a simple causal model of homicide like that depicted in Figure 3.1.[10] This model implies that age and sex are important "background" variables, that have direct relations with homicide (that is, the younger and the more males in a population, the higher the homicide rate), that age and sex are positively (indicated by + in Figure 3.1) related to socioeconomic status, which in turn is negatively (indicated by − in Figure 3.1) related to frustration and the homicide rate, and that frustration is positively related to the homicide rate.[11]

Statistics can never tell us which variables must be included in a causal model. Neither can statistics tell us which way to draw the arrows. However, once a causal model (say, of a specific social problem) has been constructed theoretically (using the best data available, hunches, insights, and so on), statistics can be used to test the model and to make inferences. For example, if we operationally defined the concepts in Figure 3.1 and calculated correlation

FIGURE 3.1 A Simple Causal Model for Homicide

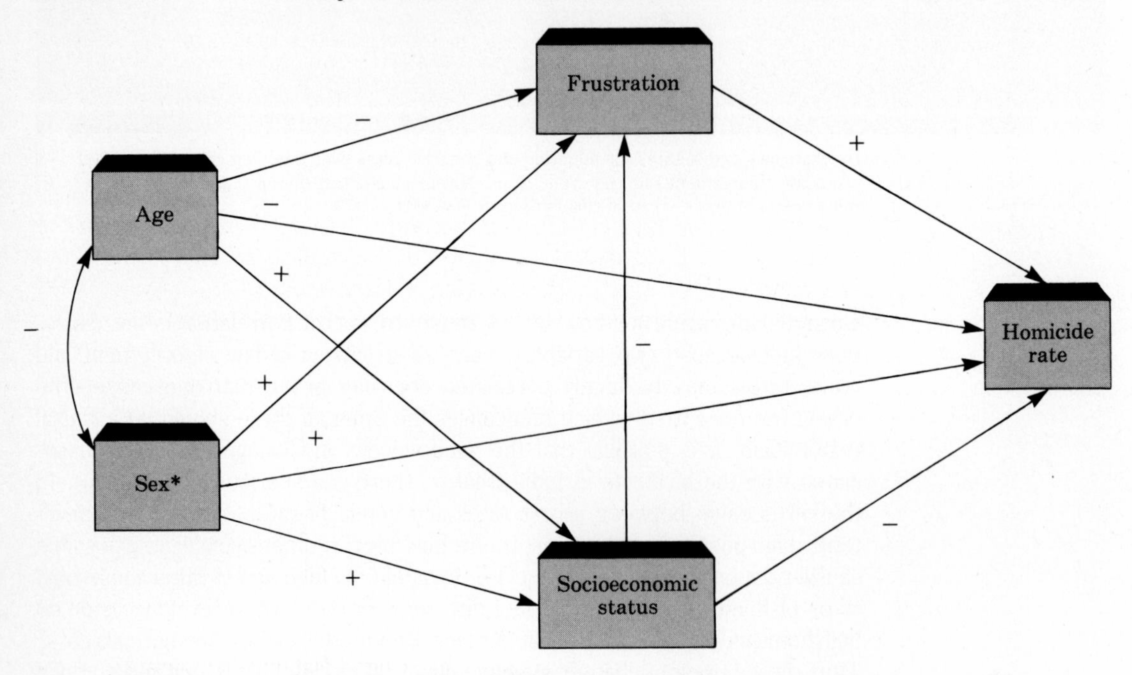

*Where male sex equals a "high" score and female sex equals a "low" score.

Source: Figure based on data from *A Study of Murder* by Stuart Palmar (Thomas Y. Crowell). Copyright © 1960 by Stuart Palmer. Reprinted by permission of Harper & Row Publishers, Inc.

coefficients for each plus and minus relationship predicted, then under a certain set of assumptions we could actually see if there were any empirical relationships, how strong they were, and if they were in fact the sign we predicted. If there were no relationships (or no statistically significant ones) between some variables or if the relationships had different signs than we expected, then we probably would need to reformulate the model.

After we had calculated correlations (actually a correlation matrix), then we could even calculate path coefficients. Path coefficients are coefficients that measure the exact influence of a specific antecedent variable (e.g., age), a specific variable presumed to be influenced (Land, 1969; Maris, 1972; Mansfield, 1986:448–503). These procedures are much more sophisticated (and even they are now somewhat outmoded) than the present text allows us to explain. The main point here, once again, is the primacy of theory or theoretical perspectives of social problems and how statistics can be used to help sharpen, shape, and refine our theories.

Four Methodological Approaches to the Study of Social Problems

It should be evident by now that to understand social problems we must examine some data. Furthermore, many theoretical perspectives in the study of social problems do not regard data only as subjective claims about what is problematic, but rather seek to go beyond subjective claims to objective conditions in society or to Durkhemian social facts (1897). Our own definition of social problems requires that we attempt to establish general patterns of human behavior or social conditions independently of whether these patterns or conditions are perceived to be problems by society. More precisely, we shall focus on recurrent patterns of social behavior or "enduring social structures."

In the chapters that follow on aging, sex or gender role conflicts, race relations, mental disorders, and so on, sociological methods will have to be applied to relevant facts. In doing this we shall be interested in four basic types of data: official records of various sorts, small-group or individual case studies, larger surveys of various populations, and social or social-psychological experiments.

Records, Documents, and Official Statistics Although we must interpret them with considerable care, one of the most valuable sources of relevant data for the study of social problems is the official statistics of various federal and state agencies (see Panel 3.2). These data tend to be presented as rates and percentages of broad social characteristics. Examples of this first type of data would include United States Census data, United Nations Demographic yearbooks, United States Vital Statistics reports, the Federal Bureau of Investigation's Uniform Crime Reports, and police or hospital records.[12] These reports contain data on both deviant and nondeviant general populations. It is also

PANEL 3.2

Sources of Official Statistics Used in the Study of Social Problems

THE UNITED STATES CENSUS BUREAU—Since 1790 the U.S. has taken a complete census every ten years. A census is a count of all of the people in a nation; of their social, economic, and demographic characteristics. The 1980 census cost about one billion dollars and asked about the size of the American population, its age and sex, rural-urban residence, racial and ethnic composition, marital status, labor force participation, occupations, educational status, and so on. Some specialized censuses of samples of the U.S. population are taken in between the decennial censuses (e.g., between 1980 and 1990).

THE UNITED STATES DEPARTMENT OF VITAL STATISTICS—Another valuable source of data for the study of social problems is that obtained through registration systems of birth, death, marriage, and divorce by civil, medical, ecclesiastical (religious), and other officials. The U.S. vital statistics permit an estimate of how the population is changing between the ten-year censuses, especially in the Monthly Vital Statistics Reports.

CURRENT POPULATION SURVEYS—Begun in the mid-1940s, the Current Population Surveys (CPS) are a source of labor-force data (e.g., employment and unemployment, income, poverty status, and so on) collected and published by the U.S. Census Bureau. The *CPS* samples one out of every 1,200 households in the country. The *CPS* conducts specialized analyses of particular population segments, such as the elderly, blacks, women, and so on. There are some variables in the *CPS* that are not in the U.S. Vital Statistics, for example, the number of children that are born.

GENERAL POPULATION SURVEYS—Population-based surveys are also conducted by private agencies like Gallup, Roper, Harris, Yankelovich, and by university survey research centers like the National Opinion Research Center (NORC) at the University of Chicago and the Institute for Social Research (ISR) at the University of Michigan. NORC has provided general social surveys of a national sample of Americans since 1972. Variables measured include work status, occupational prestige, marital status, educational status, residence, ethnicity, income, political preference, opinions about race and sexual preference, drug use, religion, traits of children, smoking behavior, preferred job traits, gun ownership, and so on.

THE FBI's UNIFORM CRIME REPORTS—The Federal Bureau of Investigation gathers statistics from nearly 16,000 city, county, and state law enforcement agencies that cover about 97 percent of the country's population. The *UCR* misses some information, such as that from campus police forces. Part I offenses (see Chapter 15) are called index crimes (e.g., murder, rape, robbery, assault, burglary, larceny, motor vehicle theft, and arson). Part I offenses tend to be very serious crimes. Part II offenses (there are 21 of them) tend to be less serious crimes (e.g., prostitution, driving under the influences, forgery, gambling, and so on). The *UCR* emphasizes crimes by low-income minority groups and tends to neglect white-collar crime and organized crime.

NATIONAL CRIME SURVEYS—The first national victimization survey was done in 1966 by NORC. Since 1972 the federal government has done national crime surveys, which measure both personal and household victimization of national samples. The NCS measured unreported crime as well as reported crime in 60,000 households (about 135,000 persons), since victims often fail to report crimes to the police the NCS data generally show more crime and higher crime rates than the FBI's *UCR*s do.

recommended that any serious student of social problems should subscribe to and read at least one major newspaper, such as the *New York Times,* the *Washington Post, The Wall Street Journal,* or the *Christian Science Monitor.* Finally, one should not overlook more personal documents like diaries, biographies, notes, and letters of various sorts. These latter types of documentary data often compensate for their obvious sampling weakness by their rich details and first-person accounts.

Of course, official statistics have been criticized by some sociologists as being potentially biased and, thus, possibly inaccurate (Douglas, 1967; Nelson et al., 1978; However, cf. Pescosolido and Mendelsohn, 1986). For example, the census bureau is often accused, usually by big-city mayors who stand to lose large sums of federal money, of undercounting minorities (Nam and Philliber, 1984:143). Other official statistics, like the *Uniform Crime Reports,* are sometimes criticized for underreporting the so-called white-collar crimes and for not being very systematic in their data gathering. Some critics do not have much faith in any third-person reports of someone else's behaviors or (especially) attitudes.

A good illustration of such sociological criticism is Douglas's objections to "official" suicide rates (1967). In an older, but important book on the *Social Meanings of Suicide* Douglas contends that there tend to be as many official statistics of suicide (i.e., rates) as there are officials. That is, each coroner or medical examiner tends to have his/her own criteria for pronouncing suicide on the death certificate. For example, one coroner is reported to have classified a death as suicide only if a suicide note were left. However, only about 25 percent of all suicides ever leave notes (Maris, 1981:275). Douglas would have us determine the meanings of suicide to the suicide individuals themselves. Of course, this process is problematic after the fact. Official statistics are also criticized for glossing over the various meanings of suicide by lumping all suicides together. Of course, others (e.g., Pescosolido and Mendelsohn, 1986; Gibbs, 1968) argue that we should use official statistics because such data have not been proven all that biased—especially compared with more subjective alternatives.

Case Studies and Participant Observation in Small Groups Much of the official statistics is concerned with groups that are too large, is not focused on actual interactions, or is not designed to provide empirical information on variables relevant to the study of social problems. For example, official statistics are usually not much help in designing and testing an exchange theory of social problems. Exchange theorists recommend that we concentrate instead on relatively small groups, thus allowing us to study face-to-face interaction, determine rewards and values more accurately (since values tend to be less complex and more homogeneous in small groups), assess rewards, costs, and profits of particular social interactions and interaction patterns better, speak more sensibly of deprivation and satiation, measure aggression and approval, and in general to examine the generation of enduring social structures, both nonproblematic and problematic.

This second broad methodological approach to social problems data gathering ranges from individual case studies to ethnographies and participant observation. Good examples of the case study approach might include the *New York Times'* descriptions of the "100 Most Needy Families" usually published just before Christmas or great cases in psychiatry like "the girl who couldn't breathe" (Freud, 1895), "the man who loved corsets" (Abraham, 1910), "the child who couldn't sleep" (Klein, 1924), or "the unknown murderer" (Reik, 1925). Ethnographies are descriptive accounts, usually by anthropologists, of life in small, often "primitive" societies. Examples here would include Malinowski's study of crime and custom among Trobriand islanders (1926) or Lewis's description of a poor Mexican family in *The Children of Sanchez* (1961). Of course, sociologists also engage in small-group or participant observation in the field. We have already had an occasion (in Chapter 1) to introduce you to Homans's description of the "Bank Wiring Observation Room." Much of the work of Erving Goffman was participant observation. To illustrate, Goffman worked as a recreation therapist in Saint Elizabeth's Hospital in Washington, D.C., to better understand the social construction of mental illnesses (1961). Other well-known classic participant observation studies include Liebow's Talley's Corner (1967), Whyte's *Street Corner Society* (1943), and Humpheys' *Tea Room Trade* (1970).

Surveys Sometimes rather than just keeping records (say of births, deaths, physician visits, army inductees, all the people in a census area, school children, and so on) or "naturalistically" observing actual small groups in action, social scientists may wish systematically to sample a specific population and then interview the sample to test particular hypotheses or gather evidence for a particular theoretical perspective. That is, we may wish to survey the behavior and/or attitudes of a segment of society.

Since many social problems concern deviant or illegal behaviors, often records do not exist and observation is difficult or even dangerous. In such a situation a survey may be called for. One thinks of Kinsey's surveys in 1948 and 1953 of the sexual behaviors of American males and females, respectively. Although the Kinsey samples were not systematic (e.g., not random), they provide some of the first detailed data ever available on patterns of sexual behaviors, normal and nonnormal. Another major survey that comes to mind is that of Srole and associates concerning mental health in midtown Manhattan (original, 1962; revised ed., 1975). Srole noted correctly that we know next to nothing about the mental health status of the general nonhospitalized population. *Mental Health in the Metropolis* showed clearly that mental illness was widespread in the general population and was highly related to low social status. Srole's survey was also instrumental in helping get President Kennedy's Community Mental Health Center Act passed in 1963.

"Bring me my pipe, my bowl, my fiddlers three, and my pollster."

Surveys are often designed to test some rather specific hypotheses, which in turn are rooted in a theoretical perspective that has been carefully thought through. All of this results in a standardized interview schedule or questionnaire that, if properly administered, provides the raw data needed to test one's research hypotheses and provide evidence for or against one's theoretical perspective. Often questionnaire items are adapted from other surveys, thus giving the researcher built-in normative comparisons with previous data on other populations. In the design phase of a survey, it is customary to explore sampling issues (such as who, how many, what age, sex, and race, and so on) and to pretest and revise the questionnaire before actually administering it to the target population.

Once the questionnaire is ready and the names and addresses of the sample have been secured, a group of interviewers is trained and assigned interviews to secure. These interviews are usually done face-to-face (i.e., door-to-door) but can also be completed via the mail or over a telephone. Routinely an interview supervisor verifies that interviews have actually been done and not just fabricated. Of course, the higher the response rate, the better. If the response rate is low, survey results are questionable. When all the interviews have been secured that can be secured, the questionnaires are ready to be coded. Coding involves translating ordinary data into numbers on magnetic computer tape. Often the same questionnaire will be coded by two different coders in an effort to minimize coding errors. Finally, the data will be statistically analyzed and interpreted in relation to specific research and theoretical arguments.

While surveys have the advantage mentioned above, they also have some distinct disadvantages. Perhaps most central among these is that survey data depend entirely on respondents. If people interviewed lie or do not know what they are talking about, then obviously the resultant survey data can be worthless. Note too that surveys tend to substitute talk for behavior. People may say (report) one thing but do another (different) thing. Standardized questionnaires by definition are also unwieldly and rigid. If the interviewer needs flexibility, ordinarily it just is not there without violating procedural mandates to administer each questionnaire the same way. Finally, surveys tend to be costly. In an era of diminished financial resources for research purposes (especially from federal government funding), to spend $100 to $200 per interview for a few thousand interviews is often prohibitive.

Experiments A final methodological approach for obtaining data relevant to the study of social problems is that of experimentation. For most of us the idea of an experiment probably conjures up images of a chemistry or physics laboratory, not a social problem. Such images are useful since one of the distinct advantages of experiments over documents, participant observation, and surveys is that causal relationships can be examined under highly controlled conditions. Often we need to know if one particular stimulus alone produces a specific outcome.

For example, suppose we wished to test the hypothesis that distributive injustice produces anger (exchange theory's fifth proposition in Panel 2.2). If we designed an experiment to test this hypothesis, traditionally we would need:

1. An experimental and a control group.
2. Before and after measurements on the dependent variable (here, anger).
3. A stimulus or treatment of distributive justice (or injustice).

Schematically, we might design our experiment crudely as in Figure 3.2:

Fortunately Thibaut (1950) has conducted a similar experiment for us already. He studied groups of boys ten to twelve years old in summer camps

FIGURE 3.2

An Experimental Design for Testing the Relation of Distributive Justice to Anger

	Before	Treatment	After
Experimental group	No anger	Distributive injustice	Anger
Control group	No anger	Distributive justice	No anger

near Boston. These boys came to him in groups of ten to twelve. Each group was subdivided into two teams of five or six members with each side including equal numbers of "popular" boys (that is, no one in the before stage had any reason to prefer being on a different team). The "treatment" consisted of playing three games in which one team consistently had the least desirable role (was hit by balls or run against as a human chain) and the other consistently had the most desirable role.

With half of the sets of teams (Thibaut does not say how many sets of two teams there were) in a fourth game the high- and low-status positions in the first three games were reversed. In the remainder in all four games the two teams were consistently either high or low status. Thus, after four games there were these four status groups:

1. Always high status.
2. Always low status.
3. One-time high, usually low status.
4. One-time low, usually high status.

Of course, distributive injustice was highest for groups 1 and 2, but with some important differences. Group 1 profited from injustice and group 2 suffered. Distributive injustice was lower for groups 3 and 4.

At the end of the experiment Thibaut measured the most popular boys out of all groups and asked them once again to choose the most popular boys out of all ten or twelve. Groups 3 and 4, the control groups, were least hostile and expressed less desire for change in their own team's composition. Group 2, as we might expect, was most angry. Group 1 tended to feel guilt, not anger. Somewhat surprisingly both groups 1 and 2 wanted changes in their teams. Group 1 wanted to be more like the central members of the high-status group, to be sure of getting rewards. Group 2 members wanted to be more like each other (made more within-group choices) to solidify their anger against Group 1. In general, the more distributive injustice, the higher the level of anger and the greater the desire for social change.

To be sure experiments have certain limits and disadvantages too when applied to human populations. One common disadvantage is that we cannot experiment easily with people, as we can with inanimate objects or even animals. Some outcomes (dependent variables) are simply too dangerous or immoral to let happen. What if outcomes were murder, heroin addiction, promiscuity, and so forth? It must also be remembered that experimental small groups are not real societies. If anything they tend to be "toy societies" comprised largely of middle-class, white, college students. In spite of these limits experiments obviously have much to tell us about social problems that previously has been largely ignored.

• Summary

In this chapter we have asked how research methods enter into the construction, elaboration, and resolution of social problems. We examined propositions (specifically, laws or axioms, definitions, empirical generalizations, theorems, and hypotheses) and how they could be linked using rules of inference to construct theories of social problems. The truth of propositions was distinguished from logical validity. An attempt was made to further specify exchange theory's concept of value into common rewards and to suggest a hierarchy of rewards following the work of Maslow. It was argued that what is rewarding needs to be established before many of our theoretical perspectives can be useful in resolving social problems.

In constructing theories of social problems broadly, one can make either logical or empirical errors. Logical errors can be further subdivided into formal or informal fallacies. Informal fallacies are errors in reasoning based in irrelevancies or ambiguities. A valid formal argument is one in which the form of the theory is such that if its premises are true, then its conclusion must be true. Rules of inference are valid arguments used to construct more elaborate arguments or theories.

Whereas logical methods are used to construct theoretical perspectives, empirical methods and statistics are used primarily to test a theory. The emphasis in this section was on facts; operationally defining them, selecting them, establishing them, interpreting them, and then using them to examine the truth or falsity of propositions. Major subsections included discussions of measurement (e.g., Type I and II errors, reliability and empirical [not logical] validity, and scales), sampling issues (e.g., simple random sampling, probability and nonprobability samples, sample sizes, and representative samples), descriptive statistics (e.g., percentages, rates, bases, measures of central tendency like the mean) and of dispersion (like standard deviation), hypothesis testing (e.g., the steps involved, the concept of association, sampling distributions, null and research hypotheses, significance levels, test statistics, and an introduction to causal inference (e.g., modeling and causation versus association)—all using propositions from and data relevant to variations on the crime argument.

Finally, Chapter 3 examined four basic methodological approaches to obtaining data for the study of social problems. These included official statistics, individual cases, surveys, and experiments. Each of these methodological approaches were elaborated and related to theories of social problems. In Chapter 4 we shall begin to use the theoretical and empirical tools assembled so carefully in the previous three chapters to attempt to understand our first substantive social problem—that of aging.

• Notes

1. Of course, emphasis on subjective social meanings need not logically entail less quantification. Some ethnomethodologists and other subjectivists are highly abstract and formal, if not mathematical, in their approach to sociology.

2. Examples are taken from Copi, 1986, passim.

3. For other purposes and types of definitions see Copi, 1986, Chapter Four.

4. Part of the genius of French sociologist Emile Durkheim (1895, 1897) was that he always took great pains to determine exactly what the social facts were to avoid explaining some condition that did not exist.

5. Actually, for the most part, we will borrow laws from others, not formulate them. One unique aspect of our approach lies in the application of exchange and structural propositions to social problems. It would be misleading to imply that exchange and structualism are new theories. They are not (cf. Turner, 1986:Ch. 12; Wilson, 1983:Ch. 3 and 4).

6. However, see my papers in the *American Sociological Review,* 1970, vol. 35 (Dec.): 1069–81 and 1971, vol. 36 (Aug.): 713–715.

7. However, to claim that whatever one does is valuable can amount to a circular definition of *value.*

8. Sometimes the seven major crimes are called Type I or index offenses to distinguish them from other crimes like embezzlement, drunkenness, disorderly conduct, arson, prostitution, and so on (Type II offenses). See Chapter 15.

9. Students wishing more detailed considerations of statistics and research methods should see Blalock, *Social Statistics,* 1979; Williamson et al., *The Research Craft,* 1982; Babbie, *The Practice of Social Research,* 1986; Mansfield, *Basic Statistics,* 1986.

10. Palmer himself did *not* construct a causal model.

11. Not all relationships in the figure have been described.

12. See, for example, (1) the U.S. Bureau of the Census, *Characteristics of the Population: 1980,* Volume I, Part I, U.S. Government Printing Office, Washington, D.C., 1983; (2) *Demographic Yearbook, 1986,* New York: United Nations; (3) *Monthly Vital Statistics Report,* National Center for Health Statistics, U.S. Department of Health and Human Services, Hyattsville, Maryland; (4) *Current Population Reports,* Population Profile of the U.S., 1985, U.S. Government Printing Office, Washington, D.C., 1986; and (5) *Uniform Crime Reports for the U.S., 1986,* U.S. Government Printing Office, Washington, D.C.

• Glossary

Argument. Any group of propositions, of which one is claimed to follow from the others, that are regarded as providing evidence for the truth of that one.

Cause. Anything producing an effect or result. A necessary condition for an effect to occur is a circumstance in the absence of which the effect cannot occur. A sufficient condition is a circumstance in the presence of which the effect must occur.

Correlation. The amount of association between two or more variables. Variables may covary without having any causal connections.

Data. Things known or assumed. Facts used to test hypotheses or assess theories.

Deductive. The premises of a deductive argument provide conclusive evidence for the truth of its conclusion. Often distinguished from inductive arguments in which premises provide some evidence for truth of its conclusion.

Empirical. Relying or based solely on fact, observation, or experiment. In philosophy the notion that knowledge arises solely out of experience or sensation. Thus, sometimes (misleadingly) contrasted with theoretical.

Error. Implies deviation from truth, accuracy, correctness, rightness, and so on. In statistics a *Type I error* is made when a true hypothesis is rejected; a *Type II error* is made when a false hypothesis is accepted.

Experiment. An investigation in which one or more variables (independent) are manipulated by an experimenter under carefully controlled conditions with the objective of demonstrating a causal connection between (or among) the independent variable(s) and a dependent variable.

Fact. Any demonstrated or demonstrable item of reality. For Durkheim, an external and constraining thing. Something that has actually happened or is true. Theories are constructed to explain facts.

Fallacy. A mistake in reasoning. Informal fallacies are errors in reasoning based on irrelevance or ambiguity. Formal fallacies violate accepted patterns of valid inference.

Logic. The study of the methods and principles used in distinguishing correct from incorrect reasoning.

Mean. A measure of central tendency in which the sum of the scores is divided by the total number of cases involved.

Null Hypothesis. States that there is no difference between several groups or no relationship between variables. Usually it is a hypothesis the researcher would like to reject.

Official Statistics. Usually a federal or state agency's tabulation of birth, death, crime, population change, mental disorder (and the like) rates; often controlling for age, sex, race, marital status, and occupation.

Participant Observation. A method of obtaining social data through firsthand observation by the researcher of relatively small face-to-face groups actually interacting. Sometimes the observer even becomes part of the group studied, sometimes not.

Probability. The likelihood, chance, or odds, that some event or outcome will occur. A probability is the proportion of a particular outcome (a "success") in the long run.

Rate. A ratio multiplied usually by 1,000 or 100,000 to avoid small decimal values. For example, the suicide rate equals the number of suicides divided by the number of the relevant population multiplied by 100,000. Or the birthrate is often given as the number of live births per 1,000 females of childbearing age.

Reliability. Evidence is reliable to the extent that we can assert confidently that similar findings would be obtained if the process of collecting evidence were repeated by independent investigators. The extent to which measures give consistent results.

Representative. A sampling plan is representative when there is a high probability that following it will produce a sample that is representative of the universe or population from which it was drawn. Refers to the correspondence of samples and universes from which samples are taken.

Research Hypothesis. A hypothesis (H_1) set up as an alternative to the null hypothesis (H_0). The research hypothesis usually predicts either a positive or negative relationship.

Rule of Inference. Standard valid argument forms used to make inferences (generate theorems) from axioms and definitions.

Sampling Distribution. Refers to the relative number of times we would expect to get certain outcomes in a very large number of experiments. The probability distribution of each possible outcome of an experiment.

Scale. A level of measurement depending on one's categorization procedures. Nominal scales are classifications. Ordinal scales permit greater or less-than comparisons (ranking). Interval scales specify exact distances among points on the scale.

Significance Level. The probability of making a Type I error (rejection of a true hypothesis) is referred to as the significance level of a test and can be set at any desired level; although .05, .01, and .001 are the most common levels.

Simple Random Sampling. Has the property of giving each individual an equal chance of being selected and also of giving each combination of individuals an equal chance of selection.

Standard Deviation. The square root of the arithmetic mean of the squared deviations from the mean. In a normal distribution 68.3 percent of all cases fall plus or minus one standard deviation from the mean and 95.5 percent of all cases within plus or minus two standard deviations from the mean.

Survey. A method of gathering data by interviewing, telephoning, or writing subjects. A systematic attempt to collect information to describe and explain the beliefs, attitudes, values, and behaviors of selected groups of people. Involves sample design, questionnaire construction and pretesting, interviewing, coding, putting data on computer tapes, and analysis.

Test Statistic. A statistic used in hypothesis testing to help one decide whether to reject or accept a hypothesis. One computes a quantity from sample data that varies in a known way according to probability theory. Then one compares its value with the test statistic's sampling distribution and makes a decision by evaluating the probability of its occurence. Common test statistics include Z, t, F, and chi-square.

Theorem. A hypothetical proposition logically derived from laws or axioms and definitions by applying rules of inference. A research result can be explained by deducing it as a theorem from axioms and definitions.

Valid. To be *empirically* valid a measure must correspond to the true position of the person or object on the characteristic being measured. To be *logically* valid an argument's premises must provide conclusive evidence for the truth of its conclusion.

• Further Reading

Babbie, Earl. *The Practice of Social Research.* Belmont, CA: Wadsworth, 1986. A proven social research textbook now in its fourth edition. It has chapters on many topics we have just discussed, including theory construction (Ch. 2), causation (Ch. 3), operationalizing (Ch. 6), sampling (Ch. 7), experiments (Ch. 8), surveys (Ch. 9), field work (Ch. 10), unobstrusive measures (Ch. 11), and scales (Ch. 15). A very useful set of appendexes is included too (e.g., an SPSS guide, glossary bibliography, how to use your library, write a research report, etc.).

Blalock, Hubert M., Jr. *Social Statistics.* New York: McGraw-Hill, 1979. A venerable textbook on social statistics by a methodology award winner, Hubert Blalock. More on scales, probability, hypothesis testing, test statistics and sampling distributions, contingency tables, correlation and regression. Several statistical exercises to practice on (for a more recent introductory statistics text, see Edwin Mansfield, *Basic Statistics,* W. W. Norton, 1986).

Copi, Irving M. *Introduction to Logic.* New York: Macmillan, 1986. Extremely readable introduction to logic complete with exercises and answers. If you are having trouble understanding rules of inference, theory construction, or evaluating logical validity, see Chapter 9. There is also a first-rate chapter on scientific explanations (13). You might also wish to look at the chapter on definitions (4).

Davis, James A. *Elementary Survey Analysis.* Englewood Cliffs, NJ: Prentice-Hall, 1971. A slim volume with the motto "Seek simplicity and distrust it" introduces the student to analyzing survey data in the tradition of Lazarsfeld and Kendall. Yule's Q and gamma test statistics figure prominently in the analysis of simple contingency tables. Emphasis is on the logic of explanation rather than pure statistics.

Selltiz, Claire et al. *Research Methods in Social Relations.* New York: Holt, Rinehart, and Winston, 1976. The nuts and bolts of doing research. Elaborates our four methodological approaches of documents, participant observations, surveys, and experiments. Also, good chapters on research design, sampling, and causal modeling. If you plan to do a research project, this is the place to start.

Weston, Louise C., ed. *Social Problems Courses: A Set of Syllabi and Related Materials.* Washington, DC: American Sociological Association, 1979. Takes a close look at empirical issues specifically related to social problems courses. Contains very useful exercises, data resources, field work projects, data reports, section on statistics and social problems (39 ff.), syllabuses of other social problems courses, and written assignments.

P·A·R·T

II

Subinstitutionally Related Social Problems

C·H·A·P·T·E·R

4

Age: Being Young and Growing Old

Exchanges with the young and the old in contemporary society tend to be costly and relatively unrewarding. Given what most human beings and societies find valuable, on the whole interaction with the aged is costly. The young tend to exchange their mostly physical advantages for money and status. Not surprisingly, then, the aged are often isolated, poor, and depressed, while adolescents and young adults routinely have sexual problems or problems related to their superior physical strength and energy (e.g., crime).

Functionalists agree that in today's society, both the young and the elderly tend to be economic and social liabilities, not assets. However, they do not see age groups as having radically different values. Rather, the young and the old have blocked opportunities to achieving basically common values. All age groups place a high value on money, security, social status, health, and so on. Conflict theorists see powerful middle-aged people oppressing the young and the old because it is advantageous to the middle aged and their interests. For example, older workers cost too much while the young work more cheaply, are less unionized, and so on. Symbolic interactionists emphasize that the meanings of age have changed with the industrial revolution and modern technology. The stereotypes of the young and the old are more negative today. Both age groups are perceived to be less useful and relatively untrained for contemporary social and work demands.

As a group middle-aged people in a society have the greatest power in large part because they have the most to offer of what the society at large finds valuable. Of course, over time these power advantages have tended to become institutionalized, sometimes in spite of what middle-aged people actually have to offer society. People usually reach their peak social effectiveness roughly between the ages thirty or thirty-five to forty-five or fifty. Problems of middle age tend to center on satiation, stress, boredom, stagnation, and repetition, rather than on disenfranchisement or lack of rewarding assets.

The large size of the younger age groups and the increasing size of aged groups in America by themselves threaten to change the power structure of U.S. society were it not for the tremendous resource advantages (e.g., of power, authority, property, political clout, money, and so on) of middle-aged elites.

◆

Age is a powerful factor in all of our lives. Often problems turn on an individual's or society's relative age. Although we will concentrate more on the elderly in this chapter (see Panel 4.1), the aging process throughout the life cycle is the fundamental social issue before us. Thus, transitions from childhood to adolescence, (for example), are just as important as those from middle age to old age. Unlike some of the more macro-level social problem topics considered later on in this book, all of the early chapters (namely, Chapters 4–9) concern social problems that are partly institutional and partly subinstitutional. For example, while ageism, sexism, racism, and so on indicate discriminatory and biased (stereotypic) social attitudes, they also grow out of real biological differences across ages, between sexes, and among races. Throughout this book we aim for a general theory of social problems based on the seven theoretical perspectives outlined in Chapter 2.[1] While most social problems texts conceive of the aged primarily as oppressed minorities (i.e., take basically a conflict or symbolic interaction perspective) and are continually reducing social situations to stereotypic "bad guys" (majority groups) and "good guys" (minority groups), we shall also look for exchange, structural, functional, and biological characteristics of the aged, (the young, and the middle aged) that help account for their social problems (See Neugarten and Neugarten, 1986:34).[2]

In trying to understand social problems related to age we must address several basic underlying issues. For one, America has an aging population, with a greater proportion of our population becoming elderly and a smaller proportion being young (Pifer and Bronte, 1986; Siegel and Taeuber, 1986). This in turn has resulted in a new economic and social dependency of the elderly on the middle aged and the young (Riley and Riley, 1986; Wayne, 1986). We shall also be concerned about how much of aging is biological, social, or cultural (Rossi, 1986; Birren, 1986). Finally, there will be several age-group

PANEL 4.1

Three Cases of Aging

Now eighty-one, **Joseph Bartlett** could look back on a long and useful life. He was living in a dusty Oklahoma town where he had lived since leaving farming and becoming a barber. He had been present at the opening of Indian Territory to white settlers and during the later oil boom. He had lost his wife and his only son ten years before. Since he had been self-employed he had no social security and was forced to turn to welfare. He was without transportation in the rural village. There were no social services, and medical care was inaccessible. His close friends and family had died, and he was too proud to ask other townspeople for the help he needed. He admitted to living in pain for a number of years but declared he would never burden anyone—"I will make do for myself."

Rose Anderson was ninety years old, wispy, and frail. She lived in a room filled with yellowed newspapers, magazines, and books; it was filthy. There were cockroaches. There was an ugly permeating stench. She was too weary to clean. She gave her energy to caring for her canary.

She had been the wife of a prominent physician but she had the "misfortune" of living to a ripe old age and outliving both the $300,000 her husband had carefully provided for her and her only child, a son, who died at the age of fifty-seven when she was seventy-six. She had given over some of her money to support her daughter-in-law and grandchildren. But most of it went for her own extensive medical expenses. She ended up living on welfare.

Professor **Frank Minkoff** a seventy-year-old Russian immigrant with a university degree in engineering, was still teaching mathematics at an evening school. He was unmarried, the only member of his family in the United States, and lived in an apartment crammed with books. Suddenly he became confused and disoriented. He was frightened and refused to leave his room. Concerned neighbors quickly called a doctor, who expressed his unwillingness to make a home visit, saying, "There is nothing I can do. He needs to be in a nursing home or a mental institution." The neighbors were unconvinced, remembering Mr. M.'s earlier good functioning. They pleaded with the doctor and, under pressure, he angrily complied and visited the home. While there he again repeated his conviction that Mr. M. needed "custodial" care. Mr. M. was coherent enough to refuse, saying he would never voluntarily go to a nursing home or mental hospital. He did agree to be admitted to a medical hospital. Admission took place and studies resulted in the diagnosis "reversible brain syndrome due to acute viral infection." Mr. M. was successfully treated and released to his home in good condition in less than a week.

Source: Excerpts from *Why Survive?* by Robert N. Butler, M.D.

The United States has an aging population. Here a Florida Jewish community center provides free lunches for the elderly. Unfortunately, most economic, social, and personal problems of the elderly are not resolved so easily. (Patricia H. Gross/Stock, Boston)

specific social issues that need to be examined. Somewhat arbitrarily we have divided these age issues into those of the young (including problems of jobs, sex, education, crime, suicide, and so on), of the middle aged (e.g., economic burdens, stress, the mid-life crisis), and of the aged (e.g., economic difficulties, isolation, work, dying, health care, and so on) (Davis, 1986; Richman and Stagner, 1986). Remember that we shall be interested in exploring these issues as they relate to both the aging of individuals and that of populations (i.e., to social structural considerations).

What better place to start than by familiarizing ourselves with the age structure of the United States and by counting the number of occupants of various age groups? As you can see from Table 4.1 and Figure 4.1, since 1900 a larger and larger proportion of the American population has become aged (See "Index of Aging" in Table 4.1). The median age was 31.2 in 1984, but is expected to be 38 by 2030. Life expectancy has increased from a little over forty years at the turn of the century to around seventy-one years now (sev-

TABLE 4.1

Percentage Distribution of Three Age Groups in the United States, 1880-1984. Index of Aging and Dependency Ratio

Year	14 Years or Under	15–64 Years	65 Years and Over	Index of Aging*	Dependency Ratio†
1984	22.0	66.1	11.9	54.1	51.3
1980	22.6	66.2	11.2	49.5	51.1
1970	28.5	61.7	9.8	34.4	61.1
1960	31.0	59.8	9.2	29.7	67.2
1950	26.8	65.3	8.2	30.6	53.5
1940	25.0	68.1	6.8	27.2	46.6
1930	29.3	65.1	5.4	18.4	53.3
1920	31.7	63.4	4.7	14.8	57.4
1910	32.1	63.4	4.3	13.4	57.4
1900	34.4	61.3	3.1	11.9	62.8
1890	35.5	60.4	3.9	11.0	65.2
1880	38.1	58.5	3.4	8.9	70.9

$$\text{*Index of aging} = \frac{\text{Population 65 years+}}{\text{Population 0–14 years}} \times 100$$

$$\text{†Dependency ratio} = \frac{\text{Population aged 0–14 and 65+}}{\text{Population 15–64 years}} \times 100$$

Source: U.S. Bureau of the Census, Census of the Population: 1970, Vol. 1, *Characteristics of the Population,* pt. 1, 1973; *Statistical Abstract of the United States*: 1979, 100th ed., p. 8; W. Petersen, *Population,* 2d ed., 1969, p. 68. (Composite data), *Statistical Abstract of the United States,* 1986:26.

enty-five for females). Death rates have been reduced largely by minimizing infant mortality and by better controlling and treating of infectious diseases. The baby-boom babies of 1947 to 1960 reach retirement age between 2012 and 2025, with fewer middle-aged population to support them (see "Index of Aging," Table 4.1 and year 2,000 in Figure 4.1).

In 1984 about 11.9 percent of the population was sixty-five years old or older, 22 percent was fourteen years old or younger, and the remainder, 66.1 percent, were in "middle" ages.[3] The sex ratio (that is, the number of males per 100 females) drops consistently with age. At conception it is about 120; at birth it is 106, between ages 15–24 it is about 98; by age 65 it drops all the way to 69. Income tends to be low at both ends of the age continuum. In 1984 the median income for males over age sixty-five was $10,450 and for females it was $6,020 versus $15,600 and $6,868 for all males and all females, respectively (cf. *Statistical Abstract of the U.S.; 1987:*441). We will have occasion to return to Figure 4.1 to attempt to unravel the various implications of the different age distributions stated there for different years.

The lives of human beings (and social units) are not just static structural phenomena, but can also be viewed as dynamic cycles of growth and development.[4] Although we may debate whether stages in the human life cycle are

FIGURE 4.1 Age Structure of the United States Population, 1900–2000*

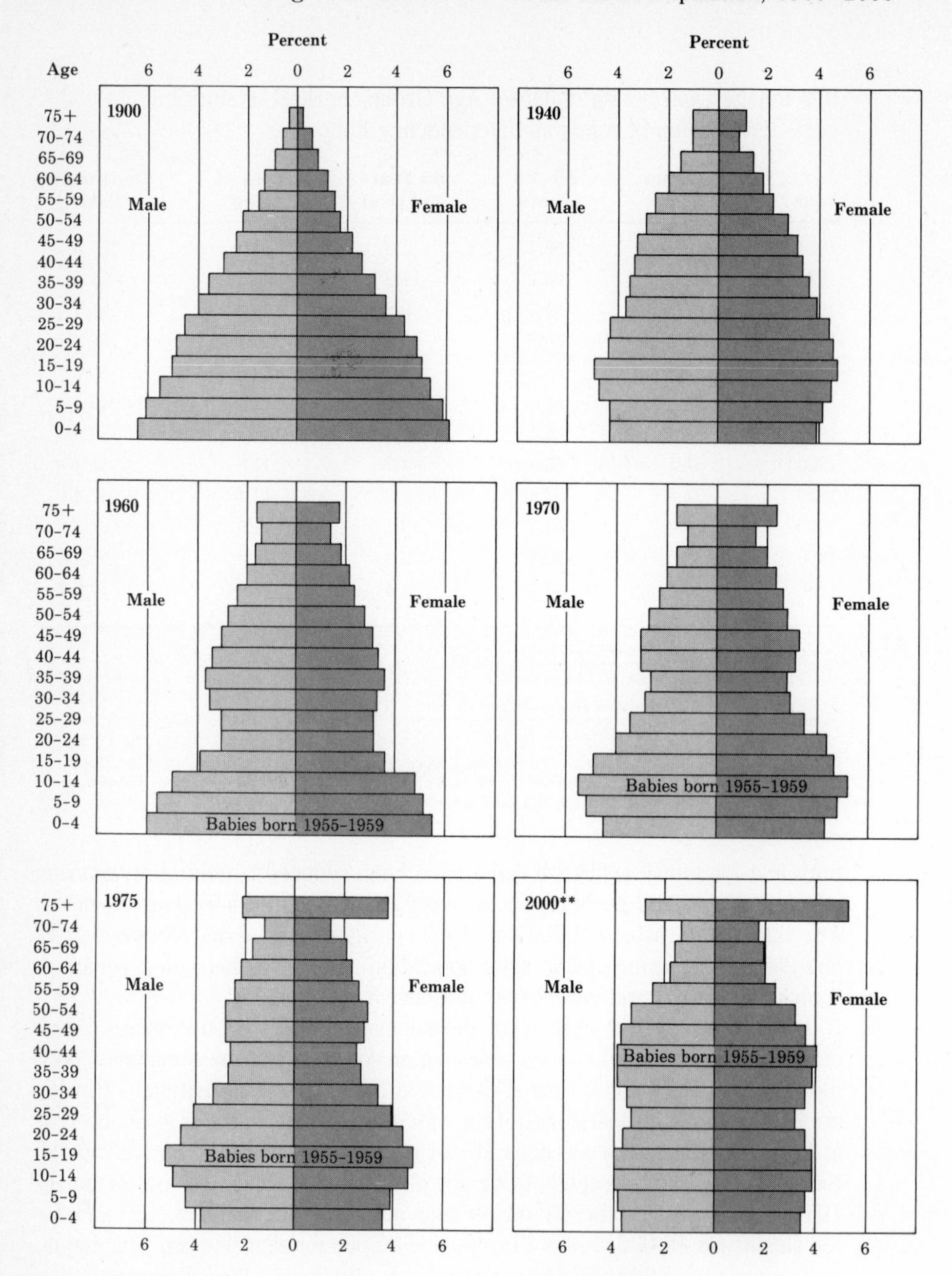

*The final band representing people 75 years and over on the pyramid includes a number of 5-year age groups, hence this band is unusually wide.

**Assuming a total fertility rate of 21, slightly improved morality and current levels of legal immigration.

Source: Charles B. Nam/Susan Gustavus Philliber, *Population: A Basic Orientation,* 2/e 1984, p. 210. Reprinted by permission of Prentice-Hall, Inc., Englewood Cliffs, N.J.

more closely associated with biological or social-cultural factors, it is generally agreed that human beings progress through various developmental changes with relatively well-defined life stages (Dannefer, 1984; Birren, 1986; Erikson, 1950). According to Erikson these life stages may be said to broadly include (see Figure 4.2):

1. Infancy (ages 0–2)
2. Toddlerhood (2–4)
3. Early childhood (5–7)
4. Middle childhood (8–12)
5. *a.* Early adolescence (13–17)
   b. Later adolescence (18–22)
6. Early adulthood (23–30)
7. Middle adulthood (31–50)
8. Later adulthood (51 +)[5]

Neugarten and Neugarten (1986), Birren (1986), and Riley and Riley (1986) emphasize that role expectations (or Figure 4.2's "developmental tasks") usually accompany these life stages and that rites of passage are often associated with moving from one role or stage to another (e.g., bar mitzvahs, graduations, marriage or funeral ceremonies). Social problems can develop because individuals, groups, or societies age chronologically but not developmentally (i.e., they stagnate). Changing social roles is like dying and successfully grieving to be able to cathect new roles.

Most theories of human development can be collapsed into at least five broad types: psychosexual and psychosocial stage or ontogenetic theories (notably those of Freud, 1905, 1940; Jung, 1963, 1964, 1968; Erikson, 1950; Levinson, 1978; and Vaillant, 1977); life-span theories (Baltes and Brim eds., 1979–1987); cognitive theories (Piaget, 1952; Cicourel, 1974); learning theories (Skinner, 1953, 1971; Bandura and Walters, 1963); and role theories (e.g., those of Parsons and Bales, 1955; Goffman, 1959; Kalleberg and Loscocco, 1983). Some of the basic issues in all theories of human development are whether the human life span can be divided into stages; what these stages are and when they occur; what crises, expectations, challenges, and so on are associated with these stages; and whether human life is teleological or ontogenetic (progresses to some natural end). Mussen, Conger, and Kagan comment as follows on the controversy concerning purposeful stages of human development (1984:34):

> When the development psychologist addresses himself to the purpose, or the adaptive value of behavior, he becomes embroiled in one of the two most controversial issues in human development, namely, does the theorist believe the child is growing toward some ideal goal? Put another way, should we conceive of psychological development as a sequence of stages that define progress toward a more "mature level" of functioning?

FIGURE 4.2 Developmental Tasks of Psychosocial Stages (after E. Erikson)

Erikson's "Eight Ages"	Life Stage	Developmental Tasks	Erikson's "Crises"
I. Oral-sensory	Infancy (birth to 2 years)	1. Social attachment 2. Object permanence 3. Sensorimotor intelligence and primitive causality 4. Maturation of motor functions	I. Basic trust vs. mistrust
II. Muscular-anal	Toddler-hood (2–4)	1. Self-control 2. Language development 3. Fantasy and play 4. Elaboration of locomotion	II. Autonomy vs. shame, doubt
III. Locomotion-genital	Early school age (5–7)	1. Sex-role identification 2. Early moral development 3. Concrete operations 4. Group play	III. Initiative vs. guilt
IV. Latency	Middle school age (8–12)	1. Social cooperation 2. Self-evaluation 3. Skill-learning 4. Team play	IV. Industry vs. inferiority
V. Puberty and adolescence	Early ado-lescence (13–17)	1. Physical maturation 2. Formal operations 3. Membership in the peer group 4. Heterosexual relation-ships	V. Identity vs. role confusion
	Later ado-lescence (18–22)	1. Autonomy from parents 2. Sex-role identity 3. Internalized morality 4. Career choice	
VI. Young adulthood	Early adult-hood (23–30)	1. Marriage 2. Childbearing 3. Work 4. Lifestyle	VI. Intimacy vs. isolation
VII. Adulthood	Middle adulthood (31–50)	1. Management of the household 2. Child rearing 3. Management of a career	VII. Generativity vs. stagnation
VIII. Maturity	Later adult-hood (51–)	1. Redirection of energy to new roles 2. Acceptance of one's life 3. Developing a point of view about death	VIII. Ego integrity vs. despair

Source: Adapted from *Childhood and Society,* 2nd. ed., by Erik H. Erikson, by permission of W. W. Norton & Company, Inc. Copyright 1950 © 1963 by W. W. Norton & Company, Inc. Copyright renewed 1978 by Erik H. Erikson.

The developmental theories of Freud, Erikson, Piaget, and recently Daniel Levinson (1978) and Dale Dannefer (1984) assume various life stages and associate them with certain expectations or developmental tasks. In some theories individual development depends on interaction with specific environmental conditions. Given a variance of about four to five years, these life stages can be dated only roughly. If one does not master the crises or challenges relevant to each life stage, then it is assumed that developmental debits will be acquired that could result in stagnation or the inability to mature normally: "At each stage of development there are certain tasks or competencies to be mastered if the individual is to maintain a normal schedule of development. If developmental tasks are not mastered at the appropriate stage, the individual suffers from immaturities and incompetencies and is placed at a serious disadvantage in adjusting at later developmental levels" (Coleman, 1984:95). In more formal sociological theories focus is often not on individual development, but rather on the normal expected life courses of whole societies or cultures (Aldrich, 1979; Lenski, 1984).

Several general points about the human life cycle need to be emphasized as a backdrop for considering the special social problems of youth, middle age, and old age. Human lives can be somewhat arbitrarily divided into periods of life stages, each with attendant roles and associated physiological changes. For our purposes life begins at conception (i.e., with a fertilized ovum possessing forty-six chromosomes and all the human genes) and ends with the stoppage of the heart, respiration, and/or a flat brain wave (EEG). Life and death are interdependent; even the sexual climaxes that result in the conception of life can be thought of as "small deaths."[6] Change makes birth and growth possible, but also necessitates aging and death. This is true physiologically and socially. Thus, aging can be thought of as a graduated series of mini-deaths and mini-rebirths. As one grows toward "the" peak of physical and social development (probably for most between the ages twenty-five and thirty-four) happiness rises (see Figure 4.3 below) and generally there is zeal for the future.

However, at some point after about age thirty-five social and physical well-being may begin to decline. One may start to live more in the past or in the futures of one's children and grandchildren. People often tend to try to hold on to what they have, rather than add to it. Resignation and life dissatisfaction become more common. Leisure activities may become more valuable than before. After ages sixty to sixty-five major reductions in income and social worth often occur, owing in part to retirement. Spouses and friends start to die. Physical strength and health wanes further. Sexual prowess and activity usually diminish (although see Botwinick, 1984:Ch. 6). One has to adjust to the inevitability and even imminence of one's own death. Paradoxically, to age appropriately one has to give up some old attachments, old valued roles and lifestyles. No wonder then that many sensitive human beings feel a sense of ambivalence and ill-defined uneasiness about even the best, longest, and healthiest of lives.

• Disenfranchised and Impotent Youth

Stating the Problem Being young in contemporary urban-industrial societies is not easy (Richman and Stagner, 1986). We tend to forget that in most preindustrial agricultural societies that childhood, adolescence, and youth were not recognized as life stages (Santrock, 1984:Ch. 1; Aries, 1962). Children tended to go directly into adulthood after an initiation ceremony marking their passage to adult responsibility. Even in the first stages of the industrial revolution marriage tended to occur very early—certainly by the teenage years—and children often went to work in factories and mines. Only recently, with expanding professionalism and greater demand for skilled labor, has adolescence emerged as a full-blown life stage characterized primarily by dormancy, latency, and prolonged preparation for adulthood. Today adolescence tends to be a time marked by marginality, confusion, and ambiguity. However, Mead argues that the Samoans did not have problems with this transition to adulthood and that the problems of adolescents in the modern West are primarily sociocultural, not physiological (1928). In fact, some have contended that the major problem of adolescence is that adolescents are freed from the responsibilities and rights of adults. As Paul Goodman put it long ago in *Growing Up Absurd* (1960), the greatest problem that young people have is their own uselessness.

Young people are expected to defer sexual gratification and meaningful employment. Although sexual maturity is reached in late childhood or early adolescence (i.e., with the puberty related changes of ejaculation and menstruation), they are expected not to act out sexually (although many do). Promiscuity, teenage pregnancy, rape, and related erotic problems are in part an outgrowth of the lack of routine, regular, acceptable sexual outlets for adolescents (Sebald, 1984:93ff.; Zelnick and Kantner, 1980). Unemployment and other economic disenfranchisements are particularly acute among teenagers. For example, the unemployment rate for black teenagers now approaches almost 50 percent (*Statistical Abstract of the U.S.*, 1986:394). Children are expected to remain in school much longer than at the turn of the century. Eighty-five percent of American youth now complete high school compared with 6 percent in 1900. Of course, delayed or blocked work opportunities can also be related to delinquency and adolescent crime (Lotz et al., 1985). Homicide is a special problem among older adolescents. Lately adolescent suicide and child abuse have also shown dramatic increases (Hendin, 1982; Maris, 1985; Gelles, 1982). Finally, many believe that drug or substance abuse among the young is related to adolescents being shut out of meaningful participation in society, as well as to the pressures and stresses of living contingently for prolonged periods of time in an achievement oriented society (Dacey, 1982).

Keniston has claimed that this period of disenfranchisement for children and adolescents has been extended to young adults (1975; Sebald, 1984:279ff.). In effect a new life stage, that of youth, has been added to the life cycle. Thus, many people ages eighteen to thirty years old are expected to remain in a dormancy period. In a very real sense then, for many (not all) young Americans, life begins at about thirty. Little wonder then that young people in our society have their own special set of social problems. Society has increasingly disenfranchised them and thereby rendered the young relatively impotent.

Both childhood and adolescence are commonly defined as having early and later periods. Early childhood extends from ages five to seven; middle childhood from ages eight to twelve. Likewise, early adolescence runs from ages twelve to seventeen and late adolescence from ages eighteen to twenty-two (see Figure 4.2; cf. Santrock, 1984). As you can see from Table 4.2, by these definitions, in 1980, there were about 35 million children in the United States (15 percent of the total population) and 42.5 million adolescents (19 percent of the population). While America still has a relatively young population—the median age was thirty years old in 1980—it is rapidly aging. For example, Americans under age fifteen constituted 31 percent of the population in 1960, 28.5 percent in 1970, but 22.7 percent in 1980. At the same time, of course, the proportions of middle-aged and elderly Americans have increased (see Table 4.1).

Since our primary concern here will be with adolescents, not children, an elaboration on adolescence as a life stage is in order. For Erikson the central life crisis for adolescents was attempting to arrive at a sense of personal identity in the midst of role experimentation, diffusion, and confusion (Figure 4.2; Santrock, 1984:50ff.).[7] In early adolescence, beginning roughly with puberty and ending with high school graduation, there is a noticeable height spurt, a maturation of the reproductive system, the development of secondary sexual characteristics (like facial and body hair), and a redistribution of body weight. Spontaneous ejaculation begins for males, as do menstruation and breast development for females. With these striking biological changes the management of sexuality in adolescence can present a major problem. This is especially the case, since (as we have seen) satisfactory routine societal outlets are usually not available. Over the last thirty to forty years we have witnessed a trend toward earlier sexual intercourse, especially for females (see Chapter 5). In 1948 Kinsey estimated that 72 percent of nineteen-year-old males and 20 percent of nineteen-year-old females had had premarital sexual intercourse. By 1973 Sorenson calculated that the figure had stayed about the same for males (i.e., 72 percent) but had risen to 57 percent for females (Kantner-Zelnik estimates 50 percent in 1979; cf. Sebald, 1984:93). Probably some of this increase for females was related to improved contraceptive technology coupled with a more liberal attitude toward premarital sexuality. Another major problem of early adolescence is drug or substance abuse. One study (Johnston et al., 1981: Santrock, 1984:611) concluded that among high school students, 93 percent used alcohol, 60 percent used marijuana, 10 percent used LSD, 32 percent used stimulants, 17 percent used cocaine, 16 percent used sedatives, and 1 percent used heroin at some time (see Chapter 9). Given the relative uselessness, stress, and frustration felt by many adolescents, drugs are often used to escape or deaden feelings.

In later adolescence the primary developmental tasks are to select an oc-

TABLE 4.2 Age and Sex Structure of the Resident Population of the United States: April 1, 1980, and April 1, 1970

Age and Sex	Population		Percent Distribution		Population Change, 1970–80	
	April 1, 1980	April 1, 1970	April 1, 1980	April 1, 1970	Number	Percent
Both sexes						
All ages	226,504,825	203,235,298	100.0	100.0	23,269,527	11.4
Under 5 years	16,344,407	17,162,836	7.2	8.4	−818,429	−4.8
5 to 9 years	16,697,134	19,969,056	7.4	9.8	−3,271,922	−16.4
10 to 14 years	18,240,919	20,804,063	8.1	10.2	−2,563,144	−12.3
15 to 19 years	21,161,667	19,083,971	9.3	9.4	2,077,696	10.9
20 to 24 years	21,312,557	16,382,893	9.4	8.1	4,929,664	30.1
25 to 34 years	37,075,629	24,922,511	16.4	12.3	12,153,118	48.8
35 to 44 years	25,631,247	23,101,173	11.3	11.4	2,530,074	11.0
45 to 54 years	22,797,367	23,234,790	10.1	11.4	−437,423	−1.9
55 to 64 years	21,699,765	18,601,669	9.6	9.2	3,098,096	16.7
65 to 74 years	15,577,586	12,442,573	6.9	6.1	3,135,013	25.2
75 to 84 years	7,726,826	6,121,627	3.4	3.0	1,605,199	26.2
85 years and over	2,239,721	1,408,136	1.0	0.7	831,585	59.1
Median age (years)	30.0	28.0				
Male						
All ages	110,032,295	98,926,204	100.0	100.0	11,106,091	11.2
Under 5 years	8,360,135	8,750,106	7.6	8.8	−389,971	−4.5
5 to 9 years	8,537,903	10,175,283	7.8	10.3	−1,637,380	−16.1
10 to 14 years	9,315,055	10,598,463	8.5	10.7	−1,283,408	−12.1
15 to 19 years	10,751,544	9,641,372	9.8	9.7	1,110,172	11.5
20 to 24 years	10,660,063	7,924,866	9.7	8.0	2,735,197	34.5
25 to 34 years	18,378,764	12,225,584	16.7	12.4	6,153,180	50.3
35 to 44 years	12,567,786	11,238,084	11.4	11.4	1,329,702	11.8
45 to 54 years	11,007,985	11,206,753	10.0	11.3	−198,768	−1.8
55 to 64 years	10,150,459	8,798,748	9.2	8.9	1,351,711	15.4
65 to 74 years	6,755,199	5,440,350	6.1	5.5	1,314,849	24.2
75 to 84 years	2,865,974	2,437,244	2.6	2.5	428,730	17.6
85 years and over	681,428	489,351	0.6	0.5	192,077	39.3
Median age (years)	28.8	26.8				
Female						
All ages	116,472,530	104,309,094	100.0	100.0	12,163,436	11.7
Under 5 years	7,984,272	8,412,730	6.9	8.1	−428,458	−5.1
5 to 9 years	8,159,231	9,793,773	7.0	9.4	−1,634,542	−16.7
10 to 14 years	8,925,864	10,205,600	7.7	9.8	−1,279,736	−12.5
15 to 19 years	10,410,123	9,442,599	8.9	9.1	967,524	10.2
20 to 24 years	10,652,494	8,458,027	9.1	8.1	2,194,467	25.9
25 to 34 years	18,696,865	12,696,927	16.1	12.2	5,999,938	47.3
35 to 44 years	13,063,461	11,863,089	11.2	11.4	1,200,372	10.1
45 to 54 years	11,789,382	12,028,037	10.1	11.5	−238,655	−2.0
55 to 64 years	11,549,306	9,802,921	9.9	9.4	1,746,385	17.8
65 to 74 years	8,822,387	7,002,223	7.6	6.7	1,820,164	26.0
75 to 84 years	4,860,852	3,684,383	4.2	3.5	1,176,469	31.9
85 years and over	1,558,293	918,785	1.3	0.9	639,508	69.6
Median age (years)	31.3	29.3				

Source: 1980 and 1970 censuses.

cupation, a marital partner, a moral code, and perhaps a political ideology. This is often a period of great turmoil as young men and women experiment to evolve and discover future identities. Traditionally for males identity centers around their occupational choices and for females identities turn more on interpersonal relations and marriage (although these sex roles are changing, especially for women). Interestingly, we are now in an era when both jobs and marriage are undergoing major changes. This makes it doubly hard for adolescents to articulate and resolve their life-stage crises. It seems absurd to many to study faithfully and diligently for a career or job that may not even exist. And it is not easy to make a commitment to marriage when you know that about 50 percent of all first marriages now end in divorce. Traditional marriage is further jeopardized by an increasing "coming out" of these individuals and groups with homosexual preferences (Santrock, 1984:484) and by larger numbers of young women who are pursuing careers first and marriage second and later, if at all.

Analyzing the Problem. The Exchange and Structural Perspectives
The relative disenfranchisement, impotency, and dormancy of young people is not only a matter of middle-age oppression, nor is it simply a noninteractive inert consequence or function of being young. Rather the problems of the young are firmly rooted in structural and interactive objective realities. According to the exchange and structural perspectives most objective conditions that restrict social interaction (with some exceptions) can cause social problems (cf., South et al., 1982).[8] If we do not interact socially with one another, then rewards, liking, and other integrative consequences cannot accrue. Thus, structurally speaking, we need to measure the heterogeneity of the young. You will recall from Chapter 2 that heterogeneity refers to the probability of outgroup associations, the probability that two randomly chosen individuals do not belong to the same group. Thus, heterogeneity tells us something of the expected rate of intergroup associations in a population, other things being equal. Using Table 4.2 we see that the percent of the American population under age twenty-four in 1980 was forty-two. Thus, heterogeneity is (see Chapter 2, footnote 20 for the computational formula):

$$1 - (.42^2 + .58^2) = 1 - (.18 + .34) = 1 - .52 = .48.$$

That is, based on the age structure alone the probability of the young interacting with the nonyoung is 48 percent. The young are not nearly as isolated as the aged. Heterogeneity for those age sixty-five or more is about .20. That is, sheer size and number do not restrict interaction chances for youth as much as they do for the aged.

Although heterogeneity tends not to account for the social problems of the young, social inequality does. As we have seen, the young tend to have no jobs or menial jobs, no or little independent income, and relatively little knowledge, experience, or skills (compared with what they will have later on). Young people tend to have low social status and little power in American society. The richest 1 percent of the population in the United States controls about 25 percent of all the social wealth (see Chapter 11). It almost goes without saying that the vast majority of the richest 1 percent are not young people. But how does age inequality arise?

From exchange theory (Homans, 1974; Chadwick-Jones, 1976; Gergen, et al., 1980; Cook, Emerson et al., 1981; Molm, 1985), we know that action and interaction depend not only on the opportunity for but also on the rewards and values of action and interaction (Panel 2.2, A1). It can be inferred from exchange theory's five propositions that the more people interact, the greater their liking for one another, provided that social interaction is not across status categories or otherwise coercive (Homans, 1974:64). Thus, although the young have relatively ample opportunity for interaction with middle-aged and older people (i.e., relatively high heterogeneity), structurally speaking that interaction tends to be across social status categories and is not very rewarding.

In fact many of the social problems of youth derive from their rationally exploiting the few interactive assets they have available to them. We have argued earlier (after Maslow, 1954, 1963) that there exists a hierarchy of human needs and rewards (as well as social needs, although there is less agreement on this point). Sleep, food, water, shelter, avoidance of pain, and reduction of sexual tension are fundamental and primary human needs. If these are met, then people can afford to be concerned with knowledge, money, careers, love, property, social status, and so forth. As George Homans says, "It is a rich man who can afford to worry about his status (1974:Ch. 9)."

If we consider some of the basic rewards that human beings can offer one another differentially by age (see Table 4.3), then two important social conclusions about the young can be drawn. First, it is not very rewarding in general to interact with young people (and if one's costs exceed one's rewards over a sufficient time, then social interaction will tend to stop). That is, as a group, Table 4.3 indicates that the young have relatively few unique interactive assets, especially compared with the middle aged. This would be even more apparent if we restricted the definition of young people to (say) teenagers. You may disagree with this conclusion, but try to understand our argument. Second, the rewards that the young excel in providing involve sex, beauty, strength, and vigor. It is precisely these areas that tend to become special social problems of the young. That is, problems like sexual acting out, violence, juvenile delinquency, and even drug abuse in part result from young people simply taking advantage of the strongest social interactive assets available to them. They are marketing their most valuable traits and the society at large (adults) is buying. In this sense we are all contributing to the very behaviors of young people that many of us paradoxically hold to be problematic (see James Kirkpatrick's moving commentary on the cocaine death of Maryland basketball star Len Bias, *The State News,* July 1, 1986).

We also know that what exchange theorists refer to as distributive injustice

Many of the social problems of young people result from them rationally exploiting their most unique interactive assets. Young males have physical strength and aggressiveness, but little money, property, job skills, or social status. Here a fifty-two-year-old man is assaulted and robbed of his recently cashed welfare check by two adolescent males. (AP/Wide World Photos)

(See exchange theory's proposition A5) is high among the young. When adolescents or young adults fail to get rewards they expected, they are likely to become angry and aggressive (Lotz et al., 1985:160ff.; Berkowitz, 1962). Juvenile delinquency, muggings, homicides, rapes and assaults, suicides, accidents, and similar behaviors are all related to the relative disenfranchisement of the young. The longer the dormancy period, the more rewards are not forthcoming, the greater the level of frustration, and the more likely young people are to become aggressive. Aggressive behavior is especially likely if

TABLE 4.3 Distribution of Basic Societal Rewards by Age

Rewards	Young* (0–29 years)	Middle Aged (30–64)	Old (65+)
Income	–	+	–
Jobs	–	+	–
Property	–	+	+/–
Physical strength, vigor, health	+	+/–	–
Sexual attractiveness, beauty	+	–	–
Self-sufficiency, independence	–	+	–
Knowledge and skills	–	+	–
Experience, wisdom	–	+/–	+
Years of productive activity left; potential	+	+/–	–

– = not very important or salient; received.
\+ = very important, salient; provided.
+/– = somewhat important, modestly common.
*Young includes early and late adolescents and young adults.

prolonged sacrifices in preparation for adulthood are not rewarded even after one becomes an adult. This can happen when the economy goes sour and new jobs are scarce or when marriages and informal relationships (e.g., living together) do not persist under severe social and economic disruption and stress.

Finally, social relations among children, adolescents, young adults, and the larger society (particularly parents) are likely to be strained, disharmonious, or imbalanced. Values are often age-specific. As we have seen, prolonged isolation in schools and the denial of full responsibilities to the young often contribute to the development of countercultures in which the young can claim radically different values from their parents and other elders.[9] If children and parents have different values, their social relationships are likely to be imbalanced and stressful. For example, if adolescents tend to place positive values on drugs and premarital sexual relationships and their parents' negative values, then precisely because children and parents care about each other the resulting small-group interactions are strained. Since values are hard to change, often disruption, conflict, and stress are inevitable in parent-child relationships. In extreme cases adolescents may run away from home or get married early to escape the stress. That is, a resolution of one set of problems viciously generates new problems for young people.

The Functional, Conflict, Symbolic Interaction, Deviance, and Biological Perspectives Of course, there are *alternative theoretical perspectives* on the social problems of youth. For example, functionalists might argue that the values of young people are not that different from those of adults. Problems like juvenile delinquency or premarital sexual acting out result more from blocked social opportunities than from different values (Merton, 1957:140ff.; Lotz et al., 1985:182; Erikson and Jensen, 1982). Much of adolescent deviance is anomic; that is, all age groups tend to share common cultural goals but the social means for realizing these goals vary by age. Deviance (Merton calls it innovation) occurs on a large scale only when the institutionalized means to achieve common societal goals are differentially distributed. That is, the young may deviate (e.g., through juvenile delinquency) because it is the only avenue to achieving important social goals open to them. In so doing, they are not primarily trying to subvert major social values. Functional theorists might also argue that one consequence of being an adolescent in an urban-industrial, technological society is to be socially disengaged and relatively useless. This would be true because of the long educational and training time required to qualify for jobs in modern urban-industrial economies (Santrock, 1984:586). Lower-class young would be expected to be particularly disadvantaged. Upper-class young adults, on the other hand, might even have some advantages (over the middle aged and the elderly), since they would tend to be the age group that had the necessary scientific and engineering university training to participate fully in an industrializing society (Lenski and Lenski, 1987:376ff., 91ff.).

Conflict theorists, on the other hand, would see young people as taken advantage of and exploited by adults (Santrock, 1984:253ff.). For example, young workers are often willing to do a job for less pay than an older worker. Young people are also less likely to be members of unions or to demand fringe benefits (such as health insurance or sick leave). Ageism is the systematic discrimination against certain groups simply based on their age. To be sure, reasonable young people would tend to resist such oppression. This is especially true as young people become stronger and in general more able physically to resist adult dominance. Conflict also refers to common everyday disagreements between parents and their adolescent children, not necessarily to parental oppression (Montemayor, 1982). Conflicts at home or with adults outside the home can lead to early marriage, sexual acting out, or crime and delinquency.

Symbolic interactionists, of course, point to the various meanings of youth's norm or law breaking. For example, delinquents sometimes are defying the parental authority of middle-class, middle-aged morality (Santrock, 1984:250; Cohen, 1955). In other cases rule or norm breaking may serve to validate one's self or identity (Cohen and Short, 1976). That is, the self is a stance-taking entity. Young people resolve their identities by opposing certain institutional prescriptions (Santrock, 1985:Ch. 10; Goffman, 1959). The symbolism of being young in contemporary society has changed as well. While youth, health, and physical vigor are highly valued, work and marriage roles today are confused. The recent dramatic rise in adolescent suicide rates (Maris, 1985) may in part be related to the depression and hopelessness felt by many young people facing high unemployment and divorce rates. To be young today means not only unusual stress, competition, and many years in school, but also the very real prospect that the future will not deliver the jobs or happy marriages and families for which young people have worked so hard.

Deviance theorists might indicate that young problems result in part from the laws or norms as much as from the behaviors of young people. Thus, changing the norms for the young could help remove some of their social problems. One thinks of examples like drinking-age laws. Simply by raising the legal drinking age from eighteen to twenty-one years (or the reverse) can have profound implications for adolescent drinking problems.

Finally, biologists or sociobiologists understandably accentuate biological changes in young people, such as the disruptive forces of puberty (Dacey, 1982). Clearly, sexuality is a less powerful factor before one is fully sexually mature. In a study by Smith (1985) on the biosocial explanation of adolescent sexual behavior, he claimed that adolescent girls with low levels of libidinal development were not likely to become sexually involved regardless of the sexual involvements of their friends. Others account for the predominance of male violence among adolescents on the basis of the sheer brute strength and larger size of most males vis-à-vis most females (van den Berghe, 1978:94–96; cf. Bryjak and Soroka, 1985:65). Biologically speaking, young people of either sex have more potential for deviance than older people based simply on their greater physical vigor.

Resolving the Problem Unlike old age, in which waiting only leads to death, adolescence does pass. Adolescence is not a terminal illness. At first glance, then, a basic strategy for resolving some youth problems would seem to be one of survival. Like the acne, with time and persistence the deprivation and dormancy should pass for most young people. Short of suicide, accidents, or rash short-term adaptations (most of them involving drugs or sex), adolescence is usually not fatal. On the other hand, we have argued that the period of youth disenfranchisement is becoming longer. And even for a period of a few years the suffering can be intense. It is all too easy for adults, who have survived and forgotten what it is like to be young, to prescribe waiting. Furthermore, socially (not individually) a certain proportion of our population will always be adolescents or young adults. A society needs to attempt to resolve the social problems of the young age group—whoever happens to be in it at the time.

A fully adequate resolution of the social problems of youth cannot be "only" psychological (Dannefer, 1984). Since youth and adolescence are related to relatively recent changes in society leading to prolonged dormancy and disengagement of the young, resolution of young people's social problems will only come from changes in work, the economy, technology, and the family. Such changes will take place slowly. Given the need for skilled laborers, technicians, and professionals, the later retirement of adult workers, and higher unemployment rates; there is even reason to believe that in the future the young will have to wait even longer to enter the adult world. It is unlikely that this training period will change any time soon. What is new is the prospect of no meaningful jobs or marriages for increasingly large numbers of young people.

"Well, whatever it is we change into, it can't come soon enough for me."

Drawing by D. Reilly; © 1973 *The New Yorker* Magazine, Inc.

It is one thing to sacrifice and postpone gratification to gain good jobs or find the "right" mate. It is quite another to be asked to do it all for nothing. There is definitely a growing sense of futility and pointlessness to the sacrifices and training of many young people.

Of course, cynically, young people could exploit their relatively unique "interactive advantages" more fully (see Table 4.3). If on the open market the young have a decided competitive advantage regarding the traits of physical vigor, beauty, and sexuality, then we might expect to see more activities among young people related to these relatively advantageous traits. The proliferation of professional sports is one good indicator that this trend is accelerating already. Still, one must realize that social adaptations that exploit sexuality, strength, or physical prowess are risky. Such adaptations also tend to be short term (for as long as you are attractive or athletic) and tend to preclude more long-term intellectual development and occupational preparation. Sexual promiscuity, sexual occupations, or even too much sexual experience are also viewed by some as detracting from opportunities for traditional marriages.

It should be noted in this context that sports and to a degree sexual activity are related to the "survival" resolution of youth problems. That is, the excess energy, libido, and frustration of young people can be discharged relatively harmlessly through sports and sex (at least until AIDS came along!). This is particularly the case with recent improvements in the technology of birth control. Management of adolescence may require some relative regular routine social mechanisms for catharsis or purging of potentially violent and destructive energies. However, most young people do not use their sexual or physical advantages as a career alternative. The idea here is still to survive until being admitted legitimately into the adult world.

A final resolution is to continue the current relative isolation and segregation of the young from the rest of society. While our definition of social problems (Table 2.2) suggests that inequality and restriction of social interaction tend to generate social problems, these effects are paradoxical. That is, social inequality has a complex relationship to social problems. As a case in point, one resolution to parent-child conflicts is for one or both sides to withdraw from interaction. For example, one would expect youth cultures, peer groups, school groups, and so on, on the whole to be more harmonious, balanced, and socially integrated than mixed age groups. However, restriction of social interaction as a permanent resolution of youth problems is unlikely to succeed. For one thing many of the rewards and opportunities needed by the young cannot be received from other young people because jobs, money, and property tend to be controlled by middle-aged or older people. Furthermore, the middle aged need to interact with the young to secure highly valued traits of beauty, strength, and so on. Of course, some cross-age social interaction is motivated by nonerotic love or altruism.

• Problems of Mid-Life

Stating the Problem *Middle age* is a vague term with many meanings (Botwinick, 1984; Dannefer, 1984). Table 4.3 implies that anyone who is not young (under thirty) or old (sixty-five or older) is in mid-life; that is, ages thirty to sixty-four. But, of course, this broad time span is too coarse to be meaningful. Erikson suggested that middle adulthood spans the years thirty-one to fifty (see Figure 4.2 above). Later Levinson (1978) recommended that Erikson's middle adulthood be subdivided into a "settling down" period in which one "becomes one's own man" or woman (roughly from ages thirty-two or thirty-three to forty or forty-one) and a "mid-life transition period" (from about ages forty to forty-five; Levinson, 1978:191ff.). Literally, if we take the life expectancies of men and women (whites here) in 1984 (71.1 and 78.3 years, respectively) and divide them by two, then mid-life for men and women is expected at about thirty-five and thirty-nine years. This is closer to Jung's (1964) definition of mid-life as roughly forty years of age. Let us agree then that mid-life occurs approximately between ages thirty-four and fifty-five, depending on one's sex and race.[10]

Although the distribution of basic societal rewards depicted in Table 4.3 would lead us to believe that middle age would be the very best time of our lives, when people were actually asked to rate their "best year," the range was between twenty-five and thirty-four years, rather than thirty-five to forty-five years (Figure 4.3). In fact both happiness and life satisfaction are rated low in advanced middle age (viz., ages forty-five to fifty-four), the only time period that this occurred (Botwinick, 1984:168).[11] More specifically, at around ages forty to forty-five marriages tended to be seen as bad, there were increased problems with children and one's own parents, health concerns rose, and it was thought to be too late to change work careers or lifestyles (Figure

4.4). In short, although mid-life ought to be one of the best times of our lives, data paradoxically indicated that on many indicators it is among the worst times of our lives.

One reason for this may be that life has a tendency to stagnate in its middle phases. In fact, Erikson felt that generation (creativity) versus stagnation was the key problem or "crisis" of mid-life (Figure 4.2; cf. Farrell and Rosenberg, 1981; Newman and Newman, 1975:318ff.). Unlike childhood, adolescence, and young adulthood, in mid-life there are fewer clear expectations or markers for achievement. In a very real sense even if you "make it," middle age is at best a plateau (Bardwick, 1986). For the most part each day is a repeat of the prior day. There will not be new jobs, new marital partners, new homes, promotions (Kalleberg and Loscocco, 1983). In fact, you may work your hardest to avoid demotion. The novelist John Updike symbolized this phase of life as a hamster running a treadmill day in, day out (1960, 1981).

One of the major changes of middle age is modifying what Levinson (1978:191–316; Dannefer, 1984:102) calls the life-dream. A large part of the task of modification is concerned with reappraising the past for what now prove

FIGURE 4.3 Mean Ratings of "Best Year" of a Person's Life as a Function of Respondent's Age (n = 76 at each age interval).

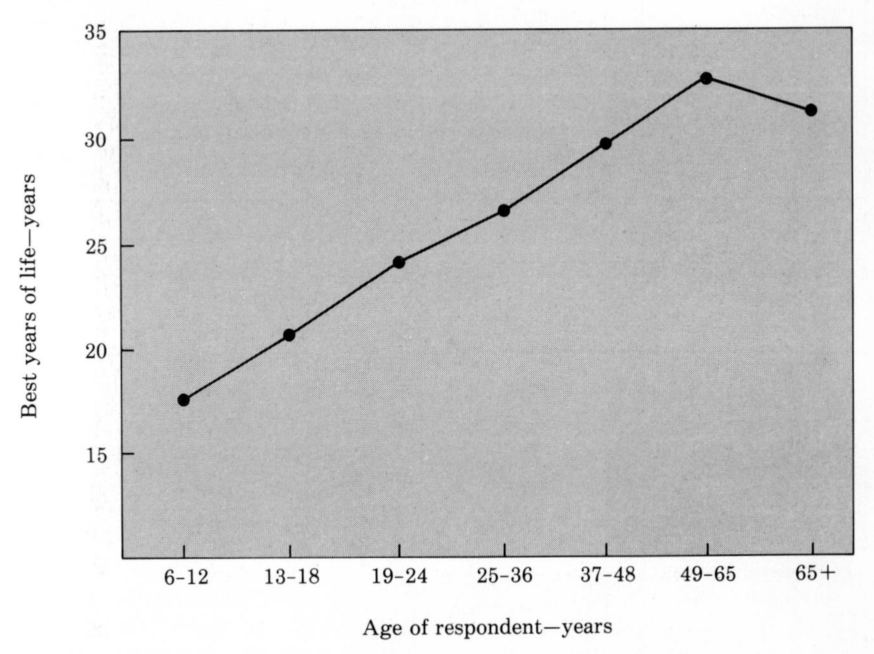

Source: Abraham Monk, *The Age of Aging: A Reader in Social Gerontology,* 1979:44. Reprinted by permission of *The Gerontologist*/the *Journal of Gerontology.* Cf., Jack Botwinick, *Aging and Behavior: A Comprehensive Integration of Research Findings,* 1984:Chapter 5; Paul Mussen et al., 1984.

FIGURE 4.4 Changing Attitudes throughout the Life Cycle

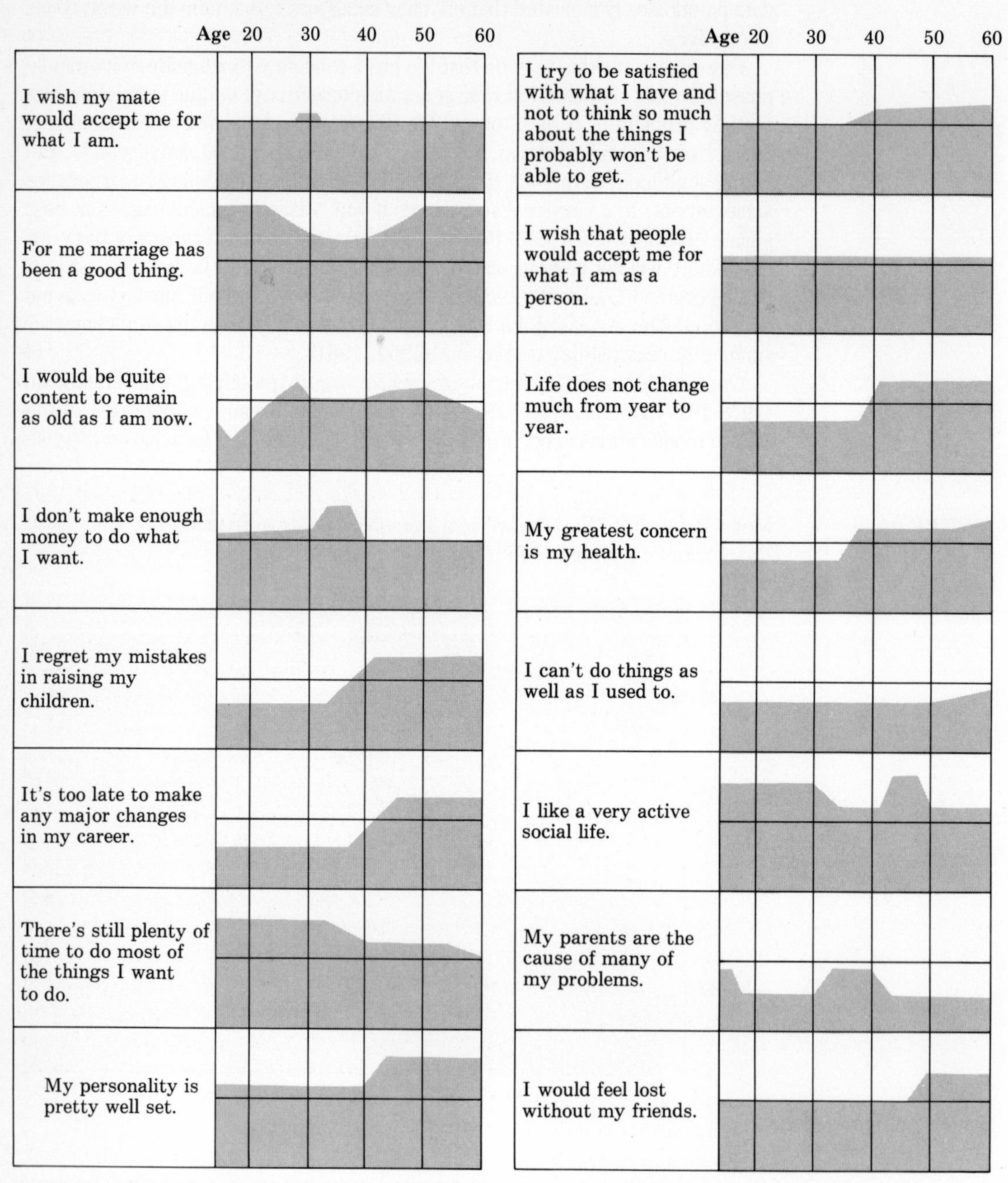

Source: Reprinted from *Psychology Today* Magazine (February 1975). Copyright © 1975, American Psychological Association, pp. 74–78; cf. Arne Kalleberg and Karyn Loscocco, "Age, Values, and Rewards: Explaining Age Differences in Job Satisfaction," 1983.

to be illusions and purging our lives of those illusions and restructuring them. Literature is full of stories of fictitious men and women who could not make these mid-life adjustments, who held on too long to young adulthood and were defeated (see Chekhov, Ibsen, Strindberg, and Eugene O'Neil).

Another part of the mid-life crisis is biological (Wantz and Gay, 1981:85). Middle-aged people have strenuous continuing responsibilities but waning physical energy. With the fatigue can come a heightened sense of one's own mortality. Often this involves resetting priorities, realizing that time is short and that everything you wanted to do is just not going to get done. Often depression can set in when one envisions long years ahead without the passion and dreams of youth. Men may experience reduction in sexual potency (especially if they are being treated for hypertension); women may go through menopause.

Accompanying these changes in biology are profound shifts in lifestyle. In one sense the middle-aged care for the young and old. It is also a time that children leave home and parents begin to die. At this time it is not unusual for divorce to occur, for extramarital affairs to become more common, for career changes to be attempted. In part these changes are a response to the routine, boredom, and excessive responsibilities just described. In part they are a consequence of opportunity. Children leave, money is more abundant, and there is often a sense of quiet desperation, of treading work and relational water until we die. "Change now or not at all," seems to be a common admonition (Gould, 1978).

Analyzing the Problem. The Exchange and Structural Perspectives Paradoxically, part of the social problems of mid-life derive from middle-aged people generally being frequently and well rewarded (Table 4.3). As Farrell and Rosenberg report, "the middle-aged themselves view this part of their lives as a 'golden period' characterized by security, diminishing external pressures and the maturity and good judgment to enjoy what life has to offer" (1981:135). What often goes unnoticed about mid-life is the accummulated effect of prolonged rewards. For example, we know from the fourth proposition of exchange theory that the more often in the recent past a person receives a reward, the less valuable any further unit of that reward becomes. It is argued here that some stagnation, apathy, unhappiness, and low life satisfaction of the middle aged curiously results from their satiation with rewards. Satiation helps account for how one can be ostensibly well-off, but subjectively miserable and dissatisfied. Satiation also helps explain mid-life changes of careers, marriages, and so on. That is, new stimuli are being sought, since the superabundant and repetitive older stimuli have ceased to be as rewarding. Of course, this cannot be the entire explanation of mid-life problems because we satiate very slowly on general reinforcers like money and social status.

Another part of the exchange explanation of mid-life problems concerns what is being exchanged. Note that exchanges tend not to be equal, or based on reciprocally intrinsic attributes. As a case in point, two robust young people might be attracted to one another on the basis of their physical appearances and thus interact sexually. On the other hand, a middle-aged person interacting sexually with a young person would most likely be exchanging his/her money, status, or power for the sexual attractiveness of the younger person. In general, middle-aged people are likely to exchange their status and power for sex, deference, strength, technical skills, knowledge, social approval, and so on. Such unequal or asymmetric exchanges are likely to be problematic for the middle-aged persons for a number of reasons. Such relationships are often excessively calculating, instrumental, and exploitative (even if they are mutual). One tends to be socially bonded not to a person, but to a person's external resources. Affectually, such relationships can be fragile and contingent (e.g., on staying attractive or having money, and so on).

Interpersonally, many middle-aged exchanges are also costly. Relationships tend to be with subordinate (competitive, younger) workers, dependent children, and aging parents. Such interactions can be threatening and depleting. Much of mid-life social interaction is a drain. It will be recalled from Chapter 2 that when interactive costs exceed interactive rewards, then social exchange ceases to be profitable and is likely itself to cease or otherwise be altered.

Structurally, it can be observed that there are relatively few middle-aged people in the American population available to support the young and the elderly.[12] Using ages thirty-five to fifty-five as middle age and referring to Table 4.2, we see that in 1980 in the United States there were about forty-six million middle-aged people, about 21 percent of the entire population. This means that roughly 79 percent of the dependent young and older population needs social and economic support from 21 percent of the middle-aged population (e.g., in social security or various child welfare benefits). Furthermore, the relative lack of out-group interaction opportunities resulting from the social classes differences of the middle aged, young, and older people is likely to encourage disliking and dissimilarity between the middle aged and other age groups. As society gets larger, relationships are increasingly hierarchical and indirect (not face-to-face). This structural condition, too, does not promote liking or social interaction.

The Biological, Symbolic Interaction, and Conflict Perspectives Other theoretical perspectives would claim that mid-life problems are related to biological or developmental factors. Of course, aging takes its toll. A lifetime of accumulated stress and responsibility is very likely related to mid-life disease and illness. Burnout is a popular concept referring to prolonged repetitive stress resulting in emotional and physical decompensation and related occupational ineffectiveness. As we have seen, women tend to go through menopause in middle age and middle-aged men often report reduced libido and even impotence in some cases. Although mid-life biological changes do not end sexual drives or interests, they often seriously alter them. If one believes that all energy is related to sexual energy, then there can be a definite diminution of life energy in mid-life for all problem solving or task resolution.

Of course, some of the middle-aged stress, burnout, overloading, and so

"Roger always lived on the edge. Then one day he fell off."

Drawing by Levin; © 1986 *The New Yorker Magazine,* Inc.

on could be symbolic. One common definition of the situation of mid-life is that it tends to involve a mid-life crisis. Researchers have found that in fact mid-life is responded to in a great variety of ways. Many mid-life men and women are not in crisis, but discover mid-life a time of new opportunities and growth (see Vaillant, 1977; Kalleberg and Loscocco, 1983; Gould, 1978; Farrell and Rosenberg, 1981).

Finally, conflict theorists remind us that the middle aged (usually white males) tend to dominate younger and older minorities. While the middle aged have disproportionate power, authority, and influence over other age groups, they do not have the right to oppress others and exploit them. Marx might contend that the depression, fear, guilt, and fatigue of many middle-aged persons derives from their keeping an unnatural and unjust control of the economy at the expense of other minority age groups. On some level the middle-aged probably fear rebellion or revolt from those age groups that they are exploiting.

Resolving the Problem Erikson (see Figure 4.2) maintains that middle-aged maturity entails learning to accept our own unique life course. And, to be sure, development itself requires aging and performing age-specific responsibilities. Achievement, success, and responsibility are never free. Some of the problems of mid-life result from the very successes and higher social status of middle-aged people. To wish not to have some mid-life problems is like wishing to be in great physical shape without dieting or exercise. Two caveats are in order. First, resignation is not the same as growth. To resolve the stagnation of mid-life one must continue to want to live and be creative. Resignation is not enough. Second, people in mid-life can profit from scaling down their aspirations and self-demands to some degree. It is probably not necessary to work as hard or in the same style once you have "arrived." This should free up some energies for other different activities.

Vaillant (1977) argues that successful life adaptors take "time off." In studying a sample of 1942–44 Harvard graduates, Vaillant found that the most successful graduates took long creative vacations and were more likely to use humor to cope. Long ago Parsons spoke not of individuals' but of society's need for latency (i.e., regeneration) (1951; cf. Lenski and Lenski, 1987:Ch. 2). One of the basic fundamental imperatives is a mechanism for recuperation, rest, and regeneration. In our instrumental, work oriented society, play has been crowded out (Maris, 1981:Ch. 6; Freud, 1899). Of course, if people in mid-life could take time off, do some different activities, break up their work patterns, then this should also help the problem of satiation with routine rewards.

One cannot as easily avoid unequal or instrumental exchanges without also changing the social structure or giving up one's status. In a movie titled *Save the Tiger* Jack Lemmon plays a prototypical small owner-businessman in the garment industry. As he ages he feels increasingly out-of-date. His business is failing, he is tired, his clients require him to be the kind of person that disgusts him, his relationships are primarily instrumental and profit oriented. In one scene he gives a young female hitchhiker a ride and, for a moment, relates to her as just another human being. But almost immediately the relationship is doomed. Their differences are too great, his commitment to his company and family can only be ignored for a short time, he is older than she is, his life experiences are too different. In the end, he returns to his own confusing, stressful, conflicted world and continues to struggle along. His resolution to problems of mid-life was a combination of time off and resignation.

Mid-life might be more manageable if some of the social responsibilities and rewards were redistributed to the young and the aged. But lately we have not been in an expanding economy. Generally, the scarcer the resources, the less likely social responsibilities and rewards will be evenly distributed. Even in the best of times this resolution is a limited alternative, since many responsibilities or social roles require knowledge, skill, training, energy, and so on that the young and the old simply often do not have. Finally, it should be noted that an expanding middle-aged population structurally would be expected to help problems of mid-life (Figure 4.1). With greater proportions (up to a point) of middle-aged people in the population, there would be more interaction potential and with it a greater probability of liking and similarity.

• The Elderly as Devalued and Unrewarding

Stating the Problem Like adolescents the elderly have been differentially evaluated in various periods of American history. Fischer, in *Growing Old in America* (1977; cf. Neugarten and Neugarten, 1986:33ff.), claims that 1607–1820 was a period of gerontophilia. During this time age was exalted. The early Puritan settlers in the United States believed that the "elect" or religiously saved were blessed with long life. Clothing styles depicted people as older than they actually were. For example, people wore white powdered wigs. Meeting house seats were assigned on the basis of age. Instead of trying to look young, people tended to overreport their ages (some people still do, e.g., to get alcoholic drinks, not because they are proud to be older). At this time in our history about 3 percent of the United States population was age sixty-five or older.

Around 1780–1820 a major shift in age values began to occur, probably associated with the American and French revolutions. From 1780 until today American society could on the whole be characterized as gerontophobic. Great value is placed on being or acting young (see Backer et al., 1982:2). As Americans moved West the 1800s' heroes were young frontiersmen and cowboys. Even President Teddy Roosevelt was "rough and ready." Associated with this frontier mentality was a changing political ideology that espoused equality for all. As major urban-industrial centers grew and farms shrunk, parents were less likely to control the economic fortunes of their children. Their offspring could now work in cities and were less dependent on inherited family property. Between 1910 and 1965 old age began to be seen as a special social problem and an elaborate system of largely federal social welfare plans and programs were instituted to deal with old age (Hendricks and Hendricks, 1981:Ch. 3). Chief among these were the Social Security Administration (1930s) and medicare and medicaid (1965).[13] By 1984 about 11.9 percent of the United States population was age 65 or older.

Of course, when we speak of the elderly we have to be careful to define terms like *aged, aging,* and *ageism.* At the turn of the century thirty-five–forty was old in that many people did not live much longer than that. Erikson (Figure 4.2) reflects this early 1900s thinking when he stops his age-stage developmental theory at age 51 and older for later adulthood. To be sure, as life expectancy has increased new life stages have emerged in the older age categories (such as young-old, old-old, and oldest old—Neugarten and Neugarten, 1986). It is important to be clear here that the upper limit of human life has not changed much; it is just that more people are living to the upper limit (especially as a result of reductions in infant mortality rates). For our purposes ages sixty-five to seventy are regarded crudely as when one is aged. Most people do not realize that sixty-five was the age that Otto von Bismarck (in 1889 as chancellor of Germany) specified as the time when government support would begin. America adopted sixty-five as the usual retirement age until recently. In 1978 Congress decreed that normally people can expect to work until age seventy.

There is considerable cultural and social variation in both who is held to be aged and how the aged are valued (Hendricks and Hendricks, 1981:31ff.). Generally where life is harsh, the elderly are regarded as burdensome. In such cases the aged are mistreated and occasionally left to die or encouraged to kill themselves. Examples here would include the Eskimos and the Ik of Uganda. For many "primitive" societies age forty or more is aged, since staying alive requires great physical prowess (cf., the Siriono of Bolivia). In some traditional, often eastern, societies the aged are highly venerated (e.g., among the Aranda of Australia or the Chinese). Remember that one of the Hebraic Ten Commandments is to "honor thy mother and father."

"Aging," contrasted with the "aged," calls our attention to the process of growing older. Aging has social or "role," behavioral, (Neugarten and Neugarten, 1986:33) and biological connotations (Botwinick, 1984:3; Birren, 1986). Social problems are likely to arise when these two somewhat different aspects of aging become confused. On the other hand, some of us act as if biological aging were not real (e.g., that age is a "state of mind"). Most emphatically aging is not only social. You can change social expectations all you want and seventy-year-old women will still not be able to conceive babies, nor will seventy-year-old men be able to run sub-four-minute miles or slam-dunk basketballs. For some curious reason we sociologists tend to forget this. On the whole as people reach about ages forty-five to fifty their bodies and minds begin to undergo significant biochemical changes. For example, aging has been related to lower metabolic rates, homeostatic imbalance, accumulation of metabolic wastes, autoimmunity (the rejection of one's own tissues increases with age), cellular aging (especially brain cells), diminished sexual potency, and accumulated disease debits (Botwinick, 1984:Ch.1).[14] On a more down-to-earth level, hair tends to turn white and fall out, teeth decay, hearing and seeing capabilities diminish, sleep is less sound, energy levels are lower, skin wrinkles, and muscles atrophy. While these age-related changes vary considerably among individuals, attempts to glorify them is ludicrous. One can accept aging without distorting it. On the other hand, it must be admitted that social roles for age are not isomorphic with biological or intellectual competencies. We have already seen that adolescents are sexually mature between ten and fourteen years old, but not allowed full sexual privileges until ages eighteen to twenty-one. Likewise not all people need to retire at sixty-five or seventy. Many sixty-five to seventy-year-old people are better workers than many thirty-five to forty year olds.

The fact that social roles for the aged are often not an accurate characterization of many older people and their capabilities has led some social scientists to introduce the concept of ageism. Ageism is the systematic stereotyping of and discrimination against people just because they are old (Botwinick, 1984:Ch. 2). These stereotypes tend to be negative. For example, the elderly are held to be all alike, disabled and sickly, not sexually active, failing in intellect, and excessively dependent. Comfort (1976) has maintained that as much as 75 percent of aging may be what he calls sociogenic. That is, only about 25 percent of aging is biologically based. Others, like Neugarten and Neugarten (1986), claim that we tend to create negative stereotypes of the aged because we fear our own decline and demise so much. Aging can be especially traumatizing for females, since societally women are often thought to age earlier but in fact live longer than men. However, while social expectations and negative stereotypes undoubtedly affect aging and how we regard it, age and its consequences are real (i.e., objective, patterned, empirical, and so on). Age is not entirely a social artifact that can be defined away.

Demographically it is clear that the United States has a rapidly aging population (Siegel and Taeuber, 1986). For example, the percent of the population age sixty-five or older has more than doubled since 1930 (Table 4.1). These changes are graphically evident in Figure 4.1. Pifer and Bronte (1986) refer to these age structure changes as the "squaring of the pyramid," since there will be roughly equal numbers of people in each age group by the year 2030. Note especially the shifts in the proportion of the population age seventy-five or more between 1900 and 2000. In the United States the ratio of the old to the young (i.e., the "index of aging") has tripled since 1930 (Table 4.1). Table 4.4 reveals that by the year 2000 there may be an increase of about three million males and three million females ages fifty-five to seventy-five compared to the year 1975 (cf. Siegel and Taeuber, 1986:82). The majority of the American elderly are women. The sex ratio for those aged sixty-five or more was about sixty-nine in 1984. About three-fourths of men over age sixty-five live with spouses but only one-third of women sixty-five or older do. American blacks tend to have lower life expectancies and thus form a lower percentage of the American elderly. In 1984 8.1 percent of all U.S. blacks were age sixty-five or over (compared to 12.6 percent for whites). Contrasted with the general population the elderly are less well educated.

Given the above social and biological conditions the elderly tend to be

TABLE 4.4

Numbers of Older Persons in U.S.A. in 1975 and in 2000 (in millions)

	1975*		**2000 (A)***		**2000 (B)†**	
	M	F	M	F	M	F
Total 55+	18.0	23.2	19.7	27.5	24.8	32.4
65+	8.9	12.8	10.2	16.3	14.4	20.8
75+	3.1	5.2	4.0	7.7	6.9	11.2
55-75	14.9	18.0	15.7	19.8	17.9	21.2

Source: Abraham Monk, *The Age of Aging: A Reader in Social Gerontology,* 1979:346. Cf. Jacob S. Siegel and Cynthia M. Taeuber, "Demographic Dimensions of an Aging Population," 1986:82.

*If age-specific death rates continue as of 1968.
†If age-specific death rates are reduced after 1970 by 2 percent per year for persons aged 20+.
Projections carried out by David D. McFarland and Grace Chiu.

PANEL 4.2

Elderly Outnumber Teens

People over 65 outnumber teenagers in the United States for the first time, and by the year 2025 the margin will increase to more than two to one, the congressional Office of Technology Assessment said Tuesday.

An agency report said the elderly population had grown from 4 percent of the total in 1900 to more than 11.5 percent in 1983.

"The number of those over 65 is projected to grow from today's 26 million to an estimated 39.3 million by 2010, when they will constitute almost 14 percent of the nation's population," it said.

In 1970, teenagers constituted 11 percent of the population, the report concluded. In 1980, they were 12 percent; in 1990 teens will constitute 9 percent of the population; 2000, 10 percent; 2025, 10 percent; and 2050, 10 percent.

Source: U.S. Congress, Office of Technology Assessment, *Technology and Aging in America,* OTA-BA-264 (Washington, DC: U.S. Government Printing Office, June 1985).

devalued. Social interaction with them is generally not seen as highly rewarding. Accordingly, the aged tend to be isolated, lonely, and depressed and to not have enough money to live well (i.e., they generally have a low quality of life). Furthermore, the elderly face special problems with failing health, a general decline in life energies, and finally, with death. As people grow older they tend to outlive their spouses and friends, children move away and start families and careers of their own, travel becomes more difficult, money is usually in short supply, extended families shrink, retirement can be forced, and people are often cut off from their jobs. The net result can be profound isolation, loneliness, and unhappiness for the aged (see Panel 4.1). Figure 4.4 shows that the elderly are by far the most unhappy of any other age group (cf. Botwinick, 1984:Ch. 5). Whereas retirement can mean a shift to exciting new roles, in fact it commonly means entrophy and waiting for death. The transition from work to retirement is hard to make, resources are low, and old habits and self-supports die slowly (Morrison, 1986).

Of course, many of the problems of the aged are economic (Palmer and Gould, 1986). The median income of people over age 65 in 1983 was $7,683 ($9,766 for men and $5,566 for women), which was only 44 percent of the median income for the U.S. population (*Statistical Abstract of the U.S.*, 1986:456). Figure 4.4 reveals that more people in the older ages say that they "don't make enough money to do what they want." Even with good retirement plans, social security, and insurance benefits the elderly are most likely to live on fixed incomes in the midst of often double-digit inflation. Most younger wage earners can get raises or "pass on" the costs of inflation to others. Rose Anderson (Panel 4.1) even outlived the $300,000 her physician husband had carefully provided for her.

The Social Security Administration was created in the 1930s and has helped the elderly cope financially (Pifer, 1986). However, in many ways social security is grossly inadequate. As the proportion of the elderly has grown and inflation mounted, social security has become extremely costly. In 1978 workers paid at a rate of 12.1 percent per year of the first $17,700 earned. By 1987 the social security rate was 14.3 percent of the first $42,600 (Barrow and Smith, 1979:Ch. 10). Even with these levels of contributions the social security system may go bankrupt (Kreps, 1979). To further complicate matters some elderly people are not covered by social security at all. These include agricultural workers, people in states with alternative retirement programs, and people who have never worked outside their homes. Lower-paid workers receive lower benefits at retirement, yet pay a greater proportion of their salaries into social security. For example, in 1987 a plumber making $42,600 and a corporate executive making $426,000 paid exactly the same social security tax. Furthermore, social security by itself is not sufficient to meet the financial needs of elderly retired persons. In fact one estimate was that we would need to save about one-third of all life income to pay for our retirement. Of course, very few people can afford to save that much (5 percent a year is about the average). In 1984 retirement payments averaged $543 per month for an individual. Payments usually begin at age sixty-five, although they can begin at age sixty-two or even earlier. Until recently social security actually punished women by paying them a little over 80 percent of what their husbands were due. Before 1977 if a woman remarried, she got nothing from her former husband's contributions.

Finally, poor health, dying, and death present special problems for the aged. Figure 4.4 indicates that the greatest concern with health is in the very oldest ages (cf. Botwinick, 1984:72, 87). Chronic diseases are particularly problematic for the aged. The number of days of restricted activity per year for the elderly is about three times the number of restricted days for the young. To help with these problems medicare and medicaid programs were created in 1965 (Davis, 1986; Barrow and Smith, 1979:334ff.). Medicare pays for about 66 percent of short-term hospital bills (the limit is sixty days). However, most routine medical needs are not covered, since the first $100 to $200 in expenses is not paid (Hendricks and Hendricks, 1981:225). For an additional $10 to $20 per month one can get optional major medical insurance. To qualify for medicaid you have to be a truly needy low-income person. Unlike medicare, medicaid does cover the costs of eyeglasses, dental work, prescription drugs, and long-term nursing care. Most nursing homes tend to provide minimal custodial care, especially for extremely aged women. These nursing homes have been known to financially exploit their clients and medicaid and to give a poor quality of care. Nursing home patients are often excessively drugged with Thorazine or Mellaril to pacify them. In some cases patients are fed cheap unnourishing food.

The rewards to the young and middle aged for interacting with the elderly are minimal. Thus, the aged tend to be isolated, lonely, and economic liabilities. The young girl, Tracie, is having trouble being heard by Mrs. Lynch. Such visits to the elderly are rare. (Elizabeth Crews/Stock, Boston)

The last main developmental problem for the elderly is to prepare for their own deaths (Backer et al., 1982; Leming and Dickinson, 1985). This is a curious responsibility that many people understandably resist. Death is something most of us have been taught to fight against. Thus, denial of one's own biological cessation is understandable. This is particularly true if you have no traditional religious beliefs and see death as the end of it all for you. Sometimes people do not fear death as much as losing control of their lives and dying alone in the cold impersonal surrounds of a health care institution. After death, survivors will find that funerals are expensive and funeral directors can exploit their vulnerability and feelings of guilt for not having done more for the deceased (Mitford, 1963). The old also realize that dying is not just another role transition. Although one can die more or less appropriately, dying is not something you do or achieve in that you do not survive it and it happens to you regardless of what you do.

Analyzing the Problem. The Exchange Perspective Much of the isolation, loneliness, and inferior economic position of the aged derives from their social exchange liabilities. As we argued in Table 4.3, the social rewards for interacting with the old are minimal. Dowd (1979:98) claims that "the aged have very little to exchange which is of any instrumental value." That is, the elderly are not likely to have much money, social position, physical attractiveness, or knowledge. Even the traits in which the aged are likely to excel vis-à-vis other age groups, like wisdom and experience, are of questionable value in an urban-industrial society. How wise or experienced can older people be in a rapidly changing, highly technical society where skills are quickly outmoded (Toffler, 1970)? Since we know from exchange theory's propositions one and three that the more rewarding and valuable something or someone is, the more action or interaction will take place, it follows that based on the principles of exchange theory, interaction with the elderly is unlikely. What old/nonold interaction there is probably is motivated primarily by love or duty, rather than by profit.

Note too that the aged have a distinct power disadvantage compared to the rest of society (Dowd, 1979:110; Pifer and Bronte, 1986:243, 329). As we have seen, power tends to accrue to the person or persons with the least interest in a social relationship (Homans, 1974:71). Since the elderly have relatively little to offer in exchange and need much, they have minimal power. Social exchange between the old and younger is costly to both sides. If the costs become too high (i.e., exceed the rewards), and they often do, then the exchange perspective predicts social disengagement (Botwinick, 1984:88–89). That is, the burdens of compliance and lost self-respect of the aged for interacting with the nonold begin to cost the old so much that, like the runaway adolescent, the aged person actually cuts him or herself off from society at large. Of course, society does not resist much, since the elderly have few valuable resources to offer society. This is not a popular, or particularly happy interpretation, but it is probably accurate for the most part. Note that power resources tend to be curvilinearly related to age. They are low for both the young and the old.

The Structural Perspective Structurally speaking, the aged have a diminished social interaction potential as well. If we calculate heterogeneity using Table 4.1 (where 11 percent of the population are age sixty-five or older), we find that heterogeneity equals 20 percent. That is, given certain assumptions, the random chance of old-nonold social interaction is crudely one in five. It will be recalled that heterogeneity for the young was much higher. Most younger people would not be expected by chance alone to have aged people with whom to interact. Since liking is positively related to interaction potential, it is not surprising that the aged tend to be negatively regarded. However, we must also note that the increasing size of the aged population, both absolutely and proportionately, should in the future reduce the structural effects limiting interaction and encouraging negative stereotypes. Siegel and Taeuber (1986:82) estimate that by the year 2030 19.6 percent of the American population will be age sixty-five or older (see Blau's theorem, 1977:21).

Inequality is another major factor in the special problems of the aged. Not only are the elderly cut off from out-group relations based on their diminished size and number, they also tend to have low social status. In fact the elderly tend to have the very lowest social status (however, see Palmer and Gould, 1986). Unlike the young (at least the very young have their parent's social status), the old are consistently low status on almost all indicators of status and have little hope of changing their status in the future (since most do not have much future). Being in the very lowest status groups, there is a great distance between elderly and society's powerful members. Structurally this distance further reduces the prospects of the aged interacting with those who could help them. Given the usual truncated diamond shape of social status hierarchies, most social interaction is one status level down (because there are usually more people below you with whom to interact). The aged have no one below them to interact with. Even though at the bottom there are more people just above you, for reasons of exchange disadvantage already cited, upward social interaction is also unlikely. Thus, based on social inequality considerations too, the aged are likely to be isolated, lonely, and depressed (if we can assume that social interaction is positively related to happiness—see Botwinick, 1984:21–22).

The Biological Perspective Of course, exchange and structure are not the only determinants of the problems of the aged. Since we have elaborated the conflict, functional, and symbolic interaction theoretical perspectives on age when considering the social problems of young people, our discussion here for the aged will be brief. Biology is also a major factor in human behavior and its problems. This is true not only for aging but also for other social problems. Biology conditions social interaction. As Homans observes (1974:74–75), the original bases for power and status are often biological. If the special problems of the elderly include isolation, economics, and health, then clearly biology plays a role. This is so because the aged tend to have less strength and energy to get out and be with others, or to work (Birren, 1986).[15] Poor health is obviously related to biological aging.

The Conflict Perspective A conflict theoretical perspective on aging might see the problems of aging as resulting from larger society's resentment of their need to support the aged economically. For example, Table 4.1 shows that the index of aging (the ratio of the old to the young) has increased almost fivefold since 1900. In recent years the middle-aged and aged American population have come into more conflict over work. Older workers cut into capitalist's profits because they command higher wages. Older workers are more likely to be members of labor unions. As for skills most elderly people do not have the scientific, engineering, or technical education to perform many jobs in a computerized, high-tech economy. Older workers tend to lose more days of work to illness than younger workers.

The Functional Perspective Functionalists might point to the objective consequences of having hordes of aged in the population. From the standpoint of societal needs one could reasonably maintain that the aged are relatively useless. As Durkheim observed as early as 1893, in a specialized division of labor society's integration is promoted by each group "filling a determinant social function" Durkheim referred to the resultant social integration as "organic solidarity" (i.e., we all tend to depend on one another). Since the aged cannot "fill a determinant function" as a group, they tend to become problematic. For example, as a whole the aged tend to be poor and socially isolated. Many of the aged drain society's scarce resources through federal and state welfare programs, social security costs, medicare and medicaid, nursing homes, hospital and health care costs and so on. One latent dysfunction of a large aged population is that the aged become economic liabilities. A latent function (and there probably are others) is that the aged could assist working mothers with the society's child-care chores.

The Symbolic Interaction Perspective Finally, symbolic interactionists would claim that aging tends to be socially defined. Sometimes our social constructions or shared beliefs about old people are not based on their actual behaviors or capabilities. The result is many stereotypes and myths about the aged (Neugarten and Neugarten, 1986). Examples of these social stereotypes might include arbitrarily labeling people old at age sixty-five; seeing all older people as alike, disabled and sickly, sexless, unintelligent or senile, and neglected; or cruel, negative jokes about elderly females (Botwinick, 1984:Ch. 2). Symbolic interactionists remind us that the meanings of being old tend to change. As we have seen, at an earlier time in American history the aged were more positively valued. However, lately we have been more likely to value youth. Did old people themselves really change all that much or do we merely see or define the elderly differently now? If it is our social definitions of age that have changed, then maybe *they* (not the elderly) are the problem. Nevertheless, while there is considerable variance in aging, and how aging is defined, old age is not a condition some dominant group invented because they were sadistic or did not care for older people.

Resolving the Problem Since social interaction with the elderly is generally costly, the federal government may have to provide financial incentives to families to care for their aged relatives (Sussman, 1979; Pifer, 1986). These incentives could take the form of a $1,000 to $2,000 tax deduction per aged relative similar to those already granted for dependent children.[16] Most grandparents could still help with child care and in so doing could gain a sense of purpose and continuity for their own lives. As the sociobiologists argue, in one's children and grandchildren at least our genes survive (Wilson, 1975; Bryjak and Soroka, 1985). Such a partial recreation of the old extended (three-generational) family would clearly minimize the elderly's isolation and loneliness, in addition to helping their economic situation. To be sure though, such a resolution is far from ideal.

For one thing most older people prefer to live by themselves if they are able to care for themselves (Sussman et al., 1979). Also, moving in with one's children often requires geographic and community disruption, since one's children have usually left their hometowns in pursuit of jobs. It may not be worth it—unless it is absolutely necessary—to give up old friends, neighbors, habits, environs, and supports to move in with your own children. Of course, having a dependent aged parent live with you is an added stress and strain as well on the children, who usually have children, jobs, and other responsibilities of their own with which to cope. It should be noted that to provide a tax deduction for caring for a dependent relative does not in itself change the intrinsic worth of that dependent. All human beings need to feel that they are lovable apart from financial inducements. Note that the structural perspective (Blau, 1977:21) predicts that the rate of out-group associations, and with it young-old prospects for mutual liking, will increase as the size of the aged population increases (Table 4.1, Figure 4.1).

The special problems of the aged are closely related to federal programs like social security, medicare, medicaid, national health insurance, and the like (Palmer and Gould, 1986; Kreps, 1979). The aged have to view with some alarm the cutting back of these programs during the period of the Reagan administration. With the population and work-life changes detailed above, in effect there are more aged with shorter work lives to prepare for longer retirements (Morrison, 1986). To have even these inadequate benefits shrink or disappear entirely is a major problem for the aged. To avoid this it is likely that retirement age will have to be raised to age sixty-eight or seventy (as it already is federally and in many states). Furthermore, some benefits will have to be reduced and more individual (nonfederal) supplemental programs initiated. The tax-deductible IRA accounts, which would have helped, were struck down in 1986. Of course, preretirement planning needs to be started early and revised periodically to accommodate changes in inflation and the economy (Monk, 1979). One recurring problem is that most people do not take their retirement needs seriously until it is too late (Morrison, 1986). Even with modest incomes something can be done if planning begins early enough and lives are relatively stable.

Since a large part of aging concerns health problems and ultimately dying and death, medicine and religion can help the aged. Modern medical technology and pharmacology have made great advances in reducing pain and suffering. Many elderly people who would have died or had chronic crippling pain only a few years ago now have hope of longer more pain-free lives. Of course, even organ transplants do not promise immortality. Nevertheless, surgery and new drugs have made it possible for more people to live more complete life spans in less pain. It is not unreasonable to expect that life expectancy itself will continue to increase. Even dying has become somewhat less dreadful with the advent of the hospice (Leming and Dickinson, 1985; Ch. 8; Saunders, 1977). The hospice is a terminal care institution originating in England and specializing in the free use of alcohol, morphine, and other drugs to aid the dying patient avoid pain. Patients are also encouraged to feel free to talk about their own deaths and to have family or friends with them if they choose.

Finally, religion should be a special resource for the aged. Most religions believe in the noncontingent sanctity of life. For example, Christian religions speak of *agapé,* a kind of nonprofit motivated love that God has for all people. Whereas in a profit-motivated impersonal, materialistic "business" world interaction with the aged may be relatively unrewarding, in most religious communities age is not a negative trait. Religions tend to value the intrinsic worth of all human beings, provided that they follow the theological codes and moral precepts of the religion. Many older people find that their relationships and values shift as they age. Some prior sensual or economic goals tend to pale with time. A new sense of community and self-worth can be discovered within the church or synagogue. Often the church can become the aged person's substitute family. Furthermore, the church as an institution is usually entrusted with the transition from living to dying. As such, elderly persons may find that preparing for their own death is more meaningful within the context of a church or synagogue. Of course, many religions do not believe that physical death or biological cessation marks the end of the individual spirit. If one shares this belief, then one of the most troubling problems of the aged can become less traumatizing.

• Summary

Age is the first of several biosocial or subinstitutional (see Chapter 10) social problems to be considered in this text. Unlike most social problems texts that tend to treat problems of age exclusively as the result of oppression (ageism) of minorities (e.g., the young and the old) by majority groups (e.g., the middle aged), the present chapter sees the problems of the young, middle aged, and elderly as also based in the sociological principles of exchange, social structure, biology-sociobiology, conflict, functionalism, and symbolic interaction. For example, the young often have special problems with sexuality and violence. It was argued that sexual attractiveness and physical strength are two of the main social interactive advantages or assets that young people enjoy vis-à-vis other age groups. In contrast, the elderly have virtually no age-specific interactive advantages over other age groups. Small wonder then that the elderly tend to be poor, isolated, and unhappy. While middle-aged people enjoy numerous interactive advantages over both the young and the old, they also tend to be satiated on their rewards. Accordingly, the middle-aged usually develop special problems from routinization, boredom, and the drain of responsibilities.

Structurally speaking, the size and number of the aged present some unique obstacles for out-group relations. Although the United States has a rapidly aging population, heterogeneity is much lower for elderly populations than for the young. For the aged the size barriers to out-group associations is compounded by the generally low social status of the aged. That is, the aged must interact across great social distances to associate with young persons. A relatively small number of middle-aged persons, on the other hand, must bear a disproportionately large share of the economic burdens for the dependent young and aged. Furthermore, both the young and the elderly age categories have expanded in modern society, since the young have longer job-training periods and the aged have greater life expectancies.

Many of the age-stage problems of social development are related to biological conditions. Obvious instances include puberty for the young and menopause for the middle aged. Problems can arise when social expectations are not synchronized with biological developments. For example, we expect adolescents not to marry or have legitimate sexual relations until several years after they are biologically mature. Jobs, which are related to marriage prospects, often can begin at age thirty or so, especially if one chooses a professional job. At the other end of the age continuum, we still expect many people to retire at age sixty-five, even if they are capable of continuing work for many years.

The resolution of age problems within the context of exchange and structural theoretical perspectives contrasts with those of conflict theory, functionalism, and symbolic interactionism. While exchange theory and structuralism realize that social inequality causes some social problems, unlike conflict theories they also contend that some social inequality may be desirable or even necessary. Social structural differentiation is often based on biological differences. Thus, while conflict theory routinely advocates social changes or even revolution to foster equality, exchange theory and structuralism are more likely to recommend resignation or modest social change. For example, resolutions of age-specific problems might focus on mechanisms helping people tolerate inevitable structural differentiations based on age. Some of these mechanisms include tension reduction (e.g., time off, sports, avocations, sexual activity), medicine and drugs, and religion. Exchange principles also suggest maximizing one's age-specific interactive advantages (e.g., sex, physical strength, money, wisdom, and so on). In cases where some age groups have little intrinsic rewards (such as the elderly) the government may need to provide monetary incentives for caring for the age groups (i.e., change the value of the age group). Of course, in a more socialistic economy different age groups should not enjoy major exchange advantages. While conflict theory advocates a more equal integrated society, exchange and structural theories acknowledge that some age-specific isolation or stratification may be necessary. A society cannot resolve all age-related subproblems simultaneously, since some resolutions produce other social problems. For example, to exploit age-specific interactive advantages ensures the persistence of social inequality based on age.

Functionalists tend to see both the young and the old as economic and social liabilities in urban-industrial society—not as assets. The young and the elderly usually have their opportunities for achieving common social values blocked. Finally, the symbolic interactionist perspective stresses that the social meanings of age have changed with the industrial revolution and the advent of modern technology. Both the young and the old are perceived as less useful and relatively untrained for contemporary social and work demands. In Chapter 5 we continue our consideration of subinstitutionally related social problems as we turn to an examination of sex roles, sexism, and sexual variation.

• Notes

1. Based on the exchange, structural, biological, conflict, symbolic interaction, functional, and social deviance theoretical perspectives sketched in Chapter 2.

2. Secondarily, we shall argue that many exchange and structural characteristics are themselves influenced by human biology.

3. Fifteen to sixty-four is not the usual definition of "middle-age." Given current life expectancies of around seventy to seventy-five years depending upon one's sex, thirty-five to thirty-eight would be middle-age, give or take a few years. Furthermore, people are often considered middle aged almost up until they retire. Thus, thirty-five to fifty-five would be a better definition than fifteen to sixty-four. If we follow Figure 4.2, the range for middle-age would be thirty-one to fifty.

4. However, human development allows for periodic stagnation and eventual death. See H. Aldrich, 1979, *Organizations and Environment* for a discussion of organizational death.

5. Many theorists break this eighth stage down into later adulthood and old age (Levinson, 1978:Ch. 2) or young-old, old-old, and oldest old (Riley and Riley, 1986).

6. Presumably because sexual orgasms have a transcendent quality in which one's self is removed, time seems to stop, a pleasurable fatigue may set in, and sleep (which itself is often considered deathlike; see Shneidman, 1985:56ff.) is likely.

7. *Crises* refer to normal conflicts of social expectation with individual development as one matures and moves through the life cycle.

8. It must be remembered that the restriction of social interaction and inequality have complex relationships with social problems (see Chapter 10). On a more sophisticated level of analysis, restriction of interaction and inequality sometimes actually inhibit social problems and may be unavoidable.

9. We say "claim" because many values are common human values that cut across age groups. Probably young people in part resent being "locked out" of the adult world whose basic values they have internalized but cannot act on. Surely adults too act out sexually (through extramarital affairs), use drugs (especially alcohol and valium), and so forth. One should not naively assume too great value differences based on age differences.

10. Life expectancy at birth in 1984 for nonwhite females was 75.2 years; for nonwhite males it was 67.3 years.

11. Life satisfaction can be high in old age because the older people are, the less they expect of life and because the gap between aspirations and perceived actuality decreases with age. That is, although older people feel "unhappy" with the quality of their lives, they nevertheless are satisfied—because life quality is not a major problem for older people.

12. There was an 11 percent gain in the thirty-five to forty-five age group in the United States between 1970 and 1980.

13. See Decker, 1980:177, Table 9.1, "Major Programs of the Federal Government that Benefit Older People."

14. It is also true that brain cells die with age and are not replaced and that blood vessels carrying vital oxygen to the brain tend to become blocked with age.

15. See note 14.

16. Senator Buckley actually introduced such a bill in Congress in 1975.

• Glossary

Adolescence. Early adolescence often begins with puberty (around age twelve) and ends with high school graduation. This stage is marked by rapid physical changes, significant conceptual maturation, and heightened sensitivity to peer approval. Later adolescence runs from about age eighteen to twenty-two and is characterized by attainment of autonomy from the family and development of a sense of personal identity.

Age Stereotype. An unvarying uniform pattern negatively portraying age groups. For example, the elderly may all be held sickly and disabled, sexually inactive, excessively dependent, unable to hold jobs, and senile.

Age Structure. A multidimensional space of different age positions among which a population is distributed.

Aged. A life period when one is in later adulthood. Most often it is the time at which one must retire from work; that is, sixty-five to seventy years old. With increasing life expectancies it may be necessary to subdivide the aged into young-old, old-old, and oldest old, in the seventy to nineties.

Aging. A process of growing older that, after a certain point in one's life, involves an increasing inability of the organism to adapt to the environment and thus to survive. Has both social and biological expectancies and competencies for various stages of aging.

Ageism. The systematic stereotyping of and discrimination against people just because they are old (or less often, because they are young).

Burnout. Prolonged repetitive stresses resulting in emotional and physical decompensation and related occupational and social ineffectiveness.

Developmental Tasks. Psychosocial expectancies associated with various life stages or age stages. Erikson felt there were eight major life stages, each with three or four associated psychosocial expectancies or developmental tasks. If development tasks relative to age stages are not mastered (i.e., the life-stage crisis resolved), then developmental stagnation can result.

Disenfranchisement. To deprive of a social privilege, right, or power.

Gerontophilia. A love of the old or being aged. Fischer (1977) claims that 1607–1820 was a period of American history marked by gerontophilia, a time when age was exalted.

Gerontophobia. A fear or dread of the old or being aged. From about 1820 until today as a whole the United States has been gerontophobic.

Hospice. An institution started in Great Britain to aid the terminally ill and dying patient. Focus is on achieving an "appropriate" death. There is a free use of pain killers and individuality is encouraged. Hospices try to avoid cold impersonal deaths and technical intensive-care heroics.

Interactive Assets/Advantages. The rewards that individuals or groups have available to them to offer in social exchanges. They include money, status, sex, physical strength, experience, property, control of work opportunities, and the like.

Life Crisis. Implies a period of role experimentation and active decision making among alternative (often opposite) choices related to developmental tasks of each major life stage. If early life crises are resolved appropriately, then the individual can progress satisfactorily into later life crises.

Life Cycle. The cycle from birth to death of human beings. Has been divided into various stages and milestones to represent major developmental life tasks and events (such as beginning school, puberty, first job, marriage, having children, death of parents, menopause, retirement, grandparenting, death). Some aspects of the life cycle are biological, others are sociocultural.

Life Stage. Various periods in human life proceeding chronologically from birth to death with associated social and biological expectations.

Medicaid. A state and federally funded medical aid program available to all recipients of public assistance and the medically needy. Covers costs for physicians, dentists, hospitals, nursing homes, outpatient services, home care, drugs, eyeglasses, and so on.

Medicare. A federal program that provides hospital insurance (Part A) for any person over age 65 who is entitled to social security. It is a deductible policy with the individual paying the first $100–$200. Part B is an optional major medical plan (mainly for physician costs) that presently costs about $20 a month.

Middle-Age. A varying span of time in the middle of the human life cycle often characterized by a crisis of creativity versus stagnation (the mid-life crisis).

Nonreciprocal Exchange. A social exchange of disparate types of rewards. The exchange may be fair or "just" but the rewards exchanged are different. Examples might include sex for money, status for youth, and so on.

Power Disadvantage. The person or group in a social relationship who has the most interest in the continuance of the relationship or who has the fewest rewards to offer the other is at a power disadvantage.

Resignation. Acceptance of one's own unique life course without great remorse. Similar to Erikson's concept of integrity. Socially to tolerate human differentiation and age-stage responsibilities without the compulsions of revolution or despair.

Social Security. A federal program of payroll deductions from the salaries of certain workers designed in the 1930s primarily to help the elderly cope financially, especially in retirement years.

Stagnation. Fixation at a particular life stage in the developmental cycle. Suggests a lack of psychological and/or social growth. May occur when routine life crises are not appropriately resolved. Often contrasted with creativity.

Youth (Young Adult). A life period following childhood and adolescence. It runs from approximately twenty-three to thirty years of age. Sometimes referred to as young adulthood.

• Further Reading

Baltes, Paul and Orville Brim, eds. *Life-Span Development and Behavior.* New York: Academic Press, 1979–1987. This multivolumed scholarly project produces an edited book every year. It usually contains the most recent studies (like annual reviews) by the best scholars. Life-span studies differ from stage theories in that they are more diverse and heterogeneous in conceptual orientation. Human development is viewed as having multiple causes and multiple outcomes.

Botwinick, Jack. *Aging and Behavior: A Comprehensive Integration of Research Findings.* New York: Springer Publishing, 1984. As the title suggests the third edition of this well-received book concentrates on research findings. There are chapters (twenty-one in all) on stereotypes, biology, the elderly's sense of well-being, sexuality, intelligence, pathological aging, creativity, and much more. The approach, like the author, is psychological.

Farrell, Michael P. and Stanley D. Rosenberg. *Men at Midlife.* Boston: Auburn House Publishing, 1981. It is hard to pick one good book on mid-life. This one reports on interviews with 300 Northeast men ages thirty-eight to forty-eight (and their families), contrasted with 150 men ages twenty-five to thirty. Farrell and Rosenberg did not find a uniform "mid-life crisis." Families, as well as work, were found to be crucial to the mid-life experience. Middle-age symbolizes our concerns about staleness, atrophy, and meaning.

Levinson, Daniel J. *The Seasons of a Man's Life.* New York: Alfred A. Knopf, 1978. A very readable book focusing on middle-age male development that was somewhat compromised by the earlier work *Passages* by G. Sheehy. Levinson claims that adults hope that life begins at forty, but actually their great fear is that it ends there.

Pifer, Alan and Lydia Bronte, eds. *Our Aging Society: Paradox and Promise.* New York: W. W. Norton, 1986. An excellent, up-to-date reader on the social, economic, and public program problems and needs of the elderly. Several (eighteen) leading social scientists (e.g., Matilda White Riley, Bernice Neugarten, Cynthia Taeuber, Alice Rossi, and so on) contribute original articles on their specialties within aging. In addition to the traditional topics there are useful chapters on blacks, hispanics, retirement, health care, and public policy.

Santrock, John W. *Adolescence: An Introduction.* Dubuque, IA: Wm. C. Brown, 1984. A good, basic textbook on adolescence, now in its second edition. Contains chapters on history, theories, biology, cognitive development, intelligence, families, peers, schools, cultural variation, the self, sex and sex roles, moral development, work, drugs, and abnormality of adolescence. Like most good texts, there is a glossary and full references. The book contains useful data and theories in a highly readable style.

C·H·A·P·T·E·R

5

Sex: Sex Roles, Sexism, and Sexual Variation

Throughout history women and men have exchanged women's unique sexual assets of childbearing, sexual gratification, and socioemotional support for the relatively unique male rewards of protection, security, money, property, and social status, most commonly through the institution of marriage. Once such exchanges between men and women become patterned and institutionalized, sexism is inevitable. Sex roles and sexism persist in part because both men and women exploit their unique interactive assets.

Conflict theorists counter that sexism persists because unequal and unfair treatment of women is especially to the advantage of males. Capitalists maximize their profits by paying women less than men and by exploiting the largely unpaid emotional and physical labor of wives at home. Functionalists and biologists point out that sex roles originally resulted from the smaller average physical size of females and their unique childbearing capabilities. These traits led to consequences of women staying at home and needing protection. Symbolic interactionists do not see sex roles as determined by biology, but rather as products of learning traditional socially restrictive stereotypes concerning the proper behaviors of women and men. Women are in fact far more versatile and capable than gender roles suggest.

Sexual variations or deviances, whatever else they are, are also human exchanges conditioned by reward, punishment, satiation, and structural opportunities. Clearly prostitution and pornography are at least exchanges of sex for money. Exclusive homosexuality is an effort to avoid the costs and punishments of heterosexual roles altogether, as well as to seek the

PANEL 5.1

Male versus Female Sexuality

A rather curious sight can be observed almost any day on a number of busy streets in New York City. A man stands on the street, and after a cursory glance at each passing pedestrian, either does or does not present the unwitting walker with a small card. A few minutes' observation ascertains that it is only male pedestrians unaccompanied by women who are given such cards. A few steps away, a woman (or sometimes a man) is going through the same performance, surveying the passing masses, but this time handing cards only to women.

The contrast in the sexual content of these cards reveals a deep split in the meaning of sexuality for males and females. The cards given to men advertise massage parlors, symbolic of sex as recreation and pleasure and the relief of insistent need apart from any entanglement with the rest of their lives. The cards offered to women, on the other hand, proffer free pregnancy testing and later abortion services, signifying the fact that for women sexuality is a much more encompassing phenomenon, difficult to separate from the reproductive cycle and entire life plan.

Female sexual identity extends far beyond the sexual act whereas male sexuality is almost totally encompassed within it. When we consider sexuality as a biological backdrop for socialization throughout the life cycle, we must concentrate on the different meanings of sexuality for men and women.

Source: From *Sex Roles: Biological, Psychological, and Social Foundations,* by Shirley Weitz. Copyright © 1977 by Oxford University Press, Inc. Reprinted by permission.

positive rewards of homosexuality. Increased heterosexual intercourse outside of marriage (e.g., premarital and extramarital sex) is also associated with several important exchange-structural factors. Birth control has made nonmarital sex less costly; effective reproduction and thus marriage are less socially necessary, and physical gratification has become more valuable and socially acceptable. Premarital and extramarital sexual activities often involve disguised or hidden exchanges.

Functionalists view nonmarital sex and homosexuality as more likely to be ends in themselves, and thus to threaten reproduction of the human species. Furthermore, society needs to provide alternatives to premarital and extramarital sex and homosexuality, since they all are presumably meeting basic social needs. Conflict theorists claim that sexual deviances like prostitution and pornography debase and exploit women (and children). Laws are passed against homosexuality and prostitution because the dominant group in society is largely married heterosexual males. Symbolic interactionists and deviance theorists believe sexually deviant identities (e.g., being a prostitute) result from repeated labeling or negative public reactions. Thus, paradoxically, often attempts to control sexual variation in fact produce it. What is defined as sexually deviant or obscene varies considerably among different social and cultural groups.

Probably more than any other social problem we shall consider in this text sexuality will be interesting to you, if not compelling. The problem of aging no doubt seems remote to most young people. If it is a problem at all, it is also one that can wait. Sex, now that's a different matter! Both because young adults are in peak biological fitness and because they need to make crucial decisions about sex, love, and marriage, the subject of human sexuality is more pressing. Think for a moment of some of the issues. How sexually intimate, how soon, with whom, how often, and with how many should we be? Is marriage an outmoded institution? Certainly a divorce rate approaching 50 percent suggests that traditional marriages are in deep trouble. Do sex-role stereotypes inhibit and compromise both men and women? If you think this is a dead issue, just remember what has happened to the equal rights amendment recently.

And what about sexual variety? Is traditional heterosexuality too limiting? Increasingly we are being forced to consider homosexuality, bisexuality, unisexuality, asexuality, androgeny, and much more. At times the options can be bewildering. Even if a traditional heterosexual relationship results in a more or less routine marriage, there probably will be temptations for extramarital affairs or even divorce (see Chapter 12). Within that marriage or other long-term relationship, what are appropriate sexual behaviors? These and other issues related to human sexuality will all be examined in this chapter.

Most social problems treatments of sexuality are either reductions of sexuality to sex or gender roles, or reductions of love and sex to their mechanics or "perversions." As a rule social problems textbooks do not even consider actual sexual behaviors any more, so severe is their preoccupation with gender roles. Seldom are the larger purposes of functions of sex in society considered. It will be recalled that social problems are general patterns of human behavior or social conditions that have become unrewarding, are no longer valuable, unjust, imbalanced, have led to social inequality, and so on. Accordingly, we need to remind ourselves what the general patterns of sexuality are and what they are intended to accomplish before we can understand how these patterns might become problematic.

Three of the major functions (not the only functions) of sexual activities are reproduction, social integration, and tension reduction or pleasure. Of course, the propagation and survival of the human species requires effective heterosexual intercourse. This has always seemed so obvious it is almost foolish to write it down. However, as we shall see in Chapter 13, generally in contemporary societies, the problem is that reproduction has become too effective.

Today there are too many people, not too few. The world population doubles every forty-one years (see Chapter 13). This means that (globally at least) sexuality is no longer related to human survival the way it once was.

Second, sexual exchanges are used to integrate society. Spouses (especially wives) are bartered to win loyalties, create family or blood ties, secure dowries and kinship bonds. Often a wife is seen as property.[1] Women are exchanged for status, security, and money both for themselves and their extended families (Weitz, 1977:117). These exchanges tend to integrate society through marriage bonds and family ties. When such exchange patterns break down or are circumvented, then social order itself is endangered at least until a new pattern emerges. Finally, sexual activity reduces tension through exertion, ejaculation, and orgasm. It is pleasurable and feels good, completely apart from its reproductive or integrative functions. The erotic potential of sexual acts also constitutes a potential basis for social anarchy. Clearly, society cannot afford to allow random narcissistic pursuit of sexual pleasure. Rape, assault, sexual dominance, aggression are all themselves special social problems.

Since we also propose a general theory of sexuality that respects objective conditions or "social facts," it is imperative that we be aware of the sex structure of the American population. It will be remembered that males and females exist in roughly equal numbers. If we define the sex ratio as the number of males per 100 females, then equal proportions of males and females in a population would result in a sex ratio of 100. Over time in the United States the sex ratio has gone down from a high of 106 in 1910 to a low of about 95 in 1980 (Zopf, 1984:137ff.; Guttentag and Secord, 1983). This downward trend is usually attributed to male losses in war, restriction of immigration, and medical advances especially beneficial to females.

As was seen in Figure 4.2, males tend to predominate at younger ages and females at older ages. However, males are more likely than females to die at all ages. For example, the sex ratio at conception is about 120, but at birth it is only 106. That is, even male fetal mortality is greater than that of females. Part of this vulnerability is due to chromosomal variation between the sexes (i.e., males are more genetically fragile). In 1983 there were about 114 million males (48.6 percent) and 120 million females (51.4 percent) of all ages in the United States, for a sex ratio of 95.

If we take these last data and calculate heterogeneity (the expected frequency of out-group associations) for the two sexes, we see that it is relatively high (.50), suggesting that heterogeneity is less important to sexual problems than inequality.[2] The chances of males and females in the American population interacting based on their size and numbers alone is in fact high.

Even though males and females occur in roughly equal numbers in the United States, they are not evenly distributed in social positions such as the labor force. Table 5.1 reveals that there is a clear division of labor in society by sex (cf. Zinn, 1986:240; Berch, 1982; Fox and Hess-Biber, 1984). Males tend to be concentrated in activities and jobs related to hunting, fishing, building, land clearing, animal herding, and so on, while females tend to be concentrated in the more domestic tasks of cooking, making clothes, gathering fuel, milking, and so on. The usual explanation for the origin of this sexual differentiation in the division of labor is that men were stronger and more aggressive than women and they were not tied to the home by pregnancy, childbirth, and child care. Of course, we shall want to actually examine in this chapter how much sexual differentiation is immutable, whether social differentiation by sex is biologically based, and how much sexual differentiation is simply a product of arbitrary sex role assignments.

TABLE 5.1 Sex Allocation in Selected Technological Activities in 185 Societies

	Number of Societies in Which the Activity is Performed by:					
Activity	**Males Exclusively**	**Males Usually**	**Both Sexes Equally**	**Females Usually**	**Females Exclusively**	**Percent Male**
Smelting of ores	37	0	0	0	0	100.0
Hunting	139	5	0	0	0	99.3
Boat building	84	3	3	0	1	96.6
Mining and quarrying	31	1	2	0	1	93.7
Land clearance	95	34	6	3	1	90.5
Fishing	83	45	8	5	2	86.7
Herding	54	24	14	3	3	82.4
House building	105	30	14	9	20	77.4
Generation of fire	40	6	16	4	20	62.3
Preparation of skins	39	4	2	5	31	54.6
Crop planting	27	35	33	26	20	54.4
Manufacture of leather products	35	3	2	5	29	53.2
Crop tending	22	23	24	30	32	44.6
Milking	15	2	8	2	21	43.8
Carrying	18	12	46	34	36	39.3
Loom weaving	24	0	6	8	50	32.5
Fuel gathering	25	12	12	23	94	27.2
Manufacture of clothing	16	4	11	13	78	22.4
Pottery making	14	5	6	6	74	21.1
Dairy production	4	0	0	0	24	14.3
Cooking	0	2	2	63	117	8.3
Preparation of vegetables	3	1	4	21	145	5.7

Source: Adapted from George P. Murdock and Caterina Provost, "Factors in the Division of Labor by Sex: A Cross-Cultural Analysis," *Ethnology,* April 1973, p. 207. Cf. Charlotte O'Kelley and Larry S. Carney, *Women and Men in Society,* 1986.

Finally, we need to be careful not to confuse sex with gender. *Sex* refers to the biological fact of maleness or femaleness. As such sex is determined by chromosomes and hormones. *Gender,* on the other hand, refers to the cultural concepts of masculinity and femininity. As such, gender can vary considerably across societies. For example, kinship and property can be matrilineal (traced through females only) or patrilineal. In the USSR physicians tend to be females, but in the USA they tend to be males. What is considered masculine or feminine is much more complicated than whether one is biologically a male or a female, although (as we shall see) gender is not all that whimsical and sexual identity is sometimes confused. It should be noted that most sociologists, understandably, concentrate on gender, rather than sex (Bleier, 1984). They act as if human sexuality could be reduced to gender roles or culture. Biology (sex) is for the most part not considered social destiny (however, see Rossi, 1984). Sexual differentiation tends to be seen as a product of sexism; as reflecting merely greed for power and arbitrary domination by males or females. We need to examine this assumption very carefully in the next section.

The Biological Roots of Sexuality

Genetics Every human cell has forty-six chromosomes, twenty-three from each parent. The twenty-third pair are the sex chromosomes, usually XX for the female and XY for the male. The male XY chromosome pair is less stable than the female XX pair. This chromosomal fragility results in greater mortality for males at all ages. It also results in sex-linked diseases or illnesses related to recessive genes, such as hemophilia or color blindness (Tavris and Offir, 1977:100). The latter are both more common among males, similar to sickle cell anemia's commonality among blacks (see Chapter 6).[3] It should be added that not all sex chromosomes are XX or XY. There are a few chromosomal abnormalities that can result in behavioral problems and, sometimes, in confused sexual identity.

Hormones The endocrine system secretes hormones essential to sexual differentiation (Bleier, 1984; Ch. 4; Hyde, 1982:54ff.). The main glands of the endocrine system are the gonads (the ovaries or testes), the adrenal, and the pituitary (which acts in concert with the hypothalamus in the brain). Generally, male hormones (especially testosterone) masculinize and female hormones (especially estrogen and progesterone) feminize.[4] Testosterone is secreted from the testes and estrogen from the ovaries. Estrogen is crucial to the development of the reproductive tract, while progesterone is essential for pregnancy. Hormonally the female is more complex than the male. Hormones are released directly into the blood stream and thus tend to affect our entire bodies. There is some evidence that testosterone is related to male aggressiveness and dominance (Maccoby and Jacklin, 1974; Ehrhart and Baker, 1974).

Sex Differences It is important to realize that there are some sexual differences that are completely independent of socialization influences or sex roles. For example, males tend to be physically larger than females even at birth, more dominant, and more resplendent (especially male animals). Male animals often engage in "epidietic" (e.g., strutting, puffing out of feathers or hair, etc.) displays toward other males to indicate claimed territory or ownership functions. Behaviorally they are saying "this is my turf" or "these are my females," and so on. Male monkeys tend to be more rough and tumble in their play than females. Female monkeys, on the other hand, are more likely to engage in grooming behavior (Hutt, 1975:58). Although males tend to have a higher basal metabolism (i.e., the lowest level of energy expenditure, often measured in terms of calories expended; 1,500 to 1,800 for the average person) and greater vital capacity, females mature earlier, talk sooner, and have lower pain and touch thresholds. On the whole it is thought that males see better, have greater variability in IQ, are better at abstract mathematics, and are more aggressive (Benbow and Stanley, 1980; however, see Bleier, 1984).

Contrary to some arguments, 99 percent of human beings have a clear sexual identity at birth. Furthermore, originally we are all females. That is, if a Y chromosome is not present, then we remain female. Female differentiation is thus "passive." It is possible to change sexual identity through administration of a combination of hormones, psychotherapy, and surgery. One can masculinize a female, but it is more difficult to feminize a male. Maleness has a certain indelibility to it (Hutt, 1975:63). The opposite is true for surgical sex changes. It is easier to surgically reconstruct a male to become a female (essentially the scrotum is used to build a vagina) than it is to surgically reconstruct a male from a female. The main problem was that until recently (about 1986) the reconstructed male's penis had to have a permanent erection to be effective for sexual intercourse.[5]

Reproduction One absolutely incontrovertible biological fact is that only women can have babies. And for thousands of years that was just about all women ages fifteen to forty-five did. Much of the domesticity of the typical female sex role grows out of the unique relationship of women to reproduction. While men could (they usually do not) care for young children, they certainly cannot get pregnant.[6] In some societies men underwent symbolic childbirth (known as couvade), but it was only symbolic. As we shall see, women's reproductive uniqueness has affected their ability to even do certain kinds of work and to compete effectively with men at work. Most women can only do "part-time" work (i.e., when they are not pregnant or not raising children). Of course, times have changed some now (not as much as you might think). Marriages come later in life, couples are less likely to have children after marriage, and completed family sizes are smaller. One reason for these changes is that children cost too much and large families are no longer needed to ensure the survival of the human species (infant mortality has been reduced, and so on). If anything, overall, there are too many people for the world's resources.

"We had that in school last week."

A major consequence of these recent social changes is that sexual relationships today are less likely to occur for the sake of reproduction and more likely to be an end in themselves (i.e., for pleasure, power, and so on). Not long ago novelist Aldous Huxley took this trend of separation of sex from reproduction to its extreme in his book *Brave New World* (1939). Huxley envisioned test-tube babies grown in a "hatchery" and raised by professionals. Sex was "just" for fun. Much of what Huxley prophesied is true only forty to fifty years later (Hyde, 1982:578). Nevertheless, for now, only women can have babies. They may choose not to, and increasingly they are, but the fact remains that if there are to be children, women tend to have to shoulder a very different burden in producing them than men do (see Panel 5.1).

Puberty, Menstruation, and Menopause Generally, sexuality is less of an issue before puberty for the obvious reasons that men and women are not sexually mature, have lower sexual drives, and cannot yet conceive children. Puberty is the time during which there is a sudden enlargement and maturation of the gonads, other genitalia, and secondary sexual characteristics (such as pubic hair, breasts, and facial hair) leading to reproductive capacity. For males puberty is signaled by their first ejaculation; for females by their first menstruation. The sex hormones described above produce major sexual changes and with them major behavioral changes. For example, menstruation can have far-reaching impacts (Bleier, 1984:86–87). Even school grades can be affected (Hyde, 1982:81). Weitz argues that women's menstrual activities are often responsible for them being regarded as "polluted" or even evil (1977: Ch. 4). The cessation of menstruation (menopause takes about two years and starts around ages thirty-five to forty-seven) can also have major impacts. Hormonal changes at menopause have been related to depression, hot flashes (sudden waves of heat from the waist up, causing perspiration, and later chills), and more painful sexual intercourse due to lubricant diminution. Once again, we see that the biology of female sexuality is quite different from that of male sexuality.

Sex and the Life Cycle Implicit in the above sections is the assumption that biological aging and its concomitants throughout the life cycle affect sexuality, especially the sexuality of females (Hyde, 1982:Chs. 10 and 11). To illustrate, the frequency of sexual intercourse is related to age. People in their twenties tend to have sexual relations two to three times a week, while people over age forty-five usually have sex only about once a week. It is also clear from other indicators that sexuality extends throughout the life cycle. We tend to forget that infants suck breasts, thumbs, and so on, or masturbate themselves; that many older widows and widowers still have relatively active sex lives. These facts should not obscure the even more powerful influences of sexuality between puberty and menopausal ages (roughly ages eight or twelve to forty-five or fifty). Thus, sexuality conditions, limits, and suggests gender roles. Gender or sex roles are not arbitrary, whimsical, fragile, social eccentricities, or capricious routines to be taken lightly. While sexual expectations and prescriptions can be changed, and in part should be changed, there are limits to those changes inherent in our biology, our history, and certainly in those institutions already in place and costly to change.

• Gender or Sex Roles?

The concept of a social role is drawn from the theater and implies that one's behavior (or even attitudes) is a performance following a script (Goffman, 1959). In the case of gender or sex roles the script is comprised of common social expectations about behavior appropriate for males and females (Doyle, 1985). More carefully stated a gender role is "a cluster of socially or culturally defined expectations that people of one gender are expected to fulfill" (Wittig, 1980; Hyde, 1982:320). When these expectations are exaggerated and based primarily on sexual preconceptions or prejudices, they become sex- or gender-role stereotypes. Most sociologists agree that men and women learn to behave

PANEL 5.2

A Female Stereotype Gone Sour

The problem lay buried, unspoken, for many years in the minds of American women. It was a strange stirring, a sense of dissatisfaction, a yearning that women suffered in the middle of the twentieth century in the United States. Each suburban wife struggled with it alone. As she made the beds, shopped for groceries, matched slipcover material, ate peanut butter sandwiches with her children, chauffered Cub Scouts and Brownies, lay beside her husband at night—she was afraid to ask even of herself the silent question—"Is this all?" . . . If a women had a problem . . . she knew that something must be wrong with her marriage, or with herself. Other women were satisfied with their lives, she thought. What kind of woman was she if she did not feel this mysterious fulfillment waxing the kitchen floor? She was so ashamed to admit her dissatisfaction that she never knew how many other women shared it. If she tried to tell her husband, he didn't understand what she was talking about. She did not really understand it herself. . . .

But on an April morning in 1959, I heard a mother of four, having coffee with four other mothers . . . say in a tone of quiet desperation, "the problem." And the others knew, without words, that she was not talking about a problem with her husband, or her children, or her home. Suddenly they realized they all shared the same problem.

Source: Betty Friedan, *The Feminine Mystique,* 1963, pp. 11–15. Reprinted by permission of W.W. Norton & Company, Inc.

more or less consistently with basic gender or sex-role expectations through a process called socialization. In keeping with our earlier distinction between sex and gender what we called sex roles are probably more aptly labeled gender roles, since they are usually culturally (not biologically) determined. One central issue in this section is how much sexuality (in the biological connotation) determines social expectations concerning male and female behavior. That is, are expectations for males and females gender or sex roles (cf. Hyde, 1982: Ch. 13; Weitz, 1977)?[7] You will notice that much of the discussion that follows is from the theoretical perspectives of symbolic interactionism and conflict sociology.

Most considerations of sexuality by sociologists tend to reduce sex to gender (Bleier, 1984; Tavris and Offir, 1977). More than this, they see gender roles as restrictive, confining, oppressive—especially of females (Greer, 1971). In modern industrial families, the wife is often viewed as the "head servant" (i.e., as a slave). Engels, in *The Origin of the Family, Private Property and the State,* writes:

> In the old communistic household, which comprised many couples and their children, the task entrusted to the women of managing the household was as

> much a public and socially necessary industry as the procuring of food by the men. With the patriarchial family, a change came. Household management lost its public character. It no longer concerned society. It became a private service; the wife became the head servant, excluded from all participation in social production. . . . The modern individual family is founded on the open or concealed domestic slavery of the wife, and modern society is a mass composed of the individual families as its molecules. (1942:65)

Given their restrictive nature gender roles are often thought to make poor use of the talents of women. Males do not escape altogether, though. They are condemned to competition, stress, and stress-related illnesses such as heart disease, hypertension, and ulcers.[8] Perhaps most disturbing (to many), male-female gender roles do not change much over time (Weitz, 1977:127). Remember that in 1982 the Equal Rights Amendment failed to be ratified by enough states to become law.

That male-female stereotypes exist is undeniable. Table 5.2 lists many of the stereotypic traits of males and females. Males are generally thought aggressive, courageous, tough, independent, ambitious, competitive, unemotional, pragmatic, and rational. Females, on the other hand, are held to be passive, submissive, gentle, dependent, family oriented, emotional, sentimental, idealistic, and intuitive (Bleier, 1984:72–73). Note that in Table 5.2 more of the male traits than the female traits are thought desirable. Weitz (1977) contends that much of the symbolism of female sex roles portrays women as evil, polluted, and witchy. Friedan, in *The Feminine Mystique* (1963), contends that the primary role of the woman is to function in the home, find fulfillment through the lives of her husband and children, rather than in a career.

Not only are women portrayed differently than men are, their place in society also tends to be depreciated or devalued (Doyle, 1985:57–63). For example, Weitzman et al. in reviewing eighteen award-winning children's books published between 1967 and 1971 found that the ratio of male to female pictures was 11:1, that boys were shown outside and girls inside the home, and that women were always depicted as mothers and wives (1972). In a book by Waller (no date) entitled *What Boys Can Be* the following occupations are listed: fireman, baseball player, policeman, cowboy, doctor, sailor, pilot, farmer, actor, president of the United States. A companion volume, *What Girls Can Be,* lists these occupations: nurse, stewardess, ballerina, model, actress, secretary, artist, schoolteacher, singer, housewife, and mother. In the Judeo-Christian religion God is a man, Eve is created from Adam's rib. Jesus is a male, and all the disciples are males. In the Torah the geneologies give the impression that only males were born or gave birth (begat). Orthodox Judaism is sex-segregated and patriarchal. Finally, virtually every film from 1966–72 that won an Academy Award had no major female role. Such negative views of women often result from and in sexism and sex discrimination (Tavris and Offir, 1977:19–23).

Since male-female gender roles and the behaviors they prescribe have been remarkably constant over long periods of time, it is naive to expect dramatic

"I laughed at the pig tie for my birthday, but then came the pig belt for Christmas, followed by the pig nightshirt for our anniversary . . ."

Drawing by Donald Reilly; © 1982 *The New Yorker* Magazine, Inc.

changes soon. Exchange and functional theories predict that behaviors that are being rewarded or have positive social consequences tend to get repeated. One interpretation of the constancy of gender or sex roles is that many people find traditional male-female gender roles rewarding or the required social changes too costly. A more cynical view is that those finding traditional gender or sex roles rewarding are relatively small in absolute numbers (e.g., middle-aged white males) but are very powerful. Probably both interpretations are partly correct.

If traditional male-female gender roles were to change, we need to ask what are some of the possible alternative outcomes and their attendant problems? Of course, one pervasive problem, since much of our society is organized around and assumes traditional sex roles, would be simple confusion, social disorganization, and lack of predictability. That is, many Americans can see gender or sex-role inequality that probably should be corrected, but at the same time are afraid of the costs of making the necessary social changes, of the disruption of their highly predictable world. Their resistance to change is thought pragmatic, not moral. Consider the relatively recent example of Title IX, which mandates that schools shall provide equal facilities and experiences

TABLE 5.2 Stereotypic Masculine and Feminine Traits

Masculine Pole Is More Desirable

Feminine	Masculine
Not at all aggressive	Very aggressive
Not at all independent	Very independent
Very emotional	Not at all emotional
Does not hide emotions at all	Almost always hides emotions
Very subjective	Very objective
Very easily influenced	Not at all easily influenced
Very submissive	Very dominant
Dislikes math and science very much	Likes math and science very much
Very excitable in a minor crisis	Not at all excitable in a minor crisis
Very passive	Very active
Not at all competitive	Very competitive
Very illogical	Very logical
Very home oriented	Very worldly
Not at all skilled in business	Very skilled in business
Very sneaky	Very direct
Does not know the way of the world	Knows the way of the world
Feelings easily hurt	Feelings not easily hurt
Not at all adventurous	Very adventurous
Has difficulty making decisions	Can make decisions easily
Cries very easily	Never cries
Almost never acts as a leader	Almost always acts as a leader
Not at all self-confident	Very self-confident
Very uncomfortable about being aggressive	Not at all uncomfortable about being aggressive
Not at all ambitious	Very ambitious
Unable to separate feelings from ideas	Easily able to separate feelings from ideas
Very dependent	Not at all dependent
Very conceited about appearance	Never conceited about appearance
Thinks women are always superior to men	Thinks men are always superior to women
Does not talk freely about sex with men	Talks freely about sex with men

Feminine Pole Is More Desirable

Feminine	Masculine
Doesn't use harsh language at all	Uses very harsh language
Very talkative	Not at all talkative
Very tactful	Very blunt
Very gentle	Very rough
Very aware of feelings of others	Not at all aware of feelings of others
Very religious	Not at all religious
Very interested in own appearance	Not at all interested in own appearance

TABLE 5.2 *(concluded)*

Feminine Pole Is More Desirable—*(concluded)*	
Feminine	Masculine
Very neat in habits	Very sloppy in habits
Very quiet	Very loud
Very strong need for security	Very little need for security
Enjoys art and literature	Does not enjoy art and literature at all
Easily expresses tender feelings	Does not express tender feelings at all easily

Source: Inge K. Broverman et al., "Sex Role Stereotypes: A Current Appraisal," *Journal of Social Issues* 28 1972. Reprinted by permission of the Society for the Psychological Study of Social Issues. The table shows the extreme poles of seven-point rating scales. Average ratings of the typical male fall toward one pole; of the typical female, toward the other pole.

for male and female students. Title IX has required vast expenditures, especially for women's athletic programs, at a time when colleges and universities are already in deep financial trouble. Most women's sports programs do not at this time generate the income men's programs do. Some universities have resolved this problem by eliminating all sports.

Many of the social problems we shall consider in the last part of this chapter (i.e., sexual deviance or variance) grow out of attempts to find alternatives to traditional sex roles (although gender problems are different from sexual problems). Some of the possibilities in a more sexually open society (i.e., freed from traditional gender-role stereotypes) include unisexuality or adrogyny (i.e., having both male and female traits), asexuality, separation of sex from the family, and homosexuality. Clearly many young people are troubled by their sexuality and seek to minimize or alter it. For some time now many students have played down their sexual differences, except for special occasions. Everyone wears jeans; everyone's hair is relatively long. Symbolically such unisexual behaviors are profound and have yet to be fully explored and understood by behavioral scientists.

On one level today's men and women may simply be taking the best traditional male and female traits and combining them. On another level they may be asking to be considered human beings and not more stereotypic sexual objects. On a still deeper level their superficial external appearance may reflect a deep ambivalence toward sexuality altogether. Indeed, one alternative to traditional sex roles is asexuality. This could result either because traditional sex roles have become too problematic or because a generation with increased sexual freedom has become satiated with sex and even grown tired of it. In some popular literature, such as Ian Fleming's James Bond novels, death or near death has replaced sex as the ultimate stimulus. Asexuality is not likely to become epidemic, since our biology is fairly constant and we recover quickly from sexual satiation (like from overeating or getting drunk).

PANEL 5.3

Changing Female Sex Roles

Women held almost a third of management, administrative, and executive jobs by 1980, up from 19 percent a decade earlier, the Census Bureau said Tuesday.

The bureau said, however, there is little change in the breakdown of men and women in occupations traditionally dominated by one group or the other. Women still hold few jobs in construction and craft, 7.8 percent, and only 1.2 percent of America's secretaries are men.

There were these other changes over the decade:

Women almost tripled their share of judgeships, from 6 percent to 17 percent, and the proportion of women lawyers grew from 5 percent to 14 percent.

Women increased their share of jobs in all the health-diagnostic fields, but still make up only a small percentage of the total practitioners. The proportion of women physicians grew from 10 percent to 13 percent, dentists from 4 percent to 7 percent, and optometrists from 4 percent to 8 percent.

Women held 10 percent or less of engineering jobs. The highest proportion of women is among industrial engineers, 10 percent, compared with 3 percent in 1970.

Source: *United Press International,* April 11, 1984. Reprinted with permission of United Press International, Copyright 1984.

Another variation in traditional gender roles would be to separate sex from love, marriage, and family. Alternatives here would include commercialization of sex, extramarital affairs, and sex for pleasure, but not reproduction. Whether such alternatives will eventually doom the American family or strengthen it is hard to tell. Some utopian novelists see marriage and the family as unnecessary, since children could be produced in laboratories and raised by professionals. In such a futuristic society men and women would tend to engage in sexual relations, if at all, simply for pleasure or tension reduction. Sexuality would not imply emotional bonding. It would be merely instrumental. Of course, it is probably just as possible to have love without sex as it is to have sex without love. Sexuality would simply not necessarily imply love. Finally, with diminished social need to reproduce ourselves, increased costs of heterosexual relations, and other factors, we probably will see more homosexuality in the future.

To summarize then, standard routinized social expectations for males and females do exist and are usually very different. Often male-female roles are stereotypic; that is, are exaggerated and based more in social prejudice or preconception than in physiology or biology. We shall examine some of the problems spawned by sexism and sexual discrimination in the next section. If male-female social-role problems are based more in cultural or value differ-

Very few women ever get to be top administrators or corporate executives even in activities dominated by women such as the public schools. The gender expectations for female workers include low-status jobs without power, such as secretaries, elementary school teachers, domestics or social service workers. (Barbara Alper/Stock, Boston)

ences, then they are problems of gender identity. However, sex roles are often just that, expectations evolved out of the basically different sexuality of men and women. Many human sexual differences are real, not merely capricious social or cultural inventions. Much of our gender identities are not incidental or accidental and cannot be toyed with as if they could be changed at will, even though many may need to be changed.

• Sexism and Sex Discrimination

Stating the Problem *Sexism* can be defined as a set of values that justifies discrimination against sex types on grounds of their (presumed) biological differences. Usually sexism connotes systematic, social, political, economic, psychological, and physical oppression of women by men (Doyle, 1985:178–185, 204–205). With sexism the sex-role stereotypes just discussed determine the life opportunity structures of women almost totally. Thus, sex discrimination is based on prejudice and preconception, rather than on the actual talents, skills, or abilities of women.[9]

Sexism is especially damaging to females' opportunities for income and work (Doyle, 1985:217–218). Table 5.3 reveals that in 1980 the annual median female income was about 60 percent that of median male income, an absolute difference of $7,415 a year between average male and female earnings. The disadvantages to females was especially large in managerial and sales types of employment. While the percentage disadvantage of women has generally improved over the years (73 = 35 percent; 77 = 59 percent; 80 = 60 percent; 82 = 63 percent; 84 = 64.3 percent), the absolute difference in male-female earnings has actually increased. The Associated Press reported November 20, 1978 that a white male who dropped out of high school actually makes more money on the average than a white female who completed college.

When women do work (and more and more are) they tend to be concentrated in low-status jobs without power, such as secretaries, elementary school teachers, domestics, and social services workers. In 1977 about 93 percent of physicians and 97 percent of lawyers in the United States were males. By 1984, 87 percent of physicians and 86 percent of lawyers still were males (see Panel 5.3). One-tenth of 1 percent of all surgeons were females. Frazier and Sadker (1973), in a study of educators, found that although 88 percent of elementary school teachers are women, only 22 percent are principals, and only two out of 1,300 are district school superintendents. Women tend not to be administrators; even in work situations they dominate in numbers. Women

TABLE 5.3 Median Annual Earnings of Full-Time Workers, 1980 (1982 and 1984)

	Median Income			
Type of Employment	**Male**	**Female**	**Difference**	**Female Income as Percent of Male**
Professional and technical	$23,026	$15,285	$ 7,741	66.4%
Managers and administrators	23,558	12,936	10,622	54.9
Clerical	18,247	10,997	7,250	60.3
Sales	19,910	9,748	10,162	49.0
Crafts	18,671	11,701	6,970	62.7
Operatives	15,702	9,440	6,262	60.1
Service workers	12,757	9,747	3,010	76.4
Laborers	13,097	7,892	5,115	60.9
Average (1980)	$18,612	$11,197	$ 7,415	60.2%
Average (1982)	$21,655	$13,663	$ 7,992	63.0%
Average (1984)	$24,004	$15,422	$ 8,582	64.3%

Source: James A. Doyle, *Sex and Gender: The Human Experience,* 1985:218; and *Statistical Abstract of the United States,* 1987.

usually work for less money because traditional sex-role stereotypes contended that women were supported by their husbands and thus did not need as much money.

> The old stereotype held that women work for pin money—extra frills and luxuries, rather than the family's meat-and-potatoes needs—or to mark time until they marry. This stereotype justified paying women less than men for the same work. "Husbands, the breadwinners, need the money more," employers could say; or "Why should I promote her? She'll just get married and quit." In fact, most women work for the same reasons men do—they need the money and they want the satisfaction. In 1973 almost two-thirds of all American working women were either heads of households (single, widowed, or divorced) or married to men whose incomes were below the poverty line. (Tavris and Offir, 1977:215*)

Since women were supposed to be dedicated primarily to their families, not to their careers, they were routinely considered "not serious" or "not dependable."

> Rose Coser and Gerald Rokoff (1971) observe, as Rossi does, that our primary role allegiances are strongly sex-typed: "A man owes to his profession what a woman owes to her family." In a sense real professional achievement requires great selfishness. If you are hot on the trail of a breakthrough in biochemistry, if you have a brilliant idea for Chapter 3 of your novel, if you have a legal brief that must be ready by 9:00 A.M. tomorrow, you must selfishly seize the time. If you are worried about feeding the family, dusting the bookshelves, or cheering up your spouse who had a lousy day, you may not finish the task. (Tavris and Offir, 1977:226*)

Economic discrimination because of sex eventually affects one's self-esteem, even one's physical health. Housewives, compared with single and married professionals have the lowest self-esteem and feel the worst about their own competence (cf. Brown and Harris, 1978). This is true even in areas where one might think they would excel, such as child care and getting along with other people. Housewives feel the least attractive, worry most about their personal identity, and most often feel lonely (Birnbaum, 1975). Although females are relatively well protected against mortality, morbidity, and illness vis-à-vis males, the pressure and stress of traditional male sex-role expectations demanding competitiveness, aggression, hard work, financial success, and so on are probably related to their greater rates of heart disease, alcoholism, suicide, and ulcers (Tavris and Offir, 1977:222ff.; Sorensen et al., 1985).

Looking briefly at the history of sexism as it applies to women and the response of women liberators we see that throughout all the social and economic changes, the subordinate position of women in Western society has remained constant (Weitz, 1977:127; O'Kelley and Carney, 1986). This is the case even though the percentage of women (of all workers) in the labor force has steadily increased from 4.6 in 1800, to 13.3 in 1900, 27.9 in 1950, 47.1 in 1977, 48.5 in 1983, and 57.3 (projected) in 1990. As a percentage of all females, in June of 1978 for the first time in history over 50 percent of all women over age sixteen were employed outside the home. (*Statistical Abstract of the United States,* 1986:398). In subsequent chapters we shall detail how significant this increased female labor force participation has been for social problems of divorce, crime, the family, and so on. Going back as far as 1595 we see that witches in early America were almost always females (Bleier, 1984:168ff.). Remy attributes this to the tendency to associate evil with women. But then women began to fight back. Mary Wollstonecraft was one of the first (1792) feminists. The first women's rights convention was held in New York in 1848. In 1871 the National Women's Suffrage Association was created and Victoria Woodhull shocked the nation by advocating "free love" for women outside of marriage.

In 1898 Charlotte Gilman wrote an influential book, *Women and Economics,* calling for women's economic independence. However, it was not until 1920 that women finally got the right to vote. In the 1920s the flappers ushered in a new era in sexual openness for women. The Great Depression of the 1930s and the two world wars marked a return to more traditional sex roles for the most part. All this was changed with Betty Friedan's book, *The Feminine Mystique* (1963), which pointed out "the problem" of a life dedicated solely to a husband, children, and a home. For some, women's liberation's ultimate revolutionary objective has not been equal opportunity for women, but the overthrowing of sex roles altogether, as illustrated dramatically in Shulamith Firestone's *The Dialectic of Sex.*

> And just as the end goal of socialist revolution was not only the elimination of the economic class privilege but of the economic class distinction itself, so that the end goal of feminist revolution must be, unlike the first feminist movement, not just the elimination of male privilege but of the sex distinction itself: genital differences between human beings would no longer matter culturally. . . . The reproduction of the species by one sex for the benefit of both would be replaced by (at least the option of) artificial reproduction: children would be born to both sexes equally, or independently of either, however one chooses to look at it; the dependence of the child on the mother (and vice versa) would give way to a greatly shortened dependence on a small group of others in general, and any remaining inferiority to adults in physical strength would be compensated for culturally. The division of labour would be ended by the elimination of labour altogether (cybernation). The tyranny of the biological family would be broken. (1970:39)

Judging by the rejection of the Equal Rights Amendment in 1982, the gender revolution is unfortunately still a ways off.[10]

Analyzing the Problem. The Exchange Perspective From the exchange perspective social interaction between sexes is different in important ways from that within sexes. It seems almost ridiculous to have to remind ourselves of this. For the 95 percent to 99 percent of the population who are heterosexual the physical rewards available to men and women differ. From exchange theory's first axiom we remember that behaviors that are rewarded tend to be repeated. Rewards can be particularly effective if we have been deprived of them for some time (Axiom 4). Table 5.4 lists basic rewards (some biological, some social-psychological) differing by sex and hints at fundamental exchange prospects. When these prospects are actualized they help create and maintain sex roles and sexism. For example, through human history women have exchanged their unique rewards of childbearing for the money, status, property, and security of males through marriage (Doyle, 1985:88ff.; Weitz, 1977:117). Obviously, only women can bear children. Until recently large families were considered an economic asset. Even today sociobiologists still claim we have strong inclinations to ensure the survival of our genes through producing children (Wilson, 1975; Bleier, 1984:Ch. 2). Furthermore, there are powerful biological supports and inducements to procreate. Sexual intercourse is usually a highly pleasurable activity.

In fact, as children have become more of an economic liability, women have increasingly exchanged their genitalia (and associated pleasure-giving abilities) for males' status, money, security, and property. Of course, it is crass, crude, and reductionistic to conceive of male-female relations this way. On the other hand, it is also undeniable that only women have female sex organs and only men have male sex organs. They have to be an interactive asset based on supply and demand alone. This is not to suggest that we reduce human relationships to sexuality; rather, we wish to suggest that sex is one important reward in social exchanges. Continuing to examine Table 5.4, the physical strength and protection that individual men offer women is less important in advanced industrialized societies with legal and police protection. Nevertheless,

TABLE 5.4 Distribution of Basic Societal Rewards by Sex

Rewards	**Females**	**Males**
Children, child-bearing potential	+	–
Female sex organs and related pleasure	+	–
Male sex organs and related pleasure	–	+
Social status, money, property, security	–	+
Physical strength, aggression, protection	–	+
Nurturance, child care, home care	+	–
Socioemotional support	+	–

– = not very important or salient, absent, received
+ = very important or salient, present, provided

it is still true that being involved with a specific male (through informal arrangements like living together all the way up to formal marriages) protects females against sexual harassment, having to date, staying attractive, and in rare cases, against rape. If you do not believe this, ask any recently separated or divorced female (or male, to a lesser extent).

In a similar way the nurturance that females have to offer males has become less valuable with the advent of child-care centers and the development of schools and other nurturing professionals. Still, wives are children's biological mothers and often their spouse's surrogate mothers. Women typically have been culturally defined as the gender group that provides socioemotional support, empathy, sensitivity, and feeling for their children and husbands (Doyle, 1985:88–89; Bleier, 1984:175ff.). Biologically it can be argued that the sexual roots of nurturance derive from giving birth, nursing, and mothering. Yet one must be careful not to reduce love, companionship, and nurturance in marital exchanges to sex-specific traits. Some of the gender attributes females are believed to have could be cultivated in males (and vice versa).

Exchange theory also reminds us that a sex group cannot have unique interactive advantages (profits) without some disadvantages as well (costs). Sex roles and sexism are a major cost of sexual differentiation. As long as some women wish to exchange children or sex for status or men wish to exchange property for sex, there will be sex roles and sexism. In a sense both men and women must get their acts together. It is not just the men who are doing the discriminating. Furthermore, the family changes (see Chapter 12) required by proposed sex-role changes like those of Firestone (above) require major, not trivial, social adjustments. Most men and many women are simply not willing to give up the traditional family.

Note too that as long as women take time out to bear and raise children, it is going to hurt their interactive value in the job market. By exchange theory's third axiom (see Panel 2.2) we would expect that fewer and fewer women would be willing to bear children or as many children as in the past. Finally, exchange theory sensitizes us to the fact that in a way male-female conflicts have nothing to do with sex. The low status and relative impotence of most women is as much of a problem as their sexuality.[11] That is, men with low power and status, who are ineffective competitors, are also discriminated against by other men. If one has power, regardless of one's sex, discrimination is less of a problem.

The Structural Perspective Structurally speaking, women as a group tend to lack proximity essential to interaction, since they are segregated from the rest of society (especially from men) by their childbearing and child-raising activities. Most of the time adult females are confined to their homes (prisons?). Even when males and females are spatially and socially proximate (a fact that should enhance interaction and liking), they tend to have unequal statuses. As we have seen, great inequality reduces interaction potential (cf. South et al. 1982:598). It should be pointed out that when women or men try to take

A typical female-male social exchange is the woman's sexual favors, childbearing, and emotional support in return for the man's money, property, security, and title (Mrs.)—usually through the institution of marriage. (Stock, Boston)

advantage of their sex-linked interactive assets (see Table 5.6), these assets themselves are structurally determined. Suppose you were sexually attractive and decided to use that advantage. How many sexually intimate two-person relationships could you simultaneously manage? How much energy do you have to be sexually active? How long can you expect to remain young and physically attractive? In a sense, sexual activity bordering on promiscuity tends to be self-defeating. For one thing, as property (here, sexual property) becomes less rare, it also becomes less valuable.

Guttentag and Secord (see Chapter 12) argue that before World War II there was always an excess of males in the United States (1983:15–16). When sex ratios are high, young adult women are highly valued and women receive more satisfaction from traditional sex roles (e.g., those of wives, mothers, and homemakers). However, in recent years sex ratios are relatively lower. There are (structurally speaking) too many women. With low sex ratios women feel more powerless and less socially valuable. They are less likely to see rewards in making commitments to traditional sex roles. Men today, on the other hand, have more freedom of choice and more control over the way they relate to women. Thus, sexism and sexual discrimination is structurally more likely in the 1980s.

The Functionalist Perspective Of course, exchange and structuralism are not the only relevant sociological perspectives on sexism and sex roles. The symbolic interactionism perspective on the problem of sexism has been considered above in the section on gender or sex roles. A functionalist perspective (see Table 2.1) would probably maintain that since sex-role differentiation and sexism have existed throughout human history, they must be meeting some basic needs of society. Thus, any attempt to eliminate sexual and gender differentiation, a part of the social system that has positive consequences contributing to social integration, is likely to be disruptive and disorganizing (Doyle, 1985:106ff.). In fact it is likely to fail unless functional alternatives are provided. Consider sex-segregated prisons. Here homosexuality (a functional alternative) replaces heterosexuality and sex roles and sexism are reproduced in prisons even though only males (or females) are incarcerated there. Functionalists might also claim that female gender roles evolve from the reproductive and child-care needs of society. The relatively long dependency needs of human children necessitates females (or someone) staying at home, nursing their offspring, and so on. Since men do not become pregnant and are usually physically stronger (indeed, they have a higher average birth weight than females), originally they could hunt and venture farther from home (cf. Bleier, 1984:Ch. 5). Eventually this leads to men being more likely to take jobs away from home. Women tend to be dependent on men for food and shelter, while bearing and raising children (Doyle, 1985:276ff.). This is not to argue that such sex-role divisions of labor could not be changed.

The Conflict Perspective Finally, conflict theorists contend that men can enjoy superior status only by oppressing others, especially women and children (Doyle, 1985:108ff.). Engels wrote:

> The first class antagonism which appears in history coincides with the development of antagonism between man and woman . . . and the first class oppression with that of the female sex by the male. . . . The well-being and development of the one group are attained by the misery and repression of the other. (Quoted in Weitz, 1977:239)

Conflict theorists argue that traditional gender roles and sexism reinforce men's dominance over women. Men control women by controlling jobs, money, and important social institutions (e.g., government). Since men benefit from sexism and sexual discrimination, they presumably have little incentive to change sex roles.

Capitalism typically exploits the relatively cheap labor of females. The profits from the female labor force are not returned fairly to women. Instead, the surplus value of female labor results in a profit for the largely male owners and managers. Some of this profit is used to expand male property, plants, machinery, inventory, and so on. Much of the rest of the profit from women's labor goes to higher incomes for male owners and managers of capital. Note too that even though more women than ever before are working outside the home (a fact that has extensive consequences for other social problems), women still are providing largely free domestic labor as wives and mothers. In effect, most working women have two jobs. The job at home provides emotional and physical service to males and children that allows them (not the supporting female mother-wives) to function better at *their* jobs and schools—to be more rested, sexually gratified, provided with a home, male offspring, and so on. Often this free mother-wives socioemotional and physical support of husbands and children comes at great personal and social expense to women. Naturally, such sexual inequities cause familial and societal conflict.

Resolving the Problem Sex roles and sexism are not going to change easily, primarily because sexual differentiation is not going to change much. Still, it would seem difficult to justify downgrading women's life chances based solely on their sexuality. Surely, society must begin to revise its sex-role stereotypes. Yet Weitz (1977: cf. O'Kelly and Carney, 1986) tells us that sex roles have remained remarkably stable for a longer time than we care to acknowledge. The problem is made worse by the organized women's groups (such as ERA opponent Phyllis Schlafly) who resist sex-role liberalization. For example, a 1971 Harris poll shows that a plurality of women were opposed to "efforts to strengthen and change women's place in society" (cf. Goldberg, 1968). It is clear now that ERA is not going to pass in the near future. Until a majority of men and women stop exchanging family, sex, and socioemotional nurturance for marriage, money, and status, sexism will remain.

In spite of the above conditions, there are social and technological changes that are going to affect sexism. First, physical strength is less important in determining social status in the era of the computer. Second, reproduction is being separated from sex and sex from marriage. Third, women are spending less time having children (about 3 percent of their total life in pregnancy and nursing) and are having fewer children. Fourth, birth control devices and techniques are freeing the sexual activity of women from the confines of marriage and childbearing (see Chapter 13). Fifth, women are becoming more class conscious and organized (e.g., they could as a group withhold sex, children, and so on). Sixth, child-care centers are growing very rapidly. Seventh, Title IX provides for equal educational facilities for men and women. Finally, hopefully many men are also becoming more sensitive to sexual inequities and will realize that it is to their own advantage to combat sexual discrimination.

One parting thought: If we could afford it, why not have multiple gender patterns (a kind of sex-role pluralism)? Certainly the United States should at least be able to support both traditional sex roles for those who choose them and careers, no marriage, no children, and so on for those who do not. In spite of some arguments presented above, there is no obvious reason why traditional sex roles have to lead to the degrading and exploiting of females. Also people should be paid for their skills, not their sexual identities. We must remember that all social stratification obscures the search for talent. Further, history teaches us that as long as there has been sexual differentiation, there has been sexism. As a rule of thumb, any difference has the potential of becoming an invidious distinction. Can you imagine a world without sexual differences?

• Heterosexual Relations Outside of Marriage

Stating the Problem Especially in the United States sexual intercourse is expected to be confined to marriage and to be primarily for the purpose of reproduction (O'Kelley and Carney, 1986:Ch. 6). Admittedly, these expectations apply to females more than males (the old "double standard"), since females have to be concerned about unwanted pregnancies (see Panel 5.1). Given America's Puritan beginnings, traditionally sex for the purpose of pleasure alone is considered suspect, if not downright sinful. Sexual relations outside of love, marriage, and the family are perceived to be threats to our traditional way of life and, perhaps, even damaging to societal integration or social order itself. Certainly it seems too chaotic and unpredictable, not to mention violent, to allow people to go around gratifying their sexual urges whenever and with whomever they choose or happen on. Such a situation conjures up animal images of males sexually abusing females, of males fighting with each other for sexual rights to females, and of children being spawned without proper care or support. Of course, it is also no small concern that as a population becomes more sexually indiscriminate venereal diseases such as AIDS, herpes, gonorrhea, and syphilis may grow out of control.

In spite of these perceived threats with better birth- and venereal-disease control techniques, heterosexual relations outside of marriage have been increasing. Hunt discovered that in 1937 and 1959, about 22 percent of the population sampled found premarital sexual intercourse acceptable (see Table 5.5). However, by 1972, 75 percent of male respondents agreed that premarital sex where "strong affection" existed was OK for men and 66 percent agreed it was OK for women (the double standard). Fifty-five percent of the females sampled felt that premarital sex was acceptable with "strong affection" for men, compared to 41 percent approving of premarital sex for women. That is, women tended to be about 20 percentage points less approving of premarital sex than men, regardless of whether men or women were having the premarital

PANEL 5.4

Cohabiting in College

In the stricter days of 1968, a Barnard College sophomore named Linda LeClair became an overnight celebrity after the public revelation that she was living off campus with a former Columbia University student. Linda's battle with school authorities made front-page news in the *New York Times* and other papers across the country. Since then, a number of researchers have investigated the phenomenon of cohabitation (living together) among college students, finding that it is an important contemporary living pattern.

Estimates of the number of students who cohabit vary from 10 percent at small liberal arts colleges that do not permit off-campus housing or overnight visits to 35 percent at large state universities that permit off-campus housing and have twenty-four hour visiting privileges. In a questionnaire answered by more than 1,000 unmarried students at Penn State, 33 percent answered yes to the question "Are you now living or have you ever lived with someone of the opposite sex?"

The sexual aspects of cohabitation should not be overdramatized. In most cases, of course, the couple have a full sexual relationship. But in about 10 percent of the cases, the couple lived together for three months or more before having intercourse. (This is a more general phenomenon in premarital sex; a couple may literally sleep together for some time before they begin having intercourse.) The motives for cohabitation seem to be more emotional than sexual.

In the Cornell study, the students gave a number of reasons for cohabiting: the loneliness of a large university, the superficiality of the "dating game," a search for more meaningful relations with others, the emotional satisfaction of living and sleeping with someone who cares about you, a desire to try out a relationship before marriage, and widespread doubts about the very institution of marriage. The single most important reason cited for choosing to live with someone was "emotional attachment to each other." Most of the relationships were monogamous.

Source: Eleanor D. Macklin. Cohabitation in College: Going Very Steady, 1974, 53–59. Reprinted with permission from *Psychology Today* Magazine. Copyright © 1974 (APA).

sex. Remember these data concern *attitudes* toward premarital sex (cf. O'Kelly and Carney, 1986:183, 192, 211).

When we turn to actual permarital sexual *behaviors* the results are conflicting. Clearly there has been some increase in premarital sexual intercourse, especially among females (see O'Kelly and Carney, 1986:171.) The question is how much of an increase (Hyde, 1982:267–277). Kinsey (1948, 1953) claimed that by age twenty-five, 33 percent of females and 71 percent of males had engaged in premarital sex. By 1972 Hunt argued that the percentages had risen to 67 percent for women and 97 percent for men. These data represent 34 percent and 26 percent gains over the Kinsey data for women and men, respectively. In a more recent study of 106,000 female readers of *Cosmopolitan*

TABLE 5.5 Percentages of People Agreeing that Premarital Intercourse Is Acceptable, 1937, 1959, 1972; Actual Premarital Partner Behavior, 1981

"Do you think it is all right for either or both parties to a marriage to have had previous sexual intercourse?"

	1937	**1959**
All right for both	22%	22%
All right for men only	8	8
All right for neither	56	54
Don't know or refused to answer	14	16

Percentages Agreeing that Premarital Coitus Is Acceptable, 1972

	Male Respondents	**Female Respondents**
For a man:		
Where strong affection exists	75%	55%
Couple in love, but not engaged	82	68
Couple engaged	84	73
For a woman:		
Where strong affection exists	66	41
Couple in love, but not engaged	77	61
Couple engaged	81	68

Percentage of *Cosmopolitan* Female Readers Having Marital and Nonmarital First Sex, 1981 (First Sex with):

Husband	5.1%
Fiancé	6.3
Steady boyfriend	63.5
Casual acquaintance	15.9
Other	9.2

Source: Morton Hunt, *Sexual Behavior in the 1970s,* 1974:115–116; Wolfe, *The Cosmo Report,* 1981:270.

magazine, Wolfe (1981) found that 95 percent of first sexual relations were not with one's spouse. However, DeLamater and MacCorquodale report actual premarital sexual intercourse in 1979 to be somewhat less, more precisely, about 75 percent for males and 65 percent for females. Of course, most of their sample was under age twenty-five. It is interesting to note that the data for actual premarital sex come closest to the male norms for premarital sex. It appears as though what the men think is appropriate actually happens. In spite of their attitudes some females are participating more in premarital sex than they think appropriate.

Looking now at extramarital sex (Table 5.6), it appears that male activity has increased in middle ages and that female participation has increased dramatically at the younger ages (Hyde, 1982:285–291). To illustrate, Kinsey (1938–1949) found 26 percent of men ages thirty-five to forty-four had had

TABLE 5.6 Incidence of Extramarital Sex among Men and Women, According to the Kinsey Study (1938-1949) and the Hunt Study (1972), the *Cosmopolitan* Study (1981), and the Blumstein-Schwartz Study (1983)

	Percentage Who Had Had Extramarital Sex			
	Kinsey (1938-1949)	**Hunt (1972)**	**Cosmo* (1981)**	**Blumstein-Schwartz (1983)**
Men				
Under 25	27	32	—	26 (all ages)
25–34	27	41	—	
35–44	26	47	—	
45–54	24	38	—	
55 and over	22	43	—	
Women				
Under 25	8	24	41	21 (all ages)
25–34	15	21	58	
25–44	17	18	66 (25–44 through 55 and over)	
45–54	9	12		
55 and over	4	15		

*Female readers of *Cosmopolitan* magazine only.

Source: Alfred Kinsey et al., *Sexual Behavior in the Human Male,* 1948, Table 54; Alfred Kinsey et al., *Sexual Behavior in the Human Female,* 1953, Table 114. Reprinted by permission of the Kinsey Institute for Research in Sex, Gender, and Reproduction, Inc. The Kinsey data are approximate; Morton Hunt, *Sexual Behavior in the 1970s,* 1974:258, 261. Reproduced with permission from Playboy Enterprises, Inc. from *Sexual Behavior in the 1970s* by Morton Hunt. Copyright © 1974 by Morton Hunt; Linda Wolfe, *Women and Sex in the '80s: The Cosmo Report,* Arbor House, 1981:312; Philip Blumstein and Pepper Schwartz, *American Couples: Money, Work, Sex,* William Morrow Co., 1983:273.

extramarital sex. By 1972 Hunt showed that the figure for that age group had risen to 47 percent. Not controlling for age Blumstein and Schwartz (1983) found a more conservative 26 percent. Among young women (under age twenty-five) the corresponding figures for extramarital sex were 8 percent (Kinsey) and 24 (Hunt) percent. In 1981, 41 percent of Wolfe's *Cosmopolitan* readers under age twenty-five reported extramarital sex. Again, not controlling for age, the Blumstein and Schwartz survey (1983) of American couples found that 21 percent of females admitted to extramarital sexual intercourse. At the same time that extramarital sex has increased for men and women in most age groups, extramarital sex for money (i.e., prostitution) has declined dramatically. Kinsey (1948) reported that 69 percent of all men had sex with prostitutes. In 1972 Hunt states that only 19 percent of the males he interviewed claimed to have had sex with prostitutes. It would seem that premarital and extramarital sex are in part replacing prostitution (cf. Blumstein and Schwartz, 1983). Another possibility is that prostitutes are being replaced by better organized, more attractive (and expensive) call girls or call boys (Greenwald, 1970).

Analyzing the Problem. The Exchange Perspective To the degree that nonmarital sex (e.g., prostitution, some affairs, and mistresses) is for money, it is a clear example of exchange. And, of course, by the first axiom of exchange theory, the more an act is rewarded, the more it will be repeated. In 1984 the median annual income of females working full time was $15,422. Hyde tells us (1982:417–418) that the annual income of call girls or boys is about $50,000 a year with no taxes.[12] Some young people must reflect why settle for $200–$300 a week in a boring, subordinate, repetitive clerical job when you can make that much in an hour or two? Like all high-paying jobs there are some risks (i.e., costs). Abuse and violence, lowered self-esteem, possible arrest (see case of the Brown University coeds who acted as prostitutes in 1985, and the prosecution of socialite Sydney Biddle Barrows in New York City as a call girl madame, *The State,* June 4, 1986), the possibility of sexually transmitted diseases, and a short career are all possible costs for selling sex. Also, not everyone can sell sex. Like the professional athlete, those who sell sex for large amounts of money must be relatively young, attractive, talented, and will only stay at their peak for a relatively short time.

But what about pre- and extramarital sex for which there is no explicit payment? Cynically, one could reply that there isn't any. Perhaps one always pays for all sex—premarital, marital, or extramarital. Even when sex is not exchanged for cold cash (although it would be interesting to calculate what the mean monetary enhancement value of most marriages is over a lifetime), it is still sex in return for companionship, social status, security, a house or property, a title (Mr., Mrs., Dr., and so on), close friendship, variety (e.g., the novelty of an extramarital affair), children, and so on. Of course, not only women provide sex for men, and other important exchanges take place in human relationships (e.g., love for love). It should be remembered that when the profit of one activity is greater than that of other activities, the profitable activity will tend to increase. This observation is relevant because the costs of nonmarital sex have declined to some degree recently due to improved birth control, less need to reproduce effectively, and more permissive values.

Other Theoretical Perspectives Structurally nonmarital sex has been encouraged by more women being in the job market (and out of the home), thus increasing the interaction prospects for all outcomes, including those for sexual intercourse. Note too that long-term marital commitments normally routinize and tend to devalue the arousal potential of sex within marriage. By exchange theory's fourth axiom (satiation) deprivation can ensue and other (nonmarital) sexual stimuli are more likely to be sought.

From the functional perspective, heterosexual intercourse within marriage is most likely to lead to reproduction and "proper" socialization and care of offspring. Nonmarital sex is more likely to be an end in itself (i.e., arousal or physical pleasure), which is potentially disruptive to the social order. Any attempt to eliminate sex for money without providing a functional alternative will tend not to work, since prostitution (and related activities) are meeting social needs marriage does not.

Obviously much pre- and extramarital sexuality is an exchange of sex for money. Here Ivy College graduate and socialite Sidney Biddle Barrows celebrates beating her felony prostitution charge for managing a classy call-girl business in New York. (UPI/Bettmann News Photos)

The deviance and symbolic interaction perspectives contend that people tend to deviate from the norm of marital sex when they have internalized a social goal (i.e., marriage or marital sex) but do not have the means or opportunities to realize this goal. Marriage to an appealing spouse is just not open to everyone. Some people are not physically attractive enough, do not have sufficient money, and so on to be able to get married. Sometimes prostitution or pornography may be a substitute for marital sex for certain groups in certain situations.

Finally, the conflict perspective states that prostitution debases (especially) women. Nonmarital sex often exploits women and children. Powerful groups in society (men) tend to meet their own sexual needs or desires only at the expense of those in lower social positions (women and children).

Resolving the Problem Some of the problems of nonmarital sexuality will resolve themselves. As effective reproduction and the traditional family become less important, nonmarital sexual activities probably will be perceived as less of a problem. As pre- and extramarital sexual activities increase, prostitution will decrease. Even the rewards for pre- and extramarital sexuality may decline, with the increase in palimony suits such as those of actor Lee Marvin or tennis pro Billy Jean King. That is, all nonmarital sexual relations may become too costly.

Pre- and extramarital sex are not likely to develop into rampant promiscuity because of health considerations (especially the AIDS problem) and interaction or structural constraints (how many people one can be sexually intimate with—except in rape situations—is severely limited) and the desire for love, loyalty, and constancy of relationships. Promiscuity destroys close relations based in love (cf. Hyde, 1982:272ff.; Hunt, 1974:151).

It is possible that much of nonmarital sex could be legalized, organized, and institutionalized. One common way to control deviant activities is to bring them out of the underworld and into local, state, and federal control. This alone makes the activities cheaper, healthier, less violent, less socially disruptive, and more positively valued. Any visit to a major European city will reveal how sexually conservative the United States is (cf. O'Kelly and Carney, 1986). As is often recommended for drugs (see Chapter 9) prostitution could be legalized. It already is in parts of the state of Nevada.

• Homosexuality

Stating the Problem A *homosexual,* obviously, is a person who is sexually attracted to or engages in sexual activities primarily with members of his or her own sex. Female homosexuals are often called *lesbians* after the Greek homosexual poetess Sappho who lived on the island of Lesbos around 600 B.C. Male homosexuals are usually referred to as *gay,* although this term is not limited to men. Occasionally the word *homophile* is used for homosexuals.

Most people regard homosexuality as inappropriate, since it inhibits reproduction and is thought to threaten the sex-role structure and the traditional family. Clearly, if enough people were exclusively homosexual, social survival would be in jeopardy. More importantly, homosexuality causes sex-role confusion. As we have seen, societies tend to be stratified by age and sex, among other traits. Sexual relations are usually with (subordinate) females. To have sexual relationships within the same-sex group confuses the power and class structure of society.

Nevertheless, Ford and Beach (1972) found that 64 percent of societies they studied allowed homosexuality for some people or even for all people some of the time. For example, among the Siwans of Africa, the Aranda of Australia, and the Keraki of New Guinea every male is expected to engage in homosexual activities as an exclusive sexual outlet during adolescence. However, in all cultures heterosexuality is the rule and homosexuality the exception.

PANEL 5.5

A Gay Couple

Tom and Brian have been living together as lovers for three years. Tom is twenty-nine, and Brian is twenty-two; they live in a medium-sized midwestern city. Tom grew up in a Roman Catholic family and attended parochial schools. His father was killed in an automobile accident when Tom was four days old. His mother remarried when he was eight years old; though he gets along well with his stepfather, he feels that he has never had a real father. When asked why he thought he was gay, he said he felt it was because of the absence of a father in his early years.

After graduating from high school, Tom joined the army and served in Vietnam and Germany. His first sexual experience was with a Japanese prostitute. Though he enjoyed the physical aspects of sex with her, he felt that something was missing emotionally. When he was twenty-three, after returning to the United States, he had his first homosexual experience with someone he met at a bar. Tom had sex with about twenty different men before meeting Brian, including one with whom he had a long-term relationship. He is currently a student at a technical college and is working toward a career in electronics.

Brian also grew up in a Roman Catholic family and attended parochial schools. He has always gotten along well with both his parents and his four siblings, and he recalls his childhood as being uneventful. He realized he was gay when he was in his early teens, but he chose to ignore his feelings and instead tried to conform to what society expected of him. He had a girlfriend when he was in high school. After he graduated from high school, he took a job; he had his first homosexual experience when he was eighteen with a man he met at work. He currently works as a salesperson at Penney's. He had sex with eight different men before meeting Tom. He has never had intercourse with a woman.

Their relationship with each other is exclusive; that is, they have an agreement that they will be faithful to each other and that neither will have sex with anyone else. Both of them said they would feel hurt if they found out that the other had been seeing someone else on the sly. They both consider casual sex unfulfilling and want to have a real relationship with their sexual partner.

Tom and Brian feel that the greatest problem in their relationship is lack of communication, which sometimes creates misunderstandings and arguments. Brian feels that the greatest joy in their relationship is the security of knowing that they love each other and can count on each other. Tom agrees, and he also says that it is important to him to know that there is someone who really cares about him and loves him.

Source: Janet Hyde, *Understanding Human Sexuality*, McGraw-Hill, 1982:370–371. Reprinted with permission.

Table 5.7 shows that only about 3 percent of males and 1 percent of females are exclusively homosexual (if we take the conservative estimates). Nevertheless, Kinsey (1953) claimed that 25 percent to 37 percent of all males and about 13 percent of all females have at least one homosexual experience to the point of orgasm. Others claim that as many as 50 percent of adolescent males have at least one homosexual experience (Sargent, 1985:310). Male

TABLE 5.7 Percentages of People in the Kinsey Data with Varying Amounts of Homosexual and Heterosexual Experience

Rating		Females (percent)	Males (percent)
0	Entirely heterosexual experience:		
	Single	61–72%	53–78%
	Married	89–90	90–92
	Previously married	75–80	
1–6	At least some homosexual experience	11–20	18–42
2–6	More than incidental homosexual experience	6–14	13–38
3–6	Homosexual as much as heterosexual experience	4–11	9–32
4–6	Mostly homosexual experience	3–8	7–26
5–6	Almost exclusively homosexual experience	2–6	5–22
6	Exclusively homosexual experience	1–3	3–16

*Ranges are given because the percentages vary depending on the age of the person, whether the person is married or single, and several other factors.

Source: A.C. Kinsey, W.B. Pomeroy, C.E. Martin, and P.H. Gebhard *Sexual Behavior in the Human Female,* 1953. Reprinted by permission of the Kinsey Institute for Research in Sex, Gender, and Reproduction, Inc.

homosexuals tend to have more partners and shorter relationships than female homosexuals. It is estimated that male homosexuals may have hundreds of sexual partners over their lifetimes, compared with five to nine partners for heterosexual males (Hyde, 1982:376).

Some people think homosexuality is perverse, pathological, and unnatural. For example, before 1973 the American Psychiatric Association labeled homosexuality an illness. After 1973 they did not (Spector and Kitsuse, 1977). In 1986 the U.S. Supreme Court ruled that even private homosexual acts were sodomous and criminal (*New York Times,* July 1, 1986). San Francisco and Seattle now have homosexual civil rights laws and elected officials who are open about their homosexual preferences. Probably negative attitudes toward homosexuality relate more to the general public's fears of sex-role confusion, disruption of the traditional family, interference with reproductive needs, and a desire to keep life simple and predictable rather than to any intrinsic perversity in homosexuality.

Analyzing the Problem: The Exchange Perspective Evidence suggests that human beings are born sexually "amorphous" with regard to sexual preference (although biologically most people are born clearly male or female). This is to say, people are just born sexual, not with hetero- or homosexual preferences.[13] Exchange theory axioms 1 and 3 suggest that this neutral sexuality of the infant (what Freud called polymorphous perversity—see Brill, 1938:592:ff) is shaped to either heterosexual or homosexual preference by differential rewards and punishments over a lifetime. Since most values exalt heterosexuality for the sake of reproductivity, social predictability, and parsimony, most often heterosexual acts are rewarded and homosexual acts are punished. Occasionally, this usual reinforcement pattern is reversed. A male may not fit the masculine stereotype, may be physically small or unaggressive (perhaps hormonally feminine), or may find heterosexual encounters aversive. Likewise, some women may find sexual relations with males assaultive, exploitative, insensitive, and so on (consider Whoopi Goldberg's character in the 1985 movie *The Color Purple*). Whatever the particulars, sometimes men and women find homosexual behaviors more rewarded and valuable than heterosexual behaviors. We probably do not know what causes homosexuality (Hyde, 1982:390). Since homosexuality is not one behavior, most likely its causes are multiple as well.

In a sensate society (Sorokin, 1957) like the United States heterosexual rewards are often given so frequently that they can lose their arousal power. Satiation can occur and alternative sexual stimuli may be sought. Some homosexuality may be engaged in because it is different, not because one has a homosexual preference. It is even possible for an individual or society to satiate (at least for a while) on all sexual stimuli. Arousal then may be sought in religion, life-risking activities, or a synergistic blending of sex and death.

Structural, Psychoanalytic, and Symbolic Interaction Perspectives Structurally note the obvious: Sex segregation (in boarding schools, the military, colleges, bathrooms, swimming pools, dormitories, prisons, hospitals, clubs, friendship groups, and so on) deriving from traditional sex roles tends to restrict heterosexual interaction. Clearly if one's sexual outlet possibilities are restricted (as they tend to be in total institutions), then on that ground alone the prospects of homosexuality will be increased. One need only think of the prevalence of homosexuality in prisons.

Psychoanalytically, in what Freud (1905) named the negative Oedipus complex, the child who later became homosexual fixated on the love of a parent of the same sex and then failed to repress this love when growing up. Symbolically Freud believed that homosexuals loved themselves, i.e., that homosexuality was a form of narcissism. Bieber et al. (1962) found that male homosexuals tended to have dominant overpowering mothers and weak or passive fathers. Wolff (1971) claimed that lesbians tended to have rejecting or indifferent mothers and absent fathers.

From a symbolic interaction perspective, if someone is labeled homosexual (Karr, 1978), this negative public reaction can restrict the alternative sexual life chances of the individual and tend to coerce him or her into a deviant (homosexual) identity. Expectations and opportunities for heterosexual activities may then change (i.e., diminish) with such successfully applied homosexual labels.

Resolving the Problem To begin with, is homosexuality really much of a social problem?[14] Probably not. Exclusive homosexual preference is very small (1 to 3 percent of the population). Generally the younger the population, the more favorable its response to homosexual rights. The gay liberation movement has made several important civil rights legal changes. In addition to those in San Francisco and Seattle, Illinois and Connecticut have repealed antihomosexual legislation. Finally, effective sexual reproduction now is less important.

Of course, society could attempt to reward heterosexuality more, but this would be of dubious value, since heterosexuality is already rewarded heavily and society has little power to change the broad social conditions (such as the lessened need to reproduce effectively) that apparently are encouraging homosexuality. To be sure, there is still considerable antihomosexual sentiment. Whereas homosexuality probably does not pose a serious threat to society, society still makes life miserable for many homosexuals. Resolutions of this problem usually include keeping one's homosexual preference discrete ("covert"), forming subgroups or communities of those people with homosexual preferences, lobbying for homosexual rights, and so on. San Francisco has been very successful in this respect.

• Summary

Like age, sex is a biosocial condition. Sex roles, sexual discrimination, and even sexual variety (some say deviancy) are not exclusively social conditions. They are at least biologically rooted. Men and women are different chromosomally, hormonally, gonadally, reproductively, and in several other sex related traits (such as weight, aggressiveness, growth patterns, musculature, basal metabolism, pain tolerance, menopause, visual acuity, age at first speaking, IQ variability, and so on—although the exact relationships of these factors to sex are still unclear). Although biology certainly does not fully determine sex roles, it plays a much more major role than we usually realize. Sex roles cannot be reduced to gender roles.

The primary issue in this chapter has been why women are treated differently than men and if this differential treatment is bad for all concerned, especially for women. No doubt, often the "culprit" is sexism, the systemic discrimination against and oppression of (usually) women by men just because they are women. As with ageism, no doubt sexism does exist and is often punitive and unjust. But the differential social treatment of men and women is much more complex than simple sexual discrimination.

When we do an exchange analysis of the social basis for the differential treatment of men and women, we see quickly that throughout history men and women have exchanged women's relatively unique rewards of childbearing, sexual gratification, and socioemotional nurturance for the relatively unique male rewards of protection, security, money, property, and status—commonly through the institution of marriage. Once such exchanges between men and women become patterned and institutionalized, some sexism is inevitable. Sexism persists in part because both men and women both mutually exploit their unique interactional assets. Feminists like S. Firestone have argued that the real hope for overcoming sexism is to eliminate the effects of sexual differentiation altogether. This extreme resolution would involve breaking up the biological family, revolutionizing reproduction, and eradicating all sexual distinctions.

Conflict theorists add that sexism persists because unequal and unfair treatment of women is especially advantageous to males. For example, capitalists maximize their profits by paying women less than men and by exploiting the largely unpaid emotional and physical labor of wives at home. Functionalists point out that sex roles originally resulted from the smaller average size of females and their unique childbearing capabilities. These traits led to consequences of women staying at home and needing protection. Symbolic interactionists do not see sex roles as determined by biology, but rather as products of learning traditional, socially restrictive gender stereotypes concerning the proper behaviors of women and men. Women are in fact far more versatile and capable than gender roles suggest.

Sexual variations from the norm of heterosexual relations within marriage can also be explained by the exchange-structural principles of pursuing rewards, avoiding punishments, finding alternatives to satiation, and social opportunities for interaction. Clearly prostitution and pornography are at least sex being exchanged for money. Even premarital and extramarital sex are "paid for" (although usually with entertainment, escape, ego-support, friendship, and diversity; not with cash), especially when those seeking it have found marital relationships satiating, unarousing, punishing, or otherwise costly. Exclusive homosexuality is rare. To the degree that homosexuality is just diffuse sexuality, the same exchange principles explain it as explain heterosexuality. Occasionally homosexuality is a sexual alternative to heterosexual roles that have become too costly for various reasons. In this sense homosexuals try (somewhat unsuccessfully) to avoid sex roles altogether.

Functionalists view nonmarital sex and homosexuality as more likely to be ends in themselves, and thus as threatening reproduction of the human species. Furthermore, society needs to provide alternatives to premarital and extramarital sex and homosexuality, since they all are presumably meeting basic social needs. Conflict theorists claim that sexual deviances like prostitution and pornography debase and exploit women (and children). Laws are passed against homosexuality and prostitution because the dominant group in society is largely married heterosexual males. Symbolic interactionists and deviance theorists believe sexually deviant identities (e.g., as a prostitute) result from repeated labeling or negative public reactions. Thus, paradoxically, attempts to control sexual variation often produce it. What is defined as sexually deviant or obscene varies considerably among different social and cultural groups. In the next chapter we examine another set of social problems that also obviously has physical and social components—that of racial and ethnic minority relations.

• Notes

1. In English law the wife was considered part of the husband's estate.

2. $H = 1 - (.48^2 + .51^2) = .501$. One must remember that heterogeneity is a population trait.

3. Of course, sickle cell anemia is almost unique to blacks.

4. Male hormones are referred to collectively as androgens.

5. This is fine, but what does one do afterward? The situation conjures up all sorts of anomalous images.

6. If you think about it for a minute, this provides a basis for women being valued more highly than men, since one man can impregnate numerous women. But a woman can only have one (usually) child every nine months or so.

7. Related issues concern how many men and women support which sex roles, how necessary traditional sex roles are for maintaining social order, how damaging or unhealthy sex-role stereotypes are for both men and women, and finally, how changeable sex roles are?

8. This may seem like a no-win situation. If women's roles become more like men's, they are freed from one set of problems only to inherit those of the male. However, this has not bothered most men.

9. To be sure, sexism to a lesser degree limits the life opportunities of men too. Men are expected to not show feelings, to be tough, to take financial responsibilities, not to nurture their children much on a daily basis, and so on.

10. This is not intended to sound unsympathetic to women's plight. Firestone may be right. That is, sexism can only change significantly if traditional sex roles are eliminated. However, our skepticism centers around the prospects for eliminating sex roles. It has only happened in science fiction novels up to now. But who knows?

11. Of course, power is related to sex roles. Arguing that male-female conflicts are really power conflicts is a naive and pointless elaboration if power is always primarily determined by sex roles.

12. She arrives at this figure assuming a minimum of $50 an hour and a twenty-hour work week.

13. Yet Kallman (1952) found perfect associations of sexual preferences among identical twins. That is, if one was homosexual, then the other always was. This was not true for nonidentical twins.

14. It may be a serious problem for some individuals.

• Glossary

Asexual. That which is not affected by or relevant to the biology of males or females; nonsexual, sexless.

Biosocial Condition. A social condition that is rooted in, partially determined by, or influenced by biological factors. Sexism is biosocial.

Chromosome. A microscopic body that contains the genes. Humans have forty-six chromosomes in every cell, twenty-three from each parent. One pair of these twenty-three determines sex.

Double Standard. A term used to indicate different norms for sexual behaviors of males and females.

Extramarital Sex. Sexual intercourse with someone other than the person to whom you are married.

Gender. The cultural concepts of masculinity and femininity. Gender roles concern social expectations associated with concepts of masculinity and femininity.

Genes. The units controlling heredity that are believed to be situated in the chromosomes.

Homosexual. A person who is sexually attracted to or engages in sexual activities primarily with members of his or her own sex.

Hormone. A chemical substance originating in a system of organs and glands (the endocrine system) that is conveyed through the blood to another part of the body, stimulating it to increased activity and secretion.

Menopause. That period (it usually occurs between ages thirty-five and fifty-eight) that marks the permanent cessation of menstrual activity.

Premarital Sex. Sexual intercourse with someone before marriage (usually before marriage of both sexual partners).

Promiscuity. Indiscriminate sexual intercourse, usually with large numbers of other partners.

Prostitution. Promiscuous sexual intercourse for money.

Puberty. The time during which there is a sudden enlargement of the gonads, other genitalia, and secondary sex characteristics leading to reproductive capacity.

Reproduction. The sexual process by which human beings produce new individuals.

Satiation. A physical, psychological, or social state or condition in which usual rewards are not presently valuable. Satiation is often contrasted with deprivation.

Sex. The biological division of human organisms into male and female. Sex roles are social expectations relevant to males or females.

Sexism. A set of values that justifies discrimination against women or men on grounds of their presumed biological differences.

Sex Rewards. The unique interactive assets of males or females deriving solely from their sexuality.

Socialization. A lifelong learning process in which each human being acquires a personality, physical, mental, and social skills, and culture.

Stereotype. A rigid mental image of a group that is applied indiscriminately to all of its members.

Stimulus. Any external agent that involves a response or causes changes in an activity of an organism.

• Further Reading

Bleier, Ruth. *Science and Gender,* New York: Pergamon Press, 1984. A highly polemical treatise by a highly competent feminist trained in the biological and medical sciences. Bleier contends that women's biological inferiority is a myth created to justify their subordinate position in Western civilization. She challenges many, if not most, of the presumed biological sexual differences.

Hunt, Morton. *Sexual Behavior in the 1970s.* Chicago: Playboy Press, 1974. A survey of 982 males and 1,044 females in twenty-four American cities bankrolled by the bunnies' employers to update Kinsey. Hunt concludes that premarital sex is more common now, the gender differences are smaller, and that social class differences are less thirty years AK (After Kinsey).

Hutt, Corinne. *Males and Females.* Middlesex, England: Penguin Books, Ltd., 1972. This is an unusual little book written by a female trained in animal ethology. The treatment is conservative in that many sexual differences are traced to biology. Hutt is skeptical of John Money's apparent belief in the malleability of sexual identity. Highly readable. Feminists will think Hutt is a heretic.

Hyde, Janet S. *Understanding Human Sexuality.* New York: McGraw-Hill, 1982. Has to be the most complete, up-to-date reference book on human sexuality available. Everything you wanted to know about sex and more. Thorough, but elementary. No integrating theoretical approach.

Kinsey, Alfred C. et al. *Sexual Behavior in the Human Male.* Philadelphia: W. B. Saunders, 1948. *Sexual Behavior in the Human Female.* Philadelphia: W. B. Saunders, 1953. The original sex surveys by Harvard-trained, Indiana University zoologist Alfred C. Kinsey and associates. Pioneering sexual histories of some 5,300 males and 5,940 females. Interviews not based on probability samples, but are highly cited in a field where potentially biased data are all there are.

Weitz, Shirley. *Sex Roles: Biological, Psychological, and Social Foundations.* New York: Oxford University Press, 1977. As the title says, an interdisciplinary approach to the study of sex roles that contains novel sections on sexual exchanges (117ff.) and on the symbolism of female sex roles (158ff.). Weitz argues that history teaches us that whatever else changes, women's sex roles do not. Thoughtful, scholarly, and complete.

C·H·A·P·T·E·R

6

Race: Racial and Ethnic Minority Relations

While there are no pure races, it is also clear that certain hereditary traits are often used to distinguish and differentiate broad subgroups of the human population. Once we admit racial or ethnic differentiation, however impure, certain social consequences are nearly inevitable. Human differentiation of any kind can encourage social isolation, disliking, and conflict. This is more probable if the racially or ethnically different group is small in size. If human groups are differentiated on any trait, these differences constitute potential bases for exchange, especially if the differences meet fundamental group needs or are held highly valuable.

Historically American blacks (and most other minorities) have exchanged their domestic labor, service, entertainment skills, and compliance for modest financial gains, protection, and security controlled by whites. Although minorities and majority groups are not biologically destined to enter into such exchanges, both blacks and whites are reluctant to alter institutional patterns that have persisted for generations, particularly when the socioeconomic costs of changing are high. Unless both blacks and whites ignore racial differences as a basis for social exchange, racism will persist.

Conflict enters racial and ethnic relations, since whites (often Anglo-Saxons), blacks, Asians, Hispanics, Jews, Puerto Ricans, American Indians, and so on, compete for scarce economic resources. Dominant whites strive to maintain their economic advantages over racial and ethnic minorities by keeping minorities poor, uneducated, out of key jobs, without property, away from elected political offices, and so on. This oppressive pattern amounts to a vicious circle of prejudice and discrimination of majority groups against minorities. Racial and ethnic conflicts may in fact be class conflicts. Minorities function as society's source of cheap labor to do its dirty service tasks, domestic work, and hard labor that no one else wants to do.

Throughout America's history the symbolism of being black has been largely negative. Derogatory racial and ethnic minority labels often are used to justify racism. Prejudiced attitudes and racial or ethnic discrimination can be a vicious cycle that actually predetermines racial and ethnic educational opportunities, income, work, health, family life, and sense of psychological well-being.

♦

Not long ago I sat next to a group of Finnish schoolgirls on a flight back to New York City from Helsinki. One of the girls was reading the Constitution of the United States in order that she might be prepared for her new life in America. The irony and naivete of such an approach to actual contemporary American life is striking. Of course, the Constitution and its amendments speak of racial, religious, political, and sexual equality.[1] Protection of the rights of individuals and minorities is labored at great length. The United States is somewhat unique in being largely a country of immigrants, many of whom fled religious and political persecution in Europe. The Statue of Liberty (rededicated on its 100th birthday in July 1986) that greeted European migrants to New York harbor invited:

> Give me your tired, your poor, Your huddled masses
> yearning to breathe free.
> The wretched refuse of your teeming shore.
> Send these, the homeless, tempest-tost to me,
> I lift my lamp beside the golden door.

For generations the United States has been seen as the "land of opportunity"; a place where those that were different or down and out could get a fresh start.[2] Consequently, America is one of the most ethnically and racially diverse countries in the world. In addition to native American Indians, Eskimos, and a large Anglo-Saxon migration originally (circa 1600) from Northern Europe, there is a sizable black population, the largest Jewish population in the world, a Hispanic population (14.6 million in 1980: *Statistical Abstract of the United States,* 1986:29) second in size only to American blacks (26.5 million in 1980), and many Asians, especially in Hawaii and California. Of course, there are also large numbers of early German, Irish, Spanish, and Italian migrants and recent refugees from Cuba, Korea, and Vietnam.

Yet in spite of its constitutional goals of racial and ethnic equality, the actual history of the United States is one of racial and ethnic prejudice and discrimination, a history ripe with majority-minority conflicts. Land, liberty, and life

PANEL 6.1

The Last Laugh

A Negro drives through a red light in a Mississippi town. The sheriff yells, "Where you think you're going?" The Negro thinks fast and answers, "Well, boss, when I see that green light come on an' all them white folks' cars goin' through, I says to myself, 'That's the white folks' light!' So I don' move. Then when that ol' red light comes on, I jus' steps on the gas. I says, 'That mus' be the niggers' light!'" The sheriff replies, "You're a good boy, Sam, but the next time you kin go on the white folks' light."

Source: From *Black Metropolis,* copyright 1945 by St. Clair Drake and Horace R. Cayton; renewed 1973 by St. Clair Drake and Susan C. Woodson, Executrix of the Estate of Horace R. Cayton. Reprinted by permission of Harcourt Brace Jovanovich, Inc.

"We're here to escape religious persecution. What are you here for?"

Drawing by Donald Reilly; © 1971 *The New Yorker* Magazine, Inc.

were forcibly wrested from the American Indians. Beginning in 1619 about 400,000 black Africans were brought to America as slaves, a practice that stopped officially about 1865, but whose discriminatory repercussions continue even today (Berry and Blassingame, 1982). Witness the inner-city black riots of the mid-1960s and the need for forced busing to achieve school integration. Similar scenarios could be written about Mexican-Americans, Puerto Ricans in New York City, Indians on reservations, Cuban refugees in Miami, Chinese, Korean, Vietnamese, and Japanese-Americans, Jews, and other American minorities. In short, the racial and ethnic ideals, laws, and moral principles of this country are in serious contradiction to the actual life experiences of most American minorities. In 1909 Israel Zangwill described America as a "melting pot."

> There she lies, the great melting pot—listen! Can't you hear the roaring and bubbling? Ah, what a stirring and seething—Celt and Latin, Slav and Teuton, Greek and Syrian, Black and Yellow—Jew and Gentile." (1909: 198–199)

Not so. Like most other nations there is a great racial and ethnic inequality in the United States (Fosset and Swicegood, 1982). Instead of assimilation, we have witnessed racial and ethnic pluralism (Simpson and Yinger, 1985:16–18; Connor, 1984). The problem is not so much that racial and ethnic groups have largely stayed separate, but rather that their life opportunities are and have remained unequal (Messner and South, 1986).

This fundamental racial and ethnic inequality raises several key issues for us that must be analyzed and, hopefully, resolved in the present chapter. For example, how can such a racially and ethnically diverse population live together without violence? What does *race* mean? Are there pure races? What are race's biological, genetic, or physiological determinants and how do they compare and contrast with its sociocultural determinants? How does the concept of race relate to having minority status? What are some of the special problems for or created by America's largest racial group, that is, black Americans? How similar are the problems of other racial and ethnic minorities (especially Hispanics and Jews) to those of American blacks? Finally, what can the theoretical perspectives of exchange, structuralism, conflict, biology, and symbolic interaction, and functionalism tell us about racial and ethnic minority relations?

We define *race* as a division of a species that differs from other divisions by the frequency with which certain hereditary traits appear among its members (Simpson and Yinger, 1985:Ch. 2; Harris and Wagley, 1985). Crudely, there are thought to be four principal races: Caucasoids (whites), Mongoloids (yellows), Negroids (blacks), and Australoids (see Figure 6.1). A *species* is a population in which any two healthy, sexually mature members of the opposing sex can mate and produce a normal and fertile offspring. Since all races can interbreed, it makes it difficult (if not impossible) to identify completely "pure" races. Still, we all know roughly what white, black, or yellow racial traits mean. Whereas race refers to inherited physical characteristics, ethnicity is a much broader concept. An *ethnic group* can be defined as any group that can be set

Like many racial minorities black teenagers tend to have high unemployment rates and low-status jobs that pay poorly. Racism keeps black Americans down through a vicious circle of prejudice and discrimination. (Peter Menzel/Stock, Boston)

off by race, religion, or national origin (Simpson and Yinger, 1985:1–11). Underlying both the concepts of racial and ethnic groups is the concept of minorities (see Simpson and Yinger, 1985:8ff.). In the United States, blacks, Hispanics, Indians, Asians, Jews, Poles, Germans, Italians, and so on, are all minority groups. Wirth (1945) defined a *minority* as "a group of people who, because of their physical or cultural characteristics, are singled out from the others in the society in which they live for differential and unequal treatment, and who therefore regard themselves as objects of collective discrimination." The existence of a minority in a society implies the existence of a corresponding dominant group with higher social status and greater privileges. Minority status carries with it the exclusion from full participation in the life of the society (Wirth, 1945:347). Thus, racism (as we shall see) has much in common with sexism and ageism. Note, that the term *minority* does not necessarily mean small in size. For example, blacks in South Africa are a minority group even though they outnumber the whites there (the same could be said of females in the United States).

The largest racial minority group is that of American blacks. In 1980 (see Tables 6.1 and 6.2) they totaled 26.5 million people or 11.7 percent of the entire population. The next largest racial or ethnic minority groups are: Jews, who number about 6 million and are concentrated especially in and about New York City; about 8.7 million Mexican-Americans who tend to be Catholic and Spanish speaking (but in 1980 there were 14.6 million Americans of Spanish origin (Hispanics) or 6.4 percent of the total U.S. population); Asians, 3.5 million people of Japanese, Chinese, Filipino, Vietnamese, Korean, Cambodian, and so on, ancestry; Puerto Ricans, about 1.9 million strong and particularly common in New York City; and American Indians, Eskimos, or Aleutians, who number about 1.4 million.

Of course, there are many other ethnic groups in the United States (some much larger than those just mentioned) that are not as visible, since they are predominantly white (do not have negroid or mongoloid physical traits) and are usually either Protestant or Catholic (i.e., non-Jewish, non-Buddhist, non-Moslem, and so on) in religious preference (see Table 6.2). Nonetheless, these white ethnics tend to have minority status in America. We refer primarily to those of German ancestry, about 49.6 million in 1980; the Irish, about 40.2 million; and those of Italian parentage or origin, about 12.2 million.[3]

In considering these American racial and ethnic minorities we should be aware of important population shifts in the last decade or so. Between 1970 and 1980 the population of whites in the United States dropped from 87.5 percent to 83.2 percent. Concurrently there has been a fairly dramatic rise in the proportion of Americans of Hispanic origin, from 4.5 percent to 6.4 percent. It is expected that Hispanics will overtake blacks as the largest racial minority group in the United States (by about the year 2000) (see U.S. Bureau of the Census, *Persons of Spanish Origin in the U.S.*, 1985). There have also been noticeable gains for Asians, from 0.8 to 1.5 percent, owing largely to our involvement in Asian wars, and a striking rise in "all other races," from 0.3 to 3.0 percent. In general, Zangwill's notion of a melting pot in which racial and ethnic groups would be assimilated and diversity reduced has not been realized. In fact America is becoming more racially and ethnically diverse. Shifts in racial and ethnic composition and intensified racial and ethnic pride and autonomy have all tended to make America more racially and ethnically pluralistic, rather than more homogeneous.

One final note before turning to a consideration of the sociobiology of race. A detailed natural history of race relations (especially of black-white relations in the United States; cf. Berry and Blassingame, 1982) will be presented later in this chapter. However, initially it is important to realize that given a broad enough time and geographic span, Negroids, Mongoloids, and Caucasoids have all had great cultures (Simpson and Yinger, 1985:56–59). A more short-sighted, ethnocentric view of the history of major racial groups might lead us to conclude erroneously that Euro-American people are superior to African, Asian, or South American peoples.

TABLE 6.1

United States Resident Population, by Race and Spanish Origin: April 1, 1980 and 1970

United States	1980	1970	Percent Distribution 1980	Percent Distribution 1970
Total	226,504,825	203,211,925	100.0%	100.0%
White	188,340,790	177,748,975	83.2	87.5
Black	26,488,218	22,580,289	11.7	11.1
American Indian, Eskimo, and Aleut	1,418,195	827,268	0.6	0.4
Asian and Pacific Islander*	3,500,636	1,538,721	1.5	0.8
Other	6,756,986	516,673	3.0	0.3
Persons of Spanish origin	14,605,883	9,072,602	6.4	4.5
Persons not of Spanish origin	211,898,942	194,139,324	93.6	95.5

*Asian and Pacific Islander groups such as Cambodian, Laotian, and Thai are included in the "other" race category. In sample tabulations, these groups will be included in the Asian and Pacific Islander category.

Source: *Statistical Abstract of the United States,* 1986:29; and 1970 Census of Population, Supplementary Report, PC(S1)–104.

TABLE 6.2

The Five Largest Ethnic Ancestry Groups in the United States, 1980

Origin*	Population (in millions)	Percent of Total Population
English, Scottish, or Welsh	49.6	22
German	49.2	22
Irish	40.2	18
Spanish	12.9	6
Italian	12.2	5

*Includes some overlap because of claimed multiple ancestry. Due to this percentages are somewhat inflated.

Source: *Statistical Abstract of the United States,* 1986:34.

• The Sociobiology of Race

Elaboration of the Concept of Race: Genes So-called racial traits (like skin color, facial features—nose, lips, eyes, and so on—skull, hair, and body shapes) are partially determined by our genetic makeup (Simpson and Yinger, 1985:Ch. 2; Wallace et al., 1981:265–350). G. Mendel (1822–84), a Czech monk who worked in a garden in Austria studying peas, did much to found the present science of genetics. Among Mendel's discoveries were that genes are units on the chromosomes (see Glossary, Chapter 5) that affect inherited characteristics. They act in pairs. The partner of any gene is called its allele. If one allele is dominant over the other, it will be expressed in the individual offspring. The allele over which it dominates is said to be recessive. The recessive allele is not expressed, although it may be expressed in a later generation.

Thus, the physical appearance of an individual does not always reveal what genes are present in the organism's chromosomes. The observable hereditary characteristics of an individual are called his/her phenotypes. The characteristics contained in his/her genes are called his/her genotype. If a person received all dominant genes, the phenotype and genotype would be the same. From what little we have discussed so far it is evident that genetic determination of racial types is very complex. Not only are some genes recessive, but genes are also polygenic; that is, inherited characteristics are produced by the additive interaction of several genes.

Pure Races Since all members of the human species (i.e., all races) can interbreed, racial traits are also influenced by isolation. Even if there are distinctive racial traits, if races do not keep physically or geographically separate, then these racial differences will change. In fact there are no pure races. It has been estimated that 80 percent of black Americans have some white ancestors and 25 percent of white Americans have some black ancestors. Just because there are no pure races it does not follow that we cannot make meaningful racial distinctions. As Simpson and Yinger conclude (1985:33): "Obviously, racial differences exist. Mongoloid Asians are visibly different from Negroid Africans and from Caucasoid Europeans."

Environment Environment also interacts with our genetic makeup to determine race. Diet, work habits, exposure (or lack of) to sun, health, temperature, and disease all affect racial traits. For example, post–World War II Japanese have gotten significantly taller, as have most other ethnic groups in America (Campbell, 1985:484).

Skin Color For many skin color is synonymous with race, the three major races being roughly white, black, and yellow. Yet, we know that the people of southern India are dark skinned and have straight hair and other Caucasoid features. The Bushmen of southern Africa have yellowish skin and Mongoloid eyefolds.

Skin (hair and eye) colors are all produced by the pigment melanin (Simpson and Yinger, 1985:30). In the lower level of the epidermis of the skin are melanocytes containing melanin pigment. The number of melanocytes is about the same across all races. However, some melanocytes produce more melanin than others. An albino's melanocytes produce no melanin. Blacks generally produce more melanin than whites. Mongoloids have a thicker surface to their skin; it conceals blood color and makes skin look yellowish.

When the skin is heavily pigmented, it is resistant to penetration of ultraviolet radiation. Thus, skin color is darkest in the tropics (Harris and Wagley, 1985; Brues, 1977:90). Yet black skin absorbs about 15 percent more heat than sunburned white skin. Thus, blacks are more prone to heatstroke than whites. Ultraviolet rays produce vitamin D in the skin. If their diets are lacking, northern peoples may have vitamin D deficiencies, which can lead to rickets.

Noses, Eyes, and Lips Caucasoids and Negroids are often thought to have distinctive noses, while Mongoloids have distinctive eyes. A projecting, sharp-edged nasal root (the part of the nose between the eyes) is characteristic of Caucasoids. Negroid noses tend to be short from top to bottom and relatively wide across the wings. Also, nostril openings commonly face forward so they are visible to a straight-ahead view. People living in cold climates tend to have smaller ears and less projecting noses. The oriental eye has a delicate fold (epicanthic fold) of skin at the inner corner of the eye that curves downward, making the eye appear slanted. The whole upper eyelid appears plump. Blacks also tend to have thick lips with strong lip inversion.

Hair Although there is great variation of hair within races, there are also hair similarities within races. Negroids tend to have bushy, tightly curled hair. In extreme cases, like the African Bushmen, there are pepper-corn curls of hair surrounded by spaces with almost no hair. Mongoloid hair tends to have a greater diameter and a greater hollow core; both traits give their hair an impressive fullness. Mongoloid hair tends to be straight. Caucasian hair (especially that from northern Europe) has greater variations of colors, but is relatively limp and fragile. Nevertheless, overall, Caucasoids are more hairy than Negroids or Mongoloids. Australoids are among the most hairy of all races.

Body Shape Caucasoids and Negroids are nearly the same in stature, with Mongoloids being smaller on the average than either whites or blacks. However, there is great variation within races (Campbell, 1985:471). For example, African pigmies average below five feet in height, while Sudanese blacks average almost six feet. Negroids tend to be long and lanky; they have a relatively short trunk and long legs and arms. Mongoloids tend to have a long trunk and short limbs. Blacks have wide shoulders and narrow hips.

Health It is well known that certain types of illness and causes of death are more common in some races than in others (Dressler, 1985). For example, sickle cell anemia (sicklemia—a condition in which red blood cells partially collapse to form a crescent or sickle shape, thereby reducing their ability to transport oxygen) is greatest among African blacks, approaching 20 percent of some populations. When the sicklemia gene is heterozygotic (inherited from only one parent), there are no pathological effects, but resistance of malaria is greatly increased (Campbell, 1985:86ff., 475). Cancer is apparently much more common among Caucasians.

Tay-Sachs disease, which leads to a progressive degeneration of the central

Drawing by Chas. Addams; © 1954 1982 *The New Yorker* Magazine, Inc.

nervous system and eventual death by age two, is caused by a single recessive gene. It is 100 times more frequent in Ashkenazic Jews (from central and east Europe) than among Sephardic Jews (from the Mediterranean areas). Some other racially related physical conditions are that American blacks are much more susceptible to frostbite; the Rh blood factor is present in about 15 percent of the European population but is virtually absent among Mongoloids; and color blindness has its greatest incidence among Caucasians (Harris and Wagley, 1985).

Intelligence Early intelligence testing (using the Stanford-Binet IQ test) showed that black schoolchildren and black soldiers in World War I scored significantly lower than white schoolchildren or white soldiers (Yerkes, 1921; Harris and Wagley, 1985). It was concluded by some that blacks were innately (i.e., biologically) less intelligent than whites (Berry and Blassingame, 1982:351ff.). In general, in army IQ tests blacks scored lower than whites.

However, when literate northern blacks were compared with literate southern whites, the IQ differences disappeared. These data suggest that culture, educational opportunity, and so forth were more related to intelligence than biology. But then A. R. Jensen (1969, 1975) claimed that controlling for social class and culture, American blacks still scored ten to fifteen IQ points below whites on a national basis (cf. Simpson and Yinger, 1985:36ff.). It was again argued that blacks were biologically inferior to whites and that as much as 80 percent of this ten to fifteen point IQ score gap could not be changed by environmental manipulation.

Critics of Jensen (e.g., Simpson and Yinger, 1985:36–39) have since argued: that since there are no pure races, one cannot even accurately measure intelligence differences among races; that the IQ gap can in fact be closed rapidly with improved learning conditions; that pre- and postnatal nutritional deficits (especially low protein and low vitamin diets) affect brain development and that blacks are most likely to have nutritional deficiencies; that IQ tests are always somewhat culturally biased; and that Jensen's twin studies were methodologically flawed.

Physical Skills When we examine the racial mix in professional athletics, it is clear that black athletes are overrepresented in major sports like basketball, football, baseball, and boxing, far in excess of their 11 to 12 percent proportion of the general population. In an early classic book Edwards documents the superiority of the black athlete.

> The degree to which Negroes have moved into pro sports is astonishing. More than half the players in the National Basketball Association are Negroes—as were 8 of the ten starters in the last NBA All-Star Game. A quarter of the players in the National Football League are Negroes, and the 1967 NFL championship team was 40 percent black. Nearly 25 percent of all players in major league baseball are American Negroes, and here too a disproportionate number of the stars are not white. For example, of the top 10 hitters in the National League for the 1967 season, only one was a Caucasian. (1973:189)

Overall it seems that there are racial differences in physical skills and that in the cases just mentioned black athletes are generally superior to white athletes. But is this superiority a result of biology, culture, or restricted social opportunities?

Some have argued that blacks as a group are especially likely to have a long body trunk, long arms, and legs. This could help their speed, reach, and jumping abilities. However, others point out that black athletes often differ more from each other than from white athletes. A few have claimed that blacks do not make good swimmers because of their low fat to muscle ratio and poor buoyancy. Similar comments have sometimes been made about black golfers and tennis players. A skeptic could reply that most American blacks have not had

PANEL 6.2

The Black Athlete

It is usually conceded today by serious analysts that the performances of black athletes are generally superior to those of white athletes. Pascal and Rapping, for instance, state that in professional baseball, "position by position, black players in the big leagues tend to outperform their white counterparts on the basis of objective measurements. This holds for veterans and rookies alike." Evidence consistent with the contention that black athletes are superior performers in sports is abundant. Consider the following:

1. In professional basketball, three of the five athletes named to the 1969–70 all-NBA team were black, as were all five of the athletes named to the all-rookie team. Blacks have won the league's most-valuable-player award twelve times in the past thirteen seasons.

2. In professional football, all four of the 1969 rookie of the year awards for offense and defense were won by black athletes; 165 of the first 250 athletes drafted into professional football in 1971 were black.

3. In professional baseball, black men have won the National League's MVP award sixteen times in the past twenty-two seasons.

4. Today there are 150 blacks out of 600 athletes in major-league baseball, 330 blacks out of 1,040 athletes in professional football, and 153 black athletes out of 180 in professional basketball. Of the athletes on professional sports 1969–70 all-star rosters 36 percent in baseball were black, 44 percent in football, and blacks comprised 63 percent of all-star talent in basketball. Boxing has practically become an all-black game of musical chairs in the high-prestige heavier weight divisions and championships. Throughout all levels of athletic competition, a similar pattern of black domination prevails wherever blacks have access in large numbers of the various sports endeavors.

Source: Harry Edwards, *Sociology of Sport,* Dorsey Press, 1973:190–191.

access to swimming pools, golf courses, or tennis courts. Probably both nature (biology) and nurture (culture, learning, and the social opportunity structure) play roles in the superiority of the black athlete in most areas and inferiority in a few others.

• Racism: Discrimination against American Blacks

Stating the Problem There is no doubt that on the whole the dominant white majority in America holds prejudged, often negative attitudes toward black American minorities and has translated these prejudices into a vicious cycle of discrimination that keeps blacks in America (and other minorities) relatively powerless. Why discrimination exists and the degree of complicity of minorities in maintaining it, as well as whether discrimination really has all that much to do with race, are questions that we have yet to answer. The answers are not simple. Discrimination is not merely a product of ignorance, greed, and hatred. There are some biological racial differences. Most importantly racial inequality is rooted in institutionalized racial exchanges that have persisted over long periods of our history and that all races are ambivalent about changing. Note that in emphasizing racism toward blacks, we do not intend to neglect or minimize similar racism toward Mexican-Americans, American Indians, Asiatics, Jews, Puerto Ricans, and so on. We will have more to say about other minorities later in this chapter. Also, much prejudice and discrimination toward blacks is similar to that directed at other American minorities.

Racism refers to the dominant members' feelings of superiority to the members of minority groups (Berry and Blassingame, 1982). Racists hate and fear minorities. Motivated by these feelings, they attempt to keep minorities relatively powerless. Racism includes not only feelings of prejudice but also acts of discrimination against minorities. While *prejudice* refers to the prejudged negative attitudes toward minority groups, *discrimination* connotes actions against minority groups on the grounds of their group membership and supposed group characteristics (Simpson and Yinger, 1985:21–23).

Prejudice and discrimination have a complex relationship with each other. For example, a person or group may be prejudiced, but may not discriminate. In 1934 La Piere studied some 250 hotels. Ninety percent of those hotels surveyed were prejudiced against minorities; that is, they said they would not serve food in their restaurants to Chinese patrons. Yet when La Piere actually showed up with Chinese customers, all but one of the 250 hotels offered service to the Chinese. That is, almost all did not in fact discriminate. Other individuals or groups may discriminate without being prejudiced. A white woman may not date black friends or marry a black man out of fear of or the prejudice of her family, friends, or larger society. Cases like these led sociologist Robert Merton to suggest that there are unprejudiced nondiscriminators, unprejudiced discriminators, prejudiced nondiscriminators, and prejudiced discriminators. While prejudiced discriminators are probably the most common type, you would probably have little trouble thinking of examples of the other types.

Prejudiced people usually have stereotypic perceptions about what blacks are like (Lieberson, 1985). It is easier to justify discrimination, if one thinks that the minorities "deserve it." You will remember from Chapter 5 that a *stereotype* is a rigid mental image of a group that is applied indiscriminately to all of its members. This mental image is usually exaggerated and erroneous. Stereotypes are overly simple reductions of reality. Racism is similar to sexism or ageism in that it is based on stereotypes. Common black stereotypes held by whites portray blacks as ignorant, lazy, superstitious, oversexed, musical, and childlike (Hamilton, 1981; Simpson and Yinger, 1985:97–109). Many older white Americans grew up with stereotypic images of blacks as people like

Advocates of white power such as the American Nazi Party, discriminate against blacks and Jews not only out of hatred, ignorance, fear, and greed. Racists often claim that they are biologically superior to minority groups. (Rich Frishman/Black Star)

Amos and Andy, Aunt Jemima, Steppin-Fetchit, Buckwheat in *Our Gang,* and Prissy in *Gone With The Wind.*

Classical stereotypes have faded some over the years (Simpson and Yinger, 1985:98). Blacks are now seen to be more rational, educated, and industrious than before. Black stereotypic traits make it easy for whites to justify their control, dominance, and exploitation of blacks. Consider, if blacks are childlike and ignorant, then they need to be taken care of; if oversexed, they have to be punished, imprisoned, segregated from white women, and so on; if lazy, then blacks deserve to be given the worst jobs or no jobs at all.

From Table 6.3 it is obvious that considerable prejudice among white Americans remains (especially for intimate personal contacts), even though in general prejudice has declined (cf. Lieberson, 1985:17–119; Schuman, Steeh, and Bobo, 1985). Over half of white Texans interviewed (in 1976) would still not like their children to have a black roommate while at college. Almost half would not want blacks to come to their homes for parties or other social events. About a third would not accept a black next-door neighbor. It should be noted that before the U.S. Supreme Court overturned the separate but equal doctrine (See *Brown* v. *the Board of Education of Topeka,* 1954) schools, housing, restaurants, swimming pools, hotels, restrooms, waiting rooms all tended to be segregated (especially in the South). So-called Jim Crow laws were passed to keep blacks from voting. For example, there were property qualifications, literacy tests, grandfather clauses, and so on, all designed to prohibit the black vote. Such acts of discrimination helped create a vicious circle of disadvantages for black Americans, one they alone have not as a group been able to break out of even today.

In 1985 Schuman, Steeh, and Bobo reviewed trends in racial attitudes in America by summarizing surveys ranging from 1942 to 1983 (see pp. 74–75, especially). Almost all attitudes of whites toward blacks have shown more approval recently of racial integration and less social distance between blacks and whites. Although there are many complexities in the Schuman et al. trends, most whites now (about 1983) favor school integration (90 percent), equal job opportunities (97 percent), elected black governmental officials (85 percent), same public accommodations for blacks (88 percent), and integrated public transportation (88 percent). However, less than half of all whites were still in favor of racial intermarriage (40 percent) and open housing (46 percent—i.e., owner cannot consider race when selling his/her home).

Discrimination as a Vicious Circle Racial discrimination and prejudice tend to push blacks into low-status jobs or unemployment (Berry and Blassingame, 1982:Ch. 6; cf. Farley, 1984). Of course, such restricted work opportunities almost guarantee that blacks will tend to have less income than the dominant white majority.[4] In turn less income means that average black parents cannot afford quality education for their children (especially in college) and cannot support their families or maintain their health as well. Poor-quality education, fewer years of education, larger and more disrupted families, and more health disadvantages all reinforce each other, feed back into poor work situations, and invigorate the original prejudice and discrimination. Thus, prejudice and discrimination constitute a vicious circle (see Figure 6.1) that blacks have great difficulty breaking out of (cf. Schaefer, 1979:25).

Jobs, Unemployment, and Income Let us look more closely at black jobs, unemployment, and income. In the United States blacks tend to be concentrated in semiskilled, domestic, and laborer occupational categories—when they have jobs at all. The average annual black unemployment rate has usually been about

TABLE 6.3 Survey of White Texans' Attitudes about Race, 1963–1971–1976–1983 (All Whites) (Percentages)

Situation in Which White Texans Accept or Approve Racial Contacts	**1963**	**1971**	**1976**	**1983***
Riding in the same section of trains and buses	49	83	90	88
Working side by side with you in the same kind of job	56	84	89	97
Eating in the same restaurants	40	80	89	—
Staying in the same hotels as you	36	76	87	88
Attending your church	46	75	80	—
Sending your children to the same schools	41	73	80	90
Attending the same social gathering outside your home	23	59	71	—
Living next door to you	23	52	64	86
Using the same swimming pools with you	19	50	62	—
Attending a social gathering in your home	13	45	58	78
Having as roommate for your son or daughter in college	8	32	41	—
Intermarriage*	4 (1957)	27	33	40

*Schuman, H. et al. *Racial Attitudes in America,* 1985:104ff. No strict comparisons can be made between Schuman et al. and Texas poll, since samples and controls differed. 1983 data = all whites, not just southern whites.

Source: Adapted from *The Texas Poll: The Statewide Survey of Public Opinion,* Report No. 875 (March 15, 1976). Conducted by Belden Associates. For data since 1976, see Simpson and Yinger, *Racial and Cultural Minorities: An Analysis of Prejudice and Discrimination,* Plenum Press, 1985:89.

twice as high as the average white unemployment rate (Farley and Bianchi, 1985:14). This unemployment rate disadvantage remains regardless of the economic conditions in American society. Recently, as unemployment has reached the highest levels since the Great Depression, blacks have been hurt the most. The unemployment rate for black teenagers is now about 50 percent. Although there have been absolute gains in black incomes vis-à-vis whites, the median black household income is still only about 60 percent that of the white median household income (*Statistical Abstract of the U.S., 1986:*445). Actually in the last few years median black household income has slipped to about 57 percent of white income. Of course, the absolute dollar difference between median white and black family incomes has actually increased substantially, from $3,124 per year in 1967 to $10,176 per year in 1984 (Table 6.4).

Education Turning to educational differences between blacks and whites, it is true that between 1940 and 1984 the percentage of blacks 25 years old or

FIGURE 6.1 A Vicious Circle of Prejudice and Discrimination against Blacks

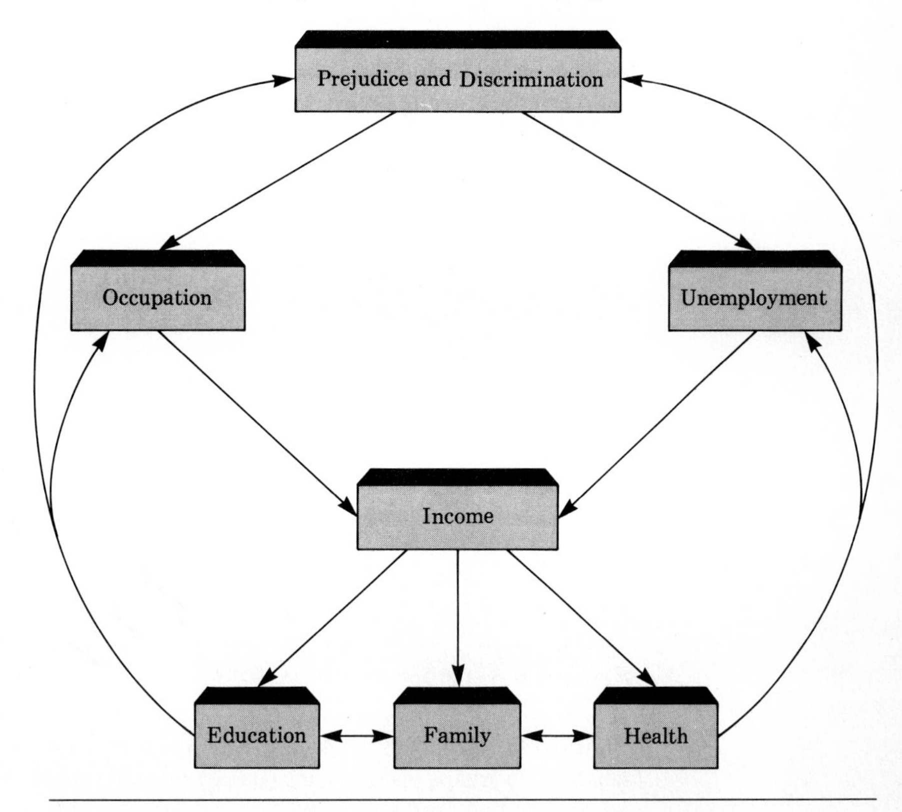

Source: Cf. George Simpson and J. Milton Yinger, *Racial and Cultural Minorities: An Analysis of Prejudice and Discrimination,* 1985:106; cf. Richard Schaefer, *Racial and Ethnic Groups,* 1979:25.

older completing high school rose from 7 percent to 59 percent (*Statistical Abstract of the U.S., 1986:*133). Also, in 1969 there were only 783 black medical students in the United States, but in 1976 there were 3,456. Yet even if they are college educated, blacks still earn only about two-thirds to three-fourths what white college graduates earn (Berry and Blassingame, 1982:293).

Family Poor economic opportunities and low income have contributed to strain and stress in black family relations (Berry and Blassingame, 1982:Ch. 3). Black male desertion rates and lack of economic support from black fathers are high. The black divorce rate is about twice as high as that of whites, 203 per 1,000 married persons for blacks in 1980 versus 92 per 1,000 for whites (Glick, 1981). Many more black families than white families are headed by mothers alone. In 1980, 44 percent of black children under eighteen years old lived with their mothers only versus only 18 percent of all families. Blacks still tend to have somewhat larger completed family sizes than whites.

TABLE 6.4 Median Income of Households by Race, 1967–1984

Year	Race: Black	Race: White	Difference	Ratio of Blacks to Whites
1967	$ 4,325	$ 7,449	$ 3,124	58%
1970	5,537	9,097	3,560	61
1971	5,578	9,443	3,865	59
1972	5,938	10,173	4,235	58
1973	6,485	11,017	4,532	59
1974	6,964	11,710	4,746	59
1975	7,408	12,340	4,932	60
1976	7,902	13,289	5,387	60
1977	8,422	14,272	5,850	59
1978	9,411	15,680	6,269	60
1979	10,133	17,257	7,126	59
1980	10,764	18,684	7,920	58
1981	11,309	20,153	8,844	56
1982	11,968	21,117	9,149	57
1983	12,443	21,886	9,443	57
1984	13,471	23,647	10,176	57

Source: Adapted from the *Statistical Abstract of the United States,* 1986:445.

Health Blacks on the whole tend to have less adequate diets, live in less sanitary conditions, and can afford quality medical care less than whites. Table 6.5 reveals that on the average in 1984 blacks could expect to live about five or six years less than whites, controlling for sex. Blacks are about four times more likely to die in childbirth, are more likely to have high blood pressure, and are more likely to die once cancer has been contracted than whites. Thus, one could argue that prejudice and discrimination not only make life unjustly hard and cause needless emotional suffering, they also literally kill black minorities at a greater rate and earlier than the dominant white majority group.

The Symbolism of Being Black Being black in America has a special meaning related to the U.S. history of slavery and the minority status of American blacks (Berry and Blassingame, 1982:Chs. 1 and 2). For example, in most of Africa being black would have a very different symbolism.[5] The first blacks came to America in 1619. In roughly twenty years about 400,000 black Africans came to the United States. It is important to note that they came as slaves. Slavery lasted until 1830 in the northern United States and until 1865 in the southern states. As we have just seen, much de facto slavery and related discrimination and oppression still remain even today.

Blackness in most places, times, and cultures has had mainly negative connotations. Just think of the expressions "blackball," "blacklist," "blackmail,"

TABLE 6.5 Life Expectancy by Race and Sex

	Black		White	
Year	Male	Female	Male	Female
1900	32.5	33.5	46.6	48.7
1950	58.9	62.7	66.5	72.2
1960	60.7	65.9	67.4	74.1
1970	60.0	68.3	68.0	75.6
1980	63.8	72.5	70.7	78.1
1984	65.5	73.7	71.8	78.8

Source: U.S. Department of Health and Human Services, *Health, United States,* 1985:40.

"black sheep," "black magic," and of the night and darkness as scary or dangerous. Evil, death, and the devil all tend to be thought of as black. The typical white's prejudice and discrimination toward blacks can be expected to damage the self-esteem and confidence of black people. Clark and Clark (1947) note that black children often described black dolls as ugly, dirty, or bad (cf. Lieberson, 1985:122). Rosenberg and Simons (1972) report that as blacks get older they and whites realize that most people rank blacks last in prestige among the four racial groups (cf. Rosenberg, 1979; Simpson and Yinger, 1985:128ff.). Recently (from about the 1970s on) blacks have made a concerted effort to portray black as beautiful to counteract majority-group stereotypes (Berry and Blassingame, 1982:419ff.).

Analyzing the Problem. The Conflict Perspective One traditional answer to the problems of prejudice, discrimination, and racism has been that of the conflict theorists (Stanfield, 1985:171; Simpson and Yinger, 1985:163–164). The conflict perspective maintains that whites in America have more wealth, power, and prestige on the average than blacks. Whites also outnumber blacks by about nine to one. Whites strive to maintain their economic advantages over blacks by keeping blacks poor, uneducated, out of key jobs, without property, away from elected governmental positions, and so forth. In short, whites (and the social structure created by some whites) oppress and exploit blacks. Some see these conflicts not as racial, but rather as disguised economic conflicts (Wilson, 1978). Prejudice is aggravated because lower-class whites compete with blacks for jobs (Smith, 1985). Prejudiced people are often found to have authoritarian personalities that promote a rigid irrational view of all blacks as inferior and gloss over deep inadequacies and fears on the part of the dominant white majority itself (Adorno et al., 1950; Simpson and Yinger, 1985:78ff.).

Conflict arises because whites, blacks, Hispanics, Jews, and so on see themselves as competing for scarce economic resources (e.g., the best jobs, educational opportunities, real estate, and so on). Thus, the economic well-

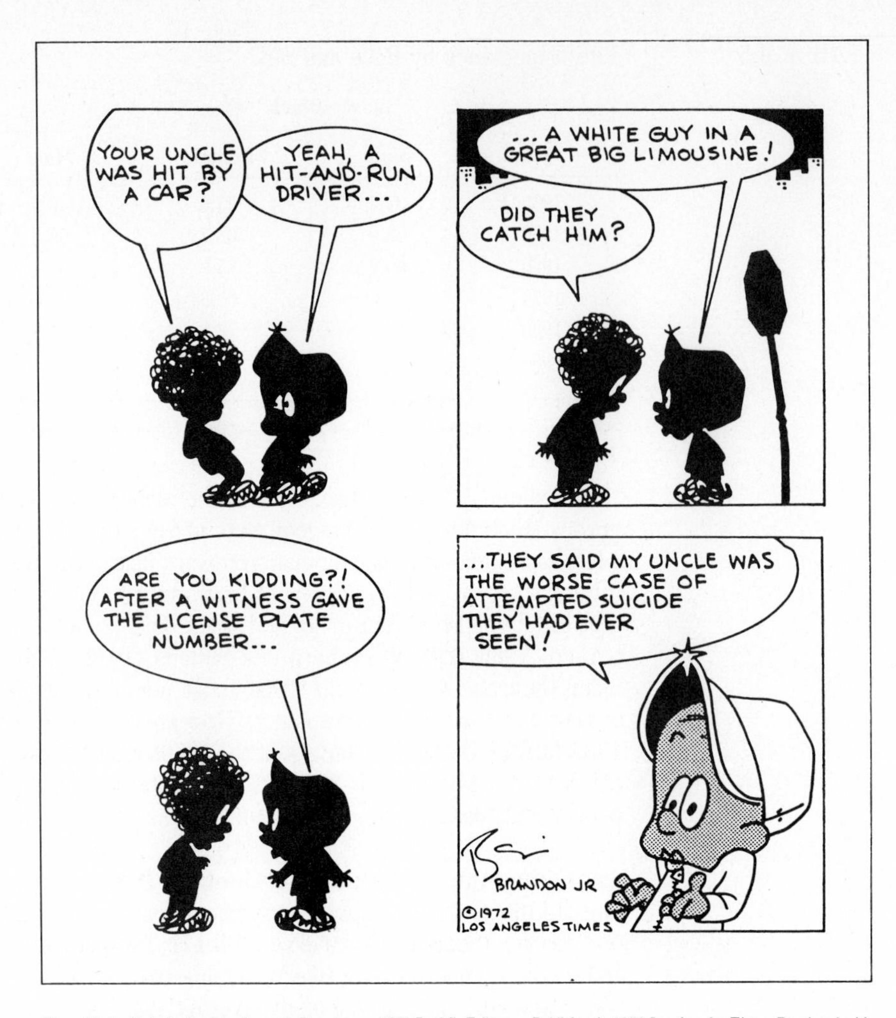

From "Outta Sight Luther" by Brumsic Brandon. © 1971 Paul S. Eriksson, Publisher in 1972 *Los Angeles Times.* Reprinted with permission of Paul S. Eriksson, Publisher.

being of one ethnic or racial group is seen to necessitate exploiting the other groups (Berry and Blassingame, 1982:Ch. 6). The conflict perspective asks "who benefits" from racial and ethnic prejudice and discrimination. Typically the dominant white majority in America is thought to take advantage of blacks and other racial or ethnic minorities by taking most of their earned profits ("surplus labor value") and paying them very low wages, by using minorities as a source of cheap labor to do dirty service and domestic work and hard labor jobs no one (including the minorities) want to do, by maintaining a backup labor force, and so on.

The Exchange Perspective Exchange theorists tend to view the conflict analysis of racial problems as overly simplistic. For example, the conflict perspective tends to assume that the differences between blacks and whites are only economic. Like sex and age differences, it is fairly easy to differentiate objectively among basic racial groups.[6] Granted there are no pure races, but it is still relatively simple to classify most people broadly as Caucasoid, Negroid, Mongoloid, or Australoid. To be sure there will be exceptions or mistakes, but for the most part it is possible to specify broad sets of genetic traits defining major racial groupings. Here one is reminded of sexual differences (see Chapter 5). That is, most people are clearly biologically either male or female; their sexual identity is usually not confused. These broad genetic differences are reinforced by cultural differences between races and cultural similarities within races. For example, in America blacks tend to have a black consciousness complete with common black values, language, lifestyle, dress, and so on (Berry and Blassingame, 1982:especially Chapter 11). That is, once one is classified or classifies oneself as black (or white, yellow, Jewish, Hispanic, and so on), one assumes certain standardized cultural traits peculiar to one's presumed race or ethnic group. Furthermore, these genetic and cultural differences are usually highly visible. Consider many of the physical traits we have already discussed, such as, skin color, hair, lips, eyes, and so on.

It will be recalled from Chapter 2 (Table 2.2) that generally anything that restricts social interaction is likely to generate social problems.[7] Racial dissimilarities do just that, because similarity is a powerful basis for social interaction. From exchange theory (Homans, 1974:64–65) we know that the more similar people are, the more likely they are to interact with and to express liking for one another. More than this, similarity is often a reward (Homans, 1974:300). That is, people express conformity by being similar to one another. Interestingly, being different, even if genetically given and relatively immutable, is often seen as deviance, and thus as something that deserves punishment. Finally, assimilation into or acceptance by a dominant group of minorities is more likely if the minority resembles the majority group (Simpson and Yinger, 1985:114).[8]

A second exchange interpretation of America's black-white relations turns on the fact that in the United States blacks originally were slaves. Many institutional arrangements perpetuating master-slave type exchanges still persist, in spite of the formal abolition of slavery itself. While not inherent in their race (that is, not a physical given), historically blacks in America have in fact been forced to exchange their domestic labor, service, compliance, entertainment, and athletic skills to dominant whites for the money, status, and predictable life course that whites usually control (Table 6.6). Finding such menial behaviors rewarded (and other more "uppity" ambitious behaviors punished), by the first axiom of exchange theory, many blacks have understandably repeated the very behaviors that paradoxically are keeping them down (this is not to blame blacks for conforming). It would be easy to construct a "payoff matrix" to demonstrate how in the short run American blacks (and other minorities) maximize their profits by complying with white dominance.

Third, not only have American blacks traditionally been subservient to whites, they have also been segregated from whites. It is well known that

TABLE 6.6 Distribution of Basic Societal Rewards by White and Black Race

Rewards	White	Black
Money, social status	+	−
Menial labor	−	+
Entertainment, sports	−	+
Compliance	−	+
Serenity and predictable life course	+	−

\+ = offers, supplies.
− = receives.

racial differences are heightened by the physical isolation of separate houses, schools, and jobs. Physical and geographical differences in turn feed back to restrict social interaction. That is, the greater the racial differences, the less the social interaction. And, as we have seen, restriction of social interaction usually generates and aggravates social problems.

For example, Messner and South (1986) found that residential segregation and relative group size (exchange and structural theory) explained robbery victimization patterns (such as blacks being most likely to rob other blacks) better than did poverty or racial inequality (conflict theory). They suggest that we need to pay close attention to structural opportunities for exchange or interaction among different racial groups. However, in a related study of Puerto Ricans Massey and Bitterman (1985) argue that racial segregation itself (here of Puerto Ricans) often results from low socioeconomic status and black ancestry.

Finally, exchange theory predicts that if expected rewards are not received, people are more likely to become angry and aggressive (axiom 5, Chapter 2). The rising social expectations of blacks in the 1960s prompted by civil rights legislation juxtaposed with persistent black-white income differentials probably increased black anger to rage and ultimately contributed to the inner-city riots in Watts, Detroit, Baltimore, and other major American cities in the late 1960s and early 1970s. In short, American blacks' sense of distributive justice was offended. Note too that aggression cost blacks relatively little, since they had few social advantages to lose. Why these urban racial disturbances have not recurred in the 1980s is an interesting social question, particularly with the recent rise of terrorism (Chapter 15).

The Structural and Functional Perspectives Based on the size alone of the American black population (completely apart from values, culture, or racial discrimination) structuralists would not expect most whites to interact much with blacks, or to like them very much. The first reason for this prediction is that blacks constitute a relatively small proportion of the American population (about 11.7 percent, according to Table 6.1). As we discussed earlier (Chapter 2), the rate of intergroup associations of a smaller group (here blacks) must exceed that of a larger group (here whites; Blau, 1977:21). Most whites in the United States will not have black friends in part because there are just too few blacks with whom whites can interact.

When we calculate the expected frequency of out-group racial associations (i.e., heterogeneity) for American blacks, it is clear that even without discrimination it is expected that only about 20 percent of all relationships will be between blacks and whites (other things being equal). Put somewhat differently, about 80 percent of all relationships are expected on the basis of size alone to be within the two major racial groups (black-black and white-white). With respect to size and heterogeneity, American blacks are similar to the American aged (see Chapter 4). Assuming that liking is generally promoted by social interaction, relatively small numbers of blacks, low heterogeneity, and the resultant low expected cross-racial interaction would predict that most whites would not like (i.e., would in fact be prejudiced against) blacks (Homans, 1974:64).

Structurally American blacks suffer from the joint effects of heterogeneity and inequality disadvantages (cf. Fossett and Swicegood, 1982). It has been documented that there is great inequality between blacks and whites (Farley, 1984). Considering income, jobs, education, health, political representation, and much more, American blacks tend to have low social status. Where great inequality exists, those with low status (blacks) are not likely to interact with those with high status (whites). It needs to be remembered that most American blacks originally came to the United States as slaves and were segregated from whites. Like wives, blacks used to be thought of as property. Blacks and other minorities function as society's source of cheap labor to do its dirty service, domestic work, and hard labor that no one else wants to do.

Finally, the interaction structure between blacks and whites in the United States is usually limited to certain approved racial exchanges (e.g., as indicated in Tables 6.3 and 6.6). Other interactions tend to be discouraged, if not prohibited. To convince yourself of this ask how many blacks (or whites, depending on your race) you work with, attend the same church or synagogue as, belong to the same club as, have as close friends, go out on a date with, have sex with, live with, or are married to. Clearly, race becomes a much more salient factor as you move through such a list of questions toward greater intimacy.

The Symbolic Interaction Perspective Earlier in this chapter we discussed the symbolism of being black. The symbolic interaction perspective contends that the names or labels that are used to describe people or groups often reflect and seek to maintain racial or ethnic minority status (Solaun and Velez, 1985). Just consider these derogatory labels: "nigger, honky, kike, wetback, chink, colored, whop, spic, mick, kraut, and limey." Labeling people in such ways has a social result of justifying discrimination against them.

Remember the Nazi's extermination of and experimentation with Jews, black

American slavery, the terrible living conditions on American Indian reservations, or housing in inner-city black ghettos. In a study by Peterson and Hagan (1984) black drug offenders were found to receive stiffer criminal penalties than white offenders for similar offenses. For example, a black man named Leroy "Nicky" Barnes of Harlem (New York City) received a life sentence without parole for a drug sale offense.

Once we apply racial or ethnic labels it is difficult for us to see beyond these stereotypes (Lieberson, 1985). We tend to confuse what is with what could be. At my university (South Carolina) black students typically have lower verbal performance skills than most white students. But this itself reflects earlier discrimination against southern blacks, not necessarily racial intelligence differences. Blacks often misperceive white attitudes toward them too. When asked how typical white college students would describe blacks, black student reports were more consistent with the attitudes of rural noncollege whites (Lieberson, 1985:119).

As we have seen, it is common in the United States to approve of blacks excelling in athletics. But what would black performance be if other social roles (e.g., those of dentists, lawyers, surgeons, business managers, and so on) were also thought appropriate for black Americans; if there were less prejudice toward certain kinds of black achievement? Clearly, it can be argued cogently that social expectations determine actual racial and ethnic achievements.

• Resolving the Problem

There are at least three basic resolutions to racism and racial discrimination. First, to open up (usually gradually) education, job, and income opportunities through legal changes (like busing or affirmative action). This usually implies that the black minority will become more similar to the white majority. Second, to break up the vicious cycle of discrimination through force, confrontation or, in the extreme, terrorist activities. And third, to peacefully coexist in a pluralistic racial society (e.g., not to especially concern oneself with [if you are black, and so on] white society or the majority group).

Changing Racial Interaction Patterns If you change interaction patterns to open up black-white social relations, the expectation is that prejudice and discrimination will be diminished. The primary reason for this expectation is that the social class of blacks is changed by better educational, job, and income opportunities. In fact some blacks (Wilson, 1978) feel that the low social class of most blacks is the real problem, not their race per se (others disagree; see Willie and Greenblatt, 1978 and Smith, 1985). Most effective social changes with regard to race relations are legal changes and they assume that over time blacks and whites will become less different from one another than they are now.

For example, one strategy has been court-ordered busing to reduce educational segregation and the resultant differential educational opportunities (Smith, 1985; McClendon and Pestello, 1983). James Coleman et al. in *Equality of Educational Opportunity* (1966, 1975) found that school integration would have positive advantages for low achievers but not for high achievers. Based on these findings and others federal courts ordered busing to achieve racial integration in schools. School integration has been relatively well accepted after the fact (Schuman et al., 1985), but has also led to some violence and to white flight to areas away from blacks (especially, to suburbia; Coleman et al., 1975). More recently the courts have begun to have their doubts about the advantages of busing (*New York Times,* November 18, 1981; May, 1986).

Some feel (Burstein, 1985; Marshall, 1982) that since blacks came to the United States as slaves and thereafter have been discriminated against, that compensation (in the form of affirmative action) should be made by requiring representation of blacks at the 11 percent to 12 percent population rate in the best schools and jobs (Simpson and Yinger, 1985:Ch. 9). Generally racial quotas have been judged legally appropriate. For example, the Supreme Court, in *United Steel Workers* v. *Weber* (1979), ruled that one can give special preferences to minority workers. But in *Bakke* v. *the Regents of the University of California* (1978), Judge Marshall and affirmative action lost five to four. Glazer (1975) says that affirmative action programs ignore individual merit in favor of racial class or group claims, especially over the group claims of all whites. Such claims by or for blacks amount to negative or reverse discrimination in the minds of many (Burstein, 1985). In 1977, 83 percent of the public (Gallup Poll) opposed affirmative action (cf. Schuman et al., 1985).

As opportunities for black jobs, income, education, and so on improve, blacks and whites should become more similar. Usually this implies that blacks will be assimilated into the dominant white majority group and its lifestyle. Race should matter less if blacks and whites have similar incomes, training, houses, lifestyles, and so on. Of course, assimilation is not the same as "passing" for white, in which case blacks do not really become more like whites, but just act "as if" they were. Both assimilation and passing should be distinguished from Uncle Tomism in which blacks played to the hilt the racist roles that were created for them.[9] Uncle Toms supported racism by "staying in their place" (Berry and Blassingame, 1982).

Force and Confrontation Blacks could meet force with force and fight racism on its own terms through riots, confrontation politics, violence, crime, demands, or terrorism. If the white majority will not give blacks equality, then blacks may have to take it. Some blacks (Carmichael and Hamilton, 1967; Berry and Blassingame, 1982:418–420) believe that black power is necessary to take what blacks in America need and deserve. Urban riots were all related to a forceful takeover and vivid display of black power and restlessness, especially by urban ghetto blacks (see the *Autobiography of Malcolm X,* 1966; see Perry, 1985 on Malcolm X; and Claude Brown's *Manchild in the Promised Land,* 1965). Recently the Reverend Jesse Jackson has organized Operation

Those in the conflict tradition feel that majority power may need to be confronted by minority power. The Reverend Jesse Jackson and Operation PUSH want to force American business and government to open up jobs for blacks and to recognize black purchasing power. (AP/Wide World Photos)

PUSH to force American businesspeople to open up jobs for blacks and to recognize black purchasing power (*New York Times,* March 9, 1980; cf. Marrett and Leggon, 1985:85, 127).

It is also well known that young black males commit more than their expected share of crimes, especially of assault and robbery (see Chapter 15; Zawitz, 1983:36–38). Black crime rates are confounded by the fact that blacks are five times more likely than whites to be arrested and that many white crimes are nonviolent white-collar crimes (like embezzlement). One could easily interpret black crime as forcibly redressing a long history of white distributive injustice and oppression. Of course, one must remember that most black crimes involve other blacks as victims (Messner and South, 1986). That is, black crime is often a form of displaced aggression, since it is not directed at the actual frustrating agent.

Force and terrorism seldom permanently resolve social problems. One reason for this is that the white majority group commonly lashes back. As cases in point, after episodes of black urban violence, Dr. Martin Luther King, Jr., was assassinated (1968) and later Urban League President Vernon Jordan was shot and nearly killed. White terrorists (like the Ku Klux Klan—see *New York Times,* February 21, 1982) have become much more vigorous lately in part in response to black aggressiveness and in part owing to our depressed economy.[10]

Racial Pluralism and Peaceful Coexistence Many observers (Stanfield, 1985:173–176; Simpson and Yinger, 1985:13–16) believe that racial pluralism (rather than racial integration, assimilation, or a new racial synthesis) is the most likely and most satisfactory resolution to America's racial problems. As long as racial minorities accentuate their differences by arguing that black is beautiful, stimulating black pride (Berry and Blassingame, 1982:52–61, 354–371), advocating black separatism, unique African roots, and so on, then pluralism is more likely than any other resolution.

Of course, pluralism may need to be supplemented by resolutions of law or force, since pluralism does not directly confront the vicious cycle of prejudice and discrimination. Pluralism implies a separate but equal goal. Since this objective has not worked well in the past (e.g., minorities have been separate but unequal), one has to question how successful it can be now. The more one emphasizes racial differences or any differences for that matter, the more one encourages lack of social interaction, disliking, and racial stereotypes.

• Other American Minorities

In many ways the other major American minority groups are similar to U.S. blacks. Most of what we have just argued about American blacks applies as well to Mexican-Americans, Puerto Ricans, Cuban Americans, American Indians, Jews, Asiatic Americans, and so on; all we have to change are the dirty names. The poverty, poor education, political exclusion, undesirable jobs, poor health, substandard housing, and so on tend to be the same for all American minorities. Usually minorities are not white Anglo-Saxon Protestants, they are relatively powerless, often poor, discriminated against, the butt of cruel ethnic jokes (e.g., jokes about Poles, "wetbacks," "Chinamen," Jews, and so on), and are concentrated mostly in unskilled jobs requiring heavy physical labor.

The other American minorities are unlike American blacks in that they are often not Protestants (they may be Catholic, Jewish, Buddhist, and so on);

From "Outta Sight Luther" by Brumsic Brandon. © 1971 Paul S. Eriksson, Publisher. in 1971 *Los Angeles Times.* Reprinted with permission of Paul S. Eriksson, Publisher.

they often do not speak English as their primary language (e.g., they often speak Spanish, Yiddish, or an Oriental language); they may not have a distinguishing skin color or have a skin color strikingly different from blacks (e.g., yellow); and they may have been in North America longer than the white majority group (consider American Indians or Mexican-Americans). Given the detail in which blacks in America have been considered above, in what follows we need only emphasize some of the unique traits of other American minorities. Space does not permit detailed analysis or resolution of their special social problems. This is not a major difficulty, since the analysis and resolutions tend to be similar to those just considered for American blacks.

Hispanics Hispanic Americans represent the second largest minority in the United States (de la Garza et al., 1985).[11] One in six U.S. citizens is of Spanish origin and of these about 60 percent are Mexican-Americans (*Statistical Abstract of the U.S., 1986*:32). By the year 2000 it is expected that Hispanics will overtake blacks as the largest American minority group. In 1985 there were about 16.9 million Hispanics in the United States. Of these 10.3 million are Mexican-Americans, 2.6 million are Puerto Ricans (mostly in New York City), and 4.1 million are Cubans and mixed Spanish origins (many in Florida). Except for many of the early Cuban migrants,[12] like black Americans, many Hispanics tend to be poor and concentrated in urban areas. Unlike most blacks, Hispanics are usually Spanish speaking and Catholic. In 1984 while only 11.5 percent of whites lived in poverty, fully 28.4 percent of Hispanics did (blacks were even higher at 33.8 percent; *Statistical Abstract of the U.S., 1986*:457; cf. Harrington, 1984).

Probably much more should be written here about Americans of Spanish origin, given the size of the minority group and its probable impact on future American social life. But space limits permit only a few additional comments about Mexican-Americans (for a good overview of Mexican-Americans see McLemore and Romo, 1985; Alvarez, 1985; de la Garza et al., 1985). Unlike blacks and Asiatics many Mexican-Americans have always lived in what is now called Texas, New Mexico, California, Arizona, Nevada, Utah, and parts of Colorado. That is, Mexican-Americans became a minority group by conquest of their own homes, most notably through the Mexican-American war of 1846–48.

Of the Mexicans who actually migrated later to the Southwest United States most found hard, dirty, and poorly paid jobs in railroading, agriculture, and mining (McLemore and Romo, 1985:14). Mexican-Americans were forced to take low wages and to live in segregated substandard housing. Although many Mexican-Americans in Los Angeles and Albuquerque have intermarried (usually to Anglos or whites) and learned English, many others (especially in Texas) have continued to speak Spanish, marry others of Mexican origin, and resist assimilation into the white majority. In the Southwest Hispanics are often illegal aliens who are exploited for their cheap labor. Since Mexico is contiguous to the United States, this problem is frequently resolved by sending Mexican-Americans "home." To combat some of this labor exploitation C. Chavez unionized migrant farm workers (Servin, 1974). In spite of some recent gains many problems remain for Mexican-Americans in the United States (see Panel 6.3; cf. de la Garza, 1985).

Jews Most people do not realize that there are more Jews in the United States than in any other country in the world (Feagin, 1984:Ch. 6). There are over six million Jews in America, about half of whom live in or about New York City. There are more Jews in the United States than in the USSR or in Israel. Most American Jews arrived in the United States after 1840 fleeing from pogroms (massacres of Jews) in Europe.[13] Of course, Jews have striking religious, language, and cultural differences from the dominant American majority group. Although Protestants, Catholics, and Jews share the Old Testament scriptures, Jews reject the idea that Jesus Christ is the promised messiah of

PANEL 6.3

A Chicano Mother in Texas Describes Her Children's Encounter with Local Bigotry

"The worst time is when the children start asking me why. I discourage them. I tell them please, stop coming at me with questions. I don't know why the Anglos are on top and we are on the bottom. I don't know why we are so many in this country and they are so few, and they control everything. I don't know why we all don't get together and start marching down the road. One child tells me that we could win, if we only fought. Another child says we wouldn't have to fight, just stand up and shake our fists, and teach them that we are going to be our own bosses. That is fine—the talk of someone who is not old enough to work, not a man or a woman, but instead drunk on a dream.

"Let them have their hope, though. I do not want to crush my children with too much of the knowledge I have picked up over the years. There is a nun I know who has helped me a lot; she has made me a better mother. She will tell me what to say, how to answer questions. I used to argue with her. I used to say that I shouldn't say anything. But she won me over. She made me see that I can't ignore my children and hope that they stay out of trouble. After all, my mother always took me aside when I was a small girl and told me things. I recall her lowering her voice, almost to a whisper; and I would go away and think about what she said. Now I do the same; I call Carlos over to me, and I tell him that he is a strong boy, and he will be a strong man, but he must not say bad things to the Anglo foreman when he walks near, and he must not wave his toy gun around and promise to kill people—the sheriff. There is a good chance that the sheriff would laugh, if he heard Carlos threaten him, but there is just as good a chance that the sheriff would begin to wonder what is going on. He and his police come through here once or twice a year; they go from house to house, 'just checking,' they tell us.

"I remember a year ago, the sheriff saw a toy pistol, and picked it up, and pretended it was real. He asked the children to put their hands up. They saw he had the toy in his hand, so they laughed. He repeated his order. They still laughed. Then he got angry. He threw the toy on the floor and shouted at the children to get against the wall and put their hands up. They did too—right away; even Carlos, only two then, knew that he had better do exactly as told. I was afraid the sheriff would pull his guns, but he didn't. He just kept his hands on them and gave us a lecture: don't we know who's boss, and don't we know how to obey the law, and don't we know how to stay out of trouble, and from now on he's going to keep a special eye out for us, and we'd better be ready at any moment for him to come around, or one of his deputies, and when they do, we'd better not get fresh, or we'd all spend the night in jail, and he'd put us in one cell, and we could stay on the floor and have bread and water, and nothing else, because he doesn't believe in spoiling prisoners. Then he told the children that he was 'only kidding!'"

Source: Robert Coles, M.D., *Eskimos, Chicanos, Indians:* vol. IV of *Children of Crisis,* Little, Brown and Company, 1977, pp. 322–24.

the Old Testament. The Jewish Torah, Bible, and prayers are in Hebrew (except for some reform Jews) and many Jewish children have a formal Hebrew education through high school age. Older European-American Jews often speak Yiddish, a Germanic language combined with some Hebrew words. Hebrew culture reflects both European and Middle Eastern traditions (e.g., keeping kosher, wearing prayer shawls, growing long hair and beards), which seems strange to most Americans. Jews tend to have a strong sense of group identity deriving in part from years of persecution and from fighting to survive. Early Christians were not allowed to be money changers, or charge interest (usury). Thus, Jews performed these functions.

Even today Jews continue to have a disproportionate involvement with finance, diamond sales, and business in general. Jews have also placed a very high value on scholarship and education. The rabbi was to be a learned man who devoted his life to God and to knowledge. Jews continue to be over-represented in education and the professions.[14] Although Jews are distinguished by their religious and ethnic traits, they are not a race. Most Jews are not distinguishable from other European or Semitic people physically. Since Israel was established as a country (1948), the large number of Jews in the United States, the typical American's lack of identification with most Arab countries (like Iran), and the religious persecution of Soviet Jews by the USSR, have all combined to encourage American support of Israel politically, financially, and militarily. However, our need for Arabic oil has probably strained this allegiance to Israel to some degree.

Asians In 1980 there were about 3.5 million Asians in the United States (about 1 percent to 2 percent of the total population) originally concentrated in California and Hawaii. These Asian-Americans were comprised of the following different nationalities: Chinese (806,000), Filipinos (774,000), Japanese (701,000), Asian Indians (361,000), Koreans (354,000), and Vietnamese (261,000) (*Statistical Abstract of the U.S.,* 1986:29). From 1850 to 1880 most Asian Americans were Chinese immigrants who worked primarily on railroad construction and in mines (cf. Current and Goodwin, 1980:464, 622). These Chinese laborers worked relatively cheaply and hard, often with the aid of opium. Their cheap labor and strange customs were deeply resented by indigenous workers. This resentment led to exploitation of Chinese laborers and eventually to the Chinese Exclusion Act of 1892. From about 1902 to 1943 virtually no Chinese laborers were admitted to the United States. Those Chinese people who were already in North America tended to be segregated in Chinatowns in part because of their strange culture, different color, bizarre religion, and unusual language (Simpson and Yinger, 1985:55ff.). Later the Japanese immigrated to Hawaii and California where they also met with much prejudice and discrimination.

After 1913 in California Japanese could not own land. In 1924 Japanese immigration was stopped. During World War II Japanese (but not Germans or Italians) were put in security camps or relocation centers. Many interned

Japanese lost their jobs and businesses during their confinement. It was not until 1952 that the Japanese could become U.S. citizens. Nevertheless most Japanese conformed to the middle-class American ethic of hard work, thrift, and self-control. Today Japanese industry (especially in electronics and automobiles) competes only too favorably with American industry. Comedian Robert Klein parodies American industry's desperation by telling us of a fictitious Ford car ad that is filmed in Pearl Harbor reconstructed to resemble the World War II bombing by Japan. Lately there have been additional migrations of Koreans, Vietnamese, and Cambodians—all displaced by American-Communist confrontations in war.

American Indians There are just under one million American Indians (1.4 million counting Eskimos), who since the Civil War (reservations started in 1830, officially) have lived mostly on federal reservations.[15] This segregation and isolation of American Indians has helped maintain their unique culture and genetic traits but has also contributed to many of the Indians' special problems (Feagin, 1984:Ch. 7). Reservations on the whole are poor and underdeveloped vis-à-vis the rest of the United States. Their unemployment rate is a towering 45 percent. Reservations also have unusually high rates of alcoholism and suicide (*U.S. News & World Report,* May 23, 1983; *New York Times,* October 29, 1973). Life expectancy on reservations is about fifty years and there is a high infant mortality rate. Exchange theorists would point to segregation and the resultant low interaction of Indians with the dominant white majority group as major factors in the whites' and Indians' disliking of each other. Of course, the displacement of American Indians by migrant Europeans has contributed to the frustration and anger of Indians toward all whites. Many Indian tribes are now suing the federal government for illegal seizure of their lands and some are receiving financial settlements (Schafer, 1979).

Other Ethnics Before 1820 most Americans were of Anglo-Saxon Protestant heritage. Even now some of the largest ethnic groups in America are virtually indistinguishable from several generation native Americans other than by their European national origin and perhaps their speaking a foreign language (see Feagin, 1984:Chs. 3–5). Included here would be those of English, Scottish, Welsh, German, Irish, Italian, or Polish national origin (see Table 6.2). For the most part these are white ethnics. The American television character, Archie Bunker, would be a good general example of those other ethnics. They tend to live in urban, working-class neighborhoods like Boston's Charlestown or Cleveland's west side. White ethnics usually resent the breaks and affirmative action advantages of blacks, Asians, Hispanics, and American Indians, with whom they compete for jobs and other scarce economic resources. We often forget the tremendous numbers of white ethnics in the United States. For example, the Germans were the largest ethnic group ever to come to America. In 1980 there were 49.2 million Americans reporting German ancestry (out of a total population of 226.5 million). Combine German ethnic

Although the largest American racial minority group is black, Hispanics, Jews, Asian-Americans, and American Indians all tend to experience problems of discrimination and prejudice similar to those of American blacks. By about the year 2000 Hispanics will be the largest racial minority group in the United States. (Peter Menzel, John R. Maher, Gary Wolinsky, John Running/Stock, Boston)

groups with 40.1 million Irish ancestry, 12.9 French ancestry, 12.2 million Italian ancestry, 10 million Scottish ancestry, 8.2 million Polish ancestry, and 6.3 million Dutch ancestry, and it is easy to see why Richard Nixon called the white ethnics in the United States the silent majority.

• Summary

Although all sexually mature healthy members of the human species can mate effectively, not all human beings share the same hereditary traits. Not only can the human population be divided in broad age and sex groups, they can also be grouped roughly by their skin color, facial features, hair, body shapes, illness propensities, and physical prowess into crude racial groups of whites, blacks, and yellows. Admittedly there are no pure races, but in fact considerable biologically based racial differences and racial inequality do exist. Sometimes racial and other groups also differ in nationality, language, religious preference, or culture. Such groups can be referred to as ethnic groups. If racial or ethnic groups lack power in a particular society, they are considered minority groups. Dominant groups in such a society are often prejudiced toward and discriminate against the racial and ethnic minority groups.

Racial or ethnic diversity are often associated with social inequality as well. For example, in the United States the black minority as a group tends to have less desirable jobs, lower average income, higher unemployment rates, fewer years of formal education, more disrupted family relations, poorer health, and shorter life expectancy rates than the typical white majority group. Minority groups in particular are likely to perceive these differential social conditions as threats, since the minority's life chances for relative well-being are diminished based on their racial or ethnic traits alone. The dominant majority group or groups, on the other hand, tend to fear the anger and potential violence of low-status minorities.

The exchange perspective reminds us that similarity is a powerful basis for social interaction. If there are biologically indicated racial differences, then, regardless of the power structure of a society, there will be differential social interaction and liking. Furthermore, as long as some blacks and whites find it rewarding to exchange domestic labor, service, compliance, entertainment, or athletic skills for the money, status, and security dominant whites tend to control, there will continue to be social inequality. Both blacks and whites share complicity in the resulting racial inequities. Also, when constitutional ideology suggests falsely that all Americans are equal, then unrealistic expected rewards tend to make minorities angry and aggressive. The American myth is that all citizens are alike or that our differences are inconsequential. The fact is that we are different in many ways—even within races—that make social differentiation and some inequality inevitable.

In the United States one undisputable racial inequality is the size of racial groups. Whites outnumber blacks about 9 to 1 and orientals about 150 to 1. Structurally this means that most American whites will not be able to have black, yellow, or nonwhite friends. The low social status of most minorities and America's history of slavery and physical segregation of minorities further discourage social interaction of whites with minorities.

Conflict enters racial and ethnic relations, since whites (often Anglo-Saxons), blacks, Asians, Hispanics, Jews, Puerto Ricans, American Indians, and so on compete for scarce economic resources. Dominant whites strive to maintain their economic advantages over racial and ethnic minorities by keeping minorities poor, uneducated, out of key jobs, without property, away from elected political offices, and so on. This oppressive pattern amounts to a vicious circle of prejudice and discrimination of majority groups against minorities. Racial and ethnic conflicts may in fact be class conflicts. Minorities function as society's source of cheap labor to do its dirty service, domestic work, and hard labor that no one wants to do.

Throughout America's history the symbolism of being black has been largely negative. Derogatory racial and ethnic minority labels often are used to justify racism. Prejudiced attitudes and racial or ethnic discrimination can be a vicious cycle that actually predetermines racial and ethnic educational opportunities, income, work, health, family life, and sense of psychological well-being.

Of course, one obvious resolution of racial or ethnic problems would be to minimize racial and ethnic differences. This is not likely to happen. People still have ethnic and racial pride and countries remain relatively autonomous units. To have one race (e.g., the human race) or one nation (e.g., earthlings) presumes at least free interaction and free interbreeding for generations. There are just too many barriers (geographic, linguistic, cultural, ideological, historical, and so on) to a unirace or uniethnicity. Assuming that racial and ethnic differences will persist, a more plausible resolution of minority problems would be to work for legal reforms that would promote educational and occupational opportunities for minorities.

Unfortunately, many minorities have found that even with similar education, jobs, or income, the white majority still considers blacks and other minorities outsiders. That is, the crucial fact may be one's race, not one's social class. To be sure, brute force could be used and has been used as a method of last recourse. But effective persistent force is just what minority groups lack in the first place. When you must display your power you are demonstrating that you do have it (and if you had it, you would not have to demonstrate it). Finally, minority force and terror usually generate an even greater repressive reaction from the white majority group. As with age and sex you cannot have the benefits of racial and ethnic differentiation without some social costs, although many question whether they must be as high as they are. In Chapter 7 we continue our examination of social problems that have physical or biosocial components in turning to physical illness and health care.

• Notes

1. Especially the First, Fifth, Sixth, Eighth, Ninth, Thirteenth, Fifteenth, and Nineteenth Amendments.

2. See the Horatio Alger Stories, such as *Ragged Dick,* 1962.

3. The Germans are the largest single immigrant group ever to come to the United States.

4. Notice that the externally enforced low social status of most blacks is a form of segregation. It has the structural consequence of restricting interaction and opportunities for blacks and other minorities (see Messner and South, 1986).

5. The major exception, of course, is South Africa.

6. Not only physically or biologically, but also socioculturally, and so on.

7. An important caveat to keep in mind is that formal organization of society into strata also resolves many problems that would accrue if all interaction had to be face-to-face in relatively small groups. That is, restriction of social interaction does not always generate social problems.

8. For example, even first generation white ethnics (such as Germans, Poles, Italians, Scots, and so on) have routinely found it easier to be perceived as "real" Americans than have second and third generation nonwhite Americans.

9. See Harriet Beecher Stowe's novel, *Uncle Tom,* 1976 ed.

10. See Chapter 15 on terrorism.

11. Just behind black Americans.

12. Most of whom were middle class.

13. The earliest Jews in America came in 1654 from Brazil.

14. While about 23 percent of all Americans are college educated, 42 percent of Jews hold college degrees.

15. American Indians, like many Mexican-Americans, are a special problem in part because they are an unassimilated defeated enemy.

• Glossary

Affirmative Action. Programs mandated largely by the federal government and courts to open up job opportunities, admission to educational institutions, and other scarce social resources to racial minorities and to women.

Assimilation. The process whereby minority group members give up their ancestral customs and adopt the culture of the majority group.

Authoritarian Personality. Personal traits, such as rigidity, moralism, and preoccupation with power and status, that often accompany prejudice.

Black Power. Self-determination and separatism of black people (their property, organizations, and culture) from the dominant (usually white) majority group, by force, confrontation, and terror.

Discrimination. Actions against minority groups on the grounds of their group membership and supposed group characteristics; granting or denying privileges on grounds rationally irrelevant to a situation.

Ethnic Group. Any group that can be set off by race, religion, or national origin.

Genotype. The hereditary characteristics contained in an individual's genes.

Hispanic. Anyone of Spanish origin.

Majority Group. The dominant group in a society that tends to have the greatest wealth, power, prestige, and privilege.

Minority Group. A group of people who, because of their physical or cultural characteristics, are singled out from the others in a society in which they live for differential and unequal treatment, and who therefore regard themselves as objects of collective discrimination.

Passing. Acting as if one were a member of a racial (or ethnic) group that one in fact is not a member of.

Phenotype. The observable hereditary characteristics of an individual.

Pogrom. An organized massacre or attack on Jewish people or a similar persecution of any minority group.

Prejudice. The prejudged negative attitudes toward minority groups; an irrational categorical like or dislike for a group of people.

Race. A division of a species that differs from other divisions by the frequency with which certain hereditary traits appear among its members; a population that through generations of inbreeding has developed more or less distinctive physical characteristics that are transmitted genetically.

Racial Pluralism. Racial groups maintaining their racial identities and differences but still coexisting peacefully and equally.

Racism. The dominant group members' feelings of superiority to members of minority groups and their use of these feelings and of the "customary way things are done in society" to keep minorities in a subordinate position.

Segregation. Laws or customs that restrict contact between (here, racial) groups, such as those with respect to housing, education, jobs, sexual relations, and marriage.

Silent Majority. The large number of white ethnics in America, such as the Germans, Poles, Irish, and Italians, that are virtually indistinguishable from "native" Americans.

Species. A population in which any two healthy sexually mature members of the opposing sex can mate and produce a normal and fertile offspring.

Uncle Tomism. A black person conforming to white racist roles and thereby supporting racism and majority-group dominance.

Vicious Circle. The interdependence of social and physical factors such that system consequences tend to feed back and reinforce system assumptions; here, those of prejudice and discrimination.

WASP. A white, Anglo-Saxon, Protestant; often considered the dominant racial and ethnic group in America.

White Backlash. The response of the dominant white majority to actions of American minorities.

White Flight. The migration of white populations away from minority-group populations, as from the central city to suburbia or from public to private schools.

• Further Reading

Berry, Mary Frances and John W. Blassingame. *Long Memory: The Black Experience in America.* New York: Oxford University Press, 1982. A book for blacks by blacks. Details the African heritage and the American oppression, complete with significant dates in black American history. Chapters on family, church, sex, politics, economics, criminal justice, education, military service, and black nationalism—all as seen by blacks.

de la Garza et al., eds. *The Mexican-American Experience.* Austin: University of Texas Press, 1985. An anthology of the best papers published in *Social Science Quarterly* (a special issue) on Mexican-Americans. The result is thirty papers designed for undergraduate understanding of an ethnic group that will soon surpass blacks as the largest American minority. Focuses on the labor market, politics, and the social and cultural context of the U.S. Mexican-American experience.

Feagin, Joe R. *Racial and Ethnic Relations.* Englewood Cliffs, NJ: Prentice-Hall, 1984. Provides in-depth reviews of various American ethnic groups not usually considered so thoroughly. Included in this review are English, Irish, Italian, Jewish, Indian, black, Mexican, Puerto Rican, and Japanese Americans. Well written, readable, and well documented.

Jakes, John. *North and South.* New York: Harcourt Brace Jovanovich, 1982. Number one best-seller (1982) from the *New York Times Sunday Review of Books.* A historical novel of two families in pre-Civil War Charlestown, South Carolina (the Mains), and Lehigh, Pennsylvania (the Hazzards). Gives an early exchange portrayal of slavery and plantation life. For example, many Southerners argued that African blacks could tolerate the southern heat and swampy lowlands (e.g., had resistance to sun and malaria) involved with rice and cotton cultivation better than whites could.

Marrett, Cora Bagley and Cheryl Leggon. *Research in Race and Ethnic Relations.* Greenwich, CN: JAI Press, 1985. This book is more advanced and technical than the others recommended. About a dozen sociologists offer hard data and empirical models focusing on socioeconomic and social stratification factors in race and ethnic relations. Some of the most recent data on race by some of our best and most well-trained young sociologists. Topics include stereotypes, affirmative action, racial terminology, social class polarization, and occupational segregation.

Simpson, George E. and J. Milton Yinger. *Racial and Cultural Minorities: An Analysis of Prejudice and Discrimination.* New York: Harper & Row, 1985. Fifth edition of the classical text on prejudice and discrimination. Chapters on the personality aspects of prejudice and minorities, intermarriage, religion, education, and art of minorities. One of the definitive sociological treatises on prejudice and discrimination. In print for over thirty years.

CHAPTER 7

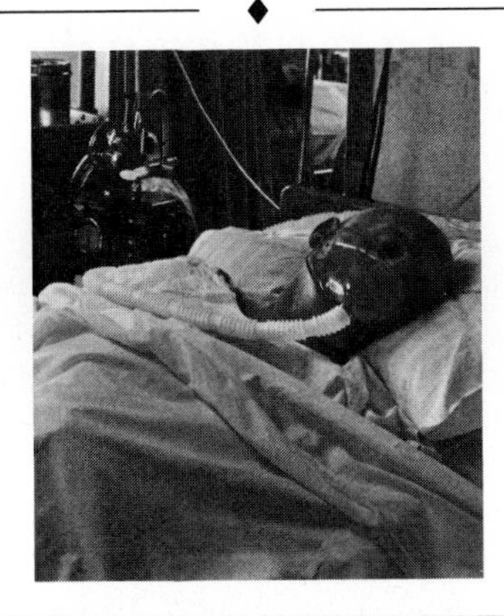

Physical Illness and Health Care

Physical health and long life are, and always have been, among the most valuable of all individual and social assets. Exchange principles remind us that those activities that are the most valuable, rewarding, and scarce will cost the most in a free society with a competitive market based on supply and demand. We will pay almost anything to avoid pain, illness, or death. Furthermore, social interaction with the ill tends not to be valuable or intrinsically rewarding. Thus, the high cost of health care in the United States is not surprising.

Structurally, most well people are unlikely to interact with sick people both because of the large numbers of healthy people and the small numbers, physical isolation, and limited activity of sick people. Bureaucratic organization, which is a must in a modern, large, dense, urban society, is costly and governed by elites. Structural factors also encourage a complex, refined division of labor, which in turn spawns costly medical specialization. The autonomy and power of the medical profession, as well as the entry of private business into medical care, have both driven costs up.

The conflict perspective argues that costs for physical illness and health care are excessively high because medical personnel, hospitals, and health insurance plans do not exist for health care, but rather for private profit. The patients' ability to pay, not their need for health care, determines the availability, quality, and promptness of medical services. Thus, the American health care system is poorly coordinated with the needs of the truly sick, who are often poor.

The picture of the American health care system that emerges from the symbolic interaction perspective is one of considerable subjectivity, arbitrariness, in which the interpretations and values of powerful interest groups hold sway. For example, the United States has twice as many surgeons per capita as Great Britain. The United States is also the only industrialized society without a national health insurance plan. The essence of the symbolic interaction approach to health care costs is that Americans have certain shared meanings or subjective perceptions about physical illness and its treatment that are not objectively required.

———— ♦ ————

It is easy to imagine physical illness being a problem for us as individuals. Being ill or injured hurts, it causes inconveniences, sometimes makes us unable to work or go to school. In the extreme case of death our entire physical life, the world as we know it, ends for us. Scary stuff! But why should physical illness trouble society? After all, none of us is socially irreplaceable. If anything, there are too many people in the world, not too few.[1] Why, in short, is physical illness a social problem (Levine, 1987)? In part the answer is that being ill simply costs too much (indeed this is the major focus of the chapter), more than it needs to, especially for the poor, minorities, and those that live in rural areas. But that is only part of the answer, and the reasons for the high costs of health are not altogether obvious.

Also, apart from the high costs of health care (especially for certain Americans), if people are sick and unable to perform their regular social roles, then society itself can be disrupted. Usually when people are ill, we give them temporary leave from their social responsibilities (Parsons, 1951; Conrad & Kern, 1986). However, if too many people are ill for too long, then this incapacitation can be a threat to the very operation of society.[2] Jobs and duties that must be done do in fact not get done. As with the individual, if enough people actually die (e.g., as in the Great Plague in London in 1665), then whole societies (or at least major social groups) can die. This possibility may appear a little far-fetched, since few, if any, societies have ever disappeared because of the physical illness and death of its members. However, it could happen in a modern nuclear war in which most of those people who were not killed by direct injury would die later of radiation poisoning or in a new plaguelike epidemic of autoimmune deficiency syndrome (AIDS; cf. Tanne, 1985).

Physical illness need not result in widespread death for there to be social problems. All that is required is for illness, aging, or death to be variable or unpredictable. As we shall see in later materials in this chapter (e.g., in Table 7.1), paradoxically, it can be a problem that people live much longer now than they did at the turn of the century. Social welfare organizations (like the U.S. Social Security Administration) react slowly to changes in the proportion of

PANEL 7.1

The High Cost of Medical Care

"The health provider industry is betting that if we cannot get competition, we're going to do nothing," said Dr. Robert J. Rubin, assistant secretary for planning and evaluation in the Department of Health and Human Services. "They are making an error," he went on, adding that if Government regulation was the only choice left, Government regulation it would be.

The expenses that patients must pay out of their own pockets have risen, of course. Usually, the bulk of the cost is not the responsibility of the patient, since insurance companies and the Government pay it.

And so, for most Americans in the last ten to fifteen years, price has been no object when it came to medical care. They have come to expect and demand the best that modern medicine can offer, whatever it costs, whether or not it is really necessary.

All too often it is not necessary, almost everyone who has analyzed the situation agrees. An army of critics charge that physicians order far too many laboratory tests, overuse medicine's wondrous but terribly expensive new technology, and put too many people in the hospital for too long.

The hidden costs of this waste are enormous. The Government deficit rises to meet the soaring cost of Medicare, which pays most medical bills for Americans sixty-five and older, and Medicaid, the health program for the poor. Workers draw lower wages than they otherwise might because their employers must pay higher health insurance premiums. Consumers pay higher prices for goods because companies pass on the higher cost of those premiums.

Almost one dollar in every ten generated by the American economy goes for medical care today, as against one dollar in twenty two decades ago. Americans spend about as much trying to stay well as they do buying and operating automobiles, and almost twice as much as they spend on clothing and jewelry.

Neither the Federal budget nor the national debt has grown nearly as rapidly as health care expenditures. By roughly doubling every six to eight years, the nation's medical bill has become a major driver of inflation. No other component of the Consumer Price Index exceeded medicine's 12.5 percent increase last year.

Moreover, when the rise in the overall inflation rate has slowed, as it has in recent months, medical costs have continued to rise as fast as ever. The Consumer Price Index in February increased at an annual rate of 3 percent. Medical costs jumped at a rate of more than 8 percent. And hospital costs, where the rise is consistently most rapid, increased by more than 11 percent. This suggests that in times of falling inflation rates and economic contraction, medical costs claim an even greater share of the gross national product, the total share of the nation's annual output of goods and services.

Source: *New York Times,* March 28, 1982.

the aged in the population. One problematic result is that the government may not be able to pay for the support of our aged population in the very near future (Kreps, 1979).

We also must realize that many physical illnesses have social causes. Agran (1979), in "Getting Cancer on the Job," demonstrates that some of the chemicals and materials workers are required to be exposed to in their jobs are known carcinogens (Bale, 1985). These include vinyl chloride (used in plastics), asbestos (used in insulation), and benzidine and benzene (used in paints). Our modern social lifestyles also contribute to certain types of physical illnesses. It is well known that cigarette smoking causes cancer. About 35 percent of American males and 30 percent of American females (1983) smoke *(Health, United States, 1985:*74). Fourteen percent of men and 24 percent of women are overweight. Obesity in the United States is related to low levels of exercise and the type of foodstuffs advertised and marketed. Rosenman et al. (1975) have argued convincingly that coronary heart disease is associated with occupational stress. Of course, in this review of social factors in physical health we do not wish to deny that the profit motives of those in the health care industry may contribute to poor health, inferior health care (for some), and poor safety policies.

It follows that the problems and issues of physical illness and health care are not one, but many. Of course, we need to determine if the medical and health care industry is exploiting the consumer; if physicians charge too much for their services, and how they manage to get away with it (cf. Starr, 1982; cf. Coser, 1984; Evans, 1984); whether the United States should have a national health insurance plan; if Americans really need all the surgery they get; and how the costs for hospital and nursing home care can be lowered. But the problems of illness and health care go beyond issues of cost and what causes them. Another important issue is: "Are the American people really all that sick"? McKeown (1978, 1980) has argued that Americans are getting healthier, completely apart from (or in some cases, in spite of) innovations in medical technology. This may not be as true for American blacks, Hispanics, the elderly, or the poor in general.

Others have suggested that our modern medical care system itself actually causes (not cures) or produces illness (Illich, 1976). *Iatrogenesis* is the creation of illness or health problems by medical care. This concept implies that many contemporary health problems are not biologically rooted, but rather are social and organizational in origin (McKeown, 1980; Dubos, 1979). Still another issue is whether the stresses, demands, and pressures of modern life experiences actually preclude health. Finally, when illness or health care results in death, there is an issue about how we react as a society. Are illness and death seen as technical failures? Are death and illness ever appropriate or should they be denied and moribund individuals kept in hospitals and nursing homes apart from their families and the rest of us? Space will preclude consideration of death and dying issues. These, then, are some of the key issues we must address

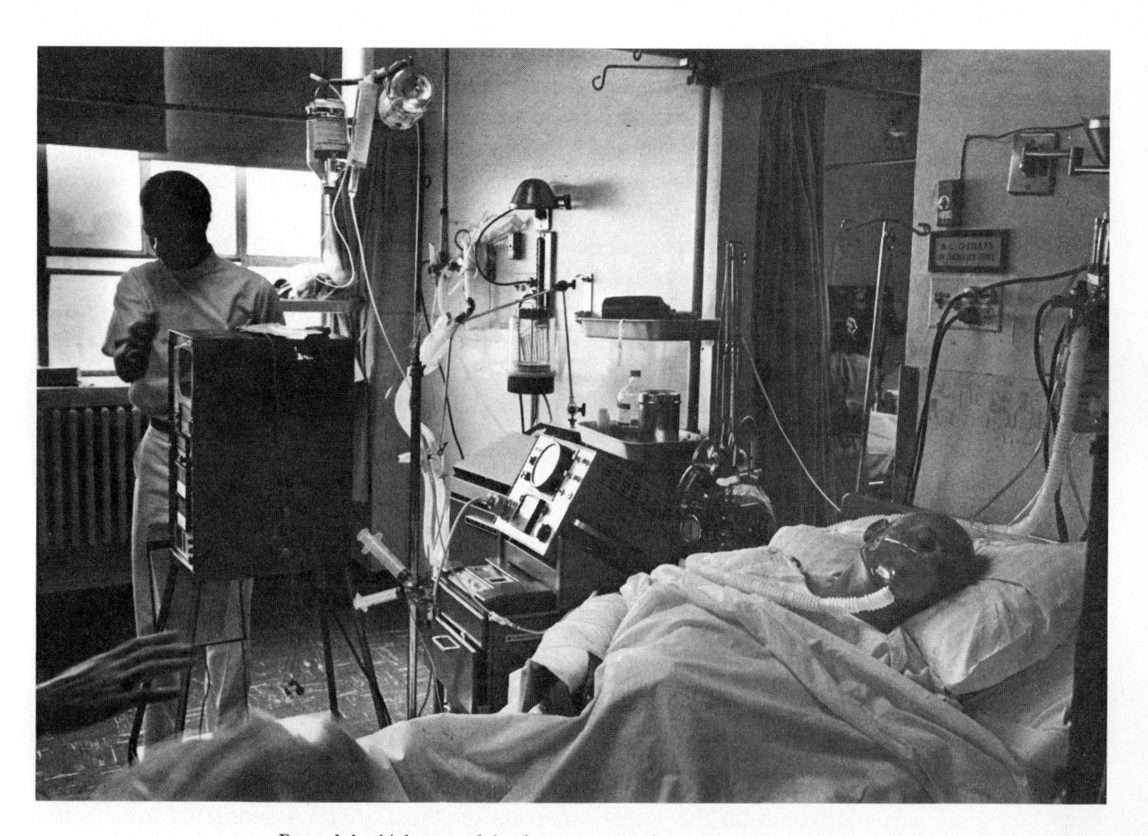

Part of the high cost of death care results from the use of modern medical technology. Respirators, heart monitors, drugs, constant nursing supervision, catheters and IVs, and so on, all push intensive care unit day costs to around $500—not to mention the costs for CAT scans, ultrasound procedures, surgery, dialysis, and so on. (George W. Gardner/Stock, Boston)

and try to resolve in the following pages. But before we move directly to these issues, we first need to attempt to be clear about what we mean when we speak of health, illness, and health care.

Health is a difficult concept to define, since it often indicates being symptom free or the absence of illness. But health is not only this. The World Health Organization's constitution defines *health* as "a state of complete physical, mental, and social well-being, not merely the absence of disease or infirmity" (Twaddle, 1974:9). According to Dubos (1979:74) *health* is "a measure of a person's ability to do and become what he or she wants to become" (cf. Illich's notion of health as a "process of adaptation"; 1976:273). Thus, we conceive of health as a positive condition going beyond the mere absence of symptoms of illness or disease. Having defined health, our definition of health care is easy. *Health care* "encompasses those activities concerned with the promotion and protection of health" (Twaddle, 1974:4).

Illness behavior is usually dichotomized into mortality and morbidity. *Mor-*

tality is the rate of death (as in Table 7.1), for example, of the leading causes of death. Notice that death is precise, relatively unambiguous, and likely to generate more accurate data than illness (Peterson, 1975:242ff.). *Morbidity,* the rate of illness(es), is vaguer and subject to more measurement problems. It is customary in describing illnesses to contrast acute disease (one that is severe or has a rapid onset and lasts less than three months, e.g., appendicitis or flu) with chronic disease (disease either lasting a long time or recurring, e.g., cancer, diabetes, ulcers, kidney or heart disease. See *Health, United States, 1985* and Table 7.3).[3]

When we take a brief look at some of these data on health and illness in the United States (the objective conditions) we see that, indeed, in many respects Americans are getting healthier (as McKeown, 1980, claimed). For example, Table 7.1 reveals that since 1900 the death rate (from all causes) has been cut roughly in half (17.2 to 8.6). Concurrently, since 1900 the overall American life expectancy has increased about 50 percent (from 49.3 to 73.3). Infant mortality rates have been reduced drastically. Since the turn of the century the leading causes of death have shifted from influenza, pneumonia, tuberculosis, and gastroenterological illnesses to heart disease, cancer, stroke, and violent death (*Health, United States,* 1985:39). Since the modern leading causes of death occur late in life and are related to aging, further declines in the death rate will be modest and slow. Today the average American loses only about 6.4 days of work per year to sickness (*Health, United States,* 1986:14).

Some have argued (McKeown, 1978, 1980) that Americans' improved health derives from the fittest surviving (in the Darwinian sense) or from better

TABLE 7.1 Death Rates and Life Expectancy by Race and Sex, 1900, 1982, and 1983

	1900 Death Rate (per 1,000 population)	**1900 Life Expectancy in Years (at birth)**	**1982 Death Rate (per 1,000 population)**	**1982 Age-Adjusted Death Rate***	**1983 Life Expectancy In Years (at birth)**
Total	17.2	49.3	8.6	5.6	74.7
Males, all races	17.9	47.9	9.5	7.4	71.0
Females, all races	16.5	50.7	7.7	4.1	78.3
Whites, both sexes	17.0	—	8.8	5.3	75.2
Males	17.7	—	9.6	7.1	71.6
Females	16.3	—	8.0	4.0	78.8
Other races, both sexes	25.0	—	8.2	7.8	71.3
Males	25.7	—	9.7	10.5	67.1
Females	24.4	—	6.8	5.7	75.3

*Age-adjustment is the application of age-specific death rates in a population of interest to a standardized age distribution to eliminate the differences in observed rates that result from age differences in population composition.

Source: *Statistical Abstract of the United States,* 1985, Tables 102 and 105. 1900 data from Bogue, 1969:593.

nutrition and hygiene (Illich, 1976), *not* from improved health care or medical technology. The conquest of tuberculosis actually took place far *before* the use of chemotherapy or vaccination (McKeown, 1980:81). However, extreme caution must be used in jumping to such conclusions, since obviously new drugs and surgical procedures (for example) have saved many lives and prolonged others that would have been lost only a few years ago (*Newsweek,* August 29, 1983).

We must also note that violent deaths (e.g., suicide, homicide, and accidents) have increased their ranks among the leading causes of death (cf. Brim et al., 1970:450), while death rates from heart disease and cancer have decreased somewhat in the last thirty years in the United States. At the same time industrial hazards and related illnesses and deaths (e.g., cancer, lung disease, and so on) have increased (Agran, 1979; *Statistical Abstract of the United States,* 1986:73).

Morbidity, as opposed to mortality, is more difficult to measure, since it is intrinsically vague, complex, and often not reported. Using days of hospital care as an indicator of U.S. morbidity prevalence, we see that not controlling for age or sex, 11 percent of hospital morbidity was for heart disease and 8 percent for cancer (in 1979). This morbidity finding is consistent with prior mortality data. Among men age sixty-five or older the percentages for days of hospital care for heart disease and cancer rise to 19 percent and 15 percent, respectively. For men and women under age fifteen pneumonia is the number one cause of hospital care. For women fifteen to forty-four years old, of course, child delivery constitutes 26 percent of all hospital care.

As we shall see shortly in following sections of this chapter, stress and our modern lifestyle are related to increased risk of heart disease, cancer, gastroenterological problems, and stroke (Rosenman and Chesney, 1980; Holmes and Rahe, 1967). Finally, it is true that the costs of illness and health care are disproportionately high and are escalating (see below). We observe in Table 7.2 that life expectancy and quality of life (PQLI) are both affected by wealth. Generally, the higher the public health expenditure per capita, the greater calorie consumption per capita per day, the more physicians per person, and the higher the gross national product (GNP) per person, then the better are a society's health and life expectancy. In what follows below we will examine (primarily) the high cost of health care in the United States, the role that physicians play in determining health care costs, and the relationship of stress to physical illness. However, before we begin to review these topics, we need to examine briefly the general biological determinants of physical illness.

• Biological and Physical Determinants of Illness

A pervasive tendency in sociology is to minimize medical technology and biological factors in illness and to exaggerate social and economic factors (Illich, 1976; Kotelchuck, 1976; Mechanic, 1979). The truth is that biology, technology, and medical science also make incredibly important positive contributions

TABLE 7.2 Inequality and Health in the Mid-1970s, International Comparisons

Country	PQLI*	IMR† 1000	Male Life Expectancy	Public Health $/Capita	Calories/ Capita/Day	Inhabitants/ Physician	GNP‡ Person	% In Absolute Poverty§
Sweden	100	9	72 years	582	2810	645	$8670	0
U.S.A.	96	15	69	218	3330	622	7890	0
Cuba	86	27	68	20	—	1153	860	0
Mexico	75	50	63	8	2580	1385	1090	10
Philippines	73	59	57	3	2260	2632	410	16
Iraq	46	27	51	6	2160	2369	1390	11
India	41	122	42	1	2210	4162	150	36
Yeman Arab Republic	27	—	44	1	2040	26,449	250	
Chad	20	160	29	1	2060	44,382	120	75

*PQLI—Physical Quality of Life Index, an average of life expectancy, infant mortality, and literacy.
†IMR—Infant Mortality Rate, the number of deaths of infants under 1 year per 1000 live births.
‡GNP—Gross National Product.
§Absolute Poverty—"poverty so stark and dehumanizing that it is inconceivable for most Western societies."

Source: *The Book of World Rankings,* by George Thomas Kurian. © 1979. Reprinted with permission of Facts On File, Inc., New York.

to our health and health care. Just remind yourself of the illnesses related to biological factors we have considered already, namely, those of age, sex, and race. For example, although people are living longer today (Figure 4.1), almost no one lives beyond 100 years.[4] A finite human life span is biologically given (Chapter 4). During our lives we all age inexorably. Biological aging entails lower metabolic rates, deterioration of cells (especially in the brain), diminished sexual potency, accumulation of metabolic wastes, accumulated disease debits, having our hair thin, turn white, and fall out, decay of our teeth, diminished hearing and seeing capabilities, wrinkling of our skin, atrophying of our muscles, sleeping less soundly, more vascular malfunctions, and lowered energy levels, just to mention a few traits. There are also age-specific illnesses. For example, males age sixty-five or older have a much higher rate of heart disease, cancer, stroke, and prostate problems (than younger men). Older females have greater rates of fractures, arthritic troubles, and eye problems (than younger women), in addition to an increased risk of heart trouble, cancer, and stroke.

In the chapter on sex (Chapter 5) we saw that males have greater mortality rates than females at all ages (even *in utero*) (Waldron, 1986). Hemophilia and color blindness are more common in men than women. Of course, the illnesses that relate to male or female reproductive organs are sexually unique. Included here would be prostatitis for males and uterine cancer, complications of childbirth, and breast cancer for females. Turning to race (Chapter 6) you will recall that sickle-cell anemia is greatest among African blacks, that cancer is much more common among whites, that Tay-Sachs disease (involving progressive deterioration of the central nervous system) predominates among central and eastern European Jews, that American blacks are more subject to frostbite than whites, and that the Rh blood factor is virtually absent among Mongoloids.

In addition to the age, sex, and race related illnesses, in the last thirty years there have been mind-boggling advances in medical technology and drugs. With the advent of modern surgical procedures many people who would have died, been crippled, disabled, or in chronic pain only a few years ago now can lead relatively productive and comfortable lives. These procedures include various surgeries from a simple appendectomy to complicated neurological procedures for a back disk removal and/or fusion. Among the most dramatic of these new surgical procedures are organ transplants (*Newsweek,* August 29, 1983). Figure 7.1 shows that although transplant operations are expensive and the mortality rate is still high in many cases, organ replacement is often the only hope remaining for many terminally ill patients (notably those with heart disease). When surgery does fail, new equipment (like kidney dialysis, respirators, heart pacemakers, and so on) allows many lives to continue. Cancer has been more intractable and resistant to medical technology. But even here genetic research (*New York Times Magazine,* October 24, 1982) has advanced to the point where microscopic segments of DNA only one gene in length can turn laboratory animals' cells cancerous. Presumably, if we can cause cancer, we should be able to reverse the causal chain and prevent cancer. Other exciting and promising research (e.g., on the two-stage development of cancer) is also underway.

The progress with modern drugs and illness prevention or cure has been nothing short of astounding. In the late 1930s and early 1940s penicillin and streptomycin appeared and allowed physicians better control of some infectious diseases that previously had damaged vital organs (such as heart valves and kidneys) and often led to death. In 1955 Jonas Salk developed an effective vaccine for polio. At about the same time phenothiazine drugs (e.g., Thorazine and Mellaril) were marketed for the treatment of psychotic disorders like schizophrenia (see Chapter 8). Lithium was found effective in managing manic-depressive illnesses (Gattozzi, 1970). More recently, the introduction of beta-blockers (e.g., Inderal, Corgard, and Tenormin) have provided new hope for sufferers of hypertensive disease, arrhythmias, migraine headaches, and anxiety. Of course, these drugs, biological factors, and medical advances represent only the tip of the proverbial iceberg. However, they should be sufficient to persuade even the most skeptical reader that illness and health care cannot be reduced to social factors alone. Having proclaimed this important caveat, let us now turn to an examination of the high costs of physical illness and health care.

• The Costs of Sickness

Stating the Problem It should come as no surprise that most of us cannot afford to get sick; it simply costs too much (*U.S. News and World Report,* August 22, 1983). This is especially true for the poor, the aged, blacks, His-

FIGURE 7.1 How Transplants Save Lives

REPLACING THE BODY'S PARTS

Using sophisticated new drugs that help prevent rejection of donated organs and more meticulous techniques for splicing the replacements, surgeons have been able to improve dramatically the success rates of transplants for a variety of organs.

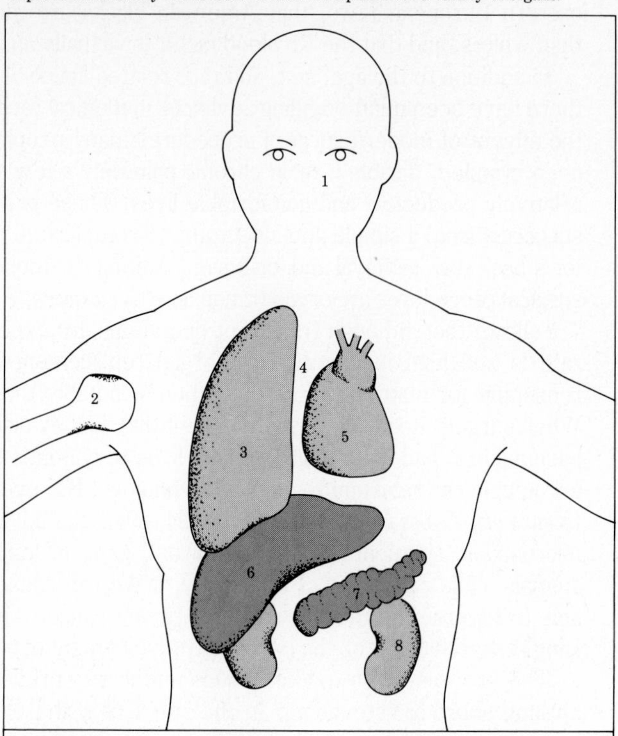

1. CORNEA

Total Transplants: 128,000

Success Rate:
90% of patients have improved vision.

Cost: $2,500–$5,000

2. BONE MARROW

Total Transplants: 2,049

Success Rate:
Terminal leukemia, 15% cured;
aplastic anemia, 80% cured;
acute leukemia in first remission, 60% cured (children), 40% cured (adults).

Cost: $60,000–$150,000

3. LUNG

Total Transplants: 36

Success Rate:
Longest surviving patient lived 10 months.

Cost: $50,000–$150,000

(Data are worldwide.)

4. HEART-LUNG

Total Transplants: 22

Success Rate:
13 patients are still living.

Cost: $78,000–$92,000

5. HEART

Total Transplants: 500

Success Rate:
78% patient survival after one year, 58% after three years, 42% after five years.

Cost: $57,000–$110,000

6. LIVER

Total Transplants: 540

Sucesss Rate:
Liver cancer, 26% patient survival after one year; noncancerous liver disease, 39% patient survival after one year.

Cost: $54,000–$238,000

(Data for U.S. and Western Europe. University of Pittsburg reports a 66% one-year survival rate after 139 liver transplants.)

7. PANCREAS

Total Transplants: 334

Success Rate:
25% of the grafts function.
Patient can survive on insulin if transplant fails.

Cost: $18,000–$50,000

(Data are worldwide.)

8. KIDNEY

Total Transplants:
No total figures available; 23,076 transplants done in the last five years.

Success Rate:
51% graft survival after one year, 40% after three years, 31% after five years.
Patient can survive on dialysis if transplant fails.

Cost: $25,000–$35,000

The number of transplants are U.S. totals unless otherwise noted. Sources: Battelle Human Affairs Research Centers; The Fred Hutchinson Cancer Research Center; University of Minnesota Medical School; Eye Bank Association of America.

Source: *Newsweek,* August 29, 1983:40. Reprinted by permission of Bob Conrad.

panics, those in lower social statuses, and other minority group members. The proportion of Americans' expenditures on physical illness and health care is larger than other items and is rising, whether we define costs as a proportion of the U.S. gross national product or the relative amount of the consumer price index spent on medical care (see Figure 7.2; cf. *New York Times,* March 28, 1982). In 1975 health care costs were more than our national defense costs (Kotelchuck, 1976:5)![5] About half of all bankruptcies are related to medical bills and serious illnesses (*New York Times,* May 7, 1978; *Time,* May 28,

FIGURE 7.2 The Growing Cost of Medical Care

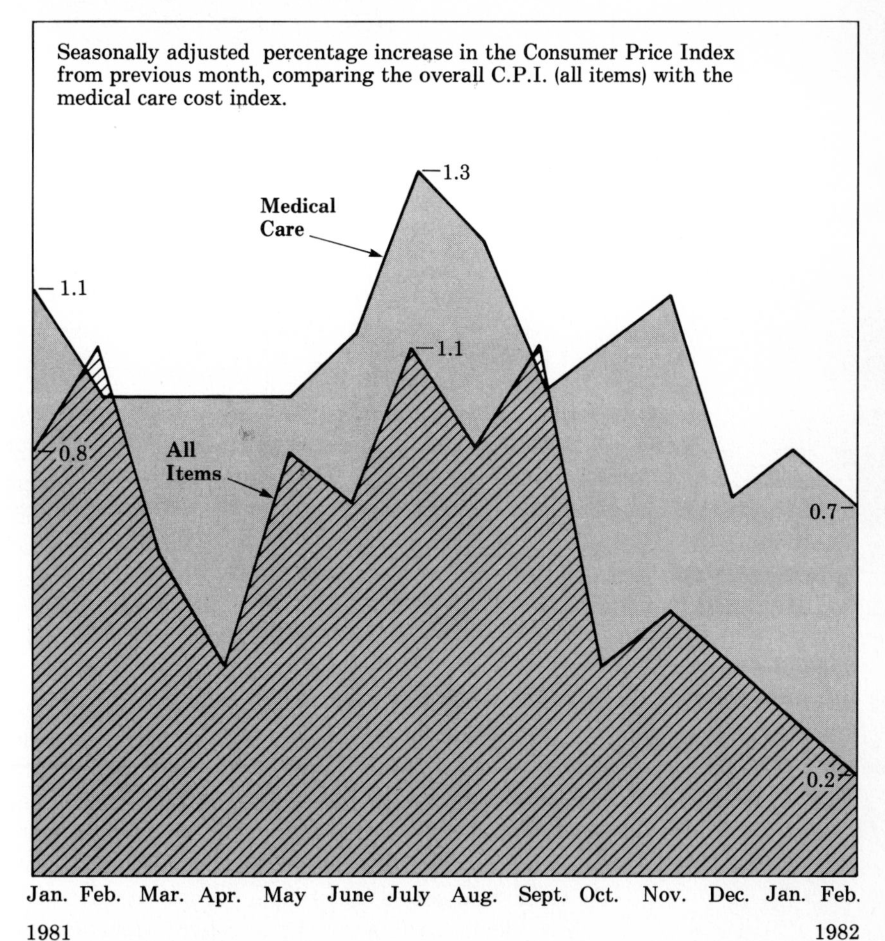

Note: The CPI measures the changes in the average price of a basket of goods and services purchased by the typical urban family—food, automobiles, housing, furniture, clothes, doctor's services, and so on.

Source: *New York Times,* March 28, 1982. Copyright © 1982 by The New York Times Company. Reprinted by permission.

1979). It is estimated that by 1990 U.S. health care costs will total $758 billion a year (*U.S. News and World Report,* September 1, 1980). In 1984 the total expenditure of $387.4 billion amounted to $1,580 for every person in the United States (*Health, United States,* 1985:128). Between 1967 and 1984 American medical care costs rose 380 percent (*Statistical Abstract of the United States,* 1986:477). By 1984 average inpatient hospital day costs were roughly $411 per day.

When we break down general health care costs into specific types of expenditures, it is apparent that most of both the total dollar output and the rise in health care costs has occurred in hospital and nursing home charges. Table 7.3 reveals that about 50 percent of each health care dollar goes for hospitals or nursing homes. This compares with about 20 percent for physician services. Hospital and nursing home percentage expenditures have increased about 34 percent and 453 percent, respectively, since 1950. Physician services and drug costs, on the other hand, have actually declined 10 percent and 51 percent in the same time period (1950–84).

If we define costs according to activity limitation (that is, restricted days, bed days, work loss, and so on) we see that about six and one-half work days per year (1983) are lost to illness; about sixteen days for men and twenty-one days for women are restricted by illness each year, and that men spend about six days in bed each year compared to about eight days for women (cf. Nathanson, 1977).

TABLE 7.3 National Health Expenditures and Percent Distribution, According to Type of Expenditure: United States, Selected Years 1950–84

Data Are Compiled by the Health Care Financing Administration

Type of Expenditure	1950	1960	1965	1970	1975	1980	1982	1983	1984
					Amount in Billions				
Total	$ 12.7	$ 26.9	$ 41.9	$ 75.0	$132.7	$247.5	$321.2	$355.1	$387.4
					Percent Distribution				
All expenditures	100.0	100.0	100.0	100.0	100.0	100.0	100.0	100.0	100.0
Health service and supplies	92.4	93.6	91.6	92.8	93.7	95.2	95.6	95.7	95.9
Personal health care	86.0	88.0	85.5	87.1	88.3	88.5	88.7	88.8	88.2
Hospital care	30.4	33.8	33.3	37.3	39.5	40.9	41.9	41.9	40.8
Physician services	21.7	21.1	20.2	19.1	18.8	18.9	19.2	19.3	19.5
Dentist services	7.6	7.4	6.7	6.3	6.2	6.2	6.1	6.1	6.5
Nursing home care	1.5	2.0	4.9	6.3	7.6	8.2	8.4	8.3	8.3
Other professional services	3.1	3.2	2.5	2.1	2.0	2.3	2.2	2.3	2.3
Drugs and drug sundries	13.6	13.6	12.4	10.7	9.0	7.5	6.8	6.7	6.7
Eyeglasses and appliances	3.9	2.9	2.8	2.6	2.4	2.1	1.7	1.8	1.9
Other health services	4.2	4.0	2.7	2.8	2.8	2.4	2.4	2.4	2.4
Expenses for prepayment	3.6	4.1	4.2	3.8	3.0	3.7	4.0	4.1	4.9
Government public health activities	2.9	1.5	1.9	1.9	2.4	2.9	2.9	2.8	2.8
Research and construction	7.6	6.4	8.4	7.2	6.3	4.8	4.4	4.3	4.1
Research	0.9	2.5	3.6	2.6	2.5	2.2	1.8	1.7	1.8
Construction	6.7	3.9	4.8	4.6	3.8	2.6	2.6	2.6	2.3

Note: The Health Care Financing Administration has made revisions in their health expenditure estimates. Data in this table may differ from those appearing in earlier volumes of *Health, United States.*

Source: Office of the Actuary: National health expenditures, 1984, by K. R. Levit, H. Lazenby, D. R. Waldo, and L. M. Davidoff. *Health Care Financing Review,* Fall 1985.

Americans also spend an inordinate amount of money on drugs and surgery. Kotelchuck claims that drug companies are among the most profitable of all industries (1976:27). In the United States patent law allows charging seventeen years of whatever the traffic will allow. It follows that the cost of drugs is not determined by the cost of production of the drugs. Typically patent name-brand drugs cost far more (sometimes twenty times more) than generic drugs having virtually the same chemical composition. For example, Barnhardt discovered that Prednisone (used for its antiinflammatory effects) sold under Schering's brand name, Meticorten, for $102.57 per 1,000 (in about 1975), but for only $4.40 per 1,000 from a wholesaler dealing in a generic brand of Prednisone. Other brand versus generic drug prices (1986 prices) include Valium (5 milligram tablet—27 cents each for brand name versus 6 cents for generic), Erthromycin (an antibiotic—14 cents for brand name versus 7 cents for generic), Aldactone (a diuretic—22 cents for brand name versus 5 cents for generic), and Amoxicillin (an antibiotic—12 cents for brand name versus 8 cents for generic).

PANEL 7.2

A Southern Medical Empire: Cool-Handed Duke

Durham, North Carolina, has one of the highest venereal disease rates in the country. The fetal death rate is nearly twice the national average. People in Durham are not very healthy, and all indications point to their getting less so.

The health problems of Durham are not due to a lack of doctors or facilities. In fact, health is the leading industry in the city. More than 9,000 people in this city of 135,000 are employed by health institutions. Together the three general hospitals have 1,141 beds. Durham County also has lots of specialized medical services. It has four times the ratio of radiologists to population as the average for the rest of the country, five times that of neurosurgeons, three times the ratio of psychiatrists, and six times that of orthopedic surgeons. However, the area has only one-seventh the ratio of general practitioners to population as the country as a whole.

In order to be a great medical center, Duke needs access to a community hospital from which to draw its teaching material and an academic hospital in which to do its research and make its money. The power structure of Durham has been obliging in both respects. A new community hospital is now under construction, and work is about to begin on the new university hospital.

Source: Bermanzohn and McGloin, *Prognosis Negative: Crisis in the Health Care System,* David Kotelchuck, ed., pp. 45–46. Copyright 1976, Random House, Inc.

Many observers of the health care scene also believe that Americans tend to have needless surgery encouraged by greedy surgeons, a technical revolution gone mad, and by a profit-hungry medical industry (*Newsweek,* October 31, 1983). To support these claims it is noted, for example, that cesarean sections in the United States increased from 6 percent to 21 percent of all births from 1965 to 1984 (Califano, 1978; *Statistical Abstract of the U.S.,* 1987:62). Between 1979 and 1983 cesarean sections rose from 599,000 to 808,000. Correcting for population size, the rate per 1,000 population rose from 4.7 (1979) to 5.9 (1983) (*Health United States,* 1985:95). The United States presently has the highest rate of elective surgery in the world (*Newsweek,* April 10, 1978; Brody, 1978). One reason for this is simply the large number of surgeons in America. For example, the United States has twice the number of surgeons per capita as England. Of course, one must remember that while surgical procedures are subject to abuse, they also offer us dramatic relief from illnesses and injuries that was previously unavailable (Kutner, 1987).

It would seem that medical insurance would help hold the costs of sickness and hospitalization down. After all, about 80 percent to 90 percent of Americans have some health insurance, if they are working (*New York Times,* May 7, 1978:69). However, cynics contend that insurance plans like Blue Cross-Blue

PANEL 7.3

Surgeon Alex Bissel on Making Money in Medicine

But I don't see anything wrong with making money. After all, the surgeon is responsible for all the suffering, injury, and even death if the surgery is performed incorrectly. The art of surgery makes it a service more valuable than that of the plumber, to my thinking, and even though plumbers are paid excessively in our society, I think surgeons should be paid more. I think that a patient actually respects the doctor who works for a reasonably high fee. He feels he's got a better doctor working for him. No patient has actually said that, but they act like that.

The classic story is the story of Steinmetz, who was asked personally by Henry Ford to come to the River Rouge plant and decide where to position the basic switches for the electrical system of the whole plant. Mr. Steinmetz said, "Do you really want me?" And Ford said yes, so Steinmetz went to the River Rouge plant and paced the length of it, looked over the whole situation, then took a pencil from his pocket and marked an X at a certain point on the wall. A week later, Mr. Ford got a bill for $50,000 and was furious. He called up Steinmetz and said, "You're billing me $50,000 for making an X on the wall of the River Rouge plant?" Mr. Steinmetz said, "Mr. Ford, for making the X on the wall of your plant, five dollars. For knowing where to put the X, $49,995. Thank you very much." And Ford paid the bill.

Source: Peter M. Rabinowitz, *Talking Medicine: America's Doctors Tell Their Stories,* W.W. Norton, 1981:140–141.

Shield, medicare, and medicaid (see Chapter 4) are intended to protect the basic income of physicians and medical institutions, not the health of individuals. Some see insurance plans as blank checks to exploitative physicians, hospitals, and nursing homes. Blue Cross, for example, provides about one-half of all hospital revenues (Kotelchuck, 1976:82). Typically medical insurance pays only part (usually about 80 percent) of "legitimate" medical expenses (after a deductible amount, which you pay all of) and sets limits for "acceptable" charges for various services and procedures. Thus, providers of medical services are guaranteed a certain fixed income and you are guaranteed to have to pay the difference between what the insurance will allow and what the physician or hospital charges. Finally, there is a limit to even the number of partial payments an insurance company will make in a given time period. Of course some physicians will accept the minimum fee for service allowed by insurance companies, but probably on the whole such doctors may be less competent and are certainly less able to provide helpful services because they need to see more patients to make the income they desire. Note that physicians (like drug companies) simply decide how much they wish to make. They are usually not regulated by anything or anyone other than their patients' ability to pay (cf. Starr, 1982:19).

PANEL 7.4

Physician Argues against Penny-Pinching

Doctors must give patients any treatment that might help them, no matter how expensive, and shouldn't try to cut the nation's $1 billion-a-day health bill by penny-pinching at the bedside of sick people, a physician concludes.

However, two economists contend that doctors will have to make some hard decisions to hold down the explosive cost of the nation's health care, now $400 billion a year.

"In caring for an individual patient, the doctor must act solely as that patient's advocate against the apparent interests of society as a whole, if necessary," Dr. Norman G. Levinsky, chief of medicine at Boston University Medical Center, wrote in one of three reports on medical costs in today's *New England Journal of Medicine.*

Levinsky said doctors may ethically make some decisions that hold down costs. They might treat people in outpatient clinics rather than admit them to hospitals, as long as the care is first-class. They may eliminate needless diagnostic tests, which sometimes are given just to make money or to avoid the chance of malpractice claims.

However, economist Victor R. Fuchs of Stanford University says that it will have to be doctors who cut costs during the day-to-day business of healing.

Another alternative is for insurance companies to write rules setting out what they will and won't pay for.

Source: *Associated Press,* December 13, 1984.

It follows that medical insurance provides few incentives for physicians or the medical industry to keep costs down (Mechanic, 1978:335–349). Some have contended (Mechanic, 1971) that a national health insurance plan would help hold costs down (cf., Gill, 1986). The United States is the only industrialized country in the world without national health insurance. On the negative side, in England, where socialized medicine (a practice vigorously resisted by the American Medical Association) has been practiced for years, there are long waiting lists for essential medical services and hospital visits and the quality of care tends to be uneven. Ehrenreich and Ehrenreich (1982) have been outspoken in their insistence that national health insurance would not solve America's physical illnesses and health care needs. They believe that national health insurance would be subject to the same abuses that Medicare and Medicaid have had.

Analyzing the Problem. The Conflict Perspective Conflict theorists (Kotelchuck, Illich, McKeown) argue that costs for physical illness and health care are excessively high because medical personnel and institutions do not exist for health care, but rather for profit. Paradoxically, health care is not the primary aim of the health care system (Kotelchuck, 1976:29). Some modern-day conflict theorists (Illich, 1976) go so far as to contend that the health care system itself actually makes us sick (iatrogenesis). If physicians, insurance plans, hospitals, nursing homes, and medical technology do not exist to make us well, then what is their objective? According to the conflict perspective the answer is that the health care system exists to secure profits for physicians and medical institutions, not primarily to take care of sick patients (McKeown, 1980).[6]

The fact that some patients may get well or be helped by the health care system is really not the point. What is important is that the patients ability to pay, not their need for health care, determines the availability, quality, and promptness of medical services (Reissman, 1986). Thus, the health care system is poorly coordinated with the needs of the truly sick, unless they happen to be rich or "lucky" enough to have interesting illnesses. Some emergency rooms and ambulance crews will actually refuse service to acutely ill or injured individuals if they are not able to pay on the spot. In doctors' offices potential clients are greeted with prominently displayed signs warning that credit cards will not be accepted and that patients must pay now and file their own insurance claims later. And to think that we used to worry about doctors not making house calls!

The Exchange Perspective A very different explanation of the high costs of health care is offered by exchange theorists. According to exchange theory (axioms 1, 2, 3, and 4; Chapter 2), those activities that are most valuable, rewarding, and scarce will cost the most in a free noncoercive market. Probably the supply and demand for costly medical services would remain, even if we tried to eliminate them (as England has learned). Health, pain and disability avoidance, and life are all highly valuable assets (see Tables 4.3 and 10.5). Health has an extremely high value to us. Consider the toasts that we make when drinking: "To your health!" "Have a happy and healthy new year!" "Long life!" Exchange theory implies that if one activity is more valuable or more rewarded than another activity, the more valuable or rewarded activity will be performed. In the case in point, put simply, money is more valuable to most people than their health or the health of others, especially if the threat to health is remote or uncertain. After all, life is not without risks and costs.

For example, sometimes you must feel that everything causes cancer. It follows that most people will undertake certain paid activities regardless of the health consequences. We must also realize that values of individuals are often different and at odds with values of societies or corporations (see Chapter 10). If industrial productivity is more valuable to society than the health or safety of a few individual workers, then the health consequences for workers will tend to be ignored (Relman, 1986). Often it costs less for a company to compensate ill workers than to make wholesale industrial changes to improve health or safety conditions (Dowie, 1985). Finally, absolutely guaranteeing industrial safety and health (if that is even possible) might destroy important industries, even a country's economy. Then how healthy would we be?

What is important is the patient's ability to pay, not the need for health care. Minorities often receive inferior health care because they cannot afford the prices physicians and hospital clinics charge and do not have health insurance or even jobs. Most minority clinics are more crowded and generally unpleasant than this one is. (Bohdan Hrynewych/Stock, Boston)

Another point, doctors and medical institutions have rare skills and services that, in a free society, they are able to exchange for large sums of money and high status. In America (and elsewhere) physicians rank second in occupational prestige only to Supreme Court justices (Hodge et al., 1964:286–302, on the NORC occupational prestige scale). Doctors make three and one-half times more money than the average professional. Of course, if physicians or medical technology fail (and they do), the exchange rule of distributive justice (see Panel 2.2, A5) would lead us to believe that medical consumers will tend to become justifiably angry. The high cost of malpractice insurance and the prevalence of legal action against doctors and hospitals support this prediction (Mechanic, 1978).

Finally, on the negative side of the interactive coin, interactions or exchanges with the ill, injured, or diseased tend not to be positive (i.e., not valuable or rewarding). Human exchange is encouraged by health, vigor, physical strength, sexual ability, self-sufficiency, and pleasure production. From the exchange perspective we would expect the sick and unhealthy to be avoided. It makes some sense then to put the sick in hospitals and nursing homes; in short, to

Human exchange is encouraged by health, vigor, physical strength, sexual prowess, self-sufficiency, and pleasure production. From the exchange perspective social interaction with the sick and unhealthy tends not to be valuable and is avoided. (AP/Wide World Photos)

isolate them from the rest of society. In the worst case the sick could make you sick (e.g., through infectious disease). Like the older person who may have to pay for sex, the physically ill have few social rewards to offer in exchange and usually must pay to have interactive partners, including medical interaction with physicians. One might reply that social workers (for example) also interact with the physically ill but do not charge as much as physicians charge their patients. The exchange answer to this objection is that the services social workers provide are less scarce and less valuable than those medical doctors provide.

The Structural Perspective It will be recalled that structuralists are not concerned primarily with a capitalistic medical industry exploiting the sick or with face-to-face human exchanges, but rather with issues of the size, number, and formal organization of relevant populations. One typical question a structuralist might ask is: "How many sick people are there and what might their size indicate about health care?" About 14 percent of the American population has chronic activity limitation in any given year (*Statistical Abstract of the United States,* 1987: Table, 167). Thus, heterogeneity for the chronically sick (one dimension of morbidity) is relatively low (.24)—about the same as that of the aged or of blacks.[7] Other things being equal this low heterogeneity structurally tends to restrict social interaction of the well with the chronically sick, and institutional confinement and their own disability restricts them further still.[8] Acute morbid conditions are more widespread. For example, about half the American population have simple colds in a year. On the average, about six workdays are lost per year to sickness. Turning to mortality (see Table 7.1), the crude death rate is 8 to 9 per 1,000. Thus, for dying patients (versus all others), heterogeneity is extremely low.[9]

Another important structural trait has been the development of medical bureaucracies in urban-industrial societies (see Chapter 10). Problems of health care are not only a health issue. In modern societies all services tend to be impersonal, rational, indirect, governed by formal rules, controlled by elites, costly, and places where social status is more important than was the case in smaller traditional societies. These are organizational problems that transcend medicine. One example of a bureaucratic problem might be that what's good for the medical industry may not be good for an individual's health (see Table 10.5 on the interests of corporate actors).

A third issue is the medical division of labor (cf. Durkheim, 1893). For example, medical specialists have increased from 17 percent of all physicians in 1930 to about 89 percent in 1983 (*Health, United States,* 1985). Specialization drives up costs, but it should improve health care. Of course, one still needs an internist or family practice physician to oversee the care of one's health in general and to coordinate all the specialists. The main point here though is that medical specialization, not simple greed for profit, generated modern hospital care, technological innovation, and new drugs. In short, a structural factor created many of our contemporary health care costs.

In a recent much-heralded and hotly debated book, *The Social Transformation of American Medicine* (1982), Paul Starr also argues for structural factors contributing to the high cost of medical care (cf. Coser, 1984; Evans, 1984). First, Starr demonstrates how medicine became a virtually autonomous power holder in American society. Institutional independence allows economic independence (1982:19). Another major factor was that corporations entered the medical field. Starr claims that from about 1965 to 1980 profit-making hospital chains grew faster than the computer industry (1982:430). For the first time managerial capitalism was introduced into American medicine on a large scale (1982:431). Now business school graduates are displacing graduates of public health schools, hospital administration, and even doctors as the top administrators of medicine (1982:448). Little wonder then that medical care has grown so expensive. The culture of health care is now dominated not by (medical) professionalism, but rather by business ethics (Coser, 1984:10; however, see Alexander et al., 1986).

Finally, we would be amiss if we did not acknowledge that structural complexities associated with contemporary urban-industrial life help generate social stress, role strain, burnout, type-A personalities, heart disease, and many related health problems. These problems will be examined in some detail in a section below on stress.

The Symbolic Interaction Perspective One could argue that the costs of health care, medical insurance, hospitals, nursing homes, drugs, surgery, and so on are socially constructed; or as McKeown puts it, most medical problems are not medical (1980). The essence of the symbolic interaction approach to health care costs is that Americans have certain shared meanings or subjective perceptions about illness and its treatment that are not objectively required (Friedson, 1970:Part III; see Table 2.1). Other, often conflicting interpretations, are equally plausible.

These symbolic subjective definitions of the American health care system begin to emerge when we compare the U.S. health situation with those in other cultures. If we look at Table 7.2 we see that Cuba puts in twenty public health dollars per capita and has a male life expectancy of age sixty-eight and a quality of life score of eighty-six. The U.S.A., on the other hand, puts in over ten times that amount per capita ($218) for a male life expectancy of sixty-nine and a quality of life score of ninety-six. Is America's ten times greater public health costs worth its modest health gains?

Consider another example we looked at earlier in this chapter. Remember that the United States has twice as many surgeons per capita as England and has the highest rate of elective surgery in the world (*Health, United States,* 1986). It is hard to believe that America's legitimate health needs objectively require the number of surgeons that we have.

We also noted that the United States is the only industrialized society without a national health insurance plan. One could argue that the perception of the superiority of a fee-for-service, nonsocialized medicine approach to health care in America is a fragile social artifact constructed by the American Medical Association and medical capitalism, not by any objective empirical proof that our health care system is better than those in countries like Great Britain or the USSR. We must remember too that physicians in England and the USSR generally are not paid as well as American medical doctors (Friedson, 1970:42). Thus, it is not self-evident that medicine and medical services have to cost what they do in America.

Notice, as well, that physicians have the power to decide when you are sick, and to label or certify you as ill. Several important consequences follow from being defined as sick. Costly health care treatment may be seen as necessary and may be prescribed. If you are defined as sick you may assume the sick role (Parsons, 1951:428–79; Siegler and Osmond, 1979) and temporarily be relieved of your normal social responsibilities. We need to ask when and under what circumstances to let people assume sick roles. Of course, the more often and longer we do, the more costly it usually is for society. It is important to realize that what is perceived as sickness varies. Some people do not even treat certain problems. For example, Zborowski in a classic 1952 study (cf. Zola, 1979) found that pain perception varied across ethnic groups. Many health professionals also doubt that traditional annual physical checkups are really necessary for most people under age forty. Tonsillectomies, which used to be performed regularly on most adolescents, are much less likely today to be seen as helpful to most individuals.

A related issue is are most people in the hospital or in outpatient clinics really sick? Scheff (1964; 1974) contends (admittedly writing mainly before deinstitutionalization) that many people in mental hospitals just broke social rules (i.e., are not really sick). Gove (1975, 1970), on the other side, counters that most hospitalized people are in fact seriously impaired. The picture of the American health care system that emerges from the symbolic interaction perspective is one of considerable subjectivity, arbitrariness, and of interpretations of powerful interest groups holding sway, not of a preordained health care system that "has to be."

Resolving the Problem It is tempting to conclude that our major cost-cutting objective should be to take social class out of health care. When someone is ill, they ought to be able to get medical treatment, even if they are poor or of a low social status. Right now, as health care exists in America, the poor both have more illnesses than the rich and are less able to afford proper care. The resolution to this problem goes far beyond the health care issue. What is required is no less than the United States having a socialistic economy, and that probably is not going to happen.

Of course, we might be able to have some socialized medicine programs and still have basically a capitalist economy. One such program that is suggested often is national health insurance. For example, in the British health service medicine is basically a public service (Mechanic, 1971). The government owns the hospitals and clinics and salaries physicians. Medical treatment is free to all citizens. In Great Britain it is estimated that physicians make about one-third less income than physicians in America. One problem with English health care is that there are long waiting lists for medical services. Another problem is that some critics (Ehrenreich & Ehrenreich, 1980) believe that a national health insurance plan would be subject to the same abuse and corruption that currently plagues medicare and medicaid. For example, with medicare, the physicians remain in charge of fees, which has led to overcharges and fake claims.

A related resolution is to develop Health Maintenance Organizations (HMOs) in lieu of fee-for-service plans (Kotelchuck, 1976:345; Kristein, Arnold, and Wynder, 1977). HMOs are prepaid group practice plans started in the 1930s (like Kaiser-Permanente) that emphasize prevention rather than medical treatment (Mechanic, 1978). HMOs have been especially effective in reducing hospitalization and surgery. In 1973 the Health Maintenance Act provided money for developing new HMOs and allowed certain employees to choose HMO plans over traditional group insurance plans. It is estimated that about 5 percent of Americans are enrolled in HMOs. One drawback is that if you do require medical treatment, you can only go to physicians participating in the plan.

Since physician services are so costly and since we must go to physicians now, it would seem reasonable to develop alternatives to and competition for physicians' services. To begin with, specialization has gotten out of control. Sometimes an individual has to go to a half-dozen or more specialists to get complete health care. Needless to say, such procedures drive up the costs of sickness. One alternative is to develop more medical generalists; that is, those physicians in family practices or internal medicine. Another is to use paraprofessionals. It can be argued that most illness complaints are medically trivial and do not require great medical expertise. In such cases nurses or physician extenders might be able to deliver essential medical services at greatly reduced costs. In fact physician assistants were certified to do just that, to provide many of the routine services physicians now offer (Light, Crain, and Fisher, 1976). As a case in point recent legislative action has tended not to allow midwives to deliver babies. This denial of legal status to the practice of midwifery forces women to have expensive hospital bills for routine child delivery or to become criminals in using an illegal service.

If we cannot get around traditional physician services, then at least we can police them and attempt to control the quality of services delivered and prevent abuses. Professional Standards Review Organizations (PSROs) were established in 1977 to review medical treatment and to sanction offenders. More precisely, PSROs are physician-run peer review bodies designed to help check medicare and medicaid fraud. If unnecessary care is found to have been given, PSROs can deny reimbursement to physicians for medicare and medicaid claims.

Other cost-cutting resolutions include the use of generic drugs, stressing preventive medicine, and home health care. Typically, brand-name drugs cost at least twice as much as generic drugs. You will recall that the brand-name drug Prednisone (discussed above) was actually twenty times more expensive than a comparable generic drug. It should also help if we spent more on prevention of illness before we needed costly cures. Hingsen et al. estimate that only about 6 percent of medical care dollars go to prevention of illness (1981:33). Given the illnesses associated with modern lifestyle changes and stress (see below), it would seem that programs of exercise, dieting, and restricted alcohol intake and smoking could do a lot to curb expensive illnesses.

An innovative concept is to actually pay people to stay healthy (*Newsweek,* August 25, 1980). In one such program $500 of Blue Shield monies was set aside each year. If employees claimed less than $500 in health insurance in a year, the difference was available for them to collect when they left their jobs.

For example, if you claimed $100 for three years and then quit, you would get $1,200 in cash. Home health care for some illnesses costs much less than hospital care. In a relevant case Norman Cousins, author and former editor of the *Saturday Review,* after becoming ill checked himself out of the hospital and into a hotel (which was cheaper and had better service). Instead of medicine Cousins took massive injections of vitamin C and watched three stooges movies (*Anatomy of an Illness,* 1979). For Cousins belly laughs for fifteen minutes were roughly equivalent in reducing pain to a standard injection of morphine.

Finally, we need more health care for chronic illness, rather than for acute illness. When we use expensive acute treatment modalities for chronic disorders like cancer and heart disease, it is often inappropriate. One result is that more needless surgery is performed. A possible resolution would be for an insurance plan to pay for a second medical opinion before surgery was done. Emphasis on acute illness methods encourages expensive heroic medical interventions (e.g., open-heart surgery or chemotherapy) and discourages prevention (e.g., reduction of stress or industrial pollutants). In the next section we examine directly the role of physicians in the high cost of illness and health care.

• Physicians

Although the proportion of health care costs for physician fees has declined (see Table 7.3) in recent years, the absolute costs for doctors' fees have gone up dramatically. It is just that hospital and nursing home care costs have gone up even more. Many students probably choose medicine not primarily to help others or to reduce suffering, but because the money is good. They know that doctors earn five times what the average wage earner brings in and three and one-half times the incomes of the average professional (*New York Times,* May 7, 1978). The gross median income of physicians in 1984 was $181,000 (of course, with specialty variation; for example, the median income for orthopedic surgeons was highest at $327,000 per year), the highest of any other occupational group (*Statistical Abstract of the United States,* 1987:93). Furthermore, physician incomes are also rising faster than those of other work groups. Physicians' services costs since 1950 rose nearly double the increase in prices generally. Part, but by no means all, of this increase in doctors' fees is attributable to physicians' need to purchase expensive malpractice insurance, which itself is growing in cost by leaps and bounds. Physicians charge several thousand dollars more each in fees every year just to cover the rising costs of their malpractice insurance.

Of course, physicians are also performing more expensive operations than ever before and the number of physicians specializing in surgery is large and growing larger. During the 1970s the number of operations rose 23 percent, while the American population grew only 5 percent. As we saw earlier, from 1965 to 1984 cesarean section births rose from 6 percent to 21 percent of all

PANEL 7.5

Being a Physician

I really love what I do, which is why I go on doing it. But there are days when I get up and know I have to give a lecture or become involved in a teaching conference or a seminar, and I feel like a goddamned trained seal, and I don't feel like doing the act that day. I just don't want to bark and roll that ball on my nose and have everybody go, "Yeaaa, look at him he's so marvelous, we can't do that." Once I get started, I'm always all right, but Jesus, I would really rather stay in bed, and I can't permit myself to do it. This is a terrible confession, but I don't think I've ever played hooky from medicine one day in my life.

We have a stereotype that's been set up and reinforced within medicine, which is that there aren't enough doctors to go around, and all the people who get sick will die immediately if some intervention doesn't occur. Now that's statistically—it's massively—untrue, but we've all bought into it. The unspoken equation is that if I don't show up for work, a human being will die, and that makes it very easy to say, "Oh my god, I've gotta be at work." So as a physician you have a degree of isolation that is unique in the world, because even if you're working with other people, you have the ultimate responsibility for a patient's welfare, and you can't share that responsibility with others.

Source: Peter M. Rabinowitz, *Talking Medicine: America's Doctors Tell Their Stories,* W.W. Norton, 1981:229–230.

births. The United States has twice the number of surgeons per capita as Great Britain and does twice the number of operations (*New York Times,* January 26, 1976).

Physicians and the American Medical Association have taken the position that competition and advertising are unethical. But we also know that competition for services of any sort tends to drive down prices. However, most physicians are not willing to be accused of behaving unethically and run the risk of losing their licenses, especially just to keep prices down for consumers. Typically, physicians set target salaries they wish and simply charge fees that will result in realization of their desired incomes. If medical insurance (like Blue Cross/Blue Shield) will not pay the physician's desired fee for service, as we have seen the patient is expected to pay the difference, often at the time of or in advance of the rendering of the service or procedure. These practices can be especially troublesome, since we cannot choose when to be ill. Physicians have a captive market whose only alternative is usually to live in pain, discomfort, or occasionally, to die.[10]

Not everyone who wants to become a physician can do so. Premedical and medical education are difficult, costly, take a long time, and are restricted primarily to white males with elite social and intellectual backgrounds (Rosengren, 1980:5). Many doctors decided on their eventual careers when they were very young (Rosengren, 1980:Ch. 5). All these physician traits tend to weigh against poor minority medical school applicants. Not only are the premedical biological and physical science course requirements demanding, the number of medical school positions, especially at the prestigious universities, are also limited and are competed for fiercely. Even after one is admitted to medical school (clearly the major step in a physician's career), the training is exhausting, often demeaning, and requires considerable persistence (Merton, 1957; Becker et al., 1961).

Although physicians comprise only about 7 percent or 8 percent of the total health care labor force (Kotelchuck, 1976:166), they tend to control health care and have considerable autonomy in doing so (Starr, 1982).[11] Friedson (1970) argues that this autonomy results in part from the presumed expertise of doctors, as well as from the right to self-determination granted to professionals. Note too that since physicians have responsibility for life and death, their profession tends to take on priestly functions. Some critics have argued that even with all this power and autonomy, physicians exert minimal control over the quality of health care (Friedson, 1970:282; Alexander, 1986). For example, physicians tend not to sanction or discipline other doctors. Interestingly, a Harris poll reveals that those people with a "great deal" of confidence in the medical profession dropped from 73 percent in 1966 to 43 percent in 1977.

Another issue often debated is, are there too few or too many physicians (Rushing, 1985; Hafferty, 1986)? There were 502,000 physicians in the United States in 1982 (542,000 in 1983). Given a population of 231 million, this amounts to about one doctor for every 460 men, women, and children, or a ratio of about 217 doctors per 100,000 population (cf. *New York Times,* May 7, 1978; *Newsweek,* May 9, 1977). The number of physicians per 100,000 is expected to rise to 239 by 1990, or roughly 600,000 (*National Center for Health Statistics,* 1980). The physician population, however, is not evenly distributed; most doctors are concentrated in affluent urban and surburban areas. The rural poor and urban ghetto minorities still do not have adequate medical care (*New York Times,* May 7, 1978).

For years the American Medical Association strictly limited the number of students admitted to medical schools in an effort to keep supply low and demand and salaries high. This policy has changed to some degree in recent years, since it now appears that having more physicians (up to a point) in the same area is related to higher, not lower, physician incomes. The more recent physicians are much more likely to be specialists (Rosengren, 1980:144). General practitioners have actually declined both absolutely (from about 50,000 to 47,000) and as a proportion of total physicians (from 15 percent to 10 percent) from 1970 to 1980 (cf. Rosengren, 1980:151). As we noted above, in 1930 specialists were only 17 percent of all physicians; today they are about 89 percent. Specialists, of course, can command higher fees, and this tends to drive up the costs of health care. Of course, neither physicians nor greedy captains of industry have much to do with some forms of illness. In large part

"Son, your mother is a remarkable woman."

Drawing by S. Gross; © 1983 *The New Yorker* Magazine, Inc.

many modern illnesses are related paradoxically to our high quality of life, affluence, and the stresses, strains, and demands of complex contemporary lifestyles, a topic to which we now turn.

• Stress

These are the times of burnout, type-A personalities, future shock (Toffler, 1970), migraines, ulcers, hypertension, heart disease, valium and librium, beta-blockers; in short, of stress and physical illness related to our contemporary, urban-industrial lifestyles. Even though we are in a sense healthier, living longer than ever before in American history, we also exist in a society with an unprecedented rate of change, bombarded by stimuli only imagined in prior generations, ultimately finite creatures in a computer and high-tech machine world where error, not self-centeredness, is the new original sin (Crichton, 1969, 1981). Is the pace, the strain and stress of it all, likely to make us sick, even kill us (Huxley, 1939)?

Before these questions can be answered we must say what we mean by *stress* (Goldberger and Breznitz, 1982). House defines *stress* as when an individual confronts a situation where his/her usual modes of behaving are insufficient and the consequences of not adapting are serious (1974:13; cf. House et al., 1986). For example, imagine a macho sport parachutist whose ripcord just malfunctioned at 2,000 feet, an ordinarily glib young woman whose car broke down in an inner-city ghetto being accosted by a dozen teenage males with rape on their minds, or a college freshman from a family with a long history of physicians who finessed high school in his/her first semester at Harvard as a premedical student. Obviously, all of these situations are stressful, but in some the failure to adapt may lead to immediate death, in others to simple discomfort, embarrassment, or role failure.

Usually, stress indicates a gradual strain on the body or mind associated with measurable physiological changes. Selye (1956, 1982) argues that stress ("any demand on the body") produces an initial lowering of bodily resistance during which a variety of infectious diseases can occur. This is followed by an activation of bodily defense mechanisms characterized by arousal of the autonomic nervous system: adrenalin discharge, increased heart rate, blood pressure, and muscle tone, and increased digestive secretion. In laboratory animals that are stressed Selye (1982) observes an alarm reaction in which the outer layer of the adrenal glands becomes enlarged and hyperactive; the thymus, spleen, and lymph nodes shrink; and deep bleeding ulcers can appear in the stomach and upper intestines. In the short run such responses are adaptive and increase the organism's survival chances (cf. Cannon, 1939), but in the long run every stressful activity and subsequent adaptation wears us down biologically, contributing to aging, disease, and eventual death (House et al., 1986).

In the 1930s Johns Hopkins psychiatrist Adolf Meyer (1958) contended that even rather routine life events like changing jobs or having children, if frequent and intense enough, could be important factors in the generation of illness. Meyers recorded such changes on his life charts and then demonstrated that these life events were associated with the development of physical and mental illnesses. More recently Holmes and Rahe (1967; Perkins, 1982) have taken many of the above concepts of stress and incorporated them into a social readjustment rating scale (SRRS) by asking subjects to rate a series of life events according to their relative degree of necessary readjustment (see Table 7.4). For example, each subject was told to assume that marriage would take 500 units (or fifty days) of adjustment and then asked to rate forty-two other events in terms of the unit adjustment (or days) s/he required compared to marriage (there are some problems of recall of events; Funch and Marshall, 1984).

Table 7.4 shows the mean values given to the forty-two life events by the subjects tested (all values were divided by ten to convert units to days). To illustrate, in Table 7.4 "death of a spouse" had the highest readjustment value (100), followed by "divorce" (73), "marital separation" (65), "jail term" (63), and so on. Notice that several *positive* events were considered stressful and required more days of adjustment than many negative events. For example,

TABLE 7.4 Social Readjustment Rating Scale

Rank	Life Event	Mean Value of Life Change Units
1	Death of spouse	100
2	Divorce	73
3	Marital separation	65
4	Jail term	63
5	Death of close family member	63
6	Personal injury or illness	53
7	Marriage	50
8	Fired at work	47
9	Marital reconciliation	45
10	Retirement	45
11	Change in health of family member	44
12	Pregnancy	40
13	Sex difficulties	39
14	Gain of new family member	39
15	Business readjustment	39
16	Change in financial state	38
17	Death of close friend	37
18	Change to different line of work	36
19	Change in number of arguments with spouse	35
20	Mortgage over $10,000*	31
21	Foreclosure of mortgage or loan	30
22	Change in responsibilities at work	29
23	Son or daughter leaving home	29
24	Trouble with in-laws	29
25	Outstanding personal achievement	28
26	Wife begin or stop work	26
27	Begin or end school	26
28	Change in living conditions	25
29	Revision of personal habits	24
30	Trouble with boss	23
31	Change in work hours or conditions	20
32	Change in residence	20
33	Change in schools	20
34	Change in recreation	19
35	Change in church activities	19
36	Change in social activities	18
37	Mortgage or loan less than $10,000	17
38	Change in sleeping habits	16
39	Change in number of family get-togethers	15
40	Change in eating habits	15
41	Vacation	13
42	Christmas	12
43	Minor violations of the law	11

*Obviously, this figure should be higher now.

Source: Reprinted with permission from *Journal of Psychosomatic Research,* 11, Thomas H. Holmes and Richard H. Rahe, "The Social Readjustment Rating Scale," Copyright 1967, Pergamon Journals, Ltd. Table 3, p. 216.

"marital reconciliation" had a value of 45, "gaining a new family member" a value of 39, and an "outstanding personal achievement," a value of 28.

In one study done by Holmes and Rahe 93 percent of 96 major health changes were associated with a clustering of life events whose individual values summed to 150 life change units (LCUs) or more in one year. Thus, a *life crisis* was defined as any clustering of life change events whose values summed to 150 LCUs or more in one year. On the average health changes followed life crises by about one year. Life crises were considered as:

Mild, if 150–199 LCUs/year
Moderate, if 200–299 LCUs/year
Major, if 300+ LCUs/year

Generally, Holmes and Rahe suggest that the greater the life changes or unit adaptive requirements, the greater the individual's vulnerability or lowering of resistance to disease, and the more serious the disease that will develop. One use of the social readjustment rating scale is to suggest the routine limits of stress an organism or individual can tolerate without risking illness, other things being equal.[12] The effects of stress vary both with actual and perceived social support (Wethington and Kessler, 1986; Lin et al., 1985).

One of the most celebrated and best-documented effects of stress is that on coronary heart disease (CHD), the leading cause of death among males thirty-five years old or older. Usually researchers have examined variables such as job stress, personality type, and heart disease. For example, House (1974) found significant negative correlations between levels of job satisfaction and heart disease mortality rates, but no correlations between job satisfaction and mortality from tuberculosis, cancer, diabetes, influenza, pneumonia, or accidents. Job pressures such as heavy work loads, high levels of responsibility, role conflicts, many deadlines, and so on were related to increased CHD. In research conducted by Columbia University (See *New York Times,* April 3, 1983) jobs with high psychological demand and low decision control (like waitresses, sales clerks, mail workers, cooks, and telephone operators) were found more likely to be associated with cardiovascular illness.

Not all people under stress react by developing coronary heart disease. Other factors such as personality traits usually act as conditioning variables (i.e., as factors that intervene between stressful stimuli and illness). For example, Rosenman et al., (1975) and Rosenman and Chesney (1982) have shown that individuals with what they call type-A personalities are two to seven times more likely to develop heart disease. Individuals with type-A personalities are characterized by excessive drive, aggressiveness, ambition, involvement in competitive activities, frequent vocational deadlines, and an enhanced sense of time urgency (see Table 7.5).[13]

Research (Kastenbaum, 1981:180–183) has shown that individuals with type-A personalities tend to be at greater risk of dying earlier than their age cohorts' life expectancy and are more likely to die from stress related illnesses or diseases such as CHD. Short of death, those with type-A personalities are

TABLE 7.5 Characteristics of the Type-A Personality

1. Speaks in a hurried and explosive style, betraying "excess aggression or hostility."
2. Moves, walks, and eats rapidly all the time.
3. Shows impatience with the tempo of people and events around him. Things are not moving fast enough or getting done quickly enough to suit him.
4. Often tries to think or do several things at the same time (to save time). This characteristic is called *polyphasic* thought or performance.
5. Always attempts to bring conversations around to topics that interest him, only pretending to listen to what others have to say when they discuss their own interests.
6. Almost always feels guilty when he relaxes or does nothing for a few days or even just a few hours.
7. Fails to observe interesting and attractive features of the environment (probably because too intent upon his own plans and schedules).
8. Does not have time to spare for enjoyment because he is preoccupied with the getting of things.
9. Operates with a "chronic sense of time urgency." He tries to do more and more in less and less time, thereby setting himself up for crises when the tight pressured schedule goes awry.
10. Behaves aggressively and competitively toward other type-A people. "This is a telltale trait," say Friedman and Rosenman, "because no one arouses the aggressive and/or hostile feelings of one type-A subject more quickly than another type-A subject."
11. Uses characteristic gestures or nervous tics that suggest he is in the midst of a continual struggle (e.g., pounding one fist into the palm of the other hand, clenching the jaw).
12. Believes that his success has been based on an ability to do things faster than others can or will, and feels he must continue to do everything as fast as he can.
13. Prefers to evaluate his own activities and those of other people in terms of numbers—how much accomplished in what period of time.

Source: From *Type A Behavior and Your Heart,* by Meyer Friedman and Ray Rosenman. Copyright © 1974 by Meyer Friedman. Reprinted by permission of Alfred A. Knopf, Inc.

also more likely to suffer from a crippled existence of a partial death-in-life. Here we refer to a whole host of psychosomatic afflictions; for example, ulcers, colitis, migraine headaches, anxiety, depression, chronic lower back pain, greater receptivity to common colds and flu, hypertension, vertigo, nausea, skin disorders, and so on (sound familiar to any of you?). Of course, type-A personalities are not all bad for us or for society. A great deal can be accomplished by high-drive, competitive, achievement oriented, aggressive individuals and groups. This raises the larger issue of what motivates us to seek stress, even when we could avoid most of it.

Samuel Klausner contends that our need to seek arousal, stimulation, and novelty requires some stress, flirting with pain, and occasionally even death (1968). There is a fundamental conflict in our lives between security and growth. Equilibrium (security) is experienced as pleasure only if it is contrasted or juxtaposed with change or disruption (stress). The principle of satiation (cf. exchange theory's Axiom 4, Chapter 2) suggests that to continue pleasure, one must increase stress. Once stress is mastered, it tends to become equi-

Contemporary urban, industrial, commercial lifestyles in an era of the computer produce high levels of stress. We are bombarded with countless demands that need to be responded to quickly and accurately. Such social stress can produce or aggravate illnesses. (Brice Flynn/Stock, Boston)

librium. For example, Klausner discusses sport parachutists who feel the need to lengthen the time of their free fall before opening their parachutes. Such stress seeking can become life threatening when we misestimate our capacity to control or tolerate it (e.g., try to canoe a white-water river that is too difficult; climb a mountain that is too icy or too steep, or even take on a job that is beyond our skills); when there are no or insufficient social control mechanisms (e.g., a fight without a referee or a war without the possibility of surrender); or when stress is too repeatedly sought or when the internal directives of the stress seeker outweigh the external checks (e.g., novelist Ernest Hemingway was probably unable to get adequate treatment for his suicide attempts given his fame and determination to die. See Hotchner, 1966).

• Summary

The primary social problems of physical illness and health care in the United States are the high costs of sickness, the roles physicians and the medical industry play in driving up these costs, our inability to fulfill important social roles due to illness or death, the fact that many illnesses have social causes (e.g., industrial pollutants or social stress), and that health care itself can make us sick (iatrogenesis). We should think of health not only as the absence of illness, but also as positive physical, mental, and social well-being. Both for morbidity (rates of illness) and mortality (rates of death), heart disease, cancer, and stroke (chronic illnesses) have been the major American health problems. In the 1980s violent unnatural deaths such as accidents, suicide, homicide, euthanasia, and abortion accounted for relatively more deaths, while infections and communicative diseases accounted for fewer deaths than in the past.

An irreducible amount of illness derives from biology and is responsive to biological, chemical, or technological treatments—if it responds to any treatment. Even though average years of life expectancy have increased, few people live beyond 100 years; aging is inescapable. We also know that men have greater mortality rates than women (from most causes) at all ages and that many diseases are relatively race specific. Great advances have been made with drugs, surgery, and the technical management of acute illness.

Nevertheless, it is still true that a major American health problem is that the proportion of our national income that we spend on health care is larger than what we spend for other goods and services and is rising at a faster rate. We have reached the point where we simply cannot afford to be sick, especially if we are out of work. Hospital and nursing home care costs have climbed far more (proportionately) than other medical costs. Medical insurance, like Blue Cross/Blue Shield, actually fuels these higher costs. Even so, many contemporary hospitals still cannot balance their budgets.

Some of the reasons for the high costs of health care no doubt center on the exploitative profit motives of the health care industry, our shared meanings of sickness (which demand more surgery, more specialists, more tests, and so on), and physicians' power to label sickness, prescribe drugs, and set their own fees as they wish. The conflict perspective argues that costs for physical illness and health care are excessively high because medical personnel, hospitals, and health insurance plans do not exist for health care, but rather for private profit. The patients' ability to pay, not their need for health care, determines the availability, quality, and promptness of medical services. Thus, the American health care system is poorly coordinated with the needs of the truly sick, who are often poor.

The picture of the American health care system that emerges from the symbolic interaction perspective is one of considerable subjectivity and arbitrariness in which the interpretations and values of powerful interest groups hold sway. For example, the United States has twice as many surgeons per capita as Great Britain. The United States is also the only industrialized society without a national health insurance plan. The essence of the symbolic interaction approach to health care costs is that Americans have certain shared meanings or subjective perceptions about physical illness and its treatment that are not objectively required.

The exchange perspective reminds us that those activities that are the most valuable, rewarding, and scarce will cost the most in a free society with a competitive market based on supply and demand. Also, interaction with the ill tends not to be valuable, or intrinsically rewarding. Structurally, most well people are unlikely to interact with sick people, both because of the small numbers of sick people and their physical isolation and limited activity. Bureaucratic organization (not just medical organization), which is a must in modern, large, dense social groups, is costly and governed by elites. Structural factors also encourage a complex refined division of labor that spawns costly medical specialization. Among the salient structural factors influencing the high cost of health care are the power and autonomy of physicians and the intrusion of private for-profit hospitals and the business world into the profession of medicine.

Some of the resolutions to problems of physical illness and health care include initiating a national health insurance plan, creating more prepaid health programs (HMOs), and using more paraprofessionals or physician extenders to do the work doctors usually do. Other health-improving, cost-cutting measures would be using more generic drugs, emphasizing preventive medicine, more home health care, paying people to stay healthy, emphasis on chronic (or acute) illness treatment, and policing the health care industry by peer review (e.g., PSROs). Part of the health care problem stems from the great autonomy of doctors. Physicians tend to set their own fees, have little or no competition, and recommend expensive tests and procedures that may not be necessary or even helpful.

Stress is another major modern health problem. Contemporary life is perhaps too fast, too demanding, and too conflicted. It may not even be possible for most of us to stay healthy in such environments. We may need to reduce the rate of our social change and lower our social expectations, while at the same time keeping the quality of life in the United States high. Modern stress and the sheer number of life events we experience are related to greater rates of illness, especially for heart disease. In Chapter 8 we continue our examination of health social problems, this time considering mental disorder and its treatment.

• Notes

1. See Chapter 13.

2. It will be recalled from Chapter 1 that a social problem is a general pattern of human behavior that is perceived to be a threat to society. In this sense widespread illness in a society certainly qualifies as a social problem.

3. There are a few major sources of data on mortality and morbidity. Among them are: (1) the *Vital Statistics of the United States,* (2) the United Nations' *Manual of the International Statistical*

Classification of Diseases, Injuries, and Causes of Death, and, in a more popular vein, (3) *Health, United States.* All three are published annually; the first and third by the U.S. Government Printing Office, and the second by The World Health Organization.

4. An exception is 1936 U.S. presidential candidate Alf Landon, who in 1983 turned ninety-six. In so doing he outlived the projected maximum age on his life insurance policies and was able to collect his own death benefits.

5. In 1975 Americans spent $104 billion for health care, compared to $88 billion for military expenditures. However, in 1984 we spent $387 billion on medical care, but $852 on defense.

6. It is not true that the health care exists merely to secure income. For example, most hospitals and physicians demand more income than Blue Cross (or other insurance plans) will allow. That is, a certain level of income resulting in the desired profit margin is the real objective.

7. Heterogeneity for the chronically sick is calculated as follows: $1 - (.14^2 + .86^2) = .24$. Once again one must be very careful not to misinterpret heterogeneity. It is a population trait.

8. Cf. Table 2.2 for the problematic effects of activity restriction.

9. Of course, to say being dead restricts social interaction sounds ludicrous. But the dying do experience similar restrictions.

10. It is well known that poor people, who cannot afford the best medical services and drugs, usually have shorter life expectancies.

11. See Kotelchuck, 1976:163:292 for an examination of the role of nurses and other workers in the health care industry.

12. Be careful not to interpret definitions of *life crises* too rigidly. Many individuals can tolerate great amounts of stress for long periods without becoming ill, especially if they are young and vigorous. For example, most college students will score fairly high on the SRRS and yet have had few serious illnesses.

13. Individuals with type-B personalities tend to be the opposite.

• Glossary

Acute Illness. A severe disease or illness with a rapid onset, but of short duration; an illness that lasts less than three months.

Arousal. The physiological or emotional stimulation of individuals or groups, as contrasted with their normal baseline states in equilibrium.

Chronic Illness. A disease or illness either lasting a long time or recurring, such as cancer, diabetes, ulcers, kidney or heart disease.

Euthanasia. An easy, good, painless death, usually of someone who is terminally ill or mortally injured. Can be active or passive, voluntary or involuntary, direct or indirect.

Fee-for-Service. A supplier's (usually a physician) method of charging for medical services to meet a desired income or profit level, rather than charging what the service is worth, what the individual can afford to pay, or what insurance companies and government agencies will allow.

Generic Drug. The common nonregistered chemical ingredients (often sold separately at greatly reduced prices) of brand name, trademark drugs.

Health. A state of complete physical, mental, and social well-being, not merely the absence of disease or infirmity.

Health Care. Those activities concerned with the promotion and protection of health.

Health Maintenance Organization. Prepaid group medical practice programs emphasizing prevention of illness and minimizing unnecessary medical expense.

Iatrogenesis. The creation of illness or health problems by medical or health care itself.

Life Crisis. Specifically, having 150 or more life-change units in a year on Holmes and Rahe's "Social Readjustment Rating Scale."

Life Events. Common positive or negative experiences that require us to adjust and, if occurring in sufficient numbers in a short time, are stressful; such as marriage, death of a spouse, trouble at work, pregnancy, and so on.

Life Expectancy. Usually the average number of years of life a newborn infant may be expected to live under the schedule of age- (sex, race, and so on) specific mortality currently in effect.

Morbidity. The rate or extent of a particular illness, injury, or disability in a defined population.

Mortality. The rate of death in a particular population.

National Health Insurance. A plan providing free medical treatment to all citizens, financed through payroll deductions (like social security) in which the national government usually owns the hospitals and clinics and salaries physicians (as in Great Britain).

Professional Standards Review Organization. Physician-run peer review bodies designed to help check medicare and medicaid fraud.

Sick Role. A social position for the sick with expectations that release ill people from normal social responsibilities and duties while they are sick.

Social Readjustment Rating Scale. A stress test developed by Holmes and Rahe that measures the adjustment days required by forty-three common life events, then scales the adjustment days (or life-change units) that each event requires, and translates the summed scale scores into no, mild, moderate, or severe life crises for a given year.

Socialized Medicine. A phrase often used by the American Medical Association to describe health care programs that limit and regulate medical costs by nationalizing health care (as in Great Britain); any program of health care that delivers medical services to all based on their need, rather than on their ability to pay.

Stress. Results when an individual confronts a situation where his/her usual modes of behaving are insufficient and the consequences of not adapting are serious; there are associated physiological changes.

Type-A Personality. Individuals who exhibit excessive drive, aggressiveness, ambition, involvement in competitive activities, have frequent vocational deadlines, have an enhanced sense of time urgency, try to do several things at the same time, and feel guilty when they relax.

• Further Reading

Mechanic, David, ed. *Handbook of Health, Health Care, and the Health Professions.* New York: The Free Press, 1983. A collection of fairly recent articles on the broad issues of the high costs of health care, medical insurance, monitoring the health care system, and health professionals by a celebrated and productive medical sociologist from the University of Wisconsin and, lately, Rutgers University.

Health, United States. An annual publication of the U.S. Department of Health and Human Services with useful tables, figures, and charts on various dimensions of illness, health care, and health care professionals and institutions. Topics include costs of medical services, days of work lost to physical illness, morbidity rates, physician specialties, hospital and nursing home data, cigarette and alcohol use, and much much more. Special health problems are emphasized each year.

Illich, Ivan. *Medical Nemesis: The Expropriation of Health.* New York: Pantheon Books, 1976. A slightly outrageous and impassioned criticism of the entire modern health care industry, focusing on the concept of iatrogenesis—illness caused paradoxically by health care. Argues that we have become healthier in spite of (certainly not because of) medical technology, surgery, doctors, and hospitals. Illich is a kind of medical Rousseau, arguing that we have the right to be sick, to treat ourselves, even to die, without interference from the medical industry or doctors.

Rabinowitz, Peter MacGarr. *Talking Medicine: American Doctors Tell Their Stories.* New York: New American Library, 1983 (cf. Conrad and Kerns, eds., 1986). First-person accounts in the Studs Terkel tradition by physicians about their education, training, practice, research, and personal lives. A readable account of what it is like to be a doctor in America today. Views of doctors on problems like health care and its high costs, as opposed to those of patient-"victims."

Goldberger, Leo and Shlomo Breznitz. *Handbook of Stress: Theoretical and Clinical Aspects.* New York: The Free Press, 1983. You have to be young and fit to even pick up this 800-page plus encyclopedic reference book of forty-six articles on the causes, responses, and treatment of stress. Several well-known experts (e.g., Selye, Janis, Lazarus, Horowitz, the Dohrenwends, and Brody) comment on the basic psychological and biological processes of stress, research and measurement problems, common and extreme stressors, and clinical conditions and treatments.

Backer, Barbara A., Natalie Hannon, and Noreen A. Russell. *Death and Dying: Individuals and Institutions.* New York: John Wiley & Sons, 1982. Three women with clinical health care backgrounds have written an excellent text on death and dying. The book is comprehensive and easy to understand. Topics are the American culture and death, the process of dying, the hospital and the dying patient, doctors, nurses, and social workers and the dying, the dying child, ethical issues, suicide, funerals, grief and bereavement, and cross-cultural perspectives. Text includes learning exercises and audio visual references.

C·H·A·P·T·E·R

8

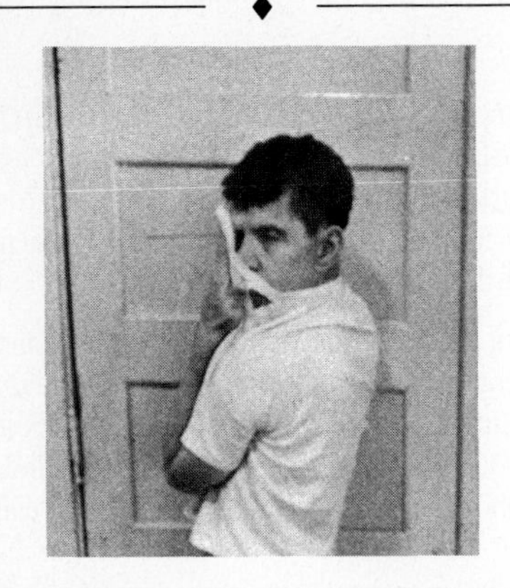

Mental Disorders and Their Treatment

Individuals or groups exhibiting strange, bizarre, eccentric, excited, aggressive, disorderly, or unpredictable behaviors are often thought to be mentally disordered and in need of confinement or treatment. From the exchange perspective the mentally disordered have learned to act crazy. Mental disorder is often rewarded. Also, social norms for noncrazy behaviors are set by reference to mentally disordered behaviors as limiting cases. Furthermore, sensitivity, creativity, and individuality are generally seen by society as positive values. However, unlike sexual, age, or racial exchanges, the mentally disordered have relatively few scarce rewards to offer larger society. Thus, punishments are usually exchanged.

Structurally, since there are relatively few psychotic people and since the psychotic tend to be segregated in state or county mental hospitals, we tend to hold negative attitudes toward the severely mentally disordered. Normal people are further distanced from the mentally disordered by the low social class and low social status of most mentally disordered people. Some of the consequences or functions of mental disorder are that people behaving eccentrically are removed from the general population, usually to state or county hospitals and are allowed or forced to assume a "sick role."

Those in the medical model tradition view mental disorder as an illness; that is, mental disorder is thought to be biologically based, to have specific organic causes and known symptoms, a known course of development, expected outcomes, durations, and responds (if at all) to technical treatments.

Like the flu or cancer, mental disorder is not believed to be heavily influenced by social relations, culture, or values.

On the other hand, sociocultural models of mental disorder (including the symbolic interaction and deviance perspectives) conceive of emotional problems as products of culture and value variation or as deviance from social norms. Sometimes people may appear crazy to us simply because they have different values or cultural expectations. Other times people become mental patients because someone else labels them crazy and the label sticks.

Conflict theorists suggest that anyone (especially if they are lower class) who seriously threatens or contests the established political and social order can be called mentally ill and locked up in state or county hospitals. Asylums are prisons for people who offend the dominant class but who have not broken any laws.

On March 30, 1981, John W. Hinckley, Jr., shot U.S. President Ronald Reagan and three other people, including presidential Press Secretary James Brady. A little over one year later a jury found Hinckley not guilty of all charges "by reason of insanity" and sent him to St. Elizabeth's Hospital in Washington instead of to prison. The nation was shocked (Kaufman, 1982). Even Hinckley himself was convinced he would at least go to prison. How could this be? An upper-middle-class young man who admitted he tried to kill at least four human beings (indeed, including the president of the United States) and who presumably knew right from wrong (although the jury verdict contradicts this) was hardly being punished at all. Presumably Hinckley's mental condition prevented him from being able to curb his murderous behavior (cf. *Behavior Today,* December 19, 1983).[1]

This was not the first time that an individual's mental condition had profound social implications. In 1972 Democratic Vice-Presidential candidate Senator Thomas Eagleton was forced to withdraw his candidacy because he had once received electroshock treatment for depressive illness. Earlier still (in 1907) Mary Baker Eddy, the founder of the Christian Science religion, narrowly escaped confinement in a mental institution owing to her then bizarre eccentric religious beliefs. These cases and others indicate fundamental issues concerning mental disorders, issues that can result in major social problems.

Of course, one absolutely basic issue is what is mental disorder (Brown, 1987)? For centuries certain individuals and groups have been seen as strange, bizarre, eccentric, mysterious, excitable, disorderly, aggressive, unpredictable—as somehow different from most of the rest of us. But are such people really crazy or does their behavior simply exceed the tolerance of other people? The first part of this question asks if mental disorder is an illness, like the flu or appendicitis. Does mental disorder result from electrical, chemical, or other organic abnormalities in the brain (Kety, 1976)? The second aspect of this

PANEL 8.1

Not Guilty by Reason of Insanity

"On March 30, 1981, I was asking to be loved. I was asking my family to take me back and I was asking Jodie Foster to hold me in her heart. My assassination attempt was an act of love. I'm sorry love has to be so painful."

Sitting alone in his prison cell awaiting what he thought would be the inevitable verdict, John W. Hinckley, Jr. penned these words as part of his "sentencing speech." Hinckley was so convinced he would be found guilty of the attempted assassination of the president and the shooting of James S. Brady, Timothy J. McCarthy, and Thomas K. Delahanty that he titled his speech "The Conviction."

The paunchy young drifter was not alone in his expectations. Most Americans thought Hinckley would be found guilty of each of the charges in the thirteen-count indictment. The jury, however, had other ideas. As Judge Barrington D. Parker successively read the verdict on each charge to a stunned and silent courtroom, the result for each count was the same: not guilty by reason of insanity.

Source: Irving R. Kaufman, *New York Times Magazine,* August 8, 1982:16.

issue asks if mental disorder is a social product (Rosenberg, 1984). Some sociologists see the mentally disordered not as ill, but as having broken important social rules (Scheff, 1975). Others believe that mental disorder can result from social stress (Wheaton, 1983).

A second issue is what should society do with the mentally disordered? Traditionally those people with serious mental illness have been locked up in state mental hospitals, even if they committed major crimes (e.g., murder or rape). But if the mentally disordered are not really sick or criminals, are we not in effect putting them away because they are troublemakers (i.e., bizarre, misfits, inappropriate, or norm violators) (Fox, 1984)? Psychiatrist Thomas Szasz claims that involuntary commitment to a mental hospital is really just social control of people we do not like (1978; Rosenfield, 1984; however, see Krauthammer, 1979). Since about 1955 (and the advent of phenothiazine drugs like Thorazine), the tendency has been to deinstitutionalize the less severely mentally disordered.

This brings us to a third issue. Can the mentally disordered get along in society at-large? If so, which kinds of mental disorder can be socially tolerated (Fox, 1984; Link and Cullen, 1986)? Here we are asking if certain kinds of mental disorder affect our very ability to be social creatures. If you hear voices, think you are Jesus Christ or Napoleon, can you perform your job or fulfill routine role expectations?[2] Clearly, most of us would not welcome a schizo-

phrenic commercial airline pilot. Often mental illness can be more debilitating than physical illness. Consider past U.S. President F. D. Roosevelt who ran the country from a wheelchair as a result of his having had polio. At the same time we worry considerably about some physically robust general who just might start World War III owing to his delusions about exaggerated communist war offensives.

Fourth, what is the difference between actual thought disorders (like schizophrenia) and religious or ethical belief systems or values that conflict with civil laws (Rosenberg, 1984)? Is it all right if you talk to God just on Sunday (or Saturday, as the case may be)? When you think about it for a minute, prayer is very strange behavior. Perhaps the danger of this issue seems a bit exaggerated. After all, is it not easy to tell when someone is crazy as opposed to just religious? Perhaps, but that is not the whole problem. What happens when one's religious values or beliefs require that s/he violate civil or criminal law? Is s/he then a criminal or mentally disordered? There is the celebrated story of Abraham and Isaac in the Judeo-Christian Bible (the book of Genesis), in which God asks Abraham to sacrifice his son Isaac to prove his religious faith. If he had actually done so, the criminal law would have considered Abraham a murderer.

Another (fifth) issue is the cost of mental disorder. You will recall that in the previous chapter the inflated costs of physical illness were one of the major issues. Although mental disorder is costly, for some reason the monetary costs of mental illness do not seem all that important to most societies. Probably one reason for this is that mental illness is usually not fatal. Also, we can suffer

People such as these obviously are difficult to interact with socially. Individuals who exhibit such bizarre, eccentric, unpredictable, or aggressive behaviors are often thought mentally disordered and in need of confinement. (Jeff Albertson/Stock, Boston)

from many types of mental disorder (especially those related to phobias, anxiety, mild depression, alcohol related disorders, and so on) and still work relatively effectively. Thus, treatment and cure of many mental disorders (although the disorders may be distressing and impairing to individuals) is not essential for social well-being.

Finally, we need to explore the use, limits, and value of psychiatric drugs, such as Thorazine, Elavil, lithium carbonate, and so on. Perhaps more than any other single factor psychopharmacology has revolutionized the treatment of mental disorders and, especially, the need to incarcerate mental patients. As we shall see, the drastic reduction of the state hospital population has resulted primarily from the introduction of new psychotropic drugs. However, critics have charged that such drugs simply mask psychiatric illnesses; they do not control underlying causes. There is also the danger of mind or behavior control abuse through using psychiatric drugs inappropriately to regulate unruly or troublesome individuals, who are not in fact mentally disordered. These then are some of the fundamental issues before us in the present chapter, issues that, if not addressed, can result in major social problems.

Of course, satisfactory resolution of issues and problems of mental disorders requires that we have some agreement on what mental illness is, on its definition. Basically, we shall follow the classification of mental disorders in the American Psychiatric Association's *Diagnostic and Statistical Manual, III,* 1980 (*DMS* III, for short), although some social and behavioral scientists object to the implied medical model in *DMS* III (a revised version, *DSM* III R, appeared in 1987). Here each of the mental disorders is conceptualized as "a clinically significant behavioral or psychological syndrome or pattern that occurs in an individual and that is typically associated with either a painful symptom (distress) or impairment in one or more important areas of functioning (disability)" (*DSM* III, 1980:6). While our definition of mental disorder is clearly sympathetic with what is called the medical model of mental disorders, we shall stop short of trying to reduce all mental disorders to chemical or electrical abnormalities in the brain (See Kety, 1976; Snyder, 1980).

Others, including sociologists, insist that mental disorder is not a biological condition, but rather a social product. For example, as we have seen, Eitzen defines *mental illness* as "behavior that exceeds the tolerance of others" (1986:456). Here the *social reaction* to, not the biological condition of, the mentally disordered is crucial (cf. McCaghy, 1976:317–318; Goffman, 1963). In a similar vein Scheff (1968:10) argues that the mentally ill break basic rules (residual rules; see below for definition) that govern social interaction. According to psychiatrist Thomas Szasz this results in "problems of living" for the mentally disordered (1978:59 and 62). Szasz believes that the mentally disordered are not sick. Rather, "psychosis is a religion we do not like." Like medical models, social-psychological models can be reduced to the point of absurdity too.[3] We shall use both medical and social explanations. Definitions of these specific types of mental disorders (alluded to in Figure 8.1) will be elaborated later on.

FIGURE 8.1 Classification of Major Mental Disorders, *DSM* III, 1980*

I. **Disorders Usually Evident in Infancy, Childhood, or Adolescence**
Mental retardation, stuttering, attention deficit, separation anxiety, anorexia, bulemia, infantile autism†

II. **Organic Mental Disorders**
Senility, alcohol or drug induced hallucinations, organic delusional syndromes

III. **Substance Use Disorders**
Abuse of or dependence on alcohol, barbiturates, amphetamines, and so on

IV. **Schizophrenic Disorders**
Withdrawal from ordinary social interaction, bizarre thought processes, paranoia, hallucinations, catatonic stupor

V. **Paranoid Disorders**
Persistent persecutory delusions or delusional jealousy not due to any other mental disorders (e.g., schizophrenia)

VI. **Affective Disorders**
Depression, elation, or exaggerated mood swings

VII. **Anxiety Disorders**
Phobias (agoraphobia, claustrophobia), panic, stress from traumatic experience (battle shock)

VIII. **Somatoform Disorders**
Hypochondria, hysteria, or conversion disorder

IX. **Dissociative Disorders**
Amnesia, fugue, multiple personality, depersonalization

X. **Psychosexual Disorders**
Transsexualism, gender identity disorder, fetishism, exhibitionism, sexual masochism, voyeurism, premature ejaculation, inhibited sexual desire

XI. **Conditions Not Attributable to Mental disorder, but Requiring Treatment**
Malingering, adult antisocial behavior, interpersonal problems, academic problems, occupational problems, noncompliance with medical treatment.

*Not all classifications are listed in Figure 8.1. Roman numerals are not used in the original.
†Not all examples are given for each classification of mental disorders.

Source: American Psychiatric Association, 1980:15–19. Reprinted with permission from the *Diagnostic and Statistical Manual of Mental Disorders, Second Edition.* Copyright 1980 American Psychiatric Association.

In passing we must note that one problem with using the *DSM* III classification of mental disorders is that the *DSM* keeps changing. For example, hysteria and homosexuality are no longer considered mental disorders. Even the concept of neurosis (as a separate category) has disappeared. Other behaviors have been added to the list of mental disorders. Cigarette smoking or caffeine addiction are now thought to be mental disorders if they cause you distress or disability. Even when the categories of mental disorder remain constant, there still exists considerable disagreement among psychiatrists and psychologists about who is or is not schizophrenic, manic-depressive, and so on (Brown, 1987; Kendell et al., 1971; Kendell, 1975; Grusky and Pollner, 1981:309–313, 319–328).

However, once we have some rough consensus on what mental disorder is, we next must ask how widespread it is. Put a little differently, are the prevalence (all cases) and incidence (new cases) of mental disorder in the United States sufficient to constitute a social problem?[4] If one uses a definition of mental disorder such as Szasz's (obviously a very broad definition) problems of living, then as many as 85 percent of the American population suffers from emotional problems (President's Commission on Mental Health, 1978, Vol. II). However, if we use the *DSM* III classifications, then about 10 percent to 20 percent of Americans have mental disorders (*Mental Health, United States,* 1985:4; *Associated Press,* October 3, 1984). Srole et al., in a classic study of a random sample of 1,700 New York City (Manhattan) adults found that 23 percent of those studied had marked or severe mental disorders (1975). However, the median or average prevalence of mental disorder in a large series of such surveys of mental disorder was found to be 15.6 percent (Dohrenwend and Dohrenwend, 1969:275–310). Thus, in 1986 roughly 36 million Americans were mentally disordered (*Mental Health, United States* 1985:4 found 29.4 million in 1980).

If we define *mental disorder* as those individuals actually treated as inpatients or outpatients, then the percentage of the American population with mental disorder shrinks from about 15 percent to 3 percent. For example, Table 8.1 reveals that in 1979 there were 6,404,000 episodes of psychiatric care (*Health, United States,* 1982:110; *Health, United States,* 1985:102). Patients in state and county hospitals have declined from about 550,000 in 1955 to about 125,000 in 1982 (*Mental Health, United States,* 1985:35). This is a 77 percent reduction in the state and county hospital patient population. Most experts attribute this inpatient decline to more effective psychiatric drugs, an increase in psychiatric outpatient services (like community mental health clinics), and new policies for deinstitutionalizing mental patients and returning them to their communities (see Figure 8.2).

A more refined method for determining the prevalence of mental disorders is to examine the frequency of specific types of *DSM* III psychiatric disorders (the actual diagnostic procedure is complex, involving decisions on five "axes"). Considering the state and county mental hospital populations we just spoke of, schizophrenia is the primary diagnosis for inpatient admissions (Figure 8.3). Alcohol related disorders are the second most common mental problem, especially for men. Depressive neurosis or affective disorder is usually the third or fourth most common mental inpatient disorder, depending upon one's sex (women tend to have a greater incidence of depressive episodes—however, see Newmann, 1986). Interestingly, a recent general psychiatric survey of the American population (see Panel 8.2) found that 13.6 percent had alcohol problems, 11.3 percent had experienced phobias (fears), and 5.7 had major depressions. Most behavioral scientists had expected depression to be the number one mental disorder in the general population.

To care for the 3 percent of the American population with treated mental disorders cost an estimated $17 billion in 1977 (*President's Commission on*

TABLE 8.1 Inpatient and Outpatient Care Episodes in Selected Mental Health Facilities, According to Type of Facility: United States, Selected Years 1965–1981.
(Data are based on reporting by facilities.)

Type of Facility	Year				
	1965	1975	1977	1979*	1981
	Number of Episodes in Thousands				
All facilities	2,637	6,409	6,393	6,404	—
Inpatient services	1,566	1,791	1,817	1,802	1,720
General hospital psychiatric service	519	566	572	—	677
State and county hospitals	805	599	574	529	499
Private hospitals†	125	165	184	197	177
Veterans Administration psychiatriac service‡	116	214	218	—	206
Federally funded community mental health centers	—	247	269	299	—
Outpatient services§	1,071	4,618	4,576	4,602	—
Federally funded community mental health center	—	1,585	1,742	1,950	—
Other mental health facilities	1,071	3,033	2,835	2,653	—

*Provisional data. 1979 data are not yet available for Veterans Administration neuropsychiatric hospital inpatient units, general hospital inpatient psychiatric units (Veterans Administration and nonfederal), and federally funded community mental health centers' (CMHCs) inpatient and outpatient services; 1978 data are used for CMHCs, and 1977 data are used for Veterans Administration psychiatric inpatient settings and for separate psychiatric inpatient and outpatient services of nonfederal general hospitals.
†Includes estimates of episodes of care in residential treatment centers for emotionally disturbed children.
‡Includes Veterans Administration neuropsychiatric hospitals and Veterans Administration general hospitals with separate psychiatric inpatient settings.
§Excludes partial care episodes and outpatient episodes of Veterans Administration hospitals and clinics.

Source: *Health, United States,* 1982:110, and *Health, United States,* 1985:102, National Institute of Mental Health: Trends in Patient Care Episodes in Mental Health Facilities, 1955–1977. *Statistical Note 154.* Public Health Service, Rockville, MD, Sept. 1980; unpublished data from the Division of Biometry and Epidemiology.

Mental Health, 1978:530ff.). This amounted to about 11 percent of the total health care bill in 1977 (which was $161 billion). However, when we add the indirect costs (costs due to death and disability, and so on), the total bill for mental disorders was more like $40 billion in 1977 (cf. *Mental Health, United States,* 1985:68–69; *Statistical Abstract of the United States,* 1987:85ff., for data up to 1985). Total direct costs for all mental health care in 1980 was $19.9 billion (*Mental Health, United States,* 1985:101). Figure 8.4 shows that in 1980 the bulk of the direct expenditures was for general hospitals, state and county mental hospitals, nursing homes, community mental health centers, and VA psychiatric services.

Mental disorder is not a new social problem. Society has always had to come to terms with bizarre, seemingly irrational, purposeless, or even unintelligible behaviors. The early Greeks and Romans thought mental illness was caused by the amount, temperature, and color of bile, blood, and phlegm

FIGURE 8.2 Percent Distributions of Inpatient and Outpatient Care Episodes in Mental Health Facilities by Type of Facility: United States, 1955 and 1973

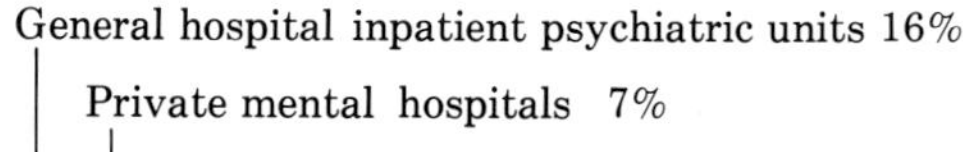

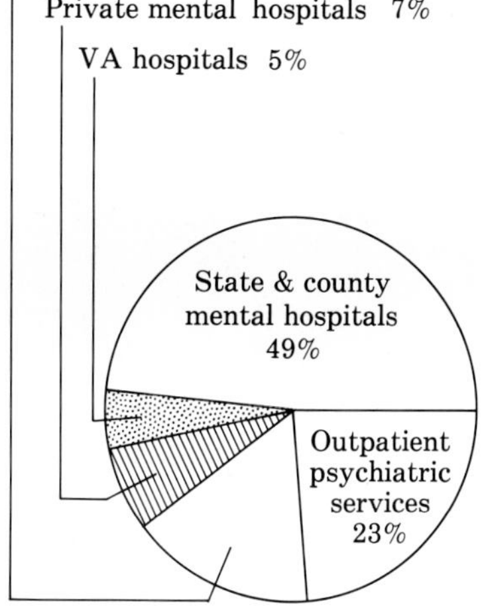

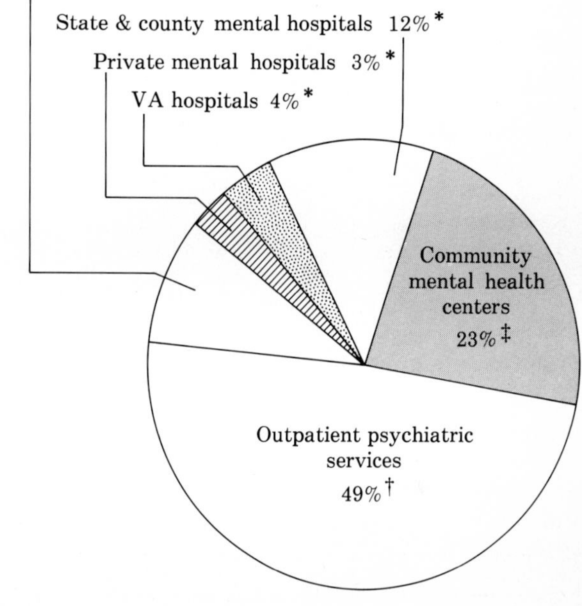

1955 (1.7 Million Episodes) **1973 (5.2 Million Episodes)**

*Inpatient services only.
†Includes free-standing outpatient services as well as those affiliated with psychiatric and general hospitals.
‡Includes inpatient and outpatient services of federally funded CMHCs.

Source: President's Commission on Mental Health, 1978:534, C.A. Taube and R.W. Redick, *Provisional Data on Patient Care Episodes in Mental Health Facilities,* 1973; *Statistical Note 124,* November 1975, Rockville, MD; Division of Biometry & Epidemiology, National Institute of Mental Health. For more recent data, see *Mental Health, United States,* 1985:9–36.

(Gallagher, 1980:7–11). For example, Hippocrates (ca., 4000 B.C.) argued that black bile caused melancholia (depression) (Cockerham, 1981:13).

In the Middle Ages (and earlier) the mentally disordered were thought to have been invaded by the devil or other evil spirits. Treatment involved either exorcism or even boring holes in the patient's head to let the evil spirits out. This practice, known as skull trepanning, was especially common in Peru 1,000 to 2,000 years ago (Cockerham, 1981:10). Many women, religious heretics, and eccentrics came to be regarded as witches (see Kramer & Springer, *Malleus Maleficarum,* "The Hammer of Witches," 1669). Witch trials began in about 1245 in France and peaked between 1450 and 1670. In Salem, Massachusetts, (1692) nineteen of twenty-five defendants accused of being witches

FIGURE 8.3 Percent Distribution of Admissions, by Selected Primary Diagnosis and Type of Inpatient Psychiatric Service: United States, 1980

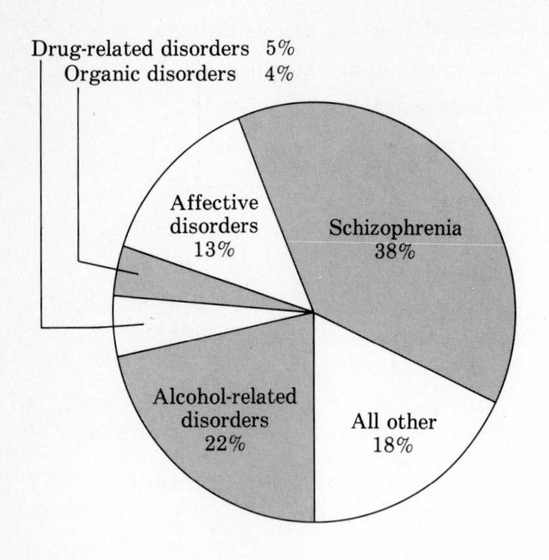

State and county mental hospitals

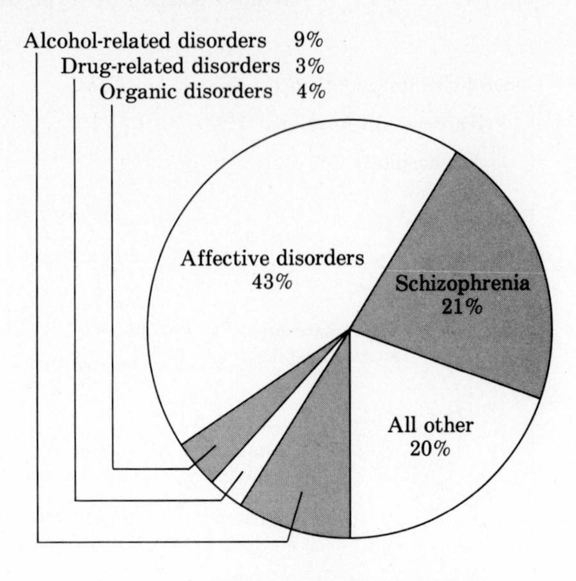

Private psychiatric hospitals

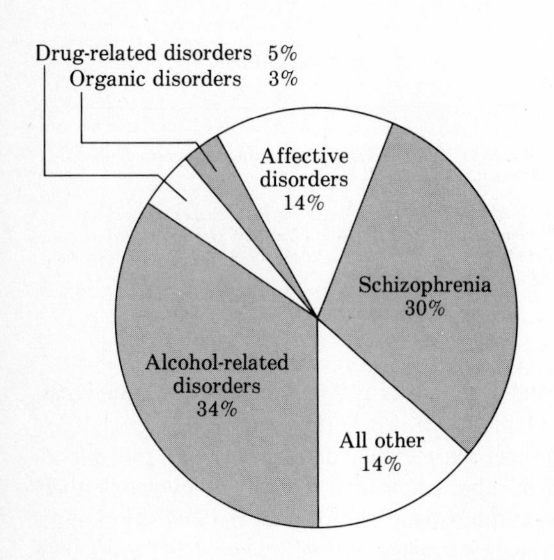

Veterans Administration medical centers

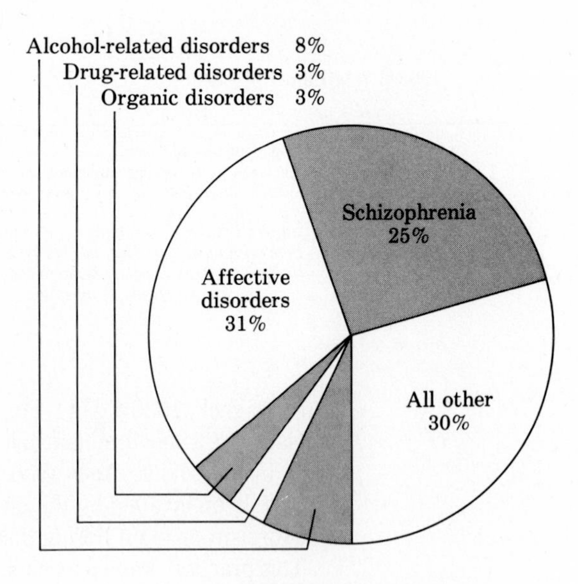

Non-Federal general hospitals

Source: *Mental Health, United States,* 1985:19.

PANEL 8.2

Alcoholism, Phobias, Most Common Mental Disorders in United States

Depression is the number one mental disorder among Americans, assume the majority of behavioral scientists. In fact, it ranks third—after alcoholism and phobias, in that order. These are some of the preliminary findings of an extensive survey of common mental disorders in the United States conducted by the National Institute on Mental Health. Of those studied, 13.6 percent had experienced alcohol abuse or dependency; 11.3 percent had experienced phobias; 5.7 percent had experienced major depression; 5.6 percent had had other drug abuse and dependency problems.

Gender related findings: Men had higher rates of psychiatric disorders than women, a higher incidence of alcoholism and antisocial personality. Women more often experienced major depression and phobias.

Age: The twenty-five through forty-four segment revealed a higher rate of psychiatric disorders. Cognitive impairment was highest among individuals over age sixty-five, but the problem was found among all age groups.

Race: There was virtually no difference in types or rankings of mental illness between blacks and whites. However, blacks tended to have slightly higher rates of phobias and drug abuse and dependency, while whites had slightly higher rates of major depression and anorexia nervosa.

Source: *Behavior Today Newsletter,* January 9, 1984. Atcom Publishing, 2315 Broadway, New York, NY 10024–4397. (212) 873–5900

and brought to court were executed (cf. Chapter 1; and Erikson, 1966:137–159).

Some of the mentally ill were put on ships (a "Ship of Fools," Foucault, 1965:11) and set to sea, only to be abandoned later on foreign soil. At the time of the American Revolution criminals, paupers, and the insane were all housed together, at first in 1727 in Connecticut. The first state hospital for the insane only was in 1773 in Williamsburg, Virginia. Starting in the 1880s and continuing until the 1940s and 1950s (actually until the present) the public was outraged by the poor care and treatment of patients in the state hospitals for the mentally disordered (see Dorothea Dix, 1820–1887). Earlier in Europe (1793) Phillippe Pinel had removed the chains from mental patients in a Paris hospital and championed more humane care of the mentally ill.

The situation in the state and county hospitals really did not improve much in the 1950s and later. What did happen was that new psychiatric drugs allowed patients to get out of the state hospitals and be treated as outpatients. Phenothiazine drugs like chlorpromazine (Thorazine) revolutionized the treatment of psychosis (especially of schizophrenia). There were also important "new" drugs for the treatment of depression, such as imipramine (Tofranil) and lithium carbonate. The effectiveness of these new drugs gave support to the medical model of mental disorder; that mental disorder was primarily a biological illness, not a social product. We now turn to a more detailed examination of this issue.

FIGURE 8.4 Estimates of Direct Costs of Mental Health Care: Health and Specialty Mental Health Sectors, United States—1980

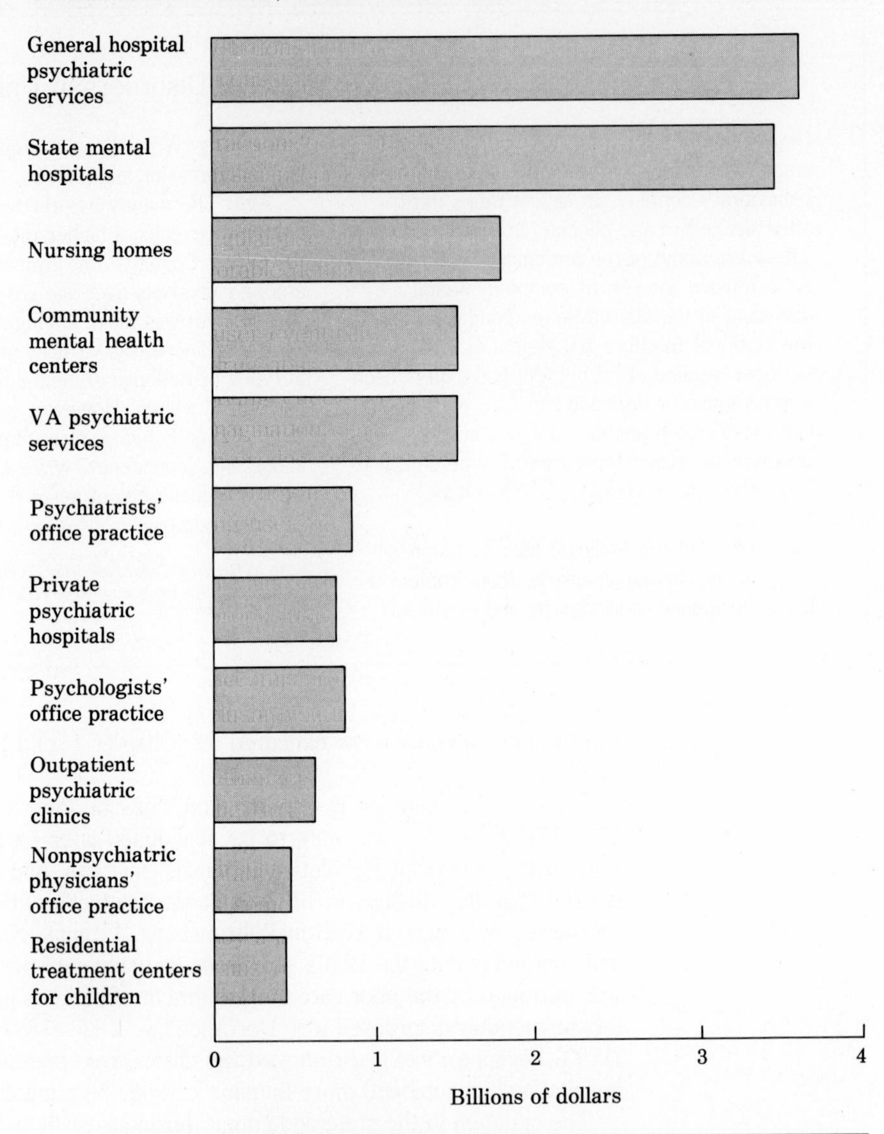

Source: *Mental Health, United States,* 1985:97.

• Contrasting Models of Mental Disorder

Unlike physical illness the causes and cures of mental disorder are less obvious. Virtually no one disputes the role of viruses or bacteria in colds, but we are less sure about biological factors in schizophrenia or depression. Somehow it seems easier to conceive of most mental illness as a social creation. In what follows we will review various contrasting theoretical models of mental disorders, including medical, sociocultural (including the symbolic interaction and deviance perspectives), conflict, exchange, and structural models.

The Medical Model Behavioral scientists like Kety (1976), Snyder (1980), and Tsuang and Vandermey (1980) tend to view mental illness as a disease. This implies that mental disorder is biologically based (including mental factors linked physically to sex, race, and age), has specific organic causes and known symptoms (for example, as in the *DSM* III descriptions), has known courses of development, expected outcomes, and durations, and responds (if at all) to technical treatments (such as psychotropic drugs, shock treatment, or psychosurgery). Like the flu or cancer in the medical model, mental disorder is not believed to be heavily influenced by social relations, culture, values, and so on. For example, an identical twin of a schizophrenic has about a 50 percent risk of becoming schizophrenic, even if removed from his/her family of origin by adoption and raised separately (Kety, 1976). In a more recent study (Associated Press, February 26, 1987) Housman et al. of the Massachusetts Institute of Technology discovered that members of a large Amish family with a defective gene (i.e., a narrow portion of chromosome #11) had an 85 percent probability of contracting manic-depressive illness sometime during their lives.

Medical model theorists, like Johns Hopkins psychopharmacologist Solomon Snyder, observe that virtually all information processing involves communication between nerve cells (i.e., neurons) via chemicals known as neurotransmitters across a synaptic cleft (the connecting gap between neurons) (Snyder, 1980, 1975). The basic hypothesis is that mental disorders are related to abnormalities in the neurotransmitters. For example, patients dying of Parkinson's disease have brains low in dopamine. Norepinephrine and serotonin synapse deficiencies are associated with depression. Finally, thorazine (chlorpromazine) helps schizophrenic symptoms apparently by blocking dopamine synapses in the brain. Thus, it seems plausible that somehow overactive dopamine synapses are related to schizophrenia.

Others in the medical model of mental illness tradition, such as Tsuang and Vandermey (1980), contend that genes cause some mental disorders. For example, in Huntington's chorea (of which folksinger Woody Guthrie died in 1967) each child of an affected parent has a 50 percent chance of sooner or later getting Huntington's disease (the usual onset is about age forty-five). The gene for Huntington's disease is dominant. That is, if it is present, the disease will always develop. As of now there is no cure for Huntington's disease. Those suffering from it gradually lose control of their minds (dementia) and bodies over a period of ten to twenty years. We also know that mood disorders like depression are ten times more likely in close relatives of depressives. Gene-linked mental disorder is suspected in alcoholism as well as in depression.

Finally, there are also psychological or psychoanalytical variations of the medical model, as seen especially in the writings of Sigmund Freud (1856–

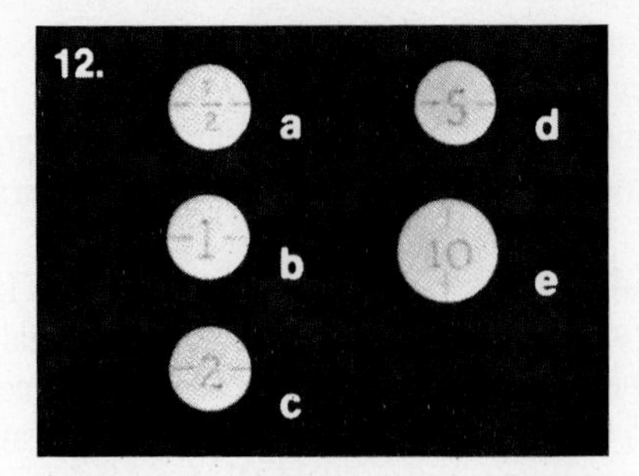

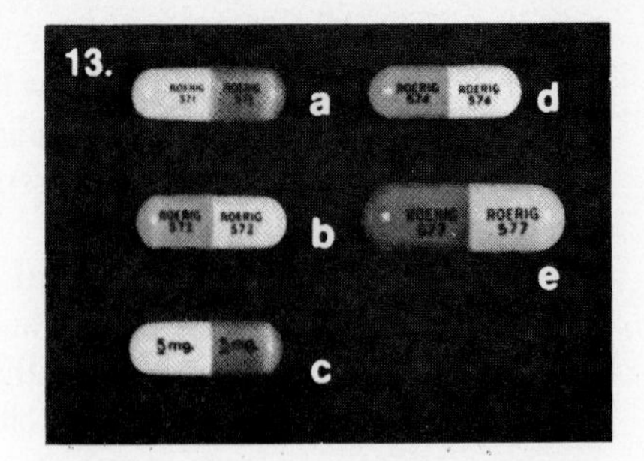

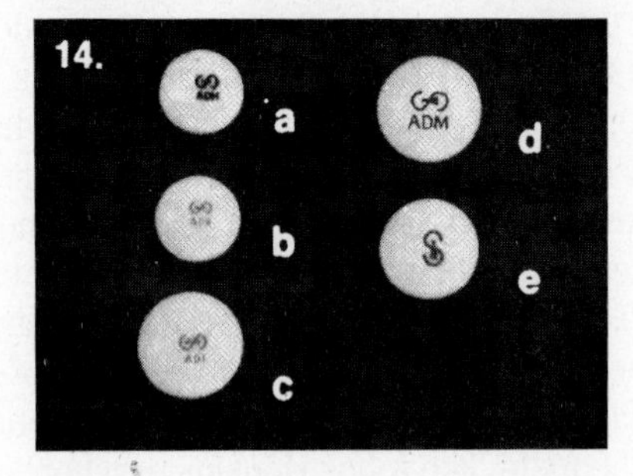

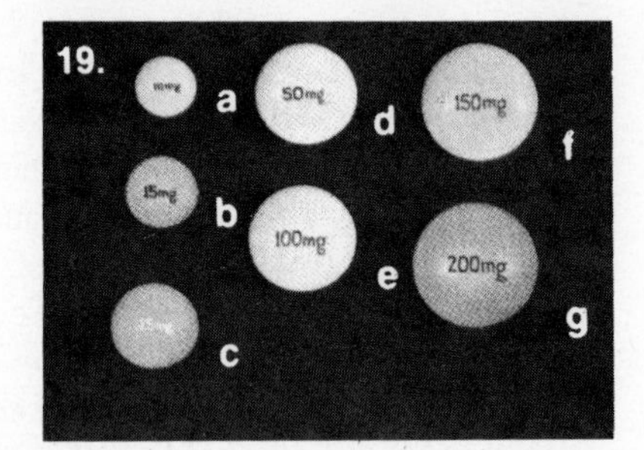

The medical model of mental illness holds that mental disorders are biochemically based and that drug or other technical treatments should be used. Pictured are common antipsychotic medications, like Haldol (12), Navane (13), Mellaril (19), Trilafon (14). (Sandoz, Inc.)

1939). An external agent or event (note the similarity to a virus or gene), usually early in one's life, is thought to cause personality or developmental abnormalities. Like the medical doctors they are, analysts treat the individual, not society. In Freud's *Mourning and Melancholia* (1953–1965; original, 1917), depression is believed to result from the loss of a love object (it could be a parent), regression of libidinal (sexual, erotic) energy into the affected person's ego, and finally the splitting of the ego. Thus, depression and suicide represent anger and murderous wishes toward significant others internalized in one's own ego. To kill them, you must kill yourself. In general, in Freud's work mental disorders result from id (a personality component for providing immediate discharge of tension or energy, seeks pleasure, avoids pain), ego, and superego (very roughly, one's conscience) conflicts. For Freud sexual conflicts were at the root of many mental disorders. For example, the old *DSM* II category of hysteria was a disorder thought to originate from repressed sexual energy.

Sociocultural Models A second major group of overlapping models of mental disorder can loosely be called sociocultural. These models tend to conceive of mental disorder as products of culture and value variation, as deviance from norms, or as being coerced into sick roles, not as diseases—organic or biological. Mental disorders are seen as problems of living in which public reactions to behavior, not the behavior itself, create mental disorder. The focus is on social interaction, not individual biology (see Rosenberg, 1984, for a symbolic interaction perspective on psychosis). The social stress and life events materials we discussed in Chapter 7 in conjunction with physical illness also fit in here—as a social model of mental illness.

Of course, sometimes people may appear crazy to us simply because they have different values or exhibit behaviors expected in one culture but anomalous in another. That is, some mental disorder is merely sociocultural variation (Gallagher, 1980:20ff.). R. Benedict found that among the Zuñi great initiative was seen as appropriate only for witches (Benedict, 1934). Hearing voices, talking to God, and so on, can be grounds for both sainthood or schizophrenia. Later in this chapter we note that psychiatrists from different countries systematically assign different *DSM* psychiatric classifications to the same patients (Kendell et al., 1971; Brown, 1987).

Another broad overlapping group of sociocultural models argues that deviant behavior and labeling produce mental disorders (Merton, 1938; Becker, 1973; Cockerham, 1981:Ch. 2; cf. Weinstein, 1983). From the deviant behavior perspective society punishes norm violators, not those that are necessarily mentally ill. Scheff (1975) says that some social rules (residual rules) are so much taken for granted (e.g., looking away 180 degrees while talking to someone or walking nude through a shopping mall) that their violation is considered insane, not just sinful or criminal. The deviance perspective points out that many of us engage in relatively harmless, transitory, crazy acts (primary deviance). Little harm results from primary deviance unless repeated negative societal reactions make us acquire a deviant (crazy) identity (secondary deviance; see Lemert, 1951, 1972; MacAulliffe and Gordon, 1974; Townsend, 1978). Others like Erikson (1966) even contend that a certain amount of crazy deviant behavior is required in a society to define what the norms are for noncrazy behavior.

Unlike physical illness, most people become mental patients because someone else labels them crazy and the label sticks (McCaghy, 1976:317–318; Scheff, 1975:9–10). Usually those people that are labeled mentally ill have broken certain important social rules and are considered troublemakers (Scheff, 1975:9–10). It is not clear that mental patients are biologically ill in the sense that cancer or heart patients are. Once the mentally ill label has been accepted, stigmatization and negative stereotypes are part of the new role (Goffman, 1963). Gove (1970:873–884) has criticized Scheff and the deviance-labeling perspective, claiming that primary deviance is more important than Scheff thinks, that Scheff is not clear on how one assumes the mentally sick role.

Applying psychiatric labels (such as schizophrenic, borderline personality, antisocial personality, manic-depressive, and so on) can be a power move by those in positions of authority to control difficult, annoying, eccentric people who are not crazy (labeling is also related to the conflict perspective of mental disorder). One powerful consequence of psychiatric labels is that they allow family, doctors, lawyers, and so on, to involuntarily commit people to mental

Drawing by Chas. Addams; © 1986 *The New Yorker* Magazine, Inc.

institutions. As renegade psychiatrist Thomas Szasz says, "psychiatry is for controlling people who have a religion we do not like" (1978:59, 62). Szasz claims that mental illness is a myth (however, see Krauthammer, *New Republic,* December 22, 1979). In fact, according to Szasz, it is the only illness a cadaver cannot have (1961). Mental illness is something one does, not something one has. You cannot see evidence of most mental disorders after the patient has died, but you can see evidence of physical illness in the bodies of dead cancer or heart patients.

Thomas Szasz, M.D., a radical psychiatrist, views society, not the individual, as mentally ill. Szasz claims that psychosis is a religion we do not like and that mental illness labels help majority groups lock up dissidents that have not committed crimes.
(Barbara Alper)

The Conflict Model Closely related to the social control model of mental disorder of Thomas Szasz is the conflict model approach of Kittrie (1973) and others (see Cockerham, 1981:38–41). In addition to being sociocultural, the conflict model of mental disorder is also socioeconomic. Both models see society, not the individual, as the real problem source. As one author put it, "mental illness is the mechanism by which one survives in a mad world" (Eitzen, 1986:456). However, the conflict model emphasizes social class and power differentials of mental patients and the sane.

Are you aware of the social class of mental patients compared to the general population? Who do you think is locked up in the state and county hospitals? Data by Hollingshead and Redlich (1953) and others (Link, Dohrenwend, Skokol, 1986) make it abundantly clear that mental patients have disproportionately low social status (Rosenfield, 1984). In fact, conflict theorists suggest that perhaps mental patients are locked up *because* of their low social status rather than because of their mental illness.

Furthermore, it is not just people with low social status who are considered mentally ill and locked up. The conflict model suggests that anyone who seriously threatens or contests the established political order can be labeled mentally ill and put away. That is, psychiatric illness is a way of controlling political dissidents. It is well known that the USSR tends to place social dissidents in mental asylums. However, we tend to delude ourselves about this practice in the United States. In fact, about 42 percent of all mental patients in the United States are committed against their will (*New York Times,* June 1, 1975). In general, if you come into conflict with powerful people in a society but are not clearly a criminal, there is still a chance that you may be labeled crazy and locked up anyway.

The Exchange Model Like labeling theory in the sociocultural model, the exchange model focuses on actual face-to-face interactions (see Link and Cullen, 1986). But the exchange model is interested in observed and measurable interactive behaviors, not in subjective meanings (Cockerham, 1981:72ff.). The exchange theory of mental disorder is closely related to learning theory (see Skinner, 1971 on operant behaviors). As such, mental disorders are seen as forms of adaptation to one's social environment (Akers, 1985). The exchange model argues that if mental disorders such as schizophrenia, depression, anxiety, and so on, exist, they have been reinforced, rewarded, made valuable and profitable (see Panel 2.2, especially exchange Propositions A1 and A3).

Like Sutherland's theory of differential association in the development of criminal behaviors (1974; cf. Chapter 15), the exchange model suggests that the mentally disordered learn to act crazy. Paradoxically, to be mentally disordered one must have the opportunity to learn how. Most obviously one could grow up with schizophrenic, depressed, alcoholic, phobic, aggressive, and so on, parents. Or society could encourage mental disorder through stress (Holmes and Rahe, 1967; Wheaton, 1983), competition (McClelland, 1953), or too great a rate of social change (Toffler, 1970).

It may seem curious to think of mental disorder as being rewarded, because in fact much so-called crazy behavior is actually punished. What are some of the rewards of mental disorder? For one, the mentally disordered are allowed not to work (see the sick role in Chapter 7), are left alone (in Kesey's *One Flew Over the Cuckoo's Nest,* 1962, the Indian chief was allowed to remain silent because of his "illness"), and are taken care of in state hospitals (fed, housed, medicated, and so on). Second, the mentally disordered often define what is normal by setting examples of the limits of acceptable behavior. Kai Erikson (1966) has argued that the "witches" in Salem, Massachusetts (1692), were valuable to society because the American pilgrims were in a normative as well as a physical wilderness. Third, once in a mental hospital patients are rewarded if they accept labels of mental illness (Goffman, 1961; Cole, 1975:141–42) and punished if they resist. Finally, the sensitivity and creativity often associated with schizophrenia and some other mental illnesses (see Kurt Vonnegut's novels, for example) are highly valued.

Still, from the perspective of the exchange model we must determine what is being exchanged between the mentally disordered and the sane, as we did with exchanges between the aged and nonaged, men and women, whites and blacks, and so on (see Tables 4.3, 5.4, 6.6). In Table 8.2 we suggest that sane-mentally disordered interactions are unlike age, sex, and racial exchanges in that few scarce interactive rewards are offered by the mentally disordered. True, food, shelter, security, and suspension of role demands are exchanged for the mentally disordered's compliance and acceptance of low social status. But for the most part (like criminals) the mentally disordered are distinguished by their inability (or refusal) to participate in routine social exchanges. Usually, punishments not rewards, are exchanged. For example, violent, aggressive, eccentric people are generally perceived to be threats to larger society and accordingly are punished by being locked up in state and county hospitals or heavily medicated to control their behavior. Thus, even though the exchange model would argue that society often rewards or finds mental disorder valuable (and helps create mental disorders), it also perceives the mentally disordered as interactively dangerous and disruptive and tends to isolate or segregate them from the rest of society in mental institutions or asylums.[5]

TABLE 8.2 Distribution of Basic Societal Punishments and Rewards by Mental Status

Punishments and Rewards	**Sane**	**Mentally Disordered**
Food, shelter security, suspension of normal role demands	+	–
Compliance, low social status	–	+
Aggression, eccentricity	–	+
Isolation	–	+

\+ = Reward or punishment present or supplied.
– = Reward or punishment absent or received.

The Structural Model As we might predict from Chapter 2, structuralists emphasize the implications of differentiated social positions for mental disorder. For example, relevant considerations would include the size and number of the mentally disordered population; the chance expectations for sane people interacting with the mentally disordered; the social class, sex, marital status, or race (distributions of the mentally disordered; see Fox, 1984); the relation of economic conditions in society and the occupational division of labor to mental disorder; the social distance or proximity of the sane from the insane; and crowding and mental status. Like the exchange model, the structural model focuses on observed, objective, measurable social patterns or behaviors. However, the structural model is more macrosociological and accordingly is less interested in individuals or small groups. Unlike the symbolic interaction or labeling and conflict models, the structural model of mental disorder places less emphasis on values, prejudices, oppression, and discrimination.

Based on our earlier discussion of the prevalence of mental disorder we know that about 15 percent of the general U.S. population (34 million) experience some classifiable mental disorder in a given year but only 3 percent (6.5 million) are actually treated. Thus, the heterogeneity[6] (the probability of out-group association) for the nontreated population is .26 and that of the treated population is .06. Considering the size of the treated mentally disordered population alone, it is extremely unlikely that most of us will ever interact with a severely mentally disordered individual. And, if interaction enhances liking and similarity, then most of us will tend to hold negative attitudes toward the mentally disordered and see them as different, strange, bizarre, and so on.

Not only are mental patients relatively rare, many of them also tend to be segregated or isolated in mental asylums. If we assume that proximity improves the chances for social interaction, then clearly mental hospitals restrict our prospects of getting to know the mentally disordered (and tends to restrict the interaction of the mentally disordered to other mentally disordered patients). Recently, segregation of the mentally disordered has been reduced by the introduction of community mental health centers (Wagenfeld and Robin, 1976), outpatient treatment, and deinstitutionalization of mental patients (Bassuk and Gerson, 1978). Some have argued that proximity to mental hospitals, not mental illness, increases one's chances of being hospitalized (see Goffman, 1961:35ff., on career contingencies of mental patients). Finally, overcrowded home living has been thought to encourage mental disorder (Galle and Gove, 1978; Brown and Harris, 1978).

In addition to physical distancing the mentally disordered tend to be distanced socially from the sane. The mentally disordered tend to have low social status or class (Hollingshead and Redlich, 1953; Srole et al., 1975; Cockerham, 1981:Ch. 5). This also restricts social interaction between the mentally disordered and nondisordered, since populations tend not to interact over great social distances. Why the mentally disordered tend to be of lower status is generally explained by their genetic heritage, their differential social stress, and the drift of the mentally disordered down the social status hierarchy. Others have pointed out that employment and mental disorder are usually negatively associated (Brenner, 1977).

For a long time it was thought that women tended to be more mentally disordered than men (Kessler, Brown, and Broman, 1981). But recent evidence suggests that women are more likely to exceed men only in manic-depressive and neurotic illnesses—if at all (cf. Fox, 1984; Newmann, 1986). In general, men have more personality disorders (Dohrenwend and Dohrenwend, 1976). In a major study of depressed women Brown and Harris (1978) contended that females' depressions were caused by low social status, major losses, or severe precipitating events—lack of employment, having no close companions, having three or more young (under fourteen) children at home, loss of their mothers in childhood, and low self-esteem (cf. Newmann, 1984; Ross and Huber, 1985). Being married usually improves mental health and race makes little or no difference (Cockerham, 1981:218ff.).

Each of these basic models (medical, sociocultural, conflict, exchange, and structural) suggests different treatments designed to control, remedy, or resolve various problems of mental disorder. As we might expect, since there is little consensus on what mental disorder or illness is, there is also considerable disagreement on how to cure, treat, or control it.

Treatment of Mental Disorder

Obviously, if you endorse the medical model, you are more likely to accept psychopharmacology than, say, social environmental therapies. Conversely, if you believe that mental disorders result primarily from labeling, you are unlikely to recommend prefrontal lobotomies for mental patients. In what follows, five basic treatment modalities corresponding roughly to the five models of mental disorder just discussed are reviewed.

Chemotherapies, Psychopharmacology, Electroshock, Somatic Therapies, Psychosurgery Most treatments grounded in the medical model see mental disorder as a physical illness, disease, or injury located in individual patients' bodies (more precisely usually in their brains), not in society itself. Basic treatments involve the chemistry, electricity, or surgery of the brain (Kaplan et al., 1980:1251). Among the most promising of the mental disorder treatments in the medical model are chemotherapy (not cancer treatment) or psychoactive drugs (i.e., those that alter the user's mood and/or behavior). First introduced in about 1954, psychopharmacological agents like the phenothiazines have revolutionized the treatment of mental disorders and have allowed many patients to be cared for in outpatient clinics (see Table 8.1; Figure 8.2).

There are at least three basic types of psychopharmacologic drugs: the antipsychotics, the antidepressives, and antianxiety agents. Drugs like Thorazine, Mellaril, Haldol, Stelazine, Taractan, and others, in addition to controlling hallucinations and delusions, also help regulate hyperactivity and aggression. Some of the major antidepressants are Elavil, Tofranil, lithium carbonate (used especially for manic-depressives), Marplan, and so on. Among the leading minor tranquilizers or antianxiety agents are Valium, Librium, and Serax.

Of course, some people have soundly criticized psychotropic drugs. Eisenberg claimed that 30 percent to 50 percent of treated schizophrenics are readmitted in one year and 60 percent to 70 percent are readmitted in five years (*U.S. News & World Report,* February 16, 1976:36). Others maintain that psychiatric drugs relieve symptoms without curing mental illness (Finkel, 1976:58–59). Sometimes the side effects of psychotropic drugs are themselves a problem. For example, phenothiazines can produce parkinsonian symptoms (or extrapyramidal effects) such as facial tics, twitching or tremors, motor discoordination (the Thorazine shuffle), and muscle limpness.

With severely depressed patients electroconvulsive treatment (ECT) is often the treatment of choice (Tanney, 1986), although we really do not know why it works (however, the same could be said of aspirin). In ECT electrodes are placed on the patient's head (see Sylvia Plath's comment on this in *The Bell Jar,* 1971) and 150–170 volts of electricity are sent into the patient's brain for one second or less. The immediate result is seizure or convulsions, loss of consciousness, and some loss of short-term memory. Although ECT is often scary and unpleasant to patients, with the use of supplemental muscle relaxants and anesthetics little permanent physical damage is done and many depressed patients improve dramatically (see Hotchner on Ernest Hemingway's ECT treatments, 1966; Tanney, 1986).

Finally, it is theoretically feasible surgically to alter parts of the brain to control specific psychopathological behaviors, although such procedures usually conjure up images of science fiction movies and mad scientists. Of course, the problem is that these psychosurgery procedures are not very refined and produce no predictable results. Given the complexities of the brain, they may never be. One popular older surgical treatment was the prefrontal lobotomy in which violent patients were "calmed" by surgically severing neural connections in the front lobes of their brains (see Kesey, *One Flew Over the Cuckoo's Nest,* 1962). Prefrontal lobotomies can be crude or precise. In either case they are highly controversial and usually a treatment of last resort. You may be astounded to learn that about 50,000 of them were done in the 1940s and 1950s in the United States.

We will probably see major advances in these medical model types of treatment of mental disorder in the future. The main reason for this is that the necessary medical technology and knowledge are increasing rapidly. Medical model treatments have received an unfair bad reputation much like early pathology, surgery, or anatomy in which it was claimed that their procedures desecrated cadavers or interfered with God's will.[7]

Psychotherapy Psychotherapies overlap with both medical and sociocultural models of mental disorder (Kaplan et al., 1980:1191ff.). To the degree that psychotherapy is based on the work of Sigmund Freud (1856–1939), the emphasis is on individual unconscious conflicts in one's personality (more precisely, id, superego, ego conflicts). Often these conflicts are dealt with somewhat inappropriately through defense mechanisms (such as, denial, repression, sublimation, projection, transference, and so on). Personality conflicts often are thought to originate in early object losses (like the death of one's mother), parent-child interactions, difficulties in sexual development, and so on.

Psychotherapeutic treatment emphasizes talking with trained therapists who listen closely and help mentally disordered patients gain insight into their unconscious conflicts through the use of dreams, slips-of-the-tongue, free associations, interpretations of current interpersonal situations in the context of one's early developmental history, and so on. Psychotherapy works best with articulate, well-educated, intelligent, upper middle-class clients who are not psychotic (that is, what used to be called neurotic patients, mainly anxious or mildly depressed patients) and who can afford the treatment (cf. Link, 1983).

Psychotherapy does not have to be conducted with individuals only. It is also used for groups or families (Satir, 1972). Often forms of psychotherapy are used to increase self-awareness and interpersonal adjustment through various techniques such as primal screams, rolfing, biofeedback, transactional analysis, sensitivity training, yoga, dieting, encounter groups, hypnosis, and psychodrama.

In spite of its popularity psychotherapy has not been proven very effective. Four basic criticisms are (1) that it does not help more than doing nothing (e.g., than just sitting in the therapist's waiting room), (2) that it does not help psychotic or organically damaged patients, (3) that it is expensive and time consuming, and (4) that its justification rests on unseen and unknowable inner forces (like the unconscious) and as such is similar to a religion (Frank, 1975; *The New Yorker,* December 5, 1983 and December 12, 1983; *Behavior Today,* February 13, 1983).

Radical Therapy What has come to be called radical therapy has grown out of both the conflict and the sociocultural models of mental disorder (Agel, 1971; Steiner, 1974). Here the cause of mental disorder is not seen as biology or the individual, but rather society's oppression of relatively powerless, lower social classes. Thus, mental disorder is seen as largely external to individuals.

It follows that treatment should be of society, not of individuals. Metaphorically speaking, society itself is crazy (and thus makes people mentally disordered). How could this be? Well, what about pollution of the air, water, food, and land as a social suicide attempt? Other examples of societal "craziness" might include entering into a nuclear arms race with the Soviet Union that could paradoxically result in world destruction; insisting that everyone work (as President Reagan does), but blocking education and employment for less privileged social groups; producing such stress and competition that it is almost impossible not to become sick, anxious, and depressed; putting those who disagree with society's basic values and goals into state hospitals or prisons; emphasizing maximum economic profit at the expense of human welfare; or allowing industry to produce known cancer-producing products (e.g., the tobacco industry).

In response to radical therapists critics have pointed out that it is difficult to change society. Radical therapists may be forced just to support individual patients, reassure them that they are not to blame, and so on. Then is radical therapy any different from traditional psychotherapy? Probably not much. Also, radical therapy ignores or minimizes individual organic factors in mental disorder, like retardation, brain tumors, senility related illnesses, even stress related to social situations that cannot be easily avoided. Included here would be problems of overwork or the strain of simply raising a family.

Behavior Modification Modifying behavior through schedules of reward or punishment assumes the exchange model of mental disorder (Brady, 1975; Stoyva, 1981). Behavior modification assumes that mental disorder originates from the learning principles of reward, punishment, deprivation, satiation, frustration, and so on (see exchange theory in Panel 2.2). If mental disorder is learned by rewarding pathological behaviors, then theoretically it can be unlearned by reinforcing more desirable responses or by punishing mentally disordered responses. For example, therapists can show a sexual deviant erotic pictures but shock him/her mildly with electricity at the same time. Or one could reward activity in depressed children.

Unlike psychotherapy or psychoanalysis, behavior modification does not concern itself with what goes on in the unconscious or the "black box" of the mind; nor does it try to change society. Behavior modification does not attribute mental disorder to genes, hormones, or other biological factors—except as they may affect learning ability.

Behavior modification techniques have been used with autistic children who are highly withdrawn and unresponsive (Mussen, Rosenzweig et al., 1977: 207ff.), in token economies of state hospitals, in systematic desensitization (for example, to phobias), in biofeedback to reward behaviors that reduce anxiety, lower blood pressure, heart rate, stomach contractions, and so on. Of course, behavior modification does not treat underlying symptoms or causes of mental disorder and cannot be used with severely retarded, grossly psychotic, or deeply depressed patients.

Social Environmental and Structural Therapy The conflict, sociocultural, and structural models all suggest that mental disorder is caused by social forces outside of the individual mental patient. Thus, treatment should focus on factors like the patient's therapeutic environment, opportunities for interacting with the mentally well, changing one's social status or group, altering macroeconomic forces, and so on (Dressler, 1985).

As we have seen, the early treatment of the mentally disordered was punitive, isolating, dreary, and custodial. Thus, improvement in mental disorder should involve improving the conditions of the treatment setting or removal of patients from asylums that cannot be reformed (deinstitutionalization; see Figure 8.2) and into community mental health centers, halfway houses, and the like (Daniels, 1975).

If segregation of the less severely mentally disordered is reduced, then more normal people will interact with the mentally disordered and their attitudes will become more favorable toward the mentally disordered (Link and Cullen, 1986). Also, perhaps it is the structural constraints on women, the poor, those in lower social classes, minorities, and so on, that contribute to their differential rates of mental disorder (Fox, 1984). For example, Brown and Harris (1978) found that structural factors heavily influence depression in females (however, see Newmann, 1986). If so, then increasing employment opportunities, helping with the raising of young, dependent children, improving self-esteem through the ERA, and so on, should reduce rates of female depression. In the next section we will consider a commonplace of much psychiatric treatment—state and county mental hospitals.

• State and County Mental Hospitals

Stating the Problem Although we have considered various concepts of mental disorder and their treatments, we have yet to examine explicitly the most frequent place for the treatment of serious mental disorder—the state or county mental hospital (*Mental Health, United States,* 1985:v). When we do, we discover that the state hospital is characterized by at least four serious problems. First, mental hospitals tend to be dreary, overcrowded, dull, and isolated (Gallagher, 1980:314). Second, state hospitals are usually custodial, not therapeutic. What care exists is often of poor quality. Third, the social organization of the state hospital is formal, hierarchical, authoritarian, and impersonal. Finally, mental hospitals paradoxically can make you "crazy." Let us expand on each of these four problems in order.

Conditions in the Mental Hospital The original purpose of the state hospital was to remove mentally disordered patients from stressful situations to a place of quiet where they would be cured (Rothman, 1971:290). As Figure 8.5 shows, this policy led to dramatic increases in the state hospital patient population until about the 1950s (cf. Figure 8.2). From a high of about 550,000 inpatients in the mid-1950s, today (1982) (with the advent of phenothiazine drugs) there are roughly 125,000 patients in state and county mental hospitals (*Mental Health, United States,* 1985:35). Of the approximately 827 mental hospitals in the United States, 277 or 33 percent are run by state or county governments—the remainder are private hospitals. (*Statistical Abstract of the United States,* 1986:113). In the last ten to fifteen years there has been a rapid increase in private mental hospitals. For example, in 1970, 57 percent of all mental hospitals were private; in 1982, 67 percent were private. DeFleur estimates that about 13 million Americans receive psychiatric care per year at the cost of $17 billion, of 11 percent of the annual health care expenditures (1986). Another estimate (*Mental Health in the United States,* 1985:96, 32, 36) puts total direct costs for mental health in 1980 at about $19 billion and total inpatient episodes at 1,779,587 and outpatient additions at 2,634,727, respectively (in 1979). Particularly from the mid-1940s to the mid-1960s state mental hospitals tended to be overcrowded, dehumanizing, and oppressive (Cockerham, 1981:279; Rothman, 1971:291). Some felt that mental hospitals were like prisons with their use of mechanical restraints, harsh punishments, and punitive treatments (Rothman, 1971:291). Others (see Weinstein, 1979) reported that patients themselves tended to have more positive attitudes toward mental hospitals. Starting in 1963 community mental health centers (CMHCs) also helped reduce the state hospital population. Today there are at least 700 CMHCs, comprising about 20 percent of all mental health facilities (*Mental Health, United States,* 1985:26). The reduction in the state hospital census has improved some, but far from all, of the adverse conditions in state mental hospitals.

Custodial Care Mental hospitals have custodial, incarcerative, and therapeutic functions (Cockerham, 1981:262). Mental patients are often perceived as dangerous deviants who need to be isolated from the rest of us, put into protective custody (Link and Cullen, 1986; Gallagher, 1980:298). Custodial and incarcerative care of the mentally disordered are thought necessary to protect society and to isolate troublesome people. Thus, mental hospitals are sometimes said to be "prisons for people who have not broken the law" (Gallagher, 1980:306). Since state hospital positions are certainly not the most rewarding ones in the mental health profession, custodial care often results by default. State hospitals are just not able to pay well enough to attract the best psychiatrists or staff. Many, if not most, state hospital physicians did not complete their psychiatric residencies (certainly not in the United States), nor were many of them board certified in psychiatry. Hills comments on both the custodial care and staff problems of the mental hospital.

> The history of mental health care in our society is a sad one. Hospitals—state and private—treat only a fraction of those committed to their care. Most hospitalization is custodial in nature, providing only food and shelter, and restraining patients from doing harm to themselves or to others. Because of inadequate budgets, most hospital staffs are so small in relation to hospital population that the notion of meaningful treatment is a permanent joke among those familiar with the problems. . . .
>
> I worked in a hospital that was built ten years after the Civil War. Most of the wards were so crowded and filthy that the staff locked itself away from the patients. Many hospitals cannot find and/or afford doctors, so they hire foreign doctors, who are not licensed in the United States, to work under a licensed director. It is not unusual for these doctors to be unable adequately to communicate with their patients because of a language barrier. . . .

FIGURE 8.5 Inpatient Population of State and County Mental Hospitals: 1900–1982

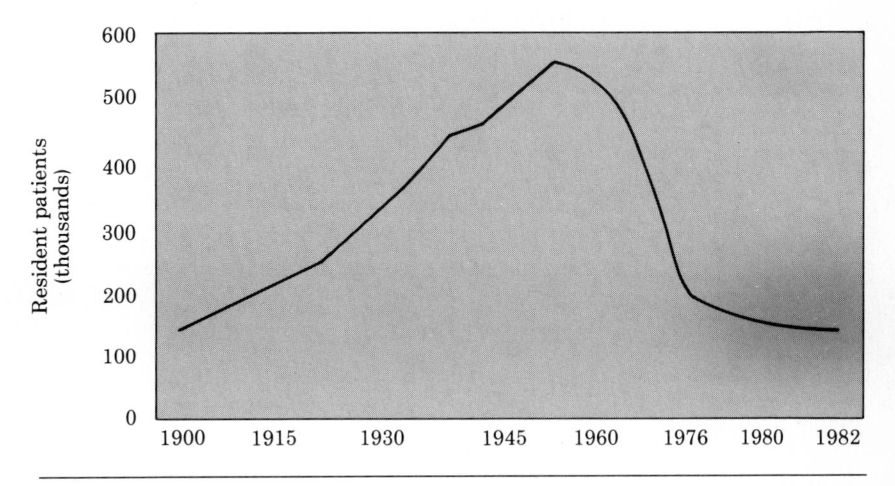

Source: *Statistical Abstract of the United States,* 1982–1983, p. 118; *Statistical Abstract of the United States,* 1986, p. 112.

> The fact is that mental hospitals simply do not and, because of costs, cannot provide treatment for the thousands of nondangerous people currently being warehoused in our giant institutions. (1977:4–9)*

For example, Rosenhan found that the average time per day that a patient in a state hospital spent with a psychiatrist was only 6.8 minutes (1973:250). Most treatment in the state hospital is largely drug (and some electroshock) therapy, not psychotherapy (Benson, 1986; Gallagher, 1980:306). In one interesting situation hospital staff found that an electroshock machine had not been working. They then compared patient improvement after the inoperative machine treatment (patients received only sedatives before shock) with machines that were working effectively. No significant differences in improvement were discovered between the two groups (Gallagher, 1980:306).[8] Clausen and Huffine (1975) have argued explicitly that just having time off, a respite from stresses outside the hospital, can be therapeutic even if care is primarily custodial.

Authoritarian Impersonal Nature of the Mental Hospital Like most bureaucratic organizations (see Chapter 10 on Weber) the state mental hospital has a strict, formal, hierarchical organization of power with the physician-psychiatrist at the top and the patient at the very bottom (Gallagher, 1980:297; Cockerham, 1981:271). Since physicians spend so little time with their patients,

*Howard Hills "Society's Outcasts," *The Center Magazine,* Vol. X, No. 4, July/August 1977, pp. 4–9. Reprinted by permission of the Center for the Study of Democratic Institutions.

in point of fact the head nurse (like Ms. Ratched in Kesey's *Cuckoo's Nest,* 1962) often actually makes the important decisions. These decisions tend to be rational, efficient, formal, and impersonal. Goffman describes the social organization of the mental hospital as a "total institution" (1961:xiii): "as a place of residence and work where a large number of like-situated individuals, cut off from the wider society for an appreciable period of time, together lead an enclosed, formally administered round of life." In total institutions like the mental hospital not only are all patients usually treated the same, they are often depersonalized (what Goffman, 1961, refers to as a stripping-of-the-self) to the point of being considered inert objects. For example, Brandt describes his admission to a mental hospital during which he was literally stripped, searched, and showered.

> During all this procedure the two aides said very little to me and later I came to see why. It wasn't because they disliked me or were trying to frighten me, although they did. It was simply that they were working. This was obviously routine procedure, a precaution they were required to take with every incoming patient to make sure he carried no drugs or weapons or other forbidden objects on his person. I was part of their work, the object they were working on, the thing to be processed. You don't normally talk to your work; if the work is routine, you don't even talk about it. You just do it.
>
> The effect on me of what they took for granted, however, was startling. I did not understand it at the time, but the meaning of the process must have been sinking in regardless. I was an object, possibly dangerous, which had to be inspected; it might be concealing something, it could not be trusted and in any case it had to be described. So they searched it. It never occurred to them to explain to the object what they were doing; you don't explain things to objects, you give them orders (1975:164).

Often if people are considered dangerous to themselves, to others, or to property, they can be committed to a mental hospital totally against their wishes (i.e., committed involuntarily; see Cockerham, 1981:268; Gallagher, 1980: 323). However, if one is not dangerous and can survive on his/her own, s/he cannot be kept in a mental hospital. Describing his own Supreme Court case (1975), Kenneth Donaldson reports on how he was committed involuntarily to the Florida State Mental Hospital at age forty-eight by his parents (1976). Donaldson got to speak with doctors about five hours in his fifteen years and roomed with fifty-nine other patients. For one entire year he was locked in a kitchen where he worked thirteen hours a day, seven days a week. The Supreme Court finally ruled that Donaldson be freed and paid $38,500 in damages.

Can a Mental Hospital Make You Crazy? Of course, Szasz, in *The Manufacture of Madness* (1970), claimed just this—that a commitment to a mental hospital (plus other psychiatric coercions) can make you mentally ill (cf. Jessica Lange in the movie *Frances* and Kesey's *Cuckoo's Nest,* 1962). In a classic study on *Asylums* (1961) Erving Goffman points out that any normal individual would resist psychiatric hospital resocialization attempts. Since there are more "crazy" people outside mental hospitals than inside, it is often your "career contingencies" that get you committed (such as living near a state hospital). In your prepatient life you have many rights that are denied you as a mental patient. Even the admission procedure can be a degradation ritual. Schwartz and Schwartz describe a typical admission (cf. Gallagher, 1980:313).

> Admission to the mental hospital is all too often a humiliating experience, reinforcing the patient's low self-esteem. In an atmosphere of impersonality and indifference, he waits for attention. He is stripped of clothes, spectacles, money, watches, wedding rings. He is put in a shower. He is given a perfunctory examination and is probably told where he is and why and what will be done to and for him and why (1964:124).

Once one is admitted to a mental hospital you may make what Goffman calls a primary adjustment. This amounts to doing what you are told, to accepting your new patient role and self-concept, to taking your drugs, to not acting aggressively, to cooperating with the staff, and so on. Or you could make secondary adjustments in which you try to perceive the vestiges of your prepatient self and social status by working the system or using what Goffman calls make-dos.[9] In both cases you resist tacitly the new patient self-concept being forced on you. Goffman argues that *any* sane person would resist hospital treatment. However, the more you resist the more crazy you are thought to be and the more harsh and punitive the treatment is. In the end the mental hospital *produces* the very mentally disordered person it presumably is trying to cure.

In a fascinating experiment D. L. Rosenhan (1973:250–258) had eight perfectly normal people admitted to a mental hospital by claiming to hear a single word (words like *thud, empty,* or *hollow*). In every other respect the pseudopatients behaved normally both before and during hospitalization. All eight were diagnosed as schizophrenics and were admitted (cf., Brown, 1987). None were ever discovered by the hospital staff as fakes. In spite of their normalcy the pseudopatients were regarded as mentally disordered. Indeed, when they were discharged it was with the diagnostic label schizophrenia, in remission. A mental hospital had in effect produced eight schizophrenics. Later, Rosenhan warned the mental hospital that more psychiatric imposters would be secretly admitted and challenged the hospital to identify them. The hospital then identified many of its patients as not crazy, only to discover later that Rosenhan had not sent any imposters the second time! In general, if patients are in a mental hospital a long enough time, they develop an institutional syndrome (Gallagher, 1980:323). Such patients become apathetic, have a lack of concern for the future, are submissive, and overdependent. Even when patients get out and are considered cured, they tend to be less likely than nonpatients to be able to find an apartment or get a job. Now that we have reviewed some of the problems of mental hospitals, we need to ask what causes them—as viewed from our major theoretical perspectives.

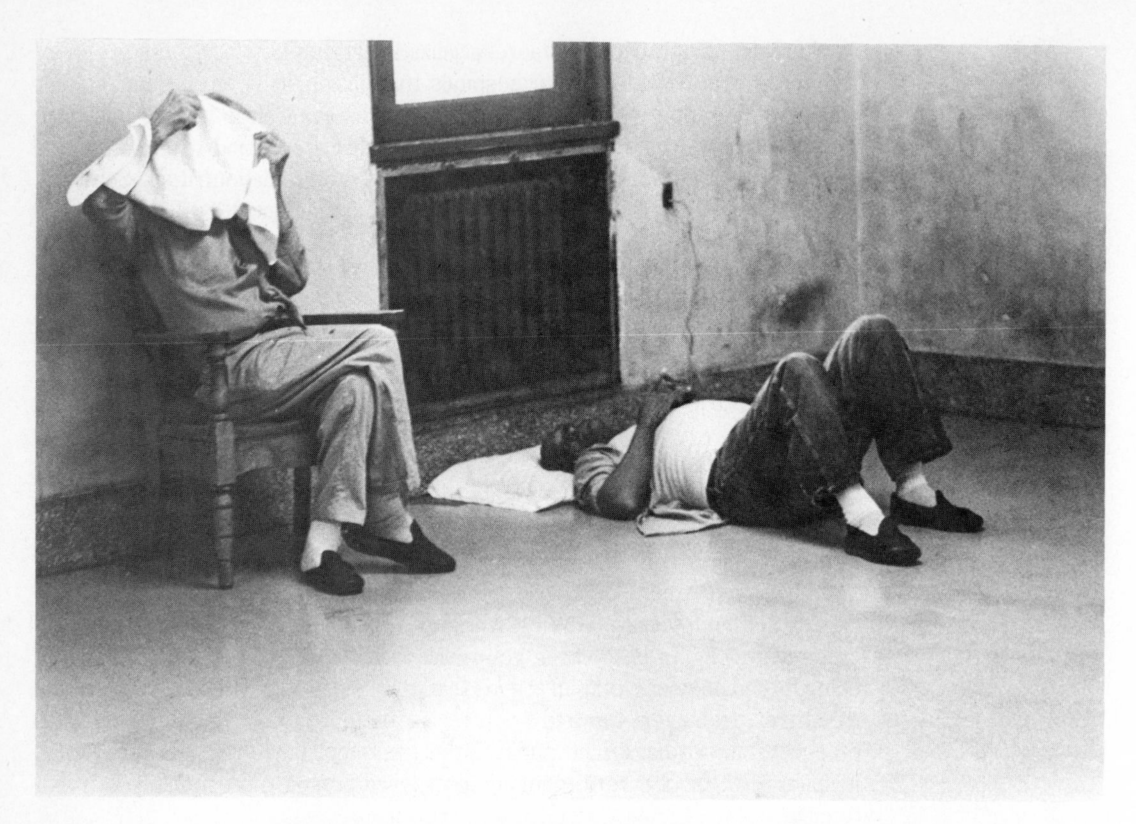

Most state and county mental hospital wards are dreary, custodial, impersonal, and can even make you crazier. Very little treatment goes on and physicians are often not board-certified in psychiatry, so it is probably better that they stay away from their patients. (Chris Maynard/Stock, Boston)

Analyzing the Problem Of course, how we view the four major types of problems of mental hospitals arising depends on our theoretical perspective. We shall look at the causes of mental hospital problems from the exchange, structural, labeling and symbolic interaction, conflict, and medical model perspectives. Within each of these major perspectives we shall analyze why hospitals are respectively dreary, overcrowded, and isolated; custodial with poor health care; impersonal, authoritarian, and formal; and places that can paradoxically make you crazy.

The Exchange Perspective From this perspective in large part the dreariness of the state mental hospital is related to the low value of interacting with the mentally disordered (see Table 8.2) the patient's relative powerlessness to reward or punish others, and the relatively low value placed on the mental health of the lower social classes in general. Remember too that some believe that the mentally disordered are being punished for breaking what Scheff (1975) calls the residual rules of social exchange. If so, why should the environment of mental patients not be dreary? We generally do not worry very much about the living conditions of prisoners (see Chapter 15).

As for the poor custodial care in state mental hospitals, typically state institutions pay less, have less expensive medical equipment, and have less desirable work conditions and environments than private institutions. For example, a fifth-year psychiatric resident typically makes about $1,000 to $1,500 less a year in stipend at a state hospital than at almost any other facility (AMA *Profile of Medical Practice,* 1980). By the first and third propositions of exchange theory (see Panel 2.2), rewards determine action. In general the more an action or behavior is rewarded, the more it will be performed. Furthermore, as Hills (1977) mentioned in the quote above, most state hospital psychiatrists are undertrained and are generally not the best doctors available. Often state hospital physicians are foreign-born and foreign-trained with incomplete psychiatric educations. If you were a board-certified psychiatrist from a prestigious medical school, would you prefer to earn $80 to $120 an hour in private practice in pleasant surroundings working with middle-class clients or $20 to $40 an hour in a dreary state hospital working with lower-class patients who may never get better and at the same time have low professional autonomy due to state governmental bureaucracy?

Also, we must remember that often people find themselves in state hospitals as the result of a long series of failed therapeutic exchanges and a general depletion of financial resources (Goffman, 1961; Cockerham, 1981:240ff.). If a psychiatrist, social worker, nurse, or other hospital staff member has not been rewarded with at least some patient improvement, the exchange perspective would predict that eventually therapeutic efforts would diminish or cease (Homans, 1961:110). That is, custody would be a rational response to failed therapy, low resources, and a poor prognosis.

The impersonality of state hospitals can also be seen to result from exchange principles (Link and Cullen, 1986). Low-status patients typically do not interact with higher-status staff. As a result the patients and staff tend not to develop liking for one another (Rosenhan, 1973:256). Thus, the mental hospital often becomes impersonal. After all, staff and patients are not equals (Cockerham, 1981:271). Note that in all institutional settings social interactions tend to be indirect, specialized, short, complex, formal, and reinforced by money and social status (see Chapter 10, Table 10.4).

Finally, how could social exchange actually make you mentally disordered or worsen your mental condition? Social interaction is related positively to similarity (Homans, 1974:127–130, 299–302; Chadwick-Jones, 1976:58) and proximity (Homans, 1974:144; Gallagher, 1980:304). The more one interacts with another, the more similar one becomes to the other. If most of the people in your total institution are mentally disordered, then it would seem to follow that over time you yourself would tend to become more mentally disordered (Townsend, 1976).[10]

Patients can also be encouraged to act "crazy" because the less one is rewarded (especially when one expects a "cure"), the greater the anger and aggressive acting-out behavior (see Panel 2.2, Proposition A5a, above; Homans, 1961:144). As for the institutional syndrome, deprivations in the state hospital lead to less activity and more apathy (Panel 2.2, Proposition A4; Homans, 1961:110; Cockerham, 1981:284ff.).

The Structural Perspective From the structural perspective both the overcrowdedness and the custodial nature of state mental hospitals can result from the rapid expansion in size of the state hospital patient population (see Figures 8.5 and 8.2). The sheer numbers of mental patients to be treated, usually in a single-state facility, contribute to custodial care completely apart from values, labels, power, and so on (Gallagher, 1980:298).

Earlier we noted that state hospital patients are, for the most part, from lower social classes. It follows that their economic, political, and other resources are usually limited. Dreary surroundings and poor health care are the rule when a population has low socioeconomic status (Szasz, 1970).

As we saw in Chapter 2 (and will see again in Chapter 10), when any group gets larger, primary group relations involving face-to-face contacts become less likely. In large groups there is an increasing occupational division of labor, hierarchical social structuring, shortened interaction time per social contact, longer spans of control, more indirect social relations, a larger part played by authority, and more emphasis on efficiency and rationality, rather than on affect. All of these structural factors tend to make state mental hospitals impersonal and formal.

Last, physically mental hospitals are not proximate, nor is access open to nonpatient populations. Mental hospital patients tend to be physically removed, segregated, and isolated from normal people (Rothman, 1971). These structural constraints, one could argue, tend to make mental illness persist, not dissipate, since most social interactions must be with other patients.

Labeling, Symbolic Interaction, and Conflict Perspectives According to these perspectives the state hospital is authoritarian, impersonal, dreary, and provides poor mental health care because the mentally disordered have broken rules (not laws) of the outside world and are being punished for it (i.e., stigmatized, defined as crazy, given negative public reactions, and so on). We control serious norm violators by confining them to state hospitals even if they are not mentally disordered. A major goal of state hospitals is not to cure, but to discipline, control, or sanction norm violators who have come into conflict with society's majority groups or dominant values. We set rule breakers apart from rule conformers. One cannot threaten dominant social values or traditional social order and get away with it, especially if one is from a lower social class and lacks the power to be eccentric (Szasz, 1975). If you make enough trouble, you can be labeled mentally disordered and be locked up.

Once in a state mental hospital you are under pressure to make what Goffman calls a primary adjustment, to accept the mentally disordered role and the accompanying prescriptions of who you are, what you should do, and be (1961).

Thus, the mental hospital pressures you to accept the label of mentally disordered (actually something more like schizophrenic or depressive) as a precondition for getting better and/or for getting out. However, once you adopt any deviant identity, your actual fate may be to get worse (here, to become mentally disordered), not better.[11] The stigma of mental disorder may be hard to shake, even after you improve and are released from the hospital.

The Medical Model It will be recalled that the medical model tends to think of all illness as diseases (Snyder, 1980). If mental disorder is a disease, others could catch it. Accordingly, one might argue that we need to remove mental patients from the general population. Furthermore, within the medical model the environment for health care is less important than the biology of health care (i.e., the drugs, shock treatments, and so on that one receives).

If there is no medical cure, then perhaps all you can do with the mentally disordered is to house and isolate them; to keep them in custody. For example, if mental disorder is genetically determined (Tsuang and Vandermey, 1980), there may be little one can do to reverse the mental condition. As for the poor quality of mental health care in state hospitals, better quality medical care is almost always very costly. Most state hospital patients simply cannot afford excellent psychiatric care. Free enterprise medical (psychiatric) capitalism might argue that you get just the health care you deserve (i.e., can afford).

Concerning the authoritarian and impersonal nature of mental hospitals, Friedson (1970) maintains that authority and related hierarchical social organizational and formal social relations are central to the medical profession. One of the main traits of the physician's lifestyle is autonomy. Also, the preferred medical model psychiatric treatments (e.g., ECT, psychotropic drugs, and so on) are in fact technical and impersonal.

Finally, if accepting the psychiatric sick role (Parsons, 1955; Siegler and Osmond, 1979) is producing more mental disorder, those in the medical model tradition might say "so be it." The medical model does not allow one to deny his/her mental illness and still improve or get well. Rather, the medical model often assumes that you must get worse before you can get better. These being the possible causes of an admittedly pretty dismal situation in state and county mental hospitals, is there anything one can do to improve the conditions and resolve some of the problems?

Resolving the Problem. Outpatient Psychiatric Care and Community Mental Health Centers Obviously, if state hospitals make us mentally ill or disordered, are dreary, overcrowded, offer poor health care, are custodial, impersonal, and authoritarian, one resolution would be to go elsewhere, to get out! This is primarily a structural resolution, since it would affect the size, proximity, and distribution of mentally disordered populations in state hospitals.[12] As we have seen (in Table 8.1 and Figure 8.2), the state and county hospital population has been largely deinstitutionalized (Huffine and Clausen, 1979) into various outpatient psychiatric settings, especially into community mental health centers (CMHCs, started in 1963; *U.S. News & World Report,* May, 1979), halfway houses, and psychiatric emergency rooms.

For example, psychiatric outpatient care episodes have increased (as a proportion of total mental health care episodes) from 23 percent in 1955 to 49 percent in 1973, and 72 percent in 1979. At the same time state hospital care episodes have been reduced from 49 percent in 1955 to only 8 percent in 1979. CMHCs in 1980 served about 27 percent to 28 percent or more of both the inpatient and outpatient psychiatric populations (*Mental Health in the United States,* 1985:27–28). Of course, some patients cannot be treated in psychiatric outpatient facilities (they must remain behind in whatever conditions state hospitals find themselves) and also we must determine if outpatient psychiatric services are really much better than state hospital inpatient services.

Deinstitutionalization and the CMHCs Bassuk and Gerson (1978) point out that deinstitutionalization has resulted in a higher turnover of mental patients staying for shorter periods of time (the median stay in 1970 was forty-one days, in 1980 twenty-three days) in state and county hospitals and in increasing numbers of psychiatric patients in nursing homes, low-cost hotels, and in CMHCs as outpatients (or even in the streets in extreme cases). Probably CMHCs have tried to do too much (Wagenfeld and Robin, 1976). For example, they tried to deliver mental health services to all segments of the population. For the most part CMHCs deal with community problems of living (such as getting a job or a divorce), rather than with the intended problems of chronic mental health patients who had been released from the state hospitals (Mechanic, 1980).

CMHCs have been beset with a host of problems. In 1980 there were 691 CMHCs, not the 2,000 planned for, and money was short even for them. Medicare provides primarily for inpatient, not outpatient, services. To make matters worse, Presidents Nixon and Reagan have cut back federal funding for CMHCs. Disappointingly, CMHC staff conditions are not better than those in the state hospitals. From 1973 to 1976 the average number of psychiatrists was down from 4.9 to 4.3 per center. Only about 6 percent of the total CMHC staff are psychiatrists (Cockerham, 1981:319–333).

To make matters worse, state hospitals continued to discharge patients as if adequate outpatient services existed. In a few cases patients were in worse straits out of the state hospital than in, as the following sad situation illustrates:

> Sheila Broughel was the victim of a particularly brutal crime. An intelligent but mentally ill twenty-six-year-old Vassar College graduate, she had worked as a secretary for *The New Yorker* magazine. She had been under psychiatric treatment for some time and had developed a deep distrust of both psychiatrists and mental hospitals. She went to Washington, D.C., to "talk with the nation's leaders about mental health" and found herself living in Washington's run-down Union Station. Usually she could be found, day or night, rain or shine, standing in the entrance to the station. Paul Hodge, a newspaper reporter for the *Washington Post,* took an interest in her.

> He was at the station covering another story, discussed her with a station policeman who told him she was "crazy" but that there was nothing he could do since she was not a danger to herself or others. Hodge bought her lunch—she said she was hungry and broke—and persuaded her to go with him to see a psychiatrist he knew at St. Elizabeth's Hospital.
>
> The psychiatrist thought she needed help and advised her to sign herself into the hospital voluntarily. She refused and asked to be taken back home—the "home" being Union Station. The reporter left her there. The next day she disappeared. Writes Hodge, "When her mutilated body, sexually assaulted and stabbed almost thirty times, was found in an abandoned garage a dozen blocks from Union Station, some of her friends and even a relative said they were not surprised and thought it to be a kind of suicide."
>
> Hodge quotes a New Haven lawyer whose firm had twice secured her release from Connecticut mental hospitals a few years earlier: He said lawyers in his office had discussed "how would we feel if something like this happened. Suppose she ends up in an alley we said. . . . Still I think we made the right decision in working to keep her out of hospitals. She was not dangerous and she passionately wanted to be free. That's what it means to have a free society, not to lock people up all the time." (Cockerham, 1981:329)*

Psychiatric Drug Therapies Another resolution (in the medical model tradition) is to use psychoactive drugs to reduce crowding in state hospitals and to avoid the poor custodial care and exacerbating effects of hospitalization (Cockerham, 1981:29–32; 78ff.). We have alluded to this strategy in several places already in this chapter.[13] For example, it was noted in Table 8.1 that starting in about 1955 (coincident with the introduction of phenothiazine drugs like Thorazine), the state hospital population was greatly reduced (Cockerham, 1981:31). Additionally, in 1955 the average state hospital stay was six months, but by 1980 it was cut to only twenty-three days. On the other hand, new state hospital admissions actually increased. Patients were just being discharged sooner. As we have seen, Eisenberg claimed that 30 percent to 50 percent of released schizophrenics were back in the state hospitals within one year (1976).

Psychiatric drugs do reduce psychotic symptoms, aggression, and anxiety. In so doing, they make social life outside the state hospital possible. But psychiatric drugs mainly control, not cure, mental disorders (Cockerham, 1981:82). In many, if not most, cases psychoactive drugs simply relieve disturbing psychiatric symptoms (Finkel, 1976).

Changing Attitudes, Values, and Laws The labeling and symbolic interaction perspectives suggest that state hospital patients are generally regarded negatively. Aviram and Segal (1973) found great resistence to having the mentally disordered released into the community (cf. Link and Cullen, 1986).

*Jonas Robitscher, "Moving Patients Out of Hospitals—In Whose Interest?" *State Mental Hospitals,* P. Ahmed and S. Plog, eds., 1976, pp. 158–59. Reprinted by permission of Plenum Publishing.

The public tends to want psychiatric patients removed and placed in state hospitals. Mental patients are perceived as dangerous, but are they (Cockerham, 1981:299ff.)? If many mental patients are not really ill or dangerous, one resolution is to remove the stigma of mental disorder (Goffman, 1963; Cockerham, 1981:288ff.). Huffine and Clausen (1979) and Link and Cullen (1986) suggest that if we would just interact with ex-patients, our negative stereotypes would begin to break down. State hospital patients tend to become incorrigible when they acquire a mentally disordered identity (see concept of secondary deviance). Critics of the labeling perspective, on the other hand, caution us that we cannot explain or define away organic brain damage.

A related resolution would be not to require mental hospitalization for some cases (Cockerham, 1981:340–375). State hospital patients are usually considered dangerous or injurious to themselves, to others, or to property. But surely not all of them are dangerous to everything all of the time. Perhaps families, the police, schools, businesses, doctors, even churches simply do not want to deal with certain types of people. Certainly the mere designation of mental illness is not sufficient to commit a person to a state hospital. In all fairness studies have shown that ex-patients often do have higher rates of robbery, assault, alcoholism, and rape (Zitrin et al., 1976).

Finally, one could argue that neither mental health nor mental illness is very important in our society. That is, to resolve state hospital problems we need to finance mental health activities better. The President's Commission on Mental Health (1978) found that only about 11 percent of the total health care dollar went for mental disorder. Clearly state hospital staff salaries and physical plant expenditures need to be increased if we are to have any hope of combating mental disorder, not to mention improving the conditions in our state mental hospitals.

• Summary

For generations individuals or groups exhibiting strange, bizarre, eccentric, mysterious, excited, disorderly, aggressive, or unpredictable behaviors have been called mentally disordered. Several issues surround the mentally disordered. For example, what should society do with them? If we leave the mentally disordered in society at large, what kinds of behaviors can or cannot be tolerated? How does society distinguish between actual thought or brain disorders and legitimate religious beliefs or simply unpopular political convictions? How costly is mental disorder to society? Finally, what are the use, value, and limits of new psychoactive drugs?

To resolve these issues we must agree on a standard definition of *mental disorder,* as well as determine how prevalent mental disorder is. Mental disorder was defined as "a clinically significant behavioral or psychological syndrome or pattern that occurs in an individual and that is typically associated with either a painful symptom (distress) or impairment in one or more important areas of functioning (disability)." While roughly 85 percent of the American population suffers from emotional problems, 10 to 20 percent actually have mental disorders (i.e., in 1986 about 36 million Americans) and only about 3 percent are ever treated for mental disorder. In state mental hospitals schizophrenia is the most common disorder, followed by alcohol related disorders and depressive neuroses or affective disorders. In nonhospital populations phobias are another common type of mental disorder. Mental disorder cost the United States about $17 billion in 1977 ($19.9 billion in 1980) or 11 percent of the total national health care bill.

Five fundamental types of models and treatments of mental disorder were discussed: medical, sociocultural (including the deviance and symbolic interaction perspectives), exchange, structural, and conflict models. The medical model tends to view mental illness as a disease. As such, mental disorder is biologically based, has specific organic causes, known courses of development, expected outcomes and durations, and responds (if at all) to technical treatments. Medical model treatments include chemotherapy or psychoactive drugs, electroconvulsive treatment (ECT, especially for depression), and (more rarely) surgical alteration of the brain (e.g., prefrontal lobotomy).

In the sociocultural model mental disorder is seen as a product of cultural or value variations, as deviance from norms, or as being coerced into mental sick roles—not as diseases. In short, mental disorders are problems of living, not primarily of biology. The focus is on social interaction and labeling. Treatment often involves psychotherapy to increase self-awareness or interpersonal adjustment. In the Freudian tradition emphasis is on resolving individual unconscious conflicts in one's own personality.

From the exchange perspective the mentally disordered are thought to have learned to act crazy. Mental disorder is often rewarded. For example, the mentally disordered do not have to work while they are ill. Also, social norms for noncrazy behavior are often set by reference to mentally disordered behaviors as limiting cases. Sensitivity, creativity, and individuality are generally seen as positive values. However, unlike sexual, age, or racial exchanges, the mentally disordered have relatively few scarce rewards to offer larger society. Thus, usually punishments (not rewards) are exchanged. One example would be locking up people who are violent or unpredictable. Treatment from the exchange perspective can involve behavioral modification schedules of reward or punishment to reinforce desired behaviors or to extinguish undesired behaviors.

Structurally, since there are relatively few psychotic people and since most of them are segregated in mental hospitals, we tend to hold negative attitudes toward the mentally disordered. Normal people are further distanced from the mentally disordered by the low social class and low status of the mentally disordered. Structural treatments might involve reducing the isolation and segregation of the less severely mentally disordered, increasing employment opportunities, helping (women especially) raise young, dependent children, improving self-esteem, and deinstitutionalizing the less impaired mental patients.

The conflict model of mental disorder emphasizes the low socioeconomic status and relative lack of power of the mentally disordered. Anyone who seriously threatens the established political order can be locked up regardless of his/her mental health. This is especially likely if a troublemaker is poor and of low social status. Radical therapy stresses that treatment should be of society, not of individuals. That is, society itself is held to be crazy and to make individuals mentally disordered.

Finally, we examined a common place for treating serious mental illness—the state or county hospital. Four serious problems were considered: the dreary, overcrowded, isolated settings of state hospitals; their custodial care; the formal, hierarchical, authoritarian, impersonal social organization of the state mental hospital; and the mental hospital as a place that makes one crazy.

From an exchange perspective the dreariness of the state hospital results in part from the low value of interacting with the mentally disordered. Custodial care is likely because state institutions are financed poorly. Custody is also a rational response to failed therapy, low resources, and a poor prognosis for patients. In all institutional settings staff and clientele are not equals, interactions tend to be indirect, specialized, short, complex, formal and reinforced by money and status. Structurally many of the problems of state mental hospitals were caused by the rapid expansion of the numbers of the hospitalized mentally disordered. We have also seen an increasing occupational division of labor and hierarchical social structuring in all of modern urban-industrial society.

The medical model of mental disorder encourages hospitalization to treat and isolate disease. Also, if mental disorder is genetic, then there is little you can do to change it. This makes custody, not cure, a primary objective. Authority and hierarchical social organization are salient traits of the medical profession, not special traits of mental hospitals. From the conflict and labeling perspectives state hospitals tend to be dreary, impersonal, authoritarian, and provide poor health care in part because patients are being punished (not treated) for breaking rules. Furthermore, once one is a mental patient one way to get out is (paradoxically) to accept that you are mentally ill. Thus, hospitalization may make you worse.

Common resolutions to the state mental hospital problems include getting out (deinstitutionalization), referring some types of patients to community mental health centers, more widespread use of psychoactive drugs, changing attitudes, values, and laws, and last, investing more public funds in state hospitals and the treatment of mental disorder. In the next chapter we consider social problems of alcohol and drug abuse before turning to more institutional or macro-level social problems.

• Notes

1. Some have argued for a guilty, but mentally ill plea, which would separate the issues of mental competence and guilt. In this case, once someone had recovered from his/her mental illness, s/he would be sent back to prison to serve the remainder of his/her sentence. The state of Michigan and others already have such a law.

2. Curiously some jobs *require* that you hear voices and talk to God. For example, most ministers have to believe in prayer and revelation to be effective in their professions.

3. As, for example, when Szasz (1974:99, 109) maintains that mental illness is not a disease because a dead body (cadaver) cannot be said to be mentally ill. However, not all physical illnesses leave clear organic signs after death (e.g., elevated blood pressure) and many mental disorders do leave signs (e.g., organic brain syndromes).

4. Remember that our definition of social problem requires that social conditions be perceived as threats by "significant numbers of the population"; that is, that social problems are (at least perceived as) relatively widespread.

5. For the most part the mentally disordered are more suicidal than homicidal. In general, mental patients are incarcerated in state hospitals because they are self-destructive, while most criminals are in prison because they are other-destructive (homicidal, assaultive, and so on). Of course, there are exceptions to both of these generalizations.

6. Heterogeneity nontreated $= 1 - (.15^2 + .85^2) = .26$.

Heterogeneity treated $= 1 - (.03^2 + .97^2) = .06$.

One has to be extremely cautious in interpreting heterogeneity coefficients.

7. It is interesting to speculate on the religious component in skepticism over the efficacy of medical treatment of the brain. Probably more than any other organ in our bodies (say kidneys, livers, hearts, lungs, and so on), the brain is godlike. Thus, tinkering with the brain is somehow sinful and irreverent.

8. I find this story hard to believe, since electroshock produces body convulsions that would have been noticed immediately with an inoperative machine.

9. A make-do is a material artifact used to support your prepatient self-concept. One example would be sparking electrical sockets to light cigarettes.

10. Conversely, if you could interact more with "normals," other things being equal, then you would expect to become more normal yourself.

11. Cf. Lemert's concept of secondary deviance (1951; cf. Higgins and Butler, 1982:171ff.).

12. See social environmental and structural therapy treatment section above.

13. Most notably in our discussions of the medical model, and chemotherapy treatments.

♦ Glossary

Affective Disorder. A disturbance of mood, accompanied by a full or partial manic or depressive syndrome.

Behavior Modification. A psychotherapeutic technique that applies the principles of learning to modify disturbed behavior, generally focusing on specific behavioral disturbances.

Community Mental Health Center. Federally supported outpatient psychiatric clinics began in 1963 to treat mental disorders in local communities, especially with the aid of new drug therapies.

Degradation Ritual. The humiliating experience of many patients when they are committed to a mental hospital, during which they are depersonalized, have their outside rights, privileges, and possessions taken away, and in effect are required to become different people.

Deinstitutionalize. To release the less severely mentally disordered state and county hospital patients into the general community, usually on an outpatient basis and supported by drug therapy.

Double-Bind Hypothesis. The thesis that schizophrena tends to develop in part because of the subjugation of children to contradictory messages from their parents and not allowing the children to ignore or withdraw from these messages.

Electroconvulsive Treatment. A treatment especially for depression or schizophrenia in which 150 to 170 volts of electricity are sent into the patient's brain for one second or less.

Institutional Syndrome. A pattern of apathy, lack of concern for the future, submissiveness, and overdependency that often develops in mental patients who have been institutionalized for a long time.

Labeling Theory of Mental Disorder. The view that mental illness is the result of a socially powerless individual committing a deviant act (or acts) and simply having the misfortune of being caught by socially powerful others who react by assigning the label of mentally ill.

Make-Do. A material artifact used to support a hospitalized mental patient's prepatient self-concept.

Mental Disorder. A clinically significant behavioral psychological syndrome or pattern that occurs in an individual and that is typically associated with either a painful symptom (distress) or impairment in one or more important areas of functioning (disability).

Milieu Therapy. A means of treating hospitalized mental patients by encouraging them to establish relationships with other patients and staff and to assume some responsibility for themselves often in a controlled physical setting.

Neuroleptics. Antipsychotic drugs like Thorazine, Stelazine, Navane, Haldol, Serpasil, Mellaril, and so on.

Neurotic. Any painful symptom (e.g., phobias, anxiety, hysteria, obsessive-compulsion) with intact reality testing.

Neurotransmitter. Chemicals (e.g., dopamine, serotonin, norepinephrine, and so on) that transmit nerve impulses from cell to cell (across the synaptic cleft) in the brain.

Psychotherapy. Forms of treatment of the mentally disordered based primarily on communication (verbal or nonverbal) between therapist and patient or client or among several individuals assuming these roles in a group setting.

Psychotic. A diagnostic term referring to a group of mental disorders in which the patient has lost contact with reality.

Psychosurgery. Surgery on the brain to relieve agitation, anxiety, or depression; such as lobotomies in which the frontal lobes of the brain are severed.

Psychotropic Drugs. Any psychoactive drug that reduces psychotic symptoms, anxiety, depressive symptoms, or other symptoms related to mental disorder.

Radical Therapy. A therapy based on the assumptions that society, not individuals, is mad, that mental illness is a myth, and that treatment should consist of understanding and reversing social oppression of those labeled mentally disordered.

Residual Rules. Conventions about expected behavior that are so basic that their violation is considered not merely deviant but crazy, as evidence of mental disorder.

Secondary Deviance. Occurs when a person continues over time to violate norms and is subsequently forced by the reactions of other people to assume a deviant role or identity.

Schizophrenia. A psychotic mental disorder that involves deterioration of a previous level of functioning, onset before age forty-five, and a duration of at least six months. Symptoms include hallucinations, delusions, thought disturbances, autism, affective disturbances, ambivalence toward persons or objects, paranoia, and withdrawal from ordinary social interaction.

Stripping-of-the-Self. A systemic process of identity resocialization that accompanies becoming a mental patient. The patient is often depersonalized; personal and social supports for one's prepatient identity are removed.

Total Institution. A place of residence and work where a large number of like-situated individuals, cut off from the wider society for an appreciable period of time, together lead an enclosed formally administered round of life.

Working the System. A nonmaterial secondary adjustment; any habitual arrangement by which a member of an organization employs unauthorized means or obtains unauthorized ends, or both, thus getting around the organization's assumptions about what he should do and get and, hence, who he should be.

• Further Reading

Cockerham, William C. *Sociology of Mental Disorder.* Englewood Cliffs, NJ: Prentice-Hall, 1981. This is a well-written overview of all of the topics we have covered in Chapter 8. The treatment is thorough, with extensive references and footnotes. Cockerham has chapters on the law, contemporary treatment, and models of mental disorder that are missing in most other texts.

Gallagher, Bernard J., III. *The Sociology of Mental Illness.* Englewood Cliffs, NJ: Prentice-Hall, 1980. Another excellent general text on the social aspects of mental disorder that is in many ways similar to Cockerham's text. However, Gallagher is even more academically thorough. He also has many more chapters on the types of mental disorders themselves than Cockerham.

Goffman, Erving. *Asylums.* New York: Doubleday Publishing, 1961. One of the true classics in the social study of mental hospitals. Goffman did participant-observation field work in St. Elizabeth's Hospital in Washington, D.C. *Asylums* argues (like Szasz) that mental hospitals help *produce* the very behaviors they are committed to treat and cure. Goffman coined phrases like "make-dos," "stripping-of-the-self," "secondary adjustments," "working-the-system," and "degradation ritual." The book is in the sociocultural model genre and reads like a novel.

Grusky, Oscar and Melvin Pollner, eds. *The Sociology of Mental Illness: Basic Studies.* New York: Holt, Rinehart, and Winston, 1981. Here are abstracts of all of the basic studies and concepts of mental disorder that you will probably want to know the details of. Writings of Freud, Mechanic, Kety, Szasz, Scheff, Gove, Hollingshead, Dohrenwend, Kohn, Brown, Goffman, Rosenhan, and many others are presented. A good basic reference work of selected and edited readings.

Snyder, Solomon H. *Biological Aspects of Mental Disorder.* New York: Oxford University Press, 1980. Elaboration of the medical model of mental disorder by a brilliant young psychopharmacologist-psychiatrist at Johns Hopkins, who is also an accomplished guitarist and therapist. Everything a first reader would need to know about affective disorders, schizophrenia, sexual disorders, alcoholism, and so on—as they all relate to neurotransmitters, the synaptic cleft, brain chemistry, genes, hormones, and so on. A little flip and careless in places, but generally well done.

Veroff, Joseph, Elizabeth Douvan, and Richard A. Kulka. *The Inner American: A Self-Portrait from 1957 to 1976.* New York: Basic Books, 1981. This empirical national survey by two psychologists and a survey researcher at the University of Michigan is a 1976 replication of their earlier 1957 survey, *Americans View Their Mental Health.* Hard data on a representative sample of 2,267 Americans concerning their feelings and sources of well-being, perception of self, marriage, parenthood, work, symptom patterns, social characteristics, and subjective mental health, and coping and social support. They find a new focus on individuals and some sense of loss of social connectedness. Also, see their companion volume, *Mental Health in America,* 1981.

C·H·A·P·T·E·R

9

Drug and Alcohol Abuse

Drug exchanges (unlike age, sex, race, and health exchanges) occur not only between people, but also between the drug abuser/user and the drugs (or their physical effects) themselves. For example, drug users and the chemical properties of drugs interact to change perception or sensation, to reduce pain, to alleviate anxiety, to produce euphoria, promote sleep, enhance sexual experiences, and so on. As such drugs and alcohol are often people substitutes. Of course, drug users/abusers also sometimes exchange their money, sexual favors, and esteem with drug suppliers for drugs.

Drugs and alcohol facilitate or enhance social exchange as well. One common effect of many different drugs is increased sociability. Since social exchange itself (e.g., work, love, play exchanges) is valuable, even necessary, drugs often make needed but potentially punishing activities possible. Drugs can also recharge or otherwise alter the rewards and values of social exchanges that have become too intense or too unrewarding. Of course, drug abuse is an exchange issue because people learn to use and abuse drugs. Also, the exchange perspective argues that behaviors that are profitable will be repeated. Obviously, the profits of drug sales by drug companies and illegal drug dealers are enormous.

Conflict theorists see drug abuse as having less to do with drugs' physical effects than with the social control of people—especially of blacks, Hispanics, and women. Many drug laws turn out to be laws against minorities, not against drugs. Laws themselves sometime cause or create drug problems by making drugs more expensive and less pure or safe.

From the functional perspective, if alcohol or drug use continues in a society, then on balance, these substances are probably meeting important social needs or providing social benefits. Drugs result in both individual and social tension reduction and increased sociability. Attempts to eliminate alcohol or drug consumption (such as by prohibition) without providing functional alternatives have tended to fail.

Symbolic interactionists argue that drug use is not intrinsically either good or bad. Physician opiate addicts or white suburban marijuana users often function well in our society and are tolerated by the criminal justice and legal system. Regular use of drugs or alcohol results from our developing an excess of favorable definitions of drug use as good or pleasurable. Drug abuse is often a result of repeated negative public reactions from which the casual drug user eventually develops a drug abuser identity.

Biologically, drug abuse may be a product of the extremely potent physically reinforcing effects of drugs. Drugs often enhance sensation, perception, or imagination. They tend to make us "feel good" and not using certain drugs can produce painful withdrawal symptoms. Some alcoholics may drink because they have low blood sugar levels (hypoglycemia). Finally, the bodies of drug users may not produce enough endorphins or other naturally occurring psychoactive drugs.

———— ♦ ————

When John Belushi, youth hero of "Saturday Night Live" and *Animal House* fame, died of a speedball (heroin and cocaine) injection on March 5, 1982, one sensed that something else died with him. The erotic, self-gratifying, infantile, drug culture of the Hollywood-New York jetsetters was dealt a blow too. Of course, other young folk champions had succumbed to drugs and the fast life before—most notably singer Janis Joplin and guitarist Jimi Hendrix. But Belushi's death was somehow different. Drug and alcohol abuse had become a *social* adaptation by a large number of Americans to attempt to cope with the stresses and strains of contemporary living. Staid Bob Woodward (*All the President's Men* and *The Brethren*) of the staid *Washington Post* was moved to write a best-selling book (*Wired,* 1984) documenting the social pressures driving increasing numbers of us to drug and alcohol abuse.

In that book John Belushi's wife Judy comments on John's social compulsion to abuse cocaine.

> Judy was concerned that drugs and music were practically synonymous. So much of the rock mystique was wrapped up in the drug culture, and having tested the waters, John was now swimming in them. He would stay up for several days, and it was interfering with their relationship and sex life.
>
> "It's my lifestyle," he said. He would try sometimes to give up cocaine, but people kept offering it to him. He'd refuse, and they would push. Belushi was no fun just watching others do it; he was funny when he joined in. Cocaine

PANEL 9.1

The Short Life and Fast Times of John Belushi

Bill Wallace, back from Memphis and his divorce, had left two messages at the Marmont saying he had returned. He and his girlfriend, Susan Morton, were driving around doing several errands during an early lunch hour, about noon. Wallace had to stop at Brillstein's and pick up a typewriter and tape recorder for John. Then Morton and Wallace drove up to the Chateau.

"Shit," Wallace said, noticing that John's car wasn't there. Wallace said he would take the typewriter in, and Morton dropped him off while she went around the corner to get gas. When Wallace got to number 3, he knocked several times. There was no answer, so he let himself in with his key. He set the typewriter down and looked along the twenty-five-foot hall to the back bedroom. It looked as though someone was in the bed. If John were sleeping, there would be snoring and wheezing. There was not even a hint of the familiar harsh, raspy breathing. The place was hot, a dry, breathless heat. The mess and squalor were John's—that particular resoluteness behind the disorder. Wallace felt a slight eeriness as he moved down the hall. Someone was clearly gathered in a tight fetal position under the covers with his head under a pillow. Wallace recognized John's form. He walked slowly up to the side of the bed, reached over, touched John's shoulder and shook it gently. "John," he said, "it's time to get up."

There was no response—no groan, no pulling back from the touch. "John," Wallace said again, "time to get up."

Nothing. Wallace pulled the pillow away carefully. John's lips were purple, and his tongue was partially hanging out. He was not moving.

Something like a flame ignited in Wallace. He had taught CPR—cardiopulmonary resuscitation—at Memphis State and recognized the signs.

Wallace flipped John's nude, heavy body over on its back. The right side, where blood had apparently settled, was dark and ghastly. Wallace, his heart leaping and racing, reached in John's mouth with trembling fingers and drew out phlegm which spilled and puddled on the bed sheet in a thick stain. There was a rancid odor. Wallace, with one near-involuntary motion, clamped his own mouth down on John's and began mouth-to-mouth resuscitation. He tried for several minutes—training and horror in each motion. The body was cold, and John's eyes contained nothing. There was no movement, not the stirring of a response, a breath, a nerve, a moan. John was dead, gone. But there was an irrational hope and a requirement that John not be dead. Tears flooded Wallace's face. He was disoriented.

Source: Bob Woodward, *Wired,* 1984:402–403.

gave him a positiveness about himself; it made everything important and intense. (Woodward, 1984:142)

Cocaine now ranks second to marijuana as the drug of choice of eighteen to twenty-five year olds (if we exclude alcohol; see *Behavior Today,* June 18, 1984, and Holtzman, 1986). Relevant to this popularity of cocaine is the trial and acquittal of auto manufacturer John Z. DeLorean for trafficking in cocaine

(*Life,* May 1984). The message of John Belushi's death was that drug and alcohol abuse and the lifestyles that usually accompany them are social adaptations that do not work—at least not if you want to live longer than thirty-five to forty years. It was a sobering thought to those who had watched Bluto frolick, overeat, and overdrink in *Animal House* and thought he (and they?) would live in excess forever.

While cocaine (and earlier heroin) may have been in the public spotlight, increasingly Americans have been attempting to break the debilitating grip of other drugs too—including alcohol, caffeine, prescription medicines (like Valium), and nicotine (see "Getting Straight," *Newsweek,* June 4, 1984). Prominent U.S. citizens like Betty Ford (see Panel 9.2) and actor Jason Robards have confessed openly to their alcoholism, even starting alcohol rehabilitation centers (cf. Franks, 1985). There have also been a spate of studies on the problem of teenage alcoholism and a related rise in adolescent suicides (Associated Press, February 2, 1984; *HEW Special Report,* 1978; Kandel, 1980; Abruzzi and Orro, 1982). It is now estimated that there are three million problem drinkers among fourteen to seventeen year olds (cf. *Health, United States,* 1985:74). Alcohol is the most popular drug on most college campuses. Even caffeine in coffee and soft drinks is emerging as a new social problem (Ray, 1978:188; Troyer and Markle, 1984).[1] There is also renewed concern about nicotine and cigarette smoking as a health hazard and as a costly drug habit (cf. U.S. Surgeon General Koop's report in *Newsweek,* June 4, 1984). It is now estimated than 10 percent of all hospital and medical costs are for the treatment of illness caused by smoking (Associated Press, March 27, 1984). Furthermore, if a person thirty-five to forty-four smokes two packs or more of cigarettes a day, cigarette related extra costs over that person's lifetime are estimated at $58,987 (in 1984).

The above discussion suggests that one of the first of several issues we must confront in the present chapter is whether drug and alcohol problems are singular and isolated or multiple and interactive. Current thinking is that the primary drug problem is what we might call polyabuse; that is, dependency on a combination of alcohol and/or drugs (*Newsweek,* June 4, 1984). According to Duncan and Gold: "Rarely does anyone take one drug at a time. The person who is taking tranquilizers may well also be a coffee drinker, an alcohol drinker, and a tobacco smoker. This use of multiple drugs is known as polydrug use" (1982:11). For example, clearly John Belushi was a polydrug abuser (Woodward, 1984:104–105).

A second, and related, issue is whether drug and alcohol abuse are necessary for us to be able to cope with the stressful demands of modern life. Perhaps our initial characterization of Belushi and his drug groupies as infantile and self-serving was unfair. The popular social scientist Alvin Toffler contends that today we live with an unprecedented rate of social stimulation and change (1970; see also the section on stress in Chapter 7). If so, little wonder then that contemporary Americans are hooked on Valium, Librium, alcohol, and cocaine (Hughes and Brewin, 1979).

Comedian John Belushi as Jake Blues of the Blues Brothers. Belushi died of a heroin and cocaine injection in 1982. Many entertainers, athletes, and professionals feel the need to use drugs to cope with the stressful demands of modern life in the fast lane. (Gerald Thomas/Stock, Boston)

Perhaps drug and alcohol abuse would not be so disturbing if they were relatively harmless. But are they? A third issue is the relation of drug abuse to crime, accidents, death, and economics. Duncan and Gold argue that 50 percent of fatal car accidents, 50 to 70 percent of homicide victims and 60 to 80 percent of homicide offenders, 25 to 35 percent of suicides, and 65 percent of child abusers involve or use alcohol (1982:112, Table 9.2). In addition to these violence costs of drug and alcohol abuse, the sheer monetary expense of drugs can be staggering.[2] Drug abuse also seems to predict work problems, such as job separation, having many jobs (work instability), and adult unemployment (Kandel and Yamaguchi, 1987). Next, are drug actions physical, social, or some combination of both? For example, does one get high or low automatically as a result of a uniform physical-chemical reaction or does one's response to drugs vary with culture, learning, ethnicity, socialization, and so on? Most importantly, what is the interaction of physical and social factors in drug abuse? From what Becker argued about marijuana use in Chapter 1, we would suspect that using drugs for pleasure is learned behavior (cf. Akers, 1985:Chs. 6–9). In a related point Glassner and Berg (1980:647) argue that religious and ethnic factors tend to discourage alcoholism among Jews, even though alcohol consumption is high. These factors include using alcohol with food, as part of rituals, and defining alcoholism as a non-Jewish trait.

Some observers (usually conflict theorists) have contended that drugs (especially heroin) are advocated by the dominant white majority in the United States to control blacks, Hispanics, and the poor or even by males to control their bored housewives and unruly children (Cafferata, Kasner, and Berstein, 1983)! Thus, a fifth issue we must consider in this chapter is the unspoken, tacit, laissez-faire social approval of certain drugs (even illegal drugs) because they function as social controls on "undesirable" segments of the population. Sometimes the social control efforts can be directed at economic castration of entire nations with undesirable religions or political ideologies (i.e., not at drugs at all). A case in point is the United States trying to persuade Thai farmers to grow Idaho potatoes, rather than poppies (for heroin)—*Newsweek,* June 25, 1984. Although historically Thailand has been friendly to the United States, America is not supportive of communism or even of Buddhism.

Still another issue is whether drug laws should be more tolerant, lax, lenient, and so on, or more strict and restrictive. It has been argued that laws, not drugs, cause social problems (Thio, 1978:302). The high cost of heroin and cocaine is due to the fact that they are illegal. Narcotic addicts are often forced into theft, violence, and prostitution to avoid painful withdrawal symptoms. In Great Britain opiates are legal drugs dispensed by physicians and pharmacies (Ray, 1978:338). Attempts to make alcohol or cigarette smoking illegal have been a dismal failure. Still another question is should we raise the legal drinking age to reduce traffic fatalities (Associated Press, October 20, 1983)?

Finally, are there natural alternatives to externally ingested drugs? Curiously, when we run or do aerobic dancing (for example), most of us stop smoking and cut back on drinking. One (not the only) reason for this is that with sustained physical exertion the body produces more norepinephrine, a natural amphetamine. The "runner's high" is just that. We also know that the brain produces natural opiates, called endorphins (Harrison, 1982) or endogenous morphine. In extreme cases people can develop pathological conditions in which they have too many endorphins and feel almost no pain. For obvious reasons most such people do not live very long. Both of these examples suggest that the body itself, when healthy and under proper conditions, can produce many, if not most, drugs that we ingest externally.

But we get ahead of ourselves. First we must be clear about what is and what is not a drug. As in previous chapters, we need to define key terms like *drug, tolerance, addiction, habituation, abuse, physical* and *psychological dependence, withdrawal, alcoholism,* and *problem drinking.* To be sure, cocaine and heroin, marijuana, LSD, PCP, Quaaludes, Valium, and Dexedrine are drugs. But what about beer, coffee, tea, Coca-Cola, cigarettes, or even airplane glue?

Following Einstein (1972:402; cf. Table 9.1), we define a *drug* as any substance that by its chemical nature alters the structure or functioning of a living organism. Our definition is more general than most dictionary definitions, which call a drug a "medicinal substance used in the treatment of a disease" (*Taber's*

"Contains glucose, dry skimmed milk, oil of peppermint, dextrose and artificial coloring."

Cyclopedic Medical Dictionary, 1970:D–46). We will concentrate on psychotropic drugs, which alter mood, perception, consciousness, or behavior (Duncan and Gold, 1982:2). By our definition alcohol, caffeine, and nicotine are all drugs.

For our purposes ***drug abuse*** exists when a person continually misuses any drug. . . , when a person has lost control over the use of the drug. . . , or when drug taking has begun to disrupt an individual's family, job, or ability to

TABLE 9.1 Drug Definitions by 1,091 Respondents

The term *drug* has been defined in many ways. Which of the following definitions do you think is most appropriate?

	n	Percent
1. A drug is any substance used as a medicine or in making medicines.	128	12
2. A drug is any chemical compound used for the relief of pain or suffering.	70	6
3. A drug is any narcotic substance, or preparation, especially one that is habit forming.	298	27
4. A drug is any substance, other than food, that by its chemical nature alters the structure of functioning of a living organism.	463	43
5. A drug is any biologically active substance used in the treatment or prevention of illness or for recreation or pleasure.	132	12

Based on the responses to this questionnaire, many respondents (43 percent) do not accept the broad scientific definition as appropriate. Interestingly, however, 27 percent of the respondents felt that only one class of substances (narcotics) are drugs. To say the least, a certain amount of confusion exists.

Source: Stanley Einstein, *Drug Forum,* 1972, 1(4):402. Copyright 1972, Baywood Publishing Company, Inc.

perform in other social roles (Duncan and Gold, 1982:11). *Drug abuse* is a vague term and can mean addiction, tolerance, physical or psychological dependence, and is often distinguished from *drug habituation.* Of course, as indicated above, drug abuse is usually polyabuse, not singular abuse.

Drug abuse in the sense of *addiction* implies a state of periodic or chronic intoxication, detrimental to the individual and society, produced by the repeated consumption of a drug. Its characteristics include an overwhelming desire or need (compulsion) to continue taking the drug and to obtain it by any means, a tendency to increase the dose, a psychological and sometimes physical dependence on the drug, and a detrimental effect on society and the individual (Snyder, 1980:84). One can be tolerant of a drug without being addicted to it. *Tolerance* simply means that with repeated administration of a drug, a larger dose is required to produce effects that earlier were produced by smaller doses (Snyder, 1980:84).

When one is addicted to a drug a *physical dependence* can result in which pronounced abstinence symptoms appear when a chronically administered drug (e.g., opiates, alcohol, barbiturates, or amphetamines) is withdrawn. These symptoms are sometimes called *withdrawal symptoms* or a withdrawal syndrome. (Duncan and Gold, 1982:16). Some people are physically dependent on drugs (e.g., hospital patients) without being drug addicts; that is, they use prescribed drugs. Thus, there is no compulsion for or self-administration of the drugs. *Psychological dependence* indicates the compelling desire or craving one has for drug effects (Duncan and Gold, 1982:16). For example, monkeys will press a lever administering intravenous injections of opiates or cocaine almost continuously until they die of starvation. Of course, heroin addicts and chain cigarette smokers also have high psychological dependence on their drugs.

Usually drug addiction is distinguished from drug habituation. *Drug habituation* is a condition resulting from the repeated consumption of a drug. Its characteristics include a desire (but not a compulsion) to continue taking a drug for the sense of well-being it engenders, little or no tendency to increase the dosage, some psychological but no physical dependence or withdrawal symptoms, and detrimental effects, if any, to the individual alone (Duncan and Gold, 1982:15; Snyder, 1980:85).

When the drug being abused is alcohol (ethanol), it is customary to differentiate alcoholism from problem drinking (Cohen, 1983:124). There are many definitions of alcoholism and none of them is entirely satisfactory. For our purposes an *alcoholic* is an excessive drinker who has lost control of his/her drinking and whose dependence on alcohol is so extreme that there is a noticeable mental disturbance or interference with his/her bodily or mental health, his/her interpersonal relations, and his/her smooth social and economic functioning. S/he is unable to refrain from drinking and to stop drinking before becoming intoxicated. S/he therefore requires treatment (Snyder, 1980:132). Some experts believe that alcoholism is a disease and that it proceeds in developmental stages (Jellinek, 1960; also see below). We regard alcoholism as addiction to alcohol, the development of tolerance, and the presence of withdrawal symptoms upon abstinence.

Problem drinking, on the other hand, may not involve addiction. *Problem drinking* refers to difficulties in living (e.g., marital, social, job, or health problems) related to repeated overdrinking (Cohen, 1983:124). Thus, problem drinking parallels the concept of drug habituation. Of course, we shall have much more to say about drug and alcohol abuse when we analyze and illustrate them in detail below. However, before we turn to those detailed analyses of specific drug and alcohol problems, we need to say a little about the general prevalence of drug use and, very briefly, sketch its history.

America, for the most part, is a prodrug society. Yet at the same time we are also conservative about drug and alcohol consumption. We tend to believe in drugs to stimulate or sedate us and to treat illness or disease. Some of our prodrug bias is the result of successful lobbying by business and medical organizations. But completely divorced of such social and economic pressures, most of us probably would use drugs to seek pleasure and avoid pain. Table 9.2 reveals that the most prevalent drug use in the United States is of what we might call "unrecognized drugs," such as coffee and tea. Coffee is the most widely used drug for adults (82 percent used it in the last year) and tea is most widely used by young people twelve to seventeen years old (55 percent). Soft drinks, like Coke and Pepsi, are not mentioned in Table 9.2, but undoubtedly they also contribute to making caffeine the drug most Americans of any age take. Given its prevalence alone we need to examine problems of caffeine abuse in some detail.

However, alcohol is most likely the greatest problem drug in the United States today (Franks, 1985; Samuelson, 1981). More money is spent on alcohol and alcohol has more violent and death related outcomes than any other drug. Americans spend about a total of $28 billion per year on alcohol and consume an average of 2.7 gallons of alcohol per person per year. Table 9.2 reminds us that 66 percent (2/3) of all adults and 51 percent (1/2) of all youths drink alcohol. Teenage alcoholism is a serious problem that has worsened in the past ten to fifteen years and deserves our careful attention (Jones and Bell-Bolek, 1986). Note too that 41 percent of all adults smoke. Marijuana use is significant primarily among young people (12 percent). Interestingly, marijuana use (mainly by young people) has about the same prevalence as adult tranquilizer (such as Valium or Librium) use (15 percent).

It should be obvious that the most abused and in a sense dangerous drugs (e.g., alcohol, nicotine, and caffeine) are all already legal. This fact alone raises further questions about the relationship of drug laws and drug abuse. If we made heroin, cocaine, and marijuana legal, would their prevalence and problems increase? Or, if we tried (again) to make alcohol and nicotine illegal, would they cease to be such social problems?[3]

To be sure, drugs have always been controversial. Now is not the time or place to give a complete history of drug use and abuse.[4] Here it must suffice for us to give a brief overview of public and governmental reactions, especially to smoking, caffeine, and alcohol. For example, as early as 1604 King James of England contended that smoking tobacco was harmful to the lungs and brain (Ray, 1978). A short time later the sultan of Turkey even had smokers put to death (smoking was forbidden in the Muslim Bible, the Koran). Smoking, or as it was known then, tobacco drinking, made its appearance in Western Europe shortly after the discovery of the new world (1492) and was at first the distinctive mark of sailors (Duncan and Gold, 1982:78).

In America, the first commissioner of the U.S. Federal Narcotics Bureau, Harry J. Anslinger, was instrumental in the passage of the 1937 Marijuana Tax Act, which outlawed marijuana smoking. Although some of Anslinger's claims about the evils of marijuana are laughable by today's standards, it is also clear that smoking marijuana, like cigarettes, is harmful to your health (Mann, 1980; Kaplan et al., 1986). In 1964 the U.S. surgeon general claimed that cigarette smoking is hazardous to one's health and in 1965 Congress passed a labeling and advertising act requiring warnings to be put on all cigarette packages and advertisements. By 1970, Congress had banned all cigarette advertising on radio or television. Recently U.S. Surgeon General Everett Koop has argued that even "second-hand" smoke (i.e., being around smokers) is dangerous and that pregnant women who smoke risk damage to their unborn children (*Newsweek,* June 4, 1984:71).

Similar negative public reactions have protested the drinking of coffee or

TABLE 9.2 Prevalence of Drug Taking (in Percent)

	Adults		Youths (12–17 Years)	
	Ever	**Past Year**	**Ever**	**Past Year**
Over-the-counter drugs				
Medical use	ND*	12.0	ND	ND
Nonmedical use	8.0	1.0	6.0	1.0
Prescription drugs				
Sedatives (medical)	ND	15.0	ND	ND
Sedatives (nonmedical)	4.0	†	5.0	1.0
Stimulants (medical)	ND	5.0	ND	ND
Stimulants (nonmedical)	6.0	1.0	5.0	1.0
Methadone	0.8	0.1	0.7	0.2
Unrecognized drugs				
Coffee	89.0	82.0†	62.0	36.0‡
Tea	85.0	55.0†	82.0	55.0‡
Glue and other inhalants	2.8	0.1	8.5	0.7
Tobacco	66.0	41.0	52.0	25.0
Alcohol	75.0	66.0	54.0	51.0
Illicit drugs				
Marijuana	19.0	7.0	23.0	12.0
LSD and other psychedelics	4.5	0.6	6.0	1.3
Cocaine	3.4	0.7	3.6	1.0
Heroin	1.3	0.1	0.6	0

*ND = no data.
†Less than 0.5 percent.
‡Use in past month.

Source: Reprinted with permission of Macmillan Publishing Company from *Drugs and the Whole Person* by David Duncan and Robert Gold. New York: Macmillan 1982:9.

alcohol. Interestingly, England's "Women's Petition Against Coffee" (1674) indicates a preference for ale (alcohol) over coffee.

> Our countrymen's pallates are become as Fanatical as their Brains; how else is't possible they should Apostatize from the good primitive way of Ale-drinking, to run a Whoreing after such variety of destructive Foreign Liquors, to trifle away their time, scald their Chops, and spend their Money, all for a little base, black, thick, nasty bitter stinking, nauseous Puddle water. (Ray, 1978:187)

In a 1984 paper Troyer and Markle reviewed the inconclusive evidence that coffee causes cancer, birth defects, and heart disease. Of course, given the violence related to alcohol and alcoholism Americans have traditionally been more concerned about alcohol problems. As early as 1773, John Wesley (the founder of the Methodist religion) called for prohibition of distilling alcohol.

Most notable, however, was the passage of the Eighteenth Amendment to the U.S. Constitution in 1919, which prohibited the manufacture, sale, or transportation of alcoholic beverages. As it turned out, prohibition was unenforceable and unpopular, leading to its repeal in 1933 (Gusfield, 1963). Still, many conservative states were slow to repeal prohibition (e.g., Mississippi did not until 1966) and to this day these states have Sunday blue laws, dry counties, and other laws limiting the sale and consumption of alcohol. Similar attempts to legislate the morality of marijuana smoking and teenage drinking also have not been successful. Many sociological lessons can be learned in these general failures of Prohibition movements, to which we shall return later.

One of the drugs getting a large share of contemporary public attention, as suggested by actor John Belushi's overdose death (Panel 9.1), the accidental burning of comedian Richard Pryor, and the auto manufacturer DeLorean's trial and acquittal for possession and sale, is cocaine (Mothner and Weitz, 1984; Anderson et al., 1985).[5] We tend to forget that cocaine has been around for a long time (*Life,* May 1984:57–68). One of the first users was psychologist-analyst Sigmund Freud, who took cocaine to combat depression and as an aphrodisiac. In 1884 (at age twenty-eight) Freud wrote: "I took for the first time 0.05 gr. of cocaine . . . a few minutes later I experienced a sudden exhilaration and a feeling of ease." In 1863 Vin Mariani, a wine laced with cocaine, was celebrated worldwide. Pope Leo XIII even awarded its producer, Angelo Mariani, a gold medal and indirectly helped sell the wine. Even Coca-Cola had cocaine as an ingredient until 1918. In fact the U.S. Food and Drug Administration actually prosecuted Coke in 1909 for *not* having enough cocaine in it (i.e., for false advertising)! You could even buy a cocaine drink for one dollar a bottle in the 1902 Sears Roebuck catalog. However, during the late 1890s concerns began to surface that cocaine would drive one into uncontrollable erotic frenzies and related acts of violence. For some reason there was special concern about cocaine-induced rapes of white women by black men. Stories circulated that standard .32 caliber police revolvers would not stop cocaine-crazed rapists, with the result that police across the nation were issued new .38 caliber pistols (Duncan and Gold, 1982:128).

Having stated several key issues, defined our terms, and discussed briefly prevalence, incidence, and the history of drugs of interest to us, we now turn to a more detailed discussion of major drug types, their respective effects (especially how various drugs act on the brain and our nervous system), and an examination of our basic theoretical perspectives as they apply to social factors in drug use.

• Physical Aspects of Drug Use

To say with Einstein (see Table 9.1) that a drug is any chemical that affects the structure or function of a living organism is not an adequate statement of the numerous types or effects of contemporary drugs. Nor is it sufficient to say that we shall focus on the so-called psychoactive drugs. There are simply too many such drugs and drug effects to stop even here.[6] For example, Usdin and Effron (1972) list 1,555 psychoactive drugs; and even Glenn's reduction to sixty psychoactive drugs is still too large and diverse (1974). Our purposes demand a classification of say four or five major drug types and their associated effects, a classification that includes alcohol, caffeine, nicotine, and unrecognized drugs.

All psychoactive drugs can be classified as (actually mainly those drugs that are usually *abused*) narcotics, depressants-tranquilizers, stimulants, hallucinogens, and *cannabis*. Alcohol is grouped with depressants, nicotine and caffeine with stimulants. Clearly our typology of drugs and effects is not perfect either. For example, Duncan and Gold (1982:6) include herbal drugs (e.g., nutmeg and catsup), over-the-counter drugs (e.g., aspirin), and other unrecognized drugs (such as airplane glue) that we omit. Ray (1978:96) combines hallucinogens and *cannabis* into a group he calls phantasticants and separates out a category of nondrug drugs (i.e., alcohol, nicotine, caffeine, and over-the-counter drugs). Other drug typologies distinguish prescription from nonprescription drugs, drugs that are legal versus illegal drugs, and call depressants "sedatives" (e.g., refer to Table 9.2 above).

Historically, we human beings have taken drugs to avoid pain (think of general anesthesia in hospitals, novocaine in the dentist's office, Brompton's Cocktail in the hospice, and Demerol for postsurgery pain);[7] seek pleasure (for example, the euphoria of opiates, the aphrodisiac effects of cocaine, or the simple tension reduction of alcohol or marijuana); treat illness or injury (consider heart disease and the so-called beta-blockers Inderal, Corgard, and Tenormin, the use of insulin for diabetes, and so on); cope with stress (Valium has become one of the most widely used modern drugs—see Hughes and Brewin, 1977. As early as 1939 Huxley in *Brave New World* recommended that the general euphoric drug soma be given with one's Friday paycheck); aid sleep and relaxation (e.g., sleeping pills like Dalmane, minor tranquilizers, or alcohol); correct natural chemical imbalances (as we saw in Chapter 8, some medical scientists believe that the brains of schizophrenics have excessive amounts of the neurotransmittor dopamine); expand consciousness or provide insight into alternative lifestyles, and so on (many college students in the 1970s felt that LSD or even marijuana made them more spiritually aware or gave them insight into everyday problems; however, some of those same students wrote their entire final examinations for their courses on the same line!); and to control groups and individuals (examples that come to mind are letting or encouraging inner-city blacks to become heroin addicts, giving Antabuse to alcoholics, or court-ordered chemical castration of male sex offenders with the drug Provera).[8]

Actual psychoactive drug effects vary broadly with the five basic types of drugs. The *narcotics* (opiates) are generally used for their analgesic, antidiarrheal, and antitussive (to suppress coughing) effects. Narcotics usually produce euphoria, drowsiness, respiratory depression, constricted pupils, and some nausea. The *depressants* or tranquilizers are used primarily as anesthetics, anticonvulsants, sedatives, hypnotics, antianxiety, or antipsychotic agents. On the whole the depressants reduce tension, enhance sociability, produce euphoria, and promote sleep.

Stimulants are used for local anesthetics, headaches, to combat fatigue or depression, hyperkinesis or hyperactivity (especially in children), narcolepsy, excess weight, and coma. They produce excitation, alertness, increased sociability, increased pulse rate and blood pressure, insomnia, and loss of appetite. *Hallucinogens* have few, if any, medical uses (although LSD has been used to prevent suicide).[9] They change perceptions of time, space, colors, and objects. The user may hope for insight, spiritual awareness, or greater understanding. Finally, *cannabis* is used to treat glaucoma and the side effects of cancer chemotherapy. Marijuana and hashish produce euphoria, relaxation, increased appetite, some disorientation, and increased sociability.[10]

Of course, one may question whether the drug effects just described are purely physical or if they are social effects. Are drug effects automatic, just chemical, or neurological reactions? Ray (1978) contends that there is no single uniform drug experience, even in the same person. You will recall that Becker (in Chapter 1) took much the same position concerning marijuana use.[11] However our position is that there are fairly consistent physical-chemical or psychopharmacological effects of major drugs (similar to our contention that there are biological differences [not only social] between young and old, male and female, black and white, sick and well, crazy and sane people).

Still, we can admit readily that drug effects also vary with dosage, tolerance, body weight, interaction with other drugs (especially with alcohol and caffeine), social expectations, and social-psychological conditions. These important qualifiers do not mean that major drugs effects are only social. Rather, there are chemical or biological reactions to most drugs that are fairly universal and independent of social expectations, contexts, culture, and so on.

• Alcoholism

Stating the Problem

> Beverage alcohol is fecal matter. Alcohol is not made of grapes or grain or other attractive foods. It is these which are devoured by the ferment germ, and the germ then evacuates alcohol as its waste product. The thought of swallowing the excrement of a living organism is not an esthetic idea but people will do such things. (Smith and Helwie, 1940:25. Quoted in Ray, 1978:124)

Alcohol is the most problematic of all drugs. More money, violence, death, and danger are associated with alcohol consumption than any other single drug (Cohen, 1983:Ch. 2; Franks, 1985). The average American drank about 35 gallons of beer (3.5 gallons of wine and 2.5 gallons of hard liquor) in 1985 (cf., *Statistical Abstract of the United States,* 1987:Table 174). The Prohibition era ran from about 1920 to 1933. All kinds of alcohol consumption was reduced by Prohibition. But Ray (1978:131) argues that hard liquor consumption actually increased during Prohibition. Since 1840 beer and wine consumption in the United States have increased dramatically; hard liquor consumption has declined. For all hard liquor, wine, and beer this translates into about 2.7 gallons of 100 percent absolute ethanol per person per year (Duncan and Gold, 1982:134ff.). From Table 9.2, we know that about two-thirds of all adults and one-half of all youth ages twelve to seventeen had at least some alcohol to drink in the past year. Recent data (see Table 9.3) show that about 37 percent of Americans do not drink at all. Of those who drink 31 percent are light drinkers, 22 percent are moderate drinkers, and 10 percent are heavy drinkers (Table 9.3). Thus, roughly 10 percent of the American population are problem drinkers (but not necessarily alcoholics). Of those problem drinkers, thirty-five to forty-five-year-old males (about 70 percent) predominate. Generally Americans drink less as they age and more as their income goes up (*Statistical Abstract of the United States,* 1987:718).

Earlier we differentiated an alcoholic from a problem drinker. An alcoholic was defined as an excessive drinker who has lost control of his/her drinking and whose dependence on alcohol is so extreme that there is a noticeable mental disturbance or interference with his or her bodily or mental health, interpersonal relations, and social and economic functioning. An alcoholic is unable to refrain from drinking or to stop drinking before getting intoxicated. Thus, treatment is required.

The National Institute of Mental Health has described the onset of alcoholism as opposed to ordinary drinking as follows:

> One of the more obvious early signs . . . is that the individual drinks more than is customary among his associates and makes excuses to drink more often. This is an indication that he is developing an insistent need—or a psychological dependence—to alcohol to help him escape from unpleasant worries or tensions.
>
> As the condition progresses he begins to experience "blackouts." He does

TABLE 9.3 Type of Drinker as a Proportion of the U.S. Adult Population (Both Sexes, 1972–1983)

	Proportion of Adult Population			
	1972	**1974**	**1976**	**1983**
Abstainer (less than one drink a year)	36	33	33	37
Light (one drink a year to three drinks per week)	32	28	38	31
Moderate (four to thirteen drinks per week)	23	28	19	22
Heavy (two or more drinks a day)	10	11	10	10

Source: Reprinted with permission of Macmillan Publishing Company from *Drugs and the Whole Person* by David Duncan and Robert Gold. New York: Macmillan 1982:106; *Health, United States,* 1985:75.

> not "pass out" or become unconscious, but the morning after a drinking bout he cannot remember what happened after a certain point. If this happens repeatedly or after taking only a moderate amount of alcohol, it is a strong indication of developing alcoholism. (1961:8)

The problem drinker, on the other hand, simply has difficulties in living (marital, social, job, health problems) related to repeated overdrinking. Problem drinking is an example of drug habituation (as opposed to drug addiction).

Foodstuffs with starch or sugar content and moisture will ferment if left standing at normal temperatures. These natural fermentation products can be distilled to get a product with an even higher alcoholic content. For example, whiskey is distilled grain beverages and brandy is distilled fruit beverages. Drunkenness is the behavior that follows the ingestion of alcoholic beverages until one's normal behavior is affected.

Usually a person is considered drunk when there is 0.1 percent ethanol (with a range of .05 percent to .02 percent) in his/her blood. A 0.1 percent blood alcohol level or blood alcohol content (BAL or BAC) means there are 100 milligrams of alcohol per 100 milliliters of blood (see Table 9.4; Cohen, 1983:3). At 0.3 percent one becomes stuporous, by 0.4 percent to 0.5 percent coma ensues, and by a BAL of 0.6 percent to 0.7 percent breathing stops and death results. Beer ranges from 3 percent to 6 percent, wine 9 percent to 14 percent, and whiskey or brandy 35 percent to 50 percent alcohol content (100-proof whiskey is 50 percent alcohol). For example, if you have a 12-ounce bottle or can of beer, then $.06 \times 12 = .72$ oz. of alcohol is consumed (one mixed drink, one beer, or four ounces of wine are all roughly equal in alcohol content. A mini-bottle usually has a slightly higher alcohol content).

Thus, if you drank a little over a six-pack of beer in less than two hours (say 8 bottles $\times$ .72 oz. alcohol = 5.76 oz. alcohol), then (other things being equal) you would be close to being legally drunk (see Table 9.4). The "other things" in drunkenness include your body weight (especially), how fast you consume the alcohol, your previous drinking history, and whether you consume alcohol in combination with food or other drugs (particularly with Valium, Librium, or antihistamine cold medicines). Of course, whiskey has more alcohol concentration and is absorbed faster in the stomach than beer.

Alcohol is a physiological depressant. It reduces tension, increases sociability, produces an intoxicated or euphoric feeling, and results in both psychological and physical dependence. Alcohol impairs the operation of the higher brain centers more rapidly than it affects the lower nervous system. Consequently, alcohol constricts reasoning and inhibition before it depresses the ability to act and express emotion. Being drunk is particularly conducive to the more or less free expression of any previously suppressed sentiments, especially violent sentiments involving assault, rape, homicide, or suicide.

Prolonged abuse of alcohol can also have serious health consequences. Cirrhosis of the liver is the ninth most common cause of death in the United States (*Statistical Abstract of the United States,* 1986:75). Alcoholism is the third leading cause of birth defects. Most alcoholics are malnourished as a result of

TABLE 9.4 Effects of Alcohol

Amounts Consumed in Two Hours, in Fluid Ounces	Percentage of Alcohol in the Blood (BAL)	Typical Effects
3	0.05	Loosening of judgment, thought, and restraint; release of tension; carefree sensation
4.5	0.08	Tensions and inhibitions lessened
6	0.10	Voluntary motor action affected; hand and arm movements, walking, and speech clumsy (officially drunk)
10	0.20	Severe motor impairment; staggering; loud, incoherent speech; emotional instability (extreme drunkenness); 100 times greater traffic risk
14	0.30	Deeper areas of brain affected; stimulus response and understanding confused; stuporous
18	0.40	Deep sleep; inability to take voluntary action (equivalent to surgical anesthesia)
22	0.50	Coma; anesthesia of centers controlling breathing and heartbeat; death

Source: Sidney Cohen, *The Alcoholism Problems: Selected Issues,* New York: The Haworth Press, Inc., 1983:1–60. Copyright 1983. Reprinted by permission.

their dietary imbalance (they don't eat right) and need B-complex vitamins and insulin. In the winter cold, skin flushing from alcohol-expanded capillaries can lead to rapid heat loss and susceptibility to pneumonia. In extreme cases of alcoholism tremors and hallucinations occur. It has been estimated that alcoholism shortens life expectancy by as much as ten to fifteen years.

Not only does alcohol abuse effect individual alcoholics, it also is highly related to the health and well-being of others through violent crime (Ray, 1979:164; Cohen, 1983:10; cf. Chapter 15). In 80 percent of all arrests for violent crimes, the offender is legally drunk (i.e., has a BAL of 0.1 percent or higher). The highest rates of alcoholism for prison inmates are among those imprisoned for sexual crimes. One-third to one-half of all rapes involve the use of alcohol by offenders. Sixty percent to 80 percent of all homicide offenders use alcohol and as many as 35 percent of suicides. Twenty percent of all alcoholics on the average eventually die by suicide (Roy, 1986). Roughly 50 percent of all highway fatalities involve alcohol. In one estimate as many as 70 percent of all deaths (regardless of cause of death) were implicated with alcohol directly or indirectly. Clearly alcohol is a very dangerous drug.

The economics of alcohol consumption indicate a financial problem of major proportions as well. About $20 to $28 billion a year is spent on alcohol. In another estimate alcohol abuse costs Americans about $50 billion annually. In 1984, $448 million was spent by distributors for beer and wine advertising alone. One possible reason the U.S. government tolerates alcohol problems is that it makes a fortune on alcohol use. At $10.50 federal tax per gallon of hard liquor, the federal government received $9.5 billion in taxes in a recent year.

Another objective condition of the alcohol consumption problem is the dramatic increase in teenage drinkers since World War II (the rate is up 70 percent; Cohen, 1983:Ch. 19). In recent years the problem of teenage alcohol use has abated somewhat (*Statistical Abstract of the United States,* 1986:118). Episodes of drunkenness in a given year by teenagers rose from 19 percent in 1966 to 45 percent in 1975 (*Third Special Report to Congress,* 1978). Six percent of all teenagers report daily use of alcohol (Associated Press, February 7, 1984). Drunken driving is the leading cause of sixteen to twenty-one year olds' deaths (Associated Press, October 20, 1983). All this has prompted most states to raise their legal drinking ages. Did it do any good? Wagenzar (1982) discovered reductions in teenage motor vehicle fatalities after the legal drinking age was raised. In Maine there was a significant drop in beer sales too after raising the drinking age.

All this is not to argue that the alcohol problem is only an objective problem or that all people have a simple unitary physical response to alcohol use. There are undoubtedly cultural, social, symbolic, and other subjective variations in drunkenness and alcoholic consumption. For example, the government of Finland operates its country's liquor sales and invests a share of its profits in research (Pittman, 1967:232ff.). In one experiment four groups of four men were observed through one-way glass. Each group went through two five-hour sessions, a few weeks apart, one session with beer and one with brandy. All men were given identical lunches and otherwise equalized. Blood tests were made every ninety minutes. Psychological tests were also administered. Control groups of nondrinkers were formed and given similar tests.

Following alcohol intake the men made more hostile, deflating, and otherwise negative remarks in their efforts to teach consensus when discussing assigned topics. More importantly, such changes were greater with brandy than with beer, even when the total alcohol absorbed into the bloodstream was the same with each beverage. This finding suggests that the social expectations associated with each of those beverages, rather than just the alcohol, affected behavior.

Drunken behavior may result, in part, from the belief that deviant behavior is morally acceptable, (cf. Kaplan et al., 1986) and perhaps even socially expected when a person has been drinking alcoholic beverages. When people think of themselves as drunk they assume—and are permitted by others—license in some social settings to engage in deviant behavior without rebuke, regardless of whether the physiological effects of alcohol actually reduce control over their behavior. One familiar indication of this is that many persons, when drinking in relatively formal and sedate social situations, behave with much more restraint after the same consumption of alcohol which, at a more informal and convivial party, would be followed by more aggressive and boisterous behavior.

Paradoxically, it sometimes also appears that where alcoholic beverages are most widely consumed, disorderly drunken behavior seems minimal (e.g., in Israel or Italy). Glassner and Berg (1980) suggest that Jews avoid alcohol problems by associating alcohol abuse with non-Jews (i.e., as not being a good Jew), drinking in association with religious rituals, restricting adult relations to other moderate drinkers, and using techniques to avoid pressure to drink heavily. Problems with violent behavior associated with heavy drinking have been more prominent in countries where alcoholic beverages are routinely consumed without food (i.e., in Ireland, Scandinavia, and the United States; cf. Strauss, 1976:187). Having specified some of the special problems of alcoholic drug abuse, we must now ask what causes such behaviors.

Analyzing the Problem. The Exchange Perspective Of course, there is a certain redundancy in analyzing the causes of alcoholism, since alcohol is after all a drug and the general causes of drug abuse are discussed separately below. Nevertheless, we shall try to emphasize what is unique about causes of alcohol problems. To avoid repeating ourselves, this section will be somewhat brief.

Exchange Propositions 1 and 3 (Panel 2.2) suggest that more rewarded and valuable activities will tend to be repeated. In the words of Akers et al. (1979:838 and 1985:141–174; cf. Cohen, 1983:88): "Whether deviant or conforming behavior is acquired or persists depends on past and present rewards or punishments for the behavior and the rewards and punishments attached to alternative behavior—(i.e., on differential reinforcement)." People learn to become alcohol users or abusers. In Kandel's studies of young people's drinking behavior she claims that the "extent of perceived drug use in the peer group, self-reported drug use by peers, and perceived tolerance for use are all strong predictors of youth's subsequent initiation into the use of alcohol (1980:269). Interestingly, parental use of hard liquor predicts adolescents' use of hard liquor . . . but not of marijuana" (cf. Kandel, 1980:271).

A second exchange perspective on alcoholism is that exchange itself is traumatic or stressful (Goffman, 1959: Roebuck and Kessler, 1972:151), even if you are being rewarded by the social exchange. For example, all exchanges entail risk. You might lose a competition, be rejected by someone you care about, look stupid or foolish, be criticized, lose money, and so on. Thus, exchange theorists maintain that alcohol is used often to cope with normal interaction anxiety (Cohen, 1983:89; Neff and Husaini, 1985).

Third, if alcoholics are exchange failures (and many are), then their relative inability to reward others in interaction and in turn to receive rewards can lead to social withdrawal (see Cloward and Ohlin's double-failures, 1959, and Merton's concept of retreatism, 1968). This exchange perspective explains teenage alcoholism especially well, since teenagers have relatively few interactive assets (see Chapter 4).

Finally, work exchanges can encourage alcohol use and abuse. If routine work exchanges cause stress, fatigue, depression, and so on, then alcohol is

A series of famous Miller Lite beer commercials by comedians (Joe Piscopo and Rodney Dangerfield) and ex-pro jocks (Dick Butkus, Bubba Smith, Bob Uker—not all pictured here) portray beer drinking as rewarding. Famous, funny, rich sports stars enjoy beer—drinking is sociable, valuable, fun, the thing our heroes do. (AP/Wide World Photos)

more likely to be used to relax, change one's mood, enhance good latency time (the time needed to rest and regenerate), and help us be able to return to productive work relations. To be sure, it does not always work out this way, for alcohol is addictive and can become an end in itself and actually subvert work relations.

The Biological Perspective For those in the biological or medical model tradition, alcoholism is seen to have genetic, biochemical, or endocrinological causes (Franks, 1985; Strauss, 1984). For example, one Danish study found that 65 percent of identical twins who had at least one alcoholic parent subsequently became alcoholics themselves, but only 25 percent of nonidentical twins with alcoholic parents did (Cohen, 1983:86; cf. Snyder, 1980:141; Ray, 1978:140). Another theory of alcoholism in the biological tradition contends that alcoholics have endocrine deficiencies that result in low blood sugar (i.e., hypoglycemia). Alcohol (often without awareness) is used to relieve the hypoglycemia (Cohen, 1983:Ch. 8).

Perhaps the most celebrated biological argument for alcoholism is Jellinek's disease concept of alcoholism (1960; cf. Cohen, 1983:Ch. 22). Jellinek maintains that alcoholics develop in three stages. First, they experience blackouts, engage in secretive drinking, and are preoccupied with alcohol use. Second, they lose control of their drinking. Finally, the alcoholic suffers prolonged intoxication and loss of alcohol tolerance (see Chapter 8, "The Medical Model," for elaboration of the concept of disease).

The Functional Perspective From the functional perspective, if alcohol use continues, then (on balance) it is probably meeting important social needs or providing net social benefits (eufunctions). With all of the obvious negative social consequences (dysfunctions) of alcohol use (e.g., more violence, accidents, antisocial behaviors, higher death rates, and so on), we tend to overlook the positive consequences of alcohol use. Obviously, alcohol does at least result in both individual and social tension reduction and increased sociability. Given the complex and trying social lives most of us live, alcohol is very useful in helping us tolerate stress and pressure. Also, alcohol is clearly highly profitable to manufacture and sell.

Social functionalists have maintained that alcoholism is more likely if cultural traditions regard drinking alcohol as a way to reduce social stress; if we occupy positions in the social structure that produce high stress; and if there are few other structural alternatives to help us deal with stress (Roebuck and Kessler, 1972). For example, lower social class black males could be claimed to fit this functional model especially well, for their social group drinking is regarded as an appropriate way to reduce stress. Many black males are in low-income groups, have high unemployment rates, and so on and have few social alternatives for dealing with stress. For example, unlike black females, black males as a group get less relief from religion. To be sure, upper socioeconomic status corporate executives may fit the structural-functional model for alcoholism too.

The Symbolic Interaction Perspective From the symbolic interaction perspective alcoholism is seen as related to our developing an excess of favorable definitions of alcohol use as good or pleasurable, as opposed to bad, unhealthy, undesirable, and so on (Sutherland and Cressey, 1978; Trice, 1984). A major factor in our acquiring such favorable definitions of alcohol use is the pressure we receive from commercial advertisers (especially beer and wine distributors) to use alcohol to be sociable, to relax, to celebrate, to feel good, and so on (Hughes and Brewin, 1979:Ch. 2; Ray, 1978:132ff.).

The symbolic interaction perspective of alcoholism is different from the biological and exchange perspectives in that it does not see alcoholism as a simple physical reaction to drugs, or as a behavior that is intrinsically rewarding or valuable. Rather, we define (or have defined for us) alcohol use/abuse as proper, appropriate, expected, good, and so on. For example, Gusfield argues that the period of 1919 to 1933—when the Eighteenth (Prohibition) Amendment was American law—represented a victory for the values and culture of middle-class ascetic Protestants over the culture of lower and upper socioeconomic groups.

Resolving the Problem It should be noted at the outset that alcohol use is already legal (except for some young people in public places). Thus, unlike (say) opiate drugs, the alcohol problem is not primarily a legal problem. Prohibition was a failure.[12] We can change the minimum drinking age, penalize drunk drivers, have Sunday blue laws that restrict Sunday alcohol sales; but the fact remains that alcohol is readily available to people of all ages and will probably stay available. Most resolutions to drinking problems fall into one of two broad types (Franks, 1985): (1) total abstinence (for example, Alcoholics Anonymous), or (2) moderation (controlled drinking; see Armor, Polich, and Stambul, 1976). At present there are roughly 7,500 treatment centers for alcoholism in the United States (Henry, 1978:337). However, alcoholism improvement rates from treatment of all sorts is probably less than 50 percent.

Since alcohol use/abuse is rewarding or valuable to alcoholics and problem drinkers, it would seem reasonable to resolve alcohol problems by changing the rewards of alcohol consumption (Cohen, 1983:113). This can be done by behavior modification or aversion therapies. The object of these alcohol treatment programs usually is for the alcoholic or problem drinker to learn to become a more moderate drinker (i.e., controlled drinking, not total abstinence). For example, in one study a hospital day room was converted to a bar. If patients ordered straight (not mixed) drinks, gulped drinks, or ordered more than three drinks at a single setting, they were given mild electric shocks in their fingers (Sobell and Sobell, 1973:599–618). Unfortunately, the association of negative stimuli with excessive drinking seems to work for only about six to eight months; then (without further treatment) the drinking problems return (*Time,* April 22, 1984). Attempts to change the rewards and values of alcohol through psychotherapy have not proven effective, in part because such treatment is too time consuming and too expensive (Armor, Polich, and Stambul, 1976).

Of course, there are drugs (like Antabuse [disulfiram] and Temposil) that cause nausea, headaches, fainting, breathing difficulties, and other unpleasant symptoms when used in conjunction with alcohol. After a while one becomes nauseous—if drinking is even contemplated (Ray, 1978:157). But who can guarantee that an alcoholic or problem drinker will or should be forced to take drugs like Antabuse? Most alcoholics will simply not take them. Furthermore, Antabuse can be dangerous as well as painful.

Once you admit you have a drinking problem, you may need detoxification and other treatment assistance. For alcoholics withdrawal symptoms (especially tremors) begin after their BAL drops below the intoxication level. Staying drunk will allow the alcoholic to avoid withdrawal symptoms. Thus, alcoholics have an understandable physical compulsion to remain alcoholics. Furthermore, the mortality from withdrawal in advanced cases of alcoholism may be as high as one in seven (Ray, 1978:154). One of the more famous alcohol treatment centers is Betty Ford's clinic, described in Panel 9.2. Such centers use trained professionals, require total abstinence from alcohol, and expect absolute conformity to rigid treatment rules. Treatment lasts for about four weeks.

A second celebrated alcoholism treatment program is Alcoholics Anonymous (AA). Unlike the Ford clinic, AA uses no trained professional therapists. It

PANEL 9.2

Inside Betty Ford's Clinic

Until just recently, movie stars and other celebrities were about as likely to go public with a drug or alcohol problem as they were to admit their age. But in 1978 former First Lady Betty Ford forever shattered that taboo with her courageous announcement that she had entered a treatment program to overcome her dual addiction to alcohol and pills. Four years later she opened the Betty Ford Center for drug and alcohol rehabilitation in Rancho Mirage, California.

The roster of public figures who have enrolled—with self-generated fanfare—in the four-week program just during the past year could head the cast of a Hollywood extravaganza: Elizabeth Taylor, Robert Mitchum, Tony Curtis, Liza Minnelli, Peter Lawford, Johnny Cash—and, most recently, Mary Tyler Moore. Like other patients, celebrities must share simply furnished rooms, make their own beds, eat cafeteria-style meals, attend two often harrowing group-therapy sessions each day and perform "therapeutic" chores, such as setting the table and taking out the garbage.

Rough

But although it is the big-name patients at the Betty Ford Center who make the headlines, 95 percent of those who sign up are more ordinary folk. The program, which costs $155 a day (far less than some hospital regimens), is based on the principles of Alcoholics Anonymous and approaches addiction as a physical disease with extensive social and psychological consequences. Because so many abusers refuse to admit their problem, group therapy can sometimes be a grueling experience. "But we never tear someone down without building them up in the same session," insists program director John Schwarzlose. "We are being tough, sure, but it is done with love." A forty-year-old housewife who recently completed the program—with some mixed feelings about it—confirms that the going can be very rough. Her account:

"You're supposed to be detoxified when you arrive at the center, but there were people who came in having had several drinks on the plane. I came in that way. They immediately go through your suitcase and take away all drugs, even aspirin, except those for special medical conditions. For the first few days you're sort of befuddled, and then it begins to seem like a nightmare. The counselors and the rules make you very dependent, like children. 'Do what we say,' they keep telling you. 'Don't ask, just do it. You were in charge of your life before and look what happened.' But they have to be harsh; they have only a month to turn you around, to make you acknowledge your alcoholism and learn to deal with your problems without drugs. Some patients say that they came to get better; the counselors tell them, 'You're full of shit. You had to come.' You won't accept their help until you admit you are helpless. Everyone found group therapy uncomfortable and embarrassing, especially when you were in 'the hot seat'—when the focus was on you.

"There was some feeling of being brainwashed, because you were so isolated from the rest of the world—no telephone calls for the first five days and after that only at certain hours, and no television except on weekends—and there was constant repetition of things you were supposed to learn. But it was benign brainwashing, toward a good end: filling you with facts and experiences that you could draw on later.

"At the beginning, I felt the place was a cross between boot camp and a POW camp; I was afraid to be honest in the letters I wrote, because I thought the counselors might

continued

PANEL 9.2—*(concluded)*

read them. They did read and make written comments on our journal entries, which we left for them in a box each night.

Sometimes a feeling of fear and paranoia developed because you couldn't understand why the counselors would be so cruel, although in the end you realized that they were being cruel to be kind. Tough love, they call it. The scariest thing I saw is something they use extremely rarely: if a patient has very strong defenses and little trust, they make him wear a blindfold—it's black and looks like a Lone Ranger mask without eyeholes—for twenty-four hours, and he has to be led around by another patient, as an exercise in developing trust. One man left because he refused to wear the mask—if you stay, you have to do what they tell you."

Ties

"One reason the center limits the TV and telephoning and even reading is that they want you to form strong ties with the group of twenty people who live in your hall, and learn how to rely on them to help you with problems. That's to prepare you for AA when you get out, and also for real-life crises, so that you'll turn to people instead of alcohol. The camaraderie and bonds you form are very intense at the time, strengthened by what they call 'circling'; before every meal and every lecture, everybody in your hall forms a big circle and puts their arms around each other and recites the alcoholic's 'serenity' prayer.

"On the morning you leave, you receive a medallion, about the size of a silver dollar. I carry mine in my wallet, and sometimes I think it's stupid, but I keep it there. In a way, the program was like having a bullet removed without anesthesia. But I also feel that the end result was a kind of miracle. I went in there at the end of my rope, in despair, needing a drink in the morning before I could leave the house—and I came out, after just four weeks, feeling optimistic, courageous, and able to cope without alcohol. They gave me back my life."

Source: Jean Seligmann with Elizabeth Bailey, *Newsweek*, September 24, 1984.

was founded in 1935 on the premise that alcoholism is a disease from which you never recover. Thus, clients are not allowed even one drop of alcohol ever again in their entire lives. AA was originally a religious organization (but is somewhat less so today) of alcoholics and ex-alcoholics assisting one another with God's help. Since AA keeps its membership anonymous, there are few if any reliable studies of the effectiveness of its programs. One suspects that total abstinence is not a reasonable objective for many people in contemporary American society.

• Drug Abuse

Stating the Problem Society can be thought of as groups of people or social units organized to pursue major common interests, as interdependent social units (e.g., involving norms, values, statuses, roles, institutions, and so on). However, both individual and social interests (values, goals, and so on) may differ widely (Homans, 1974:27; Hobbes in *Leviathan,* 1982 [original, 1651]). Group life is only possible if we can all roughly subscribe or submit to certain common expectations and values (such as hard work, rationality, control of sensuality—Williams, 1951) and endorse a common culture (Rousseau, 1712–78, *Social Contract*). In a sense to be social then is to be able to will that our own personal behavior and attitudes could become universal standards.

But psychoactive drugs can affect our very ability to be social creatures by contributing to aggressive behavior, excessive docility, inappropriate eroticism, misperception of reality, and so on. For example, heroin turns us inward (makes us asocial), lowers sexual energies, and is a "down" drug. However, since heroin is illegal, it can also prompt violence or sexual acting out to pay for this very expensive habit and to avoid withdrawal pain. LSD distorts perception of external reality and can invoke delusions and hallucinations. Cocaine stimulates erotic sensations and heightens sexual urgency. Amphetamines, like Dexedrine and Benzedrine, produce short-term euphoria followed by extreme fatigue and even clinical depression when abused. Some have argued (Mann, 1980) that THC, the active ingredient in marijuana, affects both male and female reproductive capabilities. Thus, drug abuse potentially disrupts many important social abilities and motivations. When it is widespread, drug abuse creates social (as well as physical) problems.

Marijuana and Cigarette Smoking As we saw in Table 9.2, marijuana is the most widely used illegal drug (Kaplan et al., 1986). In 1975, 23 percent of young people twelve to seventeen years old had used marijuana. Table 9.5 reveals that by 1979 young people's marijuana use had risen to 31 percent. After 1980 marijuana use declined sharply (to about 16 percent to 17 percent) among young people (Institute of Social Research Newsletter, 1983). More males than females smoke marijuana and its use is uncommon among those over age thirty-five. Given the past hysteria and federal repression of marijuana smoking, it is hard to get a clear understanding of its health consequences. Marijuana does seem to help glaucoma patients and relieve the nausea of cancer patients being treated by chemotherapy (Duncan and Gold, 1982:135ff.). However, like cigarette smoking, long-term use of marijuana is probably also associated with increased respiratory problems, bronchitis, and even cancer. Others have argued that marijuana affects the reproductive system (as we have seen), may induce genetic mutations, and lowers the testosterone levels of males (Mann, 1980). Finally, marijuana impairs learning and driving ability, increases the heart rate, may cause atrophy of the brain, and affects our immune system. It will probably be years before we fully understand all the health results of smoking marijuana.

Nicotine and carbon monoxide consumption through smoking cigarettes are much more dangerous than marijuana smoking. For one thing more people smoke cigarettes. Table 9.2 shows that 66 percent of adults and 52 percent

TABLE 9.5 Marijuana and Hashish Use, 1979 and 1982 (Percentages)

All Youth (1982) (12–17) 1979	Ever Used (27) 31	Current Use* (12) 17	Young Adults (18–25)	Ever Used (64) 68	Current Use* (27) 35	Older Adults (26 and Over)	Ever Used (23) 20	Current Use* (7) 6
Age			Age			Age		
12–13	8	4	18–21	69	40	26–34	48	17
14–15	32	17	22–25	68	30	35 and over	10	2
16–17	51	28						
Sex			Sex			Sex		
Male	34	19	Male	75	45	Male	26	9
Female	28	14	Female	61	26	Female	14	3
Race			Race			Race		
White	31	17	White	69	36	White	19	6
Nonwhite	31	15	Nonwhite	62	34	Nonwhite	26	8

*Use in past month.
Source: P.M. Fishburne, H.I. Abelson, and I. Cisin, *National Survey on Drug Abuse,* 1980: 45–47. Cf. *Behavior Today,* November 26, 1984; *Health, United States, 1985:74*; *Statistical Abstract of the United States,* 1986:118.

of young people have smoked cigarettes (41 percent and 25 percent in the last year). Data from 1982 (*Statistical Abstract of the United States,* 1986:118) confirm that 79 percent of adults and 50 percent of youth have smoked cigarettes at some time (35 percent and 15 percent, respectively, are current users). Chemically, nicotine is a stimulant that, when used to excess, can cause nausea, dizziness, general weakness, and a decrease in the oxygen-carrying capabilities in the blood (because of the gas—carbon monoxide—in cigarettes). In fact, the increase in carbon monoxide in the blood is similar to breathing extremely polluted industrial or city air (see Panel 9.3).

Unlike marijuana smoking, cigarette smoking is clearly harmful to one's health (Koop in *Newsweek,* June 2, 1984). It is estimated that cigarette smoking costs $28 billion per year in health care costs. In the United States there are about 340,000 smoking related deaths each year. As many as 129,000 of 430,000 annual cancer deaths are tied to cigarette smoking (*The Wall Street Journal,* February 23, 1982). Smokers are twice as likely to die of a heart attack as nonsmokers of the same age, twice as likely to die of cancer, and three times more likely to die of lung cancer (Duncan and Gold, 1982:88, cf. Ray, 1978:Ch. 8). Even when the health consequences are severe and preventable, as in the following example of "Berger's Disease," many smokers develop strong physical and psychological dependence on nicotine, such that they seem unable to stop smoking.

> If a patient with this condition continues to smoke, gangrene may eventually set in. First a few toes may have to be amputated, then the foot at the ankle, then the leg at the knee, and ultimately at the hip. Somewhere along this gruesome progression gangrene may also attack the other leg. Patients are strongly advised that if they will only stop smoking, it is virtually certain

"Don't worry. If it turns out tobacco is harmful, we can always quit."

that the otherwise inexorable march of gangrene up the legs will be curbed. Yet surgeons report that it is not at all uncommon to find a patient with Berger's disease vigorously puffing away in his hospital bed following a second or third amputation operation. (Brecher,1972:216)*

Cocaine According to Table 9.2, roughly 3 percent to 4 percent of youth ages twelve to seventeen and adults have tried cocaine. As many as 10 million Americans have tried cocaine sometime in their lives and about 4.1 million actually used the drug in 1982 (*Behavior Today,* June 18, 1984, *Newsweek,* June 4, 1984; *Newsweek,* February 25, 1985), down slightly from 4.5 million

*From *Licit and Illicit Drugs* by Edward M. Brecher and Editors of Consumer Reports.

PANEL 9.3

Composition of Tobacco Smoke

The smoke inhaled by smokers contains approximately 1,200 gases, vapors, and small particles. This particulate matter may be found in concentrations as high as 5 billion particles per cubic millimeter—an enormously high number when we consider that the air in our most polluted cities contains similar particles in concentrations of approximately 10,000 particles per cubic millimeter. When these particles are condensed, they form a thick, brown, sticky substance referred to as cigarette tars. These tars contain substances identified as carcinogens (or cancer-producing chemicals, such as benzopyrene), cocarcinogens (substances that do not cause cancer directly but that may combine with other substances to form cancer-producing mixtures, such as phenols), and various other substances that do not cause cancer and are not considered cocarcinogens, but are potentially dangerous in other ways (nicotine is an example).

The tars, however, account for only about 8 percent of the volume of cigarette smoke; the remaining 92 percent is composed of gas and vapor mixtures. Among the most dangerous of these gases found in smoke is carbon monoxide (which is found in concentrations more than 400 times higher than is considered safe). Carbon monoxide reduces the ability of the blood to carry oxygen. Perhaps the most distressing fact concerning the composition of tobacco smoke is that smokers are exposed to all of these substances at the same time.

Source: Reprinted with permission of Macmillan Publishing Company from *Drugs and the Whole Person* by David Duncan and Robert Gold. New York: Macmillan 1982:84.

users in 1979. Another report (Anderson, 1983) claims that 11 percent of U.S. adults have tried cocaine. One cocaine user profile reports that 67 percent were male, 85 percent were white, that the mean use per week was 6 grams, 61 percent took cocaine intranasally (21 percent free-based and 18 percent were intravenous users), 68 percent used cocaine in conjunction with alcohol, and 73 percent were unable to control their cocaine usage (i.e., had a strong psychological dependence—see *Behavior Today,* June 18, 1984).

Pharmacologically cocaine is classified as a short-acting stimulant. Among its major effects are the reduction of fatigue and the reproduction of feelings of euphoria. Some people use cocaine as an aphrodisiac (including Sigmund Freud—see *Life* magazine, May 1984). Cocaine is a crystalline alkaloid extracted from the leaves of the coca plant that grows in the Andes Mountains of South America at 1,500 to 6,000 feet above sea level (Duncan and Gold, 1982:127). It is an extremely expensive drug (although the derivative crack is cheaper). In 1986 cocaine sold for about $100 to $150 a gram (about one teaspoonful) or $2,000 an ounce. Because cocaine probably does not cause physical dependence, some claim it is a harmless drug. Crack is free-base

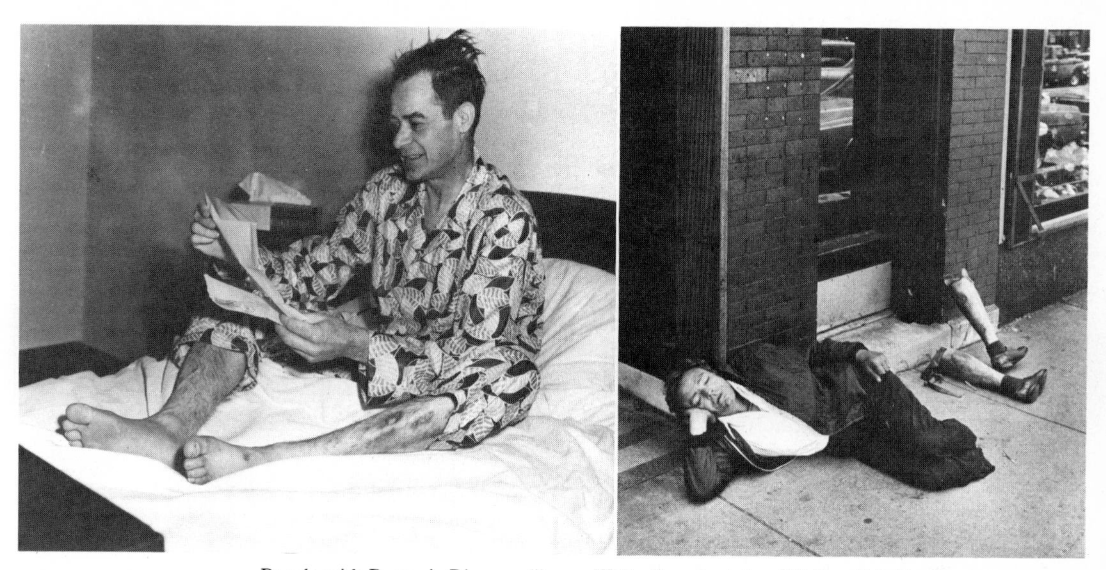

People with Berger's Disease, like ex-White Sox shortstop Bill Cissell (left) can get gangrene from the disease. Often legs have to be amputated (right). If the patient would only stop smoking, the progressive gangrene would stop. (Left—AP/Wide World Photos; Right—Thom O'Conner/Black Star)

cocaine, consumed as a smoke pellet, which sells for only about $10 a gram. Its effects are very rapid and it is addicting (Holtzman, 1986).

However, psychological dependence on cocaine is certainly intense. Many users develop a compelling desire or craving for cocaine and would do almost anything to get the drug. For example, experimental rats pushing levers at will to get cocaine continue this activity to the exclusion of all other activities until they die (Holtzman, 1986). In addition to the celebrities we have already mentioned as psychologically dependent on cocaine (e.g., Belushi, Pryor, Freud, and so on), Sir Arthur Conan Doyle (the author of Sherlock Holmes novels) abused cocaine, inventor Thomas Edison injected cocaine to help him stay up long hours without sleep, and countless professional athletes have ruined their careers in part because of their cocaine abuse. For example, in 1984 professional basketball star David Thompson was released by the Seattle Supersonics because of his repeated cocaine abuse (see Ray, 1978:Ch. 13; Duncan and Gold, 1982:128; HBO Special, "The Nightmare of Cocaine," 1984).[13]

Caffeine The most widely used (and often unrecognized) drug is caffeine. For example, 82 percent of all adults drank coffee in the past year and 55 percent of young people drank tea (see Table 9.2). In 1983 people in the United States consumed 10.2 pounds of coffee per person compared with a worldwide average of about 1.6 pounds per year per person. Over the last twenty to twenty-five years coffee consumption has gone down and soft drink consump-

PANEL 9.4

Hot-Lining for Cocaine Help

Running on empty, they dial.

"800-COCAINE, may I help you?"

Some hang up, most hang on. Twenty-four hours a day they light up the phone bank on the second floor of Fair Oaks Hospital with toll-free, nameless renditions of the cocaine blues. Half are actual coke abusers looking for medical advice, hospital referrals or a nonjudgmental ear; the rest are stumped health-care professionals or traumatized family members like the ten-year-old who recently called the Summit, N.J., hot line to say his tooted-up father would not stop beating his mother. Most callers start haltingly.

"Yeah . . . uhm . . . I'm into freebasing and I want to stop. I've been hitting the pipe for two months. I've been trying to stop on my own, but it's not working."

Last May Dr. Mark Gold, chief of research at Fair Oaks (a psychiatric and drug-dependency hospital), set up the hot line to provide public information on cocaine abuse and treatment. A room was set aside, a phone plugged in and a small computer programmed with the names and numbers of 700 doctors and drug-treatment centers across the country. "At first," says drug counselor and phone-bank supervisor Jeffrey Shore, "we figured we'd just have someone near the phone in case it rang."

It did. Originally, the hot-line staff thought they would receive 10,000 calls a year. Soon after the first line was operational, however, 1,000 calls a day began streaming into the tiny room. "We never slept," says Shore of the old times when only he and a skeleton staff were on board. "We just kept answering the phone." Now, with a better sense of how badly they are needed (and a concurrent rise in grants and donations), the not-for-profit phone bank has expanded a bit. Still squeezed into the three-desk, two-ashtray office, the hot line now boasts a mostly volunteer pool of twenty-five, three to five of whom man phones during the day. During the after-midnight hours, when the hard-core abusers traditionally call in, one counselor is on call. Many on the hot-line staff are former abusers.

tion has gone up. Of all the popular beverages, coffee has by far the highest concentration of caffeine; about 80 to 150 milligrams per five-ounce serving.

Caffeine is a member of the xanthine family, the oldest known stimulant. Caffeine is found in the seeds of coffee plants, the leaves of a South American evergreen shrub, the North American holly bush, the West African kola nut, the Brazilian soapberry plant, and of course, in tea leaves (Duncan and Gold, 1982:70–71). Blood levels for caffeine peak in about thirty to sixty minutes and have a half-life of three hours.[14] At levels of 150 to 300 milligrams caffeine offsets fatigue and makes sleep more difficult. One does become physically dependent on caffeine and will incur withdrawal symptoms if caffeine ingestion is stopped (Ray, 1978:196). Caffeine increases the consumption of oxygen (thus, it helps asthmatics) and speeds up metabolism. The health effects of caffeine are unclear at this time, but there is concern that caffeine contributes

PANEL 9.4—*(concluded)*

"Whattaya, snorting? Smoking? How much? You got health insurance? They had to lock me up five times before I got straight."

Unsurprisingly, the hot line logs more calls from New York and Los Angeles than anywhere else. Still, callers frequently dial from the Midwest and small towns. Recent surveys show that 85 percent of the callers are white, one in seven makes over $50,000 a year, 63 percent consider themselves addicted and four of five suffer from severe depression. But to those who answer the phones it's the voices, not the numbers, that haunt.

"There was this state trooper despondent on cocaine," remembers Richard Jensen, hospital coordinator for the phone bank. "He said, 'I've got my revolver in one hand and the phone in the other. It's up to you to make me decide which to use.' We kept him on for awhile, but he never told us who or where he was." Although those handling the phones are trained in crisis intervention, Jensen says 800-COCAINE's main function is education, not suicide prevention. "Only one of eight of the abusers who calls here," he remarks, "is looking for treatment. Some want to talk about how the drug is affecting them; others want to confess; they feel better after they talk about it."

One of Jensen's most disturbing calls came from a 23-year-old woman who said she had just sold her baby for $5,000 worth of cocaine. "I could hear her mother in the background saying, 'Don't tell them, it's none of their business'," details Jensen. Pausing, he muses over the 350,000 calls the hot line has received in the year it has been in operation. "We want people to know," he finishes, "that they can talk to us, and we can get them help." The message is out: on the second floor, the buttons glow.

"Yeah, listen, how long after you take cocaine does it stop showing up in your urine? Ya see, they're going to be testing us at work in 35 days and I only did it twice and . . . . Ya sure?"

Source: Neal Karlen, *Newsweek*, June 4, 1984:64.

to heart disease, anxiety, and general nervousness (see "Shunning Caffeinated Coffee," *Newsweek*, October 22, 1984; Troyer and Markle, 1984).

Valium and "Minor" Tranquilizers About 15 percent of the adult population uses (medical) sedatives in any recent given year (Table 9.2). The so-called benzodiazepines—including Valium, Librium, Dalmane, and Serax—are muscle relaxants that tranquilize and reduce anxiety. They are usually distinguished from antipsychotic or "major tranquilizers" (such as Thorazine, Stelazine, Haldol, Navane, and Mellaril). Valium, Librium, and Dalmane account for more than half of all psychotropic drug sales (all three drugs are manufactured by the Hoffman-LaRouche drug firm; see *New York Times*, February 5, 1979, "Beyond Valium"). In 1978 Hoffman-LaRouche made about $100 million in profits from the sale of minor tranquilizers alone (Hughes and Brewin,

1979:5). In fact Valium was the largest selling prescription drug in the country. Sales of Valium worldwide totaled $2 billion. In 1979 Valium cost 24 cents per hundred to produce and sold for about $7.25 per 100; obviously a very profitable venture (Prather, 1980).

Valium has much the same effects as alcohol (a fact that teenage drinkers may quickly point out to their self-righteous mothers and fathers!). It reduces anxiety, relaxes the muscles, enables one to tolerate stressful social encounters, makes you sleepy, and so on. Alcohol and Valium have interactive synergistic effects; they potentiate each other. In a famous case, Karen Anne Quinlan went into an irreversible coma and eventual death from mixing alcohol and Valium (Hughes and Brewin, 1979:42). However, for the most part, Valium is a relatively safe drug. Other things being equal, a lethal dose of Valium is about 1,600 five-milligram tablets—that is, about 1,600 times the therapeutic dose.

This does not mean that Valium is a safe drug. As little as forty milligrams of Valium a week taken for a period of several weeks can cause a clinical depression or paradoxical rage reactions. Instead of treating possible underlying depressions or actually changing stressful real-life situations, minor tranquilizers simply make the depression or stress more tolerable without curing them (as Panel 9.5 illustrates). Valium can be thought of as social discriminatory punishment for certain social groups. For example, women are twice as likely to be prescribed Valium as men. Tranquilizers in general (especially major tranquilizers in state hospitals) can be thought of as "chemical solitary confinement" (Hughes and Brewin, 1979:142). Finally, we should be aware that the greatest number of actual drug deaths is from barbiturates, not from minor tranquilizers (DAWN, 1977 in De Fleur, 1983:71), although many people do overdose on Valium and find themselves in hospital emergency rooms.

Of course, there are other important problematic aspects of drug abuse that we have not emphasized here, but could have (e.g., heroin addiction, methadone abuse in clinics, hallucinogens like PCP and LSD, and many more). Heroin is an especially dangerous drug because its effective dose is relatively close to its lethal dose. Some of the drugs we have neglected are deadly, but are engaged in by relatively small proportions of the general population. We have chosen to emphasize widespread, often unrecognized, problems of drug abuse. Having stated a few major problems, we now must ask what explains these patterns of drug abuse.

Analyzing the Problem. The Exchange Perspective Our analysis of prior social problems clearly involved the exchange of relatively unique interactive assets of different groups of people (e.g., of the young and old, men and women, blacks and whites, the sane and mentally disordered, and so on). Here, however, since drugs are not people, one realizes immediately that the exchange perspective has to be modified to some degree. What is being exchanged? Table 9.6 suggests that there are at least two levels of exchange with drugs. First, there is the drug itself interacting (physically, chemically,

PANEL 9.5

Librium Junkie

"So I talked, and I still do talk, about how I became a prescription junkie, which all started so—well, innocently. I remember my first tranquilizer prescription. I had just turned twenty-two and had just come back from my first international flight. I was tired, a little strung out, and on edge. I had a doctor's appointment that same day, just a routine checkup, and when the checkup was over, the doctor asked me how I was feeling. And I told him I was edgy and a bit tense. I complained about how mixed up, yet wonderful my life was and how I had a difficult time coping with the time changes, a full plane, and my lack of sleep."

"The doctor listened for about five minutes, nodded in that ever-so-wise way doctors have, reached for a prescription pad, and said, 'Take these, dear, whenever you feel a bit anxious or under stress.' 'These' turned out to be a prescription—refillable—for ten milligrams of Librium. I rushed out of his office to get the prescription filled because I was still a little nervous, walked out of the drugstore, popped a pill, and I tell you—what a wonderful feeling I had about an hour later. I thought that the world around me had turned all warm and mellow. Colors became softer and more diffuse. I felt like I had been wrapped up in a wonderfully protective coating of foam rubber that insulated me from the dirt, the grime, the madness, and the noise of New York."

Source: From *The Tranquilizing of America,* copyright 1979 by Richard Hughes and Robert Brewin. Reprinted by permission of Harcourt Brace Jovanovich, Inc.

and so on) with the drug user; second, drug users interacting with drug suppliers (e.g., with drug companies, physicians, illicit drug dealers, and so on).

Both drugs and drug suppliers exchange their direct or indirect ability to reward drug users with changed sensation or perception (e.g., euphoria, pain reduction, sleep, relaxation, and so on) usually for money, sex, or status. For example, drug users sometimes exchange sex or violence for the money or property of straight nondrug users. Parenthetically, since drugs are not people, one might suspect that drugs can function as people substitutes. For example, the heroin addict may fantasize about sexual relations or develop sexual associations with syringe injections (penetration) and the resultant euphoric rush (orgasm).

If we cannot speak unequivocably about the exchange between drugs themselves and people, this does not mean that the exchange perspective does not account for drug behaviors. Perhaps drugs facilitate social exchanges. You will recall that one common effect of diverse drugs was increased sociability. Sociologist Erving Goffman (1959) has argued that all social exchange is stressful, potentially dangerous, and unrewarding. From exchange theory's success proposition we know that if activities are not rewarding or rewarded, they will tend to cease. Since social exchange itself (e.g., work, love, play exchange) is

TABLE 9.6 Distribution of Basic Societal Rewards or Punishments by Drug Status

Rewards or Punishments	Drug Users*	Licit or Illicit Drug Suppliers or Drugs Themselves
Ability to chance sensation, perception, and so on of external or internal reality	−	+
Money	+	−
Sexual favors	+	−
Confer status, give esteem	+	−

+ = reward or punishment present or supplied.
− = reward or punishment absent or received.
*Drug users also interact with straight, nondrug users basically by exchanging sex or violence (actual or threatened) for the money or property of nondrug users. Of course, drug use or abuse and nondrug use is not a simple dichotomy. Drug use and abuse are highly complex behaviors along a continuum.

valuable, even necessary, drugs often make needed but potentially punishing activities possible.

In a related vein, drugs may also facilitate social interaction by recharging the rewards and values of social exchange. We remember from exchange theory's fourth proposition that human activities can lose their prior rewards through the principle of satiation. It is possible to think of (for example) having sexual relations accompanied by cocaine, watching a film or rock concert after smoking marijuana, giving a public speech having taken Valium, or counteracting depressive effect with the drug Elavil as changing the values of interactive rewards, or as making previously punishing or less rewarding acts more valuable and thus more likely.

Of course, drug abuse is also an exchange issue because people learn to use and abuse drugs (Akers, 1985; McAuliffe et al., 1984). Drug abusers interact or exchange with significant others (role models) who themselves have defined drug use and abuse as rewarding (Goode, 1972). Examples that come to mind readily include inner city blacks' use of heroin, teenagers' use of marijuana (cf. Kaplan et al., 1986), artists' and performers' use of cocaine, even workers and their coffee breaks. Conversely, when negative attitudes are held toward particular drug behaviors (such as cigarette smoking), we usually see a decline in that form of drug abuse. The concept of balance is also relevant in this context. If you like or are similar to other people and you and the others both have favorable definitions of drug abuse, then there is an added reinforcement effect of consistent, harmonious, multiple exchanges.

Finally, the exchange perspective argues that behaviors that are profitable will be repeated (Homans, 1974:119ff.). Obviously the profits of drug sales by drug companies and illegal dealers are enormous. In the preceding section we saw that cocaine and Valium both return high profits (Hughes and Brewin, 1979:20ff.). It has been estimated that heroin that brings $225,000 on the street could be purchased from a farmer in (say) the country of Turkey for $300 (Ray, 1978:326ff.; cf. *Newsweek,* September 28, 1981). The alert reader might object that profits to drug companies are not the same as profits to drug users and abusers. Of course, the answer to this objection is that major corporations (like Lilly, Robins, Squibb, or even Philip-Morris) have tremendous power to influence our consumption behavior, even if that drug consumption is not in our best interests (as U.S. Senate hearings on tobacco in 1986 indicate).[15]

The Conflict Perspective According to conflict theorists drug abuse has less to do with drug effects than with the social control of certain types of people. Drug laws tend to be laws that discriminate against certain groups of people, not drugs. For example, the white, Anglo-Saxon, Protestant, physician opiate addicts are tolerated, but violent inner-city black heroin addicts are not (Karmen, 1980). Historically, drug laws were for the social control of minorities and the working classes (e.g., of Chinese, Mexicans, blacks, and even women). The first drug laws in the United States censured Chinese laborers (California, 1875), not opiates. The conflict perspective contends that we punish those minority groups that are economically, politically, or socially threatening or otherwise objectionable to majority groups (Morgan, 1978; Szasz, 1975). As a case in point, marijuana smoking was widely disapproved of and strongly censured when it was practiced originally by the Mexican working class. But when white middle-class teenagers adopted marijuana, in most states it quickly became a misdemeanor rather than a felony to possess small amounts (about 1970).

Paradoxically, laws themselves cause or create some drug abuse (Reasons, 1975). For example, the Harrison Narcotics Act of 1914 converted addicts to criminals. Furthermore, illegal drugs such as heroin or cocaine are expensive (because they are illegal) and force theft, prostitution, and violence to support drug habits. On the other hand methadone (in legal clinics) is cheap, readily available, and avoids much deviance. Drug laws make those who share the problems of obtaining drugs interact with each other, thus perpetuating and aggravating many problems of drug abuse.

The conflict perspective also argues that drugs are often used to defy or protest dominant values, power, or authority. Thus, drug abuse is resistance or avoidance of common expectations that may not be appropriate or even possible for all social groups (Miller, 1958; Merton, 1968). Self-actualization may require being different. Thus, if a dominant social class does not use drugs, minorities may feel compelled to use drugs (or different drugs) as an act of social self-determination. For example, if productivity and rationality are the majority norms, then consumptive gratification may be the minority reaction.

The Symbolic Interaction Perspective It can be argued from the symbolic interaction point of view that drug use and abuse in and of themselves are not

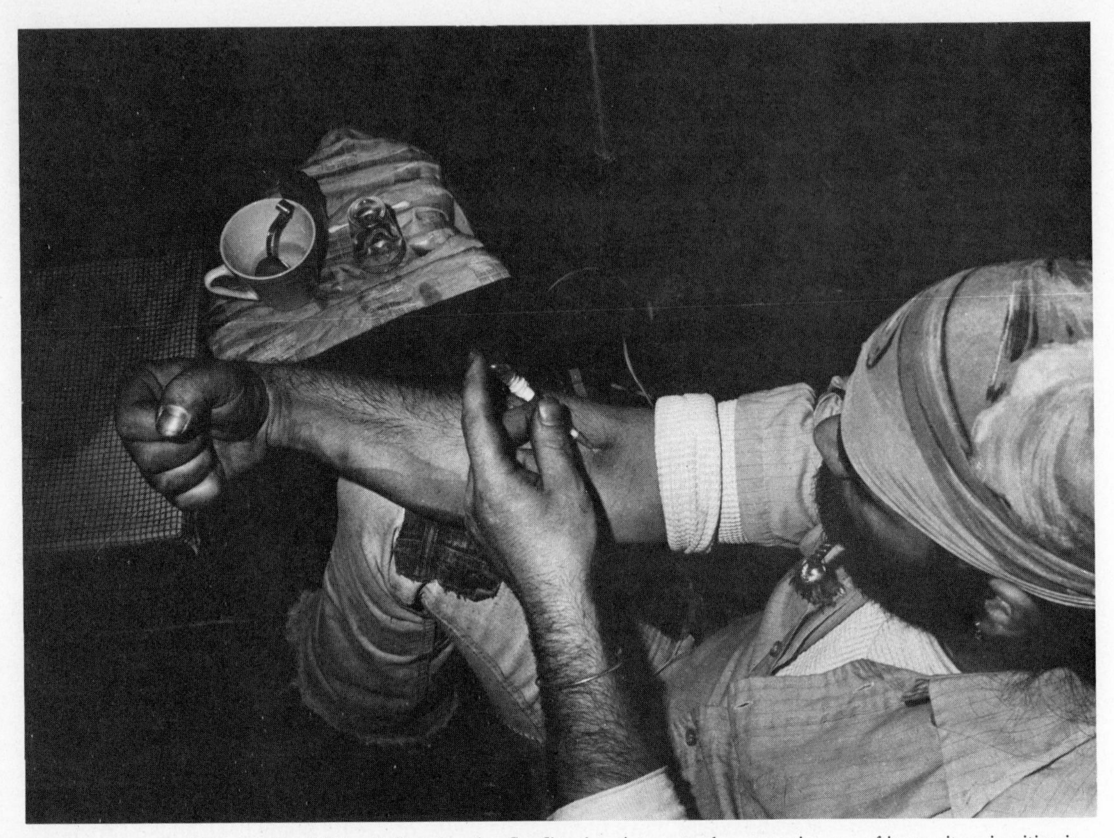

An addict mainlines heroin. Conflict theorists note that narcotics use of inner-city minorities is often tacitly supported, since heroin addiction reduces one's libido. Drugs are indirectly used by majority groups to control minorities—including suburban wives on Valium and Librium. (Charles Gatewood/Stock, Boston)

intrinsically good or bad. Drugs can be perceived in many different ways. For example, Sutherland and Cressey claim that people use or abuse drugs because their exposure to favorable definitions of drug use (see differential association) has been greater than their exposure to unfavorable definitions (1978; Ausebel, 1980:4; Becker in Chapter 1; Becker, 1980:180–190). Lindesmith (1968) also emphasizes the role of learning opiate addiction through symbolic interaction with others (cf. Lindesmith, 1980:34ff.).

In 1967 Lemert coined the phrase secondary deviance. He indicated that labeling a person a drug addict or drug abuser may restrict his/her nondrug alternatives for dealing with life problems, such that drug abuse is his/her basic or only coping strategy. Secondary deviants are those whose life and identity are organized around their deviance. In the context of the present topic, they have a drug abuser identity. Thus, drug abuse is a result of repeated negative public reactions (cf. Goffman's 1963 concept of stigma) and is not transitory.

The Biological Perspective Scholars trained in the biological perspective might contend that drug abuse occurs (e.g., opiate addiction) because of extremely potent physical reinforcing effects of drugs (McAuliffe and Gordon, 1974, 1980:137ff.). For example, opiate drug abuse produces euphoria, avoids painful withdrawal effects (Lindesmith, 1968), and has major analgesic properties.[16] From the biological perspective, drug abuse is common because "it feels good" (euphoria) (cf. Bejerot, 1980:246ff.). Drugs enhance sensation, perception, or imagination. They can intensify good feelings.

It may also be that drugs are abused because the body is not producing enough endorphins or other needed psychoactive drugs (Martin, 1980; Simon, 1980:303ff.). Hypophoria, the opposite of euphoria, is an affective disorder shared by many drug addicts. This suggests that some drug abuse could result from deficiencies or hyperactivities in the neurotransmitters of drug abusers (see Table 8.2). One must be careful here not to falsely attribute the dysphoria of drug addicts to the drugs they take. For example, Goode (1973:42) contends that "all of the diseases of addicts result from the way they live and not directly from the drug that they take."

Finally, Hochhauser suggests that chronobiological rhythms may be such that more of certain drugs are needed in some circumstances or times (1980:262ff.). For example, we know that morphine affects rats differently in periods of light or dark (diurnal rhythms). These being some of the major causes of drug abuse, we must now ask how drug problems could be reversed.

Resolving the Problem Three fundamental types of resolutions will be considered. These include alternative addictions, legalizing drugs and control issues, and finally, treatment programs. Before considering these resolutions, a caveat is in order. The issue of temperate recreational drug use is just as important as drug abuse. Drug users probably outnumber drug abusers about nine to one (Duncan and Gold, 1982:177). There is such a thing as rational, temperate, nonabusive drug consumption for some drugs. For example, many physicians use recreational drugs (even opiates) with few apparent negative consequences. Furthermore, it can be argued that individuals have inalienable rights to manipulate the pleasure or pain levels of their own bodies, as long as they do not harm others (Bayer, 1978). Drug education can be extremely helpful in promoting rational drug use (Ray, 1978:430ff.).

Alternative Addictions Although the concept of an addictive personality is questionable (Ray, 1978:333),[17] there can be little doubt that it is often difficult to change the social, work, interpersonal, biological, and personality conditions giving rise to drug abuse, addiction, or psychological compulsion to use drugs (cf. Kaplan, et al., 1986). Of course, primary prevention would attempt to keep drug abuse and its multitudinous circumstances from developing in the first place (Duncan and Gold, 1982:Ch. 15). However, primary prevention of drug problems is often not practical, since it requires major social changes that themselves would have great costs and take a long time. As a compromise, perhaps one could substitute more positive addictions for drug abuse—get the rewards and benefits of drugs from other sources?

It is easy to think of alternative addictions. As we shall see below, methadone is often substituted for heroin addiction. Running and exercise apparently increase the natural stimulant norepinephrine and allow people to stop smoking. Meditation, biofeedback, and other relaxation techniques can have many of the same cardiovascular effects as minor tranquilizers like Valium and Librium. Less caffeinated drinks can be substituted for the usual morning coffee. Religious ecstasy and what the Greeks called *agape* (nonerotic love) can even reduce the craving for sexual promiscuity and cocaine. For example, one cannot help but observe that many born-again fundamentalist Christians were drug abusers and/or sexual deviants before they converted.

Clearly, it would be better if we could all slow down, relax, minimize the stresses and pressures of contemporary social and work life, be more physically healthy, less narcissistic, and so on. But these changes are not likely to occur any time soon, if ever. Since we cannot easily change our social and personal circumstances that generate drug problems, perhaps the most we can hope for are better coping strategies or alternative "addictions" that allow us to tolerate the givens with less damage.

Legalizing Drugs, Control Issues The traditional response to problems of drug abuse has been to increase federal and state penalties (Anderson, 1983). There is some evidence that drug use in rituals or regulated drug use does discourage abuse (Duncan and Gold, 1982:181). However, a cogent argument could be made that drugs are abused and problematic in part precisely because they are illegal. That is, the primary problem is not with the chemical properties of drugs but rather with society's efforts to control the use of drugs (Ray, 1978:Ch. 2; Duncan and Gold, 1982:Ch. 14). For example, making heroin, marijuana, cocaine, and so on illegal, or restricting the manufacture and sale of Valium, amphetamines, and so on drives up the costs of these drugs. This makes it immensely profitable to sell drugs and to produce addicts. Also, the need to avoid painful withdrawal symptoms can increase theft and prostitution rates. Thus, perhaps one resolution to drug problems is not to change drugged individuals, but instead to alter the social circumstances that makes drug sales so profitable. Szasz has recommended that we legalize all dangerous drugs with only moderate controls (1975). Would this not help the drug problem (Bunker, 1979)?

Perhaps it would help to some degree, but we must remember that many of the most dangerous drugs are already legal. For example, repealing Prohibition did little to solve alcohol problems. Making alcohol, cigarettes, and caffeine legal allows society to license and tax their use, but does not guarantee control of their consumption. Thus, legalization of drugs might decrease *some* problems, but certainly not all of them. One area in which legislation might help is in the treatment and control of heroin use.

Treatment Programs Once drug users become addicted to or psychologically dependent on their drugs, treatment programs (rather than prevention programs) become mandatory (Ray, 1978:25–27). Two of the most common drug treatment programs are methadone maintenance and detoxification. Other programs include drug free programs like Synanon (Ray, 1978:333–334), crisis intervention programs, supervisory deterrent programs (e.g., programs that send drug abusers to jail if they are not compliant), educational programs, and antagonist programs (e.g., using the narcotic antagonist naltrexone to counteract the effects of heroin).

Methadone is a synthetically produced heroin substitute that can be administered orally to outpatients (Snyder, 1980:94; Duncan and Gold, 1982:205; Ray, 1978:335–337). Although methadone maintenance constitutes a new addiction, it is longer lasting, cheaper, has milder withdrawal symptoms, and is better controlled than heroin. The majority of heroin users maintained on methadone stay with their families, have steady jobs, pay taxes, and so on. Crime by former heroin users is reduced by as much as 90 percent. With methadone maintenance opiate addiction is converted from crime to illness (Bunker, 1979).

Finally, detoxification programs aim to eliminate physical dependence on the drug(s) to which one is addicted (Newman, 1979; Snyder, 1980:95). In such programs drugs are used in smaller and smaller doses over time to minimize withdrawal symptoms. Usually, the detoxification process takes about ten days for heroin addicts.

• Summary

Drug abuse occurs when a person continually misuses any drug, when a person has lost control over the use of a drug, or when drug taking disrupts the individual's family, job, or other important social roles. This general definition of *drug abuse* is reasonably accurate for alcohol abuse too, although formal definitions of *alcoholism* were given.

One who is addicted to drugs has a compulsion to take the drug(s), a psychological dependence on the drug(s), and the addiction has a detrimental effect both on the individual and society (addiction includes the concept of alcoholism). Drug habituation, on the other hand, includes a desire for the drug(s), (not a compulsion), no tendency to increase the drug dosage, no physical dependence, and few detrimental effects either on society or the individual (drug habituation parallels the concept of problem drinking).

Drug abuse includes alcohol, nicotine, caffeine, and prescription or drugstore abuse, as well as abuse of opiates, tranquilizers, cocaine, hallucinogens, and marijuana. A drug is any substance that affects the structure or function of a living organism (especially psychotropic drugs). For our purposes drugs were classified into five basic types: (1) narcotics; (2) depressants/tranquilizers; (3) stimulants; (4) hallucinogens; and (5) *cannabis*. Alcohol is a type 2 drug.

We use drugs to avoid pain, to seek or maximize pleasure, to treat illness and injury, to cope with stress, to aid sleep and relaxation, to correct chemical imbalances, to expand consciousness or insight, and to control groups and individuals. Drug effects are achieved through biochemical activities in the nervous system, which the drugs reach via the bloodstream.

Several basic issues related to drug abuse were considered. For example, does drug abuse involve one drug or many? Most drug abuse is polyabuse, involving the use of several different drugs simultaneously. Given the stress of modern life, some drug abuse is socially induced. But drug abuse is not harmless. Drug abuse, especially alcohol, is highly related to crime, accidents, and economic costs. Drugs actions are both physical and social. Some believe drugs (like prisons and mental asylums) are used to control minorities or those in lower social classes. Finally, legalizing drugs (such as marijuana, cocaine, and heroin) might help resolve some drug problems, but the most dangerous drugs (e.g., alcohol and nicotine) are already legal.

Unlike problematic age, sex, race, or mental illness exchanges, drug exchanges occur not only between people,[18] but also between the drug abuser/user and the drugs (or their effects) themselves (i.e., drug users and drugs interact to change perception or sensation, to reduce pain, to produce euphoria, and so on), as such drugs are often people substitutes. Of course, drug abusers/users still exchange money, sex, and esteem for drugs. Drugs can also function to facilitate and recharge the rewards of social exchange. Conflict theorists tend to see drug abuse as control or sedation of minorities (i.e., of blacks, Hispanics, women, and even children) and argue that drug laws themselves tend to cause social problems. Symbolic interactionists emphasize that drug abuse is learned (a trait they share with exchange theorists) and defined as good, while those adopting the biological perspective contend that drug abuse occurs primarily to achieve the real pharmacological effects of euphoria, pain reduction, tension release, and so on. Functionalists contend that drug use that persists over time generally has more socially positive than socially negative consequences. These functional explanations are about the same for drugs in general as they are for alcoholism in particular.

Resolutions to problems of drug abuse range from primary prevention (e.g., never started abusing drugs) to secondary and tertiary prevention programs such as detoxification, moderation, total abstinence from drugs, unlearning drug abuse (e.g., through behavioral modification), achieving alternative (positive) addictions (such as work, religion, and exercise), legalizing drugs, and finally, to special treatment programs for drug problems (like AA or methadone maintenance).

Having examined six social problems (namely, age, sex, race, mental illness, physical illness and drug abuse) involving some institutional factors but primarily concerning face-to-face exchanges in relatively small groups, we now turn in Chapter 10 (and the subsequent five chapters) to a new topic of macrosocial problems at the institutional level, which involves problems in more formal groups with more indirect, impersonal, and complex social exchanges.

• Notes

1. Witness the bewildering array of new carbonated drinks—Diet Coke, Diet Coke without caffeine, regular Coke without caffeine but *with* sugar, Tab with or without nutra-sweet, 7UP-caffeine, "never had it, never will," similar packages by Pepsi, and so on ad nauseum.

2. If there were 100,000 heroin addicts (say, in New York City) with $200-a-day habits, each would need to steal about $1,200 a day (equals $120 million a day or $43.8 billion a year) to meet his/her drug needs (Eitzen, 1986:513). Fencing $1,200 of stolen goods would bring only about one-sixth their actual value, or roughly $200.

3. Remember that our definition of social problems insists that problems be patterns of human behavior or social conditions perceived to be threats to society (usually) *by significant numbers* of the population. It follows that alcoholism and cigarette smoking are probably going to be more likely to be conceived of as social problems (than, say, heroin addiction) because more people use alcohol and cigarettes.

4. For a more complete discussion of the history of drug use, see Duncan and Gold, 1982:38–41; 50–52; 78–82; 100–106; 131–134; 190–192; 200–202; cf. Ray, 1978:128–132; 162–169; 186–195; 245–248; 271–273; 277–279; 299–309; 353–356; 392–398.

5. Other famous Americans who have had serious problems with cocaine include actor Richard Dreyfuss (who starred in the movie *Whose Life Is it, Anyway?* and others), Denver Nugget's and Seattle Supersonic's NBA basketball star, David Thompson, and many more professional athletes. See 1984, Home Box Office special, "The Nightmare of Cocaine."

6. *The Physician's Desk Reference,* 1987 lists approximately 2,000 prescription drugs from the major drug companies. Psychotherapeutic drugs are usually classified into minor tranquilizers or antianxiety agents, major tranquilizers or antipsychotic agents, antidepressants, and anti-Parkinsonian agents (for tremors, tics, and other extrapyramidal effects).

7. Brompton's Cocktail is a mixture of heroin, cocaine, gin, Thorazine, and sugar given to relieve the pain of terminally ill patients in Great Britain's St. Christopher's hospice.

8. Conflict theory cynics might also add a ninth effect of taking drugs, namely, to make money for the drug companies. Obviously, this is not a drug effect, but it does explain why as a society we tend to seem callous and uncaring about the effects of many potentially harmful drugs, including those of alcohol and nicotine—as well as those of illegal drugs. That is, the *health of the social body* (especially of the elites that control society) is more important than the health of individuals.

9. During the 1970s LSD was used sometimes to counteract the rigid, compulsive, self-destructive behaviors of potential suicides. Experimental programs existed at the Spring Grove State Hospital in Maryland and occasionally at the Los Angeles Suicide Prevention Center under the supervision of psychiatrist Robert Litman. Such procedures were always risky and considered a treatment of last resort in patients with otherwise high acute suicide risk.

10. The alert reader may wonder how drugs with basically different effects can all enhance sociability. Part of the answer lies in the differences in individuals inhibiting their sociability. Obviously, nervous, excited, anxious people need to calm down to be comfortable socially, while depressed individuals need more energy, excitation, and so on. Erving Goffman (1959) has argued that all social interaction is threatening. Unfavorable self-images, competition, violence, sexual aggressiveness, even death, may all result from social encounters. Little wonder then that we may need drugs to even *be* social creatures.

11. Compare Becker's 1967 paper on LSD use and changing social expectations.

12. The failure of Prohibition and the continuance of alcohol problems after prohibition should make us suspicious of claims that legalizing heroin, marijuana, cocaine, and so on would resolve those drug problems. Most dangerous drugs are already legal and are no less dangerous because they are legal (especially alcohol and nicotine).

13. Other professional athletes who have had problems with cocaine include George Rodgers of the New Orleans Saints and Washington Redskins, Kellen Winslow of the San Diego Chargers, Mercury Morris, formerly with the Miami Dolphins, and many many more.

14. Half-life refers to the time it takes for 50 percent of a drug's effect to be depleted. Since drug effects are curvilinear, the whole life of caffeine is not six hours; usually the whole life of a drug is far longer than twice its half-life.

15. Another answer is that the costs of drug abuse are not that high to many abusers. Exchange theory defines *cost* as the value of foregone alternatives. Many drug abusers are not meaningfully employed, do not have significant social relations, and so on. In short, they are not sacrificing much by giving their lives over to drugs. In fact the short-term drug euphoria may be better than their misery and isolation without drugs.

16. McAuliffe and Gordon (1974) argue that drug abuse cannot occur just for the purpose of avoiding withdrawal, since the addicts in their study spent 2.4 times more money on drugs than they needed in order to avoid withdrawal symptoms.

17. Duncan and Gold (1982:181) claim that drug abusers tend to have lower self-esteem and more stressful life conditions than nondrug abusers.

18. Except the obvious case of drug abusers/users interacting with drug dealers.

♦ Glossary

Addiction. A compulsion to take a drug, a tendency to increase the dosage, a psychological and (sometimes) physical dependence on the drug, and a detrimental effect on the individual and society.

Alcoholic. An excessive drinker who has lost control of his/her drinking and whose dependence on alcohol is so extreme that there is a noticeable mental disturbance or interference with his/her bodily or mental health, his/her interpersonal relations, and his/her smooth social and economic functioning. S/he is unable to refrain from drinking and to stop drinking before becoming intoxicated.

Alternative Addiction. A more positive compulsion for another nondrug activity (e.g., work, religion, exercise, and so on) or taking a less harmful drug (methadone) that is (presumably) less detrimental to the individual or society.

Blood Alcohol Level (BAL). The number of grams of alcohol per 100 milliliters of blood expressed as a percentage. Thus, 100 milligrams of alcohol in 100 milliliters of blood equals a BAL of 0.1 percent. One usually acts drunk when attaining BALs of 0.05 percent to 0.2 percent.

Cannabis. A plant (actually three) from which marijuana and hashish are produced. Its psychoactive ingredient (THC) results in euphoria and tension reduction when smoked or eaten.

Depressant/Tranquilizer. Any drug that sedates the central nervous system and thereby reduces mental tension and anxiety.

Detoxification. A process of administering smaller and smaller doses of a drug to eliminate physical dependence on that drug while minimizing withdrawal symptoms.

Drug. Any substance, other than food, that by its chemical nature alters the structure or functioning of a living organism.

Drug Abuse. When a person continually misuses any drug, has lost control over the use of the drug, or when drug taking has begun to disrupt an individual's family, job, or ability to perform in other social roles.

Drug Habituation. A desire (not compulsion) to take a drug, no tendency to increase the dosage, a psychological (but not physical) dependence on the drug, with detrimental effects (if any) to the individual alone.

Effective Dose. The dose that would elicit a certain response in a specified percentage of the population receiving that dose.

Endorphin. The natural opiate produced in the brain; endorphin is short for endogenous morphine.

Hallucinogen. A drug that produces unpredictable sensory distortions, fantastic visions, and other psychic (sometimes psychotic) effects.

Lethal Dose. An "LD 50" of a drug means that if 100 laboratory animals were all given a specific dose of 100 milligrams of a particular drug, 50 of the animals would die.

Narcotic. A drug that in moderate doses depresses the central nervous system, thus relieving pain and producing sleep, but that in excessive doses produces unconsciousness, stupor, coma, and possibly death.

Physical Dependence. When use of a drug has so altered an individual's physiology that s/he must continue to use the drug for his/her physical system to continue to function more or less as it did *before* the drug was first used.

Polyabuse. A dependency on a combination of alcohol and/or other drugs.

Problem Drinking. Refers to difficulties in living (e.g., marital, social, job, or health problems) related to repeated overdrinking, but usually stopping short of addiction or alcoholism.

Psychological Dependence. The compelling desire or craving one has for drug effects, which is not caused by physical dependence and does not result in withdrawal symptoms without the drug.

Psychotropic Drug. A drug that alters mood, perception, or consciousness.

Stimulant. Any drug that increases the activity of the central nervous system, raising the heart rate and blood pressure.

Synergistic Effect. The interactive potentiating effect (often unrecognized) of one drug on another, such as the combined effect of Valium and alcohol.

Tolerance. With repeated administration of a drug, a larger dose is required to produce effects that earlier were produced by smaller doses.

Unrecognized Drug. Any substance having significant chemical or psychotropic effects that go undetected by the user and are not associated with the substance. Coffee, tea, carbonated drinks, and food additives are often not considered drugs.

Withdrawal Syndrome. The intense distress or symptoms that accompany abstention from a drug to which one is addicted.

• Further Reading

Cohen, Sidney. *The Alcoholism Problems: Selected Issues.* New York: Haworth Press, Inc., 1983. Thirty-one brief, highly readable chapters on most aspects of alcoholism by a former director of NIMH's division of narcotic administration and drug abuse. A comprehensive and popular, but somewhat sensational, dramatic, and superficial coverage of BAL, teenage drinking, liver problems, auto accidents, hangovers, withdrawal syndromes, fetal alcohol syndrome, alcohol and women, alcohol-drug interactions, the pharmacology of drug abuse, and moderation in drinking.

Duncan, David and Robert Gold. *Drugs and the Whole Person.* New York: John Wiley & Sons, 1982. As the title suggests, Duncan and Gold emphasize the interaction of drugs with the whole person, give historical perspectives of drug issues, argue that drug abuse has no simple solution, and contend that all drug use is emphatically not abuse. A well-written recent overview of the prevalence of drug use, physiology of drug actions, unrecognized drugs, tobacco, alcohol, opiates and cocaine, marijuana, psychedelics, sex and drugs, drugs and the law, and prevention and treatment of drug abuse.

Fishburne, Patricia et al. *National Survey on Drug Abuse: Major Findings, 1979.* Rockville, MD: National Institute on Drug Abuse, 1980. A national sample (N = 7,224) of drug abuse of five groups of illicit substances (marijuana, hallucinogens, cocaine and heroin, psychotherapeutics, and alcohol and cigarettes). The five types are examined by percent ever used and percent used in the last month, controlling for age. Marijuana was the most commonly used psychoactive drug. About 90 percent of the sample had used alcohol, 83 percent of young adults had used cigarettes, and about 66 percent of all young adults had tried at least one illicit drug.

Lettieri, Dan J. et al. *Theories on Drug Abuse: Selected Contemporary Perspectives.* Rockville, MD: National Institute on Drug Abuse, 1980. A basic theoretical reference work with forty-three chapters by most of the celebrities in the field of drug abuse; broken down into four sections (Part I)—self, others, society, nature. The theory components are then applied (in Part II) to drug initiation, continuation, use to abuse, cessation, and relapse. A very extensive and thorough bibliography is also provided. Makes the reader aware of the diversity of views on problems of drug dependence. Once again, drug abuse is seen as a complex problem with no simple unitary resolution.

Ray, Oakley. *Drugs, Society and Human Behavior.* St. Louis: C. V. Mosby, 1978. A somewhat more scholarly overview of drugs in social and behavioral contexts than Duncan and Gold, but in the same genre. Ray is professor of psychology and pharmacology at Vanderbilt University. He collaborates with twelve other drug experts in this volume. Good chapters on the nervous system and physical aspects of drugs, the deleterious effects of drugs, what Ray calls nondrug drugs (alcohol, nicotine, over-the-counter drugs), psychotherapeutic drugs, narcotics, and phantasticants (LSD, MJ, and so on). Excellent historical materials and fifty-seven illustrations.

Woodward, Bob. *Wired: The Short Life and Fast Times of John Belushi.* New York: Simon and Schuster, 1984. Moving, fast-paced account of actor John Belushi's demise from cocaine and heroin abuse (actually from polydrug abuse). Provides insight into the stress, temptations, and indulgence of Hollywood and New York acting scenes. Interviews with Dan Aykroyd, Candice Bergen, Chevy Chase, Jane Curtain, Carrie Fisher, Gordon Lightfoot, Jack Nicholson, Carly Simon, Cathy Smith, Steven Spielberg, and others about drugs, work, and sex in the comedy industry. Should cure you of wanting to be like your heroes in the movies and television.

P·A·R·T

III

Institutional and Macrosocial Problems

C·H·A·P·T·E·R

10

Power Inequality

Once social groups get to be large, dense, complex, urban, and industrialized, inevitably a small number of business, governmental, and military elites rules the society and makes most of its important decisions. Such concentrations of power are subject to abuse, especially since few guard the guardians of society or would have the power to control them even if they did. The Ford Motor Company's design of the Pinto car is a good example of the abuse of unequal power.

In part the social problems related to power inequality are a result of the unique social structure of large, formal, urban-industrial societies. The very indirectness, impersonality, shortened and transitory exchanges, capital-consuming interactions, and the heightened importance of money and status in institutional social organization tend to generate social problems. Also, social exchanges occur not only between individuals, but also among corporate actors and even entire societies. The values, rewards, meanings of deprivation and satiation, the sense of distributive justice all vary with the type of actor. Thus, macrolevel social problems tend in part to arise simply because social exchange has different and more complex meanings at the institutional level of society.

Functionalists argue that social inequality of both power and wealth are inevitable and desirable. This is true because some social positions in any society are more important than others and require special skills. Only a few people have the talents that can be converted to these skills. This conversion of talent to skill requires training and sacrifice. To motivate the few capable individuals to undergo these sacrifices and training, they must be offered inducements of special access to society's scarce rewards. Society's scarce rewards consist of the social esteem and monetary rights and privileges built into the social positions for which they are training. Thus, giving differential access to the basic rewards of a society for some people necessarily results in social inequality.

For conflict theorists the critical factors in social stratification are not important positions needing to be matched with talented or gifted individuals who have sacrificed to get proper training, but rather what place a group has in the organization of production. In a capitalist society workers never have the opportunity to fill important social positions and thus suffer increasingly worse economic, physical, and psychological deprivations. Conflict theorists argue that big business, big government, and big military really control America, routinely abuse their power, and operate in their own interests. The conflict perspective questions the inevitability and desirability of oligarchies such as the Ford Motor Company.

♦

Unlike problems of age, sex, race, health, and drugs, which are tied in part to physical or biological factors, other social problems seem related more to the large size of the groups involved, the formal organization of their social structure, the complexity of modern society, or the unaccountability of small groups of elites to the masses. The institutional or macrosystem social problems to be considered in Chapters 10 to 15 are reflected in such events as the Iran-Contra improprieties of Lt. Colonel North and deceased CIA Director Casey, the Watergate abuse of power by ex-U.S. President Nixon and several key members of his staff and cabinet, the Lockheed Corporation offering a $7 million bribe to a single individual in Japan to secure a contract for airplanes (cf. Panel 10.2),[1] the potential bankruptcy of the Social Security Administration, the threat of an international thermonuclear war, a divorce rate approaching 50 percent for first marriages, the highest unemployment rate in the United States since the 1930s, air that is unfit to breathe in Los Angeles and other major American cities, oil and natural gas shortages and wild price fluctuations, and starvation not just in India but even in Detroit.[2]

Understanding of these macrosocial problems requires us to introduce some new explanatory principles, notably those offered by social structuralists, functionalists, and conflict theorists. However, we must remember that even institutional patterns in a society are ultimately rooted in the subinstitutional behavior of flesh and blood individuals. Like individuals and small groups, big governments, giant corporations and powerful special interest groups have common values, agree on basic rewards, can be deprived of or satiated on certain rewards, and can become frustrated in their basic expectations. Admittedly, exchange theory does not work as well for institutional-level social prob-

PANEL 10.1

Life in the Corporate Power Structure

When the individual reaches the vice presidency or he's general manager, you know he's an ambitious, dedicated guy who wants to get to the top. He isn't one of the gray people. He's one of the black-and-white vicious people—the Leaders, the ones who stick out in the crowd.

As he struggles in this jungle, every position he's in, he's terribly lonely. He can't confide and talk with the guy working under him. He can't confide and talk to the man he's working for. To give vent to his feelings, his fears, and his insecurities, he'd expose himself. This goes all the way up the line until he gets to be president. The president really doesn't have anybody to talk to, because the vice-presidents are waiting for him to die or make a mistake and get knocked off so they can get his job.

We always saw signs of physical afflictions because of the stress and strain. Ulcers, violent headaches. I remember one of the giant corporations I was in, the chief executive officer ate Gelusil by the minute. That's for ulcers. Had a private dining room with his private chef. All he ever ate was well-done steak and well-done hamburgers.

There's one corporation chief I had who worked, conservatively, nineteen, twenty hours a day. His whole life was his business. And he demanded the same of his executives. There was nothing sacred in life except the business. Meetings might be called on Christmas Eve or New Year's Eve, Saturdays, Sundays. He was lonesome when he wasn't involved with his business. He was always creating situations where he could be surrounded by his flunkies, regardless of what level they were, presidential, vice-presidential . . .. It was his life.

You say, "Money isn't important. You can make some bad decisions about money, that's not important. What is important is the decisions you make about people working for you, their livelihood, their lives." It isn't true.

To the board of directors, the dollars are as important as human lives. There's only yourself sitting there making the decision, and you hope it's right. You're always on guard. Did you ever see a jungle animal that wasn't on guard? You're always looking over your shoulder. You don't know who's following you.

The most stupid phrase anybody can use in business is loyalty. If a person is working for a corporation, he's supposed to be loyal. This corporation is paying him less than he could get somewhere else at a comparable job. It's stupid of him to hang around and say he's loyal. The only loyal people are the people who can't get a job anyplace else. Working in a corporation, in a business, isn't a game. It isn't a collegiate event. It's a question of living or dying. It's a question of eating or not eating. Who is he loyal to? It isn't his country. It isn't his religion. It isn't his political party. He's working for some company that's paying him a salary for what he's doing. The corporation is out to make money. The ambitious guy will say, "I'm doing my job. I'm not embarrassed taking my money. I've got to progress and when I won't progress, I won't be here." The shnook is the loyal guy, because he can't get a job anyplace else.

Source: Studs Terkel, *Working: People Talk about What They Do All Day and How They Feel about What They Do,*

PANEL 10.2

Buying Corporate Influence

Over 520 American corporations have admitted paying bribes or other "questionable" payments to public officials at home and abroad. These are some of the bigger spenders:

Ashland Oil, Inc. Admits paying $800,000 to senators, members of Congress, and other political figures in the U.S.

Boeing. Admits spending $50.4 million in "questionable payments" to foreign officials.

Exxon Corp. Admits paying $59.4 million to government officials and others in fifteen countries

Gulf Oil Corp. Admits giving $5 million in payments, mostly illegal, to U.S. public officials.

R. J. Reynolds. Admits paying $24.6 million to foreign officials in bribes and other questionable payments.

Source: *Newsweek,* December 8, 1975, "Washington Money-Go-Round." Allan J. Mayer with Rich Thomas, Bernice Buresh in Washington. *Newsweek,* February 19, 1979, "Business Without Bribes." David Pauly with Jon Lowell in Detroit, Pamelo Ellis Simons in Chicago, Ron Moreau in Cairo, John Walcott in Washington and Bureau reports.

lems. However, if macrosocial units can be thought of as corporate actors (Coleman, 1974), then exchange principles should still be part applicable for institutions as well as for subinstitutional behavior (see Baron, 1984; Chadwick-Jones, 1976). In the present chapter we shall examine one major aspect of macrosocial problems—the concentration and potential abuse of the power of elites, especially in big business.

Specifically we will consider the decision by the Ford Motor Company and Lee Iacocca to continue with the production of the Pinto automobile, even though they knew in advance that it would explode and burn after only modest rear-end collisions. How was Ford able to use its power to burn 500–900 innocent people to death and why did Ford not care enough to prevent these deaths? Before we can hope to give adequate answers to these questions we must define *power* and *status.*

In one of the most celebrated definitions of *power,* German sociologist Max Weber (1864–1920) argued that power was "the chance of a man or a number of men to realize their will in a communal action even against the resistance of others who are participating in the action" (1925:Ch. 4). Of course, Weber's definition of power leaves unanswered why some people can realize their wills routinely and others never seem to have their way. Karl Marx (1848) and later conflict theorists claimed the ability to enforce your will on others ultimately rested in economic factors, such as the amount of private property you owned or the control of scarce resources, such as factories, machines, and capital.

Ultimately, power may be rooted in physical force (Lenski, 1984), especially in the ability to take or give life. In spite of the popularity of Weber's definition of power, it has a disadvantage in naively assuming that power is rooted in force (Wrong, 1979). One reason economic factors are so important (see Chapter 11) in determining power is that money translates into food, shelter, health—in short, into both the quality and possibility of life. While power may ultimately depend on force, this should not be the case by definition. Thus, Wrong (1979) and Domhoff (1986:9) prefer to conceive of power as "the ability to produce intended and foreseen effects on others." This ability may be rooted in persuasion, the law, and so on, as well as in force.

Survival issues are crucial not only for individuals but also for societies. The life and prosperity of social units depend on how efficiently they can respond to various external threats such as war, hunger, climate, disease, and so on. It is just too cumbersome to have everyone deciding every issue. Thus, small groups (elites) or powerful leaders tend to arise. Inequality is also a function of the size of the surplus a society produces as well (Lenski, 1984:44). As long as societies produce just enough (food, industrial products, or whatever) to ensure their survival and to support needed production, social products tend to be shared relatively equally. However, when societies produce a surplus beyond that needed to guarantee society's continuance, that surplus will tend to be distributed in accordance with who has the power (not who is the neediest), and in the process increase social differences. Thus, social inequality is related to the economic surpluses generated in a society (cf. Lenski and Lenski, 1986).

George Homans and exchange theory argue that the bases for power lie in the differential rewards received from interpersonal exchanges (cf. Molm, 1985; 1986). Those who are "effective at realizing their wills over the resistance of others" will tend to be those who are least interested in or least dependent on the outcome of a given exchange. Thus, if others will be rewarded more by an exchange with a person (P) than P is, and as a result the others change their behavior, then power has been exercised by P (Homans, 1974:83).[3] Of course, Homans does not say explicitly in this definition why powerful people can afford to be less interested in the outcomes of exchanges with less powerful people. Blau (1977) warns us not to interpret power too simply when considering it as a property of individual social relationships (cf. Baron, 1984). For one thing great power is often exercised indirectly or not exercised at all (Blau, 1977:218). Also, in opposition to Marx's understanding of the dichotomous nature of power, Blau claims that there often is no clear line between rulers and the ruled. In complex societies most of us are both rulers and ruled.

Social class differences result from and are defined by not only unequal power but also by status and economic differences.[4] Thus, Weber (1925:631–40) argues that social inequality is a complex function of wealth, power, and prestige (he actually called them "class, party, and status"; cf, Walton, 1986:Ch. 4). We shall have a great deal to say about problems of social class

"Give me more angels and make them gladder to see me."

arising from and perpetuated by economic factors, but will reserve that discussion until Chapter 11. For exchange theorists *status* is defined simply as the rank of a person in a group (Homans, 1974:193; cf. Emerson, 1972; for measurements of status, see Powers, 1982). Individuals or groups tend to have high status if they give more (the most important factor) in exchanges of scarce goods and receive more of plentiful goods (Homans, 1974:195). For example, physicians can save lives in return for money and social approval, generals can guarantee security from external threats of aggression in return for social compliance and large defense budgets, corporation heads may offer jobs and salaries in return for productive labor and loyalty. Of course, the scarce goods provided must not only be rare but also must be valuable. Homans mentions the case of the virtuoso whistler, the best there was, who gave concerts to which no one came.

High status also affects communication or conversation patterns (Molotch and Boden, 1985; Ridgeway, Berger, and Smith, 1985). Typically a high-status person does not initiate communication with a low-status person. One reason for this is structural (cf. Kollock, Blumstein, and Schwartz, 1985). If elites comprise only 1 percent of the population, there simple are not enough of them to interact with the other 99 percent of the society. Most people have never met celebrities, such as the governor of their home states, the president of the United States, people whose net assets total $100 million or more, the chairman of the board of directors of General Motors, and so on. Remember that social interaction tends to increase liking and similarity.

In passing it should be mentioned that some individuals or groups are not consistently high status with respect to power, prestige, and wealth. The instant multimillionaire Arabs or older Texas cowboy oilmen, or lottery winners come readily to mind (they had wealth, but often little education or social status). This has an important implication for social exchange. Namely, when an individual or group has inconsistent or incongruent status, we may not know how to respond to them in social exchanges. Do we respond to their great wealth or to their uncouth social behavior, to the fact that they have a gun or to their stupidity, to their past privileged life experiences or to their recent bankruptcy? Since we agree with Lenski (1984) that status is a function of power, as important as status is, we shall have little more to say about it specifically, except as status is reflected in power and wealth inequality.

The concept of power needs to be refined further to differentiate various sources of power and to distinguish power from authority and influence.[5] The ability to force your will on recalcitrant others, to get them to change their behaviors, to be able to be less interested in social outcomes—in short, power—can derive from coercive or physical force (Homans, 1974:74; Blau, 1977:220), the large size or numbers of people, expert knowledge, ownership of property, and money or economic resources, to mention only a few of the more salient factors.[6] When one's ability to change behavior comes from legitimate rights outside of the values of interpersonal exchanges themselves, such as holding a lofty position in a large formal organization, then one is said to have *authority*. Authority is power that people recognize as legitimate.[7]

Weber contends that there are three main types of authority: legal/rational, charismatic, and traditional. Legal/rational authority derives from a system of explicit rules defining legitimate power. Charismatic authority derives from the exceptional personal attributes of individuals (such as Jesus Christ, Malcolm X, Hitler, and so on). Finally, traditional authority rests on the assumption that the way societies have always done things is appropriate or even sacred. Influence is much more subtle than authority (Domhoff, 1986:8–9). *Webster's* dictionary defines *influence* as "the act or the power of producing an effect without apparent force or direct authority." According to Lenski, influence is a form of social pressure applied through exercise of one's resources and rights, an ability to manipulate the social situation of others (1984:57). As such, influence is more related to social prestige than to pure brute force or to formal rational authority.

Finally, power varies by the type of society, its organization, and its distributive system.[8] Historically, we can conceive of human social evolution based on four basic types of roughly chronological distribution systems: hunting and gathering, horticulture, agrarian, and industrial systems (Lenski and Lenski, 1986). In most primitive societies distribution of resources is based on need, but in the more technologically advanced societies distribution is based on power (Lenski, 1984:46). It is important to understand that social interests are almost never identical to individual interests. French sociologist Emile Durkheim said much the same thing when he claimed that the individual conscience cannot be the same as what he called the collective conscience (1897). Even more importantly, when there are conflicts of interest with respect to important social decisions, men or women almost always choose their own individual or small-group interests.[9]

In most industrial societies there is sufficiently advanced technology to generate increased production, which in turn results in surpluses of goods and resources. Since surpluses are distributed in relation to power, not need, and since elites tend to follow their own interests (actually everyone does), social inequality tends to vary directly with the size of a society's surplus (Lenski, 1984:85). Interestingly, some have argued that agrarian societies are more elitist than industrial societies, since industrial societies are highly variable with respect to the concentration of power in elites. Others claim that industrial societies are run by corporate managers and experts (Kantner, 1984), not by propertied owner-entrepreneurs anymore. Ownership and control are said to be diffused throughout corporate stockholders.

Before we turn to the Ford Motor Company's Pinto car as our example of power inequality, we need to say a little more about social inequality in general (including both power and economic inequality). In the next section we examine how two functional sociologists (Davis and Moore) see social inequality developing. They actually believe that social inequality is inevitable and desirable.

Our skylines reflect institutional power differences. In America's rural, preindustrial past, church steeples dominated the horizon (top). But in contemporary urban-industrial megalopolises (bottom) monuments to finance and secular values (World Trade Center, Empire State, Chrysler Buildings) dwarf all others. (Top–Owen Franken/Stock, Boston; Bottom–Ellis Herwig/Stock, Boston)

Then we shall discuss C. Wright Mills's contention that a very small power elite group (usually no more than 1 percent of American society) controls most of the important decisions in the United States.

• Principles of Social Stratification

Social strata of differing power, wealth, and prestige tend to emerge when small, relatively homogenous groups interacting informally and affectually become unworkable. This usually happens when societies become larger, develop technologically, begin to produce economic surpluses through industrialization, undergo a marked division of labor and specialization, begin to be densely concentrated in large urban areas, become more ethnically, racially, or religiously diverse, and so on. Under these social conditions it seems that fewer and fewer people or social positions control more and more of society's scarce resources and make more and more of its important decisions. But is such social inequality in power and wealth inevitable? And if social inequality is inevitable, is it desirable?

In a now famous and ancient article titled "Some Principles of Stratification," sociologists Kingsley Davis and Wilbert Moore argued that there must be something both inevitable and "functional"[10] or socially desirable about social inequality (1945; cf. Turner, 1986:Part I). Stratification of individuals into ranked groups or social classes has been present in every known society (Walton, 1986:Ch. 3; see Figure 10.1). Notice that Davis and Moore were addressing the issue of social inequality, not particularly power inequality. Their comments are just as relevant (or more) to economic inequality, which is considered in Chapter 11. Davis and Moore's argument can be summarized as follows:

1. Certain positions in any society are (functionally) more important than others and require special skills for their performance.

For example, religious, governmental, economic, and technical positions in a society are all relatively important and require special skills. Religious positions are important because social integration depends on most people having certain common values. As long as religions determine society's moral values relevant to daily life conduct, those persons (positions) who transmit these values are themselves going to be important. In contrast to religious positions governmental positions exist to organize society in law and authority. Government makes and enforces social laws and norms, arbitrates conflicting interests, plans the overall direction of social development, and conducts war and diplomacy. Other positions, such as presidencies of major business corporations, command high salaries, shares of company stock, and so on because they are economic positions important to the well-being of society. Technical positions, because they require special skills, are given fairly high rewards (namely, much wealth, power, and prestige) but never the highest, since they

FIGURE 10.1 Social Stratification in the United States

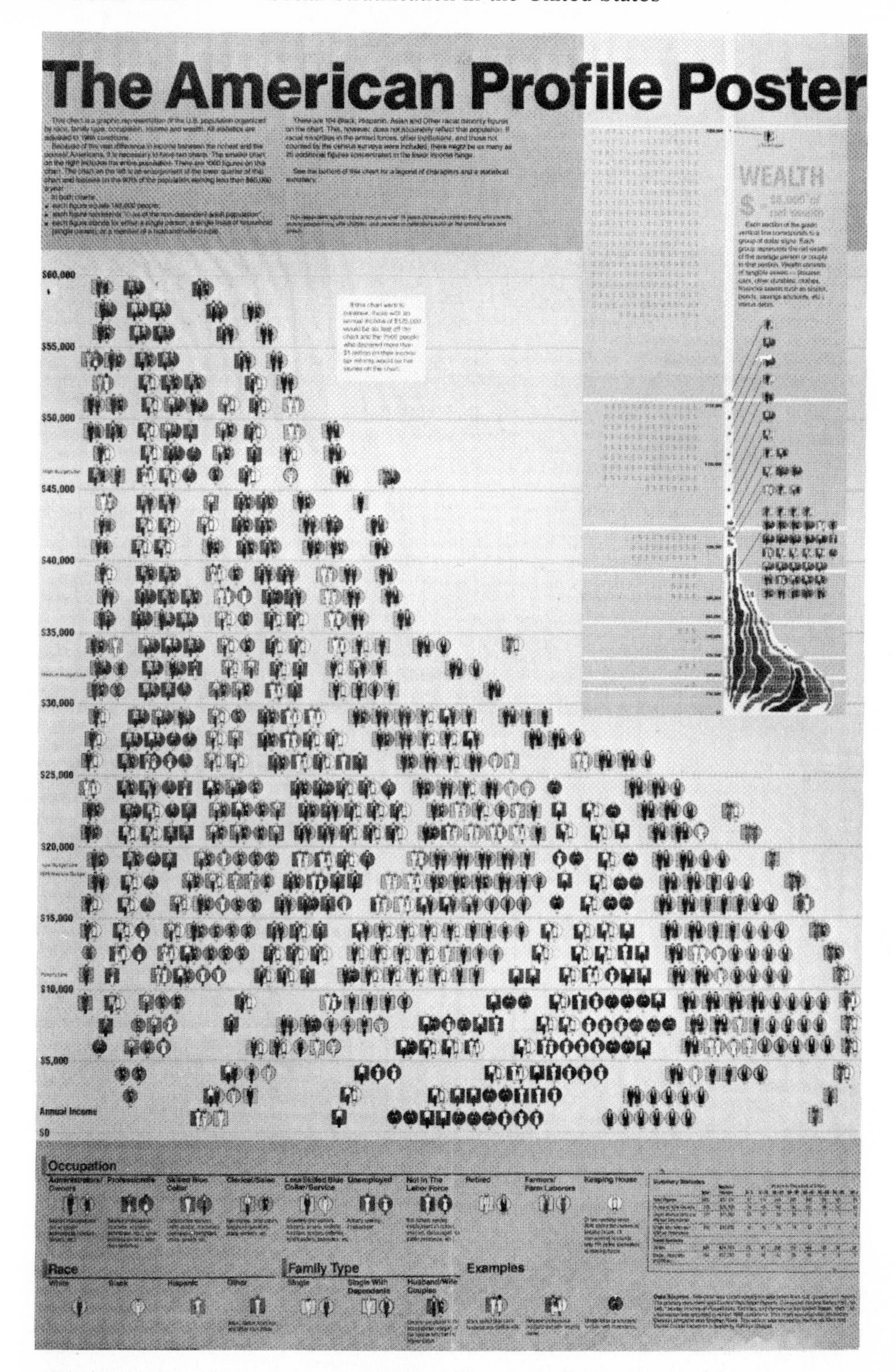

Source: Stephen J. Rose and Dennis Livingston, 1983, Social Graphics Co., 553 18 Avenue East, Seattle, Washington 98112.

are concerned with finding means to achieving goals specified by others, not with determining the social goals themselves.

2. Only a limited number of individuals in any society has the talents that can be trained to acquire the skills appropriate to these positions.

Not everyone has the intelligence, natural ability, aggressiveness, strength, or other talents required to fill functionally important positions in a society. For example, clergymen/women must be picked from those who have "been called" and are especially patient with and skilled at human relation problems. Government officials are most successful if they come from the proper family background, have sufficient organizational backing, graduate from the right law school, are of the appropriate race, religion, and so on (Unseem and Karabel, 1986). Also, clearly not everyone can become a corporation head or even a chemical engineer or nuclear physicist.

3. The conversion of talents into skills involves a training period during which sacrifices of one kind or another are made by those undergoing the training.

The deferred gratification (i.e., putting off social and economic rewards while in training) pattern of those pursuing skills essential to attaining important social positions is well known. For example, meager short-term wages and foregone potential income, postponed marriages and children, and psychological and physical stress and strain (e.g., from being in a subordinate position and from being on trial) are all part of obtaining educational or professional skills. For example, the cleric often takes vows of asceticism and chastity, works with the disadvantaged or the poor, has to learn Greek, Latin, and Hebrew, vicariously suffers others' disappointments and failures, and so on. The politician must spend years in law school and as a junior member of a firm or organization (such as the courts) has to spend his/her own money and put in long hours in campaigns to be elected to office, and is subject to the whims of the electorate. On the way up the corporate worker has to spend several years in college or business school, may be transferred frequently to undesirable locations, may have to curb his/her own opinions in favor of the company line, may be passed over in spite of all his/her sacrifices while less competent individuals are promoted. One could also consider the many sacrifices made by all graduate and professional students.

4. To induce talented persons to undergo these sacrifices and acquire the training, their future positions must carry an adequate inducement value in the form of differential, that is, privileged and disproportionate access to the scarce and desired rewards that the society has to offer.

5. These scarce and desired goods consist of rights and perquisites attached to or built into the social positions and can be classified into those things that contribute to *(a)* sustenance and comfort, *(b)* humor and diversion, and *(c)* self-respect and ego expansion.

Specifically, the most important positions in a society generally command the highest salaries, the most power, and the greatest prestige or honor. An important social position usually has more status consistency; that is, it routinely offers high levels of wealth, power, and prestige. Positions of lesser importance (e.g., those of policemen) often allow high power (police officers may carry a gun), but lower incomes and/or less prestige.

6. This differential access to the basic rewards of the society has as a consequence the differentiation of prestige and esteem that various social strata acquire. This may be said, along with the rights and perquisites of social positions, to constitute institutionalized social inequality, that is, social stratification.

7. Therefore, social inequality among different social strata in the amounts of scarce and desired goods and the amounts of prestige and esteem that they receive is both inevitable and functional (desirable) in any society.

If society wishes to motivate rare talented individuals to fill important social positions, it must be prepared to reward them differentially with its scarce resources. If it does not do this, society may not survive or at least may not operate at optimum efficiency. Once it does reward social positions differently, social inequality is unavoidable. So much for our brief review of Davis and Moore's argument about social inequality.

Of course, not everyone agrees with Davis and Moore that social inequality is necessary and fewer still believe that social inequality is desirable or functional. For example, sociologists in the broad tradition of conflict theory have consistently argued against positions like those of Davis and Moore (Marx and Engels, 1848; Turner, 1986:Part II). Taking each of Davis and Moore's numbered arguments (premises) in order, conflict theorists attempt the following rebuttal.

(1) Sooner or later the occupants of all social positions need to be motivated to perform their roles. For example, a strike by New York City garbage workers can cause a serious social problem too. One cannot always simply fire or replace less skilled workers. Modern unions can protect their workers. If unskilled workers are fired, they may become a social welfare burden. To be sure there are humane considerations of firing less skilled workers just because they defy orders. (2) If a society is rigidly stratified, then a full search for talented individuals will be restricted. Social inequality can lead to unequal opportunity for talented (notably those in lower social strata) individuals to be discovered. Thus, inequality can affect the motivation of talented lower-status individuals to achieve.

(3) Conflict theorists also question whether the sacrifices in converting raw talent into skill are that great. After all, one's parents usually pay most of their children's educational costs. Furthermore, most workers in high-status positions (such as physicians, lawyers, businesspeople, and engineers) can earn back any lost income during training within a few years after starting to work. One should not forget that to be in training for a lofty social position is itself prestigious or honorable. (4) Also, do we always need to motivate talented people with scarce economic rewards (e.g., high salaries or property)? What about the intrinsic rewards of the kind or quality of work one does? Should we

not fill some positions out of social duty or for praise and honor (which are relatively plentiful)?

(5 and 6) Why must we give equal amounts of all three types of specific social rewards? In some societies high economic rewards are considered in bad taste. For example, physicians in the USSR and Great Britain make far less in salary than physicians in the United States. Conversely, even if one does have power and property, these rewards alone do not guarantee high prestige or esteem. (7) Certainly social inequality is never only positive and desirable. In fact inequality has several negative consequences or dysfunctions. It limits the discovery of talent, legitimates the status quo, tends to make people in lower social positions have less self-respect, encourages hostility among social classes, promotes social disloyalty in lower classes, and discourages lower-status individuals from participating fully in the society. In short, conflict theorists contend that while some social inequality may be inevitable, it is not without social costs. These costs may even lead to the disruption and violent overthrow of the entire social order.

• Is There a Power Elite in America?

Once we admit that social positions can be grouped into strata of rulers and oppressed (Marx, 1848), order givers and order takers (Collins, 1975), white- and blue-collar workers (Mills, 1956), upper-upper, lower-upper, upper-middle, lower-middle, upper-lower, lower-lower social classes (Warner, 1949), and so on,[11] at least three important questions remain: how small is the upper-status group, how much power does it yield, and how interconnected or interlocked are the very powerful (or their positions) in American society? Although the United States is supposedly democratic (i.e., holds open elections, and so on) and egalitarian, many (mainly in the conflict theory tradition) have claimed that America is in fact run by a power elite comprised primarily of a few very large business corporations tied into the military and the federal government (Mills, 1956; Domhoff, 1978, 1986; Dye, 1976; Dahl, 1982; Parenti, 1978; Zeitlin, 1978).

For example, Zeitlin (1978) points out that 200 of the largest American corporations (e.g., ITT, IBM, GM, Ford, Xerox, Goodyear, General Electric, Philip Morris, Procter & Gamble, Alcoa, and so on—see Table 10.1) own 60 percent of all industrial assets in American industry (cf. *Fortune,* April 30, 1984). Other facts about who owns America include (1) 1 percent of the population holds 25 percent of the net worth of American society; (2) 1 percent of the population holds as much as 76 percent of all privately held stock (Domhoff, 1986:58); (3) 5 percent of the Americans with the highest incomes take in about 50 percent of all income from property; in fact, that in the top-income brackets almost all income is dividends, rents, royalties, and interest (not salaries); and (4) at the other end of the power continuum, about 75 percent of the American population (in 1983) made less than $25,000 a year *(Statistical Abstract of the United States,* 1986:456).

For many social scientists it is not surprising that small groups of upper-status elites control most of modern society. German political scientist Robert Michels (1915) argued that as societies and organizations grew in size and complexity that government by the few (i.e., oligarchy) was inevitable (thus, oligarchy was an iron law). As a case in point, in small primary groups (such as in Lenski's hunting and gathering societies, 1984, 1987), interaction can be face-to-face, but as groups get larger and societies become more complex interaction must be indirect and hierarchical (as is implied in Homans's concept of a social institution). If large organizations are to achieve their objectives, then Michels argued that power must be delegated to a few elites at the very top of organizations. One consequence of this delegation of power is that organizational response time to external threats (e.g., acts of war, hostile takeovers, and so on) or internal problems is shortened and leadership is much more efficient.

Agreeing in part with Davis and Moore, Michels felt that those individuals that became organizational leaders had superior talents for public speaking (see Collins's concept of social class as conversational skill, 1975; cf. Kollock, Blumstein, and Schwartz, 1985), persuasion, organization, and public relations. Furthermore, once in power, elites were at a central locus in organizations, which in turn facilitated their information gathering and their ability to influence others within their organization. If we agree with Lenski (1984) that self-interest almost always wins out over group interest, it is easy to see how leaders are both able and willing to perpetuate their own power. Since leaders of organizations have the motivation and the authority necessary for self-preservation, Michels contended that elites tended to promote only junior organization members who supported them and shared their basic values. Since ordinary members of an organization lacked the time, position, and knowledge to watch over, check, and balance organizational leaders, they had only a partial commitment to the organization, and tended to revere organizational leaders; resistance to oligarchy was minimal. Even when a Marxian-type overthrow of elites did occur, Michels thought that the end result was simply transplanting the old elite with a new one. Thus, for Michels "whoever says organization says oligarchy." Michels would conclude that not only is modern urban-industrial society unequal, but also a very small number of people and positions at the very top of society (about 1 percent) control a very large amount of society's scarce resources, give most of its orders, garner most of its prestige, and make almost all of its important decisions.

Like Michels sociologist C. Wright Mills (1914–1959; see Horowitz, 1983) agrees that a power elite controls America (1956; cf. Domhoff, 1978, 1986). The top echelon of American society is comprised of the corporate heads of large organizations (such as those listed in Table 10.2): the generals, admirals, and top pentagon officials in the military establishment; and the top politicians in the United States (the U.S. senators, state governors, and so on). But Mills goes beyond Michels in claiming that the positions of America's power elite are so interlocked (see Figure 10.2) and interrelated that democracy has in

The late C. Wright Mills argued that in fact a power elite of business, governmental, and military heads really controls all the important decisions in America. Participatory democracy is largely a myth. Such unchecked power of elites is often abused. (Yaroslava/AP/Wide World Photos)

fact become a sham (Dye, 1976). When we look closely at the very powerful, says Mills, it is apparent that they all tend to be white, Anglo-Saxon, Protestant males, from old American families, who attended the same Ivy League schools and belong to the same exclusive clubs (cf. Domhoff, 1986; Ch. 2). Moreover, power elites are not only alike, they actually exchange social positions frequently. That is, the retired general or famous military man becomes an executive for Boeing or Lockheed Corporation or becomes president of the United States (Eisenhower) or a U.S. senator (Glenn of Ohio); the business corporation head is recruited for a cabinet or agency post in Washington (McNamara).

Business funds governmental campaigns and can profit from favorable legislation, defense contracts, and so on. The government needs a healthy economy and sound national defense to protect itself. In some countries, if the military is not pleased with government actions, the government officials can simply be executed or put in prison and replaced with generals. Mills does not necessarily suggest a conspiracy of power elites; he simply observes their incestuous interlocking relationships and cautions us about the abuse of such unguarded power. To compound matters, Mills believes that special-interest (or lobby) groups exist between the masses and the power elite, making it all the more likely that elites will not be responsive to the general public.

Several studies have supported Mills's claim that a power elite runs America (Domhoff, 1986; Dye, 1976; Parenti, 1978). For example, Parenti, in *Democracy for the Few* (1983) argues that public policies favor large corporate interests (a kind of corporate welfare). At the same time that welfare is being withdrawn from the poor, aged, and minorities, it is actually being increased for the military and business. President Reagan's 1984 budget recommended no cuts in 1983 military spending and contained several increases. Reagan's 1985–89 proposed military budget of $1.3 trillion would cost the average American family $30,996. The United States already has 100 times more nuclear force than needed to kill any potential enemy (McNamara and Bethe, 1985). Parenti also claims that electoral and representative activities are only symbolic. The real substantive political system involves government giveaways to the powerful. For example, the first 22 percent of income from gas and oil is tax exempt and drilling expenses are tax deductible. But ask yourself, how many oil wells do *you* have? Parenti concludes that since wealth is so crucial to any society, the goals of business tend to become the goals of government. Furthermore, power does not allow for pluralism (pluralists argue that power is or should be dispersed among a variety of competing interests) or social reform, since those interested in social change do not have the power to change society and corporations are interested in private profit (not social reconstruction).

Of course, not everyone agrees that there is a power elite running America. According to Greeley (1986) the real problem is the *lack* of concentration of power. There is no establishment, no one elite in charge of the United States. If there were, the universally unpopular social enterprises, like the Vietnam War, would have been over with far more quickly than they in fact were, and benign social reforms to which virtually everyone agreed would be more common than they are. This is not to deny that certain groups of men can have decisive power on specific issues (e.g., to invade the Bay of Pigs in Cuba) or that certain groups (veto groups or special-interest groups, like lobbyists) are very effective in preventing things from happening. Greeley believes that the real problem is that power is too diffused, not too concentrated. Thus, if we wish to change society the most appropriate political strategy would be to seek allies to form coalitions of individuals with common interests. Even though Greeley may be correct that power elites are loosely organized, poorly integrated, and less able to initiate action than to block action, the bulk of evidence

FIGURE 10.2 Interlocking Directorates among the Core Institutions in the Rockefeller Group

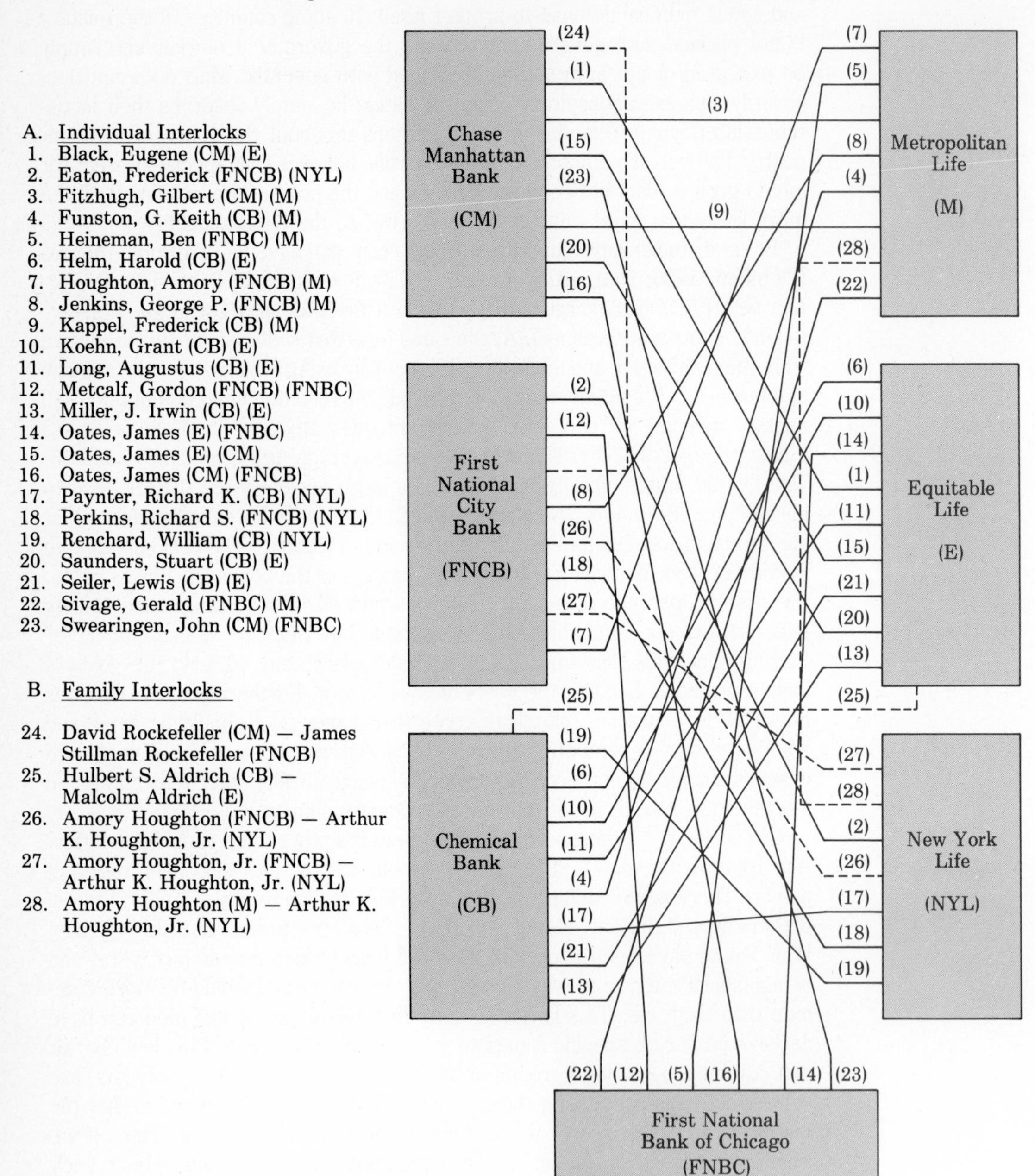

Source: James C. Knowles, "The Rockefeller Financial Group," Warner Modular Publications, 1973, p. 5.

suggests that power elites tend to run every country, everywhere. The next section will explore one of the social problems related to power inequality in corporate industry.

Power Inequality in Big Business and Big Government

Stating the Problem In the twentieth century in the United States we have witnessed several fundamental social changes that in turn helped forge the unique character of the largely institutional social problems to be considered in the last part of this text. Among the most obvious are the transitions from small to large populations, from rural to urban life, from agrarian to industrial economies, from homogeneity to heterogeneity, and from informal to formal social organization. Homans (1974:3) and Lenski (1984:Ch. 5; 1986) remind us that for millenia human societies were composed of relatively small groups of hunters and gatherers. Originally it took about 60,000 years to double the world population; now it doubles every thirty-five to forty years. In 1930 there were about two billion people in the world. That number had grown to four billion by 1975 and is expected to be eight billion by 2005–15 (see Chapter 13).

As social groups have grown larger, they have simultaneously become more urban. For example, in the United States between 1820 and 1984 the farm population shrank from 72 percent to 2 percent. In 1970 there was only one city in the world with a population over 10 million (Shanghai); by 1985 there were seventeen such cities (see Chapter 13). With increased technology our economy has become more industrially based (Lenski, 1984). In these large, urban-industrial populations, common values and relatively few occupations have now given way to diverse values and highly specialized occupations. Homogeneity has tended to be supplanted by heterogeneity of ethnicity, race, religion, values, and so on. Finally, informal social organization has for the most part been replaced by formal bureaucratic social organization.

As these basic social changes take place, concurrently they force a switch from an emphasis on subinstitutional social behavior and organization to institutional social organization, including new social problems related to social hierarchies dominated by elites; indirectness of social interaction; shortened social interaction time; an emphasis on efficiency and rationality (and a deemphasis on emotion and affect); the complexity of social organization; the high division of labor and increased occupational specialization; and the increased importance of money, status, and other generalized reinforcers (rewards that can be exchanged for other rewards).

The special institutional social problems related to these social changes can be illustrated by problems in big business corporations and big governmental organizations. Today American business is controlled by a few large corporations (see Table 10.3). General Motors, the largest American industrial corporation, had net sales of $96.3 billion in 1985. The annual budget at General

Motors is larger than those of most other nations in the world (except, obviously, the United States and the USSR). Furthermore, the largest 100 corporations in the United States (which make up only .01 percent of all corporations) control more than 50 percent of all the nation's manufacturing assets. This trend toward elite corporate control is also evident among individuals. That is, a few very wealthy individuals control most of the nation's wealth. For example, the richest 1 percent of adult individuals control about 75 percent of all corporate stock in America (Domhoff, 1986:58–59). It is true that in more recent years the elite control of personal-sector assets has actually diminished to some degree. Nevertheless, it remains that a dominant group of business corporations and a relatively few wealthy individuals still control a disproportionate share of U.S. wealth and the power associated with it.

Given the complexity, diversity, size, and occupational specialization of modern society, big federal and state government is also required to regulate and supervise society and to provide services. Big government as the central social authority functions to maintain order, collect taxes, and to administer social policies. At the end of the eighteenth century the total U.S. federal budget was only $4.3 million, but by 1985 it was $959 billion. Today about three million people work for the federal government versus about five thousand 150 years earlier. Federal regulatory agencies (such as the Food and Drug Administration, the Securities and Exchange Commission, the Environmental Protection Agency, the Occupational Safety and Health Administration, and so on) provide a classic example of the growth of big government. There are over 65,000 pages of federal regulations and federal regulatory agencies spending over $5 billion each year.[12]

In addition to business, governmental, and military elites, a few special-interest groups have disproportionate power in American society (Lenski, 1984:35ff.). As Domhoff points out, although special-interest groups tend to represent the goals of the power elite, they are not actually members of the power elite themselves.

> If the process itself (i.e., the "special-interest" process) is fairly obvious in its general outlines, most of the men and women who operate within it are neither well known nor prominent. They usually are not chairpersons of major corporations, partners in Wall Street law firms, presidents of large foundations, or highly regarded research experts from major universities. Instead, they are lesser members of the power elite—corporate managers two or three rungs from the top, lawyers who have risen from middle-level backgrounds on the basis of their experience in specific government agencies and former politicians who have been hired by corporations or trade associations because of their connections. Of 124 registered lobbyists whose social backgrounds were investigated . . . , none were from the ruling class. (1978:26; cf. 1986:129–131)*

TABLE 10.1 The Twenty-Five Largest American Industrial Corporations (Ranked by Sales), 1985

Rank 1985	Rank 1984	Company	Sales (in thousands)	Assets (in thousands)	Rank	Net Income (in thousands)	Rank
1	2	General Motors (Detroit)	$96,371,700	$63,832,800	2	$3,999,000	3
2	1	Exxon (New York)	86,673,000	69,160,000	1	4,870,000	2
3	3	Mobil (New York)	55,960,000	41,752,000	4	1,040,000	14
4	4	Ford Motor (Dearborn, Mich.)	52,774,400	31,603,600	8	2,515,400	4
5	6	International Business Machines (Armonk, N.Y.)	50,056,000	52,634,000	3	6,555,000	1
6	5	Texaco (White Plains, N.Y.)	46,297,000	37,703,000	7	1,233,000	12
7	11	Chevron (San Francisco)	41,741,905	38,899,492	6	1,547,360	10
8	8	American Tel. & Tel. (New York)	34,909,500	40,462,500	5	1,556,800	9
9	7	E. I. du Pont de Nemours & Co. (Wilmington, Del.)	29,483,000	25,140,000	12	1,118,000	13
10	9	General Electric (Fairfield, Conn.)	28,285,000	26,432,000	10	2,336,000	5
11	10	Amoco (Chicago)	27,215,000	25,198,000	11	1,953,000	6
12	12	Atlantic Richfield (Los Angeles)	22,357,000	20,279,000	14	(202,000)	464
13	14	Chrysler (Highland Park, Mich.)	21,255,500	12,605,300	23	1,635,200	8
14	13	Shell Oil (Houston)	20,309,000	26,528,000	9	1,650,000	7
15	15	U.S. Steel (Pittsburgh)	18,429,000	18,446,000	15	409,000	43
16	16	United Technologies (Hartford)	15,748,674	10,528,105	29	312,724	54
17	17	Phillips Petroleum (Bartlesville, Okla.)	15,676,000	14,045,000	10	418,000	41
18	19	Tenneco (Houston)	15,400,000	20,437,000	13	172,000	91
19	18	Occidental Petroleum (Los Angeles)	14,534,400	11,585,900	26	696,000	18
20	20	Sun (Radnor, Pa.)	13,769,000	12,923,000	22	527,000	30
21	29	Boeing (Seattle)	13,636,000	9,246,000	34	566,000	25
22	22	Procter & Gamble (Cincinnati)	13,552,000	9,683,000	32	635,000	20
23	23	R.J. Reynolds Industries (Winston-Salem, N.C.)	13,533,000	16,930,000	18	1,001,000	15
24	24	Standard Oil (Cleveland)	13,002,000	18,330,000	16	308,000	55
25	21	ITT (New York)	12,714,276	14,272,499	19	293,501	58

Source: From *Fortune* magazine's list of the 500 largest corporations; *Fortune*, April 28, 1986.

Special-interest groups operate to get tax breaks, favors, subsidies, and procedural rulings favorable to the power elite. The most obvious example of special-interest activities is lobbying in state and federal government to influence legislation favorable to big business. For example, in the 1970s the American Petroleum Institute had an annual budget for lobbying of about $16.5 million and employed 200 lobbyists, compared with the Consumer Federation's (which represented the mass consumer) budget of about $35,000 and 3 employees. Another example of special-interest activity is big business corporations giving disguised political contributions or outright bribes to big government (see Panel 10.2). Such differential power representing the interests of elites increases the probability that the interests of the ordinary citizens will not be represented, or figure prominently in shaping the broad directions of larger society (its goals, values, programs, laws, and so on), even though nonelites, by definition, constitute an overwhelming numerical majority of American society.

More importantly, such concentrated and unequal power among business and governmental elites is often abused. You readily can think of examples such as ex-President Nixon and the Watergate affair (Current and Goodwin, 1980), President Reagan and the Iran arms-for-hostages deal (1986), the suppression of American subways, trains, and similar public transportation by General Motors (Snell, 1985), the attempt by ITT to bring down a Marxist government in Chile (Sampson, 1973), or the intentional marketing of the firetrap Pinto automobile by the Ford Motor Company (Dowie, 1985). To illustrate the problem of the abuse of power by big business we shall examine the case of the Ford Pinto in some detail.

> One evening in the mid-1960s, Arjay Miller was driving home from his office in Dearborn, Michigan, in the four-door Lincoln Continental that went with his job as president of the Ford Motor Company. On a crowded highway, another car struck his from the rear. The Continental spun around and burst into flames. Because he was wearing a shoulder-strap seat belt, Miller was unharmed by the crash, and because his doors didn't jam he escaped the gasoline-drenched, flaming wreck. But the accident made a vivid impression on him. Several months later, on July 15, 1965, he recounted it to a U.S. Senate subcommittee that was hearing testimony on auto safety legislation. "I still have burning in my mind the image of that gas tank on fire," Miller said. He went on to express an almost passionate interest in controlling fuel-fed fires in cars that crash or roll over. He spoke with excitement about the fabric gas tank Ford was testing at that very moment. "If it proves out," he promised the senators, "it will be a feature you will see in our standard cars.
>
> Almost seven years after Miller's testimony, a woman, whom for legal reasons we will call Sandra Gillespie, pulled onto a Minneapolis highway in her new Ford Pinto. Riding with her was a young boy, whom we'll call Robbie Carlton. As she entered a merge lane, Sandra Gillespie's car stalled. Another car rear-ended hers at an impact speed of twenty-eight miles per hour. The Pinto's gas tank ruptured. Vapors from it mixed quickly with the air in the

Three teenage girls from Elkhart, Indiana, were killed in 1978 when this Ford Pinto was struck from behind and burst into flames. The Ford Motor Company was indicted for responsibility due to a defective design of Pinto's fuel tank. (AP/Wide World Photos)

> passenger compartment. A spark ignited the mixture and the car exploded in a ball of fire. Sandra died in agony a few hours later in an emergency hospital. Her passenger, thirteen-year-old Robbie Carlton, is still alive; he has just come home from another futile operation aimed at grafting a new ear and nose from skin on the few unscarred portions of his badly burned body. (This accident is real; the details are from police reports.)
>
> Why did Sandra Gillespie's Ford Pinto catch fire so easily, seven years after Ford's Arjay Miller made his apparently sincere pronouncements—the same seven years that brought more safety improvements to cars than any other period in automobile history? (Dowie, 1985:22–23)

To begin with, profit is the primary value in business. Cars are engineered to make money. If safety features cost too much, they will be resisted or ignored. The situation with Ford's Pinto was complicated because the Pinto was rushed into production to compete with the Volkswagen and Japanese models. Lee Iacocca (most recently head of Chrysler Corporation and instrumental in restoring the Statue of Liberty) was in charge of producing the Pinto. Iacocca had risen fast at Ford on the success of the Mustang. Iacocca set the

Pinto production schedule at twenty-five months; the normal production time was forty-three months. Given this compacted schedule, when a defective design in the Pinto gas tank and its placement were discovered, tooling had already begun. That is, it was too late to make changes without considerable costs. Thus, even though preproduction crash tests showed that Pinto's weak gas tank, placed next to a soft rear end and bumper, would rupture and burn easily, the decision was made to produce the car without design changes anyway.

Ford's engineers estimated that it would cost about $11 per car to prevent most rear-end Pinto collisions resulting in fires. A simple U-joint deflector could be placed between the fuel tank and the differential or the gas tank could be lined with a rubber bladder (see Figure 10.3). Ford calculated the savings for making these changes by assuming Ford Pintos would result in 180 burn deaths, 180 burn injuries (nondeaths), and 2,100 burned cars (see Panel 10.3).[13] Ford staff also estimated that each human life was worth about $200,000 in 1971 (at least double that now, using the same assumptions; see Panel 10.4). Using such estimates the benefits of making the fuel tank modification totaled $49.5 million. However, assuming sales of 11 million cars and 1.5 million trucks, the costs of making even an $11 repair on each vehicle was $137 million. Given this crude cost-benefit analysis, obviously it would not be profitable to make the Pinto's fuel tank safer. *So Ford did not make the change.*

The story does not end here. For eight years after the production of Pinto, Ford lobbied against a key government standard that would have forced them to change the Pinto's fuel tank (Standard 301). In that time 500 to 900 people burned to death in Pinto crashes. It was cheaper for Ford to settle out-of-court lawsuits with the estates of all burn victims after the fact than to recall all Pintos and fix the fuel tanks. In 1977, Standard 301 was passed and Ford was forced to make design changes. It turned out that a $1 plastic baffle (not $11) per car was enough to make the fuel tank safe on Pintos. Some 500 to 900 deaths and millions of dollars of profit later, those baffles are standard on all post-1977 Pintos.

Analyzing the Problem. The Exchange Perspective In analyzing the Ford Pinto controversy and power inequality we must first be clearer about how social problems in small face-to-face groups differ from those in large, complex, formal social organizations. It is easy to see how exchange principles (such as value, reward, satiation, deprivation, and distributive justice) operate when we interact directly with one or only a few other people in small-group social situations. It is more difficult to imagine exchange principles explaining social problems on the institutional or macrosocial system level. These next several pages are going to be unusually abstract and dry. But stick with it. Mastering these new concepts will help you to understand all of the remaining chapters. We promise to ask this favor of you just once.

What do we mean when we say that in this chapter (and the remainder of

FIGURE 10.3 Initial Design of Fire-Prone Pinto Compared with Eventual Modified Pinto Design

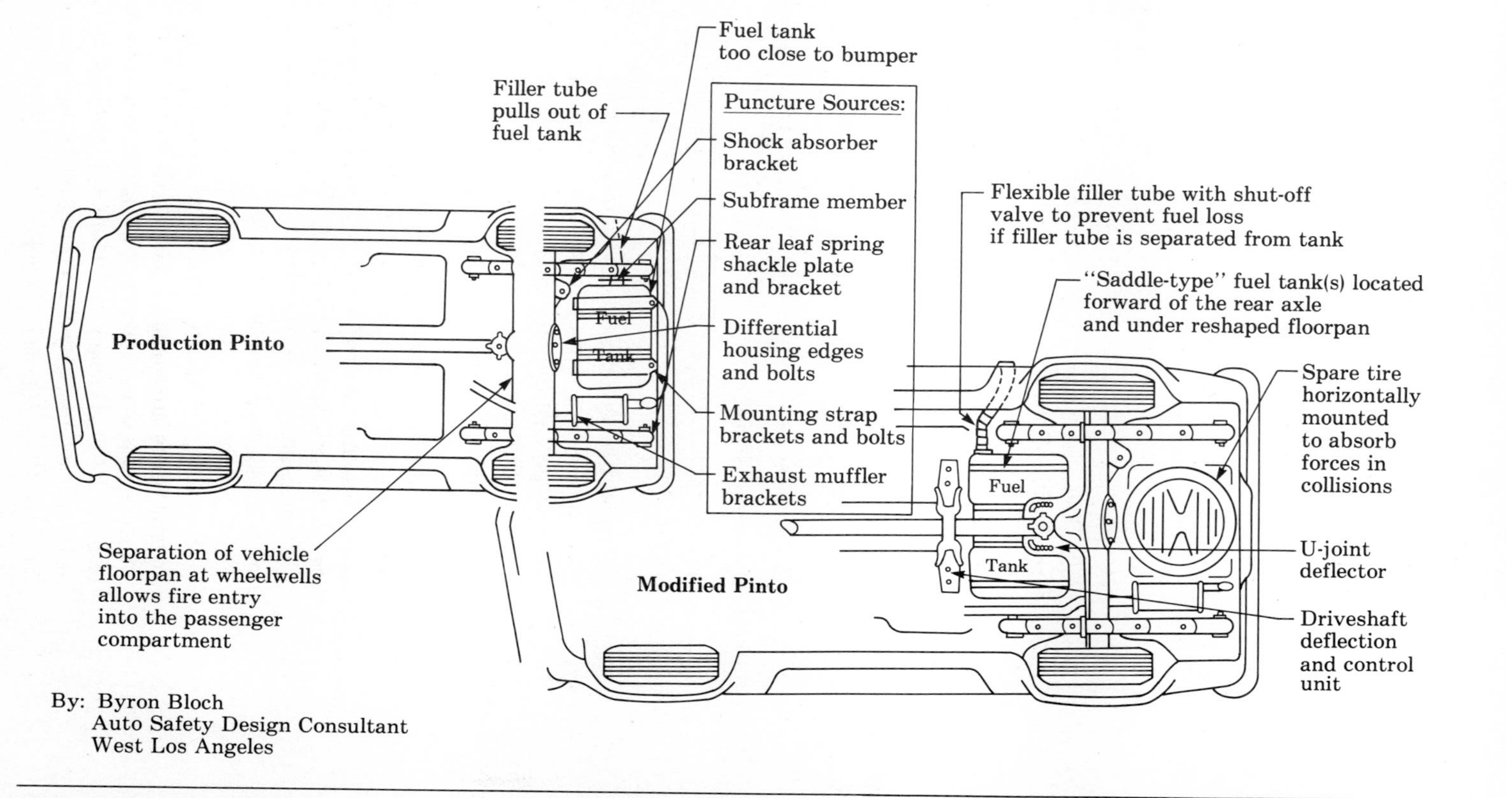

By: Byron Bloch
Auto Safety Design Consultant
West Los Angeles

Source: M. Dowie, 1985:146–147.

PANEL 10.3

$11 versus a Burn Death

Benefits and Costs Relating to Fuel Leakage
Associated with the Static Rollover
Test Portion of FMVSS 208

Benefits

Savings: 180 burn deaths, 180 serious burn injuries, 2,100 burned vehicles.
Unit Cost: $200,000 per death, $67,000 per injury, $700 per vehicle.
Total Benefit: 180 × ($200,000) + 180 × ($67,000) + 2,100 × ($700) = $49.5 million.

Costs

Sales: 11 million cars, 1.5 million light trucks.
Unit Cost: $11 per car, $11 per truck.
Total Cost: 11,000,000 × ($11) + 1,500,000 × ($11) = $137 million.

From Ford Motor Company internal memorandum: "Fatalities Associated with Crash-Induced Fuel Leakage and Fires."

Source: Mark Dowie, "Pinto Madness," 1985:35.

the book) that we shall be moving more toward considerations of institutional social problems and away from subinstitutional social problems? In part, we mean simply that the problems of power, the economy, population, the environment, the family, war, and so on can best be understood in the context of large, formal, complex, specialized, rational, impersonal social patterns.[14] This does not mean that subinstitutional social behavior or exchange theory is not relevant to macrosocial problems. What it does mean is that institutional social behavior is in important ways different from the face-to-face behaviors of small primary groups, although always rooted in them and their interactive principles.[15] However, we readily admit that exchange theory is less useful in explaining institutional-level social problems and that in Chapters 10 to 15 we will need to rely more heavily on our other theoretical perspectives (most notably on conflict theory, structuralism, and functionalism).

Earlier we defined an institution as a cluster of social roles (usually designed to resolve recurring general social problems) and said that subinstitutional social behavior concerned the principles governing actual face-to-face interaction of individuals (cf. Homans, 1974:Ch. 16). A much more elaborate list of characteristics of institutional and subinstitutional social behavior is now provided in Table 10.2. This table is important for your understanding of much of the

PANEL 10.4

What's Your Life Worth?

Societal Cost Components for Fatalities,
1972 NHTSA Study

Component	1971 Costs
Future productivity losses	
Direct	$132,000
Indirect	41,300
Medical costs	
Hospital	700
Other	425
Property damage	1,500
Insurance administration	4,700
Legal and court	3,000
Employer losses	1,000
Victim's pain and suffering	10,000
Funeral	900
Assets (lost consumption)	5,000
Miscellaneous accident cost	200

Total Per Fatality: $200,725

Here is a chart from a federal study showing how the National Highway Traffic Safety Administration has calculated the value of a human life. The estimate was arrived at under pressure from the auto industry. The Ford Motor Company has used it in cost-benefit analyses arguing why certain safety measures are not "worth" the savings in human lives. The calculation above is a breakdown of the estimated cost to society every time someone is killed in a car accident. We were not able to find anyone, either in the government or at Ford, who could explain how the $10,000 figure for "pain and suffering" had been arrived at.

Source: Mark Dowie, "Pinto Madness," 1985:30.

rest of this textbook. Take some time and make sure you comprehend the concepts presented in it. Perhaps the best way to comprehend these different characteristics is to consider two concrete examples. Think of your own family (i.e., mother, father, brothers, and sisters) as a subinstitutional social unit and the U.S. federal government as an institutional social unit. While no examples are perfect, these two will do nicely.

Your own family is a small group, usually no more than three to six people. Everyone communicates directly with everyone else; in fact you actually live

TABLE 10.2 Characteristics of Subinstitutional and Institutional Social Behaviors

Subinstitutional Social Behavior	Institutional Social Behavior
1. Face-to-face, direct exchanges	1. Indirect exchanges
2. Simple elementary social relations	2. Complex social relations
3. Small groups	3. Large groups
4. Informal expectations	4. Formal external rules
5. Social homogeneity	5. Division of labor and social specialization
6. Personal	6. Impersonal
7. Shorter spans of control, longer exchanges	7. Longer spans of control, shorter exchanges
8. Satisfaction of basic values, for example, work for food, shelter, or approval	8. Generalized reinforcers, for example, work for pay or status
9. Primitive societies	9. Contemporary, urban-industrial societies
10. Status and power earned (achievement)	10. Status and power inherited (ascription)
11. Capital building*	11. Capital consuming
12. Stable	12. Precarious

**Capital* means anything that allows people to postpone actions leading to some immediate reward to undertake other actions whose rewards, though potentially greater, are both uncertain and deferred.

Source: *Social Behavior: Its Elementary Forms,* by George C. Homans, copyright © 1974 by Harcourt Brace Jovanovich, Inc. Reprinted by permission of the publisher. Chapter 16.

together much of your life. Families tend to exchange basic rewards, such as effort for love or approval. Few tasks are performed for pay. Often family members will exert great energy out of love without asking to be rewarded (in the usual sense of reward) at all. Although there are some social roles in families, they remain fairly simple. Expectations tend to be informal; for example, clean your room, take out the garbage, cut the grass, respect your parents. Family members tend to be alike, socially equal. They usually are of the same race, religion, financial status, and have very similar basic values. Social relations in the family are primary, affective, personal, and far-reaching (diffuse). Family members usually give a great deal of time to each other. Families tend to last, remain cohesive, even after children marry or leave home.

The U.S. federal government, on the other hand, has about three million employees and expenditures of $786 billion (1983–84). The government is comprised of many different branches (e.g., the executive, legislative, and judicial), each with its own functions and subagencies. The government is a vast complex of social hierarchies with civil services and other classifications and rankings. Federal employees exchange work for pay, the classical institutional arrangement. If they do not consider their benefits adequate, workers may quit their jobs in protest (strikes are usually prohibited by law for federal employees). The federal bureaucracy has a complex division of labor and much role specialization. Social positions are governed by explicit rules and elaborate regulations. The military provides us with a good example. Here the rights and duties of positions vary tremendously by rank. In the federal government social relations tend to be impersonal, formal, and rational. Communications are usually indirect through memorandums and other written formal documents. A given interaction in the federal bureaucracy tends to last a relatively short time and spans of control are long. Federal agencies and positions are precarious. It is not uncommon for whole agencies or departments (such as the Department of Energy) to be abolished or reduced in size.

One of the key questions here is whether exchange principles, such as Homans's five exchange propositions, can even be appropriate explanations at all for institutional-level social problems (like the Ford Pinto case). Obviously if you are a structuralist and contend with French sociologist Emile Durkheim that external and constraining social facts are qualitatively different from individual behavior, then sociology can never be reduced to (Skinnerian) psychology. For most structuralists and conflict theorists, social problems cannot be reduced to the dynamics of small-group interactions. At the very least exchange theorists have problems explaining institutional behaviors subinstitutionally. Consider Homans's five propositions (see Panel 2.2). Who are the relevant actors (person and other) in a large impersonal corporation like Ford Motor Company? If values are diverse in heterogeneous groups, whose values determine particular exchanges? If social exchanges are indirect and complex, who is interacting with whom? Can one ever satiate on generalized reinforcers like money or status? When there is a wide variety of rewards available, which ones determine given social interactions? Cannot many institutions operate for long periods of time based on their norms, laws, moral codes, and so on without any recourse to subinstitutional rewards or so-called basic values? Do we not need to focus on social characteristics that transcend individual variation (such as the crime rate, the size of a population, and the organization of authority) to account for macrosocial phenomena?

To be blunt, yes, these are all serious problems for a general exchange perspective of institutional social problems. Exchange theory certainly does need to be supplemented by more structural, functional, and conflict explanations. At the same time exchange principles remain relevant to institutional analyses of social problems. For one thing, why should there be any social norms at all? Exchange theorists maintain that institutions (consider the Prohibition amendment) that are not subinstitutionally rewarding will not persist indefinitely. Their capital will in effect be used up eventually. In the end we must admit that society is comprised of flesh and blood people. Is it so far-fetched to conceive of business, military, or government elites (for example, the leaders of the major American corporations listed in Table 10.3) as if they were individuals in a fairly small group? In fact, Coleman's concept of corporate actors (1974) suggests just this. Perhaps institutions in large urban-industrial societies are not as complex as we think. Maybe we do not need to take all

Institutional corporate actors like General Motors are extremely powerful. GM has a larger annual budget than most other countries in the world. The interests of corporations are not the same as those of individuals. For corporations profit is almost all that matters. (UPI/Bettmann News Photos)

individuals (their rewards, values, anger, and so on) into account. Could the interests of a powerful few explain much of contemporary social structure? Coleman has argued that norms arise through the actions of men rationally calculating their own self-interests and that men try to extend their power to actions in which they have the most interest. If only a few powerful elites control modern society and its institutions, then perhaps *their* values assume eminence. For example, clearly profit making determines much of modern corporate social behavior.

We must also remember that institutional social structure emerges from subinstitutional behavior and to a large extent is governed by subinstitutional principles (see Chapter 2). One view of the evolution of contemporary society from small groups goes something like this: Initially people interacted relatively randomly (biology dictated much of social interaction) in fairly small hunting and gathering societies (Lenski and Lenski, 1987). Some of these relatively random social configurations persisted, since they were more rewarding than others, more balanced, and so on. As the size of social groups increased, even if groups were balanced (and had at least some differences), cliques tended to emerge based on similarity, frequency of interaction, common values, and propinquity. These cliques themselves were then ranked into social strata or classes. Those few social groups that provided the most socially valuable skills and had the scarcest social resources tended to become higher in social status. This higher status was then used to gain a disproportionate share of the social surplus generated in industrial societies. The end result was that a very few powerful elites tended to have great power in modern society. What's important to note here is that such institutional social advantages have subinstitutional roots. Institutions cannot be appropriately or completely understood apart from the actual exchanges of at least some individuals in a society.

This is not to argue that social problems at the institutional or macrosocial system level do not have some special traits. The characteristics of institutional social behavior listed in Table 10.2 suggest that institutional analyses of social problems indeed are different from subinstitutional analyses. In effect there are additional social issues deriving from the special social structure of large formal social organizations. Some of the new issues we shall need to address in the remainder of this book include the hierarchical social structure of institutions making face-to-face interaction uncommon, the resultant indirectness of social interaction (see Connor and Maris, 1976:164), the shortened interaction time with increases in population size and social density and their effects on communications (Mayhew and Levinger, 1976), the necessity of efficiency and rationality to ensure group survival, the complexity of large groups, the high division of labor (Durkheim, 1893) and the resultant changes in the basis of social integration from social likeness to mutual dependency, and the increased importance of generalized reinforcers like money and status and the lessened importance of basic social rewards—just to name some of the crucial recurring new institutional issues.

To understand power inequality and the so-called abuse of power by big business or big government from the exchange perspective, it is also necessary to elaborate and expand the concept of social actors. In subinstitutional settings we have relatively small groups of individuals in face-to-face interaction. James Coleman refers to such flesh-and-blood real-life persons as natural individuals (1974:14ff.). However, in institutional settings, such as those in big corporations (like Ford) or big government (like the U.S. federal government), exchanges do not occur simply between natural individuals (Coleman, 1974). There are also juristic persons or corporate actors. Corporate actors are intangible entities that exist only in abstraction. They have no fixed life, no body, and cannot be imprisoned. Examples of corporate actors include corporations, churches, labor unions, professional associations, clubs, lobby groups, and so on.[16] One could also further distinguish societal actors, namely, those positions or organizations that tend to represent whole societies or nations. For example, the president of the United States to a degree represents America, champions its constitution, is commander in chief of its military, and so on.

Thus, in our expanded concept of actors in institutional settings there are at least the following types of social exchanges:

1. Natural individuals with natural individuals (NI-NI).
2. Natural individuals with corporate actors (NI-CA).
3. Natural individuals with societal actors (NI-SA).
4. Corporate actors with corporate actors (CA-CA).
5. Corporate actors with societal actors (CA-SA).
6. Societal actors with societal actors (SA-SA).

Most of the exchange analyses of social problems in Chapters 1 through 9 assumed type-one exchanges; that is, individual (NI-NI) exchanges. Analysis of institutional-level social problems requires that we introduce new types of social exchange (types 2–6, above) and that we acknowledge changes even in interactions between natural individuals (e.g., more indirection, shorter exchanges, longer spans of control, use of more generalized reinforcers, more explicit rules governing interaction, more impersonal exchanges, and so on). These differences between institutional and subinstitutional interaction and social problems have led some to argue that exchange theory is not at all relevant to macrosocial problems. However, as we shall see, this is not our position. Exchange theory must be modified to account for institutional patterns and problems and complemented by other theoretical perspectives, but not abandoned. One major modification is that exchanges tend to occur among corporate actors (type 4, CA-CA), rather than between natural individuals. Nevertheless, they are still social exchanges and exchange principles still apply.

Another major change at the institutional level is that individual, corporate, and societal interests are not the same (see Table 10.3). This means that the values and rewards for type 2 through 6 exchanges are different than those for type 1 exchanges (cf. Lenski, 1984:35–42). To understand this is crucial. Usually societal or corporate interests are in maximum production, regardless of the harm that these interests may do to individuals (Lenski, 1984:41; however, see Kantner, 1984). For example, corporations value profit (Lenski, 1984:36) but are not especially concerned about the health (or even the death) of any particular individual (Braithwaite, 1984; Ermann and Lundman, 1982) so long as the corporation's life itself is not threatened. Thus, in NI-CA-type exchanges, such as that between consumers and the Ford Motor Company, Ford's values (not the consumers') will determine the basis of exchange (because Ford is more powerful) and 180 Pinto burn deaths a year will be acceptable *to Ford.* To complain that these deaths are not acceptable to the 180 who died, to their families, to Ralph Nader, and so on (even though this is obviously true), is to misunderstand the basis for NI-CA-type exchanges. Specifically, it is to confuse NI-CA exchanges with NI-NI exchanges.[17]

TABLE 10.3 A Comparison of Societal or Corporate and Individual Interests

Societal or Corporate Interests*	Individual Interests†
Maintenance of the status quo, social equilibrium	Survival, shelter, food, drink, health
Maximum production	Physical growth
Latency	Sleep
Population reproduction	Sexual gratification
Profit-making, expand national boundaries	Income, property
Technical skill, expertise	Knowledge
Order, harmony	Love
Social prosperity, avoid war defeat	Creature comfort, avoid pain and death
Power	Social status

Source: *Gerhard E. Lenski, *Power and Privilege: A Theory of Social Stratification,* 1984:35–42; Talcott Parsons in Max Black, *The Social Theories of Talcott Parsons,* 1961:100ff.
†Gerhard E. Lenski, *Power and Privilege: A Theory of Social Stratification,* 1984; A.H. Maslow, 1954, *Motivation and Personality,* 1963.

Not only can a modified exchange theory help us see why Ford went ahead with the sale of the Pinto even though they knew it could explode on collision, it can also explain why the Pinto continued to be produced for eight years. Considering the deprivation-satiation proposition (A4 in Chapter 2), we realize that all actors (and especially corporate actors) satiate slowly on money and status. However, exchanges between natural individuals are usually shorter than NI-CA or CA-CA type exchanges, in part because individuals are more likely to exchange rewards such as sex, food, shelter, and so on, and one satiates more quickly on these rewards than on generalized reinforcers.

From the consumer perspective the Pinto exchange situation violates the principle of distributive justice (A5 in Chapter 2), as it seems like an unfair exchange of natural individuals with corporate actors to not get car safety in return for their purchase price. You do not expect to pay large amounts of money for a product that is known beforehand to explode in modest rear-end collisions. In fact, anger from all NI-CA-type exchanges is likely, since corporate elites will tend to protect their own interests (which do not concern the deaths of a relatively small number of anonymous individuals), and their power will allow them to get away with it. Also, according to Marx, workers always put more labor into an industrial corporation than the corporation returns to the worker in salary or benefits (cf. Shepelak and Alwin, 1986).

From the corporate producer's perspective it might be noted that exchanges of natural individuals with corporate or societal actors are not *only* costly or exploitative. In advanced industrial societies corporations provide highly technical specialized products that natural individuals cannot offer to one another. The automobile is one such product. Corporations can produce machines that reduce our labor, make life more comfortable, longer, healthier, and so on. In short, there are considerable benefits (as well as costs) to NI-CA-type exchanges for everyone.[18] As we shall see in the next section, all types of social exchanges are affected by the structure of large, formal, bureaucratic organizations (Connor and Maris, 1976).

The Structural Perspective A large part of the problem with big business or big government originates from the special nature of institutional social organization in large, urban-industrial societies—what German sociologist Max Weber (1864–1920) referred to as bureaucracy—not just from the greed, perversity, or other personal traits of individual elites (Walton, 1986:61, 90). Writing originally in 1925 Weber described bureaucratic social structure as an ideal type (that is, how a given type of behavior would operate on a strictly rational basis, unaffected by errors or emotion, if it were directed to a single goal).[19] For Weber bureaucracy is a goal oriented type of social behavior, legal in its authority, rational in its actions, and societal in its social structure (Gerth and Mills, 1958). As such, bureaucratic social structure is characterized by:

1. *Defined positions* in which there is a division of labor of various officials who have limited specialized duties to perform.
2. *Hierarchical order,* which is pyramidal in shape. Each official takes orders from above and then supervises immediate subordinates.
3. *Explicit rules* that guide the daily functioning of the formal organization. All decisions are based on these rules, regulations, and procedures.
4. *Selection and treatment by competence.* Officials remain emotionally detached (impersonal) in order to not let feelings distort their rational judgments.
5. *Tenure.* Employees tend to make a lifelong career of service in the organization. Promotion is based on merit or seniority, not favoritism or nepotism.
6. A *specialized administrative staff* whose duties are to maintain files, records, accounts, and internal communications.

Although Weber felt that the growth of bureaucracy in the form of big business and big government was probably inevitable from the structural-functional perspective, it did not always contribute to the adjustment or adaptation of the social system. In short, in many instances bureaucracy was dysfunctional (Merton, 1957:Ch. VI; Merton, 1975; Boudon, 1981). Bureaucrats could be said to have trained incapacities in which they were unable to respond to people or problems in any way other than that which their bureaucratic rules prescribed; instrumental values often became terminal values; sentiment and personality tended to become misshaped by bureaucratic social structure; and social relations were likely to become highly impersonal.

Of course, structuralism has come a long way since Max Weber and his elementary descriptive concept of bureaucracy. One of the leading contemporary structuralists, Peter Blau (1977:Ch. 9; 1975; Blau and Merton, 1981), reminds us that inequality in power is greater than any other form of inequality, including income inequality (1977:228). Furthermore, the bigger a business or a government, the more authority must be concentrated. This concentration of authority in turn increases the insulation of the lower and upper social classes. From a structuralist's perspective power is its own protection (Blau, 1977:238). Thus, Ford can get away with a flammable Pinto because consumers lack the power necessary to challenge big business. To wish it otherwise, as consumer advocate groups do, probably requires no less than a total restructuring of contemporary industrial society. The question remains, is that price too high?

Another leading structuralist, Bruce Mayhew (1976, 1981), has quantified, operationalized, and generalized the earlier largely theoretical work of Mosca (1939), Michels (1915), Weber (1925), and Blau (1977). In so doing, Mayhew and structuralism have moved away from the notion of subjective understanding in Weber and from social-psychology in general to a more formal empirically falsifiable theory of large organizations (see Blau and Merton, 1981; Baron, 1984). Mayhew contends that all personal traits (e.g., the greed for profit of elites, the tendency for elites to form conspiracies to gain advantage over nonelites, and so on) tend to be irrelevant to understanding problems of power inequality in big business or big government.

For example, Mayhew has shown that power tends to become more unequal (to polarize) as group size increases and to become more equal as the sequence length of acts (e.g., talking, exerting control, and so on) increases. The expected relative size of the controlling component (e.g., elites) is a decreasing function of group size. That is, as groups grow larger, the ruling component grows smaller (cf. Mosca, 1939). Mayhew has also demonstrated that the density of interaction (i.e., the number of contacts one would expect to occur by chance alone) increases with population size and that the expected proportion of time per contact decreases with size. Thus, in large urban areas or the bureaucratic social structures of big business there will be more and more transitory social interactions, which in turn, suggests why social relations in a bureaucracy, as Weber claimed, will tend to be impersonal.

The Conflict Perspective Conflict theorists, such as Marx, tend to have a view of social inequality almost diametrically opposed to that of structural-functionalists like Davis and Moore (Turner, 1986:Part II; Wacquant, 1985). For example, Marx maintained that bourgeois capitalists held onto their power in society not because they were filling functionally more important positions or were more talented than their workers (proletarians), but mainly because of their economic advantages over workers. Marx argued that throughout human history there have always been ruling and oppressed social classes (for example, masters and slaves, feudal lords and their serfs, capitalists and proletarians). The ruling classes, Marx contends, owe their power to their ownership of land and raw materials (e.g., iron, coal, gas); their control of means of production (i.e., tools, factories, skills, knowledge); and to the institutional rules governing production (the mode of production) and distribution of wealth (Wilson, 1983:Chs. 11 and 12).

"Here is the way it works: We take from the rich and give to the poor—keeping only enough for salaries, travel, equipment, depreciation, and so on, and so on."

Drawing by Ross; © 1968 *The New Yorker* Magazine, Inc.

For conflict theorists the critical factors in social stratification are not important positions needing to be matched with talented or gifted individuals who have sacrificed to get proper training, and so on, but rather what place a group has in the organization of production. As we have seen, Marx believed there were really only two social classes, the rulers and the oppressed (cf. Collins, 1975, order givers and order takers). Marx thought that every society that was not socialistic eventually exploited its workers. Like Lenski (1984), Marx observed that as industrial societies produced economic surpluses *(mehrwert),* the workers did not share proportionately in these profits with the owners. The rulers or owners of property, factories, and tools took more than their fair share of the surplus. Thus, Marx concluded, capitalism existed for the private profit of the owners of capital. Eventually conflict over the distribution of the surplus was inevitable (cf. Spaeth, 1985).

In a capitalist society workers never get the opportunity to fill important social positions and thus suffer increasingly worse economic, physical, and psychological insults (see Mirowsky, 1985). Conflict theorists believe that the ordinary worker's life is marred by exploitation and escalating deprivation. In effect, entry into the ruling class is blocked for proletarians; even the number of ruling elites grows smaller and smaller with time. The result of capitalist society is a caste system; that is, a system of social inequality in which there is no possibility of movement—especially into the important social positions of the upper social class that rules. Notice that for Marx income does not determine social class, since one can have money without being an owner or ruler. Also, an owner and a worker with the same incomes would be in two different social classes.

Marx contends that there is a growing alienation of labor (1906:709) inherent in capitalistic society, since the lot of the worker must gradually worsen (Leontieff, 1985). Ultimately workers become appendages of the machines of industry (Marx, 1848:396–397). If the proletarian masses are physically concentrated (for example, in cities), enjoy good communications with one another, develop solidarity, political awareness, and organization, and a few bourgeoisie defect to the workers' cause, a revolution can occur in which the capitalist mode of production itself is overthrown (Marx and Engels, 1848:19). The goal of an emergent new socialistic order is to avoid repeating history by instituting a classless society.

Conflict theorists tend to agree with Mayhew and Levinger (1976) and Domhoff (1986) that America is run by the interests of a few powerful elites. Mayhew and Levinger go so far as to claim that democracy is a form of propaganda set in place to head off social revolts (1976), since people can hardly revolt against themselves. Thus, democracy functions to maintain the illusion of equality (the democratic mirage) and participation by the mass electorate in important social decisions. Domhoff (1967, 1978, 1979, 1986), Mills (1956), Parenti (1983), Dye (1976), and of course, Marx (1848) object to the hypocrisy of American democracy, and the claim of the inevitability of oligarchy in big business and big government.

Most conflict theorists argue that big business, big government, and big military really control America, routinely abuse their power, and operate in their own interests (What's good for Ford or GM is good for the country). As modern industrial societies generate surpluses and conflicts arise over surplus distribution, the interests of the powerful few win out (Domhoff, 1986). Marx (1848) and Lenski (1984) both contend that the economically dominant class is always politically dominant. It is hypocritical under such social conditions to claim that America is a participatory democracy, is egalitarian, that elections mean very much, and so on. For example, President Reagan cynically opposes individual welfare ("let them work") and social services, but gives away millions in "corporate welfare" to big business and the military. In the particular case under discussion of the Ford Pinto, it is hypocritical to say let the stockholders at Ford vote Iacocca out, let consumer advocate groups like that of Ralph Nader challenge Ford in court, or let consumers not purchase Pintos; since stockholders, consumer advocate groups, and consumers usually lack the political clout to make any effective protest.

The conflict perspective also questions the inevitability and desirability of oligarchies such as the Ford Motor Company and other representatives of big business. In part, Marx felt that big business or big government power inequality would self-destruct, and in part that it would be overthrown by organized social resistance movements or proletarian workers and a few bourgeoise defectors, as in the Russian revolution of 1917. The real problem with situations like the Ford Pinto (say conflict theorists) is that a *true* democracy must be established in which the interests of all citizens are considered. Ultimately capitalism must be replaced by socialism (for example, as in Cuba, although Cuba's socialism is totalitarian), private property abolished, social class distinctions eliminated or greatly reduced, corporations and other major institutions nationalized, and all resources and wealth shared equally according to need, not according to privilege or power.

Structuralists and exchange theorists for the most part are skeptical of the feasibility of such radical social changes. Perhaps oligarchy and power inequality are inevitable, regardless of the political superstructure?[20] Are the USSR, East Germany, or Cuba really socially very different from the United States? Often it seems as though the more political or economic forms (e.g., capitalism, socialism, and so on) change, the more society remains the same. Minimally (short of social revolution), conflict theorists would advocate that citizen groups (like those of Nader and Common Cause) resist big business in court, and reorganize and consolidate big government and government agencies like the Government Accounting Office (GAO) to police other organizations routinely exempt from any social control (as was the case with the FBI under J. Edgar Hoover). All of this leads us directly into the last major section of this chapter: how to resolve the problem of power inequality.

Resolving the Problem Any attempt to socially redefine power inconsistently with the actual (economic, political, physical, and so on) bases for power is likely to fail or, at least, to be very fragile. Even if power inequality is not inevitable, perhaps oligarchical capitalist society cannot be too different from the way it is. If so, the resolution to power inequality turns on checking obvious abuses of power but routinely allowing elites to do their jobs, make their decisions, and so on. It does not make much sense to try to eliminate all power and privilege to correct an occasional abuse. Of course, if you cannot join the roughly 1 percent of the population who are in control of society or are not particularly adept at resignation, you may wish for other resolutions to the problem of the abuse of unequal power.

Another strategy to correct abuse of power by business, governmental, or military elites would be to maximize competing interests. This approach is probably most appropriate for business corporations. Encouraging competition tends to make corporations more responsible. Since Ford, GM, and Chrysler have had virtual monopolies on the American automobile market, they have been able to act with impugnity. Snell (1985) says that Ford, GM, and Chrysler account for 97 percent of American automobile production. Over the years GM systematically forced electric mass transit and railroads out of major U.S. cities in favor of buses and then automobiles because buses and automobiles were more profitable. Now, compared to almost any major European city, many American cities are almost devoid of mass transit systems. By the economics of supply and demand, increasing competition forces changes in supply. Witness the changes in automobiles (small size, high mileage, diesel power, and so on) wrought by allowing Japanese and German manufacturers to compete for the American car market.

One mechanism for increasing corporate competition is to pursue antimonopoly legislation. Large American corporations tend to become larger, to drive out or cannibalize competitors (as in hostile takeovers), and eventually to become multinational. The more this trend progresses, the more likely is abuse of power. A good case illustration of the abuse of power by a monopolistic multinational corporation is Sampson's exposé of *The Sovereign State of ITT* (1973). Between 1972 and 1976, ITT tried to bring down the democratically elevated government in Chile. Charges against ITT by the U.S. Justice Department were dropped just after a subsidiary of ITT, Sheraton Hotels, made a $400,000 campaign donation to the Republican national convention in San Diego. Nixon himself ordered the case dropped. Of course, maximizing competition is less appropriate for the federal government and the military, since they operate virtually unopposed. Nevertheless, we could theoretically have a vigorous two (or even three) party system, clearly separate executive, legislative, and judicial functions of state, encourage competition among branches of the military, and ensure accountability of the military to Congress.

When elites do not control themselves, it may be necessary to police abuse of power through such vehicles as watchdog commissions and unions. Sutherland's classic *White Collar Crime* (1949) documents price fixing, embezzlement, restraint of trade, misrepresentations in advertising, and so on of major American corporations (cf. Clinard and Yeager, 1980; Wheeler and Rothman, 1982). Sutherland found that 60 percent of seventy large corporations had been convicted in criminal courts and had an average of four convictions each (could be considered habitually criminal). The Federal Trade Commission has proved useful in ferreting out and censuring such white-collar crimes. Ralph Nader and his consumer advocate groups have accused GM of putting profits before safety. Nader also won legislative battles concerning use of cyclamates, meat contamination, car safety, artificial oil shortages, and many more.

Unions have helped keep corporations honest and responsible. Recently union members have been appointed to the boards of directors of major corporations (Logue, 1981). The General Accounting Office has helped eliminate waste in federal programs, shown that wheat sales to the USSR were mismanaged, and proven that some military equipment was not combat ready. Other important policing groups include Common Cause and the Securities

Exchange Commission. Finally, Watergate and the Iran arms deals have raised public consciousness and congressional scrutiny of governmental operations. Previously many executives functioned almost without challenge. For example, former FBI director J. Edgar Hoover had nineteen of twenty-two budgets he submitted to Congress approved without change.

Of course, society is not only a rational, bureaucratic, impersonal, profit-taking phenomenon. Sociologist Max Weber indicated that social groups, especially in traditional societies, are also associational or communal. One resolution to power inequality is to take refuge in smaller more traditional groups. At first blush this resolution seems naive, since it does not change society and there may be few places to which to run. That is, can one really get away from power inequality and its abuse? Probably not entirely. Still, many argue that the work ethic is declining; leisure activities are increasing; the workweek is becoming shorter; and avocations, voluntary associations, and hobbies are all becoming more salient. In short, many people are insulating themselves from big impersonal bureaucracies by participating in smaller, more primary, largely avocational associations. To repeat, this does not change bureaucratic society, but it does provide some relief. To a degree religion has always offered such relief by being a social institution in which the rules are presumably different, where money and material achievements should not mean as much, where love and altruism are more important than greed and power, and where one is accepted in spite of what s/he is or has done. Unhappily, even a few churches and religious organizations have become big businesses and thereby compromised some of their own basic principles.

Finally, there is always the ultimate recourse of overthrowing the unequal power structure itself and substituting a more egalitarian (most often socialistic) regime in its place. Such radical social change usually involves violence or confrontation of some sort in which wealth, property, and other scarce resources are redistributed more equally. In some instances the military (a military coup) ousts the government; in others the government seizes (nationalizes) corporations or banks (see *New York Times,* January 15, 1983, in which Chile nationalized eight banks);[21] while in still others corporations take control of the stock of other corporations, influence governments, or infiltrate the military (by hiring ex-military officers as corporation officers). In Poland Lech Walesa and masses of workers challenged the government itself. Sometimes small bands of terrorists or mercenaries, instead of the military, are contracted with to make key assassinations in an effort to tumble governments or neutralize corporate influence (see Chapter 15). Overthrowing unequal power structures can either result in replacing them with different but still unequal power structures or in substituting a form of socialism for capitalism. Only in the last case is there the possibility of a real social change. Even here there is considerable evidence that social inequality tends to persist in socialistic governments. One also has to remember that violence usually breeds further violence, with one result being a highly unstable and unpredictable social order.

• Summary

In considering power inequality and its abuse we have moved from a predominantly subinstitutional level of analysis of social problems (in Chapters 4 through 9) to a more institutional level of analysis (which will continue in Chapters 11 through 15). Although institutional social problems are always rooted in subinstitutional behavior and principles (appropriately modified exchange theory is still relevant to institutional-level social problems), at the same time they also require somewhat different levels of analysis; namely, those of structuralism, conflict, functionalism, and so on. Social problems like power inequality tend to involve larger groups, more indirect exchanges, and more formal external rules. They are more complex and diverse, and more precarious, involve longer spans of control, are based more on generalized reinforcers such as money and status, and are more capital consuming.

If others are rewarded more by exchange than a person and as a result these others change their behavior, then that person may be said to have power over the others. Usually a person with power is less interested in and less dependent on the outcome of social exchanges because the powerful person already has scarce social resources. Inequality refers to social positions that vary by rank-ordered gradations. Power can be differentiated from authority in which change in behavior is based on legitimate rights outside of actual interactions or exchanges. Power can also be distinguished from influence. Unequal power is necessitated by social stratification that, according to functionalists Davis and Moore, is both inevitable and desirable to motivate talented individuals to fill important social positions. Tumin, Marx, Domhoff, Mills, and others object to the desirability and inevitability of power inequality.

According to conflict theorists one of the undesirable consequences of power inequality is that a power elite comprised of big business, generals in the military, and top federal government officers can exercise disproportionate control of the society (Mills). Opponents of power inequality argue for a more pluralistic society in which power is dispersed among competing interests, or a socialistic economy in which resources and wealth are divided more evenly according to need rather than power. Some (Michels) contend that government by a few elites (oligarchy) is inevitable as society grows in size and complexity. Others (Domhoff, Parenti, Dye) point out that in a capitalistic oligarchy public policies tend to favor big business interests to the systematic disadvantage of the masses.

A concrete example of big business' abuse of unequal power was Ford Motor Company's construction of the Pinto automobile. The Pinto was found highly flammable subsequent to even modest rear-end collisions. Ford refused to repair Pinto's unsafe fuel tank because it was cheaper to settle in court for damages than to fix all Pintos. In analyzing the Pinto case, exchange theorists note that not only are there natural individuals but also there are corporate and societal actors (Coleman). The rewards, values, satiation-deprivation schedules, notion of justice, interests, and so on are different for each type of actor. Thus, social problems tend to arise when exchanges occur across types of actors. Structurally big businesses like Ford are organized formally or bureaucratically (Weber). With such large complex social organizations this means, among other traits, a high division of labor with clearly defined social positions; pyramidal social hierarchies dominated by elites and special-interest groups; emphasis on explicit rules, efficiency, and rationality; indirectness of social interaction; and shortened interaction time. Structural sociologists (Mayhew) operationalize and generalize these traits of large formal organizations' social structure and show how special social problems can be expected to arise from them. Blau notes that power is more unequal than any other kind of inequality.

For conflict theorists the critical factors in social stratification are not important positions needing to be matched with talented or gifted individuals who have sacrificed to gain proper training, but rather what place a group has in the organization of production. In a capitalist society workers never get the opportunity to fill important social positions and thus suffer increasingly worse economic, physical, and psychological deprivations. Conflict theorists argue that big business, big government, and big military really control America, routinely abuse their power, and operate in their own interests. The conflict perspective questions the inevitability and desirability of oligarchies such as the Ford Motor Company.

Resolutions to power inequality include accepting it as inevitable and not all that bad; stimulating competing interests; policing obvious abuses with watchdog commissions, governmental controls, and so on; taking refuge in smaller more traditional often avocational social groups; or overthrowing power inequality and putting a new (often socialistic) more egalitarian sociopolitical organization in its place. In the next chapter we shall continue to explore inequality, but now we shall turn our attention to problems arising from or generating economic inequality.

• Notes

1. Hougan, "The Business of Buying Friends", *Harpers* (December 1976), 43–62.

2. *The State Newspaper,* Columbia, SC, January 30, 1983.

3. Compare with Collins's (1975) or Dahrendorf's (1959) argument that there are basically two classes of people in modern society, the order givers (the powerful) and the order takers (the powerless).

4. Weber (1925) argues that *status* refers to honor and is concerned with what he calls lifestyle, not with economic determinants of class. Cf. Turner, 1986:146ff.

5. Compare with Chapter 1.

6. Note that many of the social sources of power have clear parallels to individual sources of power (cf. Homans, 1974:74–75). That is, powerful individuals in small groups tend to be the most aggressive, the strongest, the biggest in size, the most intelligent, the fastest, and those with the most money.

7. That is, in authority situations persons with authority do not provide the reward (or punishment) themselves.

8. The following comments draw heavily from the work of G. Lenski, 1984 edition (original, 1966), in his book *Power and Privilege.* Cf. Lenski and Lenski, 1986.

9. That is, do not behave altruistically.

10. *Functional* means having consequences contributing to the adjustment or adaptation of the social system and thus being desirable for the equilibrium of society.

11. For readers on social stratification see Bendix and Lipset, 1966 or Powers, 1982. W. L. Warner held that there were six basic social classes: upper-upper, lower-upper, upper-middle, lower-middle, upper-lower, and lower-lower. The U.S. Census Bureau recognizes about twelve occupational groupings. Thus, the number of fundamental social classes varies somewhere between two and twelve.

12. The Environmental Protection Agency alone had a $1.6 billion "super fund" that was apparently abused, leading to the resignations and dismissals of several top officials *(New York Times,* March 11, 1983).

13. It turns out that all of these estimates are too low, especially the assumption that the number of injuries and deaths would be the same.

14. To be sure, social problems of age, sex, race, health, and drugs could be (and were) analyzed institutionally. However, they also lend themselves readily to subinstitutional analysis.

15. Homans (1974:367) claims that subinstitutional behavior and its principles are always relevant, even in institutional settings, since norms never completely prescribe behavior. Subinstitutional behavior is to institutions as a vine is to a trellis.

16. Actually the chairmen of their boards, their boards of directors, managers, major stockholders, elected or appointed officials, and so on.

17. If there were 580 deaths, 580 injuries, and 6,300 vehicles (i.e., about three times the Panel 10.3 benefits), Ford might have changed the Pinto's fuel tank. However, they would have made the change because it was profitable to them to do so—not because people were dying.

18. Yet we recall (Chapter 1) that the automobile costs us 45,800 American lives each year. How do we decide if automobiles in exchange for 45,800 American lives per year is "worth it"?

19. When real (not ideal) bureaucratic organizations are observed (see Blau, *The Dynamics of Bureaucracy,* 1955; Baron, 1984), several departures from the six main traits of bureaucracies can be noted.

20. See Boris Pasternak's novel *Dr. Zhivago,* 1958.

21. In many Persian, Arabic (e.g., Iran, Iraq), and South American countries, foreign oil companies have been seized.

• Glossary

Authority. The ability to change behavior coming from legitimate rights outside of the values of interpersonal exchanges themselves.

Bureaucracy. A social or organizational structure that is hierarchically ordered and governed by formal explicit rules in which officials have limited specialized duties, and perform these duties in a rational impersonal manner to maximize the efficiency of the organization.

Corporate Actor. Intangible abstract entities that represent corporations, labor unions, professional associations, lobby groups, churches, clubs, and so on. A corporate actor is a juristic person, not a flesh and blood person.

Corporate Interest. The goals or objectives of corporate actors. These include, among others, social equilibrium, maximum production, profit making, technical skill, latency, and population reproduction.

Corporate Welfare. Government subsidies or public policies that favor large corporate interests.

Division of Labor. The increasing occupational specialization and interdependency that is characteristic of bureaucratic organizations in modern urban-industrial societies.

Elites. The top 1 percent or so of the population in big corporations, the federal and state government, and the military that commands most of the power in society and makes most of society's important decisions.

Generalized Reinforcers. Rewards such as money and social status that tend to be exchanged among corporate actors, that can be exchanged for other rewards, and upon which satiation is slow.

Ideal Type. How a given type of behavior would operate on a strictly rational basis, unaffected by errors or emotion, if it were directed to a single goal.

Indirect Social Interaction. Interaction through intermediaries, networks, or interlocked social positions in large formal organizations that are complex and hierarchically ordered; not the direct face-to-face interaction of elementary social behavior.

Influence. The act or power of producing an effect without apparent force or direct authority.

Natural Individual. An actual flesh-and-blood, real-life person interested in food, drink, sleep, sexual gratification, avoidance of pain, shelter, and so on.

Oligarchy. Government or rule by the few; power exercised by elites.

Pluralism. A governmental form in which power is dispersed among a variety of competing interests.

Principle of Least Interest. The actor least interested in or dependent on the outcome of a given exchange has the most power.

Rationality. The impersonal, objective, efficient, nonaffectual, goal-directed traits of modern formal social structures like bureaucracy.

Revolution. The usually violent overthrow of ruling elites and their government with another form of government taking their place—as in the French revolution of 1789 or the Russian revolution of 1917.

Socialism. The system of the ownership and operation of the means of production and distribution by society at large rather than by private individuals, with all members of the society sharing in the work and the products of the work.

Societal Actor. The position or organization that represents an entire society or nation.

Special-Interest Group. An organization or lobby created to influence decisions that directly concerns its members.

Surplus. The social product of goods and services above and beyond the minimum level needed to ensure the continuation of production and to meet the basic needs of workers.

• Further Reading

Braithwaite, John. *Corporate Crime in the Pharmaceutical Industry.* London: Routledge & Kegan Paul, 1984. Examines bribery, unsafe drugs, antitrust actions, sale of drugs to the underworld, and so on among major drug companies. Illustrates concept of the corporate actor and structural factors allowing or promoting corporate power abuses. Power abuse in drug corporations is easier because decision makers are separated from victims. Shows how Hoffman-LaRoche made massive profits by selling heroin and morphine to the underworld. Compare with earlier book by Ermann and Lundmann, *Corporate and Governmental Deviance,* 1978.

Coleman, James. *Power and the Structure of Society.* New York: W. W. Norton, 1974. A short interesting little paperback that introduces the important concept of corporate actors or juristic persons, among other things. Coleman points out that the interests of corporate actors are not identical with those of natural persons and discusses how one might control corporate actors.

Domhoff, G. William. *Who Rules America Now: A View for the '80s?* New York: Simon & Schuster, 1986 (hardback edition, 1983). As in his 1967 book, Domhoff still argues that a fixed group of privileged people continue to dominate American economy and government. In the tradition of C. W. Mills's earlier *Power Elite,* Domhoff illustrates how about one-half of 1 percent of the American population controls the corporate community and the government through the processes of special-interest lobbying, policy planning, and candidate selection.

Kantner, Rosabeth Moss. *The Change Masters: Innovation and Entrepreneurship in the American Corporation.* New York: Simon & Schuster, 1984 (hardback edition, 1983). Attempts to define the corporate circumstances under which innovation can flourish. Examines the relationship between natural individuals and corporate actors, especially the idea that individuals are important to any renaissance of American corporations. Argues that many of problems of corporations derive from the withering of employee grass roots.

Lenski, Gerhard E. *Power and Privilege: A Theory of Social Stratification.* New York: McGraw-Hill, 1984 (original edition, 1966). A classic statement on the origins and meanings of social inequality. Examines the broad socioevolutionary historical development of hunting and gathering, horticultural, agrarian, and industrial societies. Lenski claims that men almost always choose their own interests over collective interests, that societal interests cannot be the same as individual interests, that distribution determines the sharing of products of labor to the extent required to ensure social survival and continued production, and that power will determine the distribution of nearly all of the surplus (especially in technically advanced societies).

Mills, C. W. *The Power Elite.* New York: Oxford University Press, 1956. The original indignant claim that a few business leaders, generals, and heads of government really run America, even though it is a purported democracy. Mills even suggests that corporations, government, and the military are interlocked by the socioeconomic background, schooling, clubs, and actual job exchanges of their leaders. Mills, like Marx, is not happy with this cozy elite arrangement. Many books in this genre have followed (e.g., Domhoff, 1967, 1978, 1986; Parenti, 1978; Dye, 1976).

C·H·A·P·T·E·R

11

Economic Inequality

From the exchange perspective the poor as individuals have relatively few interactive assets (perhaps a self-fulfilling prophecy) and thus are not very rewarding or valuable to associate with. On a more institutional level corporate actors need poverty and the poor (e.g., cheap labor). Accordingly, corporate actors profit from exchanges with poor natural individuals. Both institutions and individuals satiate more slowly on general reinforcers like money. It follows that those with power will take more money than others may consider their fair share (i.e., more than they need).

Many structural-functionalists argue that economic inequality is inevitable and desirable to fill important social positions with scarce talent and highly trained individuals. Most people are not gifted, have not been trained, do not have functionally important positions, and do not (therefore) deserve to be affluent. The small size and low power of the American poor work to their structural disadvantage in mounting effective political challenges to the wealthy.

Conflict theorists argue that in all previous societies there have always been rulers (usually rich) and the oppressed (usually poor). Conflict exists over the distribution of the scarce and valued resources in society. Those with power, property, and authority expropriate more than their fair share of profits to serve their own interests—way beyond their actual needs or labor costs. The conflict perspective emphasizes that capitalism's primary objective is individual gain and profit, not collective need or social welfare. Thus, in any capitalistic society the poor are victims.

From the symbolic interaction perspective many used to view poverty as God's will. Thus, the poor were seen as deserving their fate. Some took the Darwinian view that poverty was nature's way of excreting unhealthy, imbecilic, slow, vacillating, faithless members of society to make room for the fit. Others spoke of a "culture of poverty" in which the poor had values and lifestyles different from the rest of society, which perpetuated their poverty. On the whole, the poor usually have been blamed for their own poverty. During the Reagan administration governmental benefits have systematically been withdrawn from the poor. Even today the poor are often seen as idle indolent malingerers. The cure for poverty is thought to be to get a job and work hard. In fact a capitalist economy may itself generate and maintain poverty.

◆

Does it bother you that 25 percent of all Americans (Panel 11.2) live in houses that have inadequate heat and are poorly insulated, have no indoor plumbing, are infested with rats, roaches, and other vermin, often sleep two to three people in a single bed and have eight to ten people for one toilet, or are badly in need of repair (some even live in cardboard boxes on the wintery streets of New York City)? Yet in Houston, Texas, (Panel 11.3) other people actually pay $3,000 for *one night* in the Celestial Suite of the Astro Village Hotel, complete with a twelve-seat jacuzzi bath, a shower for six, and even a small baseball field! One could conclude that something is wrong in a society with such economic contrasts.[1]

We continue in this chapter to look at social problems arising from social class differences. Like power inequality, economic inequality is also primarily an institutional social problem and, as such, requires a somewhat different level of social explanation than the more subinstitutional social problems considered earlier in this text. That is, problems of economic inequality tend to arise from the social interaction of corporate actors, involve complex social relations, large groups, indirect exchanges, are couched in formal rules, reflect a highly specialized division of labor, are impersonal, have longer spans of control, shorter exchanges, and use generalized reinforcers (like money—see Table 10.4).

Usually, social class is said to be determined by wealth, power, and prestige. Of those perhaps power is the most crucial, since it can be, and usually is, translated into income or wealth inequality (although obviously, sometimes great wealth leads to power). Esteem or prestige is fairly easy to give or get, since it is not a very scarce resource—although given the lack of praise most of us experience routinely, you might easily doubt this! Still, income, or wealth inequality, is also important because our economic condition determines both the quality and even the length of our lives.

In considering economic inequality there are several basic issues we must

PANEL 11.1

Super-Rich Americans Pay No U.S. Income Tax

A handful of America's super-rich—229 couples and individuals with incomes totaling $149 million—paid no federal income tax in 1982. They claimed enough deductions, credits, and investment losses to wipe out their U.S. tax liability, although 146 of the 229 paid a total of $23.5 million to foreign governments. The 229 were among 207,291 couples and individuals with incomes above $200,000 who filed U.S. tax returns for 1982. The 229 paying no U.S. tax compared with 304 in the previous year and 114 in 1979, the Internal Revenue Service said.

The latest of the IRS reports on taxpaying habits of high-income Americans is for income earned in 1982 and reported on returns filed in 1983. The IRS said 207,291 couples and individuals reported incomes above $200,000 in 1982, up 18 percent from 1981 and up 70 percent from 1979.

On the other hand, 153 of the high earners paid no income tax to either the United States or any other country. Of 64 of the returns, the deduction for casualty and theft losses was the largest tax-saving item. In fact, one of every ten high-income returns reported a casualty or theft loss, an average of $4,366 per return. That trend prompted Congress in 1982 to restrict severely such deductions.

Source: Associated Press, January 10, 1985.

PANEL 11.2

Facts about Wealth and Poverty

In 1982, 229 people with incomes over $200,000 paid no federal income tax.

Only about 1 percent of the people on welfare are unemployed males.

Eighteen percent of all children in America live in poverty.

Only about 150 men and women are worth $100 million or more.

Thirty-three percent of a poor family's income goes for food, compared to 11 percent of a wealthy person's family income.

A realistic poverty line in the USA included about thirty-four million in 1984 (14 percent of the U.S. population).

The poorest 20 percent of the nation receives .3 percent of the country's annual incomes; the richest 20 percent receives 50.2 percent.

One of every four Americans lives in substandard housing.

Seventy million people a year worldwide are starving.

Source: From various *Statistical Abstracts of the United States* and studies considered in the present textbook.

PANEL 11.3

Contrasts—Rich versus Poor

One does not have to be a Rockefeller to live luxuriously; however, there are enough super-rich people to fill luxury condominiums like Olympic Towers on New York's Fifth Avenue, which has its own indoor block-long park, a three-story waterfall, two floors of shops, a private wine cellar, and a health club, among other amenities. When it opened in 1979, a nine-room duplex with wood-burning fireplace, circular staircase, private elevator, and sauna cost $750,000, plus a monthly maintenance fee of $1,000. Only 8 percent of the building's 230 apartments were financed; the remaining 92 percent were paid for in cash.

The luxurious surroundings of the wealthy are not limited to their homes. When they travel, they can stay at plush establishments like Astro Village Hotel in Houston. If they like, they may stay in the Celestial Suite for a mere $3,000 a night (coffee not included), where they can enjoy a twelve-seat Jacuzzi bathtub, a shower with a room for six, a mini-Astrodome rumpus room, complete with a small-scale baseball diamond and electronic scoreboard.

Gladys Miller says her after-tax Wildcat check is $83, and she gets $60 a month in food stamps. Her monthly rent is $150. "They clip me, I clip them," Gladys says of the welfare bureaucracy. "I go in and tell them I didn't receive my food stamps, even though I did." As a former heroin addict, Gladys is also enrolled in a methadone-maintenance program. Since she no longer needs either drug, she says, she sells her methadone doses for $120 a week.

Source: J. Julian and W. Kornblum, *Social Problems,* 4th ed., © 1983 p. 235–236. Reprinted by permission of Prentice-Hall, Inc., Englewood Cliffs, New Jersey.

raise. Obviously, some of these issues overlap with one another and not all of them can be addressed or resolved in this chapter. First, should America have a socialist or capitalist economy? This turns out not to be a simple question with an obvious answer, even with our current clearly capitalist economy in the USA. Accordingly, we shall devote the next rather lengthy section to examining this issue. For now suffice it to say that various socialist economists and social scientists like Karl Marx (1906) and John Kenneth Galbraith (1976) have argued forcefully for collective governmental solutions to problems of economic inequality, while more conservative capitalist economists like Milton Freidman (1962) and George Gilder (1981:4, 26, 38) counter that a vital economy needs individual entrepreneurs, taking risks, and working hard, unfettered by excessive governmental controls. Gilder goes so far as to claim that socialism is dead, in large part because the masses cannot be creative.

Second, is economic inequality good or bad? As we saw in Chapter 10, Davis and Moore maintained that social inequality in general is both necessary and inevitable (cf. Hurst, 1979). The so-called trickle-down theory claims that if elites or corporations are affluent, then everyone under them eventually will tend to benefit economically (Turner and Starnes, 1976). Furthermore, if the poor do not survive, perhaps that is the economy's way of purging society of the relatively "unfit" (Barnet, 1985). Yet, Marx believed that the poor were less well off because of the exploitation by capitalist elites (cf. Ryan, 1981). That is, the poor are not to blame for their poverty. Poverty is a structural problem. The capitalist view of poverty seems hard-hearted at best. But remember that equality (i.e., fairness) need not imply equal income.

Third, how central is economic inequality to other social problems? Of course, social scientists like Marx (1906), Eitzen (1986), Skolnick and Currie (1985), and others would answer, "very." For Marx, economic differentiation was *the* central social factor, a factor that conditioned all other life experiences. This is especially true if by economic inequality we mean wealth. Most wealthy people do not get their great economic advantages from salaries, but rather from stocks, bonds, and other property—much of which is inherited (Wonnacott and Wonnacott, 1982:770; Gilder, 1981:Ch. 5). *Income* means cash and enabled leisure and is not nearly as important in determining economic inequality as wealth.

Fourth, how should the nation's resources be distributed? As we have seen and will continue to see below, a very small number of individuals and corporations control a very large proportion of America's financial resources. For example, the richest 1 percent of Americans have 25 percent of the nation's income. The richest 20 percent have about 50 percent of the income (see Table 11.1; Wonnacott and Wonnacott, 1982:772). In a celebrated quote, economist Paul Samuelson writes (Blumberg, 1980:34): "If we made an income pyramid out of child's blocks with each layer portraying $1,000 of income, the peak would be far higher than the Eiffel Tower, but almost all of us would be within a yard of the ground." At present the federal government redistributes about one-third of this "naturally" occurring economic inequality in the United States through social security, welfare, taxes, and so on (Wonnacott and Wonnacott, 1982:773).[2] Is this redistribution desirable, and if so, how extensively should the government intervene? Some scholars claim that the less government intervention, the more productive the economy (see Gilder, 1981:44).

Fifth, what about the special problems of work and unemployment? Subquestions here will include: Who are the unemployed? For example, the Census Bureau claims (1983) that only about 13 percent of the unemployed could have worked, even if they had wanted to. What is the unique history of the work ethic in the United States? Are there enough jobs (a structural consideration) for those who want them and are qualified to fill them? What major changes have we witnessed recently in work and unemployment? One striking development is that while in 1940 only 14 percent of all wives worked, in 1979 the proportion had risen to 50 percent (Blumberg, 1980).

Sixth, what are the sources of poverty and is poverty all that undesirable? Of course, poverty is a fundamental issue and we must go to some lengths to define it carefully and measure its prevalence. Depending on one's criteria for poverty, estimates of the number of American poor range from 10 percent to as high as 30 percent of the American population. Harrington argued (in 1963; cf. Table 11.4), that 25 percent of Americans were living in poverty. The poor are especially likely to be single and divorced, female, very young or very old, and blacks and Hispanics (*Statistical Abstract of the United States,* 1987:442ff.). While many maintain that poverty is created by capitalistic exploitation of lower-status workers (Marx), others believe that there is a "culture of poverty," that propagates poverty somewhat apart from prevailing economic conditions (Lewis, 1966). More will be said about this later.

Seventh, is welfare a wise policy or should we have more "workfare"? Welfare encompasses all the government subsidies to the poor, disabled, infirm, and so on. Included in welfare would be social security, aid for dependent children (AFDC), housing supports, unemployment insurance, food stamps, medicaid, health care, and so on. One estimate is that forty-three cents of every federal dollar goes into one form of welfare or another (Greider, 1981). However, the Reagan administration has made big cuts in welfare spending (see *Newsweek,* January 4, 1982) and has argued that welfare discourages potential workers from getting a job (Bethell, 1980). Some have claimed that those on federal support (including employed government workers) should work for their money (thus the concept of workfare). Typically, capitalists contend that we must supply (e.g., work) to be given (paid) (Gilder, 1981:124ff.). Yet others point out that there are many government subsidies to the rich (what we will call wealthfare or corporate welfare; see *New York Times,* May 6, 1976).

Eighth, how can be cope more effectively with inflation and stagflation? Until recently (circa 1985), inflation (a rise in the average level of prices) has been a (if not *the*) major American economic problem (Thurow, 1980). In 1980 the inflation rate was 12.4 percent. High interest rates kill or retard economic development and investment. For the lower social classes and people on fixed incomes their very physical survival is at stake. With stagflation there is high inflation, high unemployment, and slow growth (Wonnacott and Wonnacott, 1982). Of course, this means that certain groups of people are even less able to manage inflation.

Finally, would more effective taxation resolve most economic inequality? Many want the rich more heavily taxed (Kinsley, 1985) to provide more economic equality (as indeed they have been by federal tax law changes starting in 1987).[3] In fact, taxation is the least effective means of income redistribution (Wonnacott and Wonnacott, 1982:773). Apparently the Reagan administration does not believe that income tax redistribution is the solution to the problem of economic inequality, since in 1981 the top income tax bracket was reduced from 70 percent to 50 percent. By 1987 this was further reduced to 33.5 percent and in 1988 the top-income groups will pay a flat 28 percent. Of course, theoretically at least, many deductions for the more affluent have been reduced as well.

To be better able to resolve these basic issues we must be clear about our

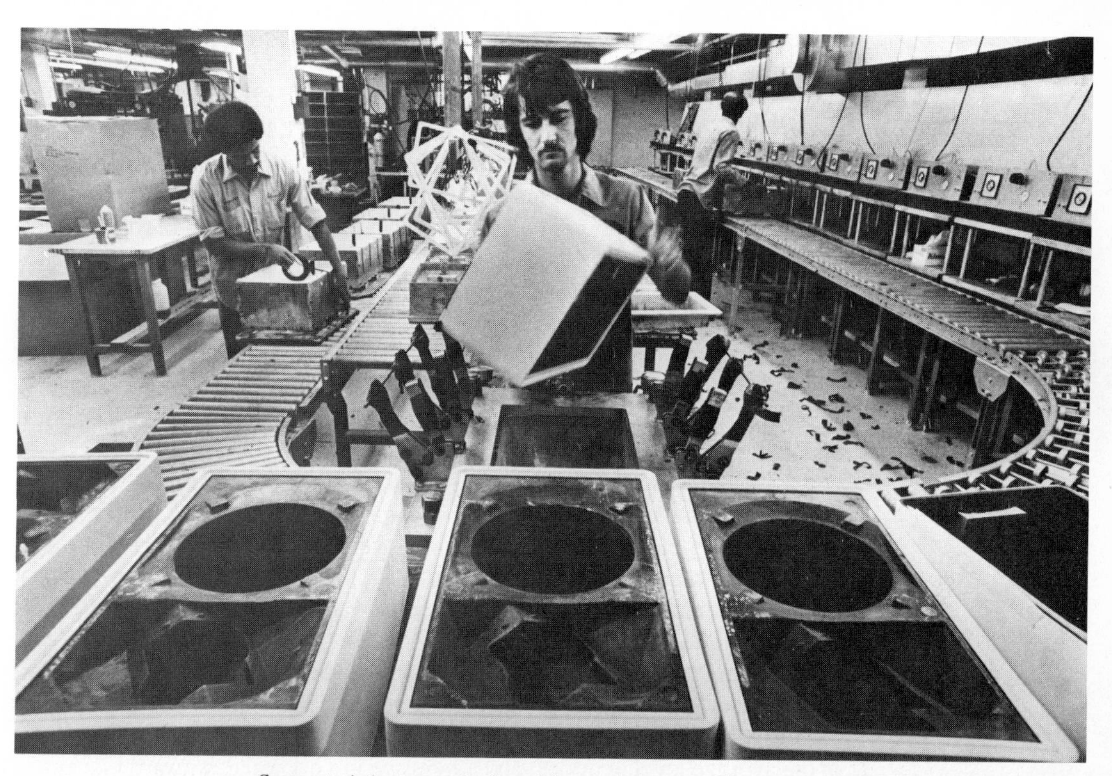

Corporate industry needs cheap labor, at least until robotics are perfected. Thus, manufacturing helps to maintain poverty, economic inequality, and blue-collar workers. However, particular individuals are not very important to industry. Here workers in Massachusetts assemble stereos. (Peter Southwick/Stock, Boston)

key terms. For example, how is economic inequality to be defined? Is it one thing or many? For our purposes there are at least three separate concepts of economic inequality. Economic inequality can be absolute, proportionate, or relative. Consider income differences. While it may be useful to know that person or group X makes $1,000 a year more income than person or group Y *(absolute inequality),* clearly this $1,000 difference is more significant if the comparison is $5,000 versus $6,000 than if it is $50,000 versus $51,000 *(relative inequality).* Thus, even though we sometimes speak of the proportion of all wealth owned by the richest 1 percent of the population *(proportionate inequality),* it is perhaps most useful to conceive of inequality as relative inequality.[4]

One measure of the concept of relative inequality is commonly known as the *Gini index* or *coefficient* (Blau, 1977:58; cf. Mayhew and Schollaert, 1980). Consider the situation depicted in Table 11.1. If 1 percent of the population has 1 percent of the wealth (or income), 50 percent has 50 percent, and 100 percent has 100 percent, wealth would be distributed equally and the Gini coefficient would have a value of zero. But if one person or a very small number of elites has all of the wealth, the Gini coefficient approaches a value of one and wealth is very unequally distributed (in Table 11.1 the highest 20 percent of the population has 50.2 percent of the total income, and so on, and the Gini coefficient is 0.48).[5-6] Gini compares the differences between actual or observed distribution of wealth (which almost always is *un*equal) with a predicted equal distribution.

We should be familiar with several other concepts. Among them are economy, poverty, wealth, gross national product, inflation, and recession. Some of these concepts (e.g., poverty) will be defined very carefully in later sections of this chapter. By *economy* we mean the allocation of scarce resources to satisfy human wants, or that complex social system that manages, develops, and distributes goods and services and rewards people for their goods and services (Wonnacott and Wonnacott, 1982:827). People are *poor* when they have inadequate income to buy the necessities of life. *Wealth,* on the other hand, includes income (both cash and leisure), savings, investments, stocks, bonds, inheritances, and properties, usually in very large amounts, such that the wealthy obviously do not have to worry about the necessities of life; in some cases they do not even have to work.

The *gross national product (GNP)* is the total consumption expenditures, plus government purchases of goods and services, plus gross private domestic investments, plus net exports of goods and services. *Inflation* is simply a rise in the average level of prices, and a *recession* is a cyclical downward movement in the economy.

Before getting into details, we also need to undertake a preliminary determination of how many Americans are rich, how many are poor, and who these two groups tend to be. It turns out that there is and always has been great economic inequality in the United States. We already know from Table 11.1 that in the United States the lowest 20 percent of the population gets only .3

TABLE 11.1 Income Distribution of United States Families in 1976, before Taxes and Transfers

Income Distribution		**Cumulative Income Distribution**	
Population	**Share of Total Income**	**Population**	**Share of Total Income**
Lowest 20%	gets 0.3%	First 20%	gets 0.3%
Second 20%	gets 7.2	First 40%	gets 0.3 + 7.2 = 7.5
Third 20%	gets 16.3	First 60%	gets 7.5 + 16.3 = 23.8
Fourth 20%	gets 26.0	First 80%	gets 23.8 + 26.0 = 49.8
Highest 20%	gets 50.2	Total	gets 49.8 + 50.2 = 100.0

Source: Congressional Budget Office, *Poverty Status of Families under Alternative Definitions of Income,* June 1977, p. 24.

percent of the nation's total income, while the highest 20 percent gets 50.2 percent of the total income. In fact, the highest 1 percent of the population holds about 25 percent of America's net worth. The richest 1 percent also owns about 75 percent of all corporate stock (see Table 10.5). This top income is almost all from dividends, rents, royalties, and interest (i.e., not from salaries). Thus, it is inappropriate to ask if the rich have good jobs because most of them do not have to work at all in any usual sense of the word *work*.

Since there are more white people in the United States, of course, most of the poor are whites. However, the rates of poverty are highest among minorities (blacks, Hispanics, the very young and very old, women, and so on—see Table 11.2). For example, the median annual family income of blacks in the United States in 1984 ($15,432) was about 56 percent that of whites ($27,686). The median female income (1983) was 64 percent that of males and

TABLE 11.2 Money Income of Families—Median Family Income in Current and Constant (1982) Dollars, by Race and Spanish Origin of Householder: 1950–1982

	Median Income In Current Dollars				Median Income In Constant (1982) Dollars				Annual Percent Change of Median Income of All Families	
Year	All Families[a]	White	Black	Spanish Origin[b]	All Families[a]	White	Black	Spanish Origin[b]	Current Dollars	Constant Dollars
1950	3,319	3,445	1,869[c]	(NA)	13,308	13,813	7,494[c]	(NA)	3.1[d]	.6[d]
1955	4,418	4,613	2,544[c]	(NA)	15,926	16,629	9,170[c]	(NA)	5.9	3.7
1960	5,620	5,835	3,230[c]	(NA)	18,317	19,018	10,528[c]	(NA)	4.9	2.9
1965	6,957	7,251	3,993[c]	(NA)	21,283	22,183	12,216[c]	(NA)	4.4	3.1
1970	9,867	10,236	6,279	(NA)	24,528	25,445	15,608	(NA)	7.5	2.9
1971	10,285	10,672	6,440	(NA)	24,513	25,435	15,349	(NA)	4.2	.1
1972	11,116	11,549	6,864	8,183	25,648	26,647	15,837	18,880	8.1	4.6
1973	12,051	12,595	7,269	8,715	26,175	27,357	15,789	18,929	8.4	2.1
1974	12,902	13,409	8,006	9,540	25,254	26,244	15,671	18,673	7.1	−3.5
1975	13,719	14,268	8,779	9,551	24,604	25,589	15,744	17,129	6.3	−2.6
1976	14,958	15,537	9,242	10,259	25,363	26,345	15,571	17,395	9.0	3.1
1977	16,009	16,740	9,563	11,421	25,500	26,684	15,232	18,192	7.0	.5
1978	17,640	18,368	10,879	12,566	26,099	27,176	16,096	18,592	10.2	2.3
1979[e]	19,587	20,439	11,574	14,169	26,047	27,150	15,391	18,842	11.0	− .2
1980[e]	21,023	21,904	12,674	14,716	24,626	25,658	14,846	17,238	7.3	−5.5
1981[e]	22,388	23,517	13,266	16,401	23,761	24,959	14,079	17,406	6.5	−3.5
1982[e]	23,433	24,603	13,598	15,227	23,433	24,603	13,598	16,227	4.6	−1.4

NA Not available. X Not applicable. Minus sign indicates decrease. [a]Includes other races not shown separately. [b]Persons of Spanish origin may be of any race. [c]For 1950–1965, black and other races. [d]Change from 1947. [e]Population controls based on the 1980 census.
Source: U.S. Bureau of the Census, *Current Population Reports,* 1983, series P-60, No. 140, and unpublished data.

the median income of people over sixty-five years old was 70 percent that of all American families. We shall have much more to say about the traits of the affluent and the poor later in this chapter.

Finally, we must look cursorily at the "natural history" of economics and economic inequality in the USA. Have there always been such great disparities in wealth? How do economic cycles differentially affect the rich and the poor? Figure 11.1 reveals that the economy varies considerably over time. Generally the economy peaks during wars and slumps after wars. The American economy responded positively to the cotton boom (circa 1840), the California Gold Rush (1850s), (especially) to World War II, and to oil price shocks. We also know that although the GNP has risen recently (except for 1973 and 1974), inflation has reduced everyone's buying power.

When economic cycles turn downward, the poor are hit particularly hard, losing jobs that are essential to their food, shelter, and psychological well-being. In very bad economic times everyone, rich and poor alike, suffer. As ex-United States President Harry Truman once said: "A recession is when your neighbor is out of work, a depression is when *you* are out of work." Government programs (such as welfare, insurance, income redistribution, and taxes) have reduced income inequality to some extent (Wonnacott and Wonnacott, 1982:773ff.), but considerable income and economic inequality remain and has been in evidence for some time in the United States. In the next section we shall examine the ideological and factual differences between ideal types of capitalism and socialism before turning to more detailed examinations of the American affluent and impoverished.

• Socialism versus Capitalism

Many issues of economic inequality turn out to be ideological debates about the worth, desirability, or efficiency of socialistic versus capitalistic economies. For example, unemployment and poverty rates are very low in socialist USSR, but innovation and concern for consumer preference are high in capitalist USA. Which trade-offs are we prepared to accept? Conversely, which economic characteristics are we *not* willing to compromise on? In the following pages we shall scrutinize these two basic economic options more closely, see how they differ, and try to understand why the United States has, and always has had, a basically capitalistic economy.

We say the United States has "basically" a capitalistic economy for the obvious reason that it is not entirely capitalistic. The U.S. government interferes with market supply and demand in many ways. Likewise, the USSR, the People's Republic of China, and Cuba are not purely socialistic economies either (see Eitzen, 1986:25). In fact the discussion that follows deals with what sociologist Max Weber (1947, original 1925–4, I, Chs. 12, 13, 15, ff.) called ideal types. Such ideal economic types as socialism or capitalism exist nowhere in pure form (cf. Gilder, 1981, 24ff.). All real economies are mixed economies.

FIGURE 11.1 Business Activity, 1835 to 1980

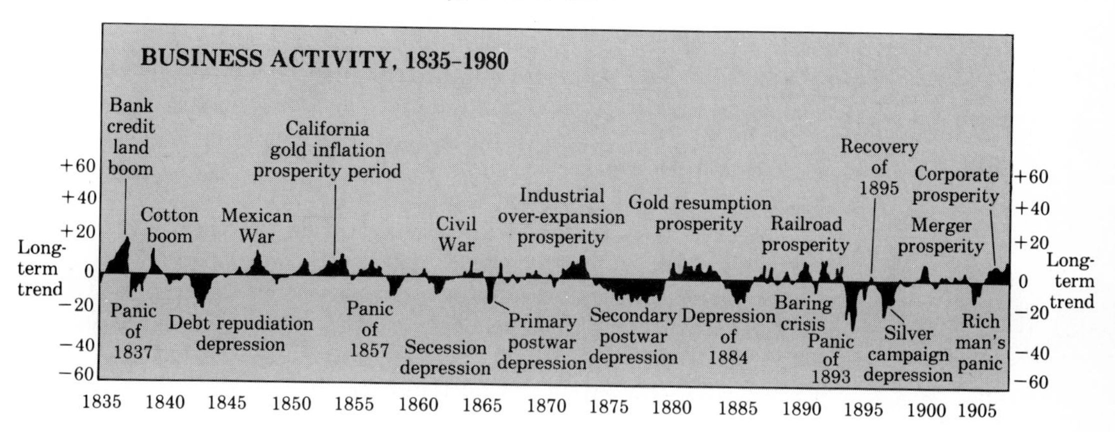

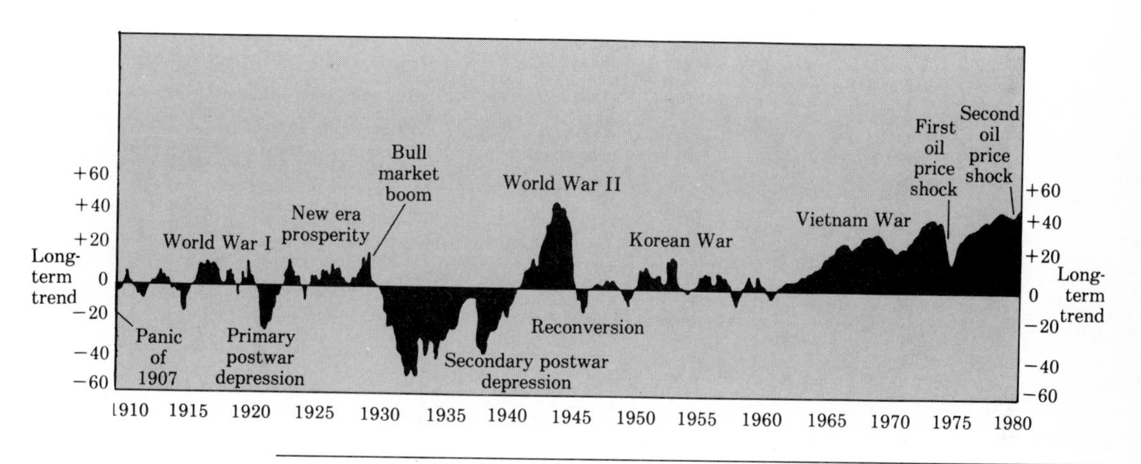

Source: Paul Wonnacott and Ronald Wonnacott, *Economics,* 1982:324–325. Courtesy, AmeriTrust Corporation, Cleveland, Ohio.

A *mixed economy* is one in which the market and the government share the decisions about what shall be produced, how, and for whom (Wonnacott and Wonnacott, 1982:44 ff.; cf. Galbraith, 1985). Thus, some of the discussion of socialism and capitalism that follows may seem somehow artificial or otherwise unconvincing to readers expecting a consideration of actual economies. We can only reply that ideal types are often very useful in understanding real empirical economic types.

Socialism and Marxism For our purposes *socialism* is an economic system in which the means of production (i.e., the capital, equipment, buildings, and land) are owned by the state (Wonnacott and Wonnacott, 1982:805; cf. Gilder, 1981:24). In most socialistic economies political power is in the hands of a political party following the doctrines of Karl Marx, as (for example) in the Soviet Union.[7] Socialism, of course, is not one thing, but has many complex connotations—as Wonnacott and Wonnacott indicate.

> *Socialism* has become an emotion-laden word that is now used loosely in a wide variety of meanings. To the campus radical, it is a tool for attacking the shortcomings of American society. To the American millionaire, it is a plot to deprive the wealthy of their hard-earned fortunes. To the Swedish politician, it means a mixed economic system, combining substantially free markets and a large degree of private ownership with a highly developed social welfare system. To Nobel prizewinner Friedrich Hayek, it represents a tragic step along "the road to serfdom." To the British Fabian socialist, it means the gradual evolution of a more humane economy, with more equal distribution of income. With such diversity on the meaning of socialism, it is little wonder people have difficulty debating its virtues and vices. (1982:805)

Since so much of the socialist economy is based on Marxist social philosophy, we need to elaborate our earlier discussion (see Chapter 10) of the general social theory of Karl Marx, with particular emphasis on the economic factor in social relations (cf. Marx, 1867; McLellan, 1973; Hook, 1955; Gilder, 1981: Ch. 3).

Marx contended that if we made a list of outstanding events in history, then we must assign the greatest weight to the "mode of economic production," that is, to the institutional rules governing production and distribution of wealth (such as slavery, feudalism, capitalism, and socialism).[8] A *social class* in Marx's terms is any aggregate of persons who perform the same function in the organization of production. Marx believed that a man's position in the production process provided his crucial life experience. This experience gained in the effort of making a living, and especially in the experience of economic conflict, would prompt members of a social class to develop common beliefs and engage in common actions.

Sooner or later, according to Marx, a point is reached in every society that is not a socialist society in which the existing economic structure hampers the full use of productive forces within it. When this happens, great masses of people suffer want and privation. Marx believed that what he called the alien-

"Enough small talk! Let's discuss money!"

Drawing by Stevenson; © 1984 *The New Yorker* Magazine, Inc.

ation of labor was inherent in capitalism and that it was a major deprivation, which would eventually lead to the proletarian (worker) revolution (Hook, 1955:25). He writes:

> Within the capitalistic system all methods for raising the social productiveness of labor are bought at the cost of the individual laborer . . .. It follows therefore that in proportion as capital accumulates, the lot of the laborer, be his payments high or low, must grow worse . . .. Accumulation of wealth at one end of the pole is, therefore, at the same time accumulation of agony of toil, slavery, ignorance, brutality, and mental degradation, at the opposite pole. (Marx and Engels, 1848)

In another place Marx asks:

> What is a working day? What is the length of time during which capital may consume the labour-power whose daily value it buys? How far may the working day be extended beyond the working time necessary for the reproduction of labour-power itself? It has been seen that to these questions

> capital replies: the working day contains the full 24 hours, with the deduction of the few hours of repose without which labour-power absolutely refuses its services again. Hence it is self-evident that the labourer is nothing else, his whole life through, than labour-power, that therefore all his disposable time is by nature and law labour-time, to be devoted to the self-expansion of capital. (There is no) time for education, for intellectual development, for the fulfilling of social functions and for social intercourse, for the free-play of his bodily and mental activity, even (for) the rest time of Sunday (and that in a country of Sabbatarians!). But in its blind unrestrainable passion, its were-wolf hunger for surplus-labour, capital oversteps not only the moral, but even the merely physical maximum bounds of the working day. (1867:290ff.)*

Marx argued that the classless society resulting from the proletarian revolution would be characterized by a higher standard of living, by greater political and cultural freedom, and by far less coercion of any kind than had been attained in all previous societies.

Capitalism Contrasted with the socioeconomic philosophy of Karl Marx and socialism is the laissez-faire (free-enterprise) capitalistic economies of Adam Smith (1937-original 1776; see Panel 11.4), Milton Freidman (1962), U.S. President Ronald Reagan (1980–1988; Reaganomics), George Gilder (1981), and others (see *Dollars & Sense,* 1986). We shall define *capitalism* as a system in which individuals are permitted to own large amounts of capital, and decisions are made primarily in private markets, with relatively little governmental interference (Wonnacott and Wonnacott, 1982:823,44; cf. Gilder, 1981:24ff.).

All capitalists tend to believe that (1) a free and competitive market will be self-regulating (e.g., if there is a demand, it will be supplied naturally; if an enterprise or an individual is not competitive, it or s/he will [should] fail, and so on); (2) the less government, the better (we must have individual freedom and dignity); (3) property (for the most part) should be privately owned; and (4) the economic system should be oriented to a goal of maximal personal profit. Note the obvious affinity of capitalism with the rugged individual entrepreneurial ethic of Henry Ford, Commodore Vanderbilt, John D. Rockefeller, the Horatio Alger stories (like *Ragged Dick,* 1867), Ayn Rand's novels (e.g., *Fountainhead,* 1943), the Benjamin Franklin ideology (as in *Poor Richard's Almanac,* 1732–57), the Darwinian notion (see *Origin of the Species,* 1859) of survival of (only) the fittest (e.g., everyone should "get a job"; there should be little or no welfare).

Economic Control by Elites in Capitalistic Economies As we saw in Chapter 10, and reemphasize here, in a capitalist economy control is exercised not just by *any* individuals. Actually a relatively few corporate heads, generals, senators, and governors direct most of the U.S. economy. In a deceptively folksy commercial for Texaco Oil Company comedian Bob Hope (himself a

*From Karl Marx, *Capital: A Critique of Political Economy,* Vol. 1 (translated by Ben Fowkes)

PANEL 11.4

Adam Smith and Classical Economics

Modern economics is often dated from 1776, the year that Adam Smith published his *Inquiry into the Nature and Causes of the Wealth of Nations.* In the same year, the Declaration of Independence was signed in Philadelphia. The timing was not entirely a coincidence. The Declaration of Independence proclaimed the freedom of the American colonies from British rule. The *Wealth of Nations* put forth the doctrine of economic freedom.

In his book, Smith argued for economic liberalism—that is, free enterprise within a country and free trade among countries. The government should interfere less in the market place; it should leave people alone to pursue their own self-interest. Smith believed that there is an "invisible hand" that causes the producer to promote the interests of society. Indeed, "by pursuing his own interest he frequently promotes that of society more effectually than when he really intends to promote it." [In advocating laissez faire (French for "leave it alone"), Smith did however recognize that government intervention might be desirable in some circumstances; for example, when the nation's defense is at stake.]

Smith was born in 1723, soon after his father died, in the small Scottish seaport of Kirkaldy, where some of the townsfolk still used nails as money. It is said that when he was 4, he was carried off by gypsies, who later abandoned him. One biographer comments: "He would have made, I fear, a poor gypsy."

He remained a bachelor throughout his life. "I am a beau in nothing but my books" was the way he described his lack of appeal for the opposite sex. He suffered from severe absentmindedness. One biographer describes how Smith, the most illustrious citizen of Edinburgh, would stroll its streets "with his eyes fixed on infinity and his lips moving in silent discourse. Every pace or two he would hesitate as if to change his direction, or even reverse it." In his mannerisms he may have been awkward, but when he picked up a pen, he became a giant; he was one of the foremost philosophers of his age.

His writing caught the eye of Charles Townshend, an amateur economist of great wit but little common sense. (As British Chancellor of the Exchequer, he was responsible for the tea tax that brought on the American Revolution.) When Townshend offered Smith the lucrative job of tutoring his ward, Smith accepted and spent four years in Switzerland and France, where he met Voltaire and other leading French philosophers. When the brother of his ward was murdered on a French street, Smith returned to Britain. There, thanks to a pension provided by Townshend, he completed *The Wealth of Nations.*

This was his second and last book. He went into semiretirement, occasionally revising his books and beginning two new ones. But he wrote that "the indolence of old age, tho' I struggle violently against it, I feel coming fast upon me, and whether I shall ever be able to finish either is extremely uncertain." He lost the struggle, dying at the age of 67—but not before he had his two unfinished works burned.

centimillionaire) quips: "Who owns Texaco?" Answer—"*You* do!" This remark is followed by cameo pictures of some ordinary looking smiling shareholders (including some toddlers, a few geriatric individuals, and so on). In fact although the United States is supposedly democratic, it is run by an economic elite. Two hundred of the largest American corporations (e.g., Xerox, IBM, ITT, GM, Ford, Goodyear, GE, Philip-Morris, Procter & Gamble, Alcoa) own over 60 percent of all industrial assets of American industry (see Table 10.3).

Other facts about who owns America include (most from Zeitlin, 1978) (1) 1 percent of the population holds 25 percent of the net worth of the society; (2) 5 percent of the Americans with the highest incomes take in about 50 percent of that income from property; (3) (in 1985) the median net worth of families was $27,735; and (4) in the top-income brackets almost all income is from dividends, rents, royalties, and interest. Clearly, in a predominantly capitalistic society economic control is in the hands of a relatively few very wealthy individuals and corporations.

Corporate Socialism (Wealthfare) At the same time welfare has been withdrawn from the poor, the aged, and minorities by the Reagan administration, it has actually been increased to the wealthy. These subsidies have been called *wealthfare* by the *New York Times* (May 1976). Let us attempt to cite some of the federal programs that in effect are welfare to corporations and wealthy individuals (and thus are a kind of corporate socialism, if you will). First, in recent years military spending has been increased, even though essential social services are not being provided and even though the USA already has 100 times more nuclear force than is needed to kill any potential enemy.[9] In 1985 the U.S. government spent $1,181 for every American on military activities (i.e., $280.7 billion ÷ 237.5 million population).

Second, in the industrial arena, the first 22 percent of income from gas and oil is tax exempt (the oil/depletion allowance). Drilling expenses are tax deductible (some of these deductions have changed recently). Foreign investments of multinational corporations lose potential taxes (and jobs) for the United States. Increasingly, products are made in countries where labor is cheap and where better tax concessions to industry are offered, such as Taiwan or Hong Kong.

Third, when we look at banking subsidies we notice that federal and state funds are deposited in certain banks and not in others at little or no interest. Of course, those funds in turn increase the total worth and capital of the favored banks. In effect this money can then be loaned to customers by the banks for sizable interest charges.

Finally, for those increasingly privileged few who can afford to own a private home, interest on their home mortgages is tax deductible (and the value of their house appreciates faster than almost any other single investment). Owning a private residence gives the average American roughly a $3,000 to $5,000 federal tax deduction each year, a deduction that renters and the unpropertied obviously do not have. These examples could be multiplied, but the reader already gets the point. To many there is a certain irony in withdrawing federal aid from the truly needy, only to increase it to those who have long ago had their basic needs met.

Is True Socialism Possible or Practical? As it turns out, most Marxist countries (like Russia, Cuba, or China) may not have truly socialist economies (nor is the United States truly capitalistic), since they are not democratic (but rather are autocratic). Central committees usually make decisions for the masses and often repress individual freedoms. This raises the intriguing question of whether a socialist economy is merely utopian, an unobtainable romantic ideal.[10] For example, could all of the people really run any sizable country? Obviously not. What then would be the mechanics of polling the people—especially to make pressing immediate decisions? There are not any; thus, elected representatives of the people are needed (and the abuse of power of these elected elites is not far behind).

Would not pure democracy ensure governance at the lowest common denominator? We tend to elect representatives who best reflect everyone else, but in fact usually have little individual excellence. Elected officials espouse what Galbraith (1976) called the conventional wisdom. Then what about Davis and Moore's argument (in Chapter 10) of the need for experts and skilled leaders? Are all people really basically the same in talent, beauty, strength, intelligence, drive, and so on? Again, obviously not (although social inequality may also disguise who is talented, bright, and so on). In fact, every society throughout human history has been socially differentiated and has had social inequality. If people are different, rewards and values will also tend to be different. In the next section we shall see that the very rich are indeed different from most of the rest of us in many ways. Often poverty and economic inequality become especially problematic because of the comparisons the poor (encouraged by the mass media—for example, in the popular television series, "Lifestyles of the Rich and Famous") make to the super-rich and the relative deprivation they may feel in making these comparisons.

• The Affluence of the Super-Rich

> Let met tell you about the very rich. They are different from you and me. They possess and enjoy early, and it does something to them, makes them soft where we are hard, and cynical where we are trustful, in a way that, unless you were born rich, it is difficult to understand. They think, deep down in their hearts, that they are better than we are because we had to discover the compensations and refuges of life for ourselves. Even when they enter into our world or sink below us, they still think that they are better than we are. They are different. (F. Scott Fitzgerald, 1926)*

*F. Scott Fitzgerald, excerpted from *All the Sad Young Men.* Copyright 1926 Charles Scribner's Sons; copyright renewed 1954 Frances Scott Fitzgerald Lanahan. Reprinted with permission of Charles Scribner's Sons, a division of Macmillan, Inc.

"On impulse, Hotchkiss bought himself a pair of jeans today, but he doesn't really understand them."

Drawing by Stan Hunt; © 1983 *The New Yorker* Magazine, Inc.

There is a world out there that most of us do not even know exists and will never experience. It is a world of power and privilege inhabited only by the very rich. A two-hour CBS television special (March 20, 1985) on the rich and famous provided a glimpse of how the wealthy are indeed different from you and me. When was the last time you took an ocean voyage on the *Royal Viking* (for one) for $54,000? Do you have your own private Amtrak railroad car? You can for only $300,000 (1985). If you travel coast-to-coast then, of course, you want to be booked on Regent Air, a wholly first-class airline on which you can have your hair styled while giving dictation to a stenographer. If you wish to stay in the best hotels in the world, then you will have to travel east. The Shangri-La in Singapore has two staff members for each guest. At the Imperial in Tokyo dinner is $500 (no tipping allowed). Or you may choose the Mandarin in Hong Kong. These are among the top three or four hotels in the world according to CBS.

Closer to home CBS recommends the Ritz-Carlton in New York City, Atlanta, or Chicago (the Chicago Ritz has its own fleet of Rolls-Royce automobiles), the Four Seasons in Washington, D.C., Copley Plaza in Boston, the Fairmont in San Francisco, the Beverly Wilshire in Los Angeles, and (if you grow tired of the New York Ritz) the Pierre in New York City.

When you travel, Portofino, Italy, is *the* place to be (says CBS). For only $80,000 you can spend the ski season at Gstaad, Switzerland. Back home, the Greenhouse Spa in Dallas, Texas, can rejuvenate your weary body. Of course, for the summer months, there are the standard vacation beaches of the rich at the Hamptons in New York, Martha's Vineyard in Massachusetts, Malibu, California, and Bermuda.[11]

It is slightly curious that social problems textbooks are much more interested in poverty than in wealth. Of course, poverty is more common and, obviously, more problematic than affluence—although one could make a sound argument that being wealthy is problematic too (both for wealthy individuals and for society). Be that as it may, in fact we know relatively little about the very wealthy.[12]

For example, when is one truly wealthy or rich? How much money, property, stocks, and so on must we have to be affluent? One crude frequently used indicator of wealth is being in the upper 1 percent of the national income distribution, the economic elite. In 1922 the top 1 percent controlled 31.6 percent of all wealth in the United States (interestingly, by 1972 this percentage shrank to 20.7 percent, *Statistical Abstract of the United States,* 1984:Table 794). As we recall from the introductory pages of this chapter, wealth is defined as the total of cash received, leisure time, savings, investments, stocks, bonds, inheritances, and properties in large amounts. Typically the wealthy are those who have inherited much of their fortune (Brittain, 1978; cf. Taylor, 1987),[13] and a few business and property owners, top corporate executives, top managers, and some professionals. The wealthy in the United States are typically male (cf. Tickamyer, 1981), Protestant, white, and older. On a more abstract level we can define *wealth* as "assets that promise a future stream of income" (Gilder, 1981:48).

But we beg the question. How much money or wealth must a person have to be considered rich? Obviously, there is no simple answer to this question, since wealth is a complex concept—often with subjective components. We do know that recently only about 150 men and women in the United States are worth $100 million (centimillionaires) or more (cf. Panel 11.5). In 1982 there were about 407,000 millionaires in the United States, mostly men (*Statistical Abstract of the United States,* 1986:463).[14] In short, a relatively small number of people are truly rich and they control a disproportionately large share of America's total wealth. For example, we saw in Table 11.1 that the highest 20 percent of the income distribution gets about 50 percent of the nation's total income (in 1976). Of those who receive salaried incomes and are wealthy, again a small number of jobs command top dollars. To illustrate, according to *Business Week* (May 11, 1981), the top twenty-five executives in the United States in 1980 made between $1,455,000 and $3,330,000.

Having great wealth means you will probably live longer and better, can

The richest 1 percent of the U.S. population controls about 20 (to 25) percent of the country's total wealth. In contrast the poorest 20 percent receive only .3 percent of American annual income. Does this seem just? (AP/Wide World Photos)

afford the best medical care, the finest education, enjoy the best materials and workmanship in your possessions, and can even influence public policy to your own advantage. If you are extremely wealthy chances are you will not even have to work *at all* in any ordinary sense of work. I have a friend in Chestnut Hill, Massachusetts, who is actually looked down on by her wealthy neighbors because her husband is a physician and has to work for a living (and be on call, at that). For the very wealthy salaries are less important, since most of their income comes from inheritance, interest, dividends, rents, and properties. Thus, trying to impress someone with your high salary is to misunderstand that the powerful and prestigious (for the most part) do not have any jobs.

Wealth is not equivalent to high status or culture in the vulgar sense. Nevertheless, great wealth does tend to breed cosmopolitan attitudes, make foreign travel more likely, provide better educational opportunities, help cultivate exotic tastes in foods and fashions, and put a higher premium on leisure activities. Of course being wealthy paradoxically allows you to keep more of

PANEL 11.5

America's Richest 400 Worth $125 Billion

Gordon P. Getty, son of oil magnate Jean Paul Getty, is the richest man in America and one of a dozen billionaires in the nation, *Forbes* magazine said Monday.

Yoko Ono was further down the list, and Michael Jackson was called an "up-and-comer."

In its annual list of the "400 richest people in America," *Forbes* said Getty, a fifty-year-old patron of the arts, is the wealthiest American even though his fortune is in the Sarah C. Getty Trust, which received $4.1 billion when Getty Oil was sold to Texaco.

The 400 richest Americans have a net worth of $125 billion, *Forbes* said, compared to the $126 billion that all individual Americans have managed to accumulate [illegible] accounts in U.S. commercial ba[illegible]

The magazine said 74 of its 4[illegible] Americans have fortunes derived principally from oil and gas, and 71 made their money mainly in real estate. Another 95 have fortunes derived from manufacturing.

Yoko Ono, widow of ex-Beatle John Lennon, is listed among the 400 richest Americans, with more than $950 million. *Forbes* classified singer Michael Jackson as an up-and-comer, and estimated his personal fortune at "just under $70 million and counting."

Source: United Press International, New York, September 18, 1984. Reprinted with permission of United Press International, Copyright 1984.

your wealth too. For example, there are many tax deductions (shelters) for the very rich (Kaiser, 1985). Social security tax stops after a certain level of income in a given year ($43,800 in 1987). Thus, social security tax amounts to a much smaller percentage of one's total income for the wealthy than for the middle and lower income groups. Of course, all of these advantages for the super-rich tend to arouse hostility, envy, curiosity, and perplexity toward the wealthy (cf. Gilder, 1981:59 and Ch. 9). Why should a small number of wealthy elites live so well while millions of others barely survive or fail to make it at all? Indeed this perceived relative deprivation of the poor vis-à-vis the super-rich may be one of the major problems of being poor in the USA. That is, in addition to being denied basic life necessities, there is also a feeling of distributive injustice. In the next section we consider less economically fortunate individuals, those who do work or at least try to (and are often unemployed or underemployed), but who receive less than they need to meet their basic life necessities—the American poor.

• Work, Unemployment, and the Social Consequences of Poverty

Stating the Problem Of course, many more Americans are poor, out of work, or underemployed than are eating caviar on leisurely $54,000 ocean cruises.[15] This has always been one of the great American ironies, indeed embarrassments, in our capitalist land of opportunity—that in fact so few hard-working bright people who did not already have wealthy families ever make it big economically. Potentially poverty is a very explosive social problem, since large numbers of hungry, poorly housed, out of work, unhealthy people in the midst of affluence seems unjustifiable, if not downright intolerable (especially to the poor themselves). It is to those issues, their prevalence, causes, and explanations, that we must now turn.

Work in America One of the first questions asked when you meet someone is "What do you do"? If the answer is nothing, we immediately feel distinctly uncomfortable with the person—especially if s/he is middle-aged. Obviously, work (secular occupational achievement or paid employment) is one of the most fundamental of American values (Williams, 1951:390; Skolnick and Currie, 1985:VIII; Maris, 1981:136ff.). Work is highly related to our social status and income levels. As Edwards noted forty to fifty years ago (forgive his sexist language), occupation tells us a great deal about one's education, income, and prestige.[16]

> The most nearly dominant single influence in a man's life is probably his occupation. More than anything else, perhaps, a man's occupation determines his course and his contribution to life. And, when life's span is ended, quite likely there is no single set of facts that will tell the kind of man he was and the part he played in life as will a detailed chronological statement of his occupation, or occupations, he pursued. Indeed there is no other single characteristic that tells so much about a man and his status—social, intellectual and economic—as does his occupation. (Edwards, 1940:xi)

Thus, not only do our jobs provide us with an income, they also do much more, for example, regulate our life activities, provide identification, association, and meaningful life experiences (Leontieff, 1985). For several excellent first-person accounts of the subjective meanings of work see *Working* (Terkel, 1974). When most workers are asked what they would do if they suddenly became wealthy (e.g., by winning a state lottery), about 80 percent replied that they would keep working (Weiss, Harwood, and Reisman, 1976; *Public Opinion 4,* August/September, 1981:21–40).

However, this does not mean that workers would necessarily continue in their same jobs. People in jobs with high autonomy (such as professors, scientists, and lawyers) tend to be relatively satisfied with their present jobs. But most blue-collar work is closely supervised, repetitious, and mindless. Not surprisingly then a 1973 HEW survey found that only 24 percent of blue-collar workers said they would choose similar work if they had a chance to start over (however, see Form, 1973; cf. Rozak, 1979). Generally, jobs with high autonomy and greater diversity of tasks are related to increased productivity and morale.

Since 1960 there have been major shifts in who works and in which jobs. For example, in 1960, 83 percent of men and 38 percent of women over age sixteen worked. By June of 1984 those percentages had shifted dramatically, with 71 percent of the men but 49.6 percent of the women now working (*Statistical Abstract of the United States,* 1986: Table 658). Between the 1960–85 time periods the labor-force unemployed jumped from 5.5 percent to 7.3 percent and those not in the labor force dropped from 41 percent to 35.3 percent. Thus, overall recently more of the population, especially more women, are working, but the unemployment rate has also risen. The increase of females in the U.S. labor force has had dramatic consequences for other social problems—such as those concerning the family, sex roles, population, crime, and so on. Industrial development initially forces women out of the labor market, but at advanced levels of development, rates of female labor-force involvement are increased (Pampel and Tanaka, 1986).

Generally there are presently more white-collar jobs (particularly for professionals, clerical workers, and managers). In 1960, 43 percent of the population was white-collar workers; in 1984, 54 percent. For blue-collar workers the percentage of jobs dropped from 37 percent (1960) to 29.7 percent (1983). The drop by 1984 was especially large for farm workers (from 8 percent to 3.4 percent—see *Statistical Abstract of the United States,* 1986: Table 680). Some observers believe that America's working force has assumed an hourglass shape, with the disappearance of many types of traditional middle-class jobs. This structural change is referred to as the shrinking middle (Currie and Skolnick, 1984:141). One result may be a kind of Marxist labor polarization, with mainly jobs for managers and a permanent underclass.

Some scholars have argued that even within blue-collar workers there is a dual-labor market (Eitzen, 1986:214; *Daedalus,* Spring 1981). For the primary core enterprises there is much capital, strong unions, high wages, and many fringe benefits. However, there are also marginal employers who pay low wages, offer few fringe benefits, hire nonskilled workers, have bad working conditions, and seek out workers who will make no demands on their employers. Of course, being satisfied or dissatisfied with your work, the kind of work you do, and so on are all very different from not having a job at all. Really crushing debilitating poverty has always been related to unemployment and unemployment rates.

Unemployment The U.S. Bureau of Labor conducts a sample survey of 65,000 American households one week out of each month of the year. The official unemployment rate is the average percent unemployment of these twelve weeklong surveys. The following types of people are counted as *unemployed:* (1) All those sixteen years old or older who had no job during the week surveyed (and tried to get one in the prior four weeks); (2) all people waiting to be called back to a job from which they had been laid off; and (3) all people waiting to report to a job within thirty days.

By this definition in June of 1985 7.3 percent of the U.S. labor force was unemployed. This unemployment rate is roughly double what it was twenty to twenty-five years earlier. Of course, the official unemployment rate is not

Who are the poor? Only about 1 percent of the unemployed poor are able-bodied males. Most are children, the elderly, women, and minorities—many of whom are unable to work and stay poor unless helped by others. (Michael Weisbrot/Stock, Boston)

the only estimate of the true prevalence of Americans out of work, nor is it clear in its meaning. For example, typically an unemployed person finds work within fifteen weeks. Those persons unemployed fifteen weeks or longer have an unemployment rate of 1 percent to 3 percent (*Fortune,* May 8, 1978). Rates for what we may call *subemployment* (after Matza and Miller, 1976:661)—namely, the unemployed plus workers employed below the poverty level (about 25 percent of workers are receiving incomes below the poverty level) plus part-time workers—are about twice the unemployment rate.

Thus, the official unemployment rate tends to underestimate unemployment. For example, part-time workers who want full-time work are not counted. Persons who desire work but are not looking for a job are not counted. If we do not take average unemployment in a given week, but count anyone who

was unemployed during the entire year, then in one year s
percent of the labor force was unemployed.

Traditionally, unemployment rates are higher for mino
Times calculated (October 13, 1975) that a 1 percent na
rate increase amounted to a 4 percent unemployment
advantaged. Black unemployment rates are generally twice white unemployment rates (in 1985, the black rate was 14 percent, compared with 6.5 percent for whites). Sixteen to nineteen-year-old black males had the highest unemployment rate of 42.7 percent (1984). Women had a rate of 7.6 percent, men a rate of 7.4 (1984). Professionals and managers had the lowest unemployment rates, about 3 percent.

While, obviously, most of the unemployed do not die or starve (there is usually unemployment insurance and eventually people find new jobs), unemployment still has far-reaching negative effects (Caplovitz, 1979; Lekachman, 1985). For example, Brenner (1977) estimated that a 1 percent increase in the unemployment rate was correlated with the following increases in human suffering:

-20,240 additional heart attack deaths.
-495 additional alcoholism deaths.
-920 additional suicides.
-648 additional homicides.
-3,340 additional admissions to state prisons.
-4,226 additional admissions to state mental hospitals.

Unemployment affects one's self-esteem, depression levels, shame, physical illness, marital problems, and promotes social isolation. The unemployed may feel alienated from society itself and thus be more likely to engage in crime and deviance. However, recent studies of collective violence and protest reveal that factors other than unemployment must be operating, since levels of public protest vary considerably even when the levels of unemployment are consistently high (Kerbo and Shaffer, 1986). In short, even if unemployment does not kill you, it can seriously color your and society's quality of life.[17]

Poverty The most common absolute definition of poverty is that used by the U.S. Social Security Administration, the so-called Orshansky definition (1969; cf. Jacobs, 1985:114). According to Orshansky *poverty* is determined by the minimum food budget multiplied by three (in part because a survey conducted by the U.S. Department of Agriculture in 1955 showed that on the average people spend about one-third of their income on food). Given this definition of poverty, Table 11.3 reveals trends in poverty in the United States since 1959. Notice that although the government's War on Poverty brought down poverty rates until about the mid-1970s, recently poverty rates have begun to creep

TABLE 11.3 Trends in Poverty, 1959–1984 (After Cash Transfers)

Year	Persons in Poverty (Millions)	Percent of Population	Poverty* Line	Median Family Income (Current Dollars)
1959	39.5	22.4	$2,973	$5,417
1966	28.5	14.7	3,317	7,500
1970	25.4	12.6	3,968	9,867
1973	23.0	11.1	4,540	12,051
1976	25.0	11.8	5,815	14,958
1979	25.2	11.6	7,412	19,587
1980	29.3	13.0	8,414	21,023
1982	34.4	15.0	9,862	23,433
1983	35.3	15.2	10,178	24,580
1984	33.7	14.4	10,609	26,433
1985	33.1	14.0	10,989	27,735

*Nonfarm family of four; Orshansky Social Security Administration Definition of poverty.

Source: U.S. Census Bureau, *Statistical Abstract of the United States, 1987,* 1986:passim.

back up again. In fact, the number of people living in poverty in 1985 (33.1 million) was about the same as in 1959 (39.5 million)—of course, there are also far more people in the United States now (cf. Panel 11.6). By the Orshansky definition, in 1985 the poverty line was $10,989 for a nonfarm family of four, putting about 14.0 percent of the American population in the poverty category.

Others (e.g., Fuchs, 1967) argue that we need a *relative* definition of *poverty.* Fuchs suggests that a meaningful definition would be any nonfarm family of four making less than half the median family income (i.e., less than $13,868 in 1985). By this somewhat higher poverty line, over 20 percent of the American population would be considered poor (cf. Table 11.4). Still another definition of poverty might be all those Americans on some form of welfare (mostly Aid for Dependent Children).

Now that we know about how many Americans are poor, we still need to determine who the poor are (Auletta, 1983). When U.S. President Reagan urges us to get tough with the unemployed poor, it is well to remind ourselves that only 1 percent to 2 percent of the poor are unemployed males. In fact, about half (49.9 percent) of the poor are children; another 12.9 percent are elderly (Panel 11.6; cf. Panel 11.2; and Harrington, 1984:85–88). Almost 50 percent of poor families are headed by females (Harrington, 1984:Ch. 8; Currie, Dunn, and Fogarty 1985). Although most of the poor are white (about 66 percent), the black poverty rate (29 percent) is higher than the white poverty rate (see Table 11.4). The poor tend to live in rural areas and urban ghettos. Finally, the poor have stayed poor; the bottom 20 percent of the population

PANEL 11.6

More Americans Living in Poverty, Census Finds

Family income in 1983 increased faster than the inflation rate for the first time in four years, the Census Bureau reported Thursday, but the number of Americans living in poverty also climbed.

The bureau's report added that wide gaps in income remain between blacks and whites and between men and women.

In its annual report on income and poverty, the Census Bureau said that the median family income in 1983 was $24,580, an increase after inflation of 1.6 percent above 1982's mark. But even with the increase, the 1983 family income was still the third lowest in 14 years, after adjustments were made for inflation.

An additional 868,000 Americans lived below the poverty level last year, the report said, raising the total of persons considered poor to 35.5 million.

The Census Bureau said the percentage of Americans living in poverty went from 15 percent in 1982 to 15.2 percent in 1983, but said the increase was not statistically meaningful.

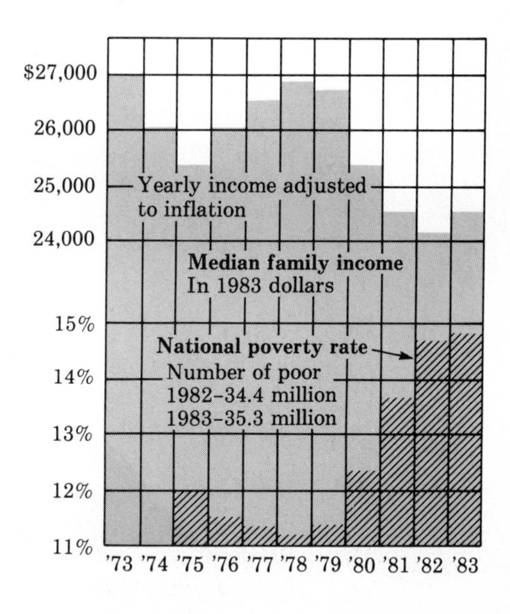

Source: Charles Green, Knight-Ridder Newspapers, July 1984.

has earned about 5 percent of the nation's income for a long time (Jacobs, 1985).

What does it mean to be poor (O'Hare, 1986; see Panel 11.7)? For openers in general, it means a shorter life expectancy, a life of less quality and more stress, poorer medical care, more child abuse, family violence and disruption, poorer housing, not having enough to eat (especially not enough protein), sending your children to less desirable schools, less justice, and a greater chance of ending up in jail or prison (Jacobs, 1985; Harrington, 1984; Currie, Dunn, and Fogarty, 1985). The poor on the average spend about 50 percent of their income on shelter (a home) and 33 percent on food; that certainly does not leave much for frills. Their homes tend to be rented (i.e., not owned),

TABLE 11.4 Total Money Income of Families, By Race, 1984 (Percent)

Income	White	Black	Spanish
Under $5,000	3.8	14.8	9.7
$5,000–$9,999	8.1	19.2	15.7
$10,000–$14,999	10.3	14.9	15.0
$15,000–$24,999	21.7	21.6	23.8
$25,000–$49,999	39.2	23.6	39.0
$50,000 and over	26.9	5.8	6.7
Total:	100.0	100.0	100.0
Median income:	$27,686	$15,432	$18,833

Source: U.S. Bureau of Census, *Statistical Abstract of the United States, 1986,* 1985: Table 751.

which means (among other things) no large deduction for federal income tax that homeowners get. When the money runs out (and it always does), it has to be borrowed at exceptionally high interest rates (Jacobs, 1985). Small wonder then that poverty is so debilitating.

Inflation Before moving on to analyze the causes of poverty and unemployment, a note is in order on the relation of inflation to economic inequality and the plight of the poor (Thurow, 1980). Of course, inflation (a rise in the average level of prices) hurts rich and poor alike. But for the poor (on fixed incomes or without income) inflation affects basic life necessities, not just discretionary purchases. This is particularly the case when the economy experiences stagflation or high inflation coupled with high unemployment and slow economic growth. The Consumer Price Index rose sharply in the 1970s (on average), but began to drop in the 1980s. Using 1959 as the base year, the highest annual percentage change was in 1980 (13.5 percent) and the lowest was in 1983 (3.5 percent). Fuel oil prices caused much of the fluctuation in prices, rising 480 percent from 1967 to 1980. We also note that in 1970 about 46 percent of the population could afford new homes, but in 1980 less than 20 percent could.

Analyzing the Problem. The Exchange Perspective In a sense the exchange problems of the poor (economic inequality, unemployment, and so on) are disguised problems of sexism, ageism, racism, and so on. That is, their salient traits are their female status, young or old age, racial minority status, and so on—not their poverty. Their poverty is a consequence of their sex, age, and race—and the social exchanges that follow from them. In general, although it sounds calloused to say so, the poor tend not to be valuable or rewarding to interact with (see Table 11.5). By definition the poor have little property or money, are relatively uneducated, and are mainly

PANEL 11.7

A Life of Poverty

Tell me something about what life was like in your family when you were growing up.

A thirty-seven-year-old woman, the second child in a family of four recalls:

It was a good family, not like a lot of others we saw. My folks cared a lot, and they were always trying. But it seems no matter how hard they tried, something went wrong, and we'd get behind. We were dirt poor most of my life. There were always money problems; sometimes there wasn't even enough food.

It seemed like every three months my father was on strike or laid off (laughing). I guess that's an exaggeration, but he really was on strike a lot. He was a laborer in construction, and he couldn't afford to be off work like that. Maybe the guys higher up got something out of the strike—you know, the carpenters and plumbers, and those workmen—but people like my dad just lost pay. They never could make it up.

Source: From *Worlds of Pain: Life in the Working-Class Family,* by Lillian Breslow Rubin.

unskilled laborers, tend to be women, very young or elderly, and racial minorities. As a group the poor tend to have socially unattractive and common traits.

For example, exchange theorists could argue that the poor tend to be physically and emotionally unhealthy, to be unclean, rigid thinking and prejudiced, local in outlook, have inadequate housing and clothing, to be religious conservatives, obese, have bad teeth, and so on (although of course one must be careful of such stereotypes). Thus, the poor tend to exchange what they have the most of, their labor—menial, physical, low-skill, dull, labor. Such labor is not a scarce commodity and just about anyone could provide it (although members of the middle and upper social classes obviously do not wish to). Thus, the poor are not paid well and the vicious cycle of poverty is perpetuated. Of course, the real issue here is whether these interactive liabilities are caused by poverty or themselves produce poverty.

We also need to remember that people satiate very slowly on generalized reinforcers like money (Homans, 1974:29). People never have enough money. If there are great economic surpluses (Lenski, 1984:44) and great power differentials, then the general rewards of money and status will be hoarded by the powerful few—producing great economic inequality. Thus, part of the explanation of economic inequality has to do with the diffuse general rewards that it offers.

Our earlier comments about the lifestyles of the rich and famous remind us

TABLE 11.5 Distribution of Basic Societal Rewards by Economic Status

	Poor	Rich
Menial, physical, domestic, service, labor	+	−
Money, property	−	+
Education	−	+
Minority status (female, young, elderly, black, Hispanic, and so on)	+	−
Health and physical attractiveness	−	+
Cosmopolitaness	−	+

\+ = Reward present or supplied.
− = Reward absent or received.

that often the poor perceive their situations as ones of great relative deprivation. That is, the poor in America may objectively enjoy much better economic conditions than even the middle classes—say in Mexico, Africa, India, and so on. However, exchange theory's fifth proposition (see Chapter 2), tells us that groups that do not get expected rewards (e.g., those of the American affluent) are especially likely to become angry and discontent. Generally, we know that one's sense of distributive justice with respect to family income is positively linked to one's material well-being satisfaction (both objectively and subjectively—Alwin, 1987). However, the relations between collective distributive justice and individual income satisfaction are complex. For example, general norms for the allocation of income of others may not be applied to one's own income (Shepelak and Alwin, 1986).

Finally, remember that the rewards and values of corporate actors and natural individuals are different (Table 10.5; Coleman, 1974). Power elites and corporations need poverty; cheap labor is valuable to them, since they are driven by a profit motive (Gans, 1972). Corporations have a vested interest in maintaining poverty. Corporately speaking, individuals can almost always be replaced. In any contest between the values of corporate actors and natural individuals, those of corporate actors almost always prevail.

The Structural-Functional Perspective You will recall from Chapter 2 that the structural-functional perspective focuses on observed objective consequences. As we have seen, from this perspective Davis and Moore offer a famous argument for economic inequality (1945; cf. Ch. 10; Hurst, 1979). They claim that certain social positions (e.g., those of physicians, lawyers, engineers, and so on) are more important to society than other positions (e.g., garbagemen) and require special aptitudes and skills, which only a few people have.

Furthermore, to convert these aptitudes into skills requires sacrifices. Thus, society must reward talented persons who undergo sacrifices and training more, especially with more income. It follows that economic inequality is inevitable.

On the negative side, most people are not gifted, have not been trained, do not have functionally important positions, and do not deserve to be affluent. Implicit in Davis and Moore's argument is that society does not really need the poor; they perform common, relatively unimportant jobs that almost anyone could and would do. Of course, Davis and Moore's position could be considered somewhat at odds with Gans's (1972) claim that the poor are useful to do society's dirty work (and create jobs for social workers). Still, the poor can have useful consequences and yet be paid little, since so many others (e.g., middle-class students) can and will do these useful cheap labor tasks.

In passing we must also observe the relatively small size of the American poor. Even at 33.7 million (1984) the poor only comprise about 14.4 percent of the U.S. population. Thus, poor-nonpoor social interactions are minimized by low heterogeneity (Blau, 1977). The poor are also low in power and education and at a disadvantage in articulating effective political protests. Physically, the poor tend to be segregated and isolated from the rich—further minimizing social interaction.

Conflict Perspective Of course, conflict theorists would argue that in all societies there have been rulers (usually rich) and the oppressed (usually poor). Conflict exists over the distribution of the scarce and valued resources in society. Those with power, property, and authority expropriate more than their fair share of profits to serve their own interests—way beyond their actual needs or labor costs (Hurst, 1979; Skolnick and Currie, 1985:Sections II and III). This structural or institutional discrimination against the poor extends to the educational system as well. Many black Americans, women, and other minorities cannot ever hope to move up the income ladder because the best jobs require a college education. Minorities lack the schools, money, and social support needed to get a college education. Industry also often fails to provide enough jobs.

The conflict perspective emphasizes that capitalism's primary objective is individual gain and profit, not collective need or social welfare. In a capitalist political economy like that in the United States, individual profit is the basic factor. This means that employers feel constrained to pay their employees as little as possible, to have a surplus of workers to lower wages, and to make decisions without regard for the economic well-being of their employees. Thus, in any capitalistic society the poor are victims (Parenti, 1978:54–55).

The Symbolic Interaction Perspective From the symbolic interaction perspective it is important to note that the meanings of poverty have changed. In the later part of the nineteenth century poverty tended to be viewed as part of God's will. Poverty was acceptable as long as those better off were charitable to the poor. Many groups of poor were seen as deserving their fate (e.g., prostitutes, beggars, idlers, and so on). Spencer (see Hofstadter, 1955) took a Darwinian view that poverty was nature's way of excreting unhealthy, imbecilic, slow, vacillating, faithless members of society to make room for the fit.

By 1966 Lewis spoke of a culture of poverty in which the poor have values and lifestyles different from the rest of society, which perpetuated their poverty (Banfield, 1974). Once again, the poor were blamed for their own poverty. Later, poverty was seen not as God's will or perpetuated by the lifestyle of the poor themselves, but rather largely as a product of big inner-city corruption. By the time of Rubin's *Worlds of Pain* (1976) (at least and probably as early as Michael Harrington's *The Other America*, [1963, cf. 1984]), it was not OK or normal to be poor (cf. Terkel's *Working* 1974:3–28, 101–118, 267–299). For example, Rubin found that working-class women had their life expectations (and frustrations) raised by the women's movement, abortion issues, E.R.A., and television lifestyles.

Symbolic interactionism stresses that how a social situation is defined and interpreted has very real consequences—often completely apart from the facts. In spite of recent definitions of the poor's situations as indefensible in the midst of affluence, many middle- and upper-class people still label the poor disreputable or deserving of their poverty (Matza and Miller, 1976). During the Reagan administration in the United States, governmental benefits have been systematically withdrawn from the poor (*Newsweek,* April 5, 1982). For example, the welfare state has been dismantled (Currie and Skolnick, 1984:141). The poor have been seen as idle indolent malingerers. The cure for poverty is to get a job and to work hard (Gilder, 1981:Ch. 6). The poor themselves may begin to see poverty as a stigma; that is, a social brand that they can never be rid of. Thus, many poor people begin to feel that their impoverished lives are hopeless and inevitable—at least in this world.

Resolving the Problem There are about a half-dozen or so basic resolutions to the problem of poverty and unemployment. First, we may simply have to accept some economic inequality. Although the amount of economic inequality varies across the type of society, there is and always has been great inequality in all societies. Since economic inequality exists in both socialist and capitalist economies, it may be inevitable and only reducible to a certain point (see Table 11.5). Having redistributed income to deal with crushing poverty, if one is still displeased, maybe the best you can hope for is that you as an individual can be upwardly mobile—can climb further out of poverty and that the prospect is there for others (Jencks, 1979).

Second, there is the resolution of supply-side economics (Gilder, 1981). From this perspective (as with that of resignation) economic inequality is good; it motivates people to work and to work hard (i.e., to compete). If we work hard, national wealth increases (e.g., the GNP rises), which then trickles down and raises everyone's lifestyles (even the poor's). The supply-side resolution

TABLE 11.6 Relative Poverty in Socialist and Capitalist Nations, 1970

	Income Share of Bottom 20 Percent	Income Share of Top 10 Percent
Socialist nations		
East Germany	10.7%	16.9%
Hungary	8.5	19.3
Capitalist nations		
France	2.3	37.2
Sweden	5.2	27.5
United Kingdom	6.6	23.9
United States	4.3	28.3
West Germany	6.1	28.6

Source: J. Shail, *Size Distribution of Income.* The World Bank, 1975.

would have us spend less on central government, cut taxes, raise national investments, and balance the federal budget. However, most of the benefits will go to the rich (deservedly).

A third resolution would be to create more jobs (see Panel 11.8 on workfare). Examples of such federal job-generating programs would be CETA (Comprehensive Employment and Training Act of 1973) and MDRC (Manpower Demonstration Research Corporation, 1980). However, CETA jobs have been criticized as bringing in wages just barely above the poverty level, almost like having no job at all. To make matters worse, in 1981 President Reagan cut 306,000 jobs in the public service sector. MDRC provided on-job training and experience to those previously regarded as unemployable (e.g., to welfare mothers, high school drop-outs, ex-addicts, and ex-criminal offenders). The only really successful groups were the welfare mothers. After nine months, 34.6 percent had a job and were off welfare.

Fourth, of course if jobs fail, there has always been the welfare resolution. With welfare the federal government (mainly) redistributes national resources and income to the poor in the form of housing subsidies, health care (medicare and medicaid), food subsidies (food stamps), job training, aid for dependent children, and unemployment insurance. Greider estimates (1981) that forty-three cents of every dollar the federal government spends goes into social security, pensions, medical assistance, and welfare. Some have criticized welfare programs. Bethell (1980) points out that in 1976 a welfare family of four received the equivalent income of $14,960 (all tax-free) and thus had little incentive to work (the so-called welfare wall).[18] Some have replied that federal programs that benefit the poor most (e.g., food stamps, Aid for Dependent Children, and medicare) are the ones that are being cut (*Newsweek,* January 4, 1982). Others (e.g., Auletta, 1983) have contended that those on welfare tend to become permanently dependent on it, a kind of parasitic underclass. If so, welfare may demoralize the poor. However, most people on welfare do

PANEL 11.8

Workfare

When Mrs. Scherer applied for food stamps in San Diego recently, she learned that the county required her to take a public service job for about twenty hours a month in return for the welfare. In a vote that foreshadowed national interest in workfare, 90 percent of the citizens of San Diego County voted that able-bodied recipients of welfare must work for their benefits. "Why not?" said Mrs. Scherer. "When you're getting something free, why not give something in return?" She helps abused and troubled children at a shelter home.

Most recipients are exempt from the workfare requirement and a good number assigned to a work site do not show up. Many have legitimate excuses, explained Sally McPherson, the project's manager, but the rest are taken off the rolls for a month. "There are two benefits to workfare," said Miss McPherson. "One is that we get the benefits of people's labor, and the other is that we reduce the food stamp rolls."

Opponents argue that workfare is punitive and does not save money, a point that Miss McPherson concedes. As Jim Bates, a Democratic county supervisor put it, "I suppose we're really dealing with symbols, with images, more than substance. If you assume social problems are worthwhile, you have to have the consent of the governed to implement the programs, and the governed obviously feel . . . that the next guy should work too."

Source: Bernard Weinraub, "Workfare in San Diego Could be Preview for U.S." *The New York Times,* May 6, 1981.

not become wards of the state, that is, most also work and do not stay on welfare (Currie and Skolnick, 1984:133).

Fifth, some have recommended that we (i.e., the government) should simply give poor people money, that is, a resolution of income maintenance (Keely et al., 1977). When this was done between 1975 to 1979 as a limited experiment, a significant number (15 percent) of female family heads dropped out of the work force (which could be good or bad, depending on your values). Most people on income maintenance bought durable goods, not more food and entertainment. A related proposal is a negative income tax in which those earning less than a specified amount are paid to bring their incomes up to that amount.

Finally, there are radical resolutions (Alperovitz and Faux, 1985:550ff.). If the wealthy or government will not stop (voluntarily) taking more than their fair share of the nation's income, the poor may redistribute income by force, violence, or law (as in the Russian revolution of 1917). Piven and Cloward (1985:428) contend that mass insurgency is required to solve the problems of poverty. They point to the increase in welfare after the 1964 to 1969 city riots in the United States. Of course, organized labor unions could also make demands on industry (Rubin, 1986; Roach and Roach, 1980). Some believe that we must have more socialist economies (see Table 11.6). Only socialist economies have come close to managing to eliminate unemployment.

• Summary

Like power inequality, economic inequality is primarily an institutional social problem and as such requires a somewhat different level of explanation. Economic inequality can be either absolute, proportionate, or most important for our purposes, relative. Generally, relative inequality can be defined as the ratio of the average status distance in a population to the average status. To measure economic inequality we introduced the concept of the Gini coefficient. Gini has a theoretical value of one when one or a small number of elites have all the wealth, and a value of zero when wealth is completely equally distributed. In the United States in recent years the Gini for income inequality is about .48.

A number of basic overlapping issues related to economic inequality were examined. Some (Gilder) argue for a capitalist economy, while others (Marx, Galbraith) argue for a more socialist economy. Trickle-down economic theory claims that inequality is good because all benefit economically from high productivity, but Marxist economic theory sees inequality as resulting in great economic, physical, and psychological exploitation of poor disenfranchised workers. Socialists tend to see economic inequality as central to all other social problems, but critics contend that power, authority, joy in work, prestige, and so on are often independent of economic issues. In America a very small economic elite controls a disproportionate share of its income (the richest 1 percent have about 25 percent of the nation's income). Socialists tend to believe that we should redistribute this unequal income and so on through taxes, welfare, and political reform.

A large part of economic inequality turns on issues of work opportunities and unemployment. For example, recently the unemployment rate has begun to creep up again and the total labor force has been expanded by larger numbers of married women working. The sources, extent, and desirability of poverty were examined. Depending on one's definition of poverty, 15 percent to 20 percent of the American population is poor, mostly the young, elderly, females, blacks, Hispanics, and single or divorced people. To combat the problem of poverty welfare benefits and differential income taxes (a socialistic resolution) commonly have been used; however, others (crudely, capitalists) contend that workfare and creating more jobs is the most appropriate resolution. Finally, we examined the special problems of inflation and stagflation.

After elaborating some of the fundamental theoretical differences between the socialist and capitalist economies to which we just alluded, we moved on to compare and contrast problems of wealth and poverty, since some of the problems of poverty derive from perceived relative deprivation. Wealth is often not thought of as a social problem; indeed, many social problems texts do not even mention wealth. Yet, the great concentration of our nation's economic resources in a small economic elite has far-ranging implications for us all. In recent years about 20 percent to 25 percent of America's total wealth was controlled by the richest 1 percent of the population. It was noted that wealth is not usually income from salaries, but rather from dividends, properties, rents, stocks, bonds, inheritances, and so on, and includes leisure-time available. The wealthy tend to live longer and better, have the best educations, the highest quality workmanship in their material possessions, the best medical care, legal and economic advisers, and enjoy more leisure time, travel, and fine food.

Poverty, on the other hand, is rightly seen as a social problem, since poverty means not being able to afford the basic necessities of life to ensure survival, as opposed to living well. If poverty is defined as the minimum food budget times three (the social security definition), then in recent years about 15 percent of the American population was poor. Only 1 percent to 2 percent of the poor are unemployed males. By far most of the poor are children, the elderly, females, blacks, and other minorities. Poverty, unlike riches, means living shorter and worse lives (on the average), not having enough to eat, inadequate housing, sending your children to less desirable schools for fewer years, experiencing more violence and stress both at home and in the larger society, and receiving poorer medical care.

Work is an especially critical life activity. It not only provides income, but also regulates and structures our lives and sense of self-worth. Obviously, the poor tend either to not have jobs at all or to have low-paying, insecure, low-status jobs. In 1985, about 7 percent of the labor force was unemployed. Clearly, many more were underemployed or subemployed, perhaps 10 percent. When there is a rise in the average level of prices (inflation) or high inflation and slow economic growth (stagflation), the poor are most directly affected. They have to give up necessities, not luxuries.

Finally, we asked how the social problems of economic inequality can be analyzed and resolved from our basic theoretical perspectives of exchange, structural-functionalism, conflict, and symbolic interaction. From the exchange perspective the poor as individuals have relatively few interactive assets (perhaps a self-fulfilling prophecy) and thus are not very rewarding or valuable to interact with. The poor tend to exchange unskilled labor for modest wages. In a sense poverty is disguised ageism, sexism, and racism, since the old, young, females, blacks, Hispanics, and so on are at particular interactive disadvantages. On a more institutional level corporate actors need poverty and the poor (e.g., cheap labor). Thus, corporate actors profit from exchanges with poor natural individuals. Another exchange explanation of economic inequality is that institutions and individuals satiate slowly on general reinforcers like money. Those with power will thus take more than others may consider their fair share (i.e., more than what they need).

Structural-functionalists, like Davis and Moore, argue that economic inequality is inevitable and desirable to fill important social positions with scarce talent and highly trained individuals. The small size and low power of the American poor works to their structural disadvantage in mounting effective political challenges to the wealthy. The conflict perspective sees capitalistic societies as emphasizing individual private profit at the expense of the poor, who are left out and abused. Those with power and control of production in a society feather their own nest. Symbolic interactionists point out that as long as the meanings of poverty include the notion that poverty is God's will, a self-perpetuating culture, a Darwinian purging of social misfits, and so on, we will continue to have poverty. For poverty to be reduced it first has to be defined as bad, unnatural, undesirable, and so on. Many of the poor are thought to be disreputable.

As for resolutions to economic inequality, the structural-functional, exchange, and some symbolic interaction perspectives encourage us to accept certain levels of economic inequality as inevitable. Thus, no resolution is seen as especially necessary. Supply-side economics also tends to see economic inequality as good because those individuals and societies without economic resources will be motivated to work harder and produce more. These greater economic products will eventually trickle down to even the poor. A more direct resolution approach would be simply to create more jobs (like the CETA and MDRC programs). The conflict perspective would suggest income redistribution through differential taxation, more federal spending, welfare, and programs such as income maintenance and negative income tax. Failing these steps, socialists suggest that more violent or politically aggressive action may be needed to forcibly wrest control of the economy from capitalists. We continue our examination of institutional or macrolevel social problems in Chapter 12 in turning to family and marital relations.

• Notes

1. See R. Barret, "No Room in the Lifeboats," *New York Times Magazine,* April 18, 1978.

2. Somewhat surprisingly, taxes are the *least* effective source of income redistribution.

3. For example, inherited wealth seems unfair to many. But these same people do not want more laws to handicap (say) smart people. Thus, inheriting intelligence is OK, but inheriting wealth is not.

4. Generally, relative *inequality* can be defined as the ratio of the average status distance in a population to the average status (Blau, 1977:57).

5. The computing formula for the Gini coefficient is $[\Sigma(X_i - 1 \cdot Y_i)] - [\Sigma(X_i \cdot Y_i - 1)]$. Thus, in Table 11.1 Gini equals $[(.20 \times .075) + (.40 \times .238) + (.60 \times .498) + (.80 \times 1.00)] - [(.40 \times .003) + (.60 \times .075) + (.80 \times .238) + (1.00 \times .498)] = 1.2092 - .7346 = .4746$.

6. It should be noted that inequality of *power* is much greater than inequality of *income.* For example, the average Gini coefficients for income are about .50, but for power are about .90 (Blau, 1977:63ff., 228).

7. Cf. Wonnacott and Wonnacott, 1982:Ch. 37, "Marxism and Marxist Economics."

8. This account draws heavily from Hook, 1955.

9. Of course, the rebuttal is always that the *relative* nuclear killing power is what is important. For example, if the USSR has *greater* nuclear power than the United States, then the fact that we could already eliminate the USSR 100 times over does not deter their aggression—at least so the argument goes.

10. The same argument could be made for Christianity.

11. See Lundberg, 1968:Ch. 16 for details on the estates and lifestyles of the Rockefellers (Pocantico Hills, New York) and Kennedys (Hyannisport, Massachusetts).

12. Perhaps they *want* it that way and have the power to guard their privacy?

13. However, Gilder (1981:55) counters that in 1978 only one-third of supermillionaires inherited a significant portion of their wealth.

14. Out of a total population of 216 million.

15. In Table 11.1 we see that the lowest 60 percent of the U.S. population get only about 25 percent of the nation's total income.

16. How much money one should expect for his/her work is a complicated matter. Some economists used to argue that if you "made your age" you were doing OK. For example, by this rule at age thirty you should expect a salary of $30,000. With inflation, this rough rule of thumb has gone up at least $1,500 per year of your life, from the original concept of $1,000 per year.

17. The suicide rate is more highly related to the unemployment rate than it is to the divorce rate (Stack, *Wall Street Journal,* May 28, 1986).

18. In effect critics like Bethell (1980) are arguing that the amount and severity of poverty is less than we think (cf. *New York Times,* April 18, 1982).

• Glossary

Capitalism. An economic system in which individuals are permitted to own large amounts of capital and decisions are made primarily in private markets with relatively little governmental interference.

Culture of Poverty. The theory by Oscar Lewis that the poor have values and lifestyles that are different from the rest of society and that perpetuate their poverty.

Economic Inequality. The distribution of people on a status dimension—here income or wealth. Economic inequality can be absolute, proportionate, or relative. Relative inequality crudely refers to the proportion of all income or wealth held by (say) the richest 1 percent of the population. More precisely, relative economic inequality is the ratio of the average status difference in a population to the average status.

Economy. The allocation of scarce resources to satisfy human wants; the complex social system that manages, develops, and distributes goods and services, and rewards people for their goods and services.

Gini Coefficient. A measure of relative inequality derived from the Lorenz curve. Gini equals one if there is complete inequality, and zero if there is complete equality.

GNP. The total product of the nation, including personal consumption expenditures, plus government purchases of goods and services, plus gross private domestic investments, plus net exports of goods and services.

Income. The cash and leisure time an individual receives.

Income Maintenance. A form of welfare in which certain individuals or families falling below standard levels of income are simply given money.

Inflation. A rise in the average levels of prices.

Poverty. A level of income insufficient to buy the necessities of life. A common official (absolute) level of poverty is the minimum food budget in a given year multiplied by three (the Orshansky social security definition for a nonfarm family of four). Relative poverty (Fuchs) is any nonfarm family of four making less than half the median family income.

Recession. A cyclical downward movement in the economy.

Socialism. An economic system in which the means of production (namely, the capital, equipment, buildings and land) are owned by the state (cf. Glossary, Chapter 10).

Stagflation. A socioeconomic condition in which there is high inflation, high unemployment, and slow growth.

Subemployment. Includes the unemployed, discouraged unemployed workers, workers employed below the poverty level, and part-time workers.

Supply-Side Economic Theory. The view that supply factors—such as the quantity of capital and the willingness to work—are the principle constraints to growth and that as national wealth increases it will trickle down to everyone.

Wealth. The total of cash received, leisure time, savings, investments, stocks, bonds, inheritances, and properties in large amounts.

Wealthfare. Government subsidies to the rich, sometimes called corporate socialism.

Welfare. Redistribution of national income and resources to the poor, disabled, infirm, and so on in the form of government housing, subsidies, health care, food subsidies, job training, aid for dependent children, and unemployment insurance.

Workfare. Work, usually part-time, in return for governmental subsidies.

• Further Reading

Blumberg, Paul. *Inequality in an Age of Decline*. New York: Oxford, 1980. Here is a book sympathetic to socialism, labor unions, and a leftist view of the American economy. Blumberg sees a weakening of American power worldwide, stagnated living standards, and growing inequality (*not* class convergence). America's exceptional economy began to erode following World War II and this erosion has begun to affect traditional American optimism. Unfortunately (for Blumberg's argument) some of the trends of the 1970s (e.g., inflation) have been reversed in the 1980s.

Galbraith, John Kenneth. *The Affluent Society*. New York: Houghton-Mifflin, 1976 (original, 1958). Contrary to economists like Keynes and Gilder, in Galbraith's influential book he claims that an expanding economy will *not* sweep away other social problems. Increased production has always been seen as an alternative to economic redistribution. In fact, great corporations are not entrepreneurial risktakers, but rather strive for economic security. Even an affluent society excludes many citizens from its benefits. Thus, Galbraith is opposed to market revival as an economic and social panacea.

Gilder, George. *Wealth and Poverty.* New York: Basic Books, 1981. One of the chief, most articulate, and persuasive of the supply-side (e.g., demand should not replace supply) and trickle-down economists. Gilder argues that the essence of capitalism is giving, not pecuniary greed. We must give in order to get. He feels the only dependable route out of poverty is work, family, and faith (in the future). Welfare reduces both the will and the reason to work. Most of us are unjustifiably hostile toward the wealthy. Afterall, the good fortune of others is finally our own (says Gilder).

Harrington, Michael. *The New American Poverty.* New York: Holt, Rinehart & Winston, 1984. In spite of Presidents Kennedy and Johnson's War on Poverty (in partial response to Harrington's earlier book, *The Other America,* 1963) "the poor are still here," claims Harrington. Poverty has a new face, but it is not gone. In 1983–84 there were more jobless than at any other time in the last fifty years. There were as many poor in 1982 as in 1965. The new poverty is multifaceted and international in scope. The hope and optimism of the 1960s has been replaced by the hopelessness of the 1980s and the generosity of Kennedy has been replaced by the meanness of Reagan.

Skolnick, Jerome H. and Elliott Currie. *Crisis in American Institutions.* New York: Little, Brown, 1985. A collection of forty essays in the socialist-Marxist tradition (see especially Chapters 4–10, 12, 15, 19, 21, 29, and 39). Argues that we have an "hourglass" economy in the United States, with winners and losers. More, not less, government intervention is needed to resolve problems of economic inequality. Essays tend to be critical of tax shelters for the rich, inherited income, and economic exploitation of the poor. In today's economy women have to be both homemakers and breadwinners, we have greater debt levels, and less chance of home ownership. New jobs tend to offer the lowest pay and not to be available to the young.

Wonnacott, Paul and Ronald Wonnacott. *Economics.* New York: McGraw-Hill, 1982. This is a comprehensive, well-written elementary economics textbook that should prove useful to students unfamiliar with many of the basic concepts and calculations of economics. Some of the more technical concepts we introduced in Chapter 11 (e.g., Gini coefficient, Lorenz curve, negative income tax, income subsidies, and so on) are presented in lucid, straightforward, easy-to-understand prose. See especially Chapters 3, 8, 19, 30, 32, 35, 36, and 37.

C·H·A·P·T·E·R

12

Family and Marital Relations

Recently there have been major changes in traditional American family and marital relations. Two of the most conspicuous of these changes in the new family are soaring divorce rates and high levels of family violence. In traditional marriages husbands tend to exchange economic security and physical protection for the wife's sexual gratification, homemaking, child production, socialization, and emotional support. However, in the 1980s basic marital rewards and exchange expectations have shifted dramatically. Traditional family values have also declined and with them there are growing conflicts in marital relations.

Structurally, when sex ratios are low (i.e., there are too many women), women and traditional marital and familial relationships are less common and alternative relationships (including divorce) are more common. Others argue that the larger the male cohort, the later marriages tend to occur, the more divorce there is, and the fewer children are born. In the 1980s working women have also been placed in closer proximity to marriage alternatives (e.g., jobs, lovers, and so on). Then too the separateness and differences of male and female sex roles and sexual socialization make eventual divorce more probable. Finally, the larger the number of children that are living at home, the greater are the rates of family violence (especially wife abuse).

Those in the functionalist camp argue that there is more divorce and family violence because the functions of the traditional family are changing. The traditional family was concerned with sexual control of its members, socialization of children, care of the aged, medical treatment of the sick and injured, providing recreation, sexual reproduction, and economic production. Many of these traditional social responsibilities or needs are now performed by other institutions. Functionalists conclude that the traditional family is less socially necessary today and divorce and family violence are more likely.

The conflict perspective tends to see traditional marriages as oppressive and restrictive of women. As women have become better organized, more economically self-sufficient, and have raised their group consciousness of marital exploitation, they have begun to rebel against male domination in traditional marriage. Divorce is the sign that women are throwing off the shackles of male domination and exploitation. One natural consequence of men and women's increased conflict over money, children, sex, housekeeping, and social activities in the traditional family is greater short-term rates of family violence. For conflict theorists, when economic equality among the sexes is greater, for a while we should expect higher divorce rates, greater sexual freedom, and even higher rates of family violence. All of these traits are signs of long-term social well-being and reform, not of social pathology.

As the case of Jeanne Buff (Panel 12.1; cf. Panel 12.2) suggests, there is a pervasive concern today that the American family is in deep trouble. Mrs. Buff is not alone. Glick (1984) estimates that about 49 percent of Americans ages twenty-five to thirty-four in 1980 either were divorced or eventually would become divorced. It is sobering to realize that the United States has one of the highest divorce rates in the world (South and Spitze, 1986). The U.S. divorce rate is two to four times higher than those of Italy, France, or Japan, and about the same as those of Sweden, England, and Canada (U.N. *Demographic Yearbook,* 1986 and 1984:720 ff.).

In fact there are a host of nested familial and marital issues. For example, when the divorce rate goes up, more preschool children need to be cared for outside the home. In 1958 outside care occurred in 31 percent of all families. By 1982 that figure had risen to a whopping 69 percent of preschool children (Cherlin and Furstenberg, 1983:229; *Statistical Abstract of the United States,* 1987:367). Family violence is also high—presumably higher than it used to be (Straus, Gelles, and Steinmetz, 1980:3). Straus, Gelles, and Steinmetz claim that there is more family violence than any other type of violence, including criminal violence (cf. Pogrebin, 1985:Ch. 5).

Boudreau (1983:443) argues that the most sweeping impact on the American family has been that of sex-role changes (cf. Panel 12.2; Finkelhor, 1985:502). The new ethic is more individual self-fulfillment, and less familial sacrifice. There are many more female-headed households today (see Figure 12.2) and more people living together outside marriage (cohabitation—Goldscheider and

PANEL 12.1

Mommy's Many Faces

On January 25, 1983, the Buffs, a demographically exemplary family of mother, father, and two young children living in a spacious three-bedroom condominium in Milwaukee, ate their last meal together. After washing the dishes, Jeanne Buff sent her three-year-old daughter Karen upstairs to read nursery rhymes with her grandmother, who was visiting. Then Jeanne and her husband Bill sat seven-year-old Andy down in the living room, held his hands, and gently told him the news. "Do you know how Mommy and Daddy don't hug and kiss anymore and fight a lot?" Jeanne asked. "Well," she said, taking a breath, "sometimes parents stop loving each other . . . Daddy's not going to live with us anymore." The next morning Bill drove away in the bitter cold, while Karen watched, sobbing from the kitchen door.

Nothing since that time has been quite as wrenching for Jeanne Buff. In the first months of running a household alone she was almost too busy to brood over the family's abruptly transformed life. The days passed in a blur of waking the kids, feeding them a breakfast of Cheerios and juice, dropping Karen and Andy at the day-care center and driving the twenty minutes to her busy job as an accountant at Blue Cross-Blue Shield. Then it was home to make dinner, read to the kids, put Karen to bed, help Andy with his homework—perhaps a little sewing, a book, to bed after midnight, and up again at dawn. There was scarcely even time to decide what her new identity was. "I felt I was Mommy, then Career Person, then I came home and was Mommy again. And when I went out on a date I was Sex Symbol."

But there were realities that made her altered status clear enough. About a year after the separation, the Buffs had to leave their expensive condominium for a rented apartment, so small that Andy sleeps on a porch separated from the living room only by a faded green blanket and with no room at all for the children's beloved pet schnauzer Leia, who was given away. Moving is not an uncommon event for female single parents. About 60 percent of them relocate to more affordable quarters within two years of a divorce.

In spite of the struggles—and the guilt, anger, and loneliness—Buff is cheerful from day to day, moderately hopeful about the future and convinced that her children, sheltered by her devotion, are reasonably happy. She has joined a local chapter of Parents Without Partners, the twenty-seven-year-old self-help group for single parents that now claims around 1,000 chapters across the country, where she gets a chance to share some of her concerns and, not incidentally, to date fellow members. She has grown staunchly independent—she hasn't yet accepted so much as a penny's worth of help from relatives. She has learned how to put up storm windows and fix shower rods. "Our lives run a lot more smoothly than they used to," she says. And she is no longer confused about her identity: at thirty-six Jeanne Buff is a divorced mother, struggling to make a life for her two children, going it alone, and learning to like it.

Source: *Newsweek*, July 15, 1985:47–48.

PANEL 12.2

Opposing Viewpoints on the American Family

Viewpoint: The American Family Is in Trouble

Some fear for the future, seeing what they interpret as symptoms of marital and familial disintegration in the rising incidence of premarital sex, higher divorce rates, and widening gaps between parents and their children. From these and other problems some people even predict the demise of the family. Others, while less pessimistic as to the final outcome, are still concerned about the trends. Our obsession with the rights of the individual, with "self-enhancement," has led up to the point, it is argued, where each marriage partner, and each child in the family is mainly concerned with his or her own personal needs and interests with little concern for the good of the whole.

Bell attributes the rise of excessive individualism to a long-term shift in American values. He sees the old-fashioned values of hard work, thrift, self-denial, and responsibility being replaced or greatly reduced by a newer "fun morality" stressing enjoyment and self-fulfillment. This new hedonism would seem to be incompatible with marriage and family stability—at least if carried very far. Individuals who develop narrowly selfish orientations may come to treat human relationships in the same way they treat cars or clothing, as things to be used for a short time and then replaced by later models. The present-day family, it is argued, has been reduced to a few specialized functions, such as affection and companionship.

Viewpoint: The American Family Is Alive and Well

There are, of course, more sanguine views on what is happening to marriage and family today. While conceding that most modern families perform fewer functions than families in earlier periods of American history, more optimistic observers point out that marriage and family today still function to meet the deepest affectional, emotional, and identity needs of most Americans, as well as society's reproductive needs. The small independent family is well adapted to modern urban-industrial society. It is mobile, for example, and thus can follow the expanding economy with its various job markets without hindrance of traditional kinship ties.

The author agrees that the American family is not going to disintegrate or be replaced by something else in the foreseeable future. Despite the many difficult issues and problems confronting the institutions of marriage and family today, it is my judgment that they will survive the present period of change and adjustment, while moving toward a more flexible marriage and family structure that should provide greater opportunities and more freedom for all family members.

Source: Everett D. Dyer, *Courtship, Marriage and Family: American Style*, The Dorsey Press, 1983:5–7.

Goldscheider, 1987). Effective sexual reproduction is less socially necessary (there are too many people, not too few) and the purely erotic aspects of sexuality are more openly pursued. Of course, these recent sex-role changes have been difficult for women, as we shall document below. Perhaps less obvious are the hardships the new American family has created for men. For example, divorce has often meant loss of a man's children and severe financial stress. Working wives have meant less emotional support for husbands, many of whom now feel suddenly less important—as not the head of the household any longer (see Pogrebin, 1985:Ch. 9, "The New Father").

The reader will recall (from Chapter 10) that an institution is a system of differentiated behavior designed to resolve recurring human problems. Traditionally the family as a social institution has been mandated with the responsibility of educating children, defending family members against violence, regulating sex and reproduction, providing love, loyalty, and noncontingent emotional support, housing, feeding, and clothing dependent members (including the elderly), and conducting religious rituals (Ogburn, 1933; cf. Boudreau, 1983:427).

One of the key issues in familial and marital relations is whether the contemporary American family still can resolve the above problems (Waite, Goldscheider, and Witsberger, 1986). For example, in our modern economy children have become monumental economic liabilities (on the average in the mid-1980s it cost about $100,000 to raise one child to independence—cf. Henslin, 1985:30). More and more families are concluding that they need two incomes to maintain the prior quality of their material life. There have also been major changes from rural living to living in large urban-industrial complexes (megalopolises—see Chapter 13). Finally with the disruption and fragmentation of the modern family one has to wonder if societal integration or cohesion itself is not put in jeopardy.

We define a *family* as "a group of persons united by ties of marriage, blood, or adoption who constitute a single household and who create and maintain a common culture" (Boudreau, 1983:423). In the past it was common for several generations of family members to live together and cooperate as an economic unit. Customarily this type of family was called an *extended family*. More recently the norm for families was simply a mother, father, and their children living together—the so-called *nuclear family*.[1] Today an increasingly common family type is the *single-parent family* (usually with a female head—see Figure 12.1). Finally, for our purposes, we may speak of *reconstituted families* in which one or both marital partners have children from previous marriages. Most American families are monogamous (comprised of one husband and one wife—at least at the same time).[2] The family in which one grows up is referred to as one's *family of orientation;* whereas the family one produces (your spouse and children) is called one's *family of procreation*. Of course, there are many other family types, but it is not necessary for our objectives to define them here.[3]

Traditionally American families have been large, a completed family size of five or six. Here we see a couple with their eleven children, grandchildren, and in-laws. The new American family is much smaller (three or four), in part because it now costs about $100,000 to raise a child to adulthood. (Michael Weisbrot/Stock, Boston)

Given these working definitions of family, and so on what is the overall prevalence and incidence of various family types and what are the general empirical dimensions of major social changes in the American family? Table 12.1 reveals that between 1980 and 1984 married couple households with children declined, while less traditional household types (e.g., female or male heads and women or men living alone) increased rapidly (while our definition of a family includes the concept of a household, a *household* simply means one or more persons occupying a housing unit—a household is not a family; see Zopf, 1984:462). Today's families are smaller and people are marrying later in life. For example, the average completed family size in 1950 was three children. By 1980 the average completed family size had shrunk to 1.9 children (*Current Population Reports,* July 1979). In 1970, 45 percent of men and 64 percent of women in their early twenties were married. By 1980, only 31 percent of men

FIGURE 12.1 Nuclear Family versus One-Parent Family

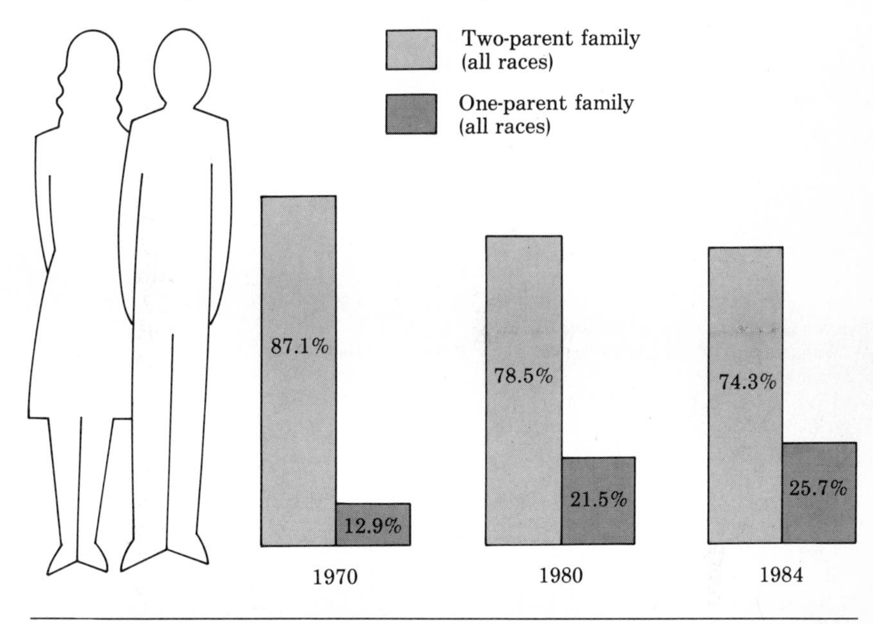

Source: *Newsweek,* July 15, 1985:46. By permission of Robert N. Conrad.

and 50 percent of women in this age group were married (Glick, 1984:22). In spite of later marriages, there is growing concern about unmarried teenaged mothers (Thompson, 1986). A 1985 estimate predicts that 40 percent of today's fourteen-year-old girls will be pregnant at least once before they reach age twenty (Wallis, *Time,* December 9, 1985).

Not only does the United States have one of the highest divorce rates in the world, its rate itself has tripled since 1960 (Blumstein and Schwartz, 1983:113). One consequence of this skyrocketing divorce rate is that there are many more female family heads. Eight out of ten single-parent families are headed by females (Boudreau, 1983:422). Table 12.2 shows that the number of children under age eighteen who live with both parents will decline rapidly over the 1980s, while the percent of children living with one parent (or in stepfamilies) will increase dramatically. Figure 12.2 indicates the percentage of all families in the United States headed by females. For all races female family heads have risen consistently. In 1970, 1980, and 1984, the percentages were 11.5, 19.4, and 22.9, respectively. For black families the proportion of female heads is even larger (Norton, 1985).

Of course, with the increases in divorce and female family heads it has also been necessary for more women to work outside their homes (Waite, Haggstrom, and Kanouse, 1986) and family violence rates growing out of this domestic turmoil have risen too (of course, married females working outside the home may itself cause or contribute to higher divorce rates—see Rubin, 1976).

TABLE 12.1 Household Change, 1980–1984

Type of Household	Households: 1980 Number (1,000)	Households: 1980 Percent Distribution	Households: 1984 Number (1,000)	Households: 1984 Percent Distribution	Households: Change, 1980–1984 Number (1,000)	Households: Change, 1980–1984 Percent	Persons in Households, 1984: Number (mil.)	Persons in Households, 1984: Percent Distribution	Persons in Households, 1984: Persons per Household, 1984
Total households	80,778	100.0	85,407	100.0	4,631	5.7	231.4	100.0	2.71
Family households	59,550	73.7	61,997	72.6	2,447	4.1	203.1	87.8	3.28
With own children under 18	31,022	38.4	31,045	36.3	23	(Z)	123.5	53.4	3.99
Without own children under 18	28,529	35.3	30,951	36.1	2,422	8.5	79.6	34.4	2.57
Married couple family	49,112	60.8	50,090	58.6	978	2.0	165.4	71.9	3.32
With own children under 18	24,961	30.9	24,339	28.5	−622	−2.5	102.3	44.2	4.20
Without own children under 18	24,151	29.9	25,750	30.1	1,599	6.6	64.1	27.7	2.49
Male householder, no spouse present	1,733	2.1	2,030	2.4	297	17.1	6.0	2.6	2.97
With own children under 18	616	.8	799	.9	183	29.7	2.4	1.0	3.00
Without own children under 18	1,117	1.4	1,231	1.4	114	10.2	3.6	1.6	2.94
Female householder, no spouse present	8,705	10.8	9,878	11.6	1,173	13.5	30.8	13.3	3.11
With own children under 18	5,445	6.7	5,907	6.9	462	8.5	18.8	8.2	3.19
Without own children under 18	3,261	4.0	3,970	4.6	709	21.7	11.9	5.1	3.00
Nonfamily households	21,226	26.3	23,410	27.4	2,184	10.3	28.2	12.2	1.21
Living alone	18,296	22.7	19,954	23.4	1,658	9.1	20.0	8.6	1.00
Male householder	8,807	10.9	9,752	11.4	945	10.7	12.9	5.6	1.33
Living alone	6,966	8.6	7,529	8.8	563	8.1	7.5	3.3	1.00
Female householder	12,419	15.4	13,658	16.0	1,239	10.0	15.3	6.6	1.12
Living alone	11,330	14.0	12,425	14.5	1,095	9.7	12.4	5.4	1.00

Z Less than .05 percent.

Source: *Statistical Abstract of the United States,* 1986:42.

TABLE 12.2

How Children Live

(The number of children under 18 who live with both parents will decline rapidly over the decade, while the number of children living with one parent or in stepfamilies will increase dramatically.)

	1981	Projection 1990	Percent Change 1981–1990
All children under 18 *(in 000s)*	62,918	58,735	– 6.6%
Percent	100.0%	100.0%	
Living with 2 parents	76.4%	69.4%	–17.9%
Living with 1 parent	20.0	26.5	23.5
Living with Mother	18.1%	24.0%	23.3%
Divorced	7.8	11.3	35.7
Married	5.6	6.3	5.8
Separated	4.9	6.1	16.8
Widowed	1.8	1.7	–13.7
Never married	2.9	4.5	47.5
Living with Father	1.9%	2.5%	25.4%
Divorced	1.0	1.5	47.7
Married	0.5	0.5	2.0
Separated	0.4	0.5	28.0
Widowed	0.3	0.2	–27.1
Never Married	0.2	0.3	49.1
All other	3.6%	4.1%	7.0%

Source: U.S. Bureau of the Census, *1980 Current Population Survey.*

FIGURE 12.2

Female Head of Family

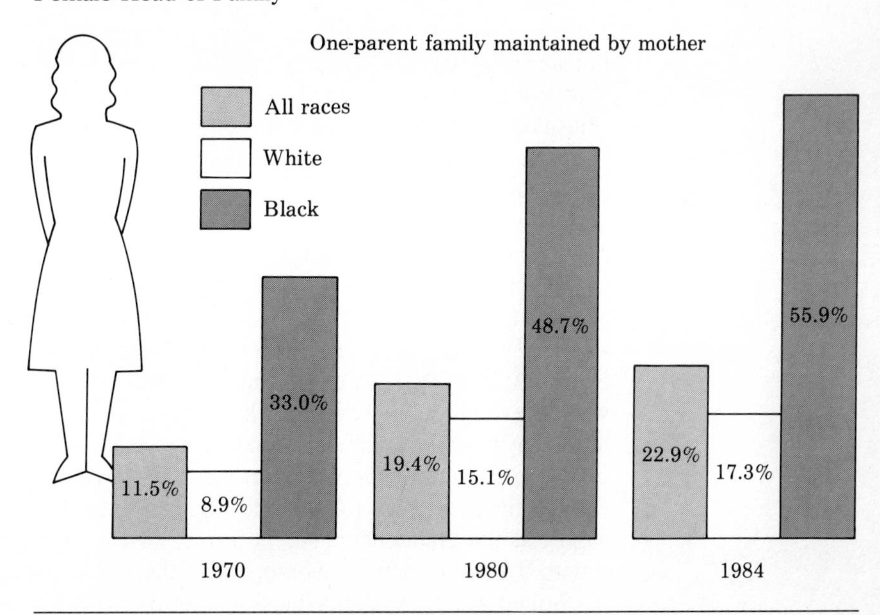

Source: *Newsweek,* July 15, 1985:46. By permission of Robert N. Conrad.

As we have seen, Cherlin and Furstenberg report that children cared for outside of the home rose from 31 percent in 1958 to 69 percent in 1982 (1983:229; *Statistical Abstract of the United States,* 1986:382).[4] As we shall see in the last section of this chapter, managing small children under duress, with domestic stress, and without adequate economic support and even modeling are all factors in increased family violence (Pines, 1985). Straus, Gelles, and Steinmetz reported that 16 percent of spouses had physically attacked their husbands or wives (1980). Many studies show that the age (not just the number), of one's children places the greatest hardship on a marriage (Rollins and Feldman, 1970:21). In a survey by Gil (1970:56) 60 percent of adults believed that almost anyone could at some time injure a child in their care. Historically, perhaps the most significant social changes in the American family have been shifts in sex roles (Boudreau, 1983:443; Rubin, 1976:215). However, as the following two sections will demonstrate, before we eulogize the traditional American family, it may be well to understand that family conditions in prior centuries probably were far worse in all aspects than they are today (McCoy, 1985:386–394).

• The Traditional American Family

We have almost a knee-jerk tendency to think of the old, large, extended, rural, self-sufficient, Bible-reading traditional American family as somehow better in every way than the new contemporary American family. Nostalgically, we mourn the passing of the traditional American family (say from 1776 to 1910) and see little but evil in today's smaller, more secular, nuclear family. But were the "good old days" of the all-American family (of "Ozzie and Harriet," "Leave it to Beaver," "Eight is Enough," "Father Knows Best," and the "Little House on the Prairie") really that different or that great?

As we saw just above, the traditional American family was socially charged with responsible reproduction, biological maintenance (feeding, clothing, and protecting members from harm), conferring (social, economic, ethnic, religious, racial, and so on) status on children, socialization of the young, emotional support and maintenance, and social control of family (Christensen and Johnsen, 1985:15 ff.). The traditional American family was a solution to the tension and stress of outside social life. The home was a family's castle (Blumstein and Schwartz, 1983:36). Or, as Lasch (1977) put it, the traditional American family was believed to be a "haven in a heartless world." Romantic love was considered the basis for traditional American marriages, and Americans were expected to stay married forever. Arranged marriages were thought un-American (Blumstein and Schwartz, 1983:36). Since the family was supposed to supply almost all the emotional needs, it also tended to become an overloaded institution. To make matters worse, today these traditional family functions are performed largely by agents (usually other social institutions) outside the family. Perhaps the only historically consistent and cross-culturally universal family function has been control of reproduction. Now even this traditional responsibility is being threatened by test-tube babies, sperm banks, surrogate spouses, and professional breeders (Lorber, 1980:527).

The older traditional extended family was typically much larger than contemporary families. Skolnick reminds us that in 1790 the average completed household size was 5.6 persons (1985:66). Theoretically the traditional family had more grandparents, aunts, and uncles living in close physical proximity to mothers, fathers, and their children. And yet, even today 50 percent of older Americans have seen their children on the previous day and about 50 percent have seen their grandchildren (Cherlin and Furstenberg, 1983:230). Blumstein and Schwartz (1983:35) claim that in fact there *never* was a strong tradition for the extended family in America (except among Afro-Americans). And in McCoy's writings on family history (as we shall see shortly) families were depicted not only as strikingly different, but also as uniformly worse (1985:387).

Economically speaking, the traditional American family in the 1700s and 1800s was rural and agrarian. The farm family supplied almost all its members' own food, clothes, and shelter (in short, the traditional American family was relatively self-sufficient). In earlier farm situations children (especially sons) were economic assets. Divorce rates in traditional families were exceedingly low. In fact, divorce was so uncommon in colonial America that records on them were not even kept before the Civil War (Dyer, 1983:231ff.). In 1867 the United States recorded 0.3 divorces per 1,000 married women fifteen years or older. By 1920 this rate had climbed to 8 or 9 per 1,000 married women. And by 1980 there were twenty-two to twenty-three divorces per 1,000 (*Statistical Abstract of the United States,* 1987:80). In the era of traditional families infant mortality rates and death in childbirth were extremely high (Skolnick, 1985:62). For example, in Plymouth Colony about 20 percent of all women died from causes related to childbirth. In seventeenth-century France, as many as 50 percent of all infants died within one year of their birth.

The treatment of children in traditional American families was also notoriously bad. Young children were not viewed as interesting and were treated with a psychological coldness and physical brutality that would horrify most of us today (McCoy, 1985:389). Working classes tended to think of children as small adults. For example, children as young as seven years old were sent off to other households to work as apprentices. Babies were not breast fed by their own mothers (but by wet nurses) and often were sent away to be nursed at the tender age of two to three days, only to return at age two years. Children were bound in tight restrictive swaddling clothes until they were about eight months old. In general, parents in traditional families actually spent less time with their children than today's nuclear families, even when both parents work outside the home (McCoy, 1985:388–391).

In the following section we ask what social, economic, and personal differences can be seen in the new American family. Are new family types worse or better than traditional American families? They certainly are different.

Drawing by Ed Arno; © 1984 *The New Yorker* Magazine, Inc.

• The New American Family

Many of us seem to fear that the new American family (especially in the 1980s) is in a pattern of fatal entropy—plagued by narcissistic self-indulgence, overemphasis on individual career gains, (too) easy divorce, high costs of living and inflationary prices, adolescents abandoned to promiscuity, alcohol, and drugs, a home devoid of God, worshipping the dollar, sensual gratification, and personal computers (Waite, Goldscheider, and Witsberger, 1986).

To begin with we need to determine how (and if) the new American family of the 1980s is different from the more traditional family of times past. What are the special traits and problems of contemporary families? We shall examine a half-dozen or so traits and then (later on in this chapter) look in detail at the special problems of divorce, child rearing, and family violence.

First, one of the most obvious and powerful social influences on the American family is economic and industrial change. With the Industrial Revolution husbands left farms; during World War II hundreds of thousands of women entered the labor force. Whereas in the 1950s in the United States 96 percent of people in their childbearing years were married; by the 1960s the marriage rate fell, the divorce rate increased, and fertility declined (Blumstein and Schwartz, 1983:38–40). Thus, modern capitalism curtailed the birthrate, turned children into economic liabilities, forced urbanization, and changed the role of women. In the 1980s family we see an increase in female household heads and the number of people living alone, a smaller household size, more women working, and higher divorce rates (Parillo, Stimson, and Stimson, 1985:358).

Second, what is the distinctive nature and quality of new American marriages? To be brief Americans are marrying later, are more likely to live alone, but still evaluate marriage as extremely important and positive (Goldscheider and Waite, 1985). Stein (1985:247) reports that between 1960 and 1983 the age of first marriage increased for women and men (respectively) from 20.3 to 22.8 and from 22.8 to 25.4. Obviously more women and men are delaying marriage (Blumstein and Schwartz, 1983:40).

Singleness and single parenting are both becoming more acceptable and more frequent (Wallis, 1985). Between 1957 and 1976 attitudes toward single people became more positive and attitudes toward the benefits of marriage less positive. Cherlin and Furstenberg chart the increased amount of singleness and disruption in a typical family of children born in the 1980s (see Table 12.3). Note too that being alone is much more common for older women than for older men. Blumstein and Schwartz point out that as people enter their forties there are 233 unattached women for every 100 men (cf. Guttentag and Secord, 1983).

However, in spite of some problems and disenchantments, the American family still flourishes today (Bates, 1984). By ages forty-five to fifty-four about 95 percent of all Americans have been married, the highest rate in history (*Statistical Abstract of the United States,* 1987:339). Further, when Caplow returned to Middletown (i.e., Muncie, Indiana), he found the new American family surprisingly strong (1982). Caplow discovered that the levels of marital satisfaction were very high (especially for men—1985:284).[5] In Thornton and Freedman's survey fully 75 percent of respondents indicated that having a good marriage and family life was very important (1982:34). Also, the vast majority of children (71 percent) in a national survey characterized their family life as close and intimate (Cherlin and Furstenberg, 1983:226; cf. Skolnick, 1985:60). These highly positive evaluations and high levels of participation in marriage and family life suggest that the new American family is simply changing form, not decaying (Glick, 1984), as some doomsayers claim (Lauer and Lauer, 1985).

Third, we need to elaborate new family trends in singlehood. As we have just seen, more Americans are delaying marriage and (later on) getting divorced after marriage. Clearly, these trends have an impact on traditional marital and familial relations. Stein (1985:250; see Table 12.4) claims that remaining single or becoming single (i.e., divorcing) increases one's career advancement, sexual experiences, life variety, and self-determination. For some of those reasons today more young and old people prefer to live alone (Brody, 1978). Even though marriage is harder on women than on men (e.g., Pogrebin, 1985:87

TABLE 12.3 Typical Sequence of Living Arrangements for Children Born in the 1980s (Especially for Females)

1. Live with both parents several years.
2. Live with mother after parents divorce.
3. Live with mother and step-father.
4. Live alone in early twenties.
5. Live with opposite sex without marriage.
6. Get married.
7. Get divorced.
8. Live alone again.
9. Get remarried.
10. Live alone again after death of spouse.

Source: Andrew Cherlin and Frank F. Furstenberg, "The American Family in the Year 2000," in *The Futurist,* June, 1983, World Future Society.

claims that marriage is a disadvantage to women, in part because they usually are both homemakers and breadwinners), young women tend to be more disappointed with singlehood than young men (Thornton and Freedman, 1982:35).

Fourth, more and more contemporary families involve single parenting (as we have demonstrated above). In 1984 less than 29 percent of all American families were constituted by a father, mother, and their children living together (Table 12.1). If we further qualify the conditions to stipulate that the father is the breadwinner and the mother is a full-time homemaker, then only 16 percent of modern American families fit the traditional stereotype of families. Glick (1979) estimates that about one-half of all children born in 1980 will grow up in single-parent households.

Fifth, in the new American family cohabitation has increased more rapidly than any other type of household (Glick and Spanier, 1980).[6] The number of unmarried couples cohabitating has increased at a rate of 15 percent a year over the last ten years (Glick, 1984:23). Sixth, as we documented in Chapter 5, the contemporary family has less control over sexuality (there is more pre-and extramarital sexual activity—see Chapter 5), birth control has been improved, and (for the most part) abortions are easier to obtain. Skolnick attributes these changes in today's family to the mid-1960s sexual revolution, the revival of feminism, and the growth of the two-worker family (1985:65). Of course, more effective birth control has also improved the opportunities for mothers to work as well as to stay working (Keniston, 1985:320). Whereas in traditional families a pregnancy meant a new child to care for and jobs foregone, today more women are aborting unwanted pregnancies.

Although we will say more about birth control (and fertility) in Chapter 13 on population, a brief aside is needed here too. There has been considerable

TABLE 12.4 Pushes and Pulls toward Marriage and Singlehood

Marriage

Pushes (Negatives in Present Situations)	**Pulls (Attractions in Potential Situations)**
Pressure from parents	Approval of parents
Desire to leave home	Desire for children and own family
Fear of independence	Example of peers
Loneliness and isolation	Romanticization of marriage
No knowledge or perception of alternatives	Physical attraction
Cultural and social discrimination against singles	Love, emotional attachment
	Security, social status, social prestige
	Legitimation of sexual experiences
	Socialization
	Job availability, wage structure, and promotions
	Social policies favoring the married and the responses of social institutions

Singlehood

Pushes (To Leave Permanent Relationships)	**Pulls (To Remain Single or Return to Singlehood)**
Lack of friends, isolation, loneliness	Career opportunities and development
Restricted availability of new experiences	Availability of sexual experiences
Suffocating one-to-one relationship, feeling trapped	Exciting lifestyle, variety of experiences, freedom to change
Obstacles to self-development	Psychological and social autonomy, self-sufficiency
Boredom, unhappiness, and anger	Support structures: sustaining friendships, women's and men's groups, political groups, therapeutic groups, collegial groups
Poor communication with mate	
Sexual frustration	

Source: Peter J. Stein, *Single,* Prentice-Hall, 1985:250.

disillusionment with almost all birth control techniques. The pill refers to a variety of chemical interferences with ovulation. If you take the pill (almost every day), it is highly effective and convenient. However, some people (e.g., those with high blood pressure) cannot tolerate the pill. Gradual hormonal changes can result in headaches, blood clots, cysts, and so on. The IUD (intrauterine device) designates several different types of mechanical devices semipermanently implanted in the uterus to prevent the female's eggs from attaching to the wall of the uterus. The IUD can cause bleeding, discomfort, and infections in many women. The diaphragm is a circular, pliable, rubber device that when fitted properly over the entrance to the uterus and used with sperm-killing jellies, or foams, prevents sperm from reaching the female's eggs (the sexist story goes that one woman kept having babies because she consumed her contraceptive jelly on her morning toast). The main problem with diaphragms (and condoms for that matter) is that they are inconvenient and interfere with spontaneous sexual intercourse. Of course, men (vasectomies) and women (tubal ligation) can be sterilized, but these procedures are usually not reversible. I had a friend who got a vasectomy at Sears. Now every time he makes love to his wife his garage door goes up. Well, not really. Finally (actually there are many other new procedures, such as Norplant—which results in self-induced menstruation), there is always abortion. More and more people regard abortion as murder. At the end of the first trimester of pregnancy, when dilation and curettage is performed, the fetus has a fully developed central nervous system as it is literally torn apart.

Seventh, the percentage of young men and women who never married has gone up strikingly since 1960. For women aged twenty to twenty-four, the never-married population doubled between 1960 and 1980. Other data from Stein reveal that the percentage of twenty-five to thirty-four year olds never marrying almost tripled between 1960 and 1982 (1985:247). However, the percentages of both the young and old who never married are at about the same levels as they were during the turn of the century.

Finally, most of these trends in the new American family have had differential effects on women and minorities (Cherlin, 1987). For example, even though women may be more concerned about long-term singlehood than men, staying single is more beneficial for women than for men (Bernard, 1982). Even after marriage, many women see divorce as liberation. When a sample of today's women were interviewed by the *New York Times* (1983:121), women valued jobs as much as they did family life. Finally, single parenting without marriage is much more common among black females (Norton, 1985). In the late 1970s two out of three black women who gave birth were unmarried (Cherlin and Furstenberg, 1983:228).

So much for our cursory review and highlighting of some salient traits of the new American family in the 1980s. We must now look more carefully at divorce as a special problem and, in particular, review sociological explanations of the causes and resolutions of problems of divorce.

• Divorce

Stating the Problem In traditional American families marriage was a religious sacrament—a union blessed by God that was supposed to last a lifetime. As we saw above, the traditional family was charged with control of reproduction, educating children, providing noncontingent love, economic support, and physical security for the wife and her children. Today, however, there have been major social and economic changes affecting the American family. Many young people have great concern about the future of marriage and the family as we know it. Will the family survive? The odds are certainly against about half of all first marriages lasting, and yet marriage and raising a family remain very attractive to the majority of Americans. And what about children scarred by divorce and a struggling economy that must support dependent children and husbandless women without the job skills necessary for productive employment?

"We had a dynamite marriage, and now we're having a dynamite divorce."

Drawing by Ziegler; © 1984 *The New Yorker* Magazine, Inc.

How extensive is the social problem of divorce? Bumpass and Rindfuss found that by age sixteen fully one-half of white children and two-thirds of black children had experienced disrupted families (1979). Figure 12.3 shows that the U.S. divorce rates peaked after the two world wars and declined during the Great Depression of 1929 (and the early 1930s). Between 1960 and 1980 the American divorce rate (per 1,000 married women) roughly doubled. In 1982 the number of divorces did drop slightly for the first time since 1962. *But* the American divorce rate is still very high. Most divorces occur in the first seven years of a marriage and the average American marriage lasts about 9.4 years.

Although in the 1980s the American people are generally more approving of divorce,[7] the consequences for both individuals and society are still serious. For adults divorce results in more household maintenance and economic problems, decreased social participation, increased sexual activity, and decreased mental well-being (Goetting, 1981). Weiss discovered that the bonds of emotional attachment formed during marriage last much longer than most divorced people expect them to (1975). Often, children's entire world is shaken (Wallerstein and Kelly, 1985:448–450). Anger lasts longer than any other single affective response to divorce. About one-half of a sample of children displayed

FIGURE 12.3 Annual Divorce Rates, United States, 1860–1978[a] and 1960–1984[b] (Divorce per 1,000 Married Women, Ages 15 and Over)

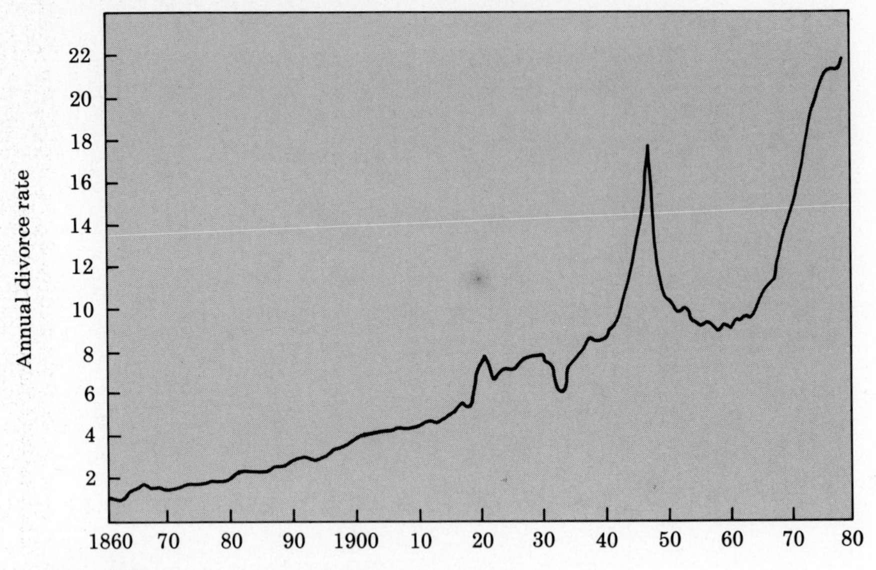

a: 1860–1978

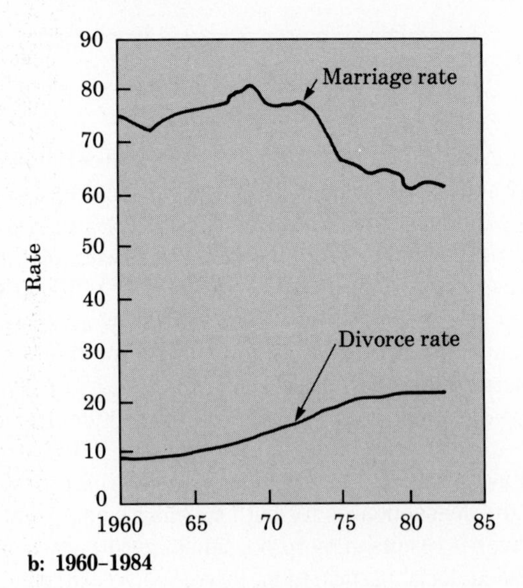

b: 1960–1984

Source: [a]Andrew Cherlin, *Marriage, Divorce, and Remarriage: Changing Patterns in the Postwar United States,* Harvard University Press, 1981:22. Reprinted by permission. 1860–1920, Paul H. Jacobson, *American Marriage and Divorce,* 1959, Table 42:1920–1967. U.S. National Center for Health Statistics, Vital and Health Statistics, series 21, no. 24, *100 Years of Marriage and Divorce Statistics,* 1973, Table 4:1968–1978. U.S. National Center for Health Stastics, Vital Statistics Report, Advance Report, vol. 29, no. 4, supplement, *Final Divorce Statistics 1978,* Table 2. [b]*Statistical Abstract of the United States,* 1986:55.

depressive behavior even a year after divorce of their parents (Wallerstein and Kelly, 1985:451).

Divorce does not affect women, children, and minorities equally. That is, divorce has differential impacts. For example, most people feel that divorce is more appropriate if there are no children involved in the marriage (*Better Homes and Gardens,* 1978). Unfortunately, about three-fifths of all marriages do involve children living at home (Cherlin and Furstenberg, 1983:227). To make matters even worse, 57 percent of divorced women received no child support from their estranged husbands in the previous year (Cherlin and Furstenberg, 1983:227). Nevertheless, more women today (even with all the hardship) see divorce as liberation. Finally, we must note (Figure 12.4) that far more black women (than white women) are separated, divorced, never married, or widowed.

Analyzing the Problem. The Exchange Perspective We must now determine what accounts for the high rates of divorce in the contemporary American family.[8] Table 12.5 (cf. Table 5.4) suggests that in traditional marriages husbands (for the most part) exchanged economic security and physical protection for the wives' sexual gratification, homemaking, child production, care, socialization, and emotional support (Guttentag and Secord, 1983; Dyer, 1983:112–113). In the traditional family children were slightly positive economic assets as farm workers but overall were not really a large part of the marital exchange. In newer marriages the wife expects to change the terms of marital exchange, to become more of an equal partner, and to work (and perhaps get sex) outside the marriage. Children have shifted from slightly positive exchange assets to major economic liabilities. In short, in today's marriages (from the exchange perspective) there are less distinctive unique interactive assets to bind husbands, wives, and children together.

Two of the most articulate advocates of new exchange-structural forces in marriage and the family in the 1980s have been Marcia Guttentag and Paul Secord (see their 1983 book *Too Many Women?).* They argue that when sex ratios are high (an excess of men), young adult women are highly valued and women receive more satisfaction from traditional sex roles (e.g., those of wives, mothers, homemakers, and so on). Before World War II there was always an excess of males in the United States (1983:15–16). However, since World War II there has always been an excess of females. With low sex ratios, women feel more powerless and less socially valuable. They are less likely to see rewards in making commitments to traditional sex roles. Thus, divorce, extramarital affairs, and many of the other traits of the new American family are more likely (1983:20–21). Today men are the scarce gender and thus have more sources of alternative satisfactions to traditional marriage than women. Men now have more freedom of choice and control over the way they relate to women—and many more are exercising this freedom of choice in the form of divorce (1983:153–161).

In support of the exchange perspective of marriage and divorce, Eckland

FIGURE 12.4 Current Marital Status of Women Aged 25–44, by Race or Color, 1950 and 1979

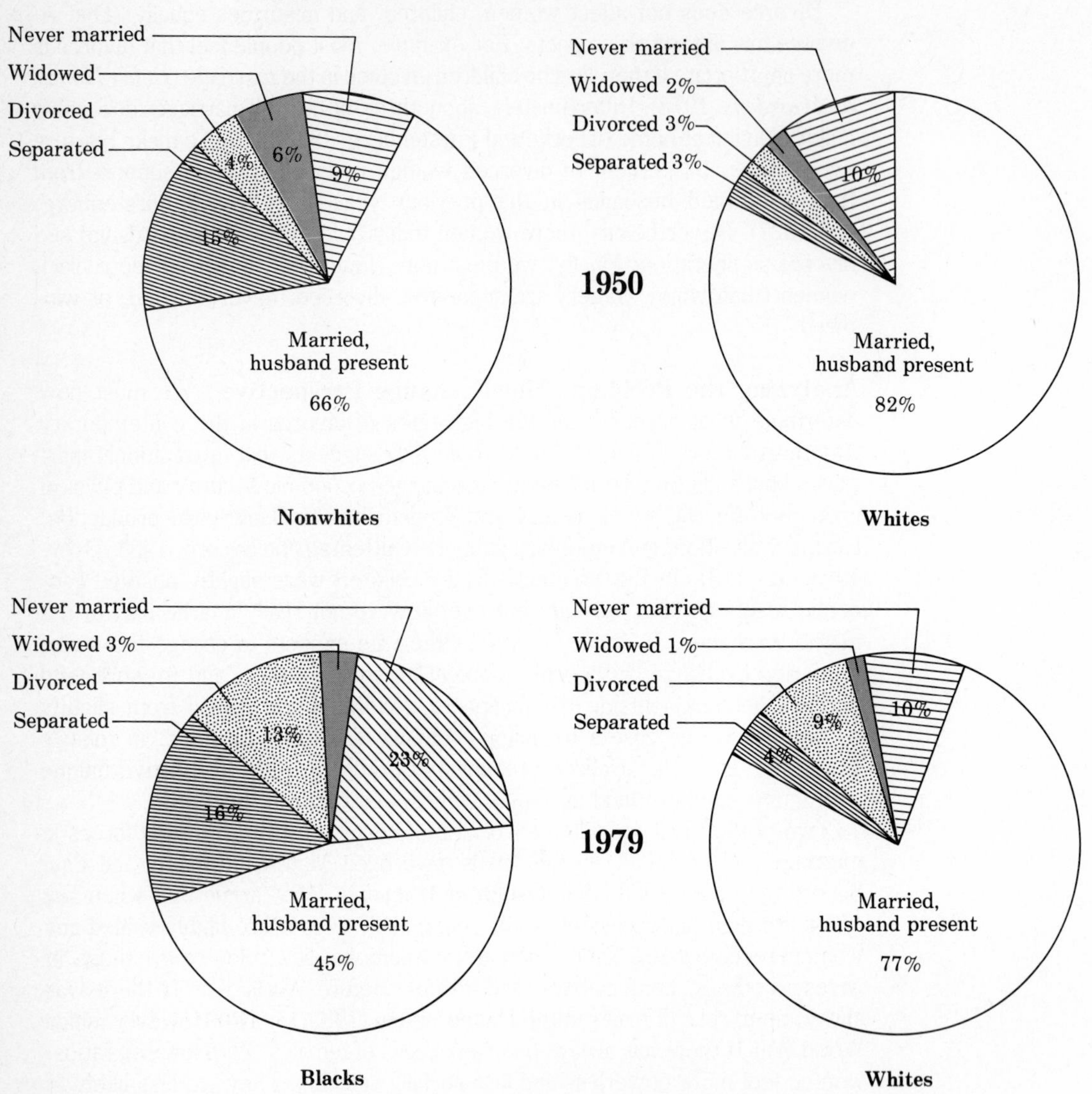

Source: Andrew Cherlin, *Marriage, Divorce, and Remarriage: Changing Patterns in the Postwar United States,* Harvard University Press, 1981:98. Reprinted by permission. U.S. Bureau of the Census. For 1979, Current Populations Report, series P-20, no. 349; for 1950, *U.S. Census of Population: 1950,* vol. IV, Special Reports, chapt. D, p. 2.

TABLE 12.5 Distribution of Basic Societal Rewards in Traditional Marriage for Husband, Wife, and Children

Rewards	Husband	Wife	Children
Economic security, monetary provision	+	−	+
Sexual gratification	−	+	−
Home care, homemaking	−	+	−
Socialization, education	−	+	−
Physical security, protection	+	−	−
Emotional support, love	−	+	−

\+ = Reward present, supplied, salient, or provided.
− = Reward absent, not supplied, minor, or received.

found that physically attractive women, even if they were mentally retarded, could still marry and marry well (1985:36). Masters and Johnson stress the fundamental exchange principle of profit in marital interaction for marriages to be sustained. They write: "The quality of marriage is determined by whether the pleasure exceeds the inevitable portion of displeasure . . . they (marital partners, especially the women) pay whatever price is required for the service to continue—for the house to be cleaned, meals prepared, children cared for, bills paid, sexual relations provided, etc." (1985:355).

To elaborate the main exchange point that in the 1980s basic marital rewards have shifted, today's women value jobs as much as they value their families (*New York Times,* 1983:21). In general, values have shifted to individualism and personal fulfillment (Boudreau, 1983:438). Blumstein and Schwartz found that in the 1980s it is uncommon (in spite of the wife being employed outside the home) for the husband to do even half the housework (1983:114; cf. Cherlin, 1987). Finally, the fact that the single most distinctive feeling divorced children have is intense anger reflects their sense of distributive injustice. Many children feel that divorce has violated their basic life expectations and that this breach of the marital agreement is grossly unfair to them (Wallerstein and Kelly, 1985:444).

The Structural Perspective Structural scholars like Easterlin (1980) emphasize the importance of cohort size for the nature of the family. Cohort size affects rates of marriage, divorce, and childbearing. Generally, the larger the male cohort, the later marriages occur, the more divorce there is, and the fewer children are born—although this argument is somewhat inconsistent with that of Guttentag and Secord (1983). Easterlin still maintains that larger male cohorts means more competition among men for qualified females to marry and more competition to stay married to attractive females.

It is also true that structurally speaking working women are placed in closer proximity to marriage alternatives. That is, women working outside the home have more economic self-sufficiency, have more frequent interaction with potential lovers, have more hired help to care for their children, and have alternative sources of emotional support. Henslin believes that the separateness and increasing differences of male and female sex roles and sexual socialization make eventual divorce more probable (1985:425).

The Functional Perspective Other family and marriage specialists in the functionalist camp argue that there is more divorce because the functions of the traditional family are changing (Boudreau, 1983:435–436). The traditional American family was concerned with sexual control of its members, socialization of children, care of the aged, medical treatment of the sick and injured, providing recreation, sexual reproduction, and economic production. Many of these social responsibilities or needs mandated to the traditional family are now performed by other institutions. Functionalists conclude that the traditional family is less socially necessary today. However, others (Curtis, 1986) suggest that family units in a society alter (often reducing social inequality) the outcome of larger society's system of economic exchanges because family units are governed more by social (not economic) exchange. In spite of this last qualification, on the whole divorce and new institutional arrangements other than the traditional family are more likely.

For example, with increased premarital and extramarital sexual activity and new birth control techniques, marriage has become less necessary and traditional families have lost much sexual control of family members. Furthermore, governmental agencies, child-care centers, and schools now do much of the childhood socialization and education that the traditional family used to do. We could go on. For example, industrialization broke up the family economic unit; the aged are now cared for more in nursing homes; sexual reproduction still takes place in the family but is threatened by sperm banks, surrogate mothers, and so on; and medical treatment has been largely transferred from the family to medical specialists. The upshot of all these social changes is that marriage and the traditional family are less functionally necessary than they used to be. Accordingly, divorce and alternatives to marriage and the traditional family are more likely.

The Conflict Perspective Finally, those in the conflict perspective maintain that traditional marriages were oppressive and restrictive especially of females (see Pogrebin, 1985:Chs. 1 and 2). As women have become better organized, become more economically self-sufficient, and raised their group consciousness of marital exploitation, they have begun to rebel against male domination in traditional marriage. In traditional marriages women tended to live in servitude to men (Dobash and Dobash, 1981). Males legally disciplined their wives and daughters through marital rights. For example, in British common law, one's wife was part of the male's private property.

Today's family is subject to much stress and conflict. Modern wives expect to be equal partners in marriage, to work outside of the home, to have help with child care and household chores. Little wonder that divorce rates have soared, with high costs to children. (Joel Gordon)

Marx and Engels (see Engels, *Origin of the Family, Private Property, and the State,* 1942) argued for the abolition of the traditional bourgeois family (McLellan, 1973:183). In traditional marriages in capitalistic societies women are forced into a subordinate position because of the superior economic productivity of males. Divorce is the sign that women are throwing off the shackles of male domination and exploitation. Thus, for conflict theorists Marx and Engels when economic equality between the sexes is greater, for a while we should expect higher divorce rates and greater sexual freedom. Both are signs of improved long-term social well-being and reform, not social pathology.

Resolving the Problem What can be done about the problems of divorce? Obviously, resolutions tend to parallel one's theoretical biases about what causes divorce. For example, one naive assumption is that since new social and economic developments have caused the divorce problem, its solution is to return to the past to reinforce the traditional family. In this regard one immediately thinks of ultraconservative females like Phyllis Schlafly (see Ihinger-Tallman, 1983:229; cf. Pogrebin, 1985:6, 8, 91, 179, 180) who oppose the Equal Rights Amendment, want to eliminate sex and death education in the schools, and put God back into the American family. Legal proposals like the Hatch Amendment (it would remove the Supreme Court 1973 abortion rights guarantee and give both Congress and the states power to restrict abortion—cf. Pogrebin, 1985:186) would make abortion murder and would result in larger families. These resolutions tend to be naive because they ignore basic social changes that are for the most part here to stay.

From the exchange perspective the obvious resolution would be to change the terms of marital exchanges. Specifically, some (obviously not all) of the problems of divorce could be resolved by prenuptial marriage contracts (see Panel 12.3). Marriage contracts stipulate in advance what is expected in a marriage, and what the terms of divorce would be. Marriage contracts are usually valid, if they were fair to start with, were contracted voluntarily, and were agreed to in good faith. If children result from a marriage, the terms of a marriage contract are normally nullified. Los Angeles divorce lawyer Marvin Mitchelson believes that most marriage contracts are in fact divorce contracts, since almost every couple who has one ends up getting divorced. A second exchange resolution is simply for married couples to make every effort to spend more time together. For example, Blumstein and Schwartz discovered that couples who have sexual relations more frequently are happier and less likely to get divorced (1983:114–115).

One obvious resolution to divorce is to remarry. Unless children are brought from the first marriage the socioeconomic status of second marriages is similar to that of the first (Jacobs and Furstenberg, 1986). Of course, the remarriage resolution to divorce tends to ignore the social factors contributing to all marital failures. Remarriages tend to be vulnerable to the same social problems as first marriages. Also, (for various reasons) one can only expect to remarry a few times.

Structural resolutions to divorce might include making divorce less easy to obtain. One suspects that no-fault divorces have encouraged couples to give up on problematic marriages too soon. Wallerstein and Kelly believe that divorce is not the solution to many people's marital unhappiness (1985). As a rule people do not feel happier until about five to ten years after divorcing. Work by the wife outside the home clearly has mixed effects on a marriage. Generally, when the wife works, couples tend to fight more (especially about how their children are being raised—see Blumstein and Schwartz, 1983:114).

If divorce is unavoidable, then we need to increase the level and regularity of child support payments and welfare aid for divorced women.[9] Panel 12.4 is encouraging. It shows that, although child support is still low, about three-fourths of those people due child support got at least some of it and about 50 percent got all of it. In 1983 the average annual child support payment was $1,740 per year (however, the *Statistical Abstract of the U.S.*, 1987:367 claims the mean child support payment in 1983 was $2,341).

PANEL 12.3

How to Write a Marriage Contract

The music is soft, the lights are low, and the ambience is perfect as you clasp the hand of your intended and talk lovingly of your future lives together. It's a rosy romantic picture. But these days marriage plans often include not just where to have the wedding and whom to invite but also when to see the lawyers and how to fill out the financial disclosure forms.

Lawyers before the wedding? Yes, indeed. Increasingly, American couples are consulting lawyers *before* they get married in order to draw up prenuptial agreements, otherwise known as marriage contracts. The rich and the famous have always had them. Jackie and Aristotle Onassis reportedly drew up a 170-point contract. Now people with thousands of dollars, not millions, are doing likewise.

Palimony lawyer Marvin Mitchelson says that, in his experience, "Everyone who signs a marriage contract ends up getting a divorce." Right now, he says, he is challenging ten prenuptial agreements. One case he handled involved a millionaire whose wife-to-be found that, on the way to church, the car detoured to a lawyer's office where, in full regalia, she was presented with a prenuptial agreement to sign. That is a classic case of coercion under the law, and, although he says it is an extreme example, Mitchelson points out that he has "never seen a prenuptial agreement that didn't have something wrong with it."

The prospective bride and groom must:

Each have a lawyer. This is a contract you are negotiating, and each of you must be represented by counsel or the contract may later be ruled invalid.

Make a full financial disclosure. Each of you will know what you are getting and what you are giving up.

Negotiate in good faith. No threats or coercion. Language like "sign it, or the wedding is off" may be grounds for invalidating a contract later.

The terms of premarital agreement can be hotly negotiated. The prospective bride, for example, may demand a specific sum—say, $20,000 for each year of marriage and for each child born in the marriage. The prospective groom may wish to keep his future wife out of all profits from a family business. If both partners work, the contract may call for contributions to household expenses to be apportioned according to income. The contract may call for one spouse to pay money to the other if they move to another city and one of them has to give up his or her job; or for the wife, if she puts her husband through professional school, to get a percentage of his annual income upon divorce.

Source: Nina Totenberg, *Parade,* December 16, 1984: 14–15.

Generally, extramarital affairs do not help save a bad marriage. Blumstein and Schwartz found in their sample (1983:115) that 26 percent of husbands and 21 percent of wives had had extramarital affairs. However, wives who had had extramarital sexual relations recently were more inclined than husbands (who had had extramarital sex recently) to feel that their marriages were not going to last. Finally, from the conflict perspective couples who did not have oppressive exploitative marriages with male domination are more likely to last.

PANEL 12.4

More Get Child Support Due Them

More than three-quarters of the women who were supposed to receive child support payments got at least part of the amount due, a slight increase that was welcomed Thursday by federal officials who have been striving to get fathers to meet their obligations.

Of the women who were due child support, 76 percent received at least some of the amount scheduled in 1983, up from 71.8 percent in 1981, the Census Bureau reported.

And the share of women who received the full amount they had been awarded, either in a voluntary agreement or a court order, increased from 46.7 percent to 50.5 percent in the same period, Census officials said.

The child support deficit in 1983 was $740 per woman, the report said. That means that the total of all payments averaged by women due payments—including those who received nothing—resulted in an average of $1,740 per woman, while the full amount due would have amounted to $2,520 per woman.

Source: The Associated Press, July 12, 1985.

For example, if couples shared control of their money, their marriages were happier, calmer, and lasted longer (Blumstein and Schwartz, 1983:113). It is always the case that children are special (and innocent) victims of divorce. In the next section we focus on what happens to children of divorce—especially what the implications (socially and individually) of divorce are for child rearing.

• Implications of Divorce for Child Rearing

Of course, one of the special problems with any divorce is the potential victimization of dependent children.[10] Levitan and Belous estimate that in recent years divorce in America involved about one million children under age eighteen per year (1981:60). Children react to divorce with shock, depression, denial, anger, lowered self-esteem, and sometimes with feelings of responsibility for their parents breaking up (Francke, *New York Times,* 1983:180). In fact, children with divorced parents are themselves about 50 percent more likely to divorce when they reach adulthood than children whose parents did not divorce. Divorce is probably hardest on children ages three to eight (Francke, 1983:182). Also, apparently boys usually take the failure of their parents' marriage harder, take longer to adjust to divorce, and show more disrupted behavior than girls. In fact, if parents have at least one male child, then they are about 18 percent more likely to remain married. The reasons for staying together because of male offspring are unclear, but presumably fathers are less willing to give up sons than they are to give up daughters.

There are a whole host of destructive negative emotions that divorced children tend to feel. Perhaps the single most salient one is conscious intense anger (Wallerstein and Kelly, 1985:444). Divorced children routinely display higher levels of anxiety, general life chaos, and disorganization (Hetherington et al., 1978:146–176). Children are especially anxious about being left by both parents (Wallerstein and Kelly, 1985:446). They even worry about their parents suiciding. Depression is another common reaction of children of divorce. About half of Wallerstein and Kelly's sample revealed depressive conflicted behavior, even at a one-year follow-up (1985:451). Zill claims that children of divorce are twice as likely as nondivorced children to need psychological counseling (1976 in Cherlin 1981). Finally, it is not uncommon for children of divorced parents to have lowered self-esteem. The children often feel rejected along with the divorced spouse or they blame themselves for the divorce (Cherlin, 1981:78; Francke, 1983:180).

Obviously, when parents get divorced most children's economic situations change dramatically (Cherlin, 1981:82). As we saw earlier, one estimate shows that 57 percent of divorced or separated women received no child support payments in the past year (Cherlin and Furstenberg, 1983:227). Who gets custody of children is an issue too. Traditionally the wife kept legal custody of children (and the husband got the bills, alimony, child support payments, and so on). Glick estimates that by 1990 only 69 percent of all children will be raised by both parents (1984:24). Increasingly courts are asking why the mother alone should have custody of divorced children. Some observers feel that same-sex custody probably works best (other things being equal—see Francke, 1983:183). More recent studies claim that joint custody works even better (*Behavior Today,* July 8, 1985). With joint custody divorced husbands tend to see their children more regularly and are more likely to pay child support.

Child problems related to divorce, but not necessarily limited to divorce, include child crime, prostitution, illegitimacy, and child-care problems. If a child is without one or both parents, clearly this increases his/her probability of turning to sexual deviance or crime for economic support (*U.S. News and World Report,* June 9, 1980). More and more women are also having children out of wedlock (see novelist John Irving's *The World According to Garp*). The rate of illegitimacy has doubled to tripled in the last thirty years (*Statistical Abstract of the United States*, 1986:62). In 1960, 5 percent of all children were born to unmarried mothers, but by 1980, 18 percent of all children were born illegitimately (Glick, 1984:23). Obviously, some illegitimate children result from divorce and many illegitimate children have problems similar to those of divorced children. Obviously, when parents are divorced and mothers work many young children are on their own from the time school lets out until mom comes home from work. These latch-key kids (children who let themselves into their homes) clearly have the potential for many problems that children with mothers at home do not have (Keniston, 1985:319ff.).

One should not conclude from this discussion that divorce is only problematic for children. Divorced children do get relief from destructive marital conflicts, arguments, even physical abuse. At least with divorce children and parents get a second chance to try to improve their life situations.[11] As hard as this transition may be on children (indeed, on all concerned), at least there is hope for improvement (Cherlin, 1981:82; Goetting, 1981). In the next and concluding section of the present chapter we examine one outcome that can happen when marital conflicts are not resolved—the problem of family violence.

• Violence in the Family

Stating the Problem

> The wife of the president of a midwestern university recently asked one of us what she could do about the beatings without putting her husband's career in danger. Japan's former Prime Minister Sato, a winner of the Nobel Peace Prize, was accused publicly by his wife of many beatings early in their married life. Ingeborg Dedichen, a former mistress of Aristotle Onassis, describes his beating her until he was forced to quit from exhaustion. "It is what every Greek husband does, it's good for the wife," he told her. (Straus, Gelles, and Steinmetz, 1980:31)

There has been growing awareness of family violence, especially of wife and child abuse (Finkelhor, 1985; Pines, 1985; Straus, Gelles, and Steinmetz, 1980; Pogrebin, 1985).[12] Perhaps one of the major changes in the new American family is the high rates of violence in it. In fact violence occurs more often among family members than among any other individuals (Straus, Gelles, and Steinmetz, 1980). Sixteen percent of all spouses have acted violently toward each other at least once in the past year (Straus, Gelles, and Steinmetz, 1980:32). Figure 12.5 gives specific percentages for various types of family violence. Not only are the types of violent acts different, there are also different types of violent offenders (e.g., lower social class alcoholics, sadistic wealthy men, psychotics, parents who themselves were battered children, sexual deviants, overly stressed parents, military authoritarians, and so on). There are an average of about twelve attacks per year per family. In an earlier study Yabraes found that about 12 percent of husbands used violence against their wives (1979).

Furthermore, 14 percent of all children are severely beaten by their parents each year (cf. Pogrebin, 1985:101; Finkelhor, 1985:501). In return children themselves are the most violent people in the family. Two-thirds of all children had attacked a brother or a sister in the last year (Straus, Gelles, and Steinmetz, 1980:Ch. 4). When we include all destructive acts (not just physical violence), Yankelovich found that 38 percent of his sample had observed at least one destructive family activity in the last year (1978 in Skolnick, 1985). The more dominant the male spouse, the more wife beating there is. The least marital violence occurs in the most democratic families (Straus, Gelles, and Steinmetz, 1980:179). Low-income families are about 50 percent more violent than high-

FIGURE 12.5 Rate at Which Violent Acts Occurred in the Previous Year and Ever in the Marriage

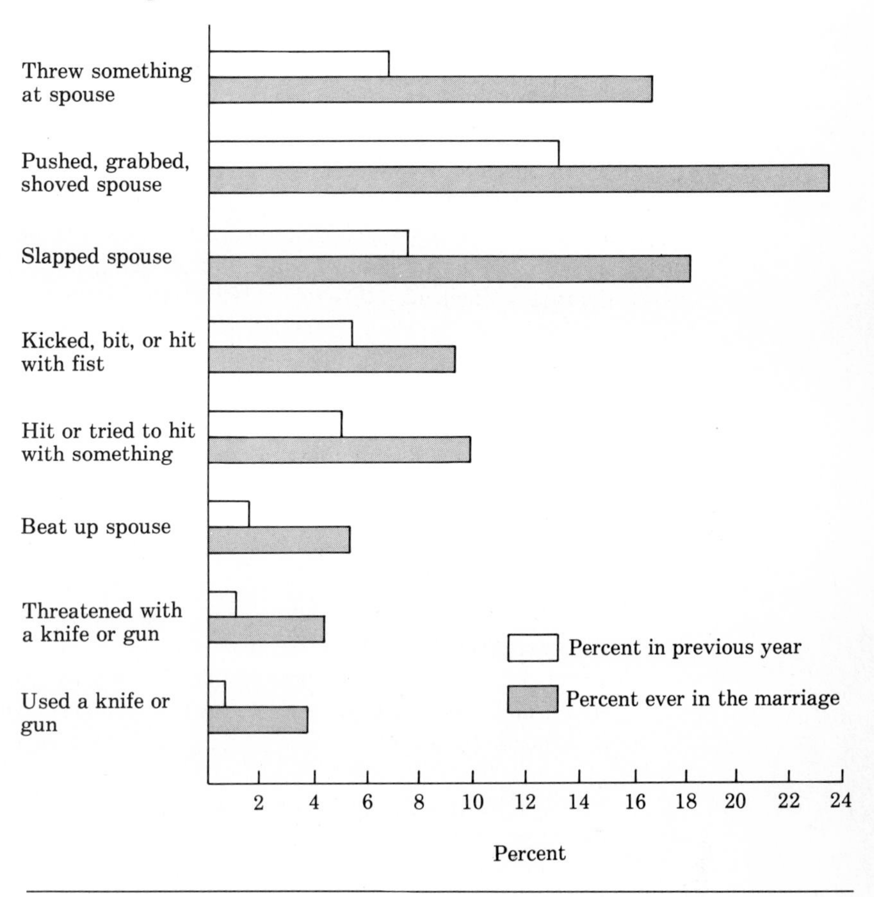

Source: From *Behind Closed Doors* by Murray A. Straus, Richard J. Gelles, and Suzanne K. Steinmetz. Copyright © 1980 by Murray A. Straus and Richard J. Gelles. Reprinted by permission of Doubleday & Company.

income families (Straus, Gelles, and Steinmetz, 1980:148), but violence can be high among highly educated families. For the most part family violence is primarily a problem in lower social class families (Finkelhor, 1985:504; Queijo, 1984:185).

It is not clear whether family violence today is greater or less than in past family situations (Straus, Gelles, and Steinmetz, 1980:6).[13] One suspects of course that family violence is not a new condition. McCoy reports that Puritan children regularly received harsh beatings from their parents (1985:392). Indeed, in seventeenth-century New England, the legal penalty for chronic disobedience of one's parents was death (Skolnick, 1985:61)!

Sexual violence of various sorts comprises a major subset of family violence.

For example, about 10 percent to 14 percent of married women have been raped by their husbands (Finkelhor and Yllo, 1983; Pogrebin, 1985:100). In a widely publicized case (Oregon, 1978) John Rideout was legally accused of raping his own wife. However, a jury found him innocent. In fact, in all but seven states a husband cannot rape his wife, since forced sex with one's wife is not considered rape (cf. Russell, *Rape in Marriage,* 1982; Pogrebin, 1985:16, 100–101, 187). Married women are often considered part of the husband's private property to do with as he wishes. The new American family has threatened many traditional husbands, some of whom now feel powerless and inadequate and take these feelings out on their wives through battering and rape. In one city hospital fully 70 percent of female visits resulted from attacks by the men in their lives (Pogrebin, 1985:100).

There are also about 100,000 cases of incest each year (Jones, Jenstrom, and MacFarlane, 1980). In one study 19 percent of women and 9 percent of men reported that they had been sexually victimized (not necessarily through incest) as children (Finkelhor, 1979). Finally, lest we forget, abortion is a form of family violence (some claim it is murder). Abortion is a complicated issue, however. Some (Straus, Gelles, and Steinmetz, 1980:235) argue that abortion should be allowed to prevent later and more extensive child and adult family violence. Others point out the obvious irony of killing a fetus to prevent violence to a child.

Analyzing the Problem We must now ask what causes child and spouse abuse. More precisely, is there something unique about the contemporary American family, marriage, and society that triggers the apparent recent surge in domestic violence?

The Exchange Perspective Look back at Table 12.5. Clearly in today's marriages both husbands and wives fail to meet traditional familial exchange expectations. For example, Straus et al. (1980:157) found that homemaking (not conflicts over money, sex, children, or social expectations) was the primary source of family conflict. Most husbands still expect their wives to be homemakers (i.e., to do the cooking, cleaning, bill paying, child care, and minor home fixings), even if they have full-time jobs outside the home (cf. Pogrebin, 1985:192 ff.; Cherlin, 1987)! In today's economy husbands are most likely to fail in their traditional economic and security functions. These failures of spouses to meet traditional marital expectations (i.e., to not provide the basic marital rewards for which the marriage was contracted) can lead to a sense of distributive injustice, anger, and eventual violence.

Note too that values have shifted more to individualism and personal fulfillment (Boudreau, 1983:438). Exchange theory maintains that the less valuable a given activity is, the less it will be performed. Traditional family values have declined and with them there are growing conflicts in marital relations. Family violence also results (from the exchange perspective) from failure in general effectiveness in routine social exchanges, that is, from interpersonal impotence. Critical cases in point are when husbands are unable to control

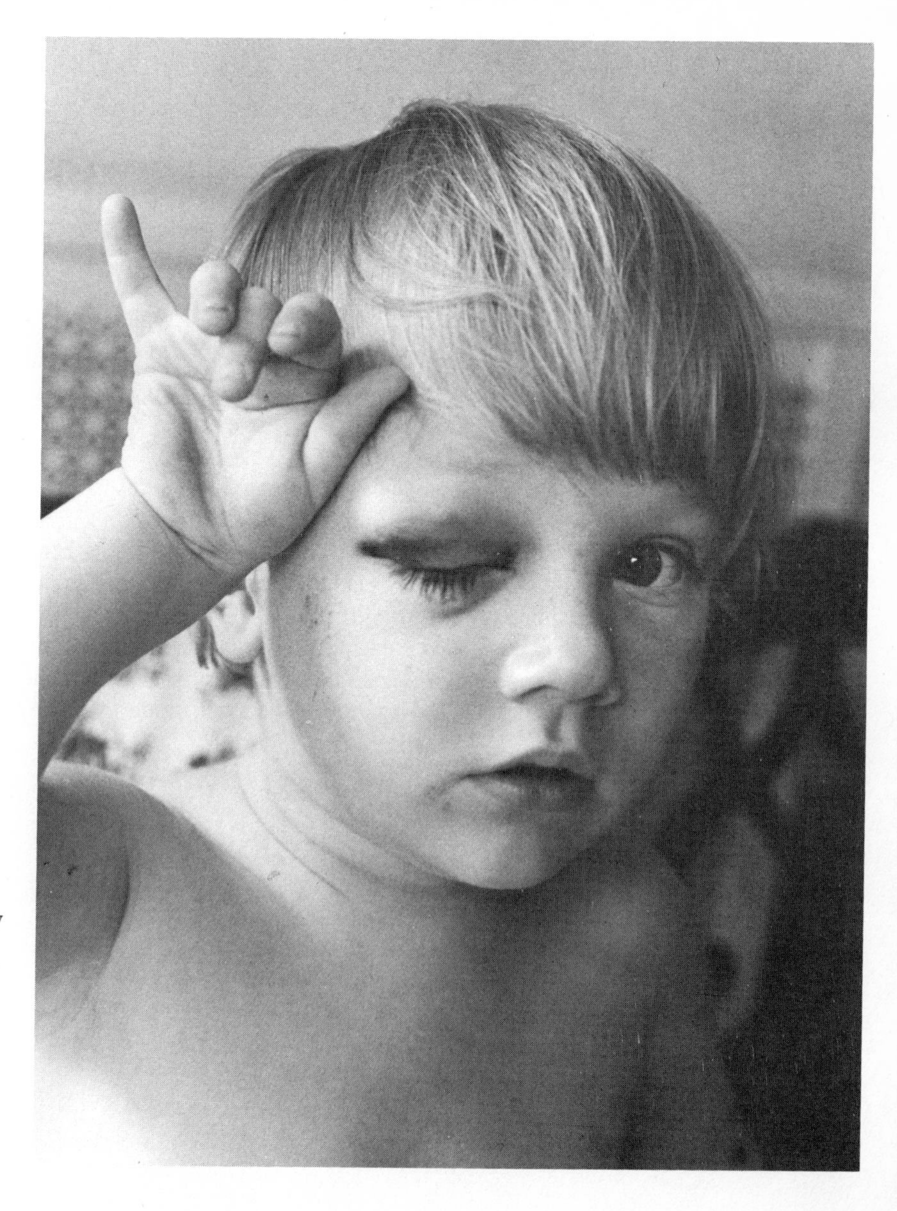

Family violence occurs more often among family members than between criminals and private citizens. About 14 percent of all children are severely beaten by their parents each year. Conflict over children leads to the most family violence. (James R. Holland/Stock, Boston)

the behavior of their wives or children. For example, when wives work outside the home many men feel as if they are no longer head of the household (Rubin, 1976:215). Modern males feel a new sense of powerlessness (Finkelhor, 1985:502). The recourse is often to violence, child, and wife abuse.

The Structural Perspective Remember that structuralism focuses on factors of size, number, and status distribution. Straus, Gelles, and Steinmetz report that conflict over children leads to the most family violence (1980:171).[14] Figure 12.6 further reveals that generally the larger the number of children living at home, the greater the amount of wife abuse. Another structural factor affecting family violence is the larger proportion of married females working outside the home. Generally, the less opportunity for interaction (i.e., the more restrictions on familial interaction), the more disliking, anger, and violence.

Guttentag and Secord (1983:153–161) add that the excess of females since about 1945 has resulted in a general devaluation of women. Since today women are less of a scarce resource, they are not as likely to be treated as well. Men in the 1980s have more freedom of choice and more control over the way they relate to women. Women have become less powerful and men more powerful. Of course, power, unfortunately, is often abused.

The Conflict Perspective The primary explanation of the classic book on family violence (*Behind Closed Doors,* Straus, Gelles, and Steinmetz, 1980) is in the tradition of conflict theory. Essentially, what Straus et al. argue is that the more conflict over money, children, sex, housekeeping, and social activities in a family, the greater the rates of family violence (1980:158–163). In an earlier work Gelles concluded that violence runs in families, is mainly a lower class phenomenon, is linked to stress, social isolation, unemployment, poverty, and social norms condoning violence, and is aggravated by alcohol abuse (1980; cf. Queijo, 1985:188).[15]

FIGURE 12.6 Wife Abuse by Number of Children Living at Home

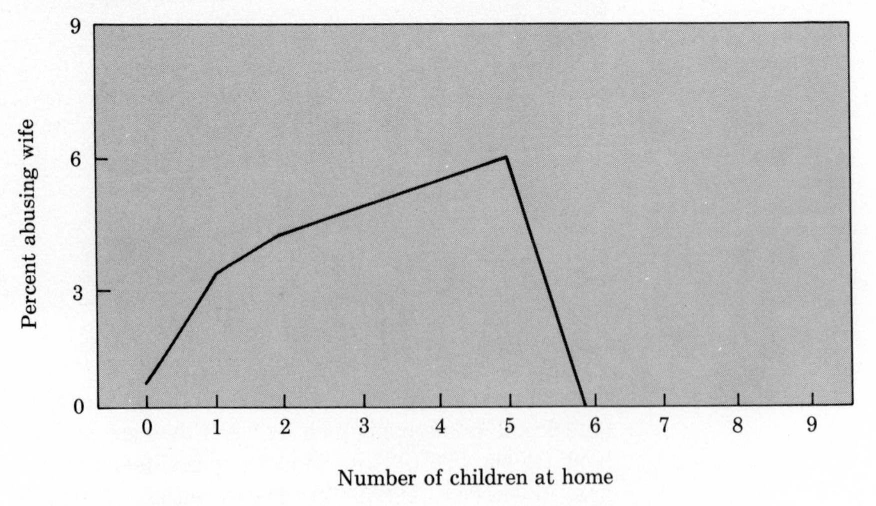

Source: From *Behind Closed Doors* by Murray A. Straus, Richard J. Gelles, and Suzanne K. Steinmetz. Copyright © 1980 by Murray A. Straus and Richard J. Gelles. Reprinted by permission of Doubleday & Company.

Resolving the Problem Having examined the problem of family violence and its causes, we must conclude by asking what can be done about them. Surely, we need not simply resign ourselves to a family violence rate of one in four or five.[16] Four concrete types of resolution are recommended. One set of resolutions turns on what G. Caplan called primary prevention (1964). It involves no less than changing society itself. First, norms condoning violence must be modified (Straus, Gelles, and Steinmetz, 1980:237). Second, sexism needs to be modified and more egalitarian marriages encouraged. It is not appropriate to exploit or hate either women or men. Third, from the exchange perspective the very basis for exchange in marriage needs to be revised (e.g., homemaking and economic responsibilities shared, although this might cause new problems too). If this is accomplished, then, hopefully, there would be less frustration, violence, and anger. Fourth, stress reduction and management are important priorities. Finally, unemployment and poverty rates need to be lowered, since both seem to spawn family violence.

A second set of resolutions is more concerned with secondary or tertiary prevention of family violence (i.e., with ameliorating the destructive effects of family violence, rather than keeping it from happening at all). For example, abused women and children need a place to go (other than running away from their homes).[17] More shelters, day-care centers, and welfare support would help (Straus, Gelles, and Steinmetz, 1980:224–227). We also need more family counseling, family planning, and divorce consultation (Straus et al., 1980:234–235). Many couples simply need to learn how to cope better in marital situations. Often the number of children a couple has needs to be reduced, especially unwanted children that the couples cannot afford. Options here include family planning, birth control, abortion, and adoption. Finally, if couples cannot live together, they need to be able to end their marriage as smoothly and nontraumatically as possible. Two last recommendations: Third, alcohol aggravates all violence; thus, we need better alcohol control. And fourth, we should train police and courts to deal more effectively and appropriately with domestic violence (Straus, Gelles, and Steinmetz, 1980:232ff.).

• Summary

As a social institution the family has been mandated with resolving recurrent human problems of regulating sexual behavior and reproduction; educating and socializing infants and young children; providing love, loyalty, and noncontingent emotional support; defending family members against violence; caring for dependent young and females (sheltering, feeding, clothing, and so on); and maintaining important cultural and religious traditions.

By the family we mean primarily the father, mother, and their children only (the nuclear family). A family is a group of persons united by ties of marriage, blood, or adoption, who constitute a single household and create and maintain a common culture. The traditional family was somewhat larger and was a more extended family (about five to six completed family size), more rural, more economically self-sufficient, with lower divorce rates and earlier marriages, more religious, more wives were homemakers, and more children got most of their basic needs met in the family itself. Infant mortality rates and death in childbirth were high.

The new contemporary American family is small (it averages two children), highly urbanized, the mother tends to work outside the home, many children are cared for in day-care centers and educated in public schools (indeed, all family life has become more secular and dependent on nonfamilial institutions), and divorce rates have skyrocketed, even though Americans are marrying later. Children have become enormously expensive to raise to maturity (about $100,000 each). Consequently, more people are remaining single. Staying single or delaying marriage allows one to pursue a career and engage in more self-development. Couples tend to cohabit for sexual gratification and companionship without getting married or having children, even though marriage is still valued highly by most Americans. Given all the stress of contemporary marriage and family life, the rate of family violence also tends to be high.

In this chapter we looked especially at the contemporary marital and familial problems of divorce and family violence. We saw that the United States has one of the highest divorce rates in the world. Furthermore, the American divorce rate has doubled since 1960. Divorce has had major social consequences, especially for women and children. One consequence seems to be increasing rates of family violence, particularly of wife and child abuse. It was estimated that about 16 percent of all spouses acted violently toward each other in the last year. Indeed, today's families display more violence than any other individuals in society.

The exchange explanation of both the problems of divorce and family violence centers on shifts in basic marital and familial rewards in recent years. In traditional marriages the husband provided economic and physical support security in return for the sexual gratification, homemaking, child production and socialization, and emotional support of the wife-mother. In contemporary marriages and families, economic, sex-role, geographic, and other social changes have made male and female rewards in marriage and the family less distinctive, less unique, and less common. Thus, today there is less reason to stay married (or even to get married). Contemporary wives tend to work outside the home, children cost more and are cared for more often by professionals, protection seems to be provided by the law and the police, and sex tends to be pursued for its own sake. With the failure of modern marriage and family to meet traditional exchange explanations, familial frustration and violence are at high levels.

Structurally, divorce and family violence vary with sex ratio size, male cohort size, the need and opportunity of wives to work outside the family, the increased proximity of married females to alternatives to marriage and family life (jobs, money, lovers, and so on), less social interaction between husbands and wives, and the size of the completed family (the larger the completed family size, the more the family violence).

Those in the functionalist camp argue that there is more divorce and family violence because the functions of the traditional family are changing. The traditional family was concerned with sexual control of its members, socialization of children, care of the aged, medical treatment of the sick and injured, providing recreation, sexual reproduction, and economic production. Many of these traditional social responsibilities or needs are now performed by other institutions. Functionalists conclude that the traditional family is less socially necessary today and divorce and family violence are more likely.

The conflict perspective tends to see traditional marriages as oppressive and restrictive of women. As women have become better organized, become more economically self-sufficient, and raised their group consciousness of marital exploitation, they have begun to rebel against male domination in traditional marriage. Divorce is the sign that women are throwing off the shackles of male domination and exploitation. One natural consequence of men and women's increased conflict over money, children, sex, housekeeping, and social activities in the traditional family is greater short-term rates of family violence. For conflict theorists when economic equality among the sexes is greater, for a while we should expect higher divorce rates, greater sexual freedom, and even higher rates of family violence. All of these traits are signs of long-term social well-being and reform, not social pathology.

Common resolutions to problems of today's marriage and family (especially those of divorce and violence) include more egalitarian marriages (e.g., sharing money, work, and child care); changing the expectations and terms for marriage (including marriage contracts); having improved second marriages; having society itself (e.g., schools, governmental agencies, and churches) assume more of the traditional marital responsibilities; in some cases allowing for more singleness, divorce, and living alone; changing norms condoning violence; and reducing stress, poverty, and alcohol abuse. Probably, trying to turn the clock back by reinforcing traditional family values and forms will not work.

Note that the concerns about marriage and family problems are social as well as personal. Traditional families performed important social tasks with major consequences for social cohesion, child care, reproduction of society, and so on—that society cannot afford to have neglected.

The next chapter (13) continues our examination of institutional-level (or macro) social problems. Most institutional-level social problems are interactive; their causes and resolutions are linked. For example, we have just seen that problems in the new American family are related closely to social changes to which we now turn in Chapter 13—namely, the urban transformation, fertility and mortality, and population growth, just to mention a few.

• Notes

1. One must be careful not to imply that the nuclear family is a modern configuration. The nuclear family dates back at least to thirteenth-century England, when it comprised as many as half of all families (McCoy, 1985:388).

2. The implied contrast is what some commentators have dubbed serial monogamy; that is, *several* spouses over a lifetime but only *one* (to speak of) at a time.

3. If you are curious, see the glossary in Lamanna and Riedmann, 1985.

4. Today about one-fourth of all women in childbearing ages will *never* have a child at all (Cherlin and Furstenberg, 1983:227).

5. Those reporting their marriages satisfying or very satisfying were business husbands, 93 percent; business wives, 93 percent; working-class husbands, 96 percent; and working-class wives, 90 percent.

6. Although unmarried cohabitating couples still account for only about 3 percent of all households.

7. For example, in studies in the Netherlands it was found that the percentage of the population believing that married people are more happy than single people declined from 60 percent to 35 percent between 1965 and 1975.

8. Remember that individual and social interests can be very different. See Chapter 10 and especially Table 10.5. For example, marriage might still be good (rewarding) for individual actors, but not for corporate actors.

9. Divorced men should also be considered to receive child support payments and child custody.

10. In one study 82 percent of survey respondents said divorce was OK if no children were involved, but only 71 percent approved if there were children (*Better Homes and Gardens,* 1978).

11. My own feeling is that two chances is also just about *all* one usually gets. With a second divorce emotional recovery, financial reorganization, and so on are much more difficult. It is also more difficult to claim that one is a victim when repeated bad outcomes accrue. Of course, some people do well after multiple disrupted relationships—but not many.

12. I say "awareness" intentionally, because it is not clear that the *rates* of family violence have actually increased. We may just be noticing what was there but unnoticed decades ago.

13. In fact, there probably is no way to measure and compare today's family violence rates with rates in past, more traditional families. Comparable data on the past simply are not available.

14. Homemaking disagreements led to the most conflict, but not to the most violence (children did).

15. Most of these factors in family violence (but not all) fit the conflict perspective—especially being lower class, stress, and social isolation.

16. A certain (unspecifiable?) level of family violence may be necessary. Some stress, competition, and social change are required to improve ourselves and our social quality of life—especially to improve the social lot of women.

17. One of the great dilemmas of modern marriage seems to be that we cannot live together, but we cannot do without each other either.

• Glossary

Cohabitation. A couple living together in an intimate sexual and emotional relationship without a traditional legal marriage.

Extended Family. A family including parents, children, grandparents, and sometimes unmarried aunts or uncles living together.

Family. A group of persons living together in an intimate interpersonal relationship, united by ties of marriage, blood, or adoption who constitute a single household and who create and maintain a common culture.

Family of Orientation. The family into which one was born, raised, and from which one's basic life orientation was received.

Family of Procreation. The family established by one's marriage that usually results in the birth of children.

Family Violence. An act carried out with the intention or perceived intention of causing physical pain or injury to another family member, including beatings, knifings, shootings, and rapes.

Illegitimacy. A birth by an unmarried woman.

Incest. Morally proscribed sexual relations between close relatives, such as brothers and sisters or parents and children.

Joint Custody. The sharing by both divorced parents of legal responsibility for making decisions about their children's upbringing and general welfare.

Monogamy. The practice or state of being married to only one person at a time.

Nuclear Family. A family group comprised of only the wife, husband, and their children.

Reconstituted Family. A family in which the husband, wife, or both partners have children from previous marriages.

Serial Monogamy. A family form in which one has several husbands or wives, but never more than one at a time.

• Further Reading

Blumsten, Philip and Pepper Schwartz. *American Couples.* New York: William Morrow and Co., 1983. In a book that received wide media attention two sociologists did in-depth research on all types of couples' relationships: married, living together (cohabitators), same sex (gay men and lesbians), urban-rural, rich-poor, all ages, with and without children, and long versus short duration with a focus on work, money, and sex lives. From over 12,000 questionnaires, 300 couples were chosen from Seattle, San Francisco, and New York for more intensive interviews.

Caplow, Theodore et al. *Middletown Families: Fifty Years of Change and Continuity.* Minneapolis: University of Minnesota Press, 1982. When Caplow, his associates, and their families went to live in and to conduct an extensive follow-up study (forty years later) of Robert and Helen Lynd's classic *Middletown* (Muncie, Indiana) studies in 1929 and 1937, Caplow found no appreciable decline in the Middletown family. Indeed, marriage and family life were stronger and more satisfying than in the 1920s.

Cherlin, Andrew J. *Marriage, Divorce, and Remarriage.* Cambridge, MA: Harvard University Press, 1981. This is a thin, lucid, first volume in a series *(Social Trends in the U.S.)* on continuity and change in society, sponsored by the Social Science

Research Council. Cherlin examines demographic trends, explanations, consequences, and black-white differences in marriage, divorce, and remarriage in the United States. A central question is: Why are marriage and divorce patterns in the 1980s so different than those in the 1950s? Familiar findings include later marriages, fewer children, higher divorce rates and increased rates of remarriage, resulting from advanced industrial society, women working outside the home, and the special consequences of the Great Depression and World War II.

Henslin, James M., ed. *Marriage and Family in a Changing Society.* New York: The Free Press, 1985. A recent reader on contemporary marriage and family life issues. Henslin has scholars provide original brief synopses of their latest theory and research. There are sections on minorities, sex roles, romance, dating and mating, marital alternatives, work and remarriage, sex, parenting, divorce, remarriage, enduring relationships, and the future. An excellent, current overview of the topic for the novice.

Lasch, Christopher. *Haven in a Heartless World: The Family Besieged.* New York: Basic Books, 1977. The family is the last refuge of love and decency from the world of commerce, competition, politics, and professionalism. Yet today's family is in a social crisis that makes it less able to be a haven. The American family has been coming apart for over 100 years as the industrial revolution took over the household and reproduction. Now the family is more and more dependent on managerial and professional classes and forces.

Straus, Murray A., Richard J. Gelles, and Suzanne K. Steinmetz. *Behind Closed Doors: Violence in the American Family.* Garden City, New York: Anchor Books, 1980. The American family may be a haven in a heartless world, but it is also the center of abusive violence. In an investigation of a national sample of 2,143 families, the New Hampshire program for Family Violence Research found that in one out of every six families the spouse hit his/her partner last year, in three out of five families parents hit their children, and in three out of five families brothers and sisters are violent toward one another. Much of this family violence goes unreported and receives no response. Authors argue for better treatment programs, especially for abused wives and children.

C·H·A·P·T·E·R

13

Population: World, National, and Urban

The world populations have recently experienced rapid growth at an accelerating rate (somewhat less in the United States), especially in most major urban areas. If unchecked, population growth could result in serious overcrowding, food shortages, deterioration of air, water, and essential nonreplenishable resources, increased violence, a generally lower quality of life, and even higher death rates. Rapid population expansion develops when fertility rates remain high while mortality rates drop sharply.

The exchange perspective suggests that historically, especially for individuals, high fertility rates have been rewarding and result from activities that we (both individuals and corporate actors) are slow to satiate on. When high fertility is too costly, birthrates invariably drop. The rapid drop in mortality rates results from a combination of high social consensus on avoiding death and the relative ease of death control vis-à-vis birth control.

Structurally, one could argue that birthrates remain high and death rates low because we are better able to support a large population through enhanced food production, advances in health and sanitation, more occupational specialization, higher socioeconomic status, more industrialized economics, and larger numbers of people living in denser areas. Some urban areas, which were originally rewarding and structurally induced, have recently become highly adversive and increasingly structurally untenable.

From a more macrosociological functional perspective (especially an ecological evolutionary worldview) fertility, mortality, and urban transformation are all variables related to societal type, technological innovation, and economic factors. To oversimplify, the move from an agrarian to an industrial era (with the latter's lowered fertility and mortality rates and increase of major cities) is related to the prevention and cure of disease (especially of communicable diseases like the flu, tuberculosis, and small pox); to technological advances (like contraceptive pills and safe methods of abortion); and to a switch from subsistence agriculture to capital-intensive industries. Dependency theories see Third-World or developing countries as less developed because of external exploitation by global capitalism. Modernization theories view population problems in Third-World countries resulting from internal conditions, such as the persistence of ideologies and institutional systems inherited from their preindustrial pasts.

The conflict and world systems perspectives conceive of large families, high birthrates, starvation diets, poor health and poor sanitation, and so on as part of a pattern engendered by economic exploitation of the developing countries by the more industrialized nations. Taking economic and political advantage of Third-World countries (such as by paying low wages, forcing exports to other countries, and charging high prices for oil) tends to keep those countries poor and technologically retarded, in short, undeveloped. Being kept industrially underdeveloped means (among other things) having high birthrates, high but falling death rates, having a large poor rural population, and undeveloped urban areas.

As recently as 1974 at the United Nation's International Conference on Population in Bucharest (Romania) the slogan of the underdeveloped countries was "development is the best contraceptive." Not so in Mexico City at the 1984 U.N. population conference. The development expected a decade before had simply not materialized and the developing countries stood in still starker contrast to the developed countries (e.g., those in North America and western Europe; Brown et al., 1985:200). Countries like China, India, Ethiopia, Mexico, Brazil (and others) are now faced with soaring population growth, overcrowding, pollution, raw sewage in the streets, resource depletion and fouling (especially of air, water, forests, and fossil fuels), diminished social services and crumbling transportation systems, starvation, violence, and even death (see Panel 13.1). The Mexican population alone is expected to grow from 70 million in 1980 to 174 million in 2025 (*Time,* August 6, 1984; Bouvier, 1984:8). Other Third-World countries (such as India) are expected to grow even more (see Figure 13.1). The present chapter is less focused on American social problems than previous chapters were, since most of the world population growth is occurring in the Third-World countries. However, obviously planet earth is finite. Population changes in Mexico, Ethiopia, China, or India have indirect but profound implications for the United States population and our own quality of life (Murray, 1985).

PANEL 13.1

Urban Apocalypse in Mexico City

When the ragged and exhausted Spanish conquistadors first beheld the lake-encircled capital of the Aztecs one November morning in 1519, they were stunned by its grandeur. A shining metropolis of some 300,000 people, far larger than any city in Europe, Tenochtitlan displayed immense stone temples to the gods of rain and war and an even more immense royal palace, where Aztec nobles stood guard in jaguar-head helmets and brightly feathered robes. In the nearby marketplace, vendors offered an abundance of jungle fruit and rare herbs and skillfully wrought creations of silver and gold. "The magnificence, the strange and marvelous things of this great city are so remarkable as not to be believed," Hernando Cortes wrote back to the imperial court of Charles V. "We are seeing things," Bernal Diaz del Castillo recalled in his memoir of the Spanish invasion, "that had never been heard of or seen before, nor even dreamed about."

A newcomer today is more apt to arrive by air, and before he glimpses the dried-up bed of Lake Texcoco, now edged with miles of slum hovels, the first thing he sees is an almost perpetual blanket of smog that shrouds the entire city. It is an ugly grayish brown. There is something strangely sinister about it—a cloud of poison. The pilot orders the seat belts tightened and announces an imminent descent into the murk and filth.

This is Mexico City, grand, proud, beautiful Mexico City, which already boasted a Spanish cathedral and a university when Washington and Boston were still woodlands. Within the past year or so this ancient metropolis has grown to about seventeen million people, and it is in the process of surpassing Tokyo as the largest city in the world. But that growth, which might once have been a point of pride, is a curse. It consists in large part of jobless peasants streaming in from the countryside at a rate of about 1,000 a day. Novelist Carlos Fuentes has called Mexico City the capital of underdevelopment; it has also become a capital of pollution and a capital of slums.

This is the city builder's dream turned nightmare. It is the supercity, the megalopolis, infected by a kind of social cancer that is metastasizing out of control. Its afflictions—a mixture of overcrowding, poverty, pollution, and corruption—are a warning to all the other great cities, particularly those in the Third World, but to New York and Los Angeles as well, that what is happening in Mexico City threatens them too.

Says one leading environmentalist: "The question is not whether we will be able to live a pleasant life a few years from now. The question is whether or not we will be able to survive." Says another, Gabriel Quadri: "If nothing is done to cleanse our home, this desert of steel and concrete will be our tomb."

Source: *Time,* August 6, 1984:26–27.

Such monumental population growth, of course, raises serious issues that we must address and hopefully resolve in this chapter.[1] First, and perhaps most obvious, is rapid unchecked population growth good or bad, helpful or disastrous, boom or bust? Thomas Malthus argued (in *An Essay on the Principle of Population,* 1798) that unchecked population growth would eventually limit

FIGURE 13.1 World Population in Millions, 1960–2025

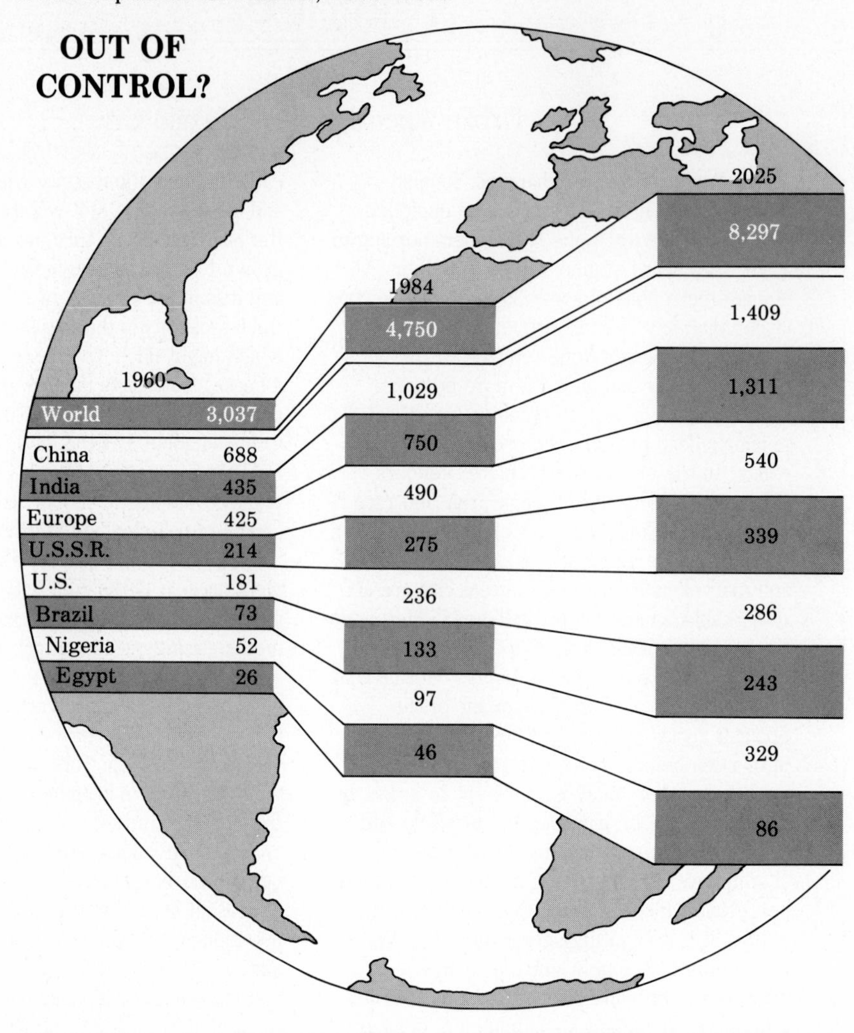

Source: *Time,* August 6, 1984. Reprinted by permission from TIME.

itself by starvation deaths, since population grows geometrically (i.e., 2,4,6,8 . . . n) while food supplies only grow arithmetically (namely, 1,2,3,4 . . . n). Most Malthusians and neo-Malthusians see disaster in eventual unchecked population growth. Others, like Simon (1981), counter that people tend to limit reproduction to fit available food, land, and so on. For example, Simon says (I could not resist), the United States has 2.3 billion acres of land. Cities, roads, railroads, airports, parking lots, and so on take up only 2.7 percent of all U.S. land.

Second, if world population growth continues unabated, will we certainly run out of food (Revelle, 1974; Philliber, 1986)? Malthusians predict mass starvation and death, such as we saw in the mid-1980s in Ethiopia (Associated Press, September 8, 1985; Bouvier, 1984:31). We tend to forget that the preoccupation of most of mankind is with obtaining enough food to eat (Hanlon, 1985). Obviously, if populations double, then food production must also double. Non-Malthusians counter that most adults in fact do not die of starvation (Simon, 1981). At worst (they say) we are experiencing a problem with the quality, not the possibility, of life. To illustrate, from 1951 to 1971 world grain production doubled, but the world population increased by only 50 percent (Paarlberg, 1981; Revelle, 1974:119). Finally, the world food problem may be one of distribution (and related political and economic issues), not of availability.

Third, will we run out of resources, such as fossil fuels, timber, fresh water, clean air, and so on? Brown et al. point out that by 1984 most countries saw forest deterioration, soil depletion (especially from overuse of nitrogen fertilizers), grassland destruction, and alteration of their hydrological cycles (1985:201; Philliber, 1986). As an example, 850 acres of timber are needed just to produce one Sunday edition of the *New York Times Magazine* (Waddington, 1978)! Fourth, will air and water become so polluted that it cannot sustain life? Since the next chapter will examine this issue in detail, no more will be said here. Fifth, will overcrowding result in violence (e.g., food wars), shortages of all kinds, and death? Clearly, unchecked population expansion will lead to land shortages (especially for certain purposes), crowding, and dense living conditions.

Sixth, what is the ethnic and political symbolism of world population growth (or decline)? If control of population growth means limiting the peoples of Africa, India, South America, China, Arabic countries, and so on, then it can be seen as genocide. Conversely, the current zero population growth (see below for definition) in countries like France, Germany (both East and West), and Austria may require fertility increases if those nations are to survive. Finally, are all population problems really urban problems, since most people now live in cities and the population problems are most severe in major world cities (*UNESCO Courier,* 1985)? What does the future hold for population growth? How accurate are projections about future population development? Before we begin to address those issues, let us once again be clear about definitions of key concepts in the study of population (a few definitions will be deferred until the relevant topic is discussed later in this chapter). These definitions will be a little dull to read and memorize, but they are important and over with reasonably quickly.

Demography can be defined as the study of the size, composition, growth, and distribution of the human population (Nam and Philliber, 1984:368). The new population of any group (country, and so on) is determined by the group's fertility minus its mortality with adjustments for migration. When we speak of the *natural increase* in a population we mean the percent excess of its births over deaths (Philliber, 1983:487). *Fertility* can be measured by the *crude birth*

"But demographic projections indicate that within twenty years, this town will be big enough for both of us."

rate, that is, the number of births per thousand population per year (Nam and Philliber, 1984:368) and *mortality* by the *crude death rate,* that is, the number of deaths per 1,000 population per year (Nam and Philliber, 1984:62). Often it is useful to adjust or control crude birth or death rates for age (or sex, religion, and so on), since young populations tend to have higher birthrates and aged populations have higher death rates.

When population growth is stable, we call this *zero population growth* (ZPG). ZPG occurs when there are about 2.1 children per completed family size. *Doubling time* is the number of years it takes a population to double in size (Philliber, 1986:488; Freedman and Berelson, 1974:3). For the world population as a whole the population now doubles every forty to forty-one years.[2] The doubling effect produces large numbers much faster than you might imagine. For example (overlook the sexism), a mythical king offered his daughter to anyone who could give him one grain of wheat for the first square of a chess board, two grains for the second, and so on until all squares were covered (i.e., sixty-four squares). To double grains until sixty-four squares were covered would require more grain than today's worldwide grain production!

Life expectancy also needs to be differentiated from life span. One's *life expectancy* is the average number of years of life predicted to be lived by a group of babies born at the same time (a cohort) (Nam and Philliber, 1984:62).[3] *Life span,* on the other hand, refers to the ultimate age to which people can live (Nam and Philliber, 1984:63). While life expectancy in the United States has almost doubled since 1900, life span has remained relatively constant at about 100 years. Finally, many populations or countries are bifurcated into two fundamentally different types. These two types of populations are usually called developed or developing (sometimes underdeveloped). *Developing countries* (constituting about 75 percent of the world population) have high crude birthrates (sometimes as high as 50), death rates that are considerably lower than their birthrates (are declining), and high population growth. Developing countries are in earlier industrial, economic, and social stages (see Lenski and Lenski, 1987; Table 13.1; and the discussion of the theory of demographic transition, below).

Developed countries have low death rates, low birthrates (but usually still somewhat higher than their death rates), and stable or zero population growth. Such developed populations have relatively high gross national products, and more industrialization, scientific, and technological development (see Table 13.1).

Now that we have defined our concepts we must take a first look at the prevalence and incidence of world and U.S. national population problems. Figure 13.1 reveals that the world population in the mid-1980s was about five billion (cf. Bouvier, 1984:10). More precisely, there were 4.85 billion people in 1985, an approximate increase per year of 81 million, resulting from 133 million births and 52 million deaths (Brown et al., 1985:203). The Population Reference Bureau estimates that in the year 2000 there will be 6.1 billion people in the world and in 2020 about 7.7 billion (Table 13.1; cf. Bouvier, 1984:23).

As we have seen, 75 percent of the world's population lives in developing countries, which have high birthrates, lowering death rates, and rapidly increasing populations (i.e., at a rate of 2 percent per year). The populations in the developing countries tend to be young, have high infant mortality rates, low life expectancy rates, and low GNPs (Table 13.1). Given these social conditions, there will be much population growth in developing countries (indeed, in the entire world), even if fertility rates are lowered (Table 13.2; Freedman and Berelson, 1974:4).

Figure 13.2 reveals that since 1650 the world population has been growing at an increasing rate (cf. Philliber, 1983:488). Today (in 1985) the world population doubles every forty-one years (Reinhold, 1979). In fact, the world population will increase as much between 1984 and 2004 as it did from the birth of Christ until 1950! That is, the growth of the world population for the first 99 percent of human history (about 990,000 years) was exceedingly small (Coale, 1974:17). The natural increase of the world population is now 1.7 percent per year (about 2 percent to 2.4 percent in the developing countries). However, most population experts agree that these high growth rates will not

TABLE 13.1 World Population Data Sheet, 1985

Region or Country	Population Estimate Mid-1985 (Millions)	Crude Birthrate	Crude Death Rate	Natural Increase (Annual, Percent)	Population "Doubling Time" in Years (at Current Rate)	Population Projected to 2000 (Millions)
WORLD	4,845	27	11	1.7	41	6,135
MORE DEVELOPED	1,174	15	9	0.6	118	1,271
LESS DEVELOPED	3,671	31	11	2.0	34	4,863
LESS DEVELOPED (EXCLUDING CHINA)	2,629	36	12	2.4	29	3,666
AFRICA	551	45	16	2.9	24	869
Northern Africa	128	41	12	2.9	24	190
Western Africa	166	48	18	3.0	23	272
Eastern Africa	159	48	17	3.1	23	258
Middle Africa	62	45	18	2.7	26	95
Southern Africa	37	36	14	2.2	31	53
ASIA	2,829	28	10	1.8	39	3,562
ASIA (Excluding China)	1,787	33	12	2.2	32	2,365
Southwest Asia	114	39	11	2.8	25	171
Middle South Asia	1,058	37	13	2.3	30	1,412
Southeast Asia	404	32	10	2.2	31	542
East Asia	1,252	18	8	1.1	65	1,437
NORTH AMERICA	264	15	8	0.7	99	297
Canada	25.4	15	7	0.8	90	29.4
United States	238.9	16	9	0.7	100	268.0
LATIN AMERICA	406	31	8	2.3	30	554
Middle America	105	33	6	2.7	26	151
Caribbean	31	25	8	1.8	39	39
Tropical South America	225	32	8	2.4	29	308
Temperate South America	46	24	8	1.6	44	56
EUROPE	492	13	10	0.3	240	509
Northern Europe	83	13	11	0.1	465	84
Western Europe	155	12	11	0.1	729	154
Eastern Europe	112	16	11	0.5	140	120
Southern Europe	143	13	9	0.4	165	151
USSR	278	20	10	1.0	71	316
OCEANIA	24	21	8	1.2	56	28

Source: Adapted from the *Population Reference Bureau, Inc.*, April 1985. Mary M. Kent and Carl Haub, 1985 *World Population Data Sheet* (Population Reference Bureau, Washington, D.C., 1985).

Population Projected to 2020 (Millions)	Infant Mortality Rate	Total Fertility Rate	Percent Population under Age 15/over Age 64	Life Expectancy at Birth (Years)	Urban Population (Percent)	Per Capita GNP, 1983 (US$)	Total Area (1000s of sq. miles)/Percent Cultivated
7,760	81	3.7	35/6	62	41	$2,760	51,720/11
1,351	18	2.0	23/12	73	72	9,380	21,344/12
6,409	90	4.2	39/4	58	31	700	30,375/10
5,121	101	5.0	41/4	56	34	880	26,670/10
1,433	110	6.3	45/3	50	31	750	11,711/6
282	97	6.0	43/4	56	42	1,190	3,291/4
454	118	6.4	47/3	48	29	580	2,372/10
452	109	6.8	47/3	49	17	300	2,454/7
163	119	6.1	44/3	48	34	420	2,553/4
82	94	5.2	39/4	53	52	2,280	1,040/6
4,340	87	3.7	37/4	60	27	940	10,659/17
3,052	103	4.6	39/4	57	31	1,360	6,954/20
253	94	5.9	42/4	61	53	3,500	1,754/10
1,834	120	5.0	41/3	52	24	260	2,620/33
702	79	4.5	40/3	59	24	710	1,735/17
1,550	35	2.1	32/5	66	29	1,360	4,551/10
330	10	1.8	22/12	75	74	13,890	7,599/12
33.1	9.1	1.7	22/10	75	76	12,000	3,851/5
296.6	10.5	1.8	22/12	75	74	14,090	3,615/20
752	62	4.2	38/5	65	66	1,890	7,935/9
211	55	4.9	43/4	65	63	1,940	963/12
51	55	3.3	35/6	67	54	—	92/26
422	70	4.2	38/4	63	66	1,860	5,446/7
67	32	3.1	30/8	70	83	2,020	1,433/12
507	15	1.8	22/13	73	73	8,200	1,881/29
83	9	1.8	21/15	74	75	9,680	608/11
144	10	1.6	20/14	74	83	10,870	383/30
127	19	2.1	24/11	71	62	—	382/45
153	18	1.9	24/12	73	69	4,810	508/37
364	32	2.4	25/10	69	64	6,350	8,649/10
32	39	2.7	29/8	71	71	8,570	3,286/6

TABLE 13.2 Current Population of Selected Countries, with Projections to Stationary State

Country	Population, 1982 (Million)	Population Size when Stationary State Is Achieved (Million)	Change from 1982 Population (Percent)
Bangladesh	93	454	+388
Brazil	127	304	+139
China	1,008	1,461	+45
Egypt	44	114	+159
Ethiopia	33	231	+600
France	54	62	+15
India	717	1,707	+138
Indonesia	153	370	+142
Japan	118	128	+8
Mexico	73	199	+173
Nigeria	91	618	+579
Pakistan	87	377	+333
Poland	36	49	+36
South Africa	30	123	+310
South Korea	39	70	+79
Soviet Union	270	377	+40
Turkey	47	111	+136
United Kingdom	56	59	+5
United States	232	292	+26
West Germany	62	54	−13

Source: From *World Development Report 1984*. Copyright © 1984 by The International Bank for Reconstruction and Development/The World Bank. Reprinted by permission of Oxford University Press, Inc.

be sustained. Eventually zero population growth will come to most countries. For the world as a whole ZPG should occur about the year 2100 (Zopf, 1984:4).

Looking specifically at American population growth we see that in mid-1985 the U.S. population was 239 million (243.5 million on June 1, 1987), the fourth largest national population in the world (Table 13.1; Zopf, 1984:81). The percent increase in the U.S. population from 1970 to 1980 was 11.4 percent; most of it was in the western and southern states (Figure 13.3). Bouvier claims that the U.S. population will stop growing at about 309 million people in the year 2050 (however, see Table 13.2) and then decline if immigration is limited to 450,000 per year (1984:5). About 75 percent of the U.S. population lives in urban areas. Recently (1985) the United States has had a crude birthrate of 15.7, a crude death rate of 8.7, and a rate of natural increase of about 0.7 to 0.9 percent. Most of the increase in the U.S. population has been natural; that is, not the result of migration.

FIGURE 13.2 World Population Growth: 1650–2000

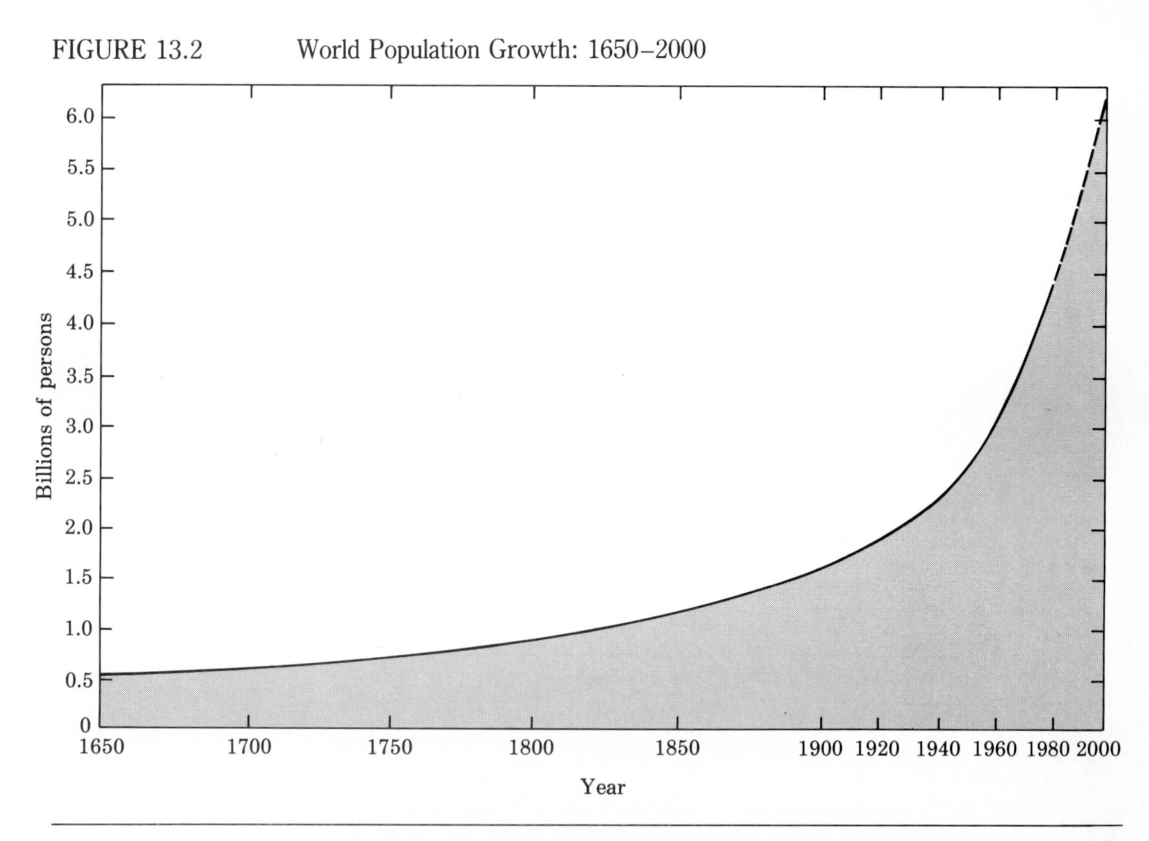

Source: Paul Zopf, Jr., *Population: An Introduction to Social Democracy,* Mayfield Publishing Co., 1984:4.

Of course, like other social problems population problems have a relevant natural history. Obviously, they did not spring full-blown in the 1980s. So-called primitive populations had crude birthrates and death rates that were both high. Thus, their rates of natural increase were low (Nam and Philliber, 1984:107). No early populations ever had total fertility rates of much more than eight births per woman. That is, they were well below the theoretical maximum of seventeen (Coale, 1974:18–19; Nam and Philliber, 1984:107). The average life expectancy in ancient populations was about twenty to thirty-five years (Nam and Philliber, 1984:63). Thus, we would expect completed family sizes of about 6.5 children, although exact records to compile accurate data to test this estimate are not available.

Perhaps the most cited historical theory of population development is called the theory of demographic transition (TDT). A simplified version of the TDT claims that there are three stages of population development: Stage I in which birth and death rates are high and population growth is low to stable; Stage II when birthrates remain high, but death rates become lower, and population growth is high (the situation in most developing countries); and Stage III in which the birthrates are lower (but usually still higher than death rates), death

FIGURE 13.3 Components of U.S. Population Change: 1960–1984

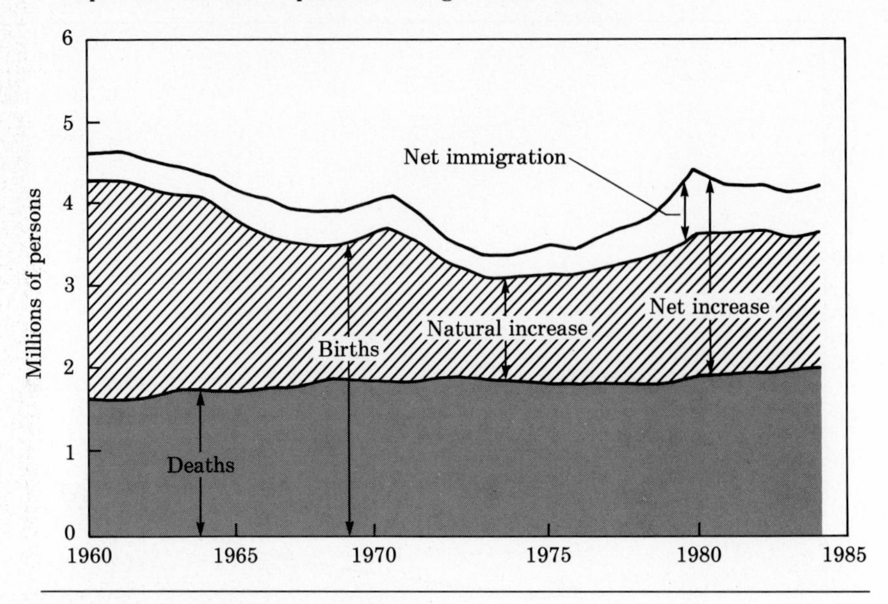

Source: *Statistical Abstract of the United States,* 1986:7.

rates are very low, and population growth is low (the situation in most developed or industrialized countries) (see Philliber, 1983:493; Coale, 1974:23). The theory of the demographic transition maintains that societal, economic, industrial, and technical changes (such as food production, vaccines, spraying DDT to control malaria, and so on) tend to cause transitions from one stage to another.

Historically, developed and developing countries have had very different population traits (see Table 13.1). As we have seen, a sizable majority of the world population lives in developing countries. Their rates of natural increase are between 2 percent to 3 percent (Demeny, 1974:105; Bouvier, 1984:7). Underdeveloped countries have populations that tend to be poorly fed. For example, they consume mostly grains, tubers, and other starchy roots, not foods high in protein (Revelle, 1974:123). More than 90 percent of the anticipated world population growth will be contributed by the developing countries (Coale, 1974:25). To be sure then, the growth of developing countries will have major implications for which races, religions, politics, ethnicities, and so on are at least in a majority, if not dominant worldwide (since Third-World countries tend to be non-Christian and nonwhite).

Having completed our overview of population problems, issues, definitions, prevalence, and incidence, and set population problems in a brief historical context, we now turn in the next section to a more detailed examination of one major aspect of population problems—that of fertility. Although we shall consider social problems of fertility, mortality, and migration in separate sections of this chapter, obviously they are related and interdependent.

• Fertility

Stating the Problem Of course the major fertility problem in an area like Mexico City (see Panel 13.1) is that fertility rates have remained high while mortality rates have been dropping, resulting in high rates of population growth (Murray, 1985). For example, Bouvier (1984:8) indicates that Mexican women still averaged six to seven births per completed family size as late as the 1950s.

High fertility rates are especially likely in the developing countries (cf. Table 13.1; Demeny, 1974:105). In fact some (Nam and Philliber, 1984:108) argue that the birthrate is the singlemost distinguishing trait of developing countries (where the mean crude birthrate is thirty-three) versus developed countries (mean birthrate is twelve). This difference has led to far greater population growth in developing countries. To illustrate, if the world population equals 100, then the developing versus developed countries had 66 percent versus 34 percent of the population in 1950. By 1985 this population difference was 75 percent and 25 percent. One of the reasons for high fertility rates is that birth control is much more difficult than death control, especially in developing countries. In spite of this growth rates have been decreasing worldwide (Reinhold, 1978).

Growth rates are calculated by subtracting death rates from birthrates and converting them to percentages (and making any necessary adjustments due to migration). For example, in the early 1970s Latin America had a birthrate of twenty-seven and a death rate of ten, for an annual growth rate of 2.7 percent (Demeny, 1974:106). Recent (1980s) world population growth rates have been about 1.7 percent (Table 13.1; Zopf, 1984:19). Every 1,000 women must give birth to roughly 2,100 children for a population just to stay constant in size, since not all children survive (*Current Population Reports*, August 1981). For the first time in 1973 the fertility rate (globally) fell below 2.1 children and remained there (Bouvier, 1984:4).

Two other fertility concepts we need to define are demographic median age and maximum fertility. The *demographic median age* is the age at which half the population is younger and half is older. Recently in developing countries the demographic median age was twenty, but in developed countries it was forty (Bouvier, 1984:14). Obviously, these age differences are reflected in different fertility rates. Age has an independent effect on fertility. For example, even if fertility rates drop, overall fertility (i.e., the number of births) will remain high if there are many young women in a population. The accepted base for maximum fertility is seventeen births per woman, as we have seen (Brown, 1985:206). Actual fertility rates are not much higher than eight births per woman (Coale, 1974:18–19).

As a result of high fertility rates and declining death rates the net increase

In Third-World or developing countries like Ethiopia birthrates have remained high while death rates initially dropped sharply. The resulting large population growth, poor public health, and food shortages have led ultimately to massive starvation deaths—especially of children. (UPI/Bettmann News Photos)

in world population from 1950 to 1975 was almost twice the size of the entire world population in 1750 (Demeny, 1974:105). In developing countries the population tripled between 1750 and 1950. In the United States between 1944 and 1958 there was (of course) a fertility spurt known as the *baby boom* (a rise in birthrates in the United States and other nations after World War II; cf. Zopf, 1984:29). Population growth at that time did not result from larger completed family size, but rather from increased fertility rates (Philliber, 1983:483).

In spite of continued population growth worldwide, the crude birthrates throughout the world have been coming down substantially since 1900 (Zopf, 1984:6; see Figure 13.4 for U.S. data). Between 1947 and 1981 the global crude birthrate declined 22 percent. Bouvier states that fertility rates will fall in the next fifty years in all regions of the world (1984:19).

There are many fascinating correlates of this long-term decline in world fertility rates. Of course, fertility rates are age-specific; the younger the population, the higher the fertility rates. Births are concentrated primarily between ages twenty and twenty-nine (Nam and Philliber, 1984:113). In older populations (like Germany, Austria, and France) there are even efforts to raise fertility rates (see the case of France in Panel 13.2; cf. Bouvier, 1984:20). At a 1 percent rate of decline, a population is reduced by half every seventy years.

FIGURE 13.4 Crude Birth and Death Rates in the United States, 1910–1980[a], 1960–1980[b]

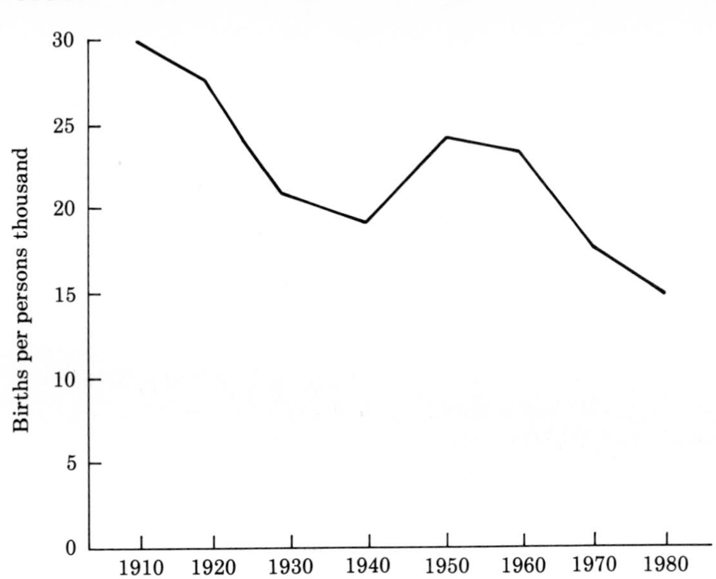

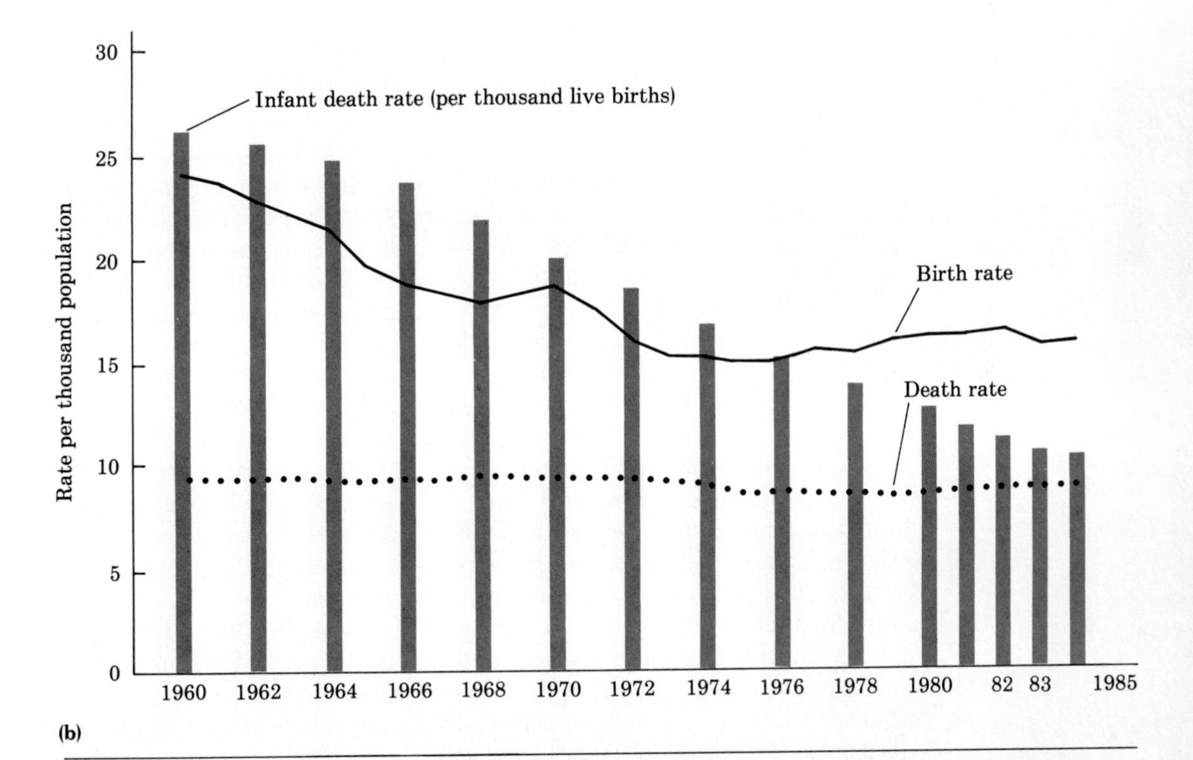

Source: [a]Susan G. Philliber, "Population Change," in *Social Problems in American Society,* Melvin DeFleur, ed. Harper & Row, 1983:484. Copyright © 1983 by Harper & Row, Publishers, Inc. Data for 1910–1970 from *Statistical Abstract of the United States, 1979,* p. 60. Data for 1980 are for January through May only and are from National Center for Health Statistics, *Monthly Vital Statistics Report,* Vol. 29, No. 6 (August 7, 1980). [b]*Statistical Abstract of the United States, 1986*:55.

This raises the specter of whole nations or races disappearing. Even Catholic fertility declined dramatically between 1960 and 1975 (Westhoff and Jones, 1979). Given those declines in fertility some demographers believe the population crisis will be limited to the twentieth century (Zopf, 1984:19; cf. Table 13.2).

Analyzing the Problem. The Exchange Perspective Exchange theorists have little trouble explaining high fertility rates and lower mortality rates. To the degree that giving birth and dying are matters of choice (and, of course, sometimes they are not), fertility is obviously more valuable and rewarding to most individuals. Copulation is pleasant most of the time and dying is often painful, disorganizing, and disturbing. Here one must be careful to distinguish the interest of individuals from those of societal or corporate actors (see Chapter 10; Demeny, 1986). High fertility is not advantageous or valuable to most societies, but it often is to individuals (Brown, 1985:214–218). Clearly, the sexual exchange that results in fertility is almost always rewarding to individuals. Furthermore, many individuals prize large families (especially, having many sons) for security of their old age, co-workers, signs of their sexual prowess, additional wage earners, shields against loneliness, and so on. Normal people tend to act in their own best interests as they see them (Demeny, 1974:113; 1986). At the same time, "untrammeled pursuit of individual interests can wreak social havoc" (Brown et al., 1985:218). The exchange perspective reminds us to ask: Who is exchanging with whom?

The decline in fertility rates we see in Figure 13.4 can also be explained by exchange principles. It would not take much imagination to construct a "payoff matrix" (à la Homans, 1974) comparing the rewards and costs of high fertility over time (especially for individuals). Such a comparison would demonstrate that profits from high fertility rates have declined dramatically in recent decades. Thus, crude birthrates would be expected to decline as well. Finally, notice that fertility rates are not up; rather, mortality rates are down. In the parlance of exchange, this suggests that the interactive costs to reduce mortality are less than those to reduce fertility (Philliber, 1983:494).

Structural-Functional Perspectives It will be recalled that the structural-functional sociological perspectives see social problems resulting from size, numbers, and objective consequences (that tend to meet societal needs). One clear cause of fertility increases has been our ability to efficiently support larger populations. For example, the number of people a single farmer could feed rose from ten in 1930 to seventy-eight in 1981 (Cochrane, 1982; McKeown, 1977). Structural-functionalists contend that population grew because of (as a result of) economic organization, improved agricultural technology, better transportation and distribution facilities, advances in public health and sanitation, and so on (Demeny, 1974:108; Lenski and Lenski, 1987).

Furthermore, since what Malthus called positive checks on fertility have

PANEL 13.2

Troisieme Enfant

Into a world in which many countries are struggling to hold families to just two children, there arrived some excellent news for France late last month in the maternity ward of St. Vincent de Paul Hospital.

First, on January 20, came Jessica Wendy Ellouk, third child of Wanda and Eddie. Then, on January 21, Camille David was born, third child of Chantal and Francois. January 22 was a very good day: Danis Mazon became the third child of Chantal and Rene, while Erwan Maquennehan became the third of Brigitte and Jean.

France, concerned about its low birthrate, not only is officially pleased with all these third children, it will pay their respective parents for having them; to be exact, $200 a month tax-free for the next two years.

It will also allow each couple to take full tax deductions for the children. And it will guarantee that the mothers—all of whom work—can have their jobs back, even if they wait as long as two years to return to work.

All over Paris last month, 789 government-sponsored sidewalk billboards appeared bearing the portrait of a newborn and urging families to consider a "troisieme enfant."

Source: Steven Twomey, *Knight-Ridder* Newspapers, February 8, 1984.

been curtailed in recent years, population has grown even more. That is, war, natural disasters, disease, and famine were all functional; they held down population growth. McKeown (1977) believes that one major factor in population growth was that the practice of infanticide virtually stopped in most countries.

From a more macrosociological functional perspective (especially an ecological evolutionary worldview) fertility, mortality, and urban transformation are all variables related to societal type, technological innovation, and economic factors (Lenski and Lenski, 1987; Hopkins and Wallerstein, 1982). To oversimplify, the move from an agrarian to an industrial era (with the latter's lowered fertility and mortality rates and increase of major cities) is related to the prevention and cure of disease (especially of communicable diseases like the flu, tuberculosis, and smallpox); to technological advances (like contraceptive pills and safe methods for abortion), and to a switch from subsistence agriculture to capital-intensive industries (Lenski and Lenski, 1987:269–272). Dependency theories see Third-World or developing countries as less developed because of external exploitation by global capitalism. Modernization theories view population problems in Third-World countries resulting from internal conditions, such as the persistence of ideologies and institutional systems inherited from their preindustrial pasts (Lenski and Lenski, 1987:395–397).

"Madame, I should have thought one of those would have been more than enough!"

The Symbolic Interaction Perspective Traditionally, many poor individuals and developing nations have defined large families as good. Having many children meant more family workers or the prospering of small minority, ethnic, or religious groups. Obviously, if a nation, group, or individual defines large families as desirable, its completed family size will tend to be larger (Demeny, 1986). Culture often operates independently from economic realities. Thus, even if children have become very expensive, the positive symbol of large families may be very slow to change. Note too that birth control is perceived as murder by many groups, whereas death control is almost universally approved of.

The Conflict Perspective As recently as 1974 developing countries like India, Iran, and China tended to see political power in the sheer size of their populations. Also, from the conflict perspective population or fertility decline is thought to be the result of societal and economic exploitation (cf. world-system dependency theory, Lenski and Lenski, 1987), resulting (for example) from starvation of the world's poor and powerless (Harrington, 1984).[4] One way to fight political oppression is to outnumber the dominant group (as, for example, blacks in South Africa do whites), then later outvote them. Thus, large families can be an instrument of social and economic change.

Large families, high birthrates, starvation diets, poor health and poor sanitation, and so on are all part of a pattern engendered by economic exploitation of the developing countries by the more industrialized nations. Taking economic and political advantage of Third-World countries (such as by paying low wages, forcing exports to other countries, and charging high prices for oil) tends to keep those countries poor and technologically retarded; in short, undeveloped. Being kept industrially underdeveloped means (among other things) having high birthrates.

The Biological Perspective This perspective overlaps somewhat with the exchange and functional perspectives, which claim that food supplies spurred fertility (Nam and Philliber, 1984:122) or that fertility is difficult to reduce because of the physical pleasure of copulation. Sociobiologists might also point to "selfish genes" and the desire for social immortality as factors in high fertility rates. Even though we as individuals cannot survive our own deaths, 50 percent of our genetic endowment is passed on to our own children. These being some of the major causes of high fertility rates and recent declines, what can societies do to reduce fertility and population growth still more?

Resolving the Problem One set of more lasting resolutions to problems of continuing high fertility focuses on transforming social institutions. Examples of this approach would include raising women's status (Brown et al., 1985:202), increasing educational and literary levels (Brown et al., 1985:208), and improving economic conditions (Zopf, 1984:160). Often those resolutions necessitate (among other procedures) government interventions, licensing, fines (e.g., for having more than one or two children), and loans. For example, Brown et al. report that China now has a one-child family policy (1985:202). Closer to home, in the United States family planning monies were increased from $13.5 million in 1968 to $279 million in 1978.

Obviously, another set of resolutions centers on contraceptive techniques of various types, including family planning and birth control. Fertility in developing countries is reduced more by delays to marriage and breast feeding than by contraception (Brown et al., 1985:208).[5] Contraceptive techniques vary by country. India tends to use sterilization, China IUDs, and the United States the pill. Worldwide, sterilization protects the most couples (Brown et al., 1985:208). However, it is also true that in virtually all countries that have stopped population growth abortion is readily available as a birth control method (Brown et al., 1985:221; Dejerassi, 1986). Historically, some countries even practiced infanticide (especially female infanticide, as in traditional China—see

Chase, 1977). Recent techniques include new drugs and surgeries. Consider Norplant, which is a self-administered menses inducer—a reversible technique that amounts to a very early abortion (see Brown et al., 1985:213).

It is also the case that no population can be fertile beyond the limits of its habitat (Zopf, 1985:18). Eventually space, famine, disease, and war will control fertility—if nothing else is done. Of course, this resolution is not pleasant and is recommended by almost no one. Most demographers contend that in time, even without much social change, zero population growth will come to most countries, anyway (Philliber, 1983:503; Zopf, 1984:23). For any particular country (but not the world, unless we consider outer space), migration is always another resolution to excessive fertility, population growth, and diminished local resources. Since population growth is always a composite consequence not only of fertility rates but also of mortality rates, in the next section we examine the dynamics of mortality.

• Mortality

Stating the Problem The world population explosion in developing countries like Ethiopia, China, Mexico, and other Third-World countries is not so much the result of high fertility rates as it is the product of drastic declines in mortality rates (Nam and Philliber, 1984:62; Zopf, 1984:211). We have noted that high fertility rates coupled with low and falling mortality rates are a special problem in developing countries (Table 13.1; Nam and Philliber, 1984:68). For example, life expectancy in the developing countries was only fifty-three years in the 1970s (Demeny, 1974:110). But by 2025 life expectancy is projected to rise to about seventy years in the developing countries (Bouvier, 1984:21).

A major reason (certainly not the only reason) for low death rates is that most people feel death control (but not necessarily birth control) is morally acceptable. That is, we tend to believe that death rates ought to be at their lowest possible level (Zopf, 1984:8). Furthermore, death controls (unlike birth controls) can be applied once, relatively cheaply, and still be very effective. Examples of such death controls would include vaccination against infectious diseases, draining malarial swamps, purifying water, or producing better varieties of grain.

If birthrates and population growth are not brought down in developing countries, then mortality rates once again will become catastrophically high. There will be mass deaths resulting from starvation and epidemics in countries like Bangladesh (Bouvier, 1984:31; Hanlon, 1985). The Sahelian zone in Africa has experienced drought, severe food shortages, and death by starvation already (Revelle, 1974:128). Of course, unchecked population growth also affects the quality of life. With lowered life quality there are partial deaths in life that are not reflected clearly in a country's crude mortality rates. For example, when a country's rate of natural increase is around 2 percent to 3 percent a year, generally there tends to be lower per capita income, higher unemploy-

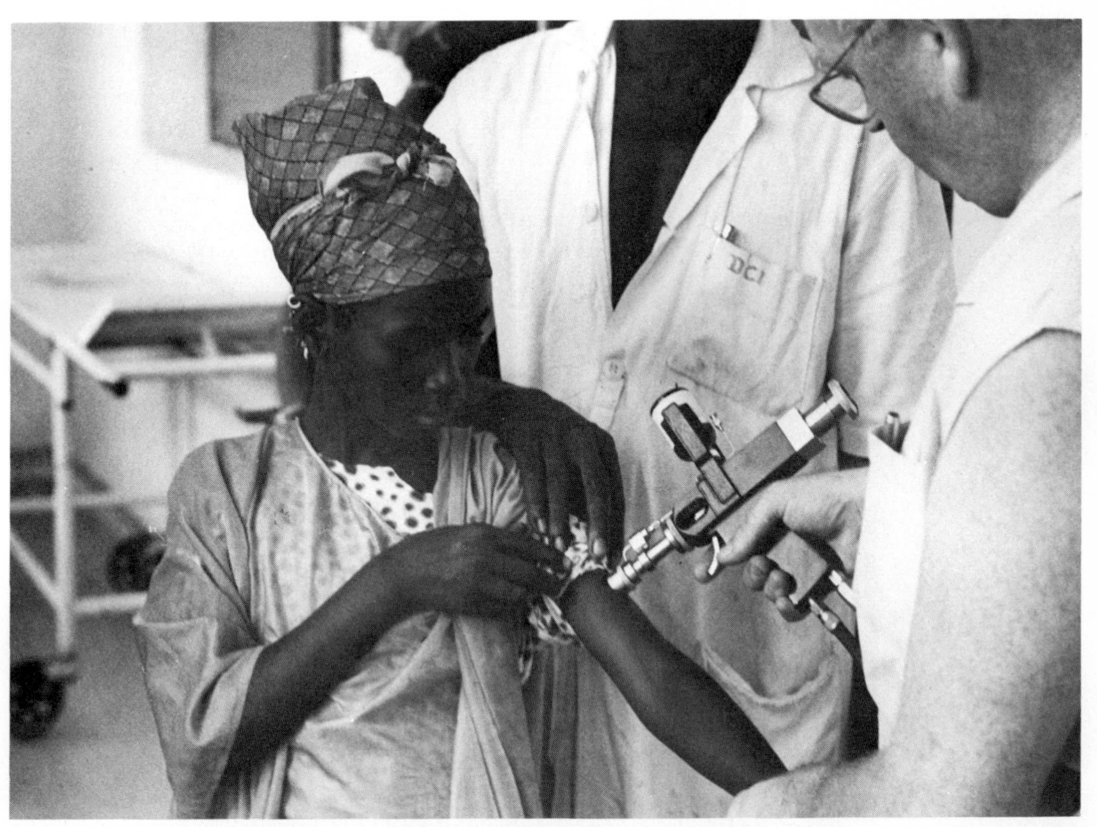

Death controls are often easier and more effective than birth controls. Death controls can be applied once, relatively cheaply, and still be effective. Unless birthrates drop too, lowered death rates cause population growth problems. Here an African is getting a smallpox vaccination. (The Bettmann Archive, Inc.)

ment, more strain on the educational system, greater political conflict, and so on. Finally, in the future there will be greater death rates from violent causes (e.g., homicide, suicide, and accidents) and from cancer, rather than from infectious diseases (see our own Chapters 7 and 15; Nam and Philliber, 1984:94).

Most of the key concepts required to state the problems of mortality have been defined above (e.g., mortality, morbidity, crude death rate). However, a few definitions remain. For example, when we speak of *death control* we mean any technique or product that reduces the death rate (Zopf, 1984:8). The *infant mortality rate* refers to the deaths of babies before their first birthday per 1,000 live births per year. Generally, the infant mortality rate is between ten to fifteen in the United States and other developed countries, but in the one hundreds in developing nations like Africa (see Table 13.1). Sometimes, when death rates decline precipitously in a short time (the opposite of a baby boom) we may call this phenomenon a *death dearth* (cf. Bouvier, 1984:7).

Figures 13.5 and 13.4 show us that the U.S death rate is down recently, but that the rate of decline has slowed. The current (i.e., mid to late 1980s) U.S. death rate is 8.5 to 9 per 1,000, versus a rate of about 11 in the world as a whole (cf. Table 13.1; Zopf, 1984:191; Nam and Philliber, 1984:66). As we saw above, some countries, like East and West Germany and Austria, actually have more deaths per year than they do births (Bouvier, 1984:4). Most observers contend that death rates are not likely to go much lower than 6 to 8 per 1,000 (Zopf, 1984:34). In all countries mortality rates are lower than birthrates and fluctuate less (Zopf, 1984:180).

In the past there were occasional episodes of massive mortality resulting from contagious diseases. Between 1348 and 1350 the bubonic plague (the black death) destroyed one-fourth to one-third of Europe's entire population—about 100 million people (Zopf, 1984:7; Nam and Philliber, 1984:78)! As recently as 1918–19 influenza killed 8 million people in India alone. However, since 1900 a greater proportion of deaths are from cancer, heart disease, and violence and a smaller proportion from infectious diseases (like flu, tuberculosis, smallpox, and pneumonia).[6]

Mortality patterns tend to be correlated with age, sex, race, social class, and other factors. Not everyone dies the same, or at the same time. As a case in point, males tend to have higher death rates than females (the male death disadvantage) from almost all causes except those related to childbirth and reproduction. Males are especially more likely than females to die from cardiovascular, neoplastic (cancer), and respiratory diseases (Nam and Philliber, 1984:80). Racial minority status does not in itself guarantee higher mortality

FIGURE 13.5 Crude Death Rates in the United States, 1910–1980

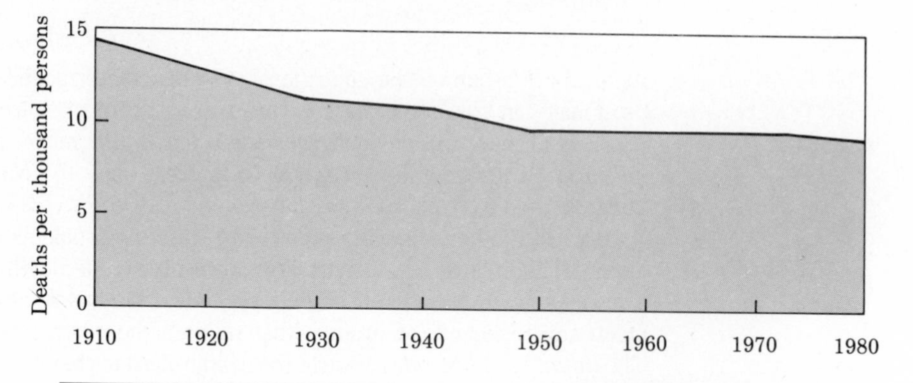

Source: Susan G. Philliber, "Population Change," in *Social Problem in American Society,* Melvin DeFleur, ed. Harper & Row, 1983:483. Copyright © 1983 by Harper & Row, Publishers, Inc. Data for 1910–1970 from *Statistical Abstract of the United States, 1979,* p. 60. Data for 1980 are for January through May only and are from National Center for Health Statistics, *Monthly Vital Statistics Report,* Vol. 29, No. 6 (August 7, 1980).

rates. Although American blacks have shorter life expectancies than whites, Chinese and Japanese Americans tend to have longer life expectancies than white Americans. Generally, socioeconomic status is inversely related to death rates at all ages. For example, the lower the social class, the higher the death rate.

Life expectancy is related to age at death. For example, if life expectancy in a population is fifty-three years, then 35 percent to 40 percent of all deaths occur to children under age five. But if life expectancy is seventy-five years, then only 5 percent to 20 percent of all deaths occur to children under five (Bouvier, 1984:8). Being under or overweight also affects death rates. Infants with low birth weights have higher death rates (Phibbs and Williams, 1981). Two-fifths of all Americans are overweight and being overweight is related to greater risk of heart disease mortality (Nam and Philliber, 1984:92–93). Of course, there are many other mortality correlates that we could have discussed, but did not (such as cigarette smoking, exercise, diet, and so on).

Analyzing the Problem Explanations of mortality problems tend to be similar to those just given for fertility. Thus, this section can afford to be brief. Remember that the theoretical perspectives presented below are not complete by themselves.

The Exchange Perspective Both individually and socially staying alive is highly valued in almost all societies. You will recall from the exchange perspective that the more valuable an act is, the more it tends to be repeated. Other things being equal, death rates tend to drop as a direct result of the very high value of avoiding death. Not only are the rewards of staying alive high, also the sociopolitical and economic costs of reducing mortality (but not fertility) are relatively low. The exchange perspective reminds us that profitable social activities tend to continue. Reducing mortality rates is at once more rewarding and less costly than reducing fertility rates. Thus, the exchange perspective would predict mortality rates would fall faster than fertility rates. Another exchange consideration in the determination of mortality rates is differential familial reinforcement (a social learning difference). Some families (and not others) reward toilet training, cleanliness, healthy diet, knowledge about mortality hazards, and so on. Those families and nations that do this will tend to have offspring that live longer (Nam and Philliber, 1984:79).[7]

The Structural and Functional Perspectives The theory of demographic transition (discussed above in some detail) fits into both the structural and functional perspectives. In Stage II of the demographic transition death rates drop rapidly, while fertility rates remain high. Said somewhat differently, structural changes in society (e.g., increased food production, concentration of large numbers of people in dense urban areas, and economic transformation from agarian to industrial economies) lower death rates. Put into functional language, lower mortality rates are the joint consequence of advances in public health, medical science, economic development, and so on (Nam and Philliber, 1984:74–75). That lower socioeconomic status (SES) is associated with higher mortality rates and is also a structural factor (Zopf, 1984:195). Countries with more rapid economic transformation and a greater relative proportion of population in mid to upper social classes will tend to have the most rapid decline in death rates—again, other things being equal.

The Conflict Perspective The major points here are the ones discussed in considering fertility. Death rates drop as a result of industrial, economic, and technological innovations (especially technological changes). In most Third-World countries it is relatively easy to lower death rates dramatically simply by vaccinating people against infectious disease, spraying DDT on malarial swamps, and growing more food. Even exploited developing countries tend to get these death rate benefits of partial industrialization or colonialization by industrialized nations. Note, however, that developing countries still never have death rates quite as low as those of the industrialized nations on which they depend. Poor, underdeveloped, unhealthy, unsanitized, rural countries still have relatively high death rates.

Another minor point is whose interests are being served by lower death rates? In a society where mortality rates are lowered, does everyone in that society benefit equally? A conflict theorist might answer that economic benefits and lower mortality rates first benefit elites and those in upper socioeconomic statuses (Rodgers, 1979:343–351; Nam and Philliber, 1984:74–75). Mortality rates tend to drop fastest in those portions of a society that are the most powerful and affluent, not evenly throughout a society. Presumably, if social transformations affected everyone's mortality rates in a society equally, those in power would be less enthusiastic in their support of social change. Thus, a conflict hypothesis of mortality might be that death rates tend to drop fastest in oligarchical societies where elites have differential access to mortality reduction benefits. However, most data do not tend to support this conflict hypothesis, since death rates tend to drop at about the same rate in all advanced urban-industrial societies independently of whether or not they are oligarchical or equalitarian.

Resolving the Problem We must remember that there is no one problem of mortality. The most common problem is that the death rates are too low. If this were the only problem and no other factors were involved, then one obvious resolution would be to raise the death rates. In fact Malthus argued that such "positive checks" on population growth as war, famine, and disease would occur naturally in the long run if population growth was unchecked (Philliber, 1983:494). In some eastern nations infanticide (especially female infanticide) has been used to raise mortality rates (or lower fertility rates, depending on how you look at infanticide) and control population growth. Such resolutions tend to be largely structural-functional results of large numbers of people and insufficient resources (especially of food).

Drawing by Lou Myers; © 1976 *The New Yorker* Magazine, Inc.

A more symbolic interaction resolution to lower mortality rates would be to change societal values to permit more euthanasia and rational suicide, particularly among the terminally ill and aged (Humphrey and Wickett, 1986; Battin and Maris, 1983). Of course, many people do not favor such death controls. For example, when is the right to die subtly transformed into the obligation to die—especially for the elderly or other "unfit" members of a society? Note too that fertility is always a part of the mortality problem. For example, if fertility rates could be brought down sufficiently, death rates would not have to be raised.

In many developing countries mortality rates (particularly infant mortality rates—see Pampel and Pillai, 1986) are still too high and the basic resolution is to lower mortality rates. This can be done by producing more food, and thus being able to support larger populations (Simon, 1981:478). In the same vein medical technology can be improved (Philliber, 1983:494). Medical and public health advances have done a great deal to control infectious diseases (like the plague or malaria). In many instances simply raising the level of sanitation can decrease death rates (Zopf, 1984:5). In some developing countries' major cities (like Calcutta or Bombay) raw human excrement accumulates on city streets because of inadequate sewage facilities. Finally, one could slow the process of aging by many of the above techniques, and surgery, organ

PANEL 13.3

A False Famine?

Africa's famine largely is a manmade calamity that could have been averted. Scientists, reaching this conclusion, fear that hunger will spread even after the drought ends, partly because of the very efforts used to fight it.

Chaotic, belated drought relief wastes uncounted lives. But officials admit that the dead—and scores of millions now desperately hungry—already were imperiled by decades of misguided development and bad policy decisions.

Nearly $10 billion in Western food aid has saved lives over ten years. But much of it came at the wrong times, in the wrong amounts, depressing prices and discouraging local production.

Food production has plummeted so dramatically since 1973 that even with normal rains, it would have dipped to its current level by 1988, according to the International Monetary Fund, or World Bank. Drought simply spurred the downward trend.

Per capita output is 220 pounds, only two-thirds of what is needed. And the United Nations expects the population to triple within forty-five years. Already, a fourth of Africa's 531 million people live entirely on imported grain.

Source: The Associated Press, September 8, 1985.

transplants, better health care, and so on (although not in most Third-World countries). Note that most of the resolutions to lower mortality rates are mainly biological or medical-technical. Although migration is not relevant to the world population problem, it does affect national population growth. Accordingly, we need to document a few of the major population migration trends in the next section of this chapter.

• Migration

It has probably occurred to you that most people do not have to keep living in overcrowded, economically underdeveloped, starving countries. Why not just leave when social conditions become intolerable? Could we not go somewhere else where there are jobs, food, water, less war, less religious persecution, and a generally higher quality of life? To a certain extent Mexican Americans, Europeans, Middle Easterners, southern blacks, and farmers have done just that in the United States. We need to remember that the natural increase of any human population is determined by the earlier population, births minus deaths, *and* plus or minus migration. In discussing migration it is customary to distinguish immigration from emigration. They refer (respectively) to in versus out migration in a specified area (usually a country's borders). Of course, there are limits to migration. For example, migration is not relevant to world population increase. Furthermore, ethnic, racial, religious, economic, and sheer physical obstacles also limit a people's migratory prospects.

In the United States there have been at least four relatively recent migratory trends. First, Figure 13.6 documents an internal migration from the North to the Southwest of the United States (cf. Philliber, 1983:485). Between 1970 and 1980 America's mountain area's population grew about 37 percent, the largest growth of any other U.S. area. The second largest growth area was in the South, which was up 22 percent in the same time period. Although Figure 13.6 does not show this, some areas of the East and Midwest (especially central cities) have actually experienced population declines.

Second, America's population is becoming increasingly more urban. Since we will discuss urban populations in the next section of this chapter, here we will make only a few observations. The urban population in the United States exceeded the percent rural around the year 1920. By the 1980s about 75 percent to 80 percent of the American population was urban (see Table 13.1).[8] Bouvier estimates that soon a majority of the entire world population will be urban (1984:23).

Third, after about 1970 the nonmetropolitan areas in the United States started to turn around (Zopf, 1984:104ff.). That is, the country's SMSAs (see definition, below) grew only 10 percent between 1970 and 1980, whereas nonmetropolitan areas (especially suburbs) grew 15 percent. Central cities did not grow at all between 1970 and 1980. Suburbanization led to serious drains on central city finances (Logan and Golden, 1986). Although American blacks have been slower than whites to leave central cities, still about 20 percent of all U.S. blacks now live in suburban areas (Sterns and Logan, 1986).

Fourth, and finally, until roughly about 1924 there were massive migrations of Western Europeans and Africans to the United States. Kingsley Davis tells us that the great period of voluntary overseas European migration was between 1840 and about 1930 (1974:58).[9] In 1924 the Immigration Act established quota systems for each nation, which drastically curtailed earlier large amounts of immigration. Thus, between 1930 and 1940 there was actually a net loss of population as a result of legal immigration. However, lately U.S. population growth as a result of legal immigration has gone back up to about 25 percent, a level it was at in the late 1880s. Recently the United States has received sizable numbers of illegal immigrants from Mexico, Cuba, and other Latin American nations (Nam and Philliber, 1984:173ff.). Illegal immigration is a special problem in the southwestern United States where many Mexican workers flee depressed Mexican economic conditions to jobs across the border in California, Arizona, New Mexico, and Texas (Zopf, 1984:236, 312). It is estimated that illegal aliens now number about three to five million or roughly 2 percent of the total U.S. population (Nam and Philliber, 1984:175).

Migration is stimulated by the technological and economic inequality between one territory and another (Davis, 1974:53). For example, migrating groups may move to escape famine, religious persecution, or to improve themselves

FIGURE 13.6 U.S. Population Makes a Southwestern Shift

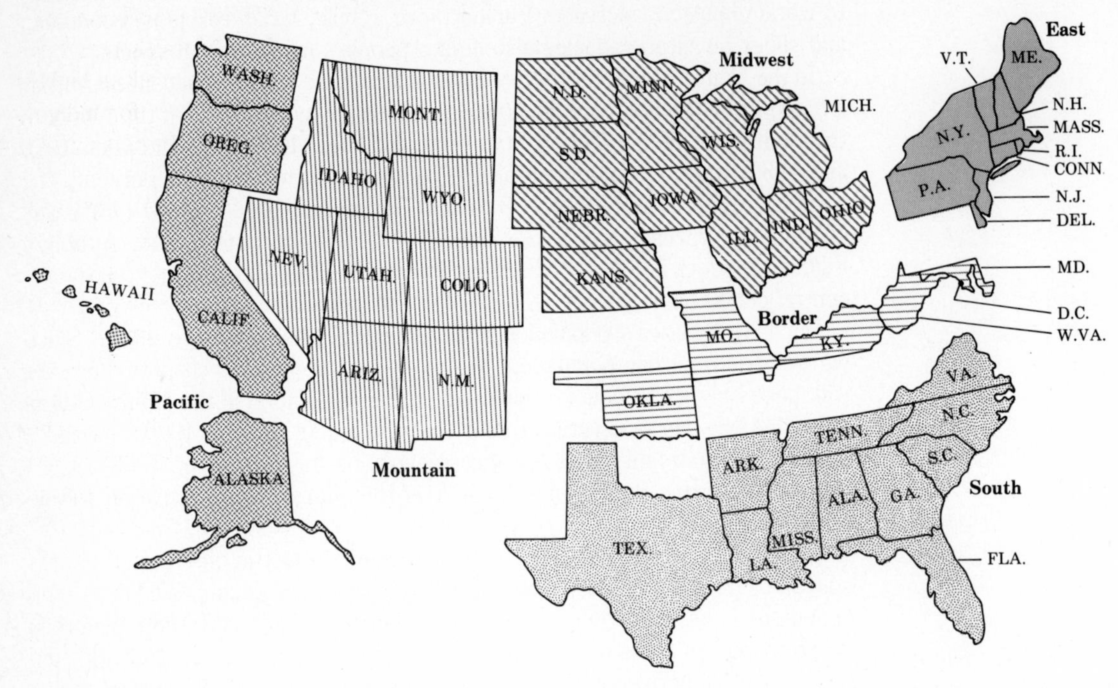

Area	Pacific	Mountain	Midwest	Border	South	East
1980 Population	31,797,000	11,368,000	53,936,000	18,408,000	61,263,000	49,732,000
1970 Population	26,548,000	8,290,000	51,913,000	16,883,000	50,060,000	49,609,000
Change since 1970	Up 19.8%	Up 37.1%	Up 3.9%	Up 9.0%	Up 22.4%	Up 0.2%

Source: Copyright, 1981, *U.S. News & World Report.* Reprinted from issue of February 16, 1981.

economically (Boswell, 1986). Obviously, advanced countries often have more jobs and pay better for those jobs. In other cases, the native population may refuse to fill low-paying, low-status jobs (consider the black African slaves' role in colonial America). Sometimes warm accessible countries can produce highly valued products not available in (say) Europe. Thus, the search for indigo, rice, cotton, spices, sugar, tobacco, coffee, tea, and so on prompted much early European migration to the Americas.

Most experts agree that the population overcrowding, food shortages, and the generally dismal quality of life in underdeveloped countries are beyond solution by emigration alone (Davis, 1974:65). Additionally, migrants tend to create problems for their host countries and cities. Just consider some of the social problems created by Castro's wholesale shipping of Cuban criminals, the insane, and other social outcasts to Florida during the Carter administration (cf. Zopf, 1984:229, 310ff.). In areas where immigration is heavy there tend to be high unemployment rates, deterioration of the environment (see Chapter 14), housing shortages, sanitation and transportation problems, racial and ethnic interbreeding, lack of adequate social services, political unrest, and urban congestion—as we shall now elaborate in the concluding major section of the present chapter (Freedman and Berelson, 1974:10).

• The Urban Transformation

Stating the Problem Not only has the world and national population grown remarkably, but also much of it has shifted from rural areas to cities (Bradshaw, 1987).[10] Industrialization usually meant urbanization, since factories were located in cities. Between 1820 and 1985 the percentage of the U.S. population on farms shrank from 72 percent to only 2.2 percent. This urban transformation altered the very character and quality of social life and spawned new social problems.

For one thing city life involved large populations in relatively small areas (think of Manhattan, New York); that is, high density and overcrowding (Zopf, 1984:70ff.; Gove and Hughes, 1983). For example, as early as 1971 Calcutta, India, had 84,896 people living in each square mile (Wilsher and Righter, 1975). In Harlem (New York City) the population density is so high that if that density rate were applied to the entire U.S. population, it would fit into just three New York City boroughs! In 1970 there was only one city with over ten million population (Shanghai), but by 1984 there were about ten such cities (see Table 13.4; *UNESCO Courier,* 1985). Table 13.3 presents the 100 biggest cities in the United States in 1980. America has six cities over one million in population (New York City, Chicago, Los Angeles, Philadelphia, Houston, and Detroit).

Second, city life often results in severe financial problems. Many large (particularly northeastern) cities have actually lost population (Frey, 1987). With population loss comes a decreasing tax base and eventually an insufficient city budget. In fact New York City was recently in danger of going bankrupt—

TABLE 13.3 America's 100 Biggest Cities, Rank Order, 1970 and 1980

1980 Rank	1980 Population	Change since 1970	1970 Rank	1980 Rank	1980 Population	Change since 1970	1970 Rank
1. New York City	7,015,600	Down 11.1%	1	51. Wichita	279,352	Up 1.0%	51
2. Chicago	2,969,570	Down 11.9	2	52. Sacramento	274,488	Up 6.8	55
3. Los Angeles	2,950,010	Up 4.9	3	53. Tampa	268,709	Down 3.2	50
4. Philadelphia	1,680,235	Down 13.8	4	54. St. Paul	268,248	Down 13.4	48
5. Houston	1,554,992	Up 26.1	6	55. Norfolk	262,803	Down 14.7	47
6. Detroit	1,192,222	Down 21.3	5	56. Virginia Beach	260,680	Up 51.5	78
7. Dallas	901,450	Up 6.8	8	57. Rochester, NY	241,539	Down 18.1	49
8. San Diego	870,006	Up 24.7	14	58. Akron	236,820	Down 14.0	52
9. Baltimore	784,554	Down 13.4	7	59. St. Petersburg	233,532	Up 8.0	61
10. San Antonio	783,296	Up 19.7	15	60. Corpus Christi	230,715	Up 12.8	62
11. Phoenix	781,443	Up 33.7	20	61. Jersey City	222,764	Down 14.4	54
12. Indianapolis	695,040	Down 7.0	11	62. Richmond	219,429	Down 12.0	57
13. San Francisco	674,063	Down 5.8	13	63. Baton Rouge	219,164	Up 32.1	83
14. Memphis	644,838	Up 3.3	17	64. Fresno	216,365	Up 30.6	84
15. Washington, DC	637,651	Down 15.7	9	65. Anaheim	214,688	Up 29.0	82
16. Milwaukee	632,989	Down 11.8	12	66. Colorado Springs	206,979	Up 52.7	104
17. San Jose	625,763	Up 36.1	29	67. Santa Ana	204,089	Up 31.1	88
18. Cleveland	572,532	Down 23.8	10	68. Lexington, KY	203,082	Up 16.5	77
19. Boston	562,582	Down 12.2	16	69. Jackson, Miss.	200,338	Up 30.1	91
20. Columbus, OH	561,943	Up 4.1	21	70. Mobile	199,392	Up 4.9	68
21. New Orleans	556,913	Down 6.2	19	71. Yonkers	194,557	Down 4.8	63
22. Jacksonville	541,269	Up 7.3	26	72. Shreveport	194,506	Up 6.8	69
23. Seattle	491,897	Down 7.3	22	73. Dayton	193,319	Down 20.5	59
24. Denver	489,318	Down 4.9	24	74. Des Moines	190,910	Down 5.2	64
25. St. Louis	448,640	Down 27.9	18	75. Knoxville	182,161	Up 4.3	76

26.	Kansas City, MO	446,562	Down 12.0	25	76.	Grand Rapids	181,602	Down 8.1	65
27.	Nashville	439,599	Up 3.2	32	77.	Montgomery	176,781	Up 32.5	107
28.	El Paso	424,522	Up 31.7	45	78.	Lubbock	174,157	Up 16.8	93
29.	Pittsburgh	423,962	Down 18.5	23	79.	Anchorage	173,992	Up 37.7	114
30.	Atlanta	422,293	Down 14.7	27	80.	Lincoln, NE	171,787	Up 14.9	92
31.	Oklahoma City	401,002	Up 8.9	37	81.	Fort Wayne	171,036	Down 3.9	72
32.	Cincinnati	383,058	Down 15.5	30	82.	Spokane	170,993	Up 0.3	80
33.	Fort Worth	382,349	Down 2.8	33	83.	Huntington Beach	170,597	Up 47.1	128
34.	Minneapolis	370,091	Down 14.8	31	84.	Madison	170,383	Down 0.8	79
35.	Honolulu*	365,114	Up 12.4	44	85.	Syracuse	170,292	Down 13.7	66
36.	Portland, OR	364,891	Down 4.0	36	86.	Riverside, CA	169,677	Up 21.1	98
37.	Buffalo	357,002	Down 22.9	28	87.	Columbus, GA	168,598	Up 8.8	89
38.	Long Beach	356,906	Down 0.5	40	88.	Chattanooga	165,328	Up 37.9	123
39.	Tulsa	355,500	Up 7.6	43	89.	Salt Lake City	162,985	Down 7.3	74
40.	Toledo	354,265	Down 7.5	34	90.	Las Vegas	162,960	Up 29.6	115
41.	Austin	343,390	Up 35.4	56	91.	Worcester, MA	161,384	Down 8.6	73
42.	Oakland	338,721	Down 6.3	39	92.	Warren, MI	161,173	Down 10.1	70
43.	Miami	335,360	Up 0.1	42	93.	Kansas City, KS	159,972	Down 4.9	81
44.	Tucson	331,506	Up 26.1	53	94.	Flint, MI	159,576	Down 17.5	67
45.	Newark, NJ	329,498	Down 13.7	35	95.	Arlington, TX	159,117	Up 76.7	177
46.	Albuquerque	328,837	Up 34.5	58	96.	Aurora, CO	158,249	Up 111.1	231
47.	Omaha	312,929	Down 9.8	41	97.	Tacoma	158,101	Up 2.4	90
48.	Charlotte	310,799	Up 28.7	60	98.	Providence, RI	156,519	Down 12.6	71
49.	Louisville	298,161	Down 17.6	38	99.	Greensboro	154,763	Up 7.4	96
50.	Birmingham	282,068	Down 6.3	48	100.	Fort Lauderdale	154,028	Up 10.3	99

*Area designated by Census Bureau. Note: Figures subject to change.

Source: Copyright, 1981, *U.S. News & World Report.* Reprinted from issue of February 16, 1981.

PANEL 13.4

New York City's Financial Crisis

September 21, 1938, was a special day for one resident of Long Island. A war was about to explode in Europe, but on this morning he was more concerned with a long-awaited package that arrived in the mail. Excitedly, he unwrapped his shiny new barometer, noticing that the needle pointed below 29, where the dial warned of "Hurricanes and Tornadoes." Ridiculous. It was a sunny day. As recounted by William Manchester in *The Glory and the Dream:* "He shook it and banged it against a wall; the needle wouldn't budge. Indignant, he repacked it, drove to the post office, and mailed it back. While he was gone, his house blew away."

Something like that happened to New York thirty-seven years later. For years, few believed the menacing storm clouds. Since 1898, New York had become America's largest and most important metropolis. Then, in the 1960s, New York stopped growing. Each year, the budget would come up short; each year, officials would devise a temporary solution by taxing a little here, borrowing a little there, fudging everywhere they could. Then, during the year and outside the normal budget review process, they would add a program here or there, and fudge some more. By 1975, city expenditures totaled $12.8 billion, while revenues totaled only $10.9 billion. New York was borrowing to close an annual operating deficit of almost $2 billion. While city and state officials tinkered and wrestled with symptoms, New York was being blown away.

Source: Ken Auletta, *The Streets Were Paved with Gold,* 1980:29. Copyright 1980, Random House, Inc.

an unthinkable prospect for the nation's financial center (*U.S. News and World Report,* May 18, 1981; cf. Panel 13.4). City budget reductions lead to deteriorating city services (such as transportation, housing, police and fire protection, and garbage removal), more poverty and hunger, rising welfare roles, crime breeding and festering in the inner city, high unemployment rates, and great occupational specialization (which makes city dwellers highly dependent on one another).[11] Banks often compound these financial problems by policies such as *redlining* (refusal of banks to lend money in areas they consider undesirable—Palen, 1981) and *deinvestment* (withdrawal of investments from undesirable areas—Taggart and Smith, 1981).

Third, city life becomes highly complex and diverse, much more so than rural or farm life. Major cities tend to be divided into racial or ethnic neighborhoods. Thus, many social issues in cities are in fact racial issues. Consider the white flight to suburbia or (more recently) back to selected areas in the center of cities *(gentrification)* (Stahara, 1987). Middle-class whites are continually being replaced by or themselves replacing urban blacks, Puerto Ricans, Mexican-Americans, and so on (Philliber, 1983:498). One result of this diversity is that large cities suffer from a lack of common values.[12]

Fourth, many radically and ethnically diverse young people in large cities form violent gangs that prey on each other and nongang city dwellers—in part acting out their elders' value differences (Rice, 1977). Sometimes city gangs generate a kind of vigilante response, as with the Guardian Angels gang in New York City. Earlier (the mid-1960s especially) there were major inner-city race riots in Detroit, Watts, Baltimore, Miami, and so on (Miller, 1975). City parents must also be concerned about school violence (O'Toole, 1978).

Fifth, large American cities tend to have highly transient populations. Historically cities have had many migrants and high mobility rates. Originally these migrants were largely Europeans (e.g., to New York City between 1880 and 1920), blacks fleeing a conservative, economically depressed, and politically oppressive old South, Mexicans, Puerto Ricans, and Jews (many in New York City). Cities also have a high professional and technical workforce turnover. All this transiency contributes to inner-city decay. In New York City alone it is estimated that 100 housing units are abandoned each day (Durant, 1979).

Sixth, cities' financial problems, high crime rates, racial and ethnic conflicts, overcrowding and transiency all lead to a lower city life quality—especially for those in lower income groups and for young couples trying to raise families. Additional factors contributing to lower city life quality are inadequate overpriced housing and poor city transportation (Rufolo, 1978).[13] A recent study (see Panel 13.5) found that the American city with the best life quality was San Francisco (the worst city overall was Fayetteville, NC). Of course, quality depends on what goods and services are offered for which group. However, some geographers warn us that measures of best and worst cities are often highly suspect and can result in unreliable results.

Finally, all these city problems taken together can lead to a feeling of urban hopelessness, a sense of cities being out of control, beyond reclamation, only able to get worse (as with Mexico City, the South Bronx or Times Square in New York, or Near-North Philadelphia). Still, some cities have apparently reversed this pervasive hopelessness and decay. Think of Baltimore's inner-city harbor development or Detroit's Renaissance Center (Williams, 1977). American cities do not have to decay and die. Why are most major European cities so much more livable? It must be remembered as well that the quality of life in major American cities is not all bad or problematic. Many of us are attracted to large cities by their higher average incomes, better public services, and cultural amenities (such as orchestras, museums, newspapers, libraries, restaurants, professional sports, ballet, and theater).

The important urban definitions we need to discuss are *city, urban area, Standard Metropolitan Statistical Area (SMSA)*. Roughly, a *city* or urban population in the United States is any population cluster of 2,500 or more (Nam and Philliber, 1984:374). An *urbanized area,* on the other hand, is a contiguous densely settled population of 50,000 or more people comprised of census areas (cf. Zopf, 1984:468). A *metropolitan* or *standard metropolitan statistical area* (SMSA) must have one city at least 50,000 in size and a total population of at least 100,000 in the SMSA area. Unlike an urban area, an SMSA may include

PANEL 13.5

Rate-a-City: Study Picks San Francisco

If you're an environmentalist, you could pick no better place to live in the United States than Sacramento, California. Individualists should head for Stamford, Connecticut, and retirees would be happiest in Harrisburg, Pennsylvania, according to a new study.

The study, conducted by Joel A. Lieske, associate professor of political science at Cleveland State University, and three of his students, examined 142 metropolitan areas of the country according to how well they satisfy human needs.

Lieske acknowledges that "quality of life" can be interpreted in different ways, but he says it is possible to find basic, objective differences in metropolitan living.

"In general, it is better to be rich than poor," Lieske said. "It is better to be safe than insecure. It is better to be well served by government than poorly served. It is better to live in a clean environment than a dirty one. And it is better to live in a community rich in amenities than one that is poor."

Using those sorts of criteria, and computing scores for each city based on a system developed by psychologist Abraham Maslow, the study ranked San Francisco as the best all-round location of the 142 cities, while Fayetteville, N.C., landed at the bottom of the list.

The best and worst areas for Lieske's population groups:

Recent college graduates: Best, New York; worst, Muskegon, Mich.

Young families: Best, Norwalk, Conn.; worst, Albuquerque, NM.

Retirees: Best, Harrisburg, Pa.; worst, Los Angeles.

Environmentalists: Best, Sacramento; worst, Pittsburgh.

Cosmopolitans: Best, New York; worst, Pine Bluff, Ark.

Communalists (those concerned with community life): Best, Binghamton, N.Y.; worst, Tulsa, Okla.

Racial minorities: Best, Rochester, Minn.; worst, Tulsa.

Business leaders: Best, Chattanooga, Tenn.; worst, Stamford.

Individualists: Best, Stamford, Conn.; worst, Lowell, Mass.

Blue collar: Best, Harrisburg, Pa.; worst, Modesto, Calif.

The five most desirable regions of the country overall, the study indicated, are Hawaii, Utah, the Pacific Northwest, New England, and the New York metropolitan area.

Hawaii is good for new college graduates, individualists, and blue-collar workers. The Mormon region rated well for retirees, racial minorities, and business leaders. The Pacific Northwest is suited to environmentalists, New England to communalists, and the New York area to cosmopolitans and young families.

Source: The Associated Press, January 28, 1985.

rural areas, since it is composed of a central city and outlying counties. Generally urban problems are worst in America's very largest cities. *Megalopolis* is a term suggested for cities that get so large that they begin to spill over into one another (Nam and Philliber, 1984:371). Examples might include referring to the Northeast coast of the United States as BOSWASH or the Pacific Southwest coast as LOSDIEGO. *Urban sprawl,* on the other hand, refers to cities devouring productive farm and forest lands; for example, paving over America with concrete (Blundell, 1980).

Just how widespread is the urban transformation? Table 13.1 tells us that the U.S. population is currently about 74 percent urban. Less developed countries are generally around 30 percent to 35 percent urban, more developed countries about 70 percent urban. The range of percent urban is from about 15 percent in Ethiopia to about 95 percent in Belgium (although Singapore is 100 percent urban). By the year 2034 approximately 65 percent of the world's population will be living in urban areas (Bouvier, 1984:23). At present one in four Americans lives in a city of 100,000 or more.

The most heavily urbanized areas in the United States (80 percent or more urban) are the Northwest, the Pacific Coast, and Florida. In 1984 there were ten urban areas of ten million population or more (including the New York City and the Los Angeles areas) and one (Tokyo) of over twenty million (Table 13.4). By 2034 there are projected to be ten urban areas of twenty million population or more—led by our old friend Mexico City at a whopping forty million (see *UNESCO Courier,* 1985)! Rapid urban growth is also expected in Beijing (Peking, China), Jakarta (Indonesia), and in several Indian cities (namely, Bombay, Dacca, Calcutta, and Madras).

TABLE 13.4 World's Ten Largest Urban Agglomerations, 1984 and 2034

1984			2034		
Rank	**Urban Area**	**Population (in Millions)**	**Rank**	**Urban Area**	**Population (in Millions)**
1.	Tokyo-Yokohama	21.3	1.	Mexico City	39.1
2.	Mexico City	18.8	2.	Shanghai	38.8
3.	New York metropolitan area	18.2	3.	Beijing	34.5
4.	Shanghai	17.0	4.	Sãȯ Paulo	32.4
5.	São Paulo	14.5	5.	Greater Bombay	30.6
6.	Beijing	14.1	6.	Dacca	29.2
7.	Los Angeles-Long Beach	10.8	7.	Calcutta	28.9
8.	Greater Buenos Aires	10.7	8.	Jakarta	26.8
9.	Rio de Janeiro	10.2	9.	Madras	23.3
10.	Seoul	9.9	10.	Tokyo-Yokohama	19.3

Source: Derived from United Nations, *Estimates and Projections of Urban, Rural, and City Populations, 1950–2025; The 1980 Assessment,* 1982, Table 8, p. 61.

These large urban areas (both worldwide and in the United States) are expected to continue to experience the following social problems in the near future: high numbers of poor people will continue living in inner cities; slum areas will remain; youth gangs and high city crime rates will persist; there will be a few city riots reminiscent of the mid-1960s; white, middle-class flight from cities to sub- and exurbia will continue; cities will continue to have severe financial problems; racial and ethnic enclaves will polarize further; and migration from the Snow to the Sunbelt will keep draining midwestern and northwestern cities (in the United States only) (*Business Week,* September 3, 1979; Rutter, 1981).

Analyzing the Problem. The Exchange Perspective One important exchange is between city dwellers and city environments or lifestyles. Initially large numbers of the population migrated to cities for jobs, the richness and accessibility of specialized goods and services, the diversity and stimulation of city life, the attractiveness of the physical site of the city (e.g., on lakes, harbors, rivers, near mountains, and so on), and the general cosmopolitanism of city life. Yet eventually the rewards of city life change and the costs increase, such that it becomes less profitable to live in large cities. In fact, eventually, living in large urban areas becomes highly adversive—particularly for the poor and minorities. Traffic congestion and general overcrowding, excessive air and water pollution, high prices, high crime rates, filth and decay in the streets and subways, health hazards, impersonality, stress and competition, lack of recreational space, insufficient facilities to raise small children, inadequate housing and slums—all dramatically alter the urban experience for the worse. Of course, all U.S. cities do not have to have all of these problems, but most of them do.

City living is also less necessary. Many alternatives to city life develop. For example, plants and factories move to suburbia or to the more rural South (Logan and Golden, 1986). One can live outside of city adversities in exurbia and commute to work. Also, many inner-city jobs disappear, making city life not only less necessary, but rather, less possible. Finally, consider the exchange principle of satiation. Large urban areas all tend to have high rates of change, shortened interaction times, much impersonality and diversity—in short, large cities are stressful (Simmel, 1902–1903). Thus, our rate of satiation with conditions in the inner city is much higher. In conclusion, since urban areas involve exchanges that are costly and less necessary, and since city dwellers often need relief from overwhelming city stimuli, one obvious resolution of urban problems (for the individual, not the city) is to simply leave. Most city problems follow from certain kinds of urban populations abandoning urban areas.

The Structural-Functional Perspective The sheer size and density of city populations also cause many urban problems.[14] For example, the need for formal organization, bureaucracies, indirect relations, shortened social interaction time, impersonality, rationality, control by elites, and so on are all products of the city's social structure.

Many of the system consequences of urbanization—consider economic and industrial development, central location of factories, having industry near waterways for commercial transport and energy generation (e.g., electricity), the ready pool of immigrant labor, the specialization of occupational skills, and so on—are positive functions for society (Ross, 1987). But there are also several unintended, maladaptive, destructive (dysfunctional) consequences of rapid urbanization. Among these dysfunctions of cities are: disorganization and social disequilibrium, crime, poverty, poor housing, exploitative work conditions, pollution, transportation breakdowns, and rural or foreign populations unfamiliar with the ways of large city life.

Burgess (1925) thought that major cities divided naturally into concentric zones, each having specialized functions. He further argued that cities have high rates of social mobility and that high mobility led to a lack of community in cities.

One of the structural issues concerning Third-World urbanization and migration to cities is whether such cities develop as a result of ecological factors like rural push (e.g., highly adversive rural working conditions) and urban pull (e.g., more favorable economic conditions in cities) or political-economic dependency on urban capitalism. While both structural factors are important, dependency world system factors are probably more predictive of urban processes than ecological factors like rural adversity (London, 1987). It seems true that the urban core dominates peripheral areas and that there is a world system of cities based on finance that transcends regional and national boundaries (Meyer, 1986).

The Conflict Perspective Of course, Marxists and neo-Marxists assume that capitalists' economic interests are served at the expense of the workers' interests (London, 1987:29). For example, it is not profitable for capitalist owners to improve inner-city slum apartments they own or to remain in city factory buildings when land prices and taxes are cheaper in suburbia and exurbia. Note too that multistoried inner-city factory buildings are not suitable for newer assembly-line manufacturing procedures. For these (conflict) reasons (and others) inner-city decay resulted. Even when there is city planning and inner-city redevelopment (such as in Detroit or Baltimore), only some downtown areas are refurbished to accommodate tourists and their economic purchasing power. Most parts of any major inner city remain undeveloped and decaying. Just step outside of Renaissance Center in Detroit, if you do not believe this!

The Symbolic Interaction Perspective Finally, the city means different experiences for different social groups (Anderson, 1978). For the urban poor the city means cutbacks in services, closed factories, high unemployment, living with crime and gangs, crowded subways, and so on. For higher status

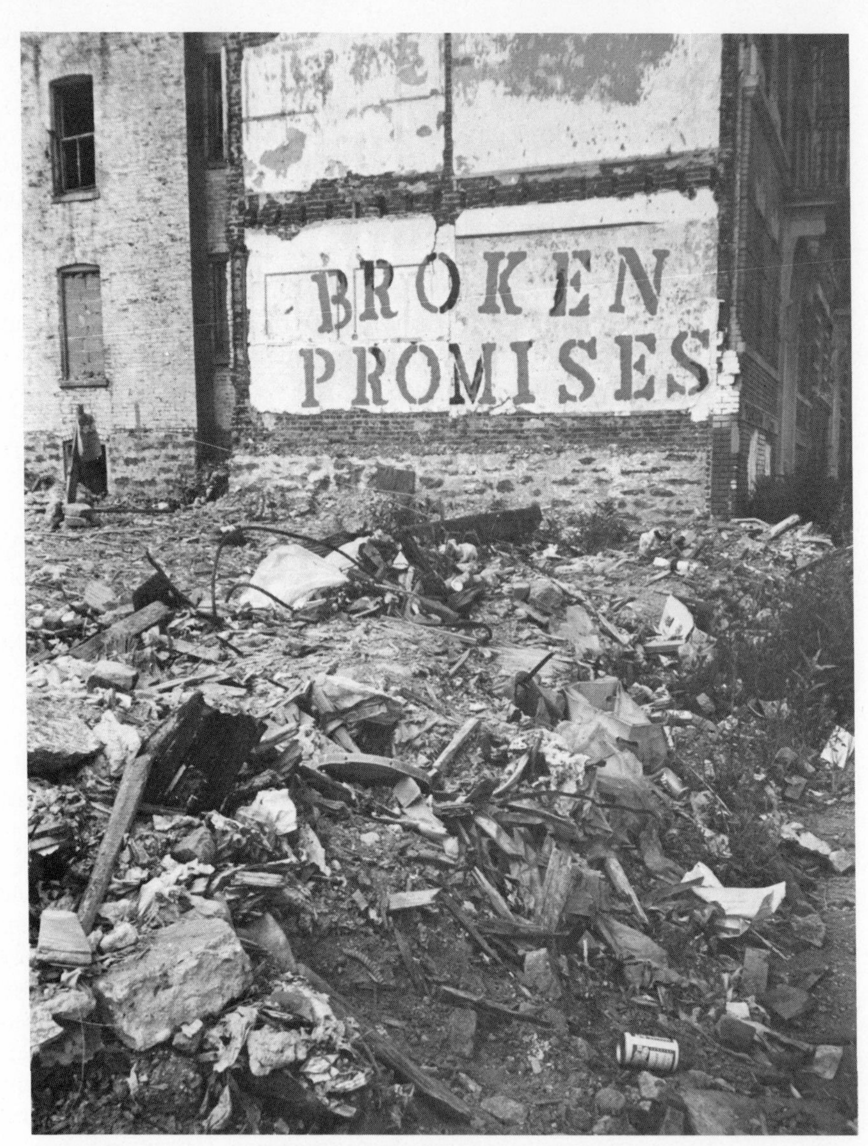

Obviously, urban living means different things for different people. For the urban poor city dwelling means blight, unemployment, high crime, cutbacks in public services, crowded subways, and danger for their children and the elderly. Pictured is an urban slum area in the South Bronx. (Barbara Alper/Stock, Boston)

corporate executives and professional technicians the city means high salaries, fine ethnic restaurants, refined arts programs, good newspapers, classical music on FM radio, and the like. In a very real sense then the city is literally perceived and experienced as a different place for the poor and the rich.

Resolving the Problem From the exchange perspective an obvious general resolution of urban problems would be to make cities more rewarding. One way of doing this would be through city enterprise zones (and other aid to cities; Walters and Angle, 1979; Philliber, 1983:502). Within enterprise zones goods are duty-free; there are little or no taxes to individuals; wage and price laws, zoning laws, rent controls, and minimum wage laws are all suspended. But child labor, pollution, health, and safety laws are all enforced (Luther, 1982).

A related proposal designed to make cities more rewarding is urban homesteading. For example, in 1973 Wilmington, Delaware, agreed to sell inner-city homes for only one dollar if the new owner would stay at least three years, and renovate the home within eighteen months. Of course, in general all city and urban planning is designed to make cities more rewarding. For one recent example of city planning see the case of Detroit's Renaissance Center. Williams (1977) argues that Detroit's planning worked. Conway (1977) counters that the Renaissance Center (and similar inner-city developments like Peachtree Center in Atlanta) are just suburban islands in a midtown ocean of decay.

From the structural perspective, if a mass exodus from the inner city reduces the city tax base and adds to city transiency,[15] a resolution would be to get the "right" populations to return to the city. Gentrification is just that process; namely, the restoration of inner-city homes by relatively affluent people (Blum, 1982). The complexity, value differences, and violence of large cities could be tempered by developing more ethnic and racial neighborhoods (Rubenstein, 1981; Schwartz, 1979). Newman (1979) suggests that cities create communities that are homogeneous by age and lifestyle. This concept could include what is called condominium in-filling; that is, efficiency units built for older populations in inner cities.

Clearly many urban problems require a strong central government. Conflict theorists argue that what is needed may be less than a socialist economy to bring urban populations under control. For an interesting example of this approach see Angotti and Dale's (1976) discussion of the renovation of Bologna, Italy. They write: "The main theoretical basis of the Bologna program is a concept of the city . . . as a public good *(bene pubblico)*. Simply stated it means that the needs of the people—all of the people—come before profit."

Finally, if nothing is done to preserve city problems, there are certain natural self-limits that may be brought on at the cost of great individual and social pain, suffering, deprivation, and even death of entire cities. Brown (1976) contends that urban population growth in Third-World countries will be checked by the impossible demands that are being made by cities for food, jobs, and energy. One resolution would be a partial return to rural life. Without such resolutions, Third-World cities will experience food, energy, and job shortages. Uncontrollable inflation, nutritional stress, dependency on external imports, growing external indebtedness, and political unrest will follow.

• Summary

Underdeveloped countries (like Mexico, Ethiopia, China, India, and Indonesia) are faced with soaring population growth, overcrowding, pollution, raw sewage in the streets, resource depletion, diminished social services, crumbling transportation systems, substandard (slum) housing, violence, starvation, and even individual and social death. What happens to populations in underdeveloped countries also clearly has implications for developed countries like the United States. These world and national population problems are primarily urban problems, since most of the growth and declining life quality has occurred in major cities.

Most observers see unchecked population growth as socially disastrous. If it continues unabated, we will run out of food and resources (such as fresh water, clean air, timber, coal, and so on); serious overcrowding and violence will follow. These problems are complicated by the racial and ethnic symbolism of population growth. That is, to control overpopulation is often interpreted as genocide for Africans, Indians, South Americans, Chinese, Arabs, and other Third-World countries.

In studying the size, compositions, growth, and distribution of the human population, we concentrated on fertility, mortality, and migration, since the new population of any group is determined by that group's fertility minus its mortality, with adjustments for migration. Several key population concepts were defined and the prevalence of problematic population patterns and trends were reviewed. These patterns were also put into historical context—with particular reference to the theory of demographic transition.

The major fertility problem is that fertility rates have remained high while mortality rates have been dropping rapidly—resulting in high rates of population growth. From the exchange perspective this pattern is no mystery, since for individuals (but not necessarily for society) copulation and high fertility rates historically have been very rewarding and are activities we are slow to satiate on. However, as the liabilities of high fertility rates in contemporary urban-industrial societies have accumulated, people have begun to limit their offspring. Large families simply cost too much. Structural-functionalists and conflict theorists view population growth as a consequence of economic organization, availability of food and agricultural technology, better transportation and distribution facilities, and advances in public health and sanitation. Fertility rates remain high because we were better able to support large populations. Resolutions of high fertility rate problems included transforming social institutions, improving contraceptive techniques, natural habitat limits, and migration.

The major mortality problem is that death rates have dropped precipitously, much more rapidly than birthrates. Exchange theory reminds us of the high value we place on avoiding pain and death. Also, the costs of death control are much less than those of birth control. Death rates can often be reduced drastically by one-time, relatively cheap social interventions—such as spraying malarial swamps with DDT. As with fertility, structurally speaking lower mortality rates result from increased food production, higher socioeconomic status, larger numbers of people living in dense urban areas, more specialized occupations, more industrialized economics, and so forth. Resolutions to low death rates include the Malthusian positive checks of war, famine, disease, and euthanasia; bringing high birthrates down; or leaving death rates low and birthrates high, but becoming more able to support these large populations (e.g., through increased food production, nonpolluting industry, and so on).

Migration was examined briefly, since it can help overcrowding in some countries. However, obviously emigration cannot solve world population problems unless we can sustain communities in outer space. We also noted major shifts in population, especially the urban transformation.

Most modern population growth has resulted from rural agrarian residents moving to a few very large urban areas. Some of the resultant special social problems of cities are high density and overcrowding, financial shortages (often from dwindling tax bases), complexity and diversity, high rates of violence and crime, transient populations, lowered quality of life, and eventual decay and hopelessness. Initially people flocked to large cities in exchange for better jobs and higher wages, the richness of specialized goods and services, the stimulation of city life, the attractiveness of the physical site, and the general cosmopolitanism of living in urban areas. Conflict theorists tend to see the urban transformation as the political economy of capitalism expropriating agricultural communities to be near inner-city factories for cheap labor. World system theories of the urban transformation were also considered.

But in the long run, most large cities became adversive and less rewarding. Jobs disappeared as business moved out of the inner city to suburbia (often out of the country). Inflation rose and specialized goods and services became unaffordable, especially for the inner-city poor, the city environment was polluted and neglected, transportation and housing deteriorated, and crime increased. What was originally a rewarding situation degenerated to costly and even profitless exchanges. People, especially upper and middle social classes, reasonably left the city—and took with them their resources. Often mainly the poor, minorities, and aged infirmed remained. Structurally major urban areas became overcrowded and underfinanced, with impersonal, superficial, formal, and indirect social relations. The bureaucratic nature of the social structure of large city organizations tended to aggravate urban problems.

One obvious resolution of urban problems from the exchange perspective would be to make city life more rewarding through enterprise zones, urban homesteading, or city planning in general. Structurally, middle- and upper-class citizens perhaps can be induced to return to the city through gentrification. The complexity and lack of social integration of big cities could be tempered by expanding and mixing ethnic, racial, and age neighborhoods—for example, through condominium in-filling. In the penultimate chapter of this text we shall examine two particularly urban social problems in some detail: the deteriorating environment and the energy crisis.

• Notes

1. Obviously population problems are institutional-level social problems, since they involve corporate and societal actors and systematic macrorelations, not just individual action.

2. The U.S. population doubles about every 100 years. The doubling time is calculated by dividing the annual growth rate (in additional persons per 1,000 population) into the number 693.

3. Look up the related concept of a life table (Zopf, 1984:422–424.

4. The recent plight of Ethiopians is a good case in point (see Panel 13.3).

5. Women are less likely to become pregnant when they are breast feeding.

6. Modern causes of death are more related to urban-industrial lifestyle and older age. Note that three of the five leading causes of middle-age deaths (twenty-five to forty-four) are violent—namely, homicide, suicide, and accidents.

7. Obviously these points could be attributed to the symbolic interaction perspective as well, since parents and families define behaviors related to lower mortality rates.

8. This should not obscure the fact that many large American inner cities have lost population to suburban areas that are still considered urban.

9. Ireland was the only country whose population declined as a result of emigration.

10. Especially related to the industrial revolution, starting about 1750 in Great Britain.

11. See Durkheim's concept of organic solidarity (1893). Cf. Blau's similar concept of penetrating differentiation (1977).

12. Reflect on the complications diverse values of cities might have for considering cities as corporate actors and applying the exchange perspective to urban societies.

13. For one reason why American ground transport (i.e., subways, electric streetcars, and so on) is so inferior to that major European cities, see Snell in Skolnick and Currie, 1985.

14. See Chapter 10, especially Mayhew and Levinger, 1976.

15. Notice that leaving the city does reduce overcrowding, but then mainly the poor and powerless remain.

• Glossary

City. Any population cluster of 2,500 or more.

Crude Birthrate. The number of births in a given year per 1,000 existing population at midyear, unadjusted for age and sex differences.

Crude Death Rate. The number of deaths in a given year per 1,000 existing population at midyear, unadjusted for age and sex differences.

Death Control. Any technique, product, procedure (e.g., nutritional, medical, or sanitary) that reduces the death rate.

Demographic Transition. A series of demographic stages through which industrialized countries have (for the most part) passed; each stage consists of a different combination of fertility and mortality, which produces different patterns of population growth or decline.

Demography. The systematic study of the size, composition, growth, and distribution of the human population.

Developed Country. Any extensively urbanized and industrialized nation with a relatively high average level of living; usually has both low birth and death rates and stable (or declining) to zero population growth.

Developing Country. A nation with a relatively low level of industrialization, a large proportion of rural population, and comparatively low levels of living; usually has relatively high birthrates, lower death rates, and a high rate of population growth.

Doubling Time. The number of years it takes a population to double in size.

Fertility. One of the three population processes (in addition to mortality and migration) indicating actual levels of reproduction.

Infant Mortality Rate. The death of babies before their first birthday per 1,000 live births per year.

Life Expectancy. The average number of years of life predicted to be lived by a group of babies born at the same time (a cohort).

Life Span. The ultimate age to which people can live.

Megalopolis. A group of large metropolitan areas clustered together.

Mortality. The number and patterns of deaths in a population, measured by the crude death rate, age-adjusted death rate, and other indexes.

Natural Increase. The (usually positive) population growth rate derived by subtracting the crude death rate from the crude birthrate; usually converted to percent increase per year.

Standard Metropolitan Statistical Area (SMSA). A large urban complex with at least one city of 50,000 or more, an urbanized area of at least 50,000 inhabitants, and a total SMSA population of at least 100,000; includes central cities and adjacent or outlying counties.

Urbanized Area. A central city of 50,000 people or more and the contiguous densely settled area; comprised of census units.

Urban Sprawl. A process in which cities devour productive farm and forest lands.

Zero Population Growth. A condition of no change in the size of a population over time because births and immigration equal deaths and emigration.

• Further Reading

Auletta, Ken. *The Streets Were Paved with Gold.* New York: Random House, 1980. A journalistic rendering of New York City's 1975 near-bankruptcy crisis by a *New Yorker* magazine writer. Examines the role of unions (the 1966 transit strike cost the city three times what it should have), banks (discusses redlining, excessive debt and borrowing practices), migration (its effects on city taxes), economic and political narcissism and anarchy (e.g., not living with a city budget; the OPEC oil shortage in 1973), federal government ($36 million went to Washington in 1975; only $29 million came back to New York City), and ethnic and racial separatism and the decline of neighborhoods. Auletta suggests that other large, especially northwestern and midwestern cities, could be vulnerable to the same problems New York City experienced in 1975.

Brown, Lester et al. *The State of the World, 1985.* New York: W. W. Norton, 1985. A recent report by the Worldwatch Institute on how to stop population growth, reduce hunger, and sustain world energy and the environment. Rapid world population growth is fueling debt crises by increasing the demand for imported food. Population growth is also related to deteriorating forests, soil, grasslands, and water cycles. An especially thorough review of fertility rates and contraceptive techniques. To control fertility we need to increase employment opportunities for women, improve education, allow abortion, and (perhaps) have more centrally planned economies (as in Cuba).

Gaines, Harold, ed. *Urban Society* 2nd ed. Guilford, CN., Duskin Publishing Group, 1982. Forty-one mostly previously published and edited short papers on various aspects of urban society. The papers are highly readable selections from scientific journals and popular magazines with relevant data and some excellent graphics. Emphasizes problems of city planning (Ch. 5), rural-urban differences (Ch. 8), slums (Ch. 11), gangs (Ch. 14), water shortages (Ch. 18), migration (Ch. 19), mass transit (Ch. 20), city finances (Ch. 24), housing decay (Ch. 25), declining neighborhoods (Ch. 35), future cities (Ch. 37), and communities in space (Ch. 41).

***Scientific American. The Human Population.* San Francisco: W. H. Freeman, 1974.** An older classical treatment by a dozen or so leading demographers of the population issues of: developed versus developing countries (Blake, Demeny, and Westhoff), food and population (Revelle), migration (Davis), fertility (Segal), and the history of population growth and the general decline in mortality rates (Coale, Freedman, and Berelson). An old but good collection of data and arguments still relevant to current population problems.

Simon, Julian L. *The Ultimate Resource.* Princeton: Princeton University Press, 1981. Upbeat, anti-Malthusian, positive, optimistic, picture of the development of the human population in the long run. Simon says that an increased need for resources usually leaves us with a permanently improved capacity to get them. Central government control of resources is counterproductive. Adding more people not only depletes world resources, but also gives us more fine, spirited minds and human beings (the ultimate resource) to resolve these problems.

Zopf, Paul E., Jr. *Population: An Introduction to Social Demography.* Palo Alto, CA: Mayfield, 1984. One of the many good recent elementary textbooks on demography. This one has an especially helpful glossary and biography. Contains chapters highly relevant to our treatment of population problems: the population explosion, zero population growth, data on the U.S. population versus the world population, age-sex profiles, fertility, mortality, migration, rural versus urban systems, racial and ethnic groups, the economy, population policies, and a helpful semitechnical section on demographic measures; e.g., of fertility, mortality, and the life table. An easy-to-read, enjoyable text on a subject that is often unnecessarily technical and dull.

C·H·A·P·T·E·R

14

Environment, Energy, and Resources

The social costs of the high level of industrial production in the United States include environmental pollution, dirty and wasted energy, and depletion of scarce natural resources. From the exchange perspective industrial corporate actors are exchanging pollution, wasted energy, and resource depletion for profit. Of course, most private citizens do not share directly in industrial profits, only in the costs (e.g., in a more contaminated environment).

Pollution and energy waste continue because they are economically profitable; because the effects of pollution, wasted energy, and resource depletion are unclear; because governmental controls are meager and often are not enforced; and because costs can be deferred to future generations. Structural-functionalists emphasize that systemic considerations are usually ignored and that it is not clear what the net functions of environmental pollution, dirty and wasted energy, and resource depletion really are. One structural fear is that we can only protect the environment at the cost of a badly crippled economy.

From the conflict perspective the essential environment-energy conflict is that between big business interests and values and the health and welfare of individuals. It is not profitable for business to conserve energy or minimize environmental pollution. Pollution control and alternative energy are expensive. The individualism ethic of the corporate world also aggravates environmental and energy problems. However, if everyone follows the logic of maximizing individual gain, in a finite environment collective ruin is a very real possibility.

Early in American history environment and energy issues were not defined (the symbolic interaction perspective) as social problems and thus little conservation or antipollution action was undertaken. The predominant Western belief was that resources were unlimited and that the future would always be better. Environmentalism produced several new laws that help define the environment as a social problem. However, some industrialists argue that the new environmentalism demands an impossibly pristine environment; that is, that environmentalism's perceptions of how clean and frugal our world ought to be are utopian and impractical.

One of the great paradoxes of the American urban-industrial social transformation is that factories and high-tech production procedures are poisoning the air we breathe, fouling the water we drink, and contaminating the soil in which our food and forests grow. At the same time modern industry is depleting unique (nonrenewable) fossil and mineral resources—especially oil and natural gas. In our quest for the highest possible material standard of living we may in fact be compromising or even destroying life for future generations of Americans.

The United States has been one of the nations most contemptuous of environmental and energy issues. Between roughly 1950 and 1985 United States energy consumption doubled, while production did not keep pace (Table 14.1; *Statistical Abstract of the United States,* 1986:556; 1987:542). Commoner (1972) reminds us that the United States has 6 percent of the world's population, but:

consumes 30 percent of the world's energy.
consumes 40 percent of the world's natural resources.
accounts for 30 to 50 percent of the world's pollution.
provides 70 percent of the world's solid wastes.

However, before we rush to condemn Americans' industrial callousness and pecuniary greed, we would do well to realize that those are several basic environmental, energy, and resource issues, which are much more complex than they may first appear.

For example, should the nation's focus be on the production and consumption of private individuals and business corporations or should we be more concerned with the collective welfare of all people and their environment or even of whole societies?[1] There can be little doubt that for the most part the United States has chosen the first option. The pervasive Western worldview has been that people differ from other creatures over which they should dominate; that human beings are masters of their own destiny; that our world has vast unlimited natural resources; and that human history is one of unilinear progress, with every problem having a technical solution (Catton and Dunlap, 1980; Buttel, 1976).

PANEL 14.1

Love Canal and the Legacy of the Hooker Chemical Company

On October 4 Jon Allen Kenny, a young boy who lived quite a distance north of the (Love Canal) evacuation zone, died of kidney failure. As the kidneys are known to be readily affected by toxicants, suspicion arose that the boy's death was related in some way to a creek that flowed behind his house and carried, near an outfall, the odor of chlorinated compounds. Because the creek served as a catch basin for a portion of the Love Canal, the state studied an autopsy of the boy, but no conclusions were reached. Jon Allen's parents, Norman, a chemist, and Luella, a medical research assistant, became discontented with the state's investigation, which they felt was "superficial." Luella said, "He played in the creek all the time. There had been restrictions on the older boys, but he was the youngest and played with them when they were old enough to go to the creek. We let him do what the other boys did. He died of nephrosis. Proteins were passing through his urine. Well, in reading the literature, we discovered that chemicals can trigger this. There was no evidence of infection, which there should have been, and there was damage to his thymus and brain. He also had nosebleeds and headaches, and dry heaves. So our feeling for now is that chemicals probably triggered it."

Source: Michael Brown, *Laying Waste: The Poisoning of America by Toxic Chemicals,* Copyright 1981, Pantheon Books, a division of Random House, Inc., pp. 44-45.

A second related issue contrasts economic considerations with those of life quality. For example *Fortune* magazine contends that environmental regulations seriously hamper the economy (Alexander, 1981:239). In 1976 the cost of complying with Environmental Protection Agency (EPA) regulations was $7.8 billion (*New Republic,* November 25, 1978; Albrecht, 1983:550). Others contend the environmental regulations aggravate inflation (Rutledge and Trevathion, 1982). In short, it may simply be too expensive to have air, water, and soil as clean as environmentalists want them.

Third, how much pollution are we as a country able or willing to trade off for the material gains of industrial production, especially of toxic chemicals and gases and radioactive wastes? Almost one ton a day per person of waste products are dumped into American skies (Auchinsloss, 1970; *National Wildlife,* 1986). As we shall see below, two of the most destructive of these aerial waste products are sulfur dioxide and various nitrogen oxides.

A fourth issue is the relationship of environmental pollution to depletion of natural resources, many of which are nonrenewable (like oil, minerals, coal, natural gas, and land). Is it the case that pollution is necessarily followed by depletion of resources (the so-called PD Day, Simon, 1981)? Certainly, if we just stop pollution, the problem of natural resource depletion remains (Albrecht, 1986:559). Domestic oil will be gone in about twenty to twenty-five years, natural gas in thirty-five to sixty years (Stobaugh and Yergin, 1982).

TABLE 14.1 World Energy Consumption, by Region and Energy Source: 1960 to 1980 (In Tons of Coal Equivalent Metric Ton = 1.1023 Short Tons*)

Region and Energy Source	Consumption (Million Metric Tons)									Percent Distribution		
	1960	1965	1970	1975	1976	1977	1978	1979	1980	1960	1970	1980
World total	3970	4971	6430	7462	7872	8076	8318	8634	8548	100.0	100.0	100.0
United States	1477	1783	2227	2284	2378	2406	2428	2470	2370	37.2	34.6	27.7
Western Europe	738	1003	1295	1407	1502	1482	1516	1619	1559	19.7	20.1	18.2
Japan	109	178	317	354	407	413	419	431	431	2.7	4.9	5.0
Centrally planned economics†	1201	1444	1783	2292	2400	2522	2630	2715	2745	30.3	27.7	32.1
Rest of world	400	563	808	1125	1185	1253	1325	1399	1443	10.1	12.6	16.9
Energy source:												
Solid fuels	1981	2070	2184	2309	2398	2448	2491	2637	2669	49.9	34.0	31.2
Liquid fuels	1311	1902	2798	3374	3603	3716	3800	3867	3709	33.0	43.5	43.4
Natural gas	593	882	1293	1556	1640	1663	1754	1842	1871	14.9	20.1	21.9
Electricity	85	116	155	223	231	248	274	288	300	2.1	2.4	3.5

*See source, p. 836, for general comments about the data.

†Includes China, Democratic People's Republic of Korea, Mongolia, Vietnam, Albania, Bulgaria, Czechoslovakia, German Democratic Republic, Hungary, Poland, Romania, and Soviet Union.

Source: *Statistical Abstract of the United States,* 1985: Table 962:560. Cf. *Statistical Abstract of the United States,* 1986:556.

This leads us directly to a fifth issue. When resources are depleted the United States becomes more dependent on foreign energy supplies—as was painfully evident in the 1973 OPEC oil blockade. North Americans consume more energy per capita than any other nation in the world and much of that energy comes from foreign imports (Table 14.2). How much energy dependency can we tolerate and still remain a strong nation with integrity? Finally, we need to get our national priorities clarified if we are to have much future. One real danger is that if pollution, resource depletion, and high energy consumption continue, future life quality may be bleak. Before we address those issues more carefully, let us define our terms; say a little more about the general prevalence of the environmental, energy, and natural resource problems; and put these problems in brief historical perspective.

By an *environment* we mean the physical and biological aspects of a specific geographical area organized into dynamic systems (Schnaiberg, 1980:9). Often we will speak of these systems as *ecosystems;* that is, as communities of living things interacting with each other and the nonliving elements around them (Albrecht, 1983:538). *Energy,* on the other hand, is the capacity for doing work and overcoming resistance; or more concretely, the physical sources (resources) of that capacity (oil, coal, gas, sun, uranium, wind, and so on). Finally, by *pollution* we mean the presence of any substances that interfere with socially desired or physically necessary uses of air, water, land, or food (Davies and Davies, 1975).

Several key energy concepts will be referred to below, especially in the data presented in tables. For example, a *BTU (British Thermal Unit)* is the amount of energy required to raise the temperature of one pound of water one

TABLE 14.2 Foreign Oil Consumption in the United States, 1960–1985

Year	Consumption (Millions of Barrels a Day)	Production (Millions of Barrels a Day)	Imports (Millions of Barrels a Day)	Imports (As a Percentage of Consumption)
1960	9.7	8.0	1.8	19%
1962	10.2	8.4	2.1	21
1964	10.8	8.8	2.3	21
1966	11.9	9.6	2.6	22
1968	13.0	10.6	2.8	22
1970	14.4	11.3	3.4	24
1972	16.0	11.2	4.7	29
1974	16.2	10.5	6.1	38
1976	17.0	9.7	7.3	43
1979 (est.)	19	10	9	47
1985 (est.)	11.8	8.9	2.9	25

Source: Robert Stobaugh and Daniel Yergin, *Energy Future,* Copyright 1982, Random House, Inc., p. 18. Cf. *Statistical Abstract of the United States,* 1986:564–565 for 1979–85 data.

degree Fahrenheit. An *exajoule* is 163 million barrels of oil or one quadrillion BTUs (cf. Table 14.3). A *kilowatt,* of course, is 1,000 watts. Other critical definitions (e.g., acid rain, the Greenhouse Effect, geothermal inversions, and so on) will be given in the proper context below.

How prevalent are general environmental, energy, and natural resource problems? Are they even really social problems at all, or are environmental pollution and purported energy shortages merely environmental hysteria? To begin with, where does environmental pollution come from? Obviously much of air and soil pollution comes from industry; especially from the burning of fossil fuels such as wood, coal, and petroleum products (including radioactive materials). For example, burning plastics produces nonbiodegradable PCBs that can cause cancer or birth defects. Chlorofluorocarbon gases (CFCs) (such as those in aerosal cans, refrigerators, computers, and so on) can damage the ozone shield around the earth, which helps filter out the sun's ultraviolet rays (Detjen, 1987).

One general consequence of industrial pollution is that the environment is becoming more acidic. Average pH levels (see glossary) of rains and snow in Central Europe and North America range between 4 and 4.5, whereas in preindustrial times the pH level was about 5.6 (Postel, 1985:101).[2] Not only is our environment becoming more acidic, it is in general becoming more toxic. *Newsweek* (November 1, 1982) claims that the environmental horror story of the 1980s is the contamination of America's ground waters by toxic chemicals (cf. Burmaster, 1982:9). One survey of ground water found that 90 percent of it was at least moderately polluted (Albrecht, 1986). Still another author claims that all water supplies (polluted or not) are expected to be down 24 percent by the year 2000 (Postel, 1985:46).

Turning to energy, wood (not oil, gas, or coal) is the primary fuel for 90 percent of the developing world (Winder, 1984:205). This means that deforestation is or will be a serious energy and environmental problem in Third-World countries. As we have seen, oil, natural gas, and coal are also in relatively short supply, and unlike wood cannot be renewed. One estimate is that the worldwide energy demand will rise from 300 exajoules in 1983 to 485 exajoules by 2000 (Chandler, 1985:148). Food also may be in short supply in the future. At current crop yields by 1997 America will need 575 million acres to feed its own population (Steinhardt, 1983:205). Unfortunately we only have 540 million acres, 51 million of which are now pasture land; 31 million are forests. Clearly the United States is going to have to increase crop yields, find alternative sources of food, reduce its population, or have many more hungry people.

We note in passing that environmental problems have always been with us. There has always been environmental destruction and disregard for energy conservation. Jacobsen and Adams (1958) remind us that the river basin of the Tigris and the Euphrates in Mesopotamia was irrigated, which left salt deposits that eventually destroyed the crops. In our own recent American history, by 1890 the wild American buffalo herds had all been slaughtered (Hayden, 1980). It was not until the late 1960s and early 1970s that America became pollution conscious. In 1967 Congress passed the Air Pollution Control Act. By 1969 the Environmental Protection Agency (EPA) had been created. In the 1970s we saw the creation of the Clean Air Act (1970), the Clean Water Act 1972, and the Toxic Substance Control Act. In 1986 the EPA declared war on asbestos (Associated Press, January 24, 1986). Yet one has to feel that all this may be too little, too late. Since President Ronald Reagan's election environmental protection and energy conservation have taken a clear back seat to industrial and economic development.

One caveat before turning to specific environmental and energy problems. Until we reach the social analysis of environmental and energy problems, much of the material may appear asociological to many students. After all, we are examining social problems in this chapter that are somewhat physical and technical. These problems are not as apparently sociological as (say) the problems of sex roles, race relations, ageism, and so on.

Yet, environmental and energy issues clearly are social too. For example, Catton (1980) conceives of environmental and energy problems as ecological concerns. He claims that human beings' socioevolutionary course is such that our culture, technology, and societies now strain the ability of the biosphere (i.e., the surface layer of planet earth and its atmosphere) to sustain life on earth. Thus, sociocultural factors determine physical problems.

Other sociologists emphasize the role of social factors in even defining energy and environmental conditions as problematic. A good example of this is the influence of the collective behavior of different sexual groups in shaping nuclear energy issues (see Brody, 1984). Still other sociologists have looked at attitudes toward environmentalism, including the benefits and costs to different groups of conservation policies (Mohai, 1985). Thus, one should not be deluded that environmental and energy issues are not social problems. Obviously, they are—probably far more than they are physical, biological, or engineering problems.

• Stating the Problem

The Deteriorating Environment? Air All living human beings and animals depend on the relatively thin elastic invisible mixture of gases (nitrogen, oxygen, hydrogen, carbon dioxide, orgon, neon, helium, and so on) that surrounds the earth. Without it we literally could not survive. Modern industrial development and the resultant pollution threaten air quality and the balance of healthful properties of the atmosphere. Here we shall examine three major aspects of air pollution: general pollution (including smog and thermal inversions), acid rain, and the so-called Greenhouse Effect.

The Pollution Standard Index (PSI) measures five common air pollutants: sulfur dioxide (SO_2), nitrogen dioxide (NO_2), ozone, carbon monoxide, and suspended particulants (solid particles in the air). If the PSI is above 100, the air is considered unhealthful to breathe. If it is above 200, it is considered hazardous. Table 14.3 shows us that most large urban-industrial areas in the United States (e.g., Los Angeles, New York City, Denver, Pittsburgh, Hous-

The Cuyahoga (Akron, Ohio) and Chicago rivers have been so polluted with oil waste that they have actually caught on fire! However, reducing industrial output may lower our quality of life. This is an oil refinery discharging industrial wastes into a bay. (Daniel S. Brody/Stock, Boston)

ton, and Chicago) have unhealthy air about one-third of each year. In Los Angeles air is unhealthy two-thirds of each year. It has been claimed that just breathing the air in New York City was the equivalent of smoking two packs of cigarettes each day (Rienow and Rienow, 1967).

On the positive side, our air quality has improved recently (*Los Angeles Times,* October 5, 1981). For example, Chicago had 240 unhealthy days in 1974 but just 48 unhealthy days in 1980 (National Wildlife Federation, 1983:85). The Environmental Protection Agency found that particulants dropped 50 percent from 1970 to 1979. SO_2 decreased 7 percent, but NO_2 increased 18 percent in the same 1970–79 time period. In spite of these recent improvements in air quality a national survey in 1986 ranked air pollution the second most important and pressing environment problem ahead of hazardous wastes, overpopulation, acid rain, and nuclear power plants (National Wildlife Federation, 1986).

Smog (a mixture of smoke and fog) is a common cause of contemporary respiratory stress, especially for the elderly, those with emphysema, tuberculosis, bronchitis, and other breathing problems. For example, smog killed

TABLE 14.3 Ranking of 40 Standard Metropolitan Statistical Areas (SMSA) by the Pollutant Standards Index (PSI), 1978–1980

Severity Level (Days with PSI Greater than 100)	SMSA	Three-Year Average of Number of Days: "Unhealthful," "Very Unhealthful," and "Hazardous" (PSI >100)	Three-Year Average of Number of Days: "Very Unhealthful," and "Hazardous" (PSI >200)
More than 150 days	Los Angeles	231	113
	San Bernardino—Riverside—Ontario	174	89
100–150 days	New York	139	6
	Denver	130	36
	Pittsburgh	119	13
	Houston	104	23
50–99 days	Chicago	93	14
	St. Louis	89	19
	Philadelphia	74	6
	San Diego	72†	3†
	Louisville	70	4
	Phoenix	70†	6†
	Gary	68	33
	Portland	62	11
	Washington	62	8
	Jersey City	58*	0*
	Salt Lake City	58	18
	Seattle	52	3
	Birmingham	50*	8*
25–49 days	Cleveland	46	11
	Detroit	39	4
	Memphis	37*	3*
	Baltimore	36	2
	Indianapolis	34	2
	Cincinnati	28	1
	Milwaukee	28	2
	Kansas City	28*	1*
0–24 days	Sacramento	22	1
	Dallas	21	1
	Allentown	21	2
	Buffalo	20†	4†
	San Francisco	18	0
	Toledo	15	2
	Dayton	15	1
	Tampa	8	1
	Syracuse	7	1

continued

TABLE 14.3 *(concluded)*

		Three-Year Average of Number of Days	
Severity Level (Days with PSI Greater than 100)	**SMSA**	**"Unhealthful," "Very Unhealthful," and "Hazardous" (PSI >100)**	**"Very Unhealthful," and "Hazardous" (PSI >200)**
0–24 days—concl.	Norfolk	6†	0†
	Grand Rapids	6*	0*
	Rochester	5	0
	Akron	4	0

*Based on 1 year of data.
†Based on 2 years of data.
Note: The Pollution Standards Index (PSI) combines the concentrations of five major pollutants (sulfur dioxide, nitrogen dioxide, ozone, carbon monoxide, and suspended particulates) into a single value.

Source: Elliott Currie and Jerome Skolnick, *America's Problems: Social Issues and Public Policy,* 1984: 386–387.

4,000 people in London in 1952. At certain times smog blocks out 25 percent of New York City's and 40 percent of Chicago's sunlight (Ehrlich and Ehrlich, 1972). Smog is particularly deadly when it is combined with thermal inversions (as it often is). With thermal inversions (in cities like Los Angeles, Denver, Phoenix, and so on) high cold air seals in lower warm air and traps pollutants in stagnate air (Carr, 1972). Populous valleys surrounded by mountains are unusually vulnerable to thermal inversions.

Lately acid rain has received a great deal of media attention (see Associated Press, March 19, 1986; La Bastille, 1986). Acid rain was first diagnosed in England in 1872. When industry and motor vehicles operate they burn oil, coal, or gas, which produces sulfur dioxide (SO_2) and nitrogen oxides (NO_x) (Postel, 1985:97). When combined with moisture in the air sulfuric and nitric acids result. Acid rain is 70 percent SO_2 and 30 percent NO_x (Postel, 1985:114). Mega-smokestacks (some in excess of 500 feet tall) and the prevailing winds usually carry these acids to the northeastern United States and Canada, where they are deposited as rain (see Figure 14.1). Acid rain kills hundreds of lakes and their fish, plants, and forests each year (Urquhart, 1982; Albrecht, 1986:546). These acid rain damages to water, flora, and fauna cost the United States $5 billion per year in the early 1980s (*Newsweek,* April 25, 1983; Postel, 1985:121). The Canadian government has grown increasingly impatient with the United States government's failure to control midwestern generated acid rain (Associated Press, March 15, 1985). Of course, northeastern U.S. acid rain means dying Adirondacks lakes and no fish caught by fishermen, but control of acid rain also means loss of midwestern jobs (Krohe, 1984:175).

A final air problem we shall discuss is called the Greenhouse Effect (Detjen,

FIGURE 14.1 Acid Rain: Sources and Destinations

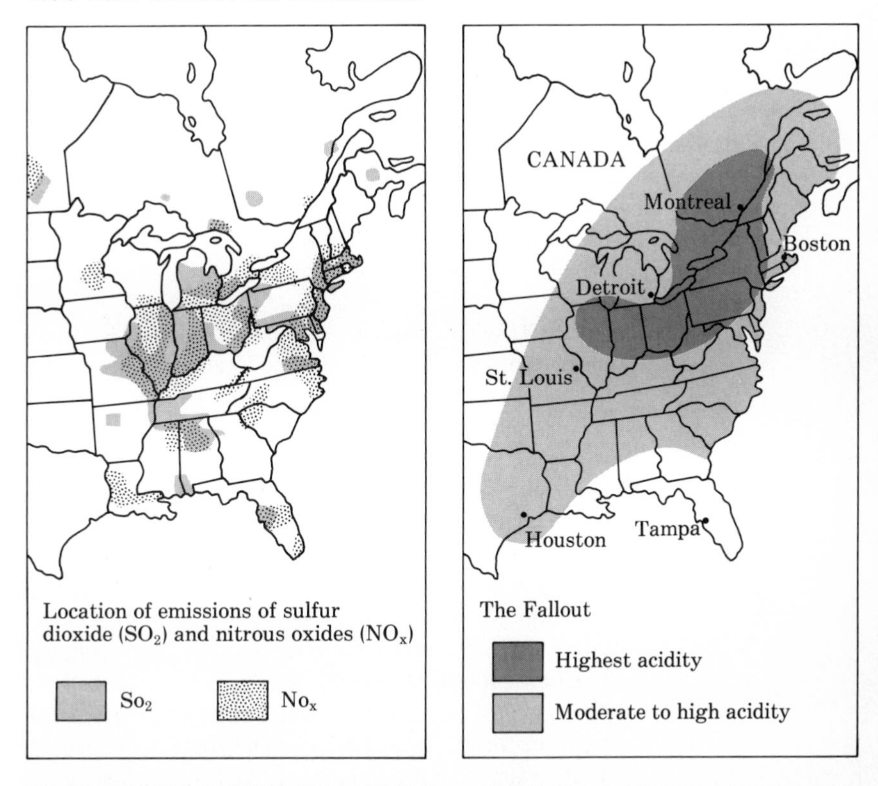

Source: Elliott Currie and Jerome Skolnick, *America's Problems: Social Issues and Public Policy,* 1984:389. For emissions, *State of the Environment 1982,* The Conservation Foundation, adapted from Environment Canada. 1982:68; for fallout, *Newsweek,* April 25, 1983:37.

1987). In 1896 it was claimed that large amounts of carbon dioxide (CO_2), injected into the earth's atmosphere when fossil fuels burn, could lead to a gradual warming trend (Rose et al., 1984:185; see Panel 14.2; cf. UPI, May 12, 1985, "Trace Gases and the Greenhouse Effect"). Carbon dioxide (CO_2) absorbs, then reradiates, heat from the surface of the earth back to earth rather than out into space. Thus, CO_2 operates like the glass on a greenhouse (Albrecht, 1983:547).

If carbon dioxide doubled from pre-1900 levels to 600 parts per million (ppm), this would produce a three-degree Centigrade rise in temperature over the entire globe—or so the theory claims (a four- to six-degree rise in the United States and Europe; Rose et al., 1984:186). With a three- to six-degree Centigrade temperature rise, the west Antarctic ice sheet might melt, flooding many lowlands and major port cities. Carbon dioxide levels increase with deforestation. However, there is no conclusive evidence that the earth's surface temperature is warming. In fact, air pollution may be blocking out some of the sun's heat. Thus, the earth could even get cooler (Bryson, 1974).

Finally, remember that the ozone layer about twenty miles above the earth's surface filters out damaging ultraviolet rays. Ozone is created when ultraviolet rays interact chemically with oxygen. Chlorofluorocarbons (CFCs) (leached into the atmosphere from refrigerators, air conditioners, computers, and so on) deplete the ozone layer by combining with oxygen and thus reducing the available oxygen to interact with ultraviolet rays (Detjen, 1987). A depleted ozone layer around the earth could lead to a major increase in skin cancers, sunburn, and overexposure.

Water Like air, water is, of course, essential for life. The 1986 survey mentioned above (National Wildlife Federation) ranked water pollution as the number one environmental priority. The two major water problems are its overconsumption and its contamination. Although water is replenishable, clearly it can be consumed faster than it is renewed with the obvious result of serious water shortages. Shortages are especially likely with large concentrated populations, under drought conditions, and where large amounts of water are being used for crop irrigation. The United States consumes two to seven times more water per person per day than any other country in the world. Most of that water (about 70 percent; Rice, 1986) is used by industry (once again industry is the environmental culprit, if there is one), followed by agricultural consumption—a distant second. As a result of this high water consumption (and other factors) the United States and several foreign countries (e.g., southern India, northern China, Mexico, and the USSR) are seriously depleting their groundwater supplies (Postel, 1985:43). Worldwide Asia and Africa have the greatest water stress and Canada the least. However, in parts of the southwestern United States the Ogallala Aquifer (underground water in the Southwest United States) is half empty and has declined 7 percent between 1978 and 1982 (see Figure 14.2). Tucson, Arizona, is the largest American city completely dependent on groundwater for its water supply and has shown other cities how water can be conserved by social programs (Postel, 1985:52).

Although water contamination is not widespread (overall only 1 percent to 2 percent of underground water is contaminated), in some specific areas contamination is high (Carey, 1984:159).[3] For example, one-half the water systems surveyed in Vermont were contaminated with chloroform. In Battle Creek, Michigan, eighteen of the city's thirty wells were laced with vinyl chloride, TCE, and benzene (Carey, 1984:167). Recently it appears that the quality of America's drinking water has actually improved (although see National Wildlife Federation, 1986). There is a major problem with sewage in water in some areas. For example, in virtually all of Latin America municipal sewage and industrial effluents are discharged into the nearest rivers or streams without treatment (Postel, 1985:51). Too much sewage in water can lead to eutrophrication or overfertilization, which consumes oxygen needed by fish (Commoner, 1972). Thus, sewage is destroying many lakes and their fish and plant

PANEL 14.2

Global Thermostat's Going Up?

The federal government warned Tuesday that a dramatic warming of the earth's climate because of the "greenhouse effect" could begin in the 1990s.

Such a warming would have potentially serious consequences for global food production, changes in rainfall and water availability, and a probable rise in coastal waters.

An Environmental Protection Agency report said that levels of carbon dioxide in the air created by the burning of fossil fuels could result in an increase of 3-6 degrees Fahrenheit by the middle of the next century and a 9-degree rise by 2100, representing "an unprecedented rate of atmospheric warming."

The condition is known as the "greenhouse effect" because carbon dioxide behaves like the glass in a greenhouse, permitting the sun's warming rays to reach the earth but not allowing the heat to escape.

The effect, the report said, is like that of a "thermal blanket" around the globe.

The report said that the warming trend will occur regardless of what steps are taken to reduce the burning of fossil fuels. Even a total ban on coal burning beginning in the year 2000—which the report called "economically and politically infeasible"—would delay by only fifteen years a 3-6-degree increase in average worldwide temperatures, the study said.

The study said a warmer climate would raise the sea level by expanding the oceans and by melting ice and snow now on land.

An increase of only two feet, the report said, "could flood or cause storm damage to many of the major ports of the world, disrupt transportation networks, alter aquatic ecosystems, and cause major shifts in land development patterns."

A global warming, the report said, could also improve climate in upper latitudes, increase rainfall for some regions, and reduce heating costs worldwide.

Drawing by Chas. Addams; © 1952 1980 *The New Yorker* Magazine, Inc.

life (Bastian and Benorado, 1983). Industrial wastes are sometimes so concentrated in some rivers (as in the Cuyahoga River in Akron, Ohio), that the rivers actually catch on fire (Slocum, 1973)! Some water pollutants could actually be put to good use. For example, industrial waste water (i.e., sludge) could be treated naturally (with the water hyacinth or with anaerobic digestion), then used for fertilizer.

Earth, Land, and Food Toxic waste products are also a common consequence of industrial development and energy use. We have already discussed some toxic gases, like sulfur dioxide (SO_2) and nitrogen dioxide (NO_2) above. Many toxic industrial chemical by-products are directly harmful to human beings. Examples would be the Love Canal, New York, site discussed above (cf. Brown, 1981). Another would be the Times Beach, Missouri, area which had to be closed due to dioxin poisoning (Currie and Skolnick, 1984:389). Figure 14.3 lists about 100 of the worst U.S. toxic dump sites in 1981. By 1983 only 5 of these sites had been cleaned up (*Newsweek,* January 3, 1983). Some of these sites are unnecessary, since many hazardous wastes can be detoxified (*Newsweek,* March 7, 1983). Recently (Associated Press, January 24, 1986) the EPA declared asbestos insulation, a known carcinogen, a top

FIGURE 14.2 The Ogallala Aquifer

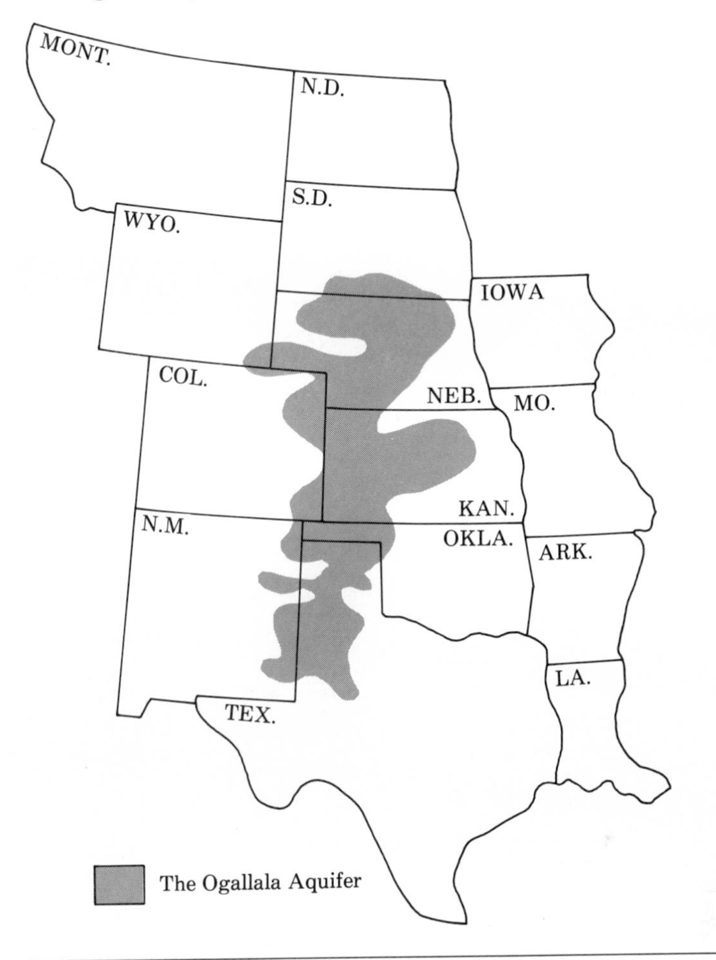

Source: James Henslin and D.W. Light, Jr., *Social Problems,* McGraw-Hill, 1983:544.

priority for removal. Radioactive wastes are not only highly toxic when stored in the ground, but they also degenerate very slowly. We shall discuss this special disposal problem when we consider nuclear energy below.

Indirectly toxic pesticides used to control insects on crops often poison the very food being produced. When these chemicals are recognized as extremely dangerous, usually they are banned from sales or distribution in the United States. However, such toxic pesticides continue to be sold to foreign countries as exports. Ironically many of the poisoned crops other countries grow (especially coffee and cocoa) are sold mainly to the United States—thus forming a "circle of poison" (Weir and Shapiro, 1980:118). At least 10 percent of America's imported food is estimated to be contaminated. Even when contam-

FIGURE 14.3 The Worst Waste Dumps: Hazardous Sites with Highest Priority for Remedial Action, 1981

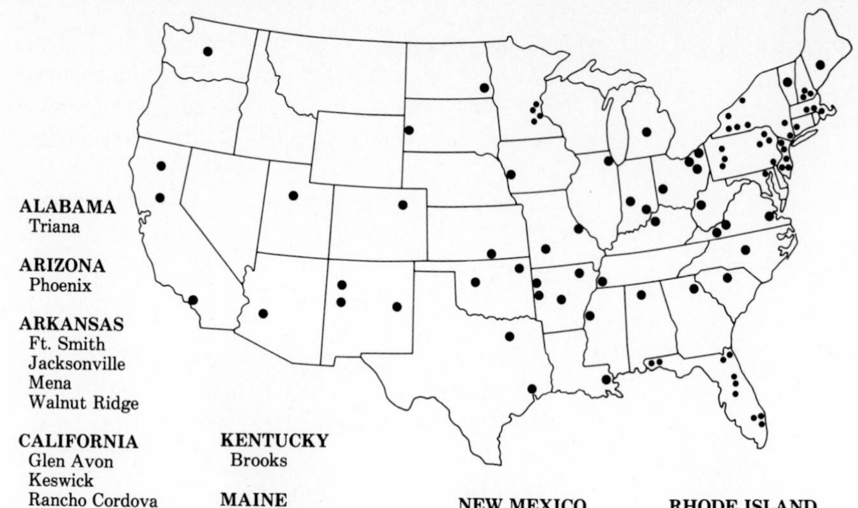

ALABAMA
Triana

ARIZONA
Phoenix

ARKANSAS
Ft. Smith
Jacksonville
Mena
Walnut Ridge

CALIFORNIA
Glen Avon
Keswick
Rancho Cordova

COLORADO
Denver

CONNECTICUT
Naugatuck

DELAWARE
Delaware City
New Castle
Red Lion

FLORIDA
Between Alford and Cottondale
Clermont
Davie
Ft. Lauderdale
Galloway
Hialeah
Jacksonville
Miami
Pensacola
Tampa
Warrington
Whitehouse
Zellwood

GEORGIA
Athens

ILLINOIS
Waukegan

INDIANA
Bloomington
Seymour

IOWA
Council Bluffs

KANSAS
Arkansas City

KENTUCKY
Brooks

MAINE
Winthrop

MARYLAND
Baltimore

MASSACHUSETTS
Ashland
North Dartmouth
Tyngsborough
Woburn

MICHIGAN
St. Louis

MINNESOTA
Andover
Oakdale
St. Louis Park
St. Paul

MISSISSIPPI
Greenville

MISSOURI
Ellisville
Springfield

NEW HAMPSHIRE
Epping
Kingston
Nashua

NEW JERSEY
Bridgeport
Edison
Elizabeth
Freehold
Hamilton
Marlboro
Monmouth County
Pitman
Pleasantville
Plumsted

NEW MEXICO
Church Rock
Clovis
Milan

NEW YORK
Batavia
Elmira
Niagara Falls
Olean
Oswego
Oyster Bay
Philipstown
Wheatfield

NORTH CAROLINA
Highway dumping in fourteen counties

NORTH DAKOTA
Rural south-eastern corner

OHIO
Ashtabula
Cleveland
Deerfield
Hamilton

OKLAHOMA
Criner
Ottawa County

PENNSYLVANIA
Bruin
Buffalo
Chester
Girard
McAdoo
Natrona Heights
Old Forge
Pittston

RHODE ISLAND
Burrillville
Coventry
Smithfield

SOUTH CAROLINA
South of Columbia

SOUTH DAKOTA
Deadwood

TENNESSEE
Memphis

TEXAS
Crosby
Grand Prairie
La Marque

UTAH
Salt Lake City

VERMONT
Burlington

VIRGINIA
West of Salem
York Country

WASHINGTON
Tacoma

WASHINGTON, D.C.

WEST VIRGINIA
Point Pleasant

Source: The Conservation Foundation, *State of the Environment 1982* p. 154.

ination is identified, about 50 percent of pesticide-infested products are sold anyway without warning labels to American customers. Even ordinary fertilizers contain nitrates, which intestinal bacteria convert to nitrite. When nitrite combines with hemoglobin, the oxygen-carrying capacity of the blood is lowered.

Some naturally occurring chemical combinations in foods are particularly dangerous. For example, nitrates can become nitroamines and cause cancer. Nitrates are in hot dogs, ham, and bacon. Amines are in beer, wine, cereal, fish, cigarettes, and so on. Thus, beer and hot dogs consumed together can be dangerous (Drummond, 1977). Food additives (like Red Dye #2) have also been shown to cause cancer.

Still another environmental concern about the earth is resource depletion. In addition to diminishing oil, natural gas, and coal supplies, the United States will also eventually run out of metals. Meadows et al. (1974) claim that the following metals are endangered:

Metal	New Domestic Supplies Gone in:
Aluminum	55 years
Copper	48 years
Gold	29 years
Mercury	41 years
Silver	42 years
Zinc	50 years

Simon (1981) replies that if these metals were really all that scarce, their prices would be higher than they in fact are.

Finally, many chemicals in the soil are destroying our trees and forests (see Figure 14.4 and Panel 14.3). Trees derive nutrition from calcium, magnesium, and potassium. Acids leech these materials from the soil (Postel, 1985:101ff). Acid makes aluminum in the soil soluble and aluminum makes tree roots less able to absorb moisture and nutrients. If trees die before maturity (when they are 80 to 130 years old), then they must be harvested. This means that excessive amounts of wood will flood the market and lower wood prices. For Canadians, one out of ten of whom have forest related jobs, the consequences are serious. Finally, the soil of America is also simply being blown, washed, and bulldozed away (Steinhardt, 1983:143). Loss of soil entails loss of agricultural productivity, less food, and more hunger. Having considered environmental problems let us now do the same for energy problems, before turning our attention to the social aspects of these problems.

Energy Sources and Crises Environment and energy are not separate issues, but in fact are inextricably interwoven. For example, excessive use of fossil fuel energy leads not only to acid rain, carbon dioxide (CO_2) warming, the extinction of some species, foul water and soil, and health problems, but also to capital shortages and the prospect of running out of fuel in the not-too-distant future (Chandler, 1985:148). America also runs the risk of becoming

FIGURE 14.4 How Forest Acreage Is Expected to Dwindle

Estimated forested area,
in millions of acres

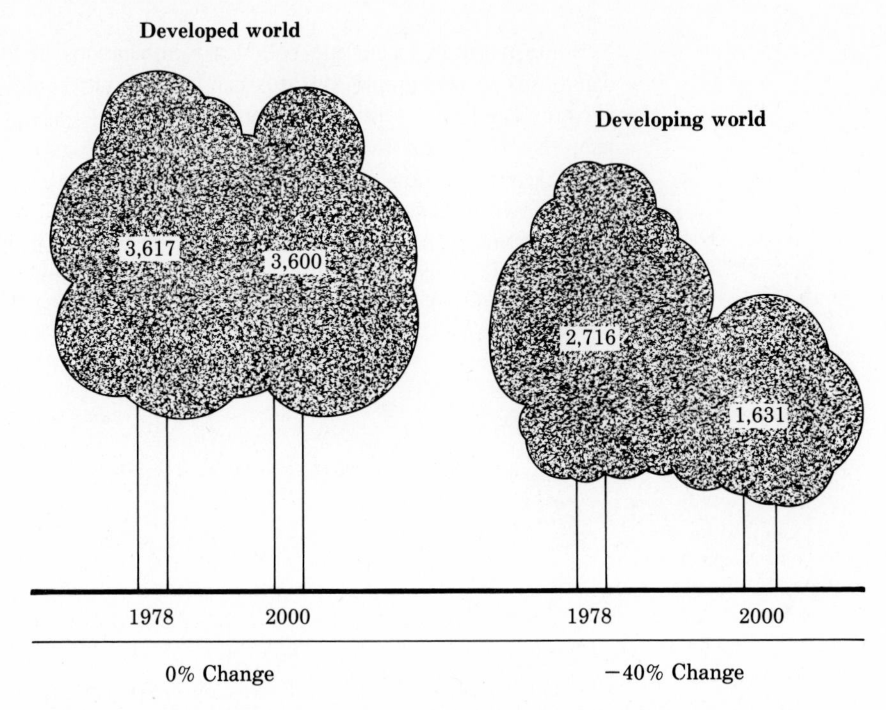

Developed world includes the Soviet Union, North America, Europe, Japan, Australia, and New Zealand. Developing world includes Latin America, Africa, Asia, and the Pacific.

Source: Council on Environmental Quality, *Global 2000 Report,* 1982 (see David Winder, "The World's Shrinking Forests," 1984).

energy dependent on hostile foreign countries like the OPEC nations (Wolf, 1986). The 1973 OPEC oil embargo forced the USA to become more energy conscious and probably marked the end of cheap and plentiful oil supplies (Brown et al., 1985:55). Other signals of energy crises include power blackouts and brownouts in the northeastern United States (especially in New York City) in 1965 and 1977, the 1978 overthrow of the Shah of Iran, and the Three Mile Island and Chernobyl nuclear reactor accidents.

Oil and Fossil Fuels Obviously the main U.S. energy crisis since 1973 has been primarily an oil crisis (or more generally, depletion of nonrenewable fossil fuels). Table 14.4 tells us that oil is the United States' primary energy source,

PANEL 14.3

Puzzling Holes in the Forest: Trees from Maine to Alabama Are Showing a Decline in Growth

In some sections of Georgia and South Carolina, yellow pine trees seem to be growing much more slowly than they once did. In southern New Jersey, patches of pitch pines have stopped growing altogether. So have parcels of spruce trees on Whiteface Mountain in New York. On Camels Hump, a major peak in Vermont's Green Mountain range, and Mount Mitchell in North Carolina, the highest peak in the East, red spruce are losing their foliage and dying, leaving barren patches on the once lush slopes. Says Botanist Hub Vogelmann of the University of Vermont: "There are some pretty big holes in the forest."

The decline, confined thus far mostly to the Eastern states, is puzzling scientists from Maine to Alabama. The mysterious selective blight may merely signal shifts in local ecological balances. Or, say the scientists, it may be the start of a trend toward devastation that could eventually engulf the entire Eastern green range. Their worry is not unfounded. An apparently similar malady has ravaged 34 percent of West Germany's wooded lands, causing an annual $509 million in damages to timber and related industries. So far, the U.S. decline has been measured mostly in aesthetic and recreational losses. But it is beginning to have an economic cost as well. Sugar Maple Harvester David Marvin, for example, has lost all the maple trees on ten acres of his 700-acre Vermont spread. A reduction in maple trees could spell disaster for the state's $10 million-a-year sugar industry. Other areas could be hit hard as well. Says Joe McClure of the Southern Region Office of the U.S. Forest Service: "Potential losses would be very significant if a long-term decline developed. Timber sales are just the beginning. The Southeast relies heavily on wood growing, transporting, and manufacturing products from it."

To gather evidence of damage, the U.S. Forest Service each decade resurveys thousands of one-acre plots, checking the diameter and height of trees and looking for portents of new growth. The ongoing survey of Southern Piedmont woodlands shows that in the past ten years the growth rate of loblolly pine, a coniferous evergreen, has been 25 percent less than expected. Botanist Vogelmann's twenty-year study of Camels Hump has shown a rapid decline in nine species of trees on the 4,083-ft. peak. The biomass (the combined weight of tree trunk, branches and foliage) has dropped sharply for several kinds of trees: 25 percent for sugar maples and beech and 34 percent for white birch. Red spruce has been the hardest hit, with a biomass decline of 71 percent.

Another clue comes from a study of 7,000 trees, sponsored by the Environmental Protection Agency. Scientists at Oak Ridge National Laboratory in Tennessee examined 14,000 core samples of the tree trunks. Their findings: beginning in 1960, in eight Eastern states, pitch and shortleaf pines and red spruce started to show narrowing growth rings, a sign of sluggish development. Similar changes have been noted in West Germany's stricken trees.

Still, most scientists agree that there is not nearly enough evidence to pin down the cause of the deterioration. Several possible suspects have been considered. Among them: insects, plant disease, poor soil condition and abnormal climatic changes. Experts note that the decline began about the time of the great Northeast drought of the early

continued

PANEL 14.3—*(concluded)*

1960s. "Drought is undoubtedly a major component of a large part of the decline," says Robert Rosenthal of the EPA. "But it doesn't explain it all. There is pretty good evidence that there are air pollution effects." Plant Pathologist Robert Bruck of North Carolina State University points out that tree growth slowed down in the early 1960s, just after extensive industrial expansion in the Ohio and Tennessee valleys. Says he: "Pollution from these industries got sent East, and the first things to intercept it were the forests at higher elevations."

Indeed, the most severe damage has occurred at high altitudes to such trees as the red spruce and Fraser and balsam firs. The summits of Camels Hump and Mount Mitchell are enshrouded for as much as a quarter of the year in clouds, which are loaded with acidic chemicals and toxic heavy metals. Says Arthur Johnson, a soil expert at the University of Pennsylvania: "Vegetation essentially combs polluted moisture droplets out of the clouds." Mountain tops at this altitude are also exposed to high concentrations of ozone and get more rain, which washes chemicals onto the trees. "Most people think of remote mountains as ideal vacation spots that are very clean, but they're not," declares Johnson. Many isolated areas in the mountains of New England have abnormally high levels of copper, zinc, nickel and cadmium. And the Green Mountains of New Hampshire, seemingly pristine, in fact rival big cities when it comes to lead pollution.

Researchers speculate that chemicals may work their damage in several ways. The excess ozone might open the pores of leaves, allowing acid rain to leach vital nutrients. Or acid rain may cause harmful changes in the chemical composition of the soil. Rain may also deposit toxic heavy metals that damage plants' root systems. Says Richard Phipps of the U.S. Geological Survey: "The darn thing is a heck of a lot more complex than we ever thought."

Solutions seem a long way off. Arboreal experts are only now beginning to assess the severity of the problem. The Forest Service, for example, has just started a study of the condition of yellow pine, the South's prime source of commercial timber. At Oak Ridge, botanists are examining samples of soil for traces of metals such as aluminum and zinc. In May, U.S. forest experts will travel to West Germany to compare notes with European scientists; in turn, German researchers will visit the United States in June. Says Fred White, staff forester with the North Carolina division of forest resources in Raleigh: "Initial answers for this phenomenon will probably be a combination of total nonsense, the truth, and lots in between."

Source: *Time,* March 19, 1984.

supplying roughly 42 percent of all energy consumed in recent years. Our oil consumption increased until about 1977–78, then declined somewhat. As we saw above, the U.S. oil problem is compounded, since we import more oil each year than any other country in the world consumes (Yergin, 1982). Note too in Table 14.4 that although the U.S. consumption/production ratio has gone down somewhat recently, America still consumes more energy than it produces. More recently (*Time,* February 3, 1986) the price of oil has dropped precipitously, to about twenty dollars (or less) per barrel of North Sea crude (although OPEC's August 1986 quotes on oil production are expected to bring oil and gas prices up again). Of course, lower oil prices will not keep oil from being used up eventually, but they will lower U.S. inflation and are expected to add two percentage points to America's GNP between 1986 and 1988. The bad news is that U.S. banks holding loans from major oil-producing countries (e.g., from Mexico) will suffer major default losses and see bank stock prices drop.

Continuing with Table 14.4, coal and natural gas together comprise (approximately) another 48 percent of the total U.S. energy source. Coal consumption has increased steadily since 1973. In the 1980s coal energy increased to about 20 percent to 25 percent of the total U.S. energy consumed. This pattern of increase is likely to persist, since oil supplies are declining while coal supplies are relatively plentiful—enough for about 400 years more of consumption (Stobaugh and Yergin, 1982). The main problem with coal energy is that it is a fairly dirty source of energy (especially from sulfur dioxide air pollution).

Given the United States' dependency on oil, coal, and natural gas, we tend to forget that for most of the world the real energy crisis is a shortage of firewood (Wolf, 1983:509). In Third-World countries (i.e., developing countries) wood or dung is the principal fuel—particularly for cooking (Chandler, 1985:161). In fact, in 1973 (after the OPEC oil crisis) even wood energy in the United States made a strong comeback. For example, wood produced more energy in 1973 (2.6 percent of all energy) than nuclear plants (i.e., 1.2 percent; see Brown et al., 1985:55).

Of course, cars, buses, trucks, and so on have both wasted gasoline and oil and contributed many nitrogen oxides (NO_x), carbon monoxide (CO), carbon dioxide (CO_2) to pollute the air. In America private cars alone use about 17 percent of our oil supplies each year (Chandler, 1985:157). American cars are also notoriously fuel inefficient. Table 14.5 reveals that U.S. automobiles are the least fuel-efficient cars in the world (mean consumption = sixteen miles per gallon). Even our new cars are the least fuel efficient (mean = twenty-two miles per gallon). If the USA car manufacturers raised auto fuel economy to (say) forty miles per gallon, it would save us as much energy as the entire country of Brazil consumes in a year (Chandler, 1985:149). This is not as far-fetched as it sounds, since cars have already been built that get ninety-three miles per gallon. Even Detroit's General Motors has seventy-eight miles-per-gallon cars ready for production, but being held off the market for economic reasons (i.e., basically they are not as profitable; Chandler, 1985:158).

In passing it should be noted that energy can be generated from waste products like animal and human excrement and garbage. Manure can be converted to methane gas (Brown et al., 1985:57). Methane digesters (devices that produce methane gas energy) consist of 10 percent human waste, 30 percent animal waste, 10 percent straw and grass, and 50 percent water. In

TABLE 14.4 U.S. Energy Production and Consumption, by Major Source: 1950 to 1984

Year	Total Production (Quad. BTU)	Percent of Production				Total Consumption (Quad. BTU)	Percent of Consumption				Consumption/Production Ratio
		Coal	Petroleum*	Natural Gas‡	Other†		Coal	Petroleum*	Natural Gas†	Other‡	
1950	34.0	41.4	33.7	20.8	4.2	33.1	37.3	40.2	18.0	4.4	.97
1955	38.7	32.0	37.2	27.3	3.5	38.8	28.8	44.4	23.2	3.6	1.00
1960	41.5	26.1	36.0	34.0	3.9	43.8	22.5	45.5	28.3	3.7	1.06
1961	42.0	24.9	36.2	34.9	4.0	44.5	21.7	45.5	29.1	3.7	1.06
1962	43.6	25.0	35.6	35.1	4.2	45.6	21.3	45.2	29.5	4.0	1.07
1963	45.9	25.9	34.8	35.4	4.0	48.3	21.6	44.9	29.8	3.7	1.05
1964	47.7	26.3	33.9	35.8	4.0	50.5	21.7	44.2	30.3	3.8	1.06
1965	49.4	26.5	33.5	35.8	4.3	52.7	22.0	44.1	29.9	4.0	1.07
1966	52.2	25.8	33.7	36.4	4.1	55.7	21.8	43.8	30.5	3.9	1.07
1967	55.1	25.1	33.9	36.5	4.4	57.6	20.7	43.9	31.2	4.2	1.05
1968	56.8	24.0	34.0	37.6	4.4	61.0	20.2	44.2	31.5	4.1	1.07
1969	59.1	23.5	33.1	38.7	4.8	64.2	19.3	44.1	32.2	4.4	1.09
1970	62.1	23.5	32.9	38.9	4.7	66.4	18.5	44.4	32.8	4.3	1.07
1971	61.3	21.5	32.7	40.5	5.3	67.9	17.1	45.0	33.1	4.8	1.11
1972	62.4	22.6	32.1	39.7	5.6	71.3	17.0	45.2	31.9	4.9	1.14
1973	62.1	22.6	31.4	39.9	6.2	74.3	17.5	45.9	30.3	5.3	1.20
1974	60.8	23.1	30.5	38.9	7.4	72.5	17.5	46.1	30.0	6.4	1.19
1975	59.9	25.0	29.6	36.8	8.6	70.0	18.0	46.4	28.3	7.3	1.18
1976	59.9	26.1	28.8	36.4	8.6	74.4	18.3	47.3	27.4	7.0	1.24
1977	60.2	26.2	29.0	36.4	8.5	76.3	18.3	48.7	26.1	6.9	1.27
1978	61.1	24.4	30.2	35.6	9.9	78.1	17.6	48.6	25.6	8.2	1.28
1979	63.8	27.5	28.4	35.0	9.1	78.9	19.1	47.1	26.2	7.6	1.24
1980	64.8	28.7	28.2	34.2	8.9	76.0	20.3	45.0	26.8	7.9	1.17
1981	64.4	28.5	28.2	34.2	9.1	74.0	21.5	43.2	26.9	8.4	1.15
1982	63.9	29.2	28.7	32.0	10.2	70.0	21.6	42.7	26.1	9.6	1.11
1983	61.2	28.2	30.1	30.6	11.2	70.5	22.6	42.6	24.5	13.2	1.15
1984, prel.	65.5	30.1	28.4	30.7	10.8	73.7	23.3	42.1	24.5	10.1	1.13

*Production includes crude oil and lease condensate. Consumption includes domestically produced crude oil, natural gas liquids, and lease condensate, plus imported crude oil and products.
†Production includes natural gas liquids, consumption excludes natural gas liquids. ‡Comprised of hydropower, nuclear power, geothermal energy, and other.

Source: *Statistical Abstract of the United States,* 1986:556.

Reprinted by permission: *Tribune* Media Services.

another related example, Munich, West Germany, gets about 12 percent of its electricity from garbage (Brown et al., 1985:56).

All fossil fuels (such as oil, coal, and natural gas) share the trait of being nonrenewable, since they take thousands of years to be generated. Figure 14.5 illustrates that fossil fuel energy consumption came into use very recently and that it will be gone just as quickly—a blip or bubble on the graph of historical energy sources. Clearly, future energy will have to come from alternatives to fossil fuels (Bacas, 1985). This is exactly what Table 14.4 shows; namely, an increasing proportion of U.S. energy supplies come from other sources (such as nuclear energy, hydroelectric power, geothermal and solar energy, and so on). Before moving on to consider these alternative energy sources and the social problems related to them, it should be stated that private residential energy consumption of oil has declined. Other residential energy sources are about constant, with electricity being the most expensive source of energy.

Nuclear Energy Although they currently supply very small amounts of energy, there was rapid growth between 1979 and 1984 of nuclear, geothermal,

TABLE 14.5 Automobile Fuel Economy, Selected Countries, 1982

Country	Autos	Fleet Average	New Cars
	(millions)	(miles per gallon*)	
Australia	6.3	19	24
Brazil	9.7	20	24
Canada	10.6	18	27
France	17.8	27	32
East Germany	2.4	27	32
Italy	17.7	24	31
Japan	39.0	31	30
Soviet Union	8.0	26	29
United Kingdom	15.6	22	28
United States	125.4	16	22
West Germany	23.2	22	28
Other	77.0	NA	NA
Total	353.0	21†	25‡

*Actual mileage on the road. Data may not be strictly comparable due to differing national testing method.
†Based on 80 percent of the cars in the world.
‡Based on 70 percent of the new cars in the world.

Source: William U. Chandler, "Increasing Energy Efficiency," *State of the World, 1985,* W.W. Norton, 1985:158.

FIGURE 14.5 Historical Perspective on Fossil Fuels

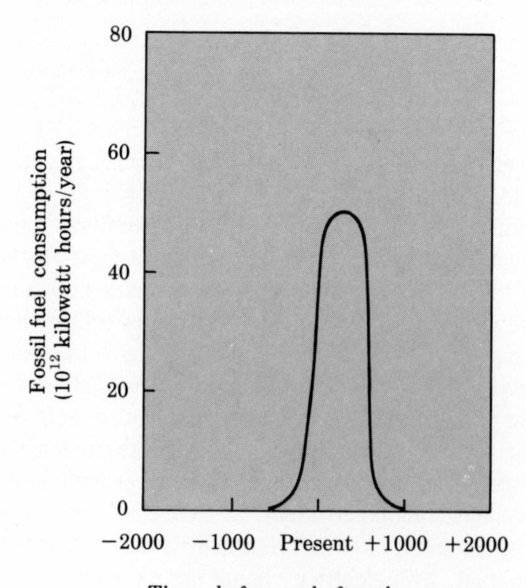

Note: The use of fossil fuels as sources of energy for human beings is of relatively recent origin and will probably not extend far into the future.

Source: M. King Hubbert, *U.S. Energy Resources, A Review as of 1972,* 1974, Figure 69.

and wind electricity, alcohol fuels (like gasohol), and solar panels. Let us consider the nuclear energy problem first.

Although nuclear energy has been much ballyhooed, heavily subsidized by the federal government, and could reduce U.S. dependence on foreign oil, it also could spread technology for nuclear war and terrorism (see Chapter 15) and imperil the environment and/or human life from shortage of hazardous radioactive waste products (Sandell, 1982:80). For these reasons (and others) the nuclear movement itself may be dying. Table 14.6 demonstrates little growth in nuclear power plants through 1984. Stobaugh and Yergin conclude that the nuclear promise has turned into the nuclear disappointment (1982:108). In about 1980 orders for new nuclear plants virtually stopped. In 1982 construction of nineteen proposed plants was canceled or postponed (*New York Times,* November 1, 1982). Much of this slowing down was the direct result of the nuclear accident at Three Mile Island, which has now cost $3 billion in direct loss. Furthermore, in 1981 alone there were 140 nuclear mishaps of major significance (*Environment,* September, 1982:21–22).

A second major setback to the development of nuclear energy plants occurred in late April and early May of 1986 when a reactor in Chernobyl, USSR, exploded and burned (Trafford and Wellborn, 1986). This accident led to strained international relations, forced Russia to shut down 50 percent of its other nuclear reactors, killed 2 people and injured at least 200 others, and sparked an international debate and protest about the global safety of nuclear reactors. This is a serious problem for countries with dense populations and no fossil fuels, such as France. In France 65 percent of all power is produced by nuclear reactors. Although only 16 percent of all U.S. power is nuclear, the United States leads the world with 101 nuclear reactors in service. Russia is second with 50 nuclear reactors. The question is whether nuclear reactors are worth the danger they pose to the world community and what alternatives exist to nuclear power.

Some nuclear fears may be unjustified. For example, nuclear energy is less expensive (1.5 cents per kilowatt hour) than coal (2.3 cents) or oil energy (4 cents) (Sandell, 1982:82). However, the start-up and investment costs to produce nuclear energy are very high. We must not forget that the environmental cost of burning coal and oil is high too because of the sulfur dioxide and acid rain generated. Some claim that the normal radiation a nuclear power plant releases (barring accidents) is less than that received yearly from dental and medical X rays (Sandell, 1982:84).

On the other hand, 100 million cubic feet of military radiation waste is now stored in South Carolina, Washington, Idaho, and New York (*U.S. News & World Report,* August 15, 1983). This waste can cause cancer, genetic defects, and death. It remains dangerous for thousands of years. For example, 154,000 residents living downwind from the Rocky Flats Nuclear Weapons Plant in Denver, Colorado, had 24 percent more cancer than those living elsewhere in Denver (Sandell, 1982:84). In a second case, the KYSHTYM nuclear disaster in the USSR in 1957 (perhaps the world's first nuclear accident) wiped out

TABLE 14.6 Nuclear Power Plants—Number, Capacity, and Generation: 1965 to 1984, United States

Item	1965	1970	1973	1975	1978	1979	1980	1981	1982	1983	1984 prel.
Operable reactors*	10	19	39	54	70	68	70	74	77	80	86
Capacity*† (mil. kWh)	.9	6.5	22.9	33.3	49.6	49.3	51.1	55.5	59.6	62.8	69.5
Electricity generated (bil. kWh)	4	22	84	173	276	255	251	273	283	294	328
Percent of total electric utility generation	.4	1.4	4.5	9.0	12.5	11.4	11.0	11.9	12.6	12.7	13.6
Capacity factor‡	NA	NA	52.9	59.7	65.7	58.7	57.1	58.4	57.2	54.8	56.5

NA = Not available.
*As of yearend.
†Net maximum dependable capacity of operable reactors.
‡Weighted average of monthly capacity factors. Monthly factors are derived by dividing actual monthly generation by the maximum possible generation for the month (hours in month times net maximum dependable capacity).

Source: *Statistical Abstract of the United States,* 1986:571. Cf. U.S. Energy Information Administration, *Annual Energy Review* and *Monthly Energy Review.*

entire towns in the Ural Mountains (Solomon and Rather, 1980; cf. Kiev [Chernobyl] nuclear accident in 1986). Thus, the nuclear energy future does not seem very promising.

Electricity and Hydropower In many ways electricity is a preferred energy source. It is environmentally clean and renewable. Unfortunately, it is also expensive, difficult to transport, and frequently generated by other energy sources (such as nuclear plants or burning coal) that themselves are dangerous, polluting, and in short supply.

One promising form of electricity is hydropower (Bacas, 1985). The first central hydroelectric plant was built in Appleton, Wisconsin, in 1882 (Brown et al., 1985:58). In a sense such small dams that generate hydroelectricity are the oil wells of the future. Of course, you must have rivers and lakes to dam before electricity can be generated. Some flat and desert areas cannot generate hydropower for obvious reasons.

A major electrical energy problem is old nonenergy-efficient electric motors. Electric motors generate about 80 percent of all electrical energy in industry. They could be made much more efficient simply by adding variable frequency drives (Chandler, 1985:155).

Solar Energy Solar energy supplies about 5 percent of America's current energy, but could supply as much as 20 percent to 25 percent by the year 2000 (Stobaugh and Yergin, 1982:183; Wolf, 1986:526). Solar energy is not depleted by consumption and is clean. Table 14.7 displays a big growth in solar heat collector shipments between 1976 and 1980, then a steady decline (noticeably in low-temperature equipment). Most solar heat energy is in residential use. In 1986 the federal government stopped giving energy tax credits for installing solar panels.

A solar energy future would entail relatively slow or zero industrial growth (Stern and Gardner, 1981). However, solar energy is a fairly effective job producer (Lerney and Posey, 1979). Of course, solar energy is not one thing. Production of solar heating panels has dropped off, but other varieties of solar electricity (e.g., photovoltaics, power towers, and solar thermals) have continued to grow or stay relatively constant since 1980 (see Table 14.8). Solar energy will be, in all probability, mainly supplemental energy, especially for cloudy cold sections of the country.

Geothermal and Wind Energy We should not forget other less discussed, smaller impact energy forms, such as geothermal energy, wind, tides, and so on. Geothermal energy means that energy generated by hot springs, geysers, molten rock, and so on. For example, in Iceland 65 percent of homes are heated by underground hot water (Brown et al., 1985:60). In coastal, lakefront, mountainous, or plains areas considerable power can be harnessed from windmills. To illustrate, the North Sea coastal town of Olfborg, Denmark, has the world's largest wind generator. Between 1973 and 1980 the U.S. Department

TABLE 14.7 Solar Collector Shipments, by Type, End Use, and Market Sector: 1974 to 1984, United States

[in thousands of square feet, except number of manufacturers. Solar collector is a device for intercepting sunlight, converting the sunlight to heat, and carrying the heat to where it will be either used or stored]

			Collector Type		End Use			Market Sector		
Year	Number of Manufacturers	Total Shipments*	Low Temperature	Medium Temperature, Special, Other	Pool Heating	Hot Water	Space Heating	Residential	Commercial	Industrial
1974	45	1,274	1,137	137	NA	NA	NA	NA	NA	NA
1975	131	3,743	3,026	717	NA	NA	NA	NA	NA	NA
1976	186	5,801	3,876	1,925	NA	NA	NA	NA	NA	NA
1977	321	10,312	4,743	5,569	6,334	1,713	1,699	7,978	1,680	105
1978	340	10,860	5,872	4,988	5,970	2,513	1,736	8,095	1,848	263
1979	349	14,251	8,395	5,857	8,551	2,958	1,722	11,387	2,015	314
1980	233	19,398	12,233	7,165	12,029	4,790	1,888	16,077	2,417	468
1981	203	20,133	8,677	11,456	9,781	7,204	2,017	15,773	2,561	1,516
1982	265	18,621	7,476	11,145	7,035	7,444	2,367	13,729	3,789	560
1983	203	16,828	4,853	11,975	4,839	9,323	2,082	11,780	3,039	1,665
1984	224	16,419	4,479	11,939	4,427	8,930	2,370	13,980	2,091	289

NA = Not available.
*Includes other end uses and market sectors not shown separately.

Source: *Statistical Abstract of the United States,* 1986:574. Cf. U.S. Energy Information Administration, *Solar Collector Manufacturing Activity,* annual.

TABLE 14.8 Actual and Projected Funding Levels for Solar Research, Development, and Demonstration,* Fiscal Years 1975–1983‡ (In Millions)

	1975	1976	1977	1978	1979	1980	1981	1982	1983
Thermal applications									
Heating and cooling of buildings	18	27	93	104	129	98	91	36	28
Agricultural and industrial process heating	—	—	8	10	11	23	19	16	16
Fuels from plants	5	5	10	20	52	79	68	72	75
Solar electric									
Solar thermal	10	15	51	60	70	80	159	237	205
Photovoltaics	8	15	59	57	91	125	151	100	100
Wind energy	7	12	21	33	51	76	90	90	90
Ocean thermal	3	4	14	35	52	110	35	68	68
Total†	49	78	258	319	455	590	613	618	582

*Estimated by solar program officials.
†Totals may not add, due to rounding.
‡Years 1975 to 1978 actual, 1979 to 1983 projected.

Source: Robert Stobaugh and Daniel Yergin, *Energy Future,* Copyright 1982, Random House, Inc., p. 206. Cf. data compiled from Government R&D Report, vol. III, no. 5, September 15, 1977:3; U.S. General Accounting Office, "Federal and State Solar Energy R&D Development and Demonstration Activities," June 19, 1975; "The Magnitude of the Federal Solar Energy Program and the Effects of Different Levels of Funding," Report of the U.S. Comptroller General, February 2, 1978.

of Energy spent nearly $200 million to develop wind turbine generators capable of producing about 200 kilowatts (Brown et al., 1985:59–60). However, at the most wind energy could supply only about 2 percent of America's total energy needs by the year 2000. In the next section we turn to various sociological perspectives on the environmental and energy problems just stated.

Analyzing the Problem

A striking trait of most conventional (especially journalistic) writing about environmental or energy issues is how much of it is totally atheoretical. Typical accounts tend to document facts or objective patterns (say, of environmental pollution or wasted energy) with little or no overt interest in how these social and physical patterns come to be or why they are considered social problems at all now but were not considered problems at some earlier time. Of course, sociological assumptions are always present, even if not articulated or elaborated. Remember that the sociological perspectives considered below are not discrete, but in fact overlap considerably.

The Exchange Perspective It would seem obvious that poisoning the air, water, and soil and depleting our scarce natural resources make no interactive sense. For example, if the social exchange is oil, coal, or gasoline burning for acid rain and other serious pollution of the air we breathe (an exchange of acts, not actors), then such an exchange could easily be considered irrational. This is especially true if there are nonpolluting nonresource-depleting alternatives—such as solar or electrical energy.

However, in an institutional context exchange relationships are indirect, complex, impersonal, more often for money, involve large numbers of actors, involve different types of actors or actions, and so on (see Chapter 10 and Table 10.3 particularly). Generally, in an institutional setting there is a multitude of social exchanges. Some of these are profitable or rewarding for some groups (and thus are rational) and with others exchange values may be undetermined, if not undeterminable. For example, burning dirty coal-producing sulfur dioxide (SO_2) is valuable to midwestern industry but not to Adirondack tourism or Canadian forestry (Krohe, 1984).

In the environment-energy controversy the basic exchange is corporate actor industrial products for economic gain (i.e., for profit). Industry (as a corporate actor) is slow to satiate on money and relatively unconcerned about environmental pollution, individual health, natural resource depletion, and so on (see the case of the Ford Pinto considered in Chapter 10). A corporation can be very healthy in spite of (or sometimes even because of) the poor health of individuals or environmental deterioration. Thus, for industry rewards typically outweigh costs and pollution will continue.

Note too that cause and effect are difficult to specify in an institutional setting. Therefore, the incentive to change (or for the government to mandate change) industrial or energy practices is low. Do nuclear plants really release dangerous amounts of radiation into the atmosphere (Sandell, 1982:84)? Is acid

Mega-smokestacks in the Midwest emit sulfur dioxide and nitrogen oxides. These gases mix with water in the air to form acids. Prevailing winds carry the acids to the Northeast and Canada and deposit them as acid rain. (Daniel Brody/Stock, Boston)

rain actually causing forests to die? (U.S. President Reagan claims that the cause of dying forests is still unclear.) Are we in fact gong to run out of fossil fuels any time soon (Simon, 1981)? Is our drinking water all that unhealthy (Carey, 1984:169)?

Environment and energy costs are also generationally deferred. You and I may not even be alive when the oil is all gone. Radiation or toxic chemical dump hazards may show up in unborn children, if at all. Thus, a certain altruism and abstraction are required to even become concerned about many environmental and energy issues. For better or worse many of us live primarily in our asocial selfish present.

Remember that the exchange perspective claims that if some act is rewarded (other things being equal) it will be repeated. But environmental and energy rewards changed dramatically with the administration of U.S. President Ronald Reagan. Consider, for example, that the federal Department of Energy was reduced greatly, that energy credits for insulation, solar heat supplements, and so on were withdrawn, and that pollution controls and environmental restriction on American industry have been relaxed. Thus, to be energy or environment conscious is not as highly rewarded as it once was, and is less likely to be common.

Finally, alternative energy sources or more environmentally benign energy is costly. Cost is the most significant exchange factor in determining environmental and energy practices (Chandler, 1985:169). Thus, understandably, car makers or industry in general are slow to switch to alternative energy sources, even though some production costs could be passed on to consumers.

The Structural-Functional Perspective The emphasis in the structural-functional perspective is on the systemic aspects of social systems and the consequences of social conditions. For example, functionalists like Commoner (1974) stress the interconnections of the ecological system. To illustrate, green plants provide oxygen and carbon dioxide (CO_2). If we add carbon dioxide to the air faster than plants or the ocean can remove it (e.g., through burning fossil fuels in industry), then the earth may gradually get warmer (the Greenhouse Effect). Commoner writes that industrialization has caused problems by breaking "the circle of life, converting its endless cycles into manmade events." A tally sheet of functions and dysfunctions of current industrial practices might tell us if they are functional and, by implication, if they are meeting a social need(s) that explains their continuation. For example, the increased GNP of the United States and our higher material standard of living is functional but the increased pollution of the environment is dysfunctional. Presumably, if a social condition or pattern had major net dysfunctions, it would be changed (consider the repeal of the Eighteenth Amendment to the U.S. Constitution concerning prohibition of alcohol). Thus, functionally speaking, the tendency is to assume that whatever is (especially over a long time), is for the best. On the other hand, latent dysfunctions are often made manifest when it is too late, that is, after considerable social or individual damage has already occurred.

One important functional dilemma is that resolution of energy problems may create new environmental problems (Basile, 1980). Thus, it can be argued that we cannot resolve or reduce all environmental and energy system problems simultaneously.

The Conflict Perspective The essential environment-energy conflict is that between big business interests and values and the health and welfare of individuals. It is not profitable for business to conserve energy or minimize environmental pollution. Individuals and even governmental agencies (like the EPA) lack both the means and the will to police environmental or energy abuses by industry.

Pollution control (e.g., coal scrubbers or electric vehicles) is expensive (Davies and Davies, 1975). Thus, if anything threatens profits, industry (and its stockholders) will resist it and resist it effectively (given industry's private ownership of the means of production). For example, 80 percent of the patents for photovoltaic cells (which convert the sun's energy to electricity) are owned by Standard *Oil,* Atlantic Richfield *Oil,* and Exxon *Oil* (Walters, 1982). Big energy corporations tend to bring out competing products. A classic case would be General Motors buying patents for carburetors that can get 70–90 miles per gallon and then keeping them off the market.[4]

The individualism ethic of the corporate world also aggravates environmental and energy problems. The individualism ethic connotes the belief that nature is inexhaustible, that technology is good, that growth and personal profit are essential, and that the highest level of materialism is desirable (Etzioni, 1975:98). In the ethos of this rugged entrepreneurial individualism, collective welfare is neglected or ignored.

The individual ethic (as obviously contrasted with a more socialistic ethic) is related to the so-called tragedy of the commons (Hardin, 1968). The main point of the tragedy of the commons is that if rewards are for maximizing individual gains, an adequate collective environment eventually will be depleted, and in the end even individuals will not be rewarded. If everyone follows the logic of maximizing individual gain, in a finite environment collective ruin is a very real possibility.

The Symbolic Interactive Perspective Early in American history environmental and energy issues were not defined as social problems and thus little conservation or antipollution action was undertaken.[5] As we have seen, the predominant Western belief was that resources were unlimited and that the future would always be better (Buttel, 1976). This mindset contributed to the near extinction of the American buffalo (in 1890) and the 1914 extinction of the passenger pigeon.

The first major environmental concerns were primarily conservation motivated, as in the creation of the American national park system by President Theodore Roosevelt (1901–1909; see Schnaiberg, 1980:378). However, conservation of wild game, sport fishing, and open woods in which to hike around are very different issues than those of air pollution, undrinkable and unswimmable water, and building homes on radioactive or chemically toxic soil.

The environmentalism movement began in the late 1960s and early 1970s (Schnaiberg, 1980:382; Courrier, 1980) because of certain undeniable events that changed public perceptions about the importance and nature of environmental and energy issues. These events included the publication of Rachel Carson's *Silent Spring* (1962, about the dangers of pesticides); the 1969 Santa Barbara oil spill; increasing air pollution (especially in Los Angeles); and the 1973 OPEC oil embargo.

Environmentalism produced several new laws that helped define the environment as a social problem. These laws included the 1967 Air Pollution Control Act; the 1969 creation of the Environmental Protection Agency (EPA); the 1970 Clean Air Act; the 1972 Clean Water Act; and the 1976 Toxic Substance Control Act.

Some industrialists argue that the new environmentalism demands an impossibly pristine environment; that is, that their perceptions of how clean and frugal our world ought to be are utopian and impractical (Schnaiberg, 1980:40ff.). United States President Ronald Reagan tended to support the industrialists' perception of the environment and energy use and accordingly has reduced federal financing for environmental programs and energy conservation.

• Resolving the Problem

Of course, resolving environmental and energy problems is no easy task. This is particularly true if the resolution requires fundamental changes in the mode of industrial production in the United States. Aside from the obvious ideological and political issues involved, such sweeping changes have profound economic and social consequences. We could end up with clean air, water, and soil only by sacrificing our current high material standard of living (including a high GNP) and world military power.

The five basic resolutions to be discussed are: changing national priorities, for example, by reducing industrial output; more federal control of industry, for example, through export regulations and fines; conservation and rationing; recycling wastes and detoxification; and new energy alternatives, and other future prospects.

Clearly, these resolutions are related to the four sociological perspectives just considered. For example, reducing industrial output is at least a conflict resolution, since it restrains profits of corporate elites. It is also a structural-functional resolution, since resetting national priorities requires specifying consequences (i.e., functions) of present environmental and energy policies and procedures. Then too priority setting also suggests symbolic interactionism, definitions, paying attention to the meanings of environment and energy issues, and so on. To resolve environmental and energy issues through fines is an exchange issue as well, since it changes the reward system of industry. Finally, note that conservation and recycling are essentially structural status-quo resolutions, which for the most part amount to living with or making do with present environmental and energy conditions.

Reducing Industrial Output Obviously, since most U.S. pollution and resource depletion comes from industry, one resolution would be to stabilize or reduce industrial output (Ehrlich and Ehrlich, 1981; Schnaiberg, 1980:Ch. 5). But how does one even begin to do this, given the rugged-individual, entrepreneurial ethos of Western capitalism? In a very real sense the suggestion almost sounds un-American. Certainly the resolution is impractical, if not simply unenforceable in the United States. Furthermore, most Third-World developing countries are trying frantically to increase their industrial production. In a highly centralized economy (e.g., Cuba's) it might be possible to slow industry, but in most countries such acts verge on being national suicide. Reducing industrial output is simply not going to work in America.

Federal Control of Industry If American industry cannot be slowed, perhaps it can be controlled in other ways. For example, Ophuls argues that many of the costs (he calls them external costs) of industrial production are not paid for by either the consumer or the producer, but instead are often quite literally dumped on society in the form of pollution and waste products (1977). Perhaps the federal government needs to do more to make American industry pay for those external costs (cf. Catton and Dunlop, 1980).

This can be done through the creation and enforcement of environmental and energy laws and agencies, such as the EPA and the federal environmental and energy legislation mentioned earlier. If price is the most important factor in energy use (Chandler, 1985:169), perhaps industry needs to pay more dearly for energy waste, resource depletion, and environmental pollution. One example of how this federal policing might work would be to stop the export of chemicals banned in the United States (Weir and Shapiro, 1985:118).

Still, it must be conceded that the federal government's record in this area has not been impressive, nor is it clear that the resolution would be good for the economy. Environmental and energy laws have often proved unpopular and difficult to apply.[6] For example, supply-side economists (see Gilder in Chapter 11) tend to argue that federal controls cause energy problems by interfering with market supply-demand patterns (Hagel, 1976). Fines tend to be modest "hand slaps" that do not correct industrial environmental and energy abuses. Given the overlap of big business, government, and military leaders (see C. W. Mills's "Power Elite" in Chapter 10), federal controls cannot be very effective. Remember too that a corporation like General Motors has the third largest annual budget of any *country* in the world (only the United States and the USSR have larger budgets).

Conservation and Rationing Probably many of America's energy and resource depletion problems could be dealt with by demand reduction, that is, by conservation (Walklet, 1979; cf. *State of the Environment, 1982*). Chandler points out that Japanese industry has been very energy efficient, but has also maintained high levels of production at the same time (1985:150). Stobaugh and Yergin predict that energy conservation measures could result in a 30 percent to 40 percent energy consumption reduction over current use (1982:136).

Consider several examples of conservation in private residences, agriculture, and industry. The average American home has a square yard of holes in it, allowing cold air in and hot air out (or vice versa, in the summer) (Lovins and Lovins, 1980:96). In fact as many as 30 percent of all American homes lack any insulation at all (Stobaugh and Yergin, 1982:170). Transportation by private cars, as opposed to mass transit, clearly wastes a great deal of oil (Chandler, 1985:157). As noted earlier, industry could conserve energy by installing regulators on electric motors and by using more cogeneration. Vast quantities of fresh water seep through unlined irrigation canals (Postel, 1985:63). Household water demands could be reduced by about 33 percent just through conservation. For example, the city of Tucson, Arizona, cut its water demand by 24 percent (Postel, 1985:67; see Panel 14.4). Recent progress in conservation is most encouraging. Between 1973 and 1982 overall the United States was 15 percent more energy efficient (Yergin, 1982:16).

PANEL 14.4

A Tale of Two Cities

Residents of Tucson use approximately 160 gallons of water per person per day. The residents of Phoenix, a little more than 100 miles to the northwest, use 260 gallons per person per day—and some of the exclusive little suburban communities around Phoenix are almost awash in 1,000 gallons of water per person per day.

Why are Arizonans so near to one another in terms of geography, but so far apart in the consumption of this resource? "Tucson has a desert mentality," says an Arizona Department of Water Resources official. "Phoenix has an oasis mentality."

Phoenix draws upon water from the Salt River and has always enjoyed the shade of mulberry trees and towering hedges. Tucson relies upon groundwater for its supplies. Its vegetation tends toward cactus and other desert plants.

But water rates make a difference too. In Phoenix, homeowners' costs for 2,350 cubic feet of water average $13.76 per month. But Tucson residents pay 76 percent more for that amount, or $24.27. Tucson's rates are part of a conservation program. Tucson manufacturers such as IBM recycle their water for efficiency and cost control.

Source: George Alexander. Reprinted from the Feb/Mar 1984 issue of *National Wildlife*.

Recycling Wastes and Detoxification Both the environment and energy use could be improved through better management of wastes and toxic materials. Recycling wastes is clearly a help to the energy problem (Brown, 1981). We have already discussed converting garbage, weeds, sawdust, excrement, and so on to fuel (see above and Brown, 1981:56–57). Waste water and sludge could be processed for use as fertilizer (Bastian and Benforado, 1983:100). Lakes soured by acid rain could be sweetened by lime applications (Allen, 1985:182). Many scarce metals, such as aluminum cans, could be recycled by reverse vending machines (see Panel 14.5) and scrap processors. Radioactive wastes probably could be managed best by isolating them in deep geological formations (Lipschutz, 1980). Finally, instead of fuel switching (e.g., from coal to some alternative fuel) acid rain and air pollution could be controlled by coal scrubbers (FDGs—Flue Gas Desulfurization Units; Krohe, 1984:177; Postel, 1985:115). While pollution and toxic substance control is often expensive (Chandler, 1985:150; Albrecht, 1983:550; Krohe, 1984:184), often the cost is less than that of lowered production and switching to alternative fuels (cf. Stobaugh and Yergin, 1982:Ch. 4).

Energy Alternatives and Future Prospects By necessity future energy use will have to move away from fossil fuels (like oil, coal, and natural gas) to renewable clean energy sources (like solar, electric, wind, and hydropower) (Kendall and Nardis, 1980; Brown et al., 1985; Bacas, 1985). Such an energy

PANEL 14.5

Reverse Vending Machines Swallow Aluminum Cans

One of the most exciting innovations in aluminum can collection is the "reverse vending machine," which brings recycling operations closer to the public.

Rather than driving across town to a scrap processor or saving up large amounts of waste for periodic community recycling drives, people can bring their empty beverage cans to conveniently located vending machines that accept small amounts of scrap and dispense payment.

According to *Resource Recycling,* the Portland, Oregon, based journal of recycling, reuse, and waste reduction, reverse vending machines were invented because of the need to reduce labor costs at recycling centers. By using machines placed in supermarkets, convenience stores, parking lots, and even video game parlors, people can redeem their beverage cans while freeing the staffs of scrap centers to handle larger amounts of cans and other recyclable materials.

Several types of reverse vending machines have been developed by different manufacturers, but, according to *Resource Recycling,* the devices share five general features. First, they accept used cans—whole or flattened, singly or in small amounts. Second, they distinguish aluminum cans from other items such as bottles and steel cans. Third, the machines count or weigh the amount of aluminum deposited; they then dispense a reward in the form of coins or redeemable coupons, tokens, or chits. Finally, the machines crush the aluminum and store it until unloaded into a truck that periodically collects the scrap.

Where used, the machines are remarkably successful. In Denver, Colorado, twenty reverse vending machines paid out more than $1 million in an eighteen-month period. Sweden reportedly will build and install an estimated 10,000 reverse vending machines as part of an effort to recover 75 percent of all aluminum cans used in the country. This would save 10,000 tons of aluminum annually (50 million cans), equal to Sweden's annual aluminum imports.

Source: William U. Chandler, "Converting Garbage to Gold: Recycling Our Materials" in *The Futurist,* February, 1984.

trend would obviously lessen carbon dioxide (CO_2) and sulfur dioxide (SO_2) environmental pollution (Rose, 1984:190). Renewable energy is also preferred because it is largely indigenous and virtually inflation proof (Brown, 1982:64). There will be a continued decline in the relative importance of nuclear energy (Brown, 1982:55). Energy conservation will be even more important in the future.

Other energy alternatives will include hydrogen from water and synfuels from weeds, garbage, and sawdust (Waddington, 1978). Cogeneration of heat produced by industrial boilers used primarily to generate electricity could also be a supplemental energy source (Larson, 1981). In the future it will be necessary to realize that all levels of society are interconnected (Humphrey and Buttel, 1982), that the environmental and energy crises are complex, that environmental problems are social problems (not just corporation or individual

Nuclear energy plants are often mentioned as an alternative to oil and coal energy. However, start-up costs are high and the danger from accidents, radiation poisoning, and waste disposal is ever present—as the recent disaster at Chernobyl, USSR, pictured here, demonstrates. (Reuters/Bettmann News Photos)

problems), that resolutions cannot afford to take a short-run approach, that new and better methodologies will be needed to assess issues, and that the scope of environmental, resource, and energy dilemmas is unprecedented in our history (Albrecht, 1983:559).

• Summary

Essentially most environmental, energy, and natural resource problems grow paradoxically out of America's advanced industrialization. In our rush to improve production and to have the highest material standard of living possible, we have run the risk of polluting our air, water, soil, depleting our scarce natural resources, and running out of cheap, clean, renewable sources.

Environmental and energy physical problems are reflections of deeper social issues. For example, should individual and private corporate interests dominate collective well-being? Is unmitigated capitalistic economic development appropriate at the cost of poor health and lowered life quality? How much pollution are we willing to accept as a society to have high industrial productivity? Can we continue to wantonly deplete scarce natural resources or should we not conserve them more? Will our energy overconsumption make us politically vulnerable to hostile foreign countries? Finally, how long can we continue with the present environmental and energy status quo before we are forced to reorder our national priorities?

Industrial development has meant pollution of America's air, water, soil, and forests. Today there is more smog, thermal inversions, acid rain, and warming (the Greenhouse Effect) than in the past. Agriculture and industry are also depleting and contaminating fresh water supplies, especially by dumping sewage and industrial wastes into rivers and lakes. Soil and forests are getting too much sulfur dioxide and nitrogen oxides. Most metals needed for industry will be used up in forty to fifty years.

As for energy, fossil fuels (especially oil) are being rapidly depleted and are nonrenewable. Cars in the United States are especially wasteful of gasoline. Nuclear energy is probably not really an alternative energy source, since it produces radioactive wastes, is only a minor supplier of energy, and is not a growing industry. Electricity is clean, but its generation often is not. Electricity is also expensive and is difficult to transport and store. Solar energy supplies only about 5 percent of America's energy and by itself would never support current industrial productivity or expansion.

From the sociological exchange perspective industrial corporate actors are exchanging pollution, wasted energy, and resource depletion for profit. Of course, most private citizens do not share directly in industrial profits, only in the social costs (i.e., in a contaminated environment and passed on production costs). Pollution and energy waste continue because they are economically profitable; because the effects of pollution, wasted energy and resource depletion are unclear; because governmental controls are modest or are not enforced; and because costs can be deferred to future generations.

Structural-functionalists emphasize that systemic considerations are usually ignored and that it is not clear what the net functions of environmental pollution, dirty and wasted energy, and resource depletion really are. One major consequence of protecting the environment could be a badly crippled economy. Conflict theorists tell us that profit is the essential concern of corporations. Big business is not particularly concerned about collective welfare (except for that of their stockholders), nor is it made to be by federal government regulations. Finally, symbolic interactionists remind us that pollution, energy waste, and resource depletion usually are not defined as social problems (or at least not as major as the problems of economic development). Thus, nothing much is done to correct pollution, waste, and depletion.

Resolutions to environmental pollution, energy waste, and national resource depletion include reducing industrial output; more federal control of industry in general (e.g., stronger export regulations and fines for industry); conservation and rationing of energy and resource; recycling and detoxification of wastes; developing new energy alternatives (like solar energy, hydro and wind power, and energy from garbage). In a sense the key resolution to environmental and energy problems is conceiving of these discrete largely physical issues as *social* problems. We all live in a finite and fragile biosphere whose well-being, even existence, turns on our collective cooperation and on recognizing and appreciating our mutual social dependencies. In the final chapter of this text we turn to social conditions that can be both problematic in themselves and desperate attempts to resolve social problems—to crime and violence.

• Notes

1. See the related discussion of the various values and interests of natural individuals, corporate actors, and social actors in Chapter 10.

2. The symbol pH is used to indicate relative acidity or alkalinity. In aqueous solutions a pH above seven represents alkalinity; below seven represents acidity.

3. However, the National Wildlife Federation (1983:76) claims that as many as 20 percent of America's drinking water systems were at least somewhat contaminated in 1978 (cf. National Wildlife Federation, 1986).

4. Cf. Snell, 1985:319, "American Ground Transport" in which it is shown how GM systematically retarded electrical mass transit systems in the United States. Cf. Brown et al., 1979: Ch. 6.

5. Remember our Chapter 2 definition of social problems speaks of social conditions or patterns that *are perceived to be threats to society* by significant numbers of the population.

6. When the EPA took photographs of the DOW chemical plant to prove pollution and force a cleanup, DOW took the EPA to federal court. The court ruled against the EPA sanction (*The Wall Street Journal,* April 21, 1982).

• Glossary

Acid Rain. Precipitation containing a high concentration of sulfuric and nitric acid (usually a pH of 4 to 4.5).

British Thermal Unit (BTU). The amount of energy required to raise the temperature of one pound of water one degree Fahrenheit.

Carbon Dioxide. A gas, CO_2, comprising about 3 percent of the earth's atmosphere, which is an end product of burning organic matter or carbon containing substances.

Chlorofluorocarbons (CFCs). Synthetic chemicals used in refrigerators, air conditioners, computers, styrofoam containers, insulation, solvents, and so on that both deplete the earth's ozone layer and contribute to the Greenhouse Effect.

Ecosystem. Communities of living things interacting with each other and the nonliving elements around them.

Energy. The capacity for doing work and overcoming resistence, including the physical sources (resources) of that capacity (e.g., oil, coal, natural gas, sun, uranium, wind, and so on).

Environment. The physical and biological aspects of a specific geographical area organized into dynamic systems.

Eutrophication. Overfertilization of a body of water whereby the growth of algae is promoted and the water's oxygen supply is deleted.

Exajoule. Energy equivalent to 163 million barrels of oil or a quadrillion BTUs.

Geothermal Energy. Energy generated by hot springs, geysers, molten rock, and so on.

Greenhouse Effect. The concentration of carbon dioxide in the atmosphere that allows sunlight to enter but inhibits the release of heat, potentially resulting in a gradual warming of the earth's climate.

Methane Digester. A piece of equipment that produces methane gas (CH_4) energy from human and animal excrement, straw, grass, and water.

Nitrogen Oxides. Gas air pollutants formed by the combination of nitrogen and oxygen, most commonly as the by-products of petroleum combustion in motor vehicles.

Ozone. A molecule of oxygen containing three oxygen atoms, which forms a shield (i.e., a layer of the earth's upper stratosphere) that protects the earth from much of the sun's ultraviolet radiation.

pH Level. A scale used to designate the degree of acidity or alkalinity, which ranges from one to fourteen; a neutral solution has a pH of seven; low pHs are acidic while pHs above seven are alkaline.

Photovoltaic. A cell that converts the sun's energy into electricity.

Pollution. The presence of any substances that interfere with socially desired or physically necessary uses of air, water, land, or food.

Pollution Standard Index (PSI). An index that measures five common air pollutants (sulfur dioxide, nitrogen dioxide, ozone, carbon monoxide, and suspended particulants); a PSI reading over 100 indicates unhealthful air; over 200, the air is said to be hazardous.

Sulfur Dioxide. A gas, SO_2, produced by burning coal, smelting, and other industrial processes that is toxic to plants and when combined with hydrogen forms sulfuric acid (H_2SO_4) and falls as acid rain.

Synfuels. Artificially synthesized fuels made from such products as weeds, garbage, and sawdust.

• Further Reading

Allen, John, ed. *Environment, 85/86.* Sluice Dock, CT: The Duskin Publishing Group, 1985. A collection of thirty-five previously published (but recent) scientific and journalistic articles divided into five sections: population and hunger, energy, pollution, resources, and biosphere. An excellent overview of all topics considered in our Chapter 14; namely, acid rain (Ch. 28), the Greenhouse Effect (Ch. 29), deforestation (Ch. 32), nuclear power (Ch. 11), solar energy (Ch. 8), toxic waste (Ch. 14), pesticides (Ch. 17), water pollution (Ch. 26), soil erosion (Ch. 23), and much more.

Brown, Michael. *Laying Waste: The Poisoning of America by Toxic Chemicals.* New York: Pantheon Books: 1981. Brown was a young journalist who took a job with the *Niagara* (New York) *Gazette,* only to discover Love Canal and the toxic dump of the Hooker Chemical Company (See *New York Times Magazine,* June 1978). In this book Brown documents the effects of toxic chemicals at Love Canal: dogs without fur, children with birth defects, and inexplicable illness (especially cancers). *Laying Waste* also reviews fish kills in Tennessee, fouled water in Massachusetts, polluted air in New Jersey, Louisiana swamps, kepone and the Allied Chemical Company, garbage, and radwaste.

Brown, Lester R., ed. et al. *The State of the World, 1985.* New York: W. W. Norton, 1985. An annual report of the Worldwatch Institute that monitors changes in the global resource base (land, water, energy, and biological support systems), focusing particularly on how changes there affect the economy. Well-written empirical chapters by Postel on managing freshwater supplies and protecting forests from acid rain, Chandler on increasing energy efficiency, and Flavin and Pollock on renewable energy.

Humphrey, Craig R. and Frederick R. Buttel. *Environment, Energy, and Society.* Belmont, CA: Wadsworth, 1982. Authors present a uniquely sociological look (what they call "environmental sociology") at energy, population, hunger, environment, and alternative energy problems. Nine chapters with a major premise that technological change, population growth, and economic production and consumption have profound effects on the biophysical basis of human societies. Problems are examined from three sociological paradigms (the conservative, liberal, and radical) rooted in the work of Durkheim, Weber, and Marx, respectively.

Schnaiberg, Allan. *The Environment: From Surplus to Scarcity.* New York: Oxford University Press, 1980. A Northwestern University sociologist who believes that environmental issues will intensify in the future, although concern has declined recently. He seeks the explanation of environmental problems in the social roots of expanded production through analysis of social institutions involved in the creation and distribution of social surplus. Specifically Schnaiberg examines population (there are too many people), technology (there has been too rapid change), consumption (there was too much consumer affluence), and production (there has been too much corporate growth).

Stobaugh, Robert and Daniel Yergin (Eds.). *Energy Future: Report of the Energy Project at the Harvard Business School.* New York: Random House, 1982. As the title indicates, this is an edited report of the energy project at the Harvard Business School. It concludes that oil, gas, coal, and nuclear energy cannot deliver the increased supplies needed by the year 2000. The United States thus has two alternatives: to import more oil or to accelerate the development of conservation and solar energy. Stobaugh and Yergin advocate the second alternative.

C·H·A·P·T·E·R

15

Crime and Violence

Often criminal activities, force, and violence are seen as the last (or only) resort in the resolution of social problems. Nations, social groups, and individuals have used illegal behaviors, violent acts, even terrorism and war to try to settle social conflicts. Of course, the prospects of even higher crime and violence rates, more random acts of terrorism, violence, or of a nuclear holocaust are especially grim.

Nevertheless, exchange principles suggest that for the most part crime and violence do pay. Young minority-group males especially have learned that criminal or violent behaviors are often rewarded and that most crimes go unpunished. Crime and violence often are generated out of social histories of frustration and inequity. For corporate actors not only are profits high, but individual controls often are ineffective. From the structural-functional perspective, crime and violence are spawned from blocked opportunities to achieve internalized common cultural goals—that is, inopportunity to achieve secular occupational success—and from having a disproportionate number of young males (the high crime-rate group) in the population.

Conflict theorists see crime and violence more as a trait of who makes the law than as the actual criminal behavior of individuals or groups. Thus, criminal law is a reflection of the interests and ideologies of the ruling class (who tend to be white, male, older, wealthier, and so on). Criminal populations are produced (especially in minority groups) because their behavior, personal qualities, and position threaten the social relations of production in capitalistic societies. Conflict theorists argue that crime, violence, terrorism, and war are all caused in large measure by sharp social and economic inequality. Crime and violence may be reasonable responses to inequity and financial deprivation. That is, they may be acts of social desperation and rage.

Differential association, labeling, and secondary deviance explanations of crime and violence are all roughly in the symbolic interaction perspective tradition. Differential association argues that criminals or terrorists acquire an excess of favorable definitions of crime or violence. Also, many crimes require skill and training. From the labeling perspective, criminals have experienced the restrictive effects of having been stigmatized and branded criminals. Negative public reactions to initial, primary, often transitory criminal deviance or violence can help manufacture secondary deviance in which a criminal or violent career may result from actually seeing oneself as criminal, that is, from developing a criminal or violent identity. The biological perspective is also reviewed, but it probably explains only a small fraction of all crime and violence.

———— ♦ ————

Violence or physical force is one obvious ultimate resolution to all of the social problems we have considered in the previous fourteen chapters. The use of violence often is immoral, but is not always criminal. As we just saw in Panel 15.1, some deviant behavior may not be considered criminal, especially if you or your social group are making the laws. Also, clearly there is some nonviolent crime. Crime and violence are social problems because they threaten lives, property, our sense of well-being, security, peace and social order, and reduce our life quality.

Just how widespread are crime and violence? About half (48 percent) of the American population is afraid to walk alone in their own neighborhoods at night (*San Francisco Chronicle,* March 11, 1982). One violent crime occurs every twenty-five seconds in the United States, a murder every twenty-eight minutes, and a forcible rape every six minutes. Lately we have even become afraid to fly in airplanes, to take vacations outside the country, to ride trains in Europe, to go shopping, or to go out to eat at restaurants in some places for fear of random criminal or murderous acts against us as innocent victims, especially for fear of terrorism (Sterling, 1981; Merari, 1985). Of course, the coup de grace of the fear of violence is the prospect of a nuclear holocaust involving the USA and Russia, a war that could end the world itself through explosion, sun blockage, radiation poisoning, freezing, and starvation (McNamara and Bethe, 1985:170; Sagan et al., 1985). Let us now review some of the issues we need to examine in this final chapter.

Do we fear crime and violence? Americans worry about crime second only to the cost of living and unemployment (Lotz, Poole, and Regoli, 1985:38ff., Currie and Skolnick, 1984:408). For us to be healthy as individuals and as a

PANEL 15.1

Three "Strikes" and William Rummel Faced Life Behind Bars—for Stealing $229

A poor person who commits a murder is far more likely to be convicted than a corporate executive who makes a decision that ends up costing many people their lives. This is well illustrated by the case of the Ford Pinto (see Chapter 10).

While the Ford executives escaped unharmed, it is interesting to compare their fate to that of William J. Rummel. On three separate occasions Rummel was convicted of crimes by Texas courts. His three convictions were for the following: (1) forging a check for $28.36; (2) obtaining $80 by fraudulent use of a credit card; and (3) taking a check for $120.75 in return for a false promise to repair an air conditioner.

Although none of these crimes involved physical injuries to the offended parties (physical injuries and deaths did occur in the Pinto case), these convictions all happened to be felonies, and under Texas law conviction for a third felony carries a mandatory sentence of life imprisonment. The constitutionality of the law was sustained by the Supreme Court. Thus, for crimes involving a total of $229.11, William Rummel faces life behind bars.

Source: George Ritzer, *Social Problems,* Random House, Inc. Copyright 1986, p. 171.

society requires a predictable life course, a sense of reasonable safety from random violence, and the knowledge that social and personal production will be rewarded. Perhaps you know someone whose child or family member was murdered, raped, assaulted, or otherwise traumatized by crime or violence. Obviously, if such violent acts become too widespread (as they have in, say, Beirut, Lebanon, Ulster, Ireland, or in some South American cities), social life itself can be put in jeopardy (Huff-Corzine, 1986).

Is crime increasing? Although we will postpone a definitive answer to this question until the prevalence of crime and violence are examined below, a few general remarks are in order here. The fear is not only that crime and violence are rampant, but rather that they are in fact getting worse. *Newsweek* claimed (March 23, 1981) that there was an epidemic of violent crime in the United States. Certainly Figure 15.1 reveals that all crime rates went up (some more than others) in the 1970s (but then dropped some in the 1980s; cf. Hagan, 1985:106). However, nonviolent property crimes still outnumber violent crimes about nine or ten to one.

Are all crimes equally serious? Obviously, not all crimes concern us equally. Some violence and crime are more threatening to society than others. For example, the National Crime Survey (NCS) (1977) showed that only a few of 204 illegal events are rated as highly serious. On a scale of 0 (not severe

FIGURE 15.1 Selected FBI Index Crimes Reported to Police, 1972–1984

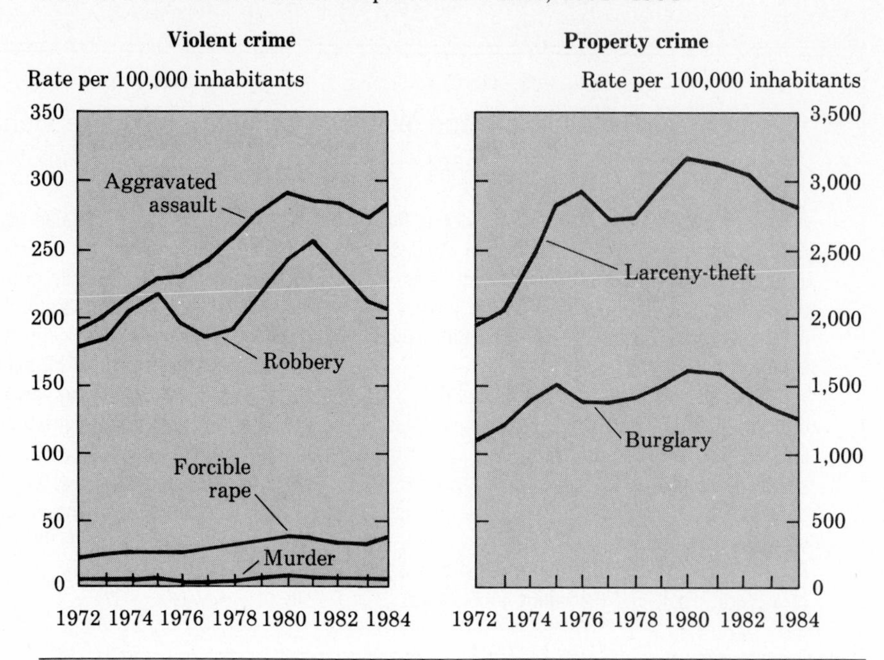

Source: *Statistical Abstract of the United States,* 1986:162. Data from FBI Uniform Crime Reports, 1972–1984.

crime) to 75 (very severe crime), the top-rated crime was terrorism, that is "planting a bomb in a public building that then exploded and killed twenty people" (severity score = 72.1). The next most serious crime was rape in which a woman died (52.8). Third was robbery of a victim, then shooting him/her to death (43.2). Interestingly, most nonviolent sexual crimes were ranked very low (i.e., were not considered serious crimes). To illustrate, female prostitution ranked about the same (2.1) in seriousness as putting large eggs in a container marked "extra large." Homosexuality (for consenting adults) and public drunkenness also ranked very low (1.3 and 0.8, respectively).

Who are crime's victims? Crime victims are disproportionately male, young, black, not married, poor, and/or live in central cities (Miethe, Stafford, and Long, 1987). Since most crimes are not reported to the police (who are the source of *Uniform Crime Report* data; Ritzer, 1986:156), victimization surveys (like NCS) generally report about twice as much crime as the FBI's *Uniform Crime Report (UCR).* For example, a victimization survey report (Zawitz, 1983:19) tells us that 5,903,440 violent crimes were committed in 1983; but Table 15.1 (below, from the *UCR*) says that there were only 1,273,280 violent crimes in 1983. The same two rape reports reveal 154,180 versus 78,920 victims in 1983. Robbery victims were 1,149,170 and 506,570, and so on.

How do race and ethnicity affect crime? Both criminal offenders and crime victims are disproportionately likely to be black or other American minorities. In part this definitely reflects the biases of the law and of the criminal justice system as much as the actual prevalence of criminal or violent behaviors (Meyers, 1987). Blacks comprise about 12 percent of the U.S. population, but 25 percent of all those arrested for crimes (*Statistical Abstract of the United States,* 1987:162) and 40 percent of the prison population. The black incarceration rate is seven times that of whites. Fully 20 percent of all blacks can expect to spend some time in jail or prison during their lives (Blumstein, 1982:1260). Blacks tend to receive more severe sentences than whites, especially for raping white women (La Free, 1980). Of 3,862 prisoners executed from 1930 to 1980, 54 percent were black (*Capital Punishment,* 1980). Three-fifths of all executions took place in the South. Thus, one important issue is, is criminal law used to control minorities—especially black males?

How costly is crime? Obviously much criminal activity is secretive, not taxed, has overpriced products, and so on. Thus, we really do not know what crime costs us. We do know that the federal government spends less than 5 percent of its annual budget on crime (Zawitz, *Report to the Nation on Crime and Justice,* 1983:99). In 1981 the federal government spent $24.7 billion on crime, but $174.6 billion on national defense. Incarceration (in prison) costs about $15,000 per year per inmate (*Time,* September 13, 1982). Green (1982) claims that illegal business operations cost the federal government $200 billion per year, whereas the average individual bank robbery netted just $3,564.

How can we control crime and violence? One widely cited study (Martinson, 1974; cf. Hagan, 1985: Ch. 10) reported that most criminal rehabilitative efforts have simply not worked. Certainly trying to "get tough" with criminals has led mainly to new laws, longer prison terms, and serious prison overcrowding (*New York Times,* December 13, 1983). For example, there were 463,866 inmates in state and federal prisons in 1985 (*Justice Assistance News,* July 3, 1985). Curiously, the solution to criminal violence often provokes a response by the law that is just as violent itself, for example, the practice of capital punishment. Note too that terrorism seems out of control to many, since police and law enforcement agencies are prohibited from using terrorist methods themselves to combat terrorism.

Are terrorism and war the final arbiters of social conflicts? Some scholars claim that war is the final arbiter of all social disputes (McNamara and Bethe, 1986:170; cf. *Atlantic Monthly,* July 1985:32–36). Of course, many Marxist and other terrorist groups are dedicated to the violent overthrow of Western capitalism by force (Clark, 1982:286). Terrorism may be the new form of traditional classical warfare, since traditional war has become too costly and does too much damage (Alexander, 1985:102). Many terrorists are supported and trained by the USSR and (probably by) the USA—who are in perennial

Force and violence are often the ultimate resolution to social problems. In Hiroshima, Japan (and Nagasaki), President Truman killed between 63,000 and 240,000 Japanese, even though World War II was virtually over before the atomic bomb was dropped. (UPI/Bettmann News Photos)

"cold war" social and ideological conflict with each other. Terrorism may even provoke a full-scale classical war (Bell, 1985:45).

As usual, before we can address these issues unambiguously and cogently, we need to be clear about what we mean by crime, violence, and other related concepts. By *crime* we mean all behaviors and actions that violate the law and are subject to formally sanctioned punishment by larger society (Zawitz, *Report to the Nation on Crime and Justice,* 1983:2).[1] Thus, human activities in and of themselves are (of course) not criminal. Crime varies with region, nation, government, culture, and so on. For example, Henslin and Light point out that pork and alcohol are illegal in Muslim countries, but polygamy (one man, many wives) is legal (1983:180). The relativity of crime can lead to the absurd conclusion that if there were no laws, then there would be no crime (see decriminalization below).

Most crimes are divided into violent events (such as homicide, rape, and assault) that may result in injury to a person and property crimes (that do not involve use or threat of force against individuals) (Zawitz, 1983:2).[2] *Juvenile delinquency* is usually regarded as the committing of an act by a minor, which would be a crime if s/he were an adult.[3] One has to be careful here. Perhaps a more accurate definition of juvenile delinquent would be anyone who has violated a juvenile code established by his or her state legislature (Vetter and Silverman, 1986). Some acts that are legal for adults are criminal for juveniles. Finally (for our purposes), in some states children that are habitually truant, disobedient, or incorrigible are labeled persons in need of supervision (PINS)—not delinquents or criminals (Lotz, Poole, Regoli, 1985:240).

Originally, *white-collar crime* was defined by Sutherland (1949) as offenses committed by a person of respectable and high social status in the course of their occupation (cf. Conklin, 1986:167 ff.). White-collar crimes can be either against corporations (e.g., embezzlement, computer fraud, or forgery) or in the name of corporations (e.g., price fixing, bribery, or tax evasion). Also, white-collar crime is sometimes defined as violations of law using a person's position of power, influence, or trust for illegal gain (Reiss and Biderman, 1980).

Organized crime usually is conspiratorial, includes acts of violence, is systemic, methodical, highly disciplined, and secretive (Omerta is the law of secrecy, violation of which results in death); isolates its top leaders from direct involvement; and is intertwined with politics and government (Zawitz, 1983:3). Classical examples of organized crime include the Mafia or Cosa Nostra (our thing), which has about 5,000 members in the United States organized into 24 "families" of 100 to 300 individuals each (*Newsday,* February 27, 1985). Typically organized crime is involved in drugs, gambling, loan sharking, prostitution, unions (e.g., dock workers), garbage removal, and so on. A *professional criminal,* on the other hand, is anyone who makes his/her living from crime. Examples would include jewel thieves, safecrackers, shoplifters, pickpockets, counterfeiters, fences, and so on.

When we speak of *terrorism* we mean the unpredictable random use of murder, violence, assault, fear, subjugation, and intimidation to disrupt the normal operations of society, which in turn are expected to result in social chaos, disorganization, and overthrow of (usually capitalistic) governments (Horowitz, 1982:288; Sterling, 1981; Merari, 1985). Finally, *war* is open, armed conflict between countries or between factions within the same country.

How much crime, violence, terrorism, and war exist in the United States (Conklin, 1986:Ch. 3)? As we said just a few paragraphs ago, generally index crimes (see Figure 15.1) went up in the 1970s. A crime index offense now occurs about once every three seconds.[4] Some specific examples are: that in 1981 almost one-third of all households were victimized by violence or theft;

PANEL 15.2

New York's Mafia Families

The five crime families named in a historic indictment Tuesday began their underworld activities at the turn of the century and gained power in the 1930s. The first "crime commission" meeting of the families came in 1931—the year federal agent Elliot Ness put Al Capone behind bars on income tax evasion charges.

Columbo Family

Gennaro "Gerry Lang" Langella, forty-six, is acting boss of the Colombo family, authorities say. Langella recently was convicted of perjury and is facing ten years in prison. Also named in the indictment was Colombo "soldier" Ralph Scopo.

The Colombo family reputedly controls funeral homes, trucking, catering and real estate firms.

It was founded by Joseph Colombo.

Genovese Family

Anthony "Fat Tony" Salerno, seventy-three, is the reputed head of the Genovese family. The Genovese gang allegedly is powerful in pornography, labor unions, the cargo industry, restaurants, seafood distributors, entertainment, and vending.

It was founded by Vito Genovese.

Gambino Family

Paul "Big Paul" Castellano, sixty-nine, is reputed head of the Gambino family—the largest and most feared mob organization in the nation. Castellano was free on $2 million bail on a racketeering indictment when he was arrested.

The Gambino family allegedly has infiltrated restaurants, food distributors, entertainment, jewelry, the garment industry, trucking, construction and waste industries. Carlo Gambino founded the family.

Bonanno Family

Phillip "Rusty" Rastelli, sixty-seven, the reputed head of the Bonanno organization, was already in jail on parole violations.

The Bonnano family allegedly controls pizza parlors, pizza supplies, expresso cafes and restaurants.

It was founded by Joseph Bonanno.

Lucchese Family

Anthony "Tony Ducks" Corallo, seventy-two, is said to be head of the Lucchese organization. Corallo already was under indictment for an alleged conspiracy to control the Long Island garbage collection industry.

The Lucchese mob reputedly controls construction and paper waste removal firms.

It was founded by Thomas Lucchese.

Source: Gerald McKelvey, *Newsday,* February 27, 1985.

that 6 percent of all households experienced at least one violent crime of rape, robbery, or assault in 1981; that there were forty-one million crime victims in 1981; and that businesses were robbed at a rate ten times higher than that of private individuals (Zawitz, 1983:7).

However, after 1980 most crime rates declined (see Figure 15.1 and Table

15.1). Although the crime index total rose 5.2 percent from 1975 to 1984, it declined 15.4 percent from 1980 to 1984. For example, between 1980 and 1984 violent crime (per 100,000) dropped from 596.6 to 539.2; murder went from 10.2 to 7.9; forcible rape from 36.8 to 35.7; robbery from 251.1 to 205.4; and aggravated assault from 298.5 to 290.2. (Cf. *Justice Assistance News,* 6–3, July 3, 1985; Kornblum and Boggs, 1984:24; United Press International, April 20, 1984; Associated Press, October 7, 1985). There was also a slight upturn in most crimes in 1985 (*Statistical Abstract of the United States,* 1987: 154).

We need to realize that in spite of recent crime-rate declines crime rates are still very high in the United States. For example, the robbery rate in New York City is 150 times the robbery rate in Tokyo (Walker, 1985:3). Remember too that violent crime is most likely to occur in the heart of major American cities. In 1983 the most violent cities in the United States were (in the order of those with the highest violent crime rates first): Detroit, Michigan (2,169 violent crimes per 100,000 population); Baltimore, Maryland (2,003); Washington, D.C. (1,915); New York City, New York (1,868); and Los Angeles, California (1,692). Finally, note that between 80 percent to 90 percent of children under eighteen years old commit some offense for which they could be arrested, but only about 3 percent are ever in fact arrested (Howell, 1985:147).

What about the prevalence of terrorism? Recently individuals, events, and groups like the IRA (Irish Republican Army), the Red Brigade, the PLO, the Hezbellah (a Shiite Muslim group), Beirut, Libya's Khadafy, the slaughter of the Jewish olympians in Munich, the bombing of an Air India plane in midflight, Carlos the Jackal, and so on have become frighteningly common. There were roughly 140 terrorist attacks between 1972 and 1982, almost all outside the United States (*New York Times,* December 29, 1983; *U.S. News & World Report,* November 7, 1983). The fear is that terrorism will spread to major American cities, as it has to London, Paris, Rome, and so on (Hirsch, 1986).

Finally, how commonplace is full-fledged war? Since 1775 the United States has been involved in nine major wars. These include the Revolutionary War, the War of 1812, the Mexican War, the Civil War, the Spanish-American War, World Wars I and II, the Korean War, and the Vietnam War (Graham and Gurr, 1969). The last major war (Vietnam) ended January 27, 1973, (although the aftermath of Vietnam continues even today). It cost Americans $330 billion, untold trauma to the living, and accomplished little or nothing. In World War II alone 14 million soldiers (322,000 Americans) and uncounted millions of civilians died—particularly European Jews—only to raise the grim prospect of the death of all humankind in a nuclear war that no one could win (Current and Goodwin, 1980:728).

Of course, crime and violence have always been with us, even if not on the scale of a nuclear catastrophe. For the most part most of us deplore crime, violence, terrorism, and war. Usually violence settles nothing and costs dearly. Yet the ultimate recourse in social conflicts is physical force or the threat of

TABLE 15.1 Index of Crime, United States, 1975–1984

Population[1]	Crime Index Total[2]	Modified Crime Index Total[3]	Violent Crime[4]	Property Crime[4]	Murder and Nonnegligent Manslaughter
Number of offenses:[5]					
1975–213,124,000	11,292,400		1,039,710	10,252,700	20,510
1976–214,659,000	11,349,700		1,004,210	10,345,500	18,780
1977–216,132,000	10,984,500		1,029,580	9,955,000	19,120
1978–218,059,000	11,209,000		1,085,550	10,123,400	19,560
1979–220,099,000	12,249,500		1,208,030	11,041,500	21,460
1980–225,349,264	13,408,300		1,344,520	12,063,700	23,040
1981–229,146,000	13,423,800		1,361,820	12,061,900	22,520
1982–231,534,000	12,974,400		1,322,390	11,652,000	21,010
1983–233,931,000	12,108,600		1,258,090	10,850,500	19,310
1984–236,158,000	11,881,800		1,273,280	10,608,500	18,690
Percent change, number of offenses:					
1984/1983	−1.9		+1.2	−2.2	−3.2
1984/1980	−11.4		−5.3	−12.1	−18.9
1984/1975	+5.2		+22.5	+3.5	−8.9
Rate per 100,000 inhabitants:					
1975	5,298.5		487.8	4,810.7	9.6
1976	5,287.3		467.8	4,819.5	8.8
1977	5,077.6		475.9	4,601.7	8.8
1978	5,140.3		497.8	4,642.5	9.0
1979	5,565.5		548.9	5,016.6	9.7
1980	5,950.0		596.6	5,353.3	10.2
1981	5,858.2		594.3	5,263.9	9.8
1982	5,603.6		571.1	5,032.5	9.1
1983	5,175.0		537.7	4,637.4	8.3
1984	5,031.3		539.2	4,492.1	7.9
Percent change, rate per 100,000 inhabitants:					
1984/1983	−2.8		+.3	−3.1	−4.8
1984/1980	−15.4		−9.6	−16.1	−22.5
1984/1975	−5.0		+10.5	−6.6	−17.7

[1]Populations are Bureau of the Census provisional estimates as of July 1, except April 1, 1980, preliminary census counts, and are subject to change.
[2]Because of rounding, the offenses may not add to totals.
[3]Although arson data are included in the trend and clearance tables, sufficient data are not available to estimate totals for this offense.
[4]Violent crimes are offenses of murder, forcible rape, robbery, and aggravated assault. Property crimes are offenses of burglary, larceny-theft, and motor vehicle theft. Data are not included for the property crime of arson.
[5]Annual totals for years prior to 1984 have been adjusted and may not be consistent with those in prior editions.
All rates were calculated on the offenses before rounding.

Source: FBI, *Uniform Crime Reports,* July 28, 1985:41.

Forcible Rape	Robbery	Aggravated Assault	Burglary	Larceny-Theft	Motor Vehicle Theft	Arson[3]
56,030	470,500	492,620	3,265,300	5,977,700	1,000,000	
57,080	477,810	500,530	3,108,700	6,270,300	966,000	
63,500	412,610	534,350	3,071,500	5,905,700	977,700	
67,610	476,930	571,460	3,128,300	5,991,000	1,004,100	
76,390	480,700	629,480	3,327,700	6,601,000	1,112,800	
82,990	565,840	672,650	3,795,200	7,136,900	1,131,700	
82,500	592,910	663,900	3,779,700	7,194,400	1,087,800	
78,770	553,130	669,480	3,447,100	7,142,500	1,062,400	
78,920	506,570	653,290	3,129,900	6,712,800	1,007,900	
84,230	485,010	685,350	2,954,400	6,591,900	1,032,200	
+6.7	−4.3	+4.9	−4.6	−1.8	+2.4	
+1.5	−14.3	+1.9	−21.4	−7.6	−8.8	
+50.2	+3.1	+39.1	−8.6	+10.3	+2.2	
26.3	220.8	231.1	1,532.1	2,804.5	473.7	
26.6	199.3	233.2	1,448.2	2,921.3	450.0	
29.4	190.7	247.0	1,419.8	2,729.8	451.9	
31.0	195.8	262.1	1,434.6	2,747.4	460.5	
34.7	218.4	286.0	1,511.9	2,999.1	505.6	
36.8	251.1	298.5	1,684.1	3,167.0	502.7	
36.0	258.7	289.7	1,649.5	3,139.7	474.7	
34.0	238.9	289.2	1,488.8	3,034.5	453.8	
33.7	216.5	279.2	1,337.7	2,863.9	430.8	
35.7	205.4	290.2	1,263.7	2,791.3	437.1	
+5.9	−5.1	+3.9	−5.5	−2.7	+1.5	
−3.0	−18.2	−2.8	−25.0	−11.9	−13.0	
+35.7	−7.0	+25.6	−17.5	−.5	−7.7	

physical force (e.g., of nuclear war). Physical force is often the underpinning of power (see Chapter 10) both for individuals and nations. The USA has in fact been and continues to be a highly violent nation (cf. Archer and Gartner, 1984). Our country was born from the Revolutionary War and grew up on rugged entrepreneurial individual heros, Western cowboys in gunfights, gangsters in New York City and Chicago, robber barons and industrial aggressors in corporations from Henry Ford to Lee Iacocca and John De Lorean. Violence in the name of social order (e.g., by the police or by characters like Charles Bronson in the movie *Death Wish* or Clint Eastwood in *Dirty Harry*) or for industrial profit is largely considered legitimate in America.

As Rose indicated years ago (in *Violence in America,* 1969:87), vigilante action from the South's Ku Klux Klan to New York City's Guardian Angels has also been tolerated in the United States. Americans' professed right to have armed private citizens is an astounding case in point. Think of the National Rifle Association's bumper stickers for pickup trucks: "When Guns Are Outlawed, Only Outlaws Will Have Guns" or "Insured by Smith & Wesson." As a country we tend to become upset only when violence is directed against innocent targets (as with terrorism) or by unauthorized agents (e.g., inner-city black male private citizens). Historically, the United States has been a very violent punitive society. For example, it was not until 1776 that prison replaced hanging as punishment for criminals. In Puritan New England the punishment for children's chronic disobedience of their parents was death (as we saw in Chapter 12). Perhaps most ominous is the delusion of many Americans that we could not possibly lose a Third World War. In the following sections we take a closer look at specific aspects of the social problems of crime and violence—especially as reflected in terrorism and war.

• Stating the Problem

Crime In this section we will examine more carefully the major categories of crime, with special attention being given to the serious crimes of homicide and rape. We will also elaborate the concept of corporate crime, and then conclude with a review of the criminal justice system.

Categories of Crime and Delinquency. Up to this point we have discussed only "serious" crimes, as represented by the eight FBI index crimes reported in the *Uniform Crime Reports* (see Table 15.1).[5] However, we have not yet defined these eight index crimes (see Zawitz, *Report to the Nation on Crime and Justice,* 1983:2–3). The index crimes are defined as follows:

Murder and nonnegligent manslaughter (homicide) is causing the death of another person without legal justification or excuse.

Rape is unlawful sexual intercourse with a female by force or without legal or federal consent.

Robbery is unlawful taking or attempted taking of property that is in the immediate possession of another, by force, or threat of force.

Assault is unlawful intentional inflicting, or attempted inflicting, of injury on the person of another. *Aggravated assault* involves inflicting bodily injury or death by means of a deadly or dangerous weapon.

Burglary is unlawful entry or breaking into any fixed structure, vehicle, or vessel . . . with or without force, with the intent to commit a felony or larceny.

Larceny (theft) is the unlawful taking or attempted taking of property (other than a motor vehicle) from the possession of another without force or deceit.

Motor vehicle theft is unlawful taking or attempted taking of a self-propelled road vehicle owned by another.

Arson is intentional damaging or destruction or attempted damaging or destruction by means of fire or explosion of the property of another without consent of the owners (cf. Ritzer, 1986:148ff.)

The first four index crimes (homicide, rape, robbery, and assault) are violent crimes, that is, crimes that may result in harm to the person. The last four index crimes (burglary, larceny, motor vehicle theft, and arson) are property crimes, that is, unlawful gaining or attempting to gain property without the use or threat of force against the individual. Property crimes outnumber violent crimes about nine or ten to one.

The criminal justice system (which varies from state to state) also distinguishes between felonies and misdemeanors (cf. Figure 15.3). *Felonies* are the most serious crimes that are punishable by a year or more in prison (e.g., homicide, forcible rape, robbery, and aggravated assault; see Ritzer, 1986:148). *Misdemeanors* are less serious crimes, usually punishable by less than one year in prison or fines (e.g., drunkenness, disturbing the peace, shoplifting, and most white-collar crime).

In addition to serious crimes there are also nonindex crimes (usually misdemeanor offenses in most states, Zawitz, 1983:2–3). These nonindex crimes include drug abuse violations, sex offenses, prostitution, fraud, drunkenness, disturbing the peace, DUI, liquor law offenses, gambling, and status offenses (i.e., acts that are illegal only if committed by a juvenile such as truancy, using alcohol before legal age, and running away from home—cf. Howell, 1985:147).

As we have seen, crudely delinquency is any act by a minor that would be a crime if the offender were an adult. Juveniles commit a disproportionate amount of crime (Cohen and Land, 1987). For example, young people ages 10 to 18 comprise 14 percent of the population (in 1982), but commit 30 percent of the robberies and 45 percent of the burglaries (Howell, 1985:147). Or consider that fifteen to seventeen-year-old males constitute only 2 percent to 3 percent of the population, but commit 13 percent of the crimes against persons and 20 percent of property crimes (*Uniform Crime Reports,* 1981; Wolfgang, 1981). Boys are arrested most often for burglary and girls most often for larceny (Howell, 1985:153). Part (and only part) of the reason for the excess of juvenile crime is that it is easier to get into trouble when you are under age eighteen, since there are more categories of criminal acts.

The most common serious (i.e., index) crime is larceny/theft. The least common serious crimes are murder and arson. The most common nonserious

"Listen, Mac, if I had the skills, I'd prefer taking this money from you in a more socially acceptable and profitable way, like plumbing or auto repair."

crimes (which are usually misdemeanors) are DUI, and drunkenness. The least common nonserious crime is embezzlement. White-collar crimes are not reported as often as street or blue-collar crimes; that is, there are not as many categories for white-collar crime. Burglary and violent crime are high on the general population's fear of crime list. Nine million American households were touched by one of these crimes in 1981 (Zawitz, 1983:7). Some of the most serious crimes, such as the serious crimes of homicide/murder and rape, deserve to be examined in greater detail.

The Problems of Homicide and Rape. Homicide and rape (as we saw above) are generally perceived as the most serious of all crimes (especially when rape is followed by murder). Even though the numbers of murders and rapes are relatively small, the public is greatly offended by them and, as a result, their arrest rates are among the very highest (about 75 percent and 50 percent, respectively). Murders are almost always reported to the police; however, a majority of rapes are not (Currie and Skolnick, 1984:410; Conklin, 1986:Ch. 4).

Homicide rates in the United States tend to drop during international wars and rise during economic depressions (*Homicide Surveillance,* 1986). For example, the U.S. homicide rate rose from about 1903 to 1933, dropped from 1934 to 1958, rose again from 1959 to 1980 (at which time the homicide rate was the highest it had been in this century), and then dropped again from 1980 to 1985 (down about 20 percent; cf. *Statistical Abstract of the United States,* 1987:155). In spite of the recent drop in homicide rates, the United States still has some of the highest homicide rates in the world (Archer and Gartner, 1984; Conklin, 1986:92). America's homicide rate is so high that American women are more likely to be murdered than European men (Currie and Skolnick, 1984:435).

Both homicide victims and offenders tend to be young (twenty to thirty years old), black, from lower social classes, and male. The homicide victim rates (1983) for race and sex are (per 100,000): black males, 51.4; black females, 11.3; white males, 8.6; and white females, 2.8 (*Statistical Abstract of the United States,* 1987:158).

Homicide is the leading cause of death for black men, ages twenty-five to forty-four (*Health, United States,* 1982:25 Currie and Skolnick, 1984:419). Blacks comprise about 12 percent of the population, but 49 percent of the homicide offenders (Blumstein, 1982:1274). Forty-four percent of murder victims were also black (Currie and Skolnick, 1984:419). Most murderers (at least 55 percent) kill their own acquaintances, friends, or relatives, not strangers (Zawitz, 1983:2; O'Brian, 1987). The most common motive for murder is an argument with someone you know (44 percent). Eighteen percent of all murders involved a felony crime (*Statistical Abstract of the United States,* 1985:171). Murders tend to be (about two-thirds) crimes of passion, with little or no premeditation (Currie and Skolnick, 1984:426; cf. Conklin, 1986:210–211, 277–278). Alcohol is often involved (at least two-thirds of the time). Thus, murder is seldom a rational planned activity.

Rape has been around for a long time as personal trouble. What is new is seeing rape as a product of the traditional social expectations for male dominance. Rape and the threat of rape are now seen (especially by feminists) more as a violent means of social control of women by men (Brownmiller, 1975). Thought of this way rape is not primarily an act of sexual passion, but rather a ritual of (male) power.[6]

Of course, not all rapists are alike (Athens, 1980). Most rapists are inadequate isolated men who dislike women, want to display their power over them, and are generally violent men. These traits help account for the physically curious situation of young men raping helpless old women. Rape serves many nonsexual needs (Groth, 1979).

As with homicide offenders, a disproportionately large number of rapists (58 percent) are either black or Hispanic (Currie and Skolnick, 1984:437). Black women are about twice as likely to be raped as white women. Most rapes involve one offender and one victim and tend to occur in the victim's home at night (between 6 P.M. and 6 A.M.; Zawitz, 1983:2).

Rapes tend not to be reported for the obvious reasons of embarrassment, fear of reprisal, and so on. Somewhat less obvious is that the criminal justice system may traumatize the rape victim as much as the rape itself. Clearly, males tend to be in a majority in police forces and in the legal system. Thus, the rape often continues symbolically by the criminal justice system. Finally, the adversary legal system can expose the female victim to excessive public humiliation and stigmatization through the process of cross-examination (Brownmiller, 1975; cf. Hyde, 1982:427 ff.).

Corporate Crime. Earlier we defined white-collar crime as violation of laws by a (usually corporate) person in a position of power, influence, or trust for illegal gain. We also observed that in recent years corporate crime cost consumers roughly $200 billion a year (Simon, 1981; Wheeler and Rothman, 1982). Since corporate crime is not violent or bloody and is committed normally by respected people in powerful positions, we often do not even think of it as crime, or punish it very harshly. The FBI, police, and the courts tend not even to recognize corporate crime as crime at all. Apparently in the corporate world, "business is business."

Yet when Clinard and Yeager (1980) studied the 582 largest U.S. corporations, they discovered that 60 percent of them had had at least one criminal violation brought against them (the mean was 4.2 acts per corporation). The worst corporate violators were the largest corporations, especially oil and pharmaceutical companies and motor vehicle manufacturers. Also, we should note that more than 100 price-fixing conspiracies were under investigation in 1979 (Green, 1982).

Corporate crime nets very large profits. For example, the mean "take" for individual offenses (circa 1980) was $5,279, but the average corporate take was a whopping $117,392 (Wheeler and Rothman, 1982:1417). It is not so far-fetched to think of corporate-induced work deaths (e.g., asbestos cancers, brown-lung deaths, or radioactive poisonings of corporate workers) as murder (Schwartz, 1985). Still, corporate executives are rarely prosecuted for criminal activities and even if they are prosecuted and convicted, at most corporate criminals suffer modest fines that are far less than their criminal profits and that are typically paid for by their corporations. Corporate criminals almost never go to jail or prison. Thus, a cogent case could be made that corporate and white-collar crime are grossly neglected areas of criminality.

The Criminal Justice System. As Panel 15.3 indicates there is a great disparity between the myths and facts about criminal justice, the police, the courts, and prisons. The notion that criminals are usually caught and appropriately and swiftly punished is largely a myth. In 80 percent of serious crimes there is not even an arrest, let alone a conviction. The police respond to only a small fraction of crimes committed (e.g., they spend just 15 percent of their time on crime itself—Zawitz, 1983:47). The criminal justice system is also notoriously slow (Glaser, 1978:87). Eighty percent of serious crimes result in guilty pleas and about 75 percent of these lead to convictions, but those convicted spend relatively little time in prison (on the average about twenty-six months). Then it's back to the streets, usually to commit more crime.

In those few cases where there is an arrest the sequence of criminal justice events is roughly as follows (see Figure 15.2; Panel 15.2; Zawitz, 1983). A hearing is held before a judge or magistrate to decide if the defendant will be released or held in jail. If the defendant is released, bail may be required. Since poor people are less likely to be able to post bail, they are more likely than those with money to spend time in jail (Lizotte, 1978:54). Ninety percent of those released before trial show up for their trial (but 10 percent of those released commit new crimes in the interim). Police gather evidence for the district attorney, who decides whether to prosecute the defendant. If there is no probable cause, the judge can dismiss the charges.

If charges remain, a grand jury (six to twenty-three citizens who do not hear the defendant) hears the charges and then decides if the evidence is sufficient to merit a trial. If it is, the grand jury will return an indictment (a true bill). The defendant may waive grand jury indictment and instead accept a service of information for the crime. Note (Figure 15.2) that crimes must be sorted into felonies, misdemeanors, petty offenses, or juvenile offenses, since these different categories of crimes are processed somewhat differently.

At arraignment the accused is told the charges, advised of his/her rights, and asked to enter a plea (three-fourths of defendants cannot afford their own lawyers and have court-appointed lawyers). Generally (80 percent) the plea is guilty.[7] Often if the defendant loses the preliminary hearing, s/he will plead guilty hoping for a reduced sentence (plea bargaining). If the crime is serious, a trial by twelve jurors is guaranteed to the defendant.

The trial involves an adversary system with two opposing counsels (plaintiff and defendant sides), a judge, and witnesses. The prosecution (i.e., the plaintiff) calls witnesses; they are cross-examined by the defendant counsel (who may bring their own witnesses too). The two counsels make final arguments and summations; then the judge instructs the jury. The jury retires and reaches a verdict. The verdict must be unanimous; otherwise the jury is hung and a mistrial is declared. Usually the judge (in some states the jury) sets the sentence. The possible sentence choices are the death penalty, incarceration in jail or prison, probation, fines, restitution, or some combination of the above. Parole, of course, is the conditional release of the prisoner before his/her sentence is completed.

Sentences usually are appealed (death penalty sentences are always appealed) on the ground of violations of due process of the law, and so on. Appellate (appeal) court calls no witnesses and has no juries. Only a few guilty verdicts are reversed.

Juvenile offenders may be diverted to other agencies or programs (such as alcohol or drug counseling, driver education, psychotherapy, and so on). Juvenile courts do not usually have juries and may remove minor children from their homes. Juveniles are often punished differently than adults. Technically juveniles are never punished, only treated. For example, about half of the juveniles are sent to open facilities (Howell, 1985:151).

PANEL 15.3

American Justice: ABCs of How It Really Works

In the wake of a serious crime, justice is swift. Police sift the clues and track down the culprit; the prosecutor throws the book at him; judge and jury do their duty, and the criminal slinks off to prison—a social menace no more.

Then the credits roll and the television show is over. Americans turn their attention back to the real world, where things are different.

The real world, where—

In four out of five cases of serious crimes, there is not even an arrest, let alone a conviction.

Of the cases in which arrests do occur, some are dropped, and just about half end in guilty pleas or convictions.

One lawbreaker might draw a stiff penalty, another a light penalty for the same offense.

Most convicts serve only a fraction of their prison terms before being put back on the street, and many of them return to crime.

The rate of violent crime has more than quadrupled during the last two decades—creating unprecedented strains. Police and prosecutors are overworked. Courts are staggering under heavy backlogs. Prisons are bursting with surplus inmates. The result: Bitter controversy engulfs almost every method by which our society struggles to cope with lawlessness. Americans are angry. Many of them believe that the institutions of law and order somehow have come unglued, exposing them and their families to a growing risk of death, injury, or property loss at the hands of thugs.

Civil proceedings are arousing fears as well. An explosion of lawsuits has made people feel more and more vulnerable to a wrathful passer-by, customer, neighbor, employee, business partner—perhaps even one's own child. The crush of litigation also has quickened concern about the fees and ethics of lawyers, whose ranks have swollen fast.

Yet how the justice system works—how it *really* works—remains a mystery to many. People's "knowledge" often boils down to a stream of half-truths and misimpressions gained from Hollywood, TV, and newspapers. This prompted *U.S. News & World Report* to prepare this . . . to help readers understand procedures that are designed not only to punish the guilty but also to protect the innocent.

A Quiz of Your Legal IQ

Here is a simple quiz to measure how much you know about the U.S. system of justice (the answers appear below).

1. How much time does the average police officer spend dealing with crime?
   A. 75 percent. B. 15 percent. C. 40 to 50 percent.

Police. The police are an important part of the criminal justice system, since they help determine (through arrest and investigation) who will enter the system at all. The police also provide us with many crime statistics and data; for example, by reporting crimes to the FBI for its *Uniform Crime Reports* (see footnote 5 for a brief discussion of what the *Uniform Crime Reports* are). The police play numerous roles in criminal justice such as law enforcement, maintenance of order, information gathering, and service activities. Since police

PANEL 15.3—*concluded*

2. The average salary of a police officer after five years on the force is:
A. $13,000. B. $22,000. C. $18,000.

3. The job of a grand jury is to:
A. Weigh the defendant's guilt or innocence. B. Determine whether inmates get parole. C. Decide whether a case goes to trial.

4. How many persons slated for trial on serious criminal charges plead guilty?
A. 60 percent. B. 10 percent. C. 80 percent.

5. The average time served in prison by a person convicted of a felony—a serious crime—is:
A. Twenty-six months. B. Six months. C. Between five and six years.

6. How many appeals are filed with the Supreme Court each year?
A. 750. B. 5,300. C. 1,500.

7. How may federal judges be removed from office?
A. Impeachment and conviction by Congress. B. Supreme Court order. C. Dismissal by the president, with Senate consent.

8. Which constitutional amendment protects citizens against unreasonable searches?
A. Fourth Amendment. B. First Amendment. C. Fourteenth Amendment.

9. Junior attorneys in law firms are paid an average salary of:
A. $15,900. B. $35,200. C. $26,600.

10. How many civil suits are brought annually in the United States?
A. About 1 million. B. Almost 37 million. C. More than 12 million.

11. Which side wins most often when a civil suit is tried?
A. The plaintiff—the person suing—wins 80 percent of the time. B. The defendant is victorious in 68 percent of cases. C. Each side wins about half the time.

12. The standard used by juries to decide a civil case is:
A. The preponderance of the evidence.
B. Guilt beyond a reasonable doubt.
C. The reasonable-man standard.

13. In most small-claims courts:
A. Lawyers are required to reduce their fees. B. Disputes under $700 are tried. C. Written evidence is excluded at all times.

Answers:
1.B; 2.C; 3.C; 4.C; 5.A; 6.B; 7.A;
8.A; 9.B; 10.C; 11.C; 12.A; 13.B.

Source: Copyright, 1982, *U.S. News & World Report.* Reprinted from issue of November 1, 1982.

departments operate twenty-four-hours a day, they often get calls for anything and everything (Hagan, 1985:236). Surprisingly, only about 10 percent of police calls are for law enforcement and only about 15 percent of their total time is spent on crime (Zawitz, 1983:47).

Most of the time the police are directing traffic, settling domestic quarrels, arbitrating landlord-tenant debates, escorting bag ladies to some agency, rescuing would-be suicides, helping deliver babies, managing various "crazies,"

FIGURE 15.2 Sequence of Events in the Criminal Justice System

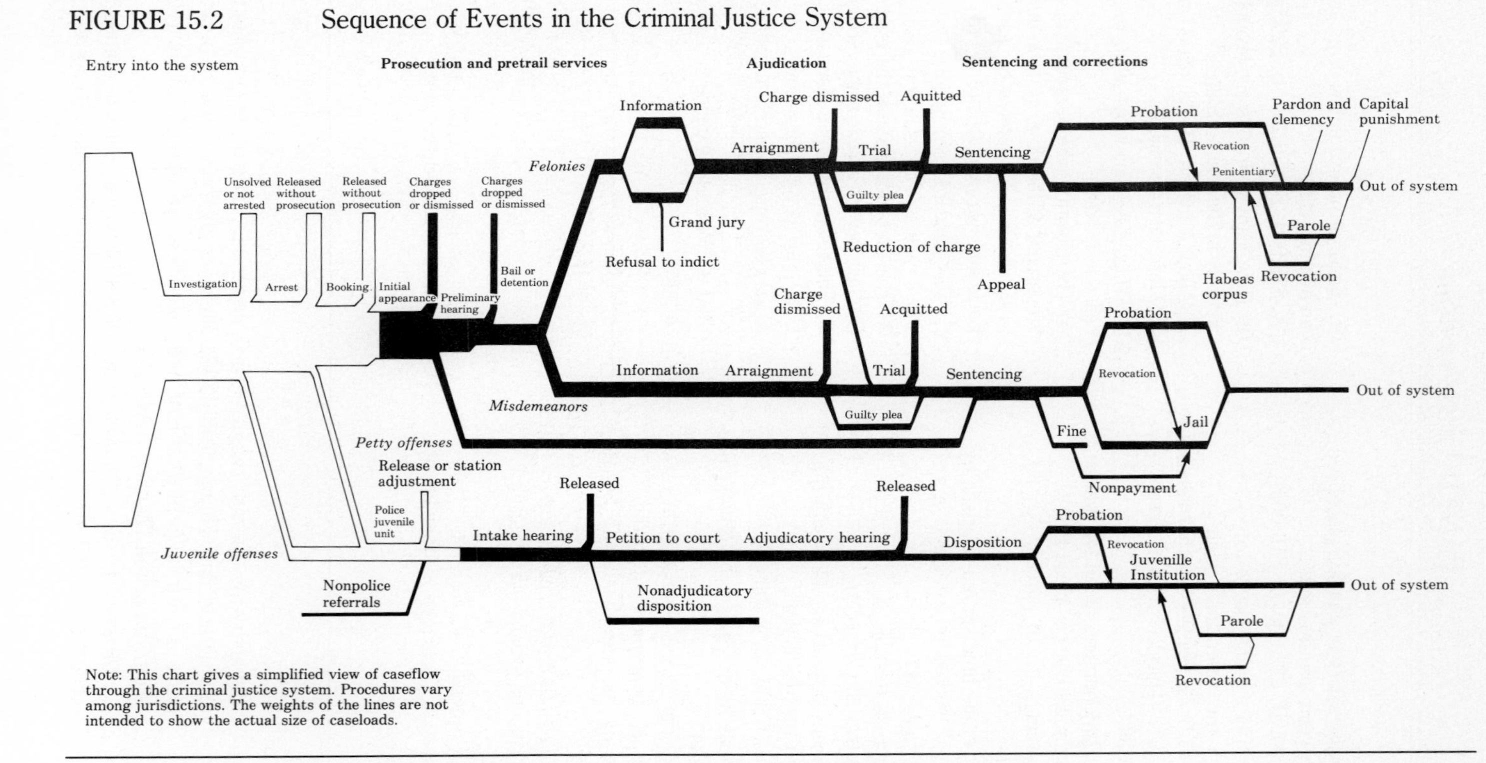

Note: This chart gives a simplified view of caseflow through the criminal justice system. Procedures vary among jurisdictions. The weights of the lines are not intended to show the actual size of caseloads.

Source: U.S. Department of Justice, Bureau of Justice Statistics, *Report to the Nation on Crime and Justice,* 1983:42–43.

or just driving around on patrol. Little wonder, then, that the police do little to reduce crime (Kelling et al., 1974). Furthermore, most police involvement in crime is reactive, not proactive (Black and Reiss, 1970). Often the police just try to keep crime from getting out of control. Certainly, they do not eliminate crime.

In 1977 there were 11,475 municipal police departments and 1,122 special police departments in the United States (Zawitz, 1983:47). This amounts to about one to three policemen or women for each 1,000 residents. By 1987 city, county, and state police departments rose to over 16,000. One salient police problem relates to their use of force and violence in trying to do their jobs. Of course, just carrying a gun gives the police officer tremendous power. At the same time the police are expected to use restraint and control in their use of force (Meridith, *Psychology Today,* May 1984; United Press International, December, 11, 1985). This causes a great deal of conflict and stress for the policeman or woman who must confront armed (often drunken) and dangerous criminals (or terrorists), who themselves have no constraints in using their weapons (see the novels and nonfiction of Joseph Wambaugh—*The Glitter Dome, The Delta Star,* or *The Onion Field*—on this problem in the Los Angeles Police Department). Westley argues that at least 40 percent of police officers believe that they have the right to use force to coerce respect for the law from the public.

Arrest, Jail, and Prisons. Although we shall have more to say about incarceration below (as a resolution to crime), we must note here that part of the problem of crime and violence is revealed in who is arrested and incarcerated. Most of those in jails and prisons are young (the mean age was twenty-five), poor (average prearrest income was $3,714 per year in 1978), uneducated (average education was 10.2 years), black, and male (94 percent). Blacks are 11 percent to 12 percent of the U.S. population, but make up 28 percent to 29 percent of those arrested (*Statistical Abstract of the United States,* 1986:173) and 41 percent of those in jails and prisons. As we saw above, jails and prisons are now bursting at the seams.

Blacks are given longer sentences than whites and are less likely to be paroled (Meyers, 1987). Thus, we must wonder if police are not agents of the state—especially of the dominant white majority—who use the law as an excuse to harass and socially control the poor and minorities (Lizotte, 1978:564). Of course, many police officers (including black and Hispanic officers) and whites would counter that the law is color blind and that minorities are in fact more likely to break the law. Clearly, the incarceration issue is a complex one.

Terrorism Recently we have witnessed an upsurge of violent political activity that lies somewhere between crime and full-scale war. Colonel Khadafy of Libya has attacked U.S. ships in international waters and the United States has retaliated with bombing raids in Libya. Bombings have increased in previously uncommon places—such as London, Paris, Rome, and New York City. Innocent passengers waiting for airplanes have been machine gunned. One may even begin to wonder about the terrorist connections of the poisoning of Tylenol capsules.

Definitions and Concepts. As we saw above, *terrorism* is unpredictable, random murder, assault, violence, fear, subjugation, and intimidation designed to disrupt the normal social and political order, until the military overthrows the government or the government (usually capitalistic) dies from disorganization (Sterling, 1981:8, 16–18, 162, 172; cf. Horowitz, 1982:288). Others have called terrorism "the reasoned, brutally violent deeds of rebels engaged in an irregular campaign" (Bell, 1985:41).

Although terrorism is certainly not limited to Marxists and the USSR, much of modern terrorism is designed to overthrow capitalistic governments (especially the United States or U.S.-sponsored governments) and to replace them with communistic governments (Alexander, 1985:101; Sterling, 1981; *New York Times Magazine,* March 1, 1981; Clark, 1982:286). Clearly, Marx and Lenin believed in the necessity of political violence to usher in socialism (Alexander, 1985:104). If violence is random, that is, if brutal death can come to anyone at any time, terrorists believe that social and political change will be demanded by the masses to stop the killing and disruption. In fact terrorism has not led to the collapse of bourgeois society—yet (Harkabi, 1985:21).

Terrorism is covert war with no fronts (Harkabi, 1985:19). It is an outgrowth of guerilla warfare (see Marighella, *Mini-Manual for Urban Guerillas,* in Sterling, 1981). Terrorism involves the use of minimum violence to achieve major po-

PANEL 15.4

Terrorism: A Question of Definition?

"One man's terrorist attack is another man's blow for freedom," said Hodding Carter, State Department spokesman under President Carter and now a journalist for public television's "Inside Story" and ABC's "This Week with David Brinkley." Carter was the first of three speakers in this year's Milton S. Eisenhower Symposium, "Terrorism: Implications for a Free Society." "If the British had used the word in 1776," the journalist noted, "George Washington could have been called a terrorist."

Carter began with a dictionary, which calls terrorism "the use of violence and intimidation, especially for political purposes." That definition leaves a great deal of room, Carter said. For example, the stereotypical image of a wild, bearded, bomb-throwing, hostage-seizing fanatic "totally without redeeming qualities," he said, is "too simplistic, too neat, and dead wrong." In fact, the most prevalent form of terrorism today is state terrorism, where governments suppress their own people, kidnapping and murdering them in the night, putting them in prison without legitimate charges, ruling them under martial law.

Source: *Johns Hopkins University Magazine*, February/April, 1985: 74–75.

litical results (Harkabi, 1985:19). Thus, often terrorism is a modern form of warfare that is less hazardous and less expensive than traditional war (Alexander, 1985:102). Modern terrorism is distinguished from earlier terrorism by indiscriminate violence with no one considered an innocent victim.

Working Within Society Versus Disruption and Overthrow of Society. Most terrorist organizations are dedicated to the disruption and overthrow of (especially capitalist) governments. Exchange theory's distributive injustice proposition reminds us that if relative inequality is fairly constant over time, but the economic situation improves somewhat, paradoxically, terrorist revolutions are more likely (as in the U.S. black urban riots of the mid-1960s). Of course, as capitalist society breaks down (see Pasternak's novel, *Dr. Zhivago*), so do social rewards. The immediate result of most terrorism is for the situation to get worse, even for the oppressed. In fact terrorism threatens the norms of all civilized society (Harkabi, 1985:21). Just think of what has happened in Italy (because of the Red Brigade), in Ulster (because of the IRA), in Beirut, Lebanon, in Iran, in Poland, and so on (cf. Bell, 1985:42–43).

The costs of disruption are very high. Many people lose their lives. Terrorism jeopardizes our most basic civil right—the right to life itself (cf. Horowitz, 1982:290). Without life all other rights are meaningless (Clark, 1982:285). Yet some oppressed people must feel that their lives are not worth much anyway under exploitative capitalistic regimes. Still, does terrorism really change society?

PANEL 15.5

Poll Uncovers Frustration over Terrorism

Most Americans think the United States should be doing more to combat international terrorism but do not back military action against terrorists or governments supporting them, a new poll released Sunday shows.

Some 55 percent of those surveyed believe the United States could be doing more to protect Americans against the threat of international terrorism. Thirty-eight percent said the U.S. government was doing enough.

The *Times* noted that most of those dissatisfied with the government's reactions to terrorism were women, blacks, less educated people and people who disapprove of President Reagan's performance.

Just 3l percent of Americans said they thought terrorism should be fought with military force if innocent people might be killed.

Forty-nine percent of those polled said it would make matters worse if the United States took military action against terrorists every time an attack affected Americans, while just 40 percent said it would reduce terrorism.

Source: United Press International, February 10, 1986.

The Terrorist Network. Who are the terrorists? Sterling argues that terrorism is an organized international strategy sponsored mainly by the Soviet Union (especially the KGB; cf. Alexander, 1985:101) and to a lesser degree by Palestine, Cuba, South Yemen, Libya, East Germany, Yugoslavia, and a few other countries (1981:15, 119, 258). Of course, the United States engages in some terrorist activities too (in part through the CIA). The United States also finances terrorist activities in many other countries. Just think of the former Shah of Iran, ousted Phillipine President Marcos, the Contras or Nicaraguan rebels. Terror can be red (i.e., left, as with Italy's Red Brigade) or black (i.e., right, as in Hitler's Nazi Germany). International centers of operation include Paris, Zurich, London, and Dublin (Sterling, 1981:53, 129), with training in South Yemen, Cuba, and Libya (1981:3, 4, 39, 41, 220) and targets in Oman, Uruguay, Italy, Vienna, Israel, Ireland, and Iran (1981:101, 106).

Many terrorists are (or were) relatively well-to-do, upper-class individuals. Examples might include Patty Hearst (of the Symbionese Liberation Army), Peruvian Carlos the Jackal, millionaire Feltrinelli in Italy (deceased), and Colonel Khadafy of Libya (Sterling, 1981:25, 131, 258). Although terrorism's basic goal is to disrupt social order and to overthrow the government, sometimes (e.g., in Uruguay) the military actually overthrows the terrorists (that is, terrorism backfires).

An irresolvable problem is that terrorism does not seem to change society much. Most terrorists end up dead or in prison at an early age. Terrorists seem to not realize that in communist countries there is still inequality (i.e.,

Some feel terrorism has replaced classical warfare, which is now too costly and disruptive. Pictured are four well-known terrorists: (1) Carlos-the-Jackal (a famous international terrorist with the Armed Arab Struggle), (2) Patricia Hearst (who was kidnapped by the SLA), (3) Seamus Costello (deceased terrorist leader of Irish Republican Socialism Party), and (4) Fusako Shingenbu (a leader of the Japanese Red Army). (AP/Wide World Photos)

socialism is not democratic either). One must be careful not to confuse social or economic reality with the political system. For example, there can be social or economic inequality in socialist countries and they can still be politically socialistic. Even organized crime opposes terrorism, since world economic stability is necessary for the profit of illegitimate as well as legitimate business. In spite of all these problems with terrorism we will probably see major increases of terrorist activities in the United States itself in coming years. However, terrorism ultimately will prove futile, will provoke vicious cycles of counter-terrorism (from the United States and other countries), and may lead to full-fledged war (Bell, 1985).

Threats of Nuclear War Of course, the ultimate act of violence is a full-fledged traditional war that could threaten the very continuance of life itself. Especially grim is the specter of a nuclear holocaust. Earlier we provided a definition of classical war and examined briefly the history, loss of life, and economic cost of war (cf. Keegan and Darracott, 1981). Here we only hope to skim some salient aspects of a contemporary type of war—nuclear conflict.

Nuclear Strategies and Killing Power. As U.S. President Ronald Reagan has said: "A nuclear war cannot be won and must not be fought" (McNamara and Bethe, 1985:170). Nuclear weapons have only one purpose, to prevent their use. Nuclear strategies are aimed at mutual deterrence. Nuclear killing power is immense. Just one of America's thirty-six nuclear submarines has more killing power than man has shot against man in all previous human history (McNamara and Bethe, 1985:171). The United States currently has about 11,000 nuclear warheads directed against 5,000 targets. Our total inventory of nuclear warheads is about 50,000. The notion of a first strike that eliminated the other side's retaliatory capability is irrational, since our nuclear submarines are constantly mobile and virtually invulnerable. And, as we shall see, a major first strike would harm the aggressor, as well as the target country.

Who Has the Bomb? Avoidance of nuclear war is increasingly unlikely as more and more countries develop the nuclear bomb. For example, Pakistan started building atom bombs in 1955 (in Kahuta—*Time,* June 3, 1985). In 1974 India exploded a nuclear device. Of course, the USA, USSR, Britain, France, and China already have nuclear capabilities. Israel and South Africa probably also have nuclear weapons; and Argentina and Brazil are not far behind. Particularly worrisome is that Libya's Khadafy provided millions of dollars for Pakistan's development of nuclear weapons. Imagine what could happen if Khadafy had nuclear weapons!

Star Wars. Lately the United States and President Reagan have advocated developing a Strategic Defense Initiative (called Star Wars), an impenetrable shield that would protect the entire nation against foreign missile attack (McNamara and Bethe, 1985:172; Tierney, 1986). The problem (in addition to its $26 billion price tag) is that even if the Star Wars shield were 99 percent effective, 1 percent of Soviet warheads could destroy every major city in America (Tierney, 1986:178). Thus, the Star Wars program is a technical folly;

it cannot work. An earlier technical folly was the nuclear airplane (Tierney, 1986:179)—theoretically an airplane that could stay aloft indefinitely without landing. After fifteen years and $1 billion of developmental expenditures U.S. President Kennedy killed the project. Among its major problems were that if it crashed accidently it could contaminate the environment and kill many innocent civilians and that it was difficult to repair a radioactive airplane.

The Aftermath of Nuclear War. A major nuclear war is an unthinkable psychotic nightmare (Sagan et al., 1985). Assuming that one-half to one-third of nuclear supplies were detonated (about 5,000 megatons), it would be pitch black initially in target zones (from soot, dust, and smoke in the air). This sun-blocking smog would be highly toxic from radioactivity. About 30 percent of northern midlatitude areas would receive roughly 250 rads—which is the mean lethal dosage of radiation. Of course, radiation causes hemorrhaging, diarrhea, lesions, anemia, immunological damage, pneumonia, and gastroenterological problems.

It would also get very cold (a base temperature of −10° F). In July the temperature in the United States would range from 0 to −20° F. Plants, animals, and human beings would literally freeze to death. The hydrological cycle would be suppressed and droughts would result. Fierce storms would occur at sea and along coastal areas. Much of ocean life would die. The only survival would be in extraordinarily deep shelters, with huge supplies of food and self-contained air supplies. At least one-half of the world population would die directly as a result of such a nuclear war.

• Analyzing the Problem

Of course, crime and violence comprise many different types of acts and are not one, simple, unitary phenomenon. Although we will now review five basic types of explanations of crime and violence, none of these theoretical perspectives can be a "perfect fit" to the data. Clearly, a world war and shoplifting, a rape-murder and littering, computer theft and blowing up a train station in Bologna, Italy, are all very different types of crimes or violence. At best we offer generic explanations in what follows. Much more detailed explanations of particular types of crime and violence are required to do a truly adequate job of explanation.

The Exchange Perspective Crime and Violence Pays. In spite of the FBI, the police, and the criminal justice system admonishments that Crime Does Not Pay, clearly it does. A fundamental exchange proposition is that the more a specific behavior is rewarded, the more it will be performed (cf. Piliavin, et al., 1986).[8] The data in this chapter show that most crimes are not even reported to the police. If they are reported, only a small proportion of them lead to arrests and fewer still of those arrested are actually convicted. Finally, many convictions do not result in jail or prison sentences—especially for the more lucrative white-collar crimes (Hagan, 1985:284).

Almost always the monetary rewards for criminal or violent activities are greater than those for noncriminal activities. So even if there is some risk, it is usually thought to be worth it. Consider shrimping versus smuggling drugs to shore or prostitution versus being a secretary. Fines against corporations are almost always less than the profits netted by the crime committed (Glaser, 1978). Terrorists are often released. In the case of human-bomb suicidal terrorists there is no individual left to punish after the crime. Finally, war is often very profitable, especially for the victor (Japan and Germany actually profited, as well, from World War II). Note too that the basic exchange between the violent or criminal offender and the victim is physical force (or threat of physical force) for money, property, or land (and other natural resources).

Interaction Patterns. Social interaction's effects on crime and violence are not consistent (Miethe, Stafford, and Long, 1987). Exchange theory suggests that the more you interact with another person or group, the more similar you will become to them and the more you will like them. This would indicate that crime and violence are more probable against strangers. In fact this is true for war, terrorism, and for certain kinds of crimes (e.g., for theft; Vetter and Silverman, 1986:40). Terrorist acts are usually against those of opposite religions (e.g., Jews versus Muslem Arabs or Irish Protestants against Catholics), nationalities (Libyans and Iranians versus Americans), races (South African whites versus blacks) or political persuasions (capitalist Americans versus socialist Russians).

On the other hand, most murders, rapes, and other violent crimes are against acquaintances, friends, relatives, and people who are similar in many aspects to the offender (O'Brian, 1987). This may simply be a result of proximity and propinquity. That is, although the stimulus for aggression is abstract and remote (e.g., the economy, unemployment, discrimination, and so on), the target is simply whomever the offender is around most of the time.

Learning Violence and Crime. Exchange principles imply that violence and crime are learned (see Akers, 1979, 1985) from a social conditioning process in which rewards and punishments shape behavior (cf. Hagan, 1985:169). Through a process of differential reinforcement criminals gradually learn to define crime and violence as more desirable than conforming behaviors. Thus, crime and violence result not just because of the absence of controls against them, but rather because (for criminals) crime and violence are positively rewarded.

Distributive Injustice. The Fifth Proposition of exchange theory (see Chapter 2, Panel 2.2) states that when individuals or groups do not receive the rewards they expected (or receive unexpected punishments), they are more likely to become angry and aggressive. Thus, exchange theory would contend that violent and criminal actors would be more likely to have life histories of social and personal frustration and inequity (Berkowitz, 1962; Conklin, 1986:142–143). Certainly, this would be the case for most black and Hispanic offenders.

Contrary to popular belief crimes often are not punished and do pay. Most crimes are not even reported to police, few criminals actually spend time in prison—especially for the more lucrative white-collar crime. (AP/Wide World Photos)

Corporate Actors. To the degree that control, negative reinforcement, and punishment (e.g., the death penalty) discourage individual actors from crime and violence, we must remind ourselves that corporate criminal actors have no body to imprison, hang, shoot, electrocute, and so on (Hagan, 1985:276–280). Individual sanctions simply do not work well on corporate actors. It follows that much corporate crime and violence may be caused by the absence of an effective control system. For example, there seems to be no end to the individual Arab terrorists who are willing to kill themselves to strike a blow for Allah or against American capitalism.

The Structural-Functional Perspective Blocked Opportunities. Structural sociologists argue that crime and deviance (including violence) often are caused not by personal traits of individual criminals or even by the rewards and reinforcements criminals have received to commit crimes. Instead, structuralists emphasize the differential social opportunities that some groups and individuals have to do what all of us need to do—viz., to make money, achieve in an occupation, secure social status and esteem, and so on.[9] For example, Merton (1986:194) stresses that all Americans have internalized the cultural goal of material economic success, but not all Americans have equal opportunities to make money, acquire property, and so on, legitimately. Thus, crime and violence (i.e., illegitimate opportunities) tend to result when legitimate means to achieving important common cultural goals are blocked. Individuals and groups who then wish to achieve these goals are forced to "innovate" through crime and violence (cf. Conklin, 1986:198 ff.; Cloward and Ohlin, 1959).

Demographic Changes. There are some relatively recent changes in the demographic structure of the American population that also probably play an important part in explaining the rise in crime and violence from 1960 to 1980. We know already that crime and violence are committed primarily by young people (Conklin, 1986:117ff.). For example, the median age for almost all crimes is less than twenty-five years old. Considering the age structure of the United States, it is not surprising then that crime rates went up in the 1960s and 1970s, or that they declined in the 1980s. The post World War II baby boomers (after 1945) reached the ages of maximum crime and violence potential in the late 1960s and early 1970s. By the mid-1980s many baby boomers were in their midthirties. Thus, both the rise and the recent decline in crime and violence can be explained in part by the age structure of the U.S. population (see Heitgerd and Bursik, 1987).

Based on age alone crime rates should stay relatively low, since (for example) the number of eighteen to twenty-four year olds in the United States will continue to decline (Cohen and Land, 1987). From 14.6 million in 1985, projections call for 13.1 million and 12.5 million eighteen to twenty-four year olds in 1990 and 2000, respectively (*Statistical Abstract of the United States,* 1986:27; cf. Easterlin, 1980). The median age of the U.S. population is slowly but continually rising. Of course, age is not the only factor, especially in terrorism and war. Other structural factors influencing crime rates include a much greater proportion of women working and thus leaving their homes unprotected during the daytime (Cohen and Felson, 1976) and organizational constraints on budgets for law enforcement (McDowall and Loftin, 1986).

The Conflict Perspective The preponderance of blacks, Hispanics, and other minorities committing crimes, being arrested, going to jail or prison, being executed—and, to a degree, acting as terrorists or waging wars—is explained by conflict theorists as a trait of the law, not of the actual criminal behavior of individuals or groups. For example, Quinney argues that criminal law is "first and foremost a reflection of the interests and ideologies of the ruling class" (who tend to be white, male, older, wealthier, and so on, 1976:192). Put somewhat differently (by Spitzer, 1975): "criminal populations are produced because their behavior, personal qualities, and/or position threaten the social relations of production in capitalistic societies."

Thus, criminal justice and the law are used by older, relatively financially well-off white males to control young, poor, minorities (Simon, 1981). The law protects the interests of the dominant group (Beirne and Quinney, 1982). The majority group tends to criminalize the behaviors of minorities and not to criminalize its own behavior (such as white-collar business activities). Like juveniles, blacks, the poor, certain females (e.g., prostitutes), and so on are more likely to be criminals because there are more laws for them to break (Hawkins, 1987).

Most conflict theorists argue that crime, violence, terrorism, and war are all caused in large measure by sharp inequality (Meyers, 1987; cf. Blau and Blau, 1982, on the cost of inequality). The poor, blacks, Hispanics, Third-World Arab countries, and so on are all socially disenfranchised. Many acts of crime and violence occur in social systems where unemployment is high, the support systems are stingy, and there is a large underclass (Currie and Skolnick, 1984:447). Crime and violence may be reasonable responses to inequity and financial deprivation; that is, they may be acts of social desperation and anger (Gordon, 1981). Even in the case of a possible World War III between the United States and the USSR social inequality (in the United States and countries the United States aids financially) is still a major issue.

The Biological Perspective Cesare Lombroso. Biological explanations of crime and violence are often treated as a joke. Part of this bad reputation of the biology of crime and violence derives from the poor empirical methods of early researchers. For example, Cesare Lombroso (1836–1909) was a prison physician (see *Criminal Man,* 1876) who conducted thousands of postmortem examinations and anthropometric studies of criminals (Lotz, Poole, and Regoli, 1985:150–151). On the basis of these studies Lombroso concluded that criminals had distinct physical and mental characteristics (Hagan, 1985:19).[10]

Some of these distinct traits included pointed ears, sloping foreheads, receding chins, close-set and shifty eyes, and so on. In fact, Lombroso believed that criminals were atavistic throwbacks to an earlier more primitive and violent evolutionary form of modern human beings. Unfortunately (for the biological perspective of crime), later research has proven that many of the "criminal" traits Lombroso claimed to have discovered were not unique to criminals. In fact Lombroso, for all his precision, never used a control or comparison group of noncriminals. What Lombroso did accomplish was to redirect attention back to individual factors in crime and violence.

Somatotypes, Illness, and Physical Injury. Others have taken Lombroso's physical perspective on crime and violence and extended it to studies of body types or somatotypes (Sheldon, 1949). Sheldon contended that juvenile delinquents tended to be more muscular and athletic (mesomorphs) than nondelinquents (Shoemaker, 1984). While this may be true, it is hardly predictive of delinquency or crime. In a related study Palmer (1960) did a controlled investigation of fifty-one murderers and their nonmurderer brothers. He found that murderers were more likely to have epilepsy, head injuries, and more serious illnesses than their nonmurderer brothers.

Genetics and Chromosomes. The old, familiar identical twin biological procedure has shown that identical twins are more alike in their criminal behaviors than are fraternal twins (Christiansen, 1974; cf. Stott, 1982). Finally, the XYY chromosomal configuration in males has been thought to be associated with violent crimes, especially with violent sexual crimes (Witkin et al., *Science,* 1976, 1978). For example, convicted mass murderer-rapist Richard Speck was thought to be an XYY male. XYY determination is a complex, time-consuming process that usually is not done. Also, as with the other biological factors, it probably explains only a small fraction of some types of crime and violence.

Symbolic Interaction Perspectives Differential Association. From this theoretical perspective criminals or terrorists have evolved an excess of favorable definitions of crime or violence (Sutherland, 1937, 1974; Conklin, 1986:241–248). Differential association (like exchange theory) claims that people learn to act like criminals, usually in face-to-face interactions with others (Conklin, 1986:Ch. 10—especially p. 242ff.). For example, many crimes require skill and training (Maurer, 1974). Just consider burglary, pickpocketing and thievery, computer crime, and so on. One does not simply commit many types of crimes without detailed training and preparation of various sorts. Juvenile delinquents may learn criminal behaviors from other delinquents (Matsueda, 1982). Also, much violence may be copied, suggested, imitated, and so on from the mass media—especially from television (Phillips, 1980, 1986). In this case face-to-face exchange may not be essential. This process is sometimes called differential identification (Conklin, 1986:244). Another variation of differential association theory adds the concept of reinforcement (see Akers, 1985). Here criminal or violent learning occurs through positive and negative reinforcement (cf. Piliavin et al., 1986). For example, the absence of rewards from attending school might help make criminal activity more attractive. A final example of differential association's effect would be white-collar crime in which executives often learn that loyalty to the corporation is more important than loyalty to the law.

The Labeling Perspective. Labels are also important in the production of crime. From the labeling perspective criminals have experienced the restrictive effects of having been stigmatized and branded as criminals (Schur, 1971; Conklin, 1986:249–256). Consider that labels (particularly those that result in prison or jail sentences) tend to limit one's social associations to other criminals, increase police surveillance, help one acquire a criminal identity, tend to affect how police treat you after arrest, and so on (Ritzer, 1986:164; Lotz, Poole, and Regoli, 1985:208–216). Such negative public reactions to initial, primary, often transitory criminal deviance or violence can help manufacture secondary deviance in which a criminal or violent career may result from actually seeing oneself as a criminal or adopting a criminal identity (Lemert, 1951, 1967; Schur, 1979; Lotz, Poole, and Regoli, 1985:210–211).

For example, Klemke (1978) found that shoplifters who were apprehended by the police were more likely to shoplift again than those who were not apprehended by the police. However, other types of criminals apparently do not undergo an identity change if apprehended by the law. White-collar criminals would be an example of those who tend not to acquire a deviant (criminal) identity (Sutherland, 1983). Also, stigmatization of delinquent criminal behavior is probably not as likely to result in a delinquent self-concept as was previously thought (Hepburn, 1977). Finally labeling is an incomplete explanation of crime or violence because it does not tell why (primary) deviance occurred in the first place (Conklin, 1986:256). In the next and final section of this chapter resolutions are suggested for the social problems of crime and violence.

• Resolving the Problem

Five basic resolutions (deterrence, incapacitation, retribution, rehabilitation, and decriminalization) are offered to the problems of crime and violence. Of course, these resolutions cut across the five causes of crime and violence just reviewed. For example, one can deter crime using any or all of the exchange, structural, conflict, biological, or symbolic interaction approaches.

Many Americans do not believe that anything can prevent crime (*Newsweek,* March 23, 1981). Typically approaches to resolving crime and violence fall into two basic types: those of conservatives or of liberals. Conservatives generally want to catch and convict more criminals, and have more severe punishments for them (Walker, 1985:6).

Conservatives believe that criminals tend to lack self-control and that poverty is no excuse for crime. Individual responsibility is stressed and crime control is modeled after the ideal of patriarchal family. Liberals ordinarily favor rehabilitation and social reform. They usually blame society and the economy for crime and violence, not the individual criminal.

Reprinted by permission: *Tribune* Media Services.

Deterrence and Prevention Obviously the preferred resolution to crime and violence would be to keep them from ever happening in the first place—what Caplan calls primary prevention (1964). As we saw above, the main strategy of nuclear weapons is to deter war, to make war unthinkable. Although the data are mixed, probably in general criminal sanctions tend to deter crime (Hagan 1985;303; cf. Piliavin et al., 1986). Conservatives argue that swift and certain punishments for crimes discourage would-be criminals (Taylor, *New York Times,* December 13, 1983). At the same time there is conflicting evidence that capital punishment actually deters homicide or other serious crimes (Hagan, 1985:304).

The police are usually ineffective in preventing crime and violence, since the police do not spend most of their time on crime. When the police are involved with crime, it is most often reactive, that is, after the fact, when it is too late to deter crime (Black and Reiss, 1970). Note that to be effective in preventing terrorism police would need special powers such as searching without warrants and detaining suspects without arrest (Clark, 1982:283; Hirsch, 1986).

True crime prevention probably requires sweeping social changes (Kornblum and Boggs, 1984). For example, the community, family, and the economy all would need to be altered (Heitgerd and Bursik, 1987)—especially in high-crime areas (Currie, 1983; Silberman, 1978). Poverty-stricken neighborhoods need a sense of purpose and internal control. Clearly, if such major social and economic changes are required to prevent crime and violence, prevention and deterrence are not likely to be workable resolutions.

Incapacitation The primary response to crime and violence has usually been to incapacitate offenders, to remove them from public circulation—especially through imprisonment and capital punishment. For example, James Q. Wilson contends that if every person convicted of a serious crime were imprisoned for three years, serious crime would be reduced by one-third (1983; cf. Kornblum and Boggs, 1984:25). Obviously, criminals in prison cannot commit public crimes.

All but two states have mandatory prison terms for some crimes (Taylor, 1983:130). But Bazelon (see Panel 15.6) and others argue that all the get-tough resolution to crime has done is to swell prison censuses to the point of bursting the available space and to harden those criminals who go there. We know that in 1985 there were 463,866 prisoners in state and federal prisons—an all-time high. The United States already has one of the harshest prison systems in the world. Our incarceration rate is two to eight times higher than those of other countries (Doleschal and Newton, 1981). Furthermore, most inmates in prisons are not violent criminals (Mullen et al., 1980). Certainly, prison does not rehabilitate criminals, as we shall see. Imprisonment tends to amount to racism, since proportionately far more blacks than whites are imprisoned and executed (Meyers, 1987; Hawkins, 1987).

Of all the incapacitating options capital punishment is the most effective. Dead men do not commit crimes. In about 1776 in the United States imprisonment replaced hanging as punishment for serious crimes (Ignatieff, 1978:154). However, over time most Americans have grown more supportive of capital punishment. For example, from 1965 to 1980 the percent of the public favoring capital punishment rose from 38 percent to 67 percent (Davis, 1980:81). About 72 percent of the public want capital punishment sentences carried out and have grown impatient with endless appeals that seem to protect murderers better than their victims (*Justice Assistance News,* July 3, 1985:4).

Some evidence does show that capital punishment deters future crime. Ehrlich concluded that each execution prevented seven to eight other murders (1975; cf. Walker, 1985:76). Still, we must also realize that pickpockets used to steal from crowds that came to see other pickpockets hung (Hibbert, 1963)! It is disturbing too that 54 percent of all prisoners executed from 1930 to 1980 were black (*Capital Punishment,* 1980).

Retribution Going back as far as the Code of Hammurabi (the eighteenth century B.C.) retributionists have felt that crime and violence must be responded to with a punishment that fits the seriousness of the offense (Conklin, 1986:Ch. 16). The *lex talionis* principle (i.e., an eye for an eye and a tooth for a tooth) states that social order is balanced only if the resolution to crime and violence is equal or proportionate to the act committed (van den Haag, 1975;

PANEL 15.6

Is Incapacitation the Answer to the Crime Problem?

Yes: James Q. Wilson, from *Thinking About Crime* (New York: Basic Books, 1975).

No: David L. Bazelon, from "Solving the Nightmare of Street Crime," *USA Today*, January 1982.

Issue Summary

Yes: James Q. Wilson argues that imprisoning everyone convicted of a serious offense for several years would greatly reduce these crimes. He contends that incapacitation is the one policy that works.

No: Judge David L. Bazelon discusses the moral and financial costs of the incapacitation approach and argues that society must attack the brutal social and economic conditions that are the root causes of street crime.

As crime has mushroomed, public indignation has intensified—particularly when spectacular cases have been brought to light about paroled convicts committing new felonies, light sentences being handed down for serious crimes, and cases being thrown out of court on legal technicalities. Over the past decade or so, there has been a dramatic increase in the number of Americans who think that the authorities should be tougher on criminals. To take a prominent example: While a majority of Americans in the 1960s favored the abolition of the death penalty, today more than 70 percent favor its use in some cases.

David L. Bazelon admits that incapacitation is a short-term solution to street crime that will deliver some results. He points out, however, its high financial and moral costs, explaining that the United States already imprisons a larger proportion of its citizens than all other developed nations, except the USSR. A three-fold increase in the prison population will not make a significant dent in the rate of serious crimes, maintains Bazelon, and the needed new prisons will cost many billions of dollars. More importantly, he says, the incapacitation approach assumes that convicted offenders will continue to commit crimes and in effect punishes them for future misdeeds. Bazelon's approach raises serious questions concerning individual justice. He believes the only satisfactory answer is to attack the social and economic conditions that are the root causes of street crime; others, such as Wilson, argue for more immediate action.

Source: *Taking Sides: Clashing Views on Controversial Social Issues*, fourth edition, George McKenna and Kurt Finsterbusch, editors. Reprinted by permission of the Dushkin Publishing Group, Inc. 1986:268–269 and 285.

Ritzer, 1986:173). Thus, murderers should be executed, serious crimes should be responded to with serious punishments, and so on. For example in Muslim law thieves often had their thieving arm cut off.

The concept of retribution requires that the state and/or the individual victim get even (i.e., get revenge) with the offender. Many people believe that crime and violence flourish because the offender (whether s/he is a Libyan terrorist or an individual murderer) is seldom punished as severely as the crime s/he committed. Even murderers have almost endless appeal rights while in prison and seldom die the horrible deaths they inflicted on their victims (Berns, 1979).

About 80 percent of white Americans think we do not deal harshly enough with certain criminals (*Public Opinion Quarterly,* April–May, 1981:40).

Nonretributionists reply that violence begets more violence. Retribution in fact may lead to a vicious cycle of crime and violence—as, for example, between the PLO and Israel or between American whites and blacks (Horowitz, 1982:291, 296). In a sense retributionists stoop to the same low level as the criminal offender when they allow and encourage capital punishment. Although one felon can be executed, perhaps many others are incited to crime and violence for the sake of the original felon's cause and his execution or by a general subculture of normative violence spawned by retributionism.

Some retributionists want restitution too. At least twenty-six states now have forms of victim compensation programs (Conklin, 1986:376–377). Most explicitly, the offender can be ordered by the court to restore the victim's loss through financial payments (Hagan, 1985:289; Johnson in Sullivan and Victor, 1985:209). Restitution alone clearly is an inadequate response to crime and violence, since only about 3 percent of those arrested are ever convicted (Heinz, *USA Today,* July 1984). Also, it is obvious that an offender cannot restore a life he took or remove a serious trauma he caused.

Rehabilitation Some criminologists contend that crime and violence are sicknesses which offenders need to be cured of (Cullen and Gilbert, 1982). Thus, their resolution to crime and violence is to rehabilitate offenders to their prior healthy state. Although there were 3,859 executions of criminals in the United States from 1930 to 1967, from 1967 to 1977 there were none (Hagan, 1985:290). For the most part the criminal justice system shifted from punishment to attempts at rehabilitation. These rehabilitative efforts were a miserable failure. Martinson (1974) reviewed 231 studies and concluded that rehabilitation had little or no effect on criminal recidivism (i.e., on being returned to the criminal justice system or prison for subsequent additional crimes or violence). For every 100 inmates released from prison about 50 are returned to prison within three years (Conklin, 1986:442).

Rehabilitation has led mainly to overcrowded prisons. By the 1970s the idea that criminals could be treated and reformed collapsed (Taylor, 1983; Blumstein, 1978; Ritzer, 1986:178). Now we have started executing criminals again rather than trying to rehabilitate them. There are several reasons for the rehabilitative failure. For one, many criminals never were healthy at any time in their lives. For another, crime and violence are social, not just individual maladies. It is much more difficult to cure a sick society than it is to cure a sick individual. We know already that very little police, court, and prison time and money are spent on rehabilitation. Most prisons in the criminal justice system are merely custodial. Finally, living in prison with other criminals tends to teach you how to be a criminal (not a noncriminal). Of course, offenders can also get very angry from the obvious frustrations and mistreatments they must face in prison.

Decriminalization and Legalization As you will recall from the very beginning of this chapter, crimes are determined in part by the law. It follows that one obvious (and sometimes somewhat absurd) resolution to crime and violence problems is to change criminal laws. In a sense, if we abolish criminal laws, technically we would also abolish crime. Of course, there would still be many activities and behaviors that would be highly problematic, even if they were not called crime.

On the other hand, decriminalization is not as ridiculous as it sounds. For example, Morris and Hawkins advocate that we make status offenses and victimless crimes legal (in *The Honest Politician's Guide to Crime Control,* 1970). They recommend that we decriminalize private sexual activities between consenting adults, prostitution, pornography, drug use, gambling, public drunkenness, and so on. Then the funds used to enforce these minor (usually moral) crimes, would be available to fight for more serious crimes.[11]

Our present criminal laws have not been very effective. For example, New York City was forced to release hundreds of prisoners jailed for minor crimes to relieve jail overcrowding (Taylor, 1983). In recent years it cost about $15,000 a year to imprison a criminal. To spend this much money to punish a criminal may seem silly, even irrational, if the crime was relatively minor. Finally, it can be argued that many laws are criminogenic; that is, they produce crime through processes of labeling, secondary deviance, and so-called crime tariffs (e.g., if you make a behavior—say prostitution—illegal, it only drives up the price; it does not prevent the behavior—cf. Walker, 1985:196).

• Summary

In a sense crime and violence were considered last in this text because often force is seen as the last resort in the resolution of social problems. Most textbooks tend to consider crime separately and earlier in the book. Although not all crime is violent or bloody in the way murder, terrorism, and war are, even embezzlement or computer crimes involve aggressive expropriation of resources that are not legally one's own. As such all crime and violence put social order in jeopardy.

Crimes—all acts that violate laws and are subject to formal sanctions—raise several important social issues. Will crime and violence give rise to social anarchy? Is crime increasing? Which crimes are more serious? Who is most likely to be victimized by crime? How do race and ethnicity affect crime? What are the costs of crime? How can crime and violence be controlled? Will we be forced into terrorism and world war to settle social conflicts?

To address these issues several key concepts were defined: violent and nonviolent crime, the FBI's eight index crimes, felonies, misdemeanors, delinquency, white-collar crime, organized crime, professional crime, terrorism, and war. The general prevalence and history of crime and violence were also reviewed. A major conclusion was that crime rates rose in the 1970s, but mostly declined after 1980. Although terrorism has become a fundamental

Victimless crimes (like prostitution, drug use, gambling or drunkenness) could be decriminalized and the criminal justice funds saved used to control more serious crimes—like murder, assault, and rape. Obviously, some behaviors would still be problematic, even if they were not called crimes. (Michael Weisbrot/Stock, Boston)

concern recently, there has been no traditional American war since 1973 (i.e., since Vietnam).

Next the problems of crime (especially homicide, rape, and corporate crime), terrorism, and war were elaborated. Property crimes (burglary, larceny, motor vehicle theft, and arson) outnumber violent crimes (homicide, rape, robbery, and assault) about nine to one. Larceny is the most common index crime and murder is the least common. Crimes tend to be committed by young males, often by minorities. Certainly the young, black, male offender is disproportionately represented among homicide and rape offenders. We observed that the United States has one of the highest homicide rates in the world and that rape often serves nonsexual needs of inadequate men to dominate women. Rape victims in a sense are raped again by the patriarchal criminal justice system. It was noted that corporate crimes often are ignored or are not even considered as crimes, but rather as overly zealous business activities. This section concluded with a review of the process and procedures of the criminal justice system, the police, and prisons.

Terrorism was defined as unpredictable, random, murder, assault, violence, fear, subjugation, and intimidation designed to disrupt the normal social and political order. The key to modern terrorism is its random and brutal nature. Often terrorism is Marxist in origin and is designed to overthrow capitalist governments and economies. Many experts feel that terrorism is a contemporary substitute for classical warfare—which has become too costly, disruptive, and devastating. Most terrorists have given up on solving social problems by working within the social system. A large amount of terrorism today is sponsored by the USSR and their communist allies, although the United States and the CIA obviously resort to some terrorism (e.g., as in the Cuban invasion). The final problem examined in the present chapter was the threat of nuclear war. Nuclear weapons are designed for deterrence, not for actual use. A nuclear war would be an unthinkable psychotic nightmare, a battle in which all sides would lose.

From the exchange perspective crime and violence persist because they "pay." Most crimes result in net profits or rewards, few criminals are arrested, and fewer still are convicted and sentenced. White-collar crimes almost always are highly profitable. Even terrorism and war have surprisingly few costs, especially for their leaders. The interaction effects on crime and violence are mixed. Although interaction usually encourages liking (maybe it increases all affects), violent acts are normally against those with whom we interact most often (as is the case with homicide). Most criminal or violent persons learn to act illegally or aggressively. Criminal and violent behaviors typically result from lifetimes of social and personal frustration and inequity. Finally, individual controls do not work very effectively on corporate actors.

Structural-functionally, crime and violence are seen to originate from blocked opportunities of certain (often disadvantaged) social groups to achieve common internalized cultural goals (e.g., that of material economic success). These blocked opportunities are aggravated by having relatively large proportions of young people in the population. Having a large number of minority males (e.g., in the U.S. South) also is related to increased rates of crime and violence.

From the conflict perspective criminal law is seen to serve primarily the interests of the ruling class. Often the law is used to try to control young, poor, minority-group males. Violence may be the only alternative to such disenfranchised social groups. Crime and violence rates are thought to be highest where there is sharp social inequality.

Biologically we examined body or somatotypes, twin studies, and XYY male chromosomes, but found little evidence for widespread biological influences on crime and violence. To conclude, the symbolic interaction perspective saw crime and violence as products of differential association and labeling. Often criminals have reduced options for any noncriminal alternative activities as a result of repeated prior negative public reactions, stigmatization, and the acquisition of criminal or violent identities.

Five basic resolutions to social problems of crime and violence were considered. They included deterrence, incapacitation, retribution, rehabilitation, and decriminalization. Except for nuclear war, deterrence has not proven very effective. Although sanctions probably help deter some crime, the police themselves spend little time on crime and prison recidivism rates are high. Some (Wilson) have argued that consistent and uniform imprisonment could reduce violent crime by up to one-third. Others point out that such practices have led mainly to overcrowded prisons and hardened criminals. Capital punishment probably deters little crime, since murderers usually do not kill a second time anyway.

Retributionists argue that the criminal sanction should match the criminal offense. Yet violence (even justified) often begets further violence. Rehabilitation for the most part simply has not worked. Decriminalization would remove minor or status offenses from the list of crimes and use the money saved to fight more serious crimes. Of course, society cannot allow itself to conclude erroneously that merely abolishing criminal laws would also abolish crime. If only it were that easy!

• Notes

1. Particular types and categories of crime will be defined below.

2. Violence is physical force used to injure, damage, or kill.

3. Note that other than providing definitions we will have relatively little else to say about delinquency, organized crime, and professional crime.

4. However, with the FBI's Crime Clocks, the time gets shorter simply as the population in the United States gets larger.

5. As of July 28, 1985, about 16,000 local, county, and state police agencies reported crimes to the FBI as sources for their *UCR*. Other sources of crime data include the *National Crime Survey* (victimization studies are involved), public opinion polls, the *Sourcebook of Criminal Justice Statistics,* and *Justice Assistance News*—just to cite a few major sources.

6. Although, obviously, there is still some sexual arousal involved in rape.

7. It can also be not guilty or *nolo contendere;* for example, the accused accepts the penalty, but does not admit guilt.

8. Conversely, acts that are punished or sanctioned effectively will be diminished or will cease.

9. Exchange theory argues that generalized reinforcers are extremely important in advanced industrialized societies that are heavily institutionalized (cf. Homans, 1974:Ch. 16).

10. Cf. the claim of underactive autonomic nervous system leading to an inadequate fear response in criminals (Mednick and Volaka, 1980).

11. Many minor crime sanctions are in fact trying to legislate morality, even though the behaviors punished do not obviously harm anyone or harm society.

• Glossary

Crime. All behaviors and actions that violate the law and are subject to formally sanctioned punishment by larger society.

Criminal Justice System. A loose confederation of agencies at all levels of government that together provide the means by which we apprehend, try, and punish criminal offenders.

Corporate Crime. See *white-collar crime.*

Decriminalization. A process by which crime is controlled by making some minor or victimless crimes legal.

Felonies. The most serious crimes, punishable by death or by a year or more in prison.

Homicide. Causing the death of another person without legal justification or excuse.

Incapacitation. A response to crime in which the public is protected by removing the offender from public circulation, especially through imprisonment or capital punishment.

Index Crime. The eight serious crimes or "street crimes" reported by the FBI in their *Uniform Crime Reports:* murder and nonnegligent manslaughter, rape, robbery, assault, burglary, larceny, motor vehicle theft, and arson.

Juvenile Delinquency. The committing of an act by a minor, which would be a crime if s/he were an adult.

Nonindex Crimes. Nonserious, usually misdemeanor criminal acts or status offenses such as prostitution, DUI, gambling, and so on.

Nuclear Winter. The cold, stormy, dark, dry, radioactive, firey conditions subsequent to a series of major nuclear explosions.

Organized Crime. An organized continuing criminal conspiracy that engages prostitution, sale of illegal drugs, loan sharking, extortion, and so on.

Professional Crime. The illegal activities of anyone who makes his/her living from crime.

Property Crime. Unlawful acts with the intent of gaining property, but that do not involve the use or threat of force.

Rape. Unlawful sexual intercourse with a female by force or without legal or factual consent.

Recidivism. Being arrested and returned to the criminal justice system or to prison for additional crimes subsequent to prior arrest and/or imprisonment.

Retribution. A procedure to control crime in which the sanction for crime is proportionate to the crime itself and attempts to restore the balance existing before the criminal act. Sometimes restitution or compensation is paid to the victim or to the state.

Star Wars. A synonym for Strategic Defense Initiative—a supposedly impenetrable shield that would protect the United States against foreign missile attack.

Terrorism. The unpredictable random use of murder, violence, assault, fear, subjugation, and intimidation to disrupt the normal operations of society, which in turn is expected to result in social chaos, disorganization, and overthrow of governments.

Violent Crime. Events, such as homicide, rape, and assault, that may result in injury to a person.

War. Open armed conflict between countries or between factions within the same country.

White-Collar Crime. Offenses committed against or for a corporation by a person of respectable and high social status in the course of their occupation; violations of the law using a person's position of power, influence, or trust for illegal gain.

• Further Reading

Barnes, Leroy W., ed. "Peace and War." In *Social Problems, 86/87.* Sluice Dock, CT: The Duskin Publishing Group, 1986:162–200. Six highly readable short essays on war by experts like Carl Sagan and Robert McNamara. Considers nuclear war; how to prevent nuclear war; the star wars project; who has the (nuclear) bomb; America's military intervention in Vietnam, El Salvador, and Lebanon; and how the United States supports dictators friendly to the United States but criticizes the Soviet Union's suppression of human rights.

Hagan, John. *Modern Criminology: Crime, Criminal Behavior, and Its Control.* New York: McGraw-Hill, 1985. A sound basic textbook on criminology. Focuses on definitions of crime, whether crime rates are increasing, class differences in criminal behavior, the male propensity for crime, corporate crime, minorities and crime, theories of criminal behavior (three long chapters), new types of crime, and the punishment, treatment, and prevention of crime. A standard, fairly current textbook with an excellent bibliography.

Merari, Ariel, ed. *On Terrorism and Combating Terrorism.* Frederick, MD: University Publications of America, 1985. This somewhat Israeli-biased seventeen-chapter volume grew out of the international seminar on political terrorism sponsored by the Jaffee Center for Strategic Studies of Tel-Aviv University in 1979. A highly current examination of the impact of the media on terrorism, problems involving hostages, the relation of terrorism to war, and the role of Germany and the Soviet Union in terrorism. Recently terrorism has increased, is more directed at people rather than property, claims more lives, is more technically sophisticated, and is more often conceived of as a tool of foreign policy.

Sullivan, John J. and Joseph L. Victor, ed. *Criminal Justice 85/86.* Sluice Dock, CT: The Duskin Publishing Group, 1985. A current sampling and editing of fifty-five short chapters from the criminal justice literature. Many pieces are journalistic and popular. They read well and are amply illustrated with graphics (pictures, tables, figures, and so on). Major sections on (1) definitions, crime fear, victimization, the criminal justice system, the mafia; (2) the police; (3) the courts; (4) delinquency and juvenile justice; and (5) corrections.

Walker, Samuel. ***Sense and Nonsense About Crime.*** **Monterey, CA: Brooks/ Cole Publishing, 1985.** An iconoclastic critical book reviewing current crime-control policies, especially those of conservatives, by focusing on robbery and burglary. Excellent at showing what does not work in reducing serious crime, but not as helpful in providing sensible crime-control alternatives. A good supplement to and elaboration of the resolution section of this chapter.

Zawitz, Marianne W., ed. ***Report to the Nation on Crime and Justice: The Data.*** **Rockville, MD: Bureau of Justice Statistics Report, 1983.** Although it is now a little dated, this thin empirical volume provides general U.S. data on how much crime there is, who it strikes, when, where, who the typical offender is, the government's response to crime, how juveniles are handled differently from adult criminals, what happens to convicted offenders, and the costs of justice. All done with first-rate color graphics, figures, and tables.

BIBLIOGRAPHY

Abraham, Karl. 1953 (original, 1910). The Man Who Loved Corsets. In *Selected Papers of Karl Abraham, M.D.* New York: Basic Books.

Abruzzi, William and Gene Orro. 1982. Drug Abuse and Suicide. *Contemporary Drug Problems* 11:145–157.

Adorno, T. W. et al. 1950. *The Authoritarian Personality.* New York: Harper & Row.

Agel, Jerome, ed. 1971. *The Radical Therapist.* New York: Ballantine Books.

Agran, Larry. 1979. Getting Cancer on the Job. In *Crisis in American Institutions.* Jerome H. Skolnick and Elliott Currie, eds., 432–442. Boston: Little, Brown.

Akers, Ronald L. 1985. *Deviant Behavior: A Social Learning Approach.* Belmont, CA: Wadsworth.

Akers, Ronald L. et al. 1979. Social Learning and Deviant Behavior. *American Sociological Review* 44:635–655.

Albrecht, Stan. 1986 (original edition, 1983). Environment. In *Social Problems in American Society.* M. DeFleur, ed., 538–561. Boston: Houghton Mifflin.

Aldrich, Howard E. 1979. *Organizations and Environments.* Englewood Cliffs, NJ: Prentice-Hall.

Alexander, Jeffrey A., Michael A. Morrisey, and Stephen M. Shortell. 1986. Effects of Competition, Regulation, and Corporatization on Hospital-Physician Relationships. *Journal of Health and Social Behavior* 27:220–235.

Alexander, Jeffrey C. 1983. *Theoretical Logic in Sociology, Volume IV.* Berkeley: University of California.

Alexander, Tom. 1981. A Simpler Path to a Cleaner Environment. *Fortune,* May 4.

Alexander, Yonah. 1985. Terrorism and the Soviet Union. In *On Terrorism and Combating Terrorism.* A. Merari, ed., 101–118. Frederick, MD: University Publications of America.

Alger, Horatio. 1962 (original, 1867). *Ragged Dick.* New York: Macmillan.

Allen, John, ed. 1985. *Environment 85/86.* Guilford, CT: Dushkin.

Alperovitz, Gar and Jeff Faux. 1985. Building a Democratic Economy. In *Crisis in American Institutions.* J. H. Skolnick and E. Currie, eds., 550–557. Boston: Little, Brown.

Alvarez, Rudolfo. 1985. The Psycho-Historical and Socioeconomic Development of the Chicano Community in the United States. In *The Mexican American Experience.* R. O. de la Garza et al., eds., 33-56. Austin: University of Texas Press.

Alwin, Duane F. 1987. Distributive Justice and Satisfaction with Material Well-Being. *American Sociological Review* 52:83–95.

American Medical Association. 1980. *Profile of Medical Practice.* Washington, DC: American Medical Association.

American Psychiatric Association. 1980. *Diagnostic and Statistical Manual of Mental Disorders, III.* Washington, DC: American Psychiatric Association.

Andersen, Kurt. 1983. Crashing on Cocaine. *Time,* April 11.

Anderson, Harry et al. 1985. Cocaine: The Evil Empire. *Newsweek,* February 25:14–23.

Anderson, Martin. 1978. *Welfare.* Stanford, CA: The Hoover Institute.

Anderson, T. W. and Stanley L. Sclove. 1978. *An Introduction to the Statistical Analysis of Data.* Boston: Houghton Mifflin.

Angotti, Thomas R. and Bruce S. Dale. 1976. Bologna, Italy: Urban Socialism in Western Europe. *Social Policy,* May/June.

Archer, Dane and Rosemary Gartner. 1984. *Violence and Crime in Cross-National Perspective.* New Haven, CT: Yale University Press.

Aries, P. 1962. *Centuries of Childhood.* New York: Vintage Books.

Armor, David J. et al. 1976. *Alcoholism and Treatment.* Washington, DC: The Rand Corporation.

Asimov, Isaac. 1982. *How Did We Find Out about the Beginning of Life?* Chicago: Walker.

Athens, Lonnie H. 1980. *Violent Criminal Acts and Actors: A Symbolic Interaction Study.* Boston: Routledge & Kegan Paul.

Auchinsloss, Kenneth. 1970. The Ravaged Environment. *Newsweek,* January 26:2–6.

Auletta, Ken. 1980. *The Streets Were Paved with Gold.* New York: Random House.

Auletta, Ken. 1983. *The Underclass.* New York: Vintage Books.

Ausubel, David P. 1980. An Interactional Approach to Narcotic Addiction. In *Theories on Drug Abuse.* Dan J. Lettieri et al., eds., 4–7. Rockville, MD: National Institute on Drug Abuse.

Aviram, U. and S. Segal. 1973. Exclusion of the Mentally Ill. *Archives of General Psychiatry* 29:126–131.

Babbie, Earl. 1986. *The Practice of Social Research.* Belmont, CA: Wadsworth.

Bacas, Harry. 1985. Energy Alternatives. *Nation's Business* July:34–35.

Backer, Barbara A., Natalie Hannon, and Noreen A. Russell. 1982. *Death and Dying: Individuals and Institutions.* New York: John Wiley & Sons.

Bale, Tony. 1985. Breath of Death: The Asbestos Disaster Comes Home to Roost. In *Crisis in American Institutions.* Jerome H. Skolnick and Elliot Currie, eds., 413–427. Boston: Little, Brown.

Baltes, Paul B. and Orville G. Brim, Jr., eds. 1979–1987. *Life-Span Development and Behavior.* New York: Academic Press.

Bandura, A. and R. H. Walters. 1963. *Social Learning and Personality Development.* New York: Holt, Rinehart & Winston.

Banfield, Edward C. 1974. *The Unheavenly City Revisited.* Boston: Little, Brown.

Bardwich, Judith M. 1986. *The Plateauing Trap.* New York: MAACOM—American Management Association.

Barnes, LeRoy, ed. Peace and War. In *Social Problems, 86/87.* L. Barnes, ed., 162–200. Guilford, CT: Dushkin.

Barnet, Richard J. 1985. No Room in the Lifeboats. In *Crisis in American Institutions.* J. H. Skolnick and E. Currie, eds., 558–566. Boston: Little, Brown.

Baron, James N. 1984. Organizational Perspectives on Stratification. In *Annual Review of Sociology, 10.* R. H. Turner and J. F. Short, Jr., eds., 37–70. Palo Alto, CA: Annual Reviews.

Barrow, Georgia M. and Patricia A. Smith. 1979. *Aging, Ageism, and Society.* New York: West Publishing.

Basile, Paul S. 1980. Energy Soothsayers Not Saying the Whole Sooth. *Bulletin of the Atomic Scientists* 39:43.

Bassuk, Ellen L. and Samuel Gerson. 1978. Deinstitutionalization and Mental Health Services. *Scientific American* 238:46–53.

Bastian, Robert K. and Jay Benforado. 1983. Waste Treatment: Doing What Comes Naturally. *Technology Review,* February/March:100–107.

Bates, Peter. 1984. The Family: An Island of Stability. *Bostonia,* July:16, 18, 19.

Battin, Margaret P. and Ronald W. Maris, eds. 1983. *Suicide and Ethics.* New York: Human Sciences.

Bayer, Ronald. 1978. Heroin Decriminalization and the Ideology of Tolerance: A Critical Review. *Law and Society Review* 12:301–318.

Becker, Howard S. 1953. Becoming a Marijuana User. *American Journal of Sociology* 59:235–242. Chicago: University of Chicago Press.

Becker, Howard S. 1967. History, Culture, and Subjective Experience. *Journal of Health and Social Behavior* 7:163–176.

Becker, Howard S. 1973. *Outsiders: Studies in the Sociology of Deviance.* New York: Free Press.

Becker, Howard S. 1980. The Social Bases of Drug-Induced Experience. In *Theories on Drug Abuse.* Dan J. Lettieri et al., eds. 180–190. Rockville, MD: National Institute on Drug Abuse.

Becker, Howard S. et al. 1961. *Boys in White: Student Culture in Medical School.* Chicago: University of Chicago Press.

Becnel, Barbara. 1979. Black Workers: Progress Derailed. In *Crisis in American Institutions.* Jerome H. Skolnick and Elliott Currie, eds., 149–159. Boston: Little, Brown.

Behavior Today. 1984. Alcoholism, Phobias, Most Common Mental Disorders in U.S. Volume 15, Number 1, January 9.

Beirne, Piers and Richard Quinney, eds. 1982. *Marxism and Law.* New York: John Wiley & Sons.

Bejerot, Nils. 1980. Addiction to Pleasure. In *Theories on Drug Abuse.* Dan J. Lettieri et al., eds., 246–255. Rockville, MD: National Institute on Drug Abuse.

Bell, J. Bowyer. 1985. Terrorism and the Eruption of Wars. In *On Terrorism and Combating Terrorism.* A. Merari, ed., 41–52. Frederick, MD: University Publications of America.

Benbow, C. and J. Stanley. 1980. Sex Differences in Mathematical Ability: Fact or Artifact? *Science* 210:1262–1264.

Benedict, Ruth. 1934. *Patterns of Culture.* Boston: Houghton Mifflin.

Benson, Paul R. 1986. The Prescription of Discretionary Antipsychotic Medication by State Mental Hospital Psychiatrists. *Journal of Health and Social Behavior* 27:28–43.

Berch, Bertina. 1982. *The Endless Day: The Political Economy of Women and Work.* New York: Harcourt Brace Jovanovich.

Berger, Peter L. and Thomas Luckmann. 1966. *The Social Construction of Reality.* Garden City, NY: Doubleday Publishing.

Berkowitz, Leonard. 1962. *Aggression: A Social Psychological Analysis.* New York: McGraw-Hill.

Berkowitz, Leonard. 1975. *A Survey of Social Psychology.* Hinsdale, IL: Dryden Press.

Bernard, J. 1982. *The Future of Marriage.* New Haven, CT: Yale University Press.

Berns, Walter C. 1979. *For Capital Punishment: Crime and the Morality of the Death Penalty.* New York: Basic Books.

Berry, Mary F. and John W. Blassingame. 1982. *Long Memory: The Black Experience in America.* New York: Oxford University Press.

Bethell, Tom. 1980. Treating Poverty. *Harpers* 260:16–24.

Better Homes and Gardens. 1978. Editorial—What's Happening to the American Family? Des Moines, IA: Merideth Publishing.

Bieber, Irving et al. 1962. *Homosexuality: A Psychoanalytic Study.* New York: Basic Books.

Bierstedt, Robert. 1974. *Power and Progress: Essays on Sociological Theory.* New York: McGraw-Hill.

Birnbaum, Judith A. 1975. Life Patterns and Self-Esteem in Gifted Family-Oriented and Career-Committed Women. In *Women and Achievement.* Martha T. S. Mednick et al., eds., 396–419. New York: Halsted Press.

Birren, James E. 1986. The Process of Aging: Growing Up and Growing Old. In *Our Aging Society.* Alan Pifer and Lydia Bronte, eds., 263–282. New York: W. W. Norton.

Black, Donald and Albert Reiss. 1970. Police Control of Juveniles. *American Sociological Review* 35:63–77.

Black, Max, ed. 1961. *The Social Theories of Talcott Parsons.* Englewood Cliffs, NJ: Prentice-Hall.

Blalock, Hubert M., Jr. 1979. *Social Statistics.* New York: McGraw-Hill.

Blau, Judith and Peter Blau. 1982. The Cost of Inequality: Metropolitan Structure and Violent Crime. *American Sociological Review* 47:114–128.

Blau, Peter M. 1955. *The Dynamics of Bureaucracy.* Chicago: University of Chicago Press.

Blau, Peter M. 1964. *Exchange and Power in Social Life.* New York: John Wiley & Sons.

Blau, Peter M. 1975. *Approaches to the Study of Social Structure.* New York: Free Press.

Blau, Peter M. 1977. *Inequality and Heterogeneity: A Primitive Theory of Social Structure.* New York: Free Press.

Blau, Peter M. and Robert K. Merton. 1981. *Continuities in Structural Inquiry.* Beverly Hills, CA: Sage Publications.

Bleier, Ruth. 1984. *Science and Gender: A Critique of Biology and Its Theories on Women.* New York: Pergamon Press.

Blum, David J. 1982. Youthful Professionals Without Any Children Transform City Areas. *The Wall Street Journal,* February 1.

Blumberg, Paul. 1980. *Inequality in An Age of Decline.* New York: Oxford University Press.

Blumer, Herbert. 1969. *Symbolic Interactionism: Perspective and Method.* Englewood Cliffs, NJ: Prentice-Hall.

Blumstein, Alfred. 1982. On the Racial Disproportionality of the U.S. Prison Populations. *Journal of Criminal Law and Criminology,* Fall.

Blumstein, Alfred, Jacqueline Cohen, and Daniel Nagin, eds. 1978. *Deterrence and Incapacitation: Estimating the Effects of Criminal Sanctions on Crime Rates.* Washington, DC: National Academy of Sciences.

Blumstein, Philip and Pepper Schwartz. 1983. *American Couples: Money, Work, Sex.* New York: William Morrow.

Blundell, William E. 1980. As World Needs Food, U.S. Keeps Losing Soil to Land Developers. *The Wall Street Journal,* October 24.

Bogue, Donald J. 1969. *Principles of Demography.* New York: John Wiley & Sons.

Boswell, Terry E. 1986. Discrimination and Chinese Immigration. *American Sociological Review* 51:430–437.

Botwinick, Jack. 1984. *Aging and Behavior: A Comprehensive Integration of Research Findings.* New York: Springer Publishing.

Boudon, R. 1980. *The Crisis in Sociology.* New York: Columbia University Press.

Boudon, Raymond. 1981. Undesired Consequences and Types of Structures of Systems of Interdependence. In *Continuities in Structural Inquiry,* P. M. Blau and R. K. Merton, eds., 255–287. Beverly Hills, CA: Sage Publications.

Boudreau, Frances A. 1983. Families and Intimate Living. In *Social Problems in American Society.* Melvin L. DeFleur, ed., 420–447. Boston: Houghton Mifflin.

Bouvier, Leon F. 1984. Planet Earth 1984–2034: A Demographic Vision. *Population Bulletin* 39:1–38.

Bradshaw, York W. 1987. Urbanization and Underdevelopment: A Global Study of Modernization, Urban Bias, and Economic Dependency. *American Sociological Review* 52:224–239.

Brady, John P. 1975. Behavior Therapy. In *Comprehensive Textbook of Psychiatry, II.* A. Freedman, H. Kaplan, and B. J. Sadock, eds., 1824–1830. Baltimore: Williams & Wilkins.

Braithwaite, John. 1984. *Corporate Crime in the Pharmaceutical Industry.* London: Routledge & Kegan Paul.

Brandon, Robert M., Jonathon Rowe, and Thomas H. Stanton. 1982. In *Crisis in American Institutions.* Jerome H. Skolnick and Elliott Curie, eds., 100–118. Boston: Little, Brown.

Brandt, Anthony. 1975. *Reality Police: The Experience of Insanity in America.* New York: William Morrow & Co.

Brecher, Edward M. 1972. *Licit & Illicit Drugs.* Boston: Little, Brown.

Brenner, M. Harvey. 1977. Health Costs and Benefits of Economic Policy. *International Journal of Health Services* 7:611.

Brill, A. A. 1938. *The Basic Writings of Sigmund Freud.* New York: Random House.

Brim, Orville G., Jr. et al., editors. 1970. *The Dying Patient.* New York: Russell Sage Foundation.

Brittain, John A. 1978. *Inheritance and the Inequality of Material Wealth.* Washington, DC: Brookings Institution.

Brody, Charles J. 1984. Differences by Sex in Support for Nuclear Power. *Social Forces* 63:209–228.

Brody, Elaine M. 1978. The Aging of the Family. *Annals of the American Academy of Political and Social Science* 438:13–27.

Broverman, Inge K. et al. 1972. Sex-Role Stereotypes: A Current Appraisal. *Journal of Social Issues* 28:59–79.

Brown, Claude. 1965. *Manchild in the Promised Land.* New York: Signet.

Brown, George W. and Tirril Harris. 1978. *Social Origins of Depression: A Study of Psychiatric Disorder in Women.* New York: Free Press.

Brown, Lester R. 1976. The Limits to Growth of Third World Cities. *The Futurist,* December.

Brown, Lester R. 1982. The Coming Solar Age. *Natural History,* February:55–64.

Brown, Lester et al. 1979. *Running on Empty: The Future of the Automobile in an Oil-Short World.* New York: W. W. Norton.

Brown, Lester R. et al. 1985. *State of the World, 1985.* New York: W. W. Norton.

Brown, Michael. 1981. *Laying Waste: The Poisoning of America By Toxic Chemicals.* New York: Washington Square Press.

Brown, Phil. 1987. Diagnostic Conflict and Contradiction in Psychiatry. *Journal of Health and Social Behavior* 28:37–50.

Brownmiller, Susan. 1975. *Against Our Will: Men, Women, and Rape.* New York: Simon & Schuster.

Brues, Alice M. 1977. *People and Races.* New York: Macmillan.

Bryjak, George J. and Michael P. Soroka. 1985. *Sociology: The Biological Factor.* Palo Alto, CA: Peek Publications.

Bryson, R. A. 1974. A Perspective on Climate Change. *Science,* May 17: 753–760.

Bumpass, Larry and Ronald R. Rindfuss. 1979. Children's Experience of Marital Disruption. *American Journal of Sociology* 85:49–65.

Bunker, Edward. 1979. A Junkie View of the Quagmire. In *Crisis in American Institutions.* J. Skolnick and E. Currie, eds., 506–513. Boston: Little, Brown.

Burgess, Ernest W. 1925. The Growth of the City: An Introduction to a Research Project. In *The City.* R. E. Park, E. W. Burgess, and R. D. McKenzie, eds., 47–62. Chicago: University of Chicago Press.

Burke, Kenneth. 1965 (originally published, 1935). *Permanence and Change.* New York: Bobbs-Merrill.

Burmaster, David. 1982. The New Pollution: Groundwater Contamination. *Environment,* March.

Burstein, Paul. 1985. On Equal Employment Opportunity and Affirmative Action. In *Research in Race and Ethnic Relations.* C. B. Marrett and C. Leggon, eds., 91–112. Greenwich, CT: JAI Press.

Butler, Robert N. 1982. The Tragedy of Old Age in America. In *Crisis in American Institutions.* Jerome H. Skolnick and Elliot Currie, eds., 436–457. Boston: Little, Brown.

Buttel, Frederick H. 1976. Social Science and the Environment Competing Theories. *Social Science Quarterly* 57:307–323.

Cafferata, Gail L., Judith Kasper, and Amy Bernstein, 1983. Family Roles, Structure, and Stressors in Relation to Sex Differences in Obtaining Psychotropic Drugs. *Journal of Health and Social Behavior* 24:132–143.

Califano, Joseph A., Jr. 1978. *Health, United States, 1978.* Washington, DC: U.S. Department of Health, Education, and Welfare.

Campbell, Bernard G., ed. 1985. *Humankind Emerging.* Boston: Little, Brown.

Cannon, W. B. 1939. *The Wisdom of the Body.* New York: W. W. Norton.

Capital Punishment, 1980, National Prisoner Statistics. Washington, DC: U.S. Department of Justice.

Caplan, Gerald. 1964. *Principles of Preventive Psychiatry.* New York: Basic Books.

Caplow, Theodore. 1982. *Middletown Families: Fifty Years of Change and Continuity.* Minneapolis: University of Minnesota Press.

Caplovitz, D. 1979. *Making Ends Meet: How Families Cope with Inflation and Recession.* Beverly Hills, CA: Sage Publications.

Carey, Jon. 1984. Is It Safe to Drink? *National Wildlife,* February/March:19–21.

Carmichael, Stokley and Charles Hamilton. 1967. *Black Power.* New York: Vintage Books.

Carr, Donald E. 1972. The Disasters. In *Society and Environment: The Coming Collision.* R. R. Campbell and J. L. Wade, eds. Boston: Allyn & Bacon.

Carson, Rachel. 1962. *The Silent Spring.* New York: Fawcett.

Castro, Janice. 1983. Prescription for Profit: Private Hospital Firms Bring Management Skills to the Bedside. *Time* July 4:42–43.

Catton, William R., Jr. 1980. *Overshoot: The Ecological Basis of Revolutionary Change.* Urbana: University of Illinois Press.

Catton, William R., Jr. and Riley E. Dunlap. 1980. A New Ecological Paradigm for Post-Exuberant Sociology. *American Behavioral Scientist* 24:15–47.

Centers for Disease Control. 1986. *Homicide Surveillance.* Atlanta: Centers for Disease Control.

Chadwick-Jones, J. K. 1976. *Social Exchange Theory: Its Structure and Influence in Social Psychology.* New York: Academic Press.

Chandler, William U. 1985. Increasing Energy Efficiency. In *State of the World, 1985.* L. R. Brown, ed., 147–171. New York: W. W. Norton.

Chase, Allen. 1977. *The Legacy of Malthus: The Social Costs of the New Scientific Racism.* New York: Alfred A. Knopf.

Cherlin, Andrew J. 1981. *Marriage, Divorce, and Remarriage: Changing Patterns in the Postwar United States.* Cambridge, MA: Harvard University Press.

Cherlin, Andrew. 1987. Politicizing the American Family. *Johns Hopkins Magazine* February: 18–24.

Cherlin, Andrew and Frank F. Furstenberg, Jr. 1983. The American Family in the Year 2000. *The Futurist,* June.

Christensen, Harold T. and Kathryn P. Johnsen. 1985. In *Marriage and Family in a Changing Society.* James M. Henslin, ed., 15–26, New York: The Free Press.

Christiansen, Karl O. 1974. Seriousness of Criminality and Concordance among Danish Twins. In *Crime, Criminology and Public Policy.* R. Hood, ed., 63–77. New York: Free Press.

Cicourel, Aaron V. 1974. *Cognitive Sociology.* New York: Free Press.

Clark, Kenneth B. and Mamie P. Clark. 1947. Racial Identification and Preference in Negro Children. In *Readings in Social Psychology.* T. M. Newcomb and E. L. Hartley, eds., 169–178. New York: Holt, Rinehart & Winston.

Clark, Richard C. 1982. Technological Terrorism. In *Taking Sides.* K. Finsterbusch and G. McKenna, eds., 282–286. Guilford, CT: Dushkin.

Clausen, John A. and Carol L. Huffine. 1975. Sociocultural and Social/Psychological Factors Affecting Social Responses to Mental Disorder. *Journal of Health and Social Behavior* 16:405–420.

Clinard, Marshall B. and Peter Yeager. 1980. *Corporate Crime.* New York: Free Press.

Clinard, Marshall B., ed. 1964. *Anomie and Deviant Behavior.* New York: Free Press.

Cloward, Richard and Lloyd Ohlin. 1959. Illegitimate Means, Anomie, and Deviant Behavior. *American Sociological Review* 24:164–177.

Coale, Ansley J. 1974. The History of the Human Population. In *The Human Population.* D. Flanagan et al., eds., 15–28. San Francisco: W. H. Freeman.

Cochrane, William. 1982. Growing Scarcities of Resources Are Future Threat. *Alton Telegraph,* March 17.

Cockerham, William C. 1981. *Sociology of Mental Disorder.* Englewood Cliffs, NJ: Prentice-Hall.

Cohen, Albert K. 1955. *Delinquent Boys: The Culture of the Gang.* Glencoe, IL: Free Press.

Cohen, Albert K. 1966. *Deviance and Control.* Englewood Cliffs, NJ: Prentice-Hall.

Cohen, Albert K. and James F. Short, Jr. 1976. In *Contemporary Social Problems.* Robert K. Merton and Robert Nisbet, eds., 47–102. New York: Harcourt Brace Jovanovich.

Cohen, Lawrence E. and Kenneth C. Land. 1987. Age Structure and Crime. *American Sociological Review* 52:170–183.

Cohen, Lawrence E. and Marcus Felson. 1979. Social Change and Crime Rate Trends: A Routine Activity Approach. *American Sociological Review* 44:588–608.

Cohen, Sidney. 1983. *The Alcoholism Problems: Selected Issues.* New York: Haworth Press.

Cole, Stephen. 1975. *The Sociological Orientation.* Chicago: Rand-McNally.

Coleman, James S. et al. 1966. *Equality of Educational Opportunity,* Washington, DC: U.S. Office of Education.

Coleman, James S. 1974. *Power and the Structure of Society.* New York: W. W. Norton.

Coleman, James S. et al. 1975. *Trends In School Segregation, 1968–1973.* Washington, DC: The Urban Institute.

Coleman, James C. and James N. Butcher. 1984. *Abnormal Psychology and Modern Life.* Chicago: Scott, Foresman.

Coles, Robert. 1977. *Eskimos, Chicanos, Indians* (Volume IV of *Children of Crisis*). Boston: Little, Brown.

Collins, Randall. 1975. *Conflict Sociology: Toward an Explanatory Science.* New York: Academic Press.

Comfort, Alex. 1976. Age Prejudice in America. *Social Policy* 17:3–8.

Commoner, Barry. 1972. *The Closing Circle: Nature, Man, & Technology.* New York: Bantam.

Conklin, John E. 1986. *Criminology* (Second Edition). New York: MacMillan.

Connor, Huell E., Jr. and Ronald Maris. 1976. Exchange, Balance, and Formal Organization in Psychotherapeutic Interactions. *Suicide and Life-Threatening Behavior* 6:150–168.

Connor, Walker. 1984. *The National Question in Marxist-Leninist Theory and Strategy.* New Jersey: Princeton University Press.

Conrad, Peter and Rochelle Kerr, eds. 1986. *The Sociology of Health and Illness.* New York: St. Martin's Press.

Conservation Foundation. 1982. *State of the Environment.* Washington, DC: Conservation Foundation.

Conway, William G. 1977. The Case against Urban Dinosaurs. *The Saturday Review,* May 14.

Cook, Karen S., R. Emerson et al. 1981. The Distribution of Power in Exchange Networks: Theory and Experimental Results. *American Journal of Sociology* 89:275–305.

Cook, Karen S., ed. 1987. *Social Exhange Theory.* Beverly Hills: Sage Publications.

Copi, Irving M. 1986. *Introduction to Logic.* New York: Macmillan.

Coser, Lewis A. 1967. *Continuities in the Study of Social Conflict.* New York: Free Press.

Coser, Rose L. 1984. American Medicine's Ambiguous Progress. *Contemporary Sociology* 13:9–11.

Courrier, Kathleen, ed. 1980. *Life After 1980: Environmental Choices We Can Live With.* Andover, MA: Brick House.

Cousins, Norman. 1979. *Anatomy of an Illness.* New York: W. W. Norton.

Crichton, Michael. 1981. *Five Patients.* New York: Avon.

Crichton, Michael. 1969. *The Andromeda Strain.* New York: Alfred A. Knopf.

Criminal Victimization in the United States, 1983. 1985. Washington, DC: U.S. Government Printing Office.

Cullen, Francis T. and Karen E. Gilbert. 1982. *Reaffirming Rehabilitation.* Cincinnati, OH: Anderson.

Current, Richard N. and Gerald J. Goodwin. 1980. *A History of the United States.* New York: Alfred A. Knopf.

Current Population Reports, Population Profile of the United States, 1985. 1986. Washington, DC: U.S. Government Printing Office.

Currie, Elliott. 1983. Crime and Politics. In *Rethinking Liberalism.* New York: Avon.

Currie, Elliott and Jerome H. Skolnick. 1984. *America's Problems: Social Issues and Public Policy.* Boston: Little, Brown.

Currie, Elliott, Robert Dunn, and David Fogarty. 1985. The Fading Dream: Economic Crisis and The New Inequality. In *Crisis in American Institutions.* Jerome H. Skolnick and Elliott Currie, eds., 94–112. Boston: Little, Brown.

Curtis, Richard F. 1986. Family and Inequality Theory. *American Sociological Review* 51:168–183.

Dacey, John S. 1982. *Adolescents Today.* Glenview, IL: Scott, Foresman.

Dahl, Robert A. 1982. *Dilemmas of Pluralistic Democracy.* New Haven: Yale University Press.

Dahrendorf, Ralf. 1959. *Class and Class Conflict in Industrial Society.* Stanford, CA: Stanford University Press.

Daniels, Robert S. 1975. The Hospital as a Therapeutic Community. In *Comprehensive Textbook of Psychiatry, II.* A. Freedman, H. Kaplan, and B. J. Sadock, eds., 1990–1994. Baltimore: Williams and Wilkins.

Dannefer, Dale. 1984. Adult Development and Social Theory. *American Sociological Review* 49:100–116.

Darwin, Charles. 1975 (original, 1859). *Origin of the Species.* Cambridge, MA: Harvard University Press.

Datel, W. E. and A. W. Johnson. 1979. Suicide in United States Army Personnel. *Military Medicine* 144:239–244.

Davies, J. Clarence and Barbara S. Davies. 1975. *The Politics of Pollution.* Indianapolis: Bobbs-Merrill.

Davis, James A. 1971. *Elementary Survey Analysis.* Englewood Cliffs, NJ: Prentice-Hall.

Davis, James A., ed. 1980. *General Social Surveys, 1972–1980: Cumulative Codebook.* Chicago: National Opinion Research Center.

Davis, Karen. 1986. Paying the Health-Care Bills of an Aging Population. In *Our Aging Society.* Alan Pifer and Lydia Bronte, eds., 299–318. New York: W. W. Norton.

Davis, Kingsley. 1959. The Myth of Functional Analysis as a Special Method in Sociology and Anthropology. *American Sociological Review* 24:757–772.

Davis, Kingsley. 1974. The Migrations of Human Populations. In *The Human Population.* D. Flanagan et al., eds., 53–68. San Francisco: W. H. Freeman.

Davis, Kingsley and Wilbert Moore. 1945. Some Principles of Stratification. *American Sociological Review* 10:242–249.

de Catanzaro, Denys. 1981. *Suicide and Self-Damaging Behavior.* New York: Academic Press.

de la Garza et al., eds. 1985. *The Mexican American Experience: An Interdisciplinary Anthology.* Austin: University of Texas Press.

Decker, David L. 1980. *Social Gerontology: An Introduction to the Dynamics of Aging.* Boston: Little, Brown.

DeFleur, Melvin L. 1986 (original, 1983). *Social Problems in American Society.* Boston: Houghton Mifflin.

Dejerassi, Carl. 1986. Abortion in the United States: Politics or Policy? *Bulletin of the Atomic Scientists* April:38–41.

DeLamater, John and Patricia MacCorquodale. 1979. *Premarital Sexuality: Attitudes, Relationships, Behavior.* Madison: University of Wisconsin Press.

Demeny, Paul. 1974. The Populations of the Underdeveloped Countries. In *The Human Population.* D. Flanagan et al., eds., 105–118. San Francisco: W. H. Freeman.

Demeny, Paul. 1986. Population and the Invisible Hand. *Demography* 23:473–488.

Demerath, N. J., III., and Richard A. Peterson, eds. 1967. *System, Change, and Conflict.* New York: Free Press.

Demographic Yearbook. 1986. New York: United Nations.

Detjen, Jim. 1987. Pollution Clouds Sky's Future. *Knight-Ridder,* March 8.

Dewey, John. 1922. *Human Nature and Conduct.* New York: Henry Holt.

Dobash, Russell P. and R. Emerson Dobash. 1981. Community Response to Violence Against Wives. *Social Problems* 28:563–581.

Dohrenwend, Barbara S. and Bruce P. Dohrenwend. 1969. *Social Status and Psychological Disorder.* New York: John Wiley & Sons.

Doleschal, Eugene and Anne Newton. 1981. *International Rates of Imprisonment.* Hackensack, NJ: National Council on Crime and Delinquency.

Dollars & Sense. 1986. Trading Woes, Trading Blows. Editorial, Jan.-Feb.:5–7.

Domhoff, G. William. 1967. *Who Rules America?* Englewood Cliffs, NJ: Prentice-Hall.

Domhoff G. William. 1978. *Who Really Rules?* New Brunswick, NJ: Transaction.

Domhoff, G. William. 1979. *The Powers That Be.* New York: Vintage Books.

Domhoff, G. William. 1986. *Who Rules America Now: A View for the '80s.* New York: Simon & Schuster.

Donaldson, Kenneth. 1976. *Insanity Inside Out.* New York: Crown Publishers.

Douglas, Jack D. 1967. *The Social Meanings of Suicide.* Princeton, NJ: Princeton University Press.

Dowd, James J. 1979. Aging as Exchange: A Preface to Theory. In *The Age of Aging.* Abraham Monk, ed., 98–118. Buffalo, NJ: Prometheus Books.

Dowie, Mark. 1985. Pinto Madness. In *Crisis in American Institutions.* Jerome H. Skolnick and Elliott Currie, eds., 22–37. Boston: Little, Brown.

Doyle, James A. 1985. *Sex and Gender: The Human Experience.* Dubuque, Iowa: W. C. Brown.

Dressler, William W. 1985. Extended Family Relationships, Social Support, and Mental Health in a Southern Black Community. *Journal of Health and Social Behavior* 26:39–48.

Drummond, Hugh. 1977. Add Poison for Flavor & Freshness. *Mother Jones* 2:13–14.

Dubos, Rene. 1979. *The Mirage of Health: Utopias, Progress, and Biological Change.* New York: Harper & Row.

Duncan, David and Robert Gold. 1982. *Drugs and the Whole Person.* New York: John Wiley & Sons.

Durant, Seymour B. 1979. Laetrile for the Urban Crisis. *Journal of the Institute for Socioeconomic Studies* 4:68.

Durkheim, Emile. 1960 (original, 1893). *The Division of Labor in Society.* New York: Free Press.

Durkheim, Emile. 1962 (original, 1895). *The Rules of Sociological Method.* New York: Free Press.

Durkheim, Emile. 1963 (original, 1897). *Suicide.* New York: Free Press.

Durkheim, Emile. 1961 (original, 1912). *The Elementary Forms of the Religious Life.* New York: Collier Books.

Durkheim, Emile. 1953 (original, 1924). *Sociology and Philosophy.* New York: Free Press.

Dye, Thomas R. 1976. *Who's Running America? Industrial Leadership in the United States.* Englewood Cliffs, NJ: Prentice-Hall.

Dyer, Everett D. 1983 *Courtship, Marriage, and Family: American Style.* Chicago, IL: Dorsey Press.

Dynes, Russell. 1974. Sociology as a Religious Movement. *The American Sociologist* 9–4:169–175.

Easterlin, Richard A. 1980. *Birth and Fortune: The Impact of Numbers on Personal Welfare.* London: Grant McIntyre.

Eckland, Bruce. 1985. Theories of Mate Selection. In *Marriage and Family in a Changing Society.* J. M. Henslin, eds., 232–241. New York: Free Press.

Edelman, Marian Wright. 1985. Growing up Black in America. In *Crisis in American Institutions.* Jerome H. Skolnick and Elliott Currie, eds., 143–161. Boston: Little, Brown.

Edwards, Alba. 1940. *Population: Comparative Occupational Statistics for the United States, 1870 to 1940.* Washington, DC: U.S. Department of Commerce, Bureau of the Census.

Edwards, Harry. 1973. *Sociology of Sport.* Chicago, IL: Dorsey Press.

Ehrenreich, Barbara and John Ehrenreich. 1982. The American Health Empire: The System Behind the Chaos. In *Crisis in American Institutions.* Jerome H. Skolnick and Elliott Currie, eds., 393–407. Boston: Little, Brown.

Ehrhardt, A. and S. Baker. 1974. Fetal Androgens, Human Central Nervous System Differentiation, and Behavior Sex Differences. In *Sex Differences in Behavior.* R. C. Friedman et al., eds. New York: John Wiley & Sons.

Ehrlich, Isaac. 1975. The Deterrent Effect of Capital Punishment: A Question of Life and Death. *American Economic Review* 65:397–417.

Ehrlich, Paul R. and Anne H. Ehrlich. 1972. *Population, Resources, Environment.* San Francisco: W. H. Freeman.

Ehrlich, Paul R. and Anne H. Ehrlich. 1981. *Extinction: Causes and Consequences of the Disappearance of the Species.* New York: Random House.

Einstein, Stanley. 1972. The Use and Misuse of Drugs in Commuter-Town. *Drug Forum* 1(4):401–416.

Eitzen, D. Stanley. 1986. *Social Problems.* Boston: Allyn & Bacon.

Emerson, Richard M. 1972. Exchange Theory, Part I: A Psychological Basis for Social Exchange. In *Sociological Theories in Progress, Vol. 2.* J. Berger et al., eds., 38–57. New York: Houghton-Mifflin.

Engels, F. 1942. *The Origin of the Family, Private Property and the State.* Moscow: Foreign Languages Publishing House.

Erikson, Erik H. 1950. *Childhood and Society.* New York: W. W. Norton.

Erikson, Kai T. 1966. *Wayward Puritans: a Study in the Sociology of Deviance.* New York: John Wiley & Sons.

Erikson, Maynard L. and Gary F. Jensen. 1982. Delinquency Is Still Group Behavior! In *Juvenile Delinquency.* Rose Giallombardo, ed., 265–277. New York: Harper & Row.

Ermann, David and Richard J. Lundman, eds. 1982. *Corporate and Governmental Deviance.* New York: Oxford University Press.

Etzioni, Amitai. 1975. A Creative Adaptation to a World of Rising Shortages. *Annals of the American Academy of Political and Social Science* 420:98.

Evans, Daryl P. 1984. Paul Starr and the Secret Sharers. *Contemporary Sociology* 13:11–13.

Faia, Michael A. 1986. *Dynamic Functionalism: Strategy and Tactics.* Cambridge: Cambridge University Press.

Farley, R. 1984. *Blacks and Whites.* Cambridge, MA: Harvard University Press.

Farley, Reynolds and Suzanne M. Bianchi. 1985. Social Class Polarization: Is It Occurring among the Blacks. In *Research in Race, Ethnic Relations.* C. B. Marrett and C. Leggon, eds., 1—32. Greenwich, CT: JAI Press.

Farrell, Michael P. and Stanley D. Rosenberg. 1981. *Men at Midlife.* Boston: Auburn House.

Feagin, Joe R. 1984. *Racial and Ethnic Relations.* Englewood Cliffs, NJ: Prentice-Hall.

Finkel, Norman J. 1976. *Mental Illness and Health: Its Legacy, Tensions, and Changes.* New York: Macmillan.

Finkelhor, David. 1979. *Sexually Victimized Children.* New York: Free Press.

Finkelhor, David. 1985. Common Features of Family Abuse. In *Marriage and Family in a Changing Society.* J. M. Henslin, ed., 500–507. New York: Free Press.

Finkelhor, David and K. Yllo. 1983. *License to Rape: Sexual Violence against Wives.* New York: Holt, Rinehart & Winston.

Finsterbusch, Kurt and George McKenna. 1986. *Taking Sides: Clashing Views on Controversial Social Issues.* Guilford, CT: Dushkin.

Firestone, Shulamith. 1970. *The Dialectic of Sex: The Case of Feminist Revolution.* New York: William Morrow.

Fischer, David H. 1977. *Growing Old in America.* New York: Oxford University Press.

Fishburne, P. M., H. I. Abelson, and I. Cisin. 1980. *National Survey on Drug Abuse, 1979.* Rockville, MD: National Institute on Drug Abuse.

Fitzgerald, F. Scott. 1926. *All the Sad Young Men.* New York: Charles Scribner.

Ford, Clellan S. and Frank A. Beach. 1972. *Patterns of Sexual Behavior.* New York: Harper Colophon Books.

Form, William H. 1973. Auto Workers and Their Machines. *Social Forces* 52:1–15.

Fossett, Mark and Gary Swicegood. 1982. Rediscovering City Differences in Racial Occupational Inequality. *American Sociological Review* 47:681–689.

Foucault, M. 1965. *Madness and Civilization.* New York: Random House.

Fox, John W. 1985. Sex, Marital Status, and Age as Social Selection Factors in Recent Psychiatric Treatment. *Journal of Health and Social Behavior* 25:394–405.

Fox, Mary F. and Sharlene Hess-Biber. 1984. *Women At Work.* Palo Alto, CA: Mayfield.

Francke, Linda B. 1983. The Sons of Divorce. *New York Times Magazine,* May 22.

Frank, Jerome D. 1975. Evaluation of Psychiatric Treatment. In *Comprehensive Textbook of Psychiatry, II.* A. Freedman, H. Kaplan, and B. J. Sadock, eds., 2010–2014. Baltimore: Williams & Wilkins.

Franklin, Benjamin. 1977 (original, 1732-1757). *Poor Richard's Almanac.* New York: Rosenbach, Mus., and Lib.

Franks, Lucinda. 1985. A New Attack on Alcoholism. *New York Times Magazine,* October 20:46–48, 50, 61, 62.

Frazier, Nancy and Mary P. Sadker. 1973. *Sexism in School and Society.* New York: Harper & Row.

Freedman, Ronald and Bernard Berelson. 1974. The Human Population. In *The Human Population.* D. Flanagan et al., eds., 3–15. San Francisco: W. H. Freeman.

Freeman, Howard E. et al., eds. 1983. *Applied Sociology.* San Francisco: Jossey-Bass.

Freese, Lee. 1980. Formal Theorizing. In *Annual Review of Sociology, Vol. 6.* Alex Inkeles et al., eds., 187–212. Palo Alto, CA: Annual Reviews, Inc.

Freud, Sigmund. 1899. The Interpretation of Dreams. In *The Standard Edition of the Complete Works of Sigmund Freud.* J. Strachy, ed., Vols. 4 and 5. London: Hogarth Press.

Freud, Sigmund. 1937 (original, 1895). The Girl Who Couldn't Breathe. In Joseph Breuer and Sigmund Freud. *Studies in Hysteria.* New York: Nervous and Mental Disease Publishing Co.

Freud, Sigmund. 1905. Three Essays on the Theory of Sexuality. In *The Standard Edition of the Complete Psychological Works of Sigmund Freud.* J. Strachy, ed., Vol. 7. London: Hogarth Press.

Freud, Sigmund. 1953–1965 (original,1917). Mourning and Melancholia. In *The Standard Edition of the Complete Psychological Works of Sigmund Freud.* J. Strachy, ed., 247–252 (Vol. 4). London: Hogarth Press.

Freud, Sigmund. 1940. An Outline of Psychoanalysis. In *The Standard Edition of the Complete Psychological Works of Sigmund Freud.* J. Strachy, ed., Volume 23:148–150. London: Hogarth Press.

Frey, William H. 1987. Migration and the Depopulation of the Metropolis. *American Sociological Review* 52:240–257.

Friedan, Betty. 1963. *The Feminine Mystique.* New York: Dell.

Friedman, Milton. 1962. *Capitalism and Freedom.* Chicago: University of Chicago Press.

Friedman, M. and R.H. Rosenman. 1974. *Type A Behavior and Your Heart.* New York: Alfred A. Knopf.

Friedson, Eliot. 1970. *Profession of Medicine.* New York: Dodd, Mead.

Fuchs, Victor. 1967. Redefining Poverty and Redistributing Income. *The Public Interest* 8:88–95.

Fuller, Richard and R. Meyers. 1941a. Some Aspects of a Theory of Social Problems. *American Sociological Review* 6:24–32.

Fuller, Richard and R. Meyers. 1941b. The Natural History of a Social Problem. *American Sociological Review* 6:320–328.

Funch, Donna P. and James R. Marshall. 1984. Measuring Life Stress: Factors Affecting Fall-Off in the Reporting of Life Events. *Journal of Health and Social Behavior* 25:453–464.

Gaines, Harold, ed. 1982. *Urban Society.* Guilford, CT: Dushkin.

Galbraith, John K. 1976. *The Affluent Society.* New York: Houghton Mifflin.

Galbraith, John K. 1985. *New York Times* (Business Section), May 25.

Gallagher, Bernard J. 1980. *The Sociology of Mental Illness.* Englewood Cliffs, NJ: Prentice-Hall.

Galle, Omer and Walter Gove. 1978. Overcrowding, Isolation, and Human Behavior: Exploring the Extremes in Population Distribution. In *Social Demography.* K. Tauber and J. Sweet, eds., 95–132. New York: Academic Press.

Gans, Herbert J. 1972. The Positive Functions of Poverty. *American Journal of Sociology* 78:275–288.

Garfinkel, Harold. 1967. *Studies in Ethnomethodology.* Englewood Cliffs, NJ: Prentice-Hall.

Gattozzi, Antionette A. 1970. *Lithium in the Treatment of Mood Disorders.* Washington, DC: U.S. Government Printing Office.

Gelles, Richard J. 1982. Domestic Criminal Violence. In *Criminal Violence.* Marvin E. Wolfgang and Neil A. Weiner, eds., 201–235. Beverly Hills, CA: Sage Publications.

Gergen, Kenneth J., Martin S. Greenberg, and Richard H. Willis. 1980. *Social Exchange: Advances in Theory and Research.* New York: Plenum Press.

Gerth, H. H. and C. Wright Mills. 1958. *From Max Weber.* New York: Oxford University Press.

Gibbs, Jack P., ed. 1968. *Suicide.* New York: Harper & Row.

Gil, D. 1970. *Violence against Children.* Cambridge, MA: Harvard University Press.

Gilder, George. 1981. *Wealth and Poverty.* New York: Basic Books.

Gill, Derek. 1986. A National Health Service: Principles and Practice. In *The Sociology of Health and Illness.* P. Conrad and R. Kern, eds., 454–467. New York: St. Martin's Press.

Glaser, Daniel. 1978. *Crime in Our Changing Society.* New York: Holt.

Glassner, Barry and Bruce Berg. 1980. How Jews Avoid Alcohol Problems. *American Sociological Review* 45:647–663.

Glazer, Nathan. 1975. *Affirmative Action: Ethnic Inequality and Public Policy.* New York: Basic Books.

Glenn, W. A. 1974. *A Compendium of Recent Studies of Illegal Drug Use.* Research Triangle Park, NC: Research Triangle Institute.

Glick, Paul. 1979. The Future of the American Family. In *Current Population Reports.* Bureau of the Census. Washington, DC: U.S. Government Printing Office.

Glick, Paul C. 1981. A Demographic Picture of Black Families. In *Black Families.* Harriette P. McAdoo, ed., 106–126. Beverly Hills, CA: Sage Publications.

Glick, Paul C. 1984. How American Families Are Changing. *American Demographics,* January: 21–25.

Glick, Paul C. and Graham B. Spanier. 1980. Married and Unmarried Cohabitation in the United States. *Journal of Marriage and the Family* 42:19–30.

Glueck, Sheldon and Eleanor Glueck. 1956. *Physique and Delinquency.* New York: Harper & Row.

Goetting, Ann. 1981. Divorce Outcome Research: Issues and Perspectives. *Journal of Family Issues,* September:243–257.

Goffman, Erving. 1959. *The Presentation of Self In Everyday Life.* Garden City, NY: Doubleday Publishing.

Goffman, Erving. 1961. *Asylums.* Garden City, NY: Anchor Books.

Goffman, Erving. 1963. *Stigma.* Englewood Cliffs, NJ: Prentice-Hall.

Goldberg, Philip. 1968. Are Women Prejudiced against Women? *Transaction* 5 (April):28–30.

Goldberger, Leo and Shlomo Breznitz, eds. 1982. *Handbook of Stress: Theoretical and Clinical Aspects.* New York: Free Press.

Goldscheider, Calvin and Frances K. Goldscheider. 1987. Moving in and out of Marriage: What Do Young Adults Expect? *American Sociological Review* 52:278–285.

Goldscheider, Frances K. and Linda J. Waite. 1986. Sex Differences in the Entry into Marriage. *American Journal of Sociology* 92:91–109.

Goode, E. 1972. *Drugs in American Society.* New York: Alfred A. Knopf.

Goode, Erich. 1973. *The Drug Phenomenon: Social Aspects of Drug Taking.* Indianapolis: Bobbs-Merrill.

Goodman, Paul. 1960. *Growing Up Absurd.* New York: Random House.

Gordon, David M. 1981. Class and Economics of Crime. *Review of Radical Political Economics* 3:51–75.

Goring, Charles. 1972 (original, 1913). *The English Convict.* Montclair, NJ: Patterson Smith.

Gould, Roger L. 1978. *Transformations.* New York: Simon & Schuster.

Gove, Walter R. 1970. Societal Reaction as an Explanation of Mental Illness: An Evaluation. *American Sociological Review* 35:873–884.

Gove, Walter R. 1975. The Labelling Theory of Mental Illness: A Reply to Scheff. *American Sociological Review* 40:242–248.

Gove, Walter R. and Michael Hughes. 1983. *Overcrowding in the Household.* New York: Academic Press.

Graham, Hugh D. and T. R. Gurr. 1969. *Violence in America: Historical and Comparative Perspectives, Volume II.* Washington, DC: National Commission on the Causes and Prevention of Violence.

Greeley, Andrew. 1986. Building Coalitions. In *Taking Sides.* K. Finsterbusch and G. McKenna, eds., 216–220.

Green, Mark. 1982. *Winning Back America.* New York: Bantam.

Greenwald, Harold. 1970. *The Elegant Prostitute.* New York: Ballantine Books.

Greer, Germaine. 1971. *The Female Eunuch.* New York: Bantam.

Greider, W. 1981. The Education of David Stockman. *The Atlantic Monthly* December: 27–54.

Groth, A. Nicholas. 1979. *Men Who Rape: The Psychology of the Offender.* New York: Plenum.

Grusky, Oscar and Melvin Pollner. 1981. *The Sociology of Mental Illness.* New York: Holt, Rinehart & Winston.

Gusfield, Joseph R. 1963. Man's Institutions. In *Modern Sociology.* Alvin W. and Helen P. Gouldner, 482–544. New York: Harcourt Brace Jovanovich.

Gusfield, Joseph R. 1963. *Symbolic Crusade: Status Politics and the American Temperance Movement.* Urbana: University of Illinois Press.

Guttentag, Marcia and Paul F. Secord. 1983. *Too Many Women? The Sex Ratio Question.* Beverly Hills: Sage Publications.

Hafferty, Frederic W. 1986. Physician Oversupply as a Socially Constructed Reality. *Journal of Health and Social Behavior* 27:358–369.

Hagan, John. 1985. *Modern Criminology: Crime, Criminal Behavior and Its Control.* New York: McGraw-Hill.

Hagel, John. 1976. *Alternative Energy Strategies: Constraints and Opportunities.* New York: Praeger.

Hamilton, David L. 1981. *Cognitive Processes in Stereotyping and Intergroup Behavior.* Hillsdale, NJ: Lawrence Erlbaum Associates.

Hanlon, Michael. 1985. Famine: A Race against Time. *World Press Review* February: 37–42.

Hardin, Garrett. 1968. The Tragedy of the Commons. *Science* 162:1243–1248.

Harkabi, Yehoshafat. 1985. Guerrilla Warfare and Terrorism. In *On Terrorism and Combating Terrorism.* A. Merari, ed., 19–23. Frederick, MD: University Publications of America.

Harrington, Michael. 1963. *The Other America.* Baltimore: Penguin.

Harrington, Michael. 1984. *The New American Poverty.* New York: Holt, Rinehart & Winston.

Harris, Marvin. 1971. *Culture, Man, and Nature.* New York: Thomas Y. Crowell.

Harris, Marvin and Charles Wagley. 1985. *Culture, People and Nature.* New York: Harper & Row.

Harrison, Joseph. 1982. A Rationale for the Use of New Data in Psychopharmacology as Applied to Current Federal Narcotic Drug Legislation. *Contemporary Drug Problems* 11:21–38.

Hawkins, Darnell F. 1987. Beyond Anomalies: Rethinking the Conflict Perspective on Race and Criminal Punishment. *Social Forces* 65:719–745.

Hayden, Tom. 1980. *The American Future: New Visions Beyond Old Frontiers.* Boston: South End Press.

Heath, Anthony. 1976. *Rational Choice and Social Exchange: A Critique of Exchange Theory.* London: Cambridge University Press.

Heider, Fritz. 1967. *The Psychology of Interpersonal Relations.* New York: John Wiley & Sons.

Heitgerd, Janet L. and Robert J. Bursik, Jr. 1987. Extracommunity Dynamics and the Ecology of Delinquency. *American Journal of Sociology.* 92:775–787.

Hempel, C. G. 1959. Explanations and Laws. In *Theories of History.* P. Gardiner, ed. New York: Free Press.

Hendin, Herbert. 1982. *Suicide in America.* New York: W. W. Norton.

Hendricks, Jon and C. Davis Hendricks. 1981. *Aging in Mass Society: Myths and Realities.* Cambridge, MA: Winthrop Publishers.

Henry, Kenneth. 1978. *Social Problems.* Glenview, IL: Scott, Foresman.

Henslin, James M. 1985. *Marriage and Family in a Changing Society.* New York: Free Press.

Henslin, James M. and D. W. Light, Jr. 1983. *Social Problems.* New York: McGraw-Hill.

Hepburn, John R. 1977. The Impact of Police Interventions on Juvenile Delinquents. *Criminology* 15:225–262.

Hetherington, E. M. et al. 1978. The Aftermath of Divorce. In *Mother-Child, Father-Child Relations.* J. H. Stevens and M. Mathews, eds. Washington, DC: National Association for the Education of Young Children.

Hibbert, Christopher. 1963. *The Roots of Evil: A Social History of Crime and Punishment.* New York: Minerva.

Higgins, Paul C. and Richard R. Butler. 1982. *Understanding Deviance.* New York: McGraw-Hill.

Hills, Howard. 1977. Society's Outcasts. *Center Magazine* 10:3–5.

Hingsen, Rolf et al. 1981. *In Sickness and in Health.* St. Louis: C. V. Mosby.

Hirsch, Daniel et al. 1986. Protecting Reactors from Terrorists. *The Bulletin of Atomic Scientists* March.

Hirschman, Charles and Morrison G. Wong. 1986. The Extraordinary Educational Attainment of Asian-Americans. *Social Forces* 65:1–27.

Hite, Shere. 1976. *The Hite Report.* New York: Macmillan.

Hobbes, Thomas. 1982 (original, 1651). *Leviathan.* New York: Penguin Books.

Hochhauser, Mark. 1980. A Chronobiological Control Theory. In *Theories on Drug Abuse.* Dan J. Lettieri et al., eds., 262–268. Rockville, MD: National Institute on Drug Abuse.

Hodge, Robert W. et al. 1964. Occupational Prestige in the United States. *American Journal of Sociology* 70:286–302.

Hodge, Robert W. et al. 1966. A Comparative Study of Occupational Prestige. In *Class, Status, and Power.* R. Bendix and S. M. Lipset, eds., 309–321. New York: Free Press.

Hofstadter, Richard. 1955. *Social Darwinism in American Thought.* Boston: Beacon Press.

Hollingshead, August B. and Frederick C. Redlich. 1953. Social Stratification and Psychiatric Disorders. *American Sociological Review* 18:163–169.

Holmes, Thomas H. and Richard H. Rahe. 1967. The Social Readjustment Rating Scale. *Journal of Psychosomatic Research* 11:213–218.

Holtzman, David. 1986. Crack Shatters the Cocaine Myth. *Insight* magazine, June 23:48–49.

Homans, George C. 1950. *The Human Group.* New York: Harcourt Brace Jovanovich.

Homans, George C. 1962. *Sentiments and Activity.* New York: The Free Press of Glencoe.

Homans, George C. 1964. Bringing Men Back In. In *American Sociological Review* 29:809–818.

Homans, George C. 1974. *Social Behavior: Its Elementary Forms.* New York: Harcourt Brace Jovanovich.

Hook, Sidney. 1955. *Marx and the Marxists.* Princeton, NJ: Van Nostrand.

Hopkins, Jerence K. and Immanuel Wallerstein. 1982. *World-Systems Analysis: Theory and Methodology.* Beverly Hills: Sage Publications.

Horowitz, Irving L. 1982. Can Democracy Cope with Terrorism? In *Taking Sides.* K. Finsterbusch and G. McKenna, eds., 288–293. Guilford, CT: Dushkin.

Horowitz, Irving Louis. 1983. *C. Wright Mills: An American Utopian.* New York: Free Press.

Hotchner, A.E. 1966. *Papa Hemingway.* New York: Random House.

House, James S. 1974. Occupational Stress and Coronary Heart Disease: A Review. *Journal of Health and Social Behavior* 15:12–27.

House, James S. et al. 1986. Occupational Stress and Health Among Men and Women in the Tecumseh Community Health Study. *Journal of Health and Social Behavior* 27:62–77.

Howell, James C. 1985. Facts about Youth and Delinquency. In *Criminal Justice 85/86.* J. J. Sullivan and J. L. Victor, eds., 146–157. Guilford, CT: Dushkin.

Hubbert, M. King. 1974. *U.S. Energy Resources, A Review as of 1972.* Washington, DC: U.S. Government Printing Office.

Huff-Corzine, Lin, Jay Corzine, and David C. Moore. 1986. Southern Exposure: Deciphering the South's Influence on Homicide Rates. *Social Forces* 64:906–924.

Huffine, Carol L. and John A. Clausen. 1979. Madness and Work: Short- and Long-Term Effects of Mental Illness on Occupational Careers. *Social Forces* 57:1049–1062.

Hughes, Richard and Robert Brewin. 1979. *The Tranquilizing of America.* New York: Harcourt Brace Jovanovich.

Humphrey, Craig R. and Frederick R. Buttel. 1982. *Environment, Energy, and Society.* Belmont, CA: Wadsworth.

Humphrey, Derek and Ann Wickett. 1986. *The Right to Die.* New York: Harper & Row.

Humphreys, Laud. 1970. *Tearoom Trade: Impersonal Sex in Public Places.* Chicago: Aldine Publishing.

Hunt, Morton. 1974. *Sexual Behavior in the 1970s.* Chicago: Playboy Press.

Hurst, Charles. 1979. *The Anatomy of Social Inequality.* St. Louis: C. V. Mosby.

Hutt, Corinne. 1975. *Males and Females.* Baltimore: Penguin Books.

Huxley, Aldous. 1939. *Brave New World.* New York: Harper & Row.

Hyde, Janet S. 1982. *Understanding Human Sexuality.* New York: McGraw-Hill.

Ignatieff, Michael. 1978. *A Just Measure of Pain: The Penitentiary in the Industrial Revolution, 1750–1850.* New York: Pantheon Books.

Ihinger-Tallman, Marilyn. 1983. Sex Discrimination. In *Social Problems in American Society.* Melvin L. DeFleur, ed., 29. Boston: Houghton Mifflin.

Illich, Ivan. 1976. *Medical Nemesis: The Expropriation of Health.* New York: Pantheon Books.

Institute for Social Research. 1983. *ISR Newsletter* (see Associated Press, February 7, 1984). Ann Arbor, MI: University of Michigan.

Irving, John. 1978. *The World According to Garp.* New York: E. P. Dutton.

Jacobs, Jerry. 1982. *The Moral Justification of Suicide.* Springfield, IL: Charles C Thomas.

Jacobs, Jerry A. and Frank F. Furstenberg, Jr. 1986. Changing Places: Conjugal Careers and Women's Marital Mobility. *Social Forces* 64:714–732.

Jacobs, Paul. 1985. Keeping the Poor Poor. In *Crisis in American Institutions.* J. H. Skolnick and E. Currie, eds., 113–123. Boston: Little, Brown.

Jacobsen, Thorkild and Robert M. Adams. 1958. Salt and Silt in Ancient Mesopotamian Agriculture. *Science,* November 21:1251–1258.

Jellinek, E. M. 1960. *The Disease of Alcoholism.* Highland Park, NJ: Hillhouse Press.

Jencks, Christopher. 1979. *Who Gets Ahead? The Determinants of Economic Success in America.* New York: Basic Books.

Jensen, Arthur R. 1969. How Much Can We Boost I.Q. and Scholastic Achievement? *Environment, Heredity, and Intelligence.* Harvard Educational Review Reprint Series 2. Cambridge, MA.

Jensen, Arthur R. 1975. Race and Mental Ability. In *Racial Variation in Man.* F. J. Ebling, ed., 80–105. New York: John Wiley & Sons.

Johnson, Leslie, 1985. Frustration: The Mold of Judicial Philosophy. In *Criminal Justice 85/86.* J. J. Sullivan and J. L. Victor, eds., 206–211. Guilford, CT: Dushkin.

Johnston, Lloyd et al. 1981. *Student Drug Use in America, 1975–1981.* Rockville, MD: National Institute on Drug Abuse.

Jones, Barbara M., Linda L. Jenstrom, and Kee MacFarlane, eds. 1980. *Sexual Abuse of Children: Selected Readings.* Washington, DC: U.S. Department of Health and Human Services.

Jones, Coryl L. and Catherine S. Bell-Bolek. 1986. Kids and Drugs: Why, When, and What We Can Do About It? *Children Today* May/June: 5–10.

Julian, Joseph and William Kornblum. 1986. *Social Problems.* Englewood Cliffs, NJ: Prentice-Hall.

Jung, Carl G. 1963. *Memories, Dreams, and Reflections.* New York: Pantheon Books.

Jung, Carl G., ed. 1964. *Man and His Symbols.* Garden City, NY: Doubleday Publishing.

Jung, Carl G. 1968. *Analytical Psychology: Its Theory and Practice.* New York: Pantheon Books.

Justice Assistance News. Published ten times a year. Washington, DC: Bureau of Justice Statistics.

Kaiser, Robert G. 1985. Gimme Shelters—And Cut My Taxes. In *Crisis in American Institutions.* J. H. Skolnick and E. Currie, eds., 133–140. Boston: Little, Brown.

Kalleberg, Arne and Karyn A. Loscocco. 1983. Age, Values, and Rewards: Explaining Age Differences in Job Satisfaction. *American Sociological Review* 48:78–90.

Kallman, Franz J. 1952. Twin and Sibship Study of Overt Male Homosexuality. *American Journal of Human Genetics* 4:136–146.

Kandel, Denise B. 1980. Drugs and Drinking Behavior Among Youth. *Annual Review of Sociology* 6:235–285.

Kandel, Denise B. and Kazuo Yamaguchi. 1987. Job Mobility and Drug Use: An Event History Analysis. *American Journal of Sociology* (January) 92:836–878.

Kantner, Rosebeth M. 1984. *The Change Masters: Innovation and Entrepreneurship in the American Corporation.* New York: Simon & Schuster.

Kaplan, Harold I. et al., eds. 1980. *Comprehensive Textbook of Psychiatry.* Baltimore: Williams & Wilkins.

Kaplan, Howard B. et al. 1986. Escalation of Marijuana Use: Application of a General Theory of Deviant Behavior. *Journal of Health and Social Behavior* 27:44-61.

Karmen, Andrew. 1980. The Narcotics Problem: Views From the Left. In *Is America Possible?* H. Etzkowitz, ed. St. Paul, MN: West Publishing.

Karr, Rodney K. 1978. Homosexual Labeling and the Male Role. *Journal of Social Issues* 34:73–83.

Kastenbaum, Robert J. 1981. *Death, Society, and the Human Experience.* St. Louis: C. V. Mosby.

Kaufman, Irving R. 1982. Not Guilty by Reason of Insanity. The *New York Times Magazine* August 8:16.

Keegan, John and Joseph Darracott. 1981. *The Nature of War.* New York: Holt, Rinehart & Winston.

Keely, Michael C. et al. 1977. *The Labor Supply Effects and Costs of Alternative Negative Income Tax Programs.* Menlo Park, CA: SRI International.

Kelling, George et al. 1974. *The Kansas City Preventive Patrol Experiment.* Washington, DC: Police Foundation.

Kemeny, John G. and J. Laurie Snell. 1962. *Mathematical Models in the Social Sciences.* Waltham, MA: Blaisdell Publishing Co.

Kendall, Henry W. and Steven J. Nardis, eds. 1980. *Energy Strategies: Toward A Solar Future.* Cambridge, MA: Ballinger.

Kendell, R. E. 1975. *The Role of Diagnosis in Psychiatry.* Oxford, England: Blackwell Scientific Publications.

Kendell, R. E. et al. 1971. Diagnostic Criteria of American and British Psychiatrists. *Archives of General Psychiatry* 25:123–130.

Keniston, Kenneth. 1975. Prologue: Youth as a Stage of Life. In *Youth.* R. J. Havinghurst and P. H. Dreyer, eds. Chicago: University of Chicago Press.

Keniston, Kenneth. 1985. Working Mothers. In *Marriage and Family in a Changing Society.* J. M. Henslin, ed., 319–321. New York: Free Press.

Kerbo, Harold R. and Richard A. Shaffer. 1986. Unemployment and Protest in the United States, 1890–1940: A Methodological Critique and Research Note. *Social Forces* 64:1046–1056.

Kesey, Ken. 1962. *One Flew Over the Cuckoo's Nest.* New York: Viking Press.

Kessler, R. C., R. L. Brown and C. L. Broman. 1981. Sex Differences in Psychiatric Help-Seeking: Evidence from Four Large-Scale Surveys. *Journal of Health and Social Behavior* 22:49–64.

Kety, Seymour S. 1976. The Biological Roots of Schizophrenia. *Harvard Magazine* 78:20–26.

Kinsey, Alfred, Wardell B. Pomeroy, and Clyde E. Martin. 1948. *Sexual Behavior in the Human Male.* Philadelphia: W. B. Saunders.

Kinsey, Alfred C. et al. 1953. *Sexual Behavior in the Human Female.* Philadelphia: W. B. Saunders.

Kinsley, Michael. 1985. High On the Hog. In *Crisis in American Institutions.* J. H. Skolnick and E. Currie, eds., 124–132. Boston: Little, Brown.

Kirkpatrick, James. 1986. Len Bias. Columbia, S.C.: *The State News* (July 1).

Kittrie, Nicholas N. 1973. *The Right to Be Different: Deviance and Enforced Therapy.* Baltimore: Penguin Books.

Klausner, Samuel Z. 1968. *Why Men Take Chances: Studies in Stress-Seeking.* Garden City, NY: Doubleday Publishing.

Klein, Melanie. 1950 (original, 1924). The Child Who Couldn't Sleep. In *The Psychoanalysis of Children.* London: The Hogarth Press.

Klemke, Lloyd. 1978. Does Apprehension for Shoplifting Amplify or Terminate Shoplifting Activity? *Law and Society Review* 12:391–403.

Klineman et al. 1980. *The Cult That Died.* New York: G. P. Putnam's Sons.

Knowles, James C. 1973. The Rockefeller Financial Group. Warner Module Publications, Module 343.

Kollock, Peter, Philip Blumstein, and Pepper Schwartz. 1985. Sex and Power in Interaction. *American Sociological Review* 50:34–46.

Kornblum, William and Vernon Boggs. 1984. New Alternatives for Fighting Crime. *Social Policy,* Winter: 24–28.

Kotelchuck, David, ed. 1976. *Prognosis Negative: Crisis in the Health Care System.* New York: Vintage Books.

Kramer, Heinrich and James Springer. 1942 (original, 1669). *Malleus Maleficarum.* Translated by Montague Summers. New York: Dover.

Krauthammer, Charles. 1979. The Myth of Thomas Szasz. *New Republic,* December 22.

Kreps, Juanita M. 1979. Social Security in the Coming Decade: Questions for a Mature System. In *The Age of Aging.* Abraham Monk, ed., 328–343. Buffalo, NY: Prometheus Books.

Kristein, Marvin et al. 1977. Health Economics and Preventive Care. *Science* 195:457–462.

Krohe, James Jr. 1984. Can We Stop Acid Rain and Who Should Pay the Bill? *Across the Board,* February:15–25.

Kurian, George T. 1979. *The Book of World Rankings.* New York: New American Library.

Kutner, Nancy G. 1987. Issues in the Application of High Cost Medical Technology: The Case of Organ Transplantation. *Journal of Health and Social Behavior* 28:23–36.

La Bastille, Anne. 1986. The International Acid Test. *Sierra* May–June:51–55.

La Free, Gary D. 1980. The Effect of Sexual Stratification by Race on Official Reactions to Rape. *American Sociological Review* 45:842–854.

Land, Kenneth C. 1969. Principles of Path Analysis. In Edgar F. Borgotta (ed.). *Sociological Methodology, 1969.* San Francisco: Jossey-Bass.

Larson, Eric. 1981. Industry Examines Profit Prospects of Selling 'Cogeneration' Energy. *The Wall Street Journal,* February 19.

Lasch, Christopher. 1977. *Haven in a Heartless World: The Family Besieged.* New York: Basic Books.

Lauer, Jeanette and Robert Lauer. 1985. Marriages Made to Last. *Psychology Today,* June:22–26.

Lekachman, Robert. 1985. The Specter of Full Employment. In *Crisis in American Institutions.* J. H. Skolnick and E. Currie, eds., 74–79. Boston: Little, Brown.

Lemert, Edwin M. 1951. *Social Pathology.* New York: McGraw-Hill.

Lemert, Edwin M. 1972 (original, 1967). *Human Deviance, Social Problems, and Social Control.* Englewood Cliffs, NJ: Prentice-Hall.

Leming, Michael R. and George E. Dickinson. 1985. *Understanding Dying, Death, and Bereavement.* New York: Holt, Rinehart & Winston.

Lenski, Gerhard E. 1984 (original, 1966) *Power and Privilege: A Theory of Social Stratification.* New York: McGraw-Hill.

Lenski, Gerhard E. and Jean Lenski. 1987. *Human Societies: An Introduction to Macro-Sociology* (Fifth Edition). New York: McGraw-Hill.

Leontieff, Wassily W. 1985. The Distribution of Work and Income. In *Crisis in American Institutions.* J. H. Skolnick and E. Currie, eds., 346–353. Boston: Little, Brown.

Lerney, L. J. and F. H. Posey. 1979. *Comparative Effects of Energy Technologies on Employment.* Sacramento, CA: California Energy Commission.

Levi-Strauss, Claude. 1963. *Structural Anthropology.* New York: Basic Books.

Levine, Sol. 1987. The Changing Terrains in Medical Sociology: Emergent Concern with Quality of Life. *Journal of Health and Social Behavior* 28:1–6.

Levinson, Daniel J. 1978. *The Seasons of a Man's Life.* New York: Alfred A. Knopf.

Levit, K. R. et al. 1985. *Health Care Financing Review* (HCFA Pub. No. 03200). Washington, DC: U.S. Government Printing Office.

Levitan, Sar A. and Richard S. Belous. 1981. *What's Happening to the American Family?* Baltimore: Johns Hopkins.

Lewis, Oscar. 1961. *The Children of Sanchez: Autobiography of a Mexican Family.* New York: Random House.

Lewis, Oscar. 1966. Culture of Poverty. *Scientific American* 215:3–9.

Lieberson, Stanley. 1985. Stereotypes: Their Consequences for Race and Ethnic Interaction. In *Research in Race and Ethnic Relations.* C. B. Marrett and C. Leggon, eds., 113–137. Greenwich, CT: JAI Press, Inc.

Liebow, Elliot. 1967. *Tally's Corner.* Boston: Little, Brown.

Light, Judy A., Mary J. Crain, and Donald Fisher. 1976. Physician Assistant: A Profile of the Profession, 1976. *The PA Journal* 7:59-81.

Lin, Nan et al. 1985. The Buffering Effect of Social Support Subsequent to an Important Life Event. *Journal of Health and Social Behavior* 26:247–263.

Lindesmith, Alfred R. 1968. *Addiction and Opiates.* Chicago: Aldine Publishing.

Lindesmith, Alfred R. 1980. A General Theory of Addiction to Opiate-Type Drugs. In *Theories on Drug Abuse.* Dan J. Lettieri et al., eds., 34–37. Rockville, MD: National Institute on Drug Abuse.

Link, Bruce. 1983. The Reward System in Psychotherapy. *Journal of Health and Social Behavior* 24:61–69.

Link, Bruce G. and Francis T. Cullen. 1986. Contact with the Mentally Ill and Perceptions of How Dangerous They Are. *Journal of Health and Social Behavior* 27:289–302.

Link, Bruce G., Bruce P. Dohrenwend, and Andrew E. Skodol. 1986. Socioeconomic Status and Schizophrenia. *American Sociological Review* 51:242–258.

Linton, Ralph. 1936. *The Study of Man.* New York: Appleton-Century.

Lipschutz, Ronnie D. 1980. *Radioactive Waste: Politics, Technology, and Risk.* Cambridge, MA: Ballinger.

Lizotte, Alan J. 1978. Extra-Legal Factors in Chicago's Criminal Courts: Testing the Conflict Model of Criminal Justice. *Social Problems* 25:564–580.

Logan, John R. and Reid M. Golden. 1986. Change in Suburbs and Satellites. *American Sociological Review* 51:430–437.

Logue, John. 1981. Toward Industrial Democracy. *The Progressive* 45:44.

Lombroso-Ferrero, Gina. 1911 (original, 1876). *Criminal Man.* Montclair, NJ: Patterson-Smith.

London, Bruce. 1987. Structural Determinants of Third World Urban Change. *American Sociological Review* 52:28–43.

Lorber, Judith. 1980. Beyond Equality of the Sexes. In *Marriage and Family in a Changing Society.* J. M. Henslin, ed. New York: Free Press.

Lotz, Roy, Eric D. Poole, and Robert M. Regoli. 1985. *Juvenile Delinquency and Juvenile Justice.* New York: Random House.

Lovins, Amory B. and L. Hunter Lovins. 1980. *Energy/War: Breaking the Nuclear Link.* San Francisco: Friends of the Earth.

Lundberg, F. 1968. *The Rich and the Super-Rich.* New York: Bantam.

Luther, Jim. 1982. Reagan Wants Enter-Price Zone Plan to Aid Cities. *Associated Press,* January 27.

Maccoby, Eleanor E. and Carol N. Jacklin. 1974. *The Psychology of Sex Differences.* Stanford, CA: Stanford University Press.

Macionis, John J. 1987. *Sociology.* Englewood Cliffs, NJ: Prentice-Hall.

Macklin, Eleanor D. 1974. Cohabitation in College: Going Very Steady. *Psychology Today* 8(6):53–59.

Malinowski, B. 1962 (original, 1926). *Crime and Custom in Savage Society.* Paterson, NJ: Littlefield, Adams.

Malthus, Thomas. 1976 (original, 1798). *Essay on the Principle of Population.* New York: W. W. Norton.

Mann, Peggy. 1980. Marijuana: The Myth of Harmlessness Goes up in Smoke. *Saturday Evening Post* July/August.

Mansfield, Edwin. 1986. *Basic Statistics.* New York: W. W. Norton.

Maris, Ronald W. 1970. The Logical Adequacy of Homans' Social Theory. *American Sociological Review* 35:1069–1081.

Maris, Ronald W. 1971. Deviance as Therapy: The Paradox of the Self-Destructive Female. *Journal of Health and Social Behavior* 12:114–124.

Maris, Ronald W. 1971. Second Thoughts: Uses of Logic in Theory Construction. *American Sociological Review* 36:713–715.

Maris, Ronald W. 1972. Reply to Hamblin et al. *Journal of Health and Social Behavior* 13:106–109.

Maris, Ronald W. 1981. *Pathways to Suicide.* Baltimore: Johns Hopkins University Press.

Maris, Ronald W. 1985. The Adolescent Suicide Problem. *Suicide and Life-Threatening Behavior* 15:91–109.

Maris, Ronald W. 1986. Basic Issues in Suicide Prevention. *Suicide and Life-Threatening Behavior* 16:326–334.

Marrett, Cora B. and Cheryl Leggon. 1985. *Research in Race and Ethnic Relations, Volume 4.* Greenwich, CT: JAI Press.

Marshall, Thurgood. 1982. Is Affirmative Action Reverse Discrimination? In *Taking Sides.* Kurt Finsterbusch and George McKenna, eds., 214–221. Guilford, CT: Dushkin.

Martin, William R. 1980. Emerging Concepts Concerning Drug Abuse. In *Theories on Drug Abuse.* Dan J. Lettieri et al., eds., 278–285. Rockville, MD: National Institute on Drug Abuse.

Martinson, Robert. 1974. What Works?—Questions and Answers About Prison Reform. *The Public Interest* 35:22–54.

Marx, Karl. 1906 (original, 1867). *Capital: A Critique of Political Economy.* New York: Random House.

Marx, Karl and F. Engels. 1969 (original, 1848). *The Communist Manifesto.* Translated by Samuel Moore. Chicago: Henry Regnery.

Maslow, A. H. 1954. *Motivation and Personality.* New York: Harper & Row.

Maslow, A. H. 1963. Self-Actualizing People. In *The World of Psychology* (Vol. 2). G. B. Levitas, ed., 174. New York: George Braziller.

Massey, Douglas S. and B. Bitterman. 1985. Explaining the Paradox of Puerto Rican Segregation. *Social Forces* 64:306–331.

Masters, William H. and Virginia E. Johnson. 1985. In *Marriage and Family in a Changing Society*. J. M. Henslin, ed., 348–357. New York: Free Press.

Matsueda, Ross L. 1982. Testing Control Theory and Differential Association. *American Sociological Review* 47:489–504.

Matza, David and Henry Miller. 1976. Poverty and the Proletariat. In *Contemporary Social Problems*. R. K. Merton and R. Nisbet, eds., 639–674. New York: Harcourt Brace Jovanovich.

Mauer, David. 1974. *The American Confidence Man*. Springfield, IL: Charles C Thomas.

Mayhew, Bruce H. 1981. Structuralism versus Individualism, Part II. *Social Forces* 59:627–648.

Mayhew, Bruce H. and Paul T. Schollaert. 1980. The Concentration of Wealth: A Sociological Model. *Sociological Focus* 13:1–35.

Mayhew, Bruce H. and Roger L. Levinger. 1976. Size and the Density of Interaction in Human Aggregates. *American Journal of Sociology* 82:86–110.

Mayhew, Bruce H. and Roger L. Levinger. 1977. Conflicting Interpretations of Human Interaction. *American Journal of Sociology* 83:445–459.

McAuliffe, William E. 1975. Beyond Secondary Deviance: Negative Labelling and Its Effect on the Heroin Addict. In *The Labelling of Deviance*. Walter R. Gove, ed., 205–242. New York: Sage Publications.

McAuliffe, William E. and Robert A. Gordon. 1974. A Test of Lindesmith's Theory of Addiction: The Frequency of Euphoria Among Long-Term Addicts. *American Journal of Sociology* 79:795–840.

McAuliffe, William E. and Robert A. Gordon. 1980. Reinforcement and the Combination of Effects: Summary of a Theory of Opiate Addiction. In *Theories on Drug Abuse*. Dan J. Lettieri et al., eds., 137–141. Rockville, MD: National Institute on Drug Abuse.

McAuliffe, William E. et al. 1984. Psychoactive Drug Use by Young and Future Physicians. *Journal of Health and Social Behavior* 25:34–53.

McCaghy, Charles H. 1976. *Deviant Behavior: Crime, Conflict, and Interest Groups*. New York: Macmillan.

McClelland, D. C. et al. 1953. *The Achievement Motive*. New York: Appleton-Century-Crofts.

McClendon, McKee J. and Fred P. Pestello. 1983. Self-Interest and Public Policy Attitude Formation: Busing for School Desegregation. *Sociological Focus* (January): 1–12.

McCoy, Elin. 1985. Childhood Through the Ages. In *Marriage and Family in a Changing Society*. J. M. Henslin, ed., 386–394. New York: Free Press.

McDowall, David and Colin Loftin. 1986. Fiscal Politics and the Police: Detroit, 1928–1976. *Social Forces* 65:162–176.

McKeown, Thomas. 1977. *The Modern Rise of Population.* New York: Academic.

McKeown, Thomas. 1978. The Determinants of Health. *Human Nature.* 1–4:60–67.

McKeown, Thomas. 1980. *The Role of Medicine: Dream, Mirage, or Nemesis.* Princeton, NJ: Princeton University Press.

McLellan, David. 1973. *Karl Marx: His Life and Thought.* New York: Harper & Row.

McLemore, S. Dale and Richardo Romo. 1985. The Origins and Development of the Mexican American People. In *The Mexican American Experience.* de la Garza et al., eds., 3–32. Austin: University of Texas Press.

McNall, Scott G., ed. 1979. *Theoretical Perspectives in Sociology.* New York: St. Martin's Press.

McNamara, Robert S. and Hans A. Bethe. 1985. Reducing the Risk of Nuclear War. *Atlantic Monthly,* July: 32–36.

McPherson, J. Miller and Lynn Smith-Lovin. 1986. Sex Segregation in Voluntary Associations. *American Sociological Review* 51:61–79.

McRandle, James H. 1965. *The Track of the Wolf.* Evanston, IL: Northwestern University Press.

Mead, George H. 1934. *Mind, Self & Society.* Chicago: University of Chicago Press.

Mead, Margaret. 1928. The Role of the Individual in Samoan Culture. *Journal of the Royal Anthropological Institute* 58:481–495.

Mead, Margaret. 1935. *Sex and Temperament in Three Primitive Societies.* New York: Mentor Books.

Meadows, Donella H. et al. 1974. The Limits to Growth: A Report for the Club of Rome's Project on the Predicament of Mankind. New York: Universe.

Mechanic, David. 1971. England's National Health Insurance. *Journal of Health and Social Behavior* 12:18–29.

Mechanic, David. 1978. *Medical Sociology.* New York: Free Press.

Mechanic, David. 1979. *Future Issues in Health Care: Social Policy and the Rationalizing of Medical Services.* New York: Free Press.

Mechanic, David. 1980. *Mental Health and Social Policy.* Englewood Cliffs, NJ: Prentice-Hall.

Mechanic, David, ed. 1983. *Handbook of Health, Health Care, and the Health Professions.* New York: John Wiley & Sons.

Mednick, Sarnoff A. and Jan Volaka. 1980. Biology and Crime. In *Crime and Justice: An Annual Review of Research, Vol. II.* N. Morris and M. Tonry, eds., 85–158. Chicago: University of Chicago Press.

Mednick, Sarnoff A. and Karl O. Christiansen, eds. 1977. *Biosocial Bases of Criminal Behavior.* New York: Gardner Press.

Merari, Ariel. 1985. *On Terrorism and Combating Terrorism.* Frederick, MD: University Publications of America.

Merton, Robert K. 1938. Social Structure and Anomie. *American Sociological Review* 3:672–682.

Merton, Robert K. 1957 (revised, 1968). *Social Theory and Social Structure.* Glencoe, IL: Free Press.

Merton, Robert K. 1975. Structural Analysis in Sociology. In *Approaches to the Study of Social Structure,* P. M. Blau, ed., 21–52. New York: Free Press.

Merton, Robert K. and R. Nisbet, eds. 1976. *Contemporary Social Problems.* New York: Harcourt Brace Jovanovich.

Messner, Steven and Scott South. 1986. Economic Deprivation, Opportunity Structure and Robbery Victimization: Intra- and Interracial Patterns. *Social Forces* 64:975–991.

Meyer, Adolf. 1958. *Psychobiology: A Science of Man.* Springfield, IL: Charles C Thomas.

Meyer, David R. 1986. The World System of Cities: Relations Between International Financial Metropolises and South American Cities. *Social Forces* 64:553–581.

Meyers, Martha A. 1987. Economic Inequality and Discrimination in Sentencing. *Social Forces* 65:746–765.

Michels, Robert. 1962 (original, 1915). *Political Parties.* New York: Crowell-Collier.

Miethe, Terance, Mark C. Stafford, and J. Scott Long. 1987. Routine Activities, Lifestyle, and Victimization. *American Sociological Review* 52:184–194.

Milgram, S. 1963. Behavioral Study of Obedience. *Journal of Abnormal and Social Psychology* 67:376.

Miller, Walter B. 1958. Lower-Class Culture as a Generating Milieu of Gang Delinquency. *Journal of Social Issues* 14:5–19.

Miller, Walter B. 1975. *Violence By Youth Gangs as a Crime Problem in Major American Cities.* Washington, DC: U.S. Government Printing Office.

Mills, C. Wright. 1956. *The Power Elite.* New York: Oxford University Press.

Mills, C. Wright. 1959. *The Sociological Imagination.* New York: Oxford University Press.

Mirowsky, John. 1985. Depression and Marital Power: An Equity Model. *American Journal of Sociology* 91:557–592.

Mitford, Jessica. 1963. *The American Way of Death.* Greenwich, CT: Fawcett Publications.

Mohai, Paul. 1985. Public Concern and Elite Involvement in Environmental-Conservation Issues. *Social Science Quarterly* 66:820–838.

Molm, Linda D. 1985. Relative Effects of Individual Dependencies: Further Tests of the Relation Between Power Imbalance and Power Use. *Social Forces* 63:810–837.

Molm, Linda. 1986. Gender, Power, and Legitimation. *American Journal of Sociology* 91:1346–1386.

Molotch, Harvey L. and Deidra Boden. 1985. Talking Social Structure. *American Sociological Review* 50:273–287.

Monk, Abraham, ed. 1979. *The Age of Aging: A Reader in Social Gerontology.* Buffalo, NY: Prometheus Books.

Montemayor, R. 1982. The Relationship between Parent-Adolescent Conflict and Amount of Time Adolescents Spend with Parents, Peers, and Alone. *Child Development* 53:1512–1519.

Morgan, Patricia A. 1978. The Legislation of Drug Law: Economic Crisis and Social Control. *Journal of Drug Issues* 8:59.

Morris, Norval and Gordon Hawkins. 1970. *The Honest Politicians Guide to Crime Control.* Chicago: University of Chicago Press.

Morrison, Malcolm H. 1986. Work and Retirement in an Older Society. In *Our Aging Society.* Alan Pifer and Lydia Bronte, eds., 341–366. New York: W. W. Norton.

Mosca, Gaetano. 1939. *The Ruling Class.* New York: McGraw-Hill.

Mothner, Ira and Alan Weitz. 1984. How to Get Off Cocaine. *Rolling Stone* June 7: 29–31.

Mullen, Joan et al. 1980. *American Prisons and Jails, Volume I.* Washington, DC: National Institute of Justice.

Murray, Anne Firth. 1985. A Global Accounting. *Environment.* July–August:7–34.

Mussen, Paul, Mark R. Rosenzweig et al. 1977. *Psychology: An Introduction.* Lexington, MA: D. C. Heath.

Mussen, Paul Henry, John J. Conger, and Jerome Kagan. 1984. *Child Development and Personality.* New York: Harper & Row.

Nam, Charles B. and Susan Gustavus Philliber. 1984. *Population: A Basic Orientation.* Englewood Cliffs, NJ: Prentice-Hall.

Nathanson, Constance A. 1977. Sex, Illness, and Medical Care: A Review of Data, Theory, and Method. *Social Science and Medicine* 11.

National Institute of Mental Health. 1961. *Alcoholism.* Washington, DC: U.S. Government Printing Office.

National Wildlife Federation. 1986. Troubling Times with Toxics. February–March:29-36.

Neff, James A. and Baqar A. Husaini. 1985. Stress-Buffer Properties of Alcohol Consumption. *Journal of Health and Social Behavior* 26:207–221.

Nelson, Franklyn, Norman L. Farberow, and Douglas R. MacKinnon. 1978. The Certification of Suicide in Eleven Western States. *Suicide and Life-Threatening Behavior* 8:75–88.

Neugarten, Bernice L. and Dail A. Neugarten. 1986. Changing Meanings of Age in the Aging Society. In *Our Aging Society.* Alan Pifer and Lydia Bronte, eds., 33–52. New York: W. W. Norton.

Newman, Barbara M. and Philip R. Newman. 1975. *Development Through Life: A Psychosocial Approach.* Chicago, IL: Dorsey Press.

Newman, Robert G. 1979. Detoxification Treatment of Narcotic Addicts. In *Handbook on Drug Abuse.* DuPont et al., eds., 21–29. Rockville, MD: National Institute on Drug Abuse.

Newmann, Joy P. 1984. Sex Differences in Symptoms of Depression: Clinical Disorder or Normal Distress? *Journal of Health and Social Behavior* 25:136–159.

Newmann, Joy P. 1986. Gender, Life Strains, and Depression. *Journal of Health and Social Behavior* 27:161–178.

Newsweek. 1978. Too Much Surgery? April 10, pp. 65–67.

Norman, Robert Z. and Fred S. Roberts. 1972. A Measure of Relative Balance for Social Structures. In *Sociological Theories in Progress, Volume 2.* Joseph Berger, Morris Zelditch, Jr., and Bo Anderson, eds., 358–392. Boston: Houghton Mifflin.

Norton, Eleanor H. 1985. Restoring the Traditional Black Family. *New Times Magazine* June 2: 43–98.

O'Brian, Robert M. 1987. The Interracial Nature of Violent Crime: A Reexamination. *American Journal of Sociology* 92:817–835.

O'Hare, William. 1986. The Eight Myths About Poverty. *American Demographics* 22:26.

O'Kelley, Charlotte G. and Larry S. Carney. 1986. *Women and Men in Society.* Belmont, CA: Wadsworth Publishing Co.

O'Toole, Patricia. 1978. Casualties in the Classroom. *New York Times Magazine,* December 10:59, 78–90.

Ogburn, W. F. 1933. The Family and Its Functions. In *Recent Social Trends.* W. F. Ogburn, ed. New York: McGraw-Hill.

Ophuls, William. 1977. *Ecology and the Politics of Scarcity.* San Francisco: W. H. Freeman.

Orshanksky, Mollie. 1969. How Poverty Is Measured. *Monthly Labor Review* 92:37–41.

Paarlberg, Don. 1981. Enough Food? Sure, If We Don't Play It Dumb. In *Will There Be Enough Food?* J. Hayes, ed. Washington, DC: U.S. Department of Agriculture.

Palen, J. John. 1981. *The Urban World.* New York: McGraw-Hill.

Palmer, Stuart. 1960. *A Study of Murder.* New York: Thomas Y. Crowell.

Palmer, John L. and Stephanie G. Gould. 1986. In *Our Aging Society.* Alan Pifer and Lydia Bronte, eds., 367–390. New York: W. W. Norton.

Pampel, Fred C. and Kazuko Tanaka. 1986. Economic Development and Female Labor Force Participation: A Reconsideration. *Social Forces* 64:599–619.

Pample, Fred C. and Vijayan K. Pillai. 1986. Patterns and Determinants of Infant Mortality in Developed Nations, 1950–1975. *Demography* 23:525–542.

Parenti, Michael. 1978. *Power and the Powerless.* New York: St. Martin's Press.

Parenti, Michael. 1983. *Democracy for the Few.* New York: St. Martin's Press.

Parrillo, Vincent N., John Stimson, and Ardyth Stimson. 1985. *Contemporary Social Problems.* New York: John Wiley & Sons.

Parsons, Talcott. 1937. *The Structure of Social Action.* Glencoe, IL: Free Press.

Parsons, Talcott. 1951. *The Social System.* Glencoe, IL: Free Press.

Parsons, Talcott and R. F. Bales, eds. 1955. *Family, Socialization, and Interaction Process.* Glencoe, IL: Free Press.

Pasternak, Boris. 1958. *Doctor Zhivago.* New York: Pantheon.

Perkins, David V. 1982. The Assessment of Stress Using Life Events Scales. In *Handbook of Stress.* L. Goldberger and S. Breznitz, eds., 320–331. New York: Free Press.

Perry, Bruce. 1985. Neither White Nor Black. *Ethnic Groups* 6–4.

Pescosolido, Bernice A. and R. Mendelsohn. 1986. The Social Organization of Suicide Rates. *American Sociological Review* 51–1:80–100.

Peterson, Ruth and John Hagan. 1984. Changing Conceptions of Race and Sentencing Outcomes. *American Sociological Review* 49:56–70.

Peterson, William. 1975. *Population.* New York: Macmillan.

Phibbs, C. and R. Williams. 1981. Newborn Risk Factors and the Costs of Neonatal Intensive Care. *Pediatrics* 68:313–321.

Philliber, Susan G. 1986 (original edition, 1983). Population Change. In *Social Problems in American Society.* Melvin DeFleur, ed., 480–505. Boston: Houghton-Mifflin.

Phillips, David P. 1980. Airplane Accidents, Murder, and the Mass Media. *Social Forces* 58:1001–1024.

Phillips, David P. and Lundie L. Cartensen. 1986. Clustering of Teenage Suicides after Television News Stories about Suicide. *New England Journal of Medicine* 315:685–689.

Physicians' Desk Reference. 1987. Oradell, NJ: Medical Economics.

Piaget, Jean. 1952. *The Origins of Intelligence in Children.* New York: International Universities Press.

Pifer, Alan and Lydia Bronte, eds. 1986. *Our Aging Society: Paradox and Promise.* New York: W. W. Norton.

Piliavin, Irving et al. 1986. Crime Deterrence and Rational Choice. *American Sociological Review* 51:101–119.

Pines, Maya. 1985. Aggression: The Violence Within. *Science Digest,* July:36–39.

Pittman, David J., ed. 1967. *Alcoholism.* New York: Harper & Row.

Piven, Francis F. and Richard A. Cloward. 1985. The Relief of Welfare. In *Crisis in American Institutions.* J. H. Skolnick and E. Currie, eds., 428–446. Boston: Little, Brown.

Plath, Sylvia. 1971. *The Bell Jar.* New York: Bantam Books.

Pogrebin, Letty. 1985. *Family Politics.* New York: McGraw-Hill.

Poloma, Margaret M. 1979. *Contemporary Sociological Theory.* New York: Macmillan.

Population Reference Bureau. *1985 World Population Data Sheet.* Washington, DC: Population Reference Bureau.

Postel, Sandra. 1985. Managing Fresh Water Supplies. In *State of the World, 1985.* L. R. Brown, ed., 42–72. New York: W. W. Norton.

Postel, Sandra. 1985. Protecting Forests from Air Pollution and Acid Rain. In *State of the World, 1985.* L. R. Brown, ed., 97–123. New York: W. W. Norton.

Powers, Mary, ed. 1982. *Measures of SES: Current Issues.* Boulder, CO: Westview.

Prather, Jane E. 1980. The Mystic of Minor Tranquilizers. In *Use and Misuse of Benzodiazephines.* Senate Hearings, 438–458. Washington, DC: U.S. Government Printing Office.

Quadagno, Jill S. 1979. Paradigms in Evolutionary Theory. *American Sociological Review* 44:100–109.

Quadagno, Jill S. 1980. Sociobiology and Paradigms in Evolutionary Theory. *American Sociological Review* 45:159–162.

Queijo, J. 1984. The Paradox of Intimacy. *Bostonia Magazine,* July:21–25.

Quinney, Richard. 1976. *Criminology.* Boston: Little, Brown.

Rabinowitz, Peter M. 1981. *Talking Medicine: America's Doctors Tell Their Stories.* New York: W. W. Norton.

Radcliffe-Brown, A. R. 1952. *Structure and Function in Primitive Society.* Glencoe, IL: Free Press.

Rand, Ayn. 1943. *Fountainhead.* New York: New American Library.

Ray, Oakley. 1978. *Drugs, Society, and Human Behavior* (2d Edition). St. Louis: C. V. Mosby.

Reasons, Charles. 1975. The Politics of Drugs: An Inquiry in the Sociology of Social Problems. *Sociological Quarterly* 15:388.

Reik, Theodor. 1959 (original, 1925). The Unknown Murderer. In *The Compulsion To Confess.* New York: Farrar, Straus & Cudahy.

Reinhold, Robert. 1978. World Population Growth Slows. *New York Times,* November 20.

Reinhold, Robert. 1979. 50 Percent Rise in World Population Forecast by Year 2000. *New York Times,* February 25.

Reiss, Albert J., Jr. 1961. *Occupations and Social Status.* New York: Free Press.

Reiss, Albert J. and Albert D. Biderman. 1980. *Data-Sources on White-Collar Law Breaking.* Washington, DC: U.S. Department of Justice.

Reissman, Catherine K. 1986. Improving Health Experiences for Low Income Patients. In *The Sociology of Health and Illness.* P. Conrad and R. Kern, eds., 399–411. New York: St. Martin's Press.

Relman, Arnold S. 1986. The New Medical-Industrial Complex. In *The Sociology of Health and Illness.* P. Conrad and R. Kern, eds., 210–218. New York: St. Martin's Press.

Revelle, Roger. 1974. Food and Population. In *The Human Population.* D. Flanagan et al., eds., 119–130. San Francisco: W. H. Freeman.

Rice, Berkeley. 1977. The New Gangs of Chinatown. *Psychology Today,* May.

Rice, Berkeley. 1986. Fresh Water Shocks of the 1980s. *Across the Board* March:17–23.

Richman, Harold A. and Matthew W. Stagner. 1986. In *Our Aging Society.* Alan Pifer and Lydia Bronte, eds., 161–180. New York: W. W. Norton.

Ridgeway, Cecilia, Joseph Berger, and LeRoy Smith. 1985. Nonverbal Cues and Status: An Expectation States Approach. *American Journal of Sociology* 90:955–978.

Rienow, Robert and Leona Train Rienow. 1967. *Moment in the Sun.* New York: Ballantine Books.

Riley, Matilda W. and John W. Riley, Jr. 1986. Longevity and Social Structure: The Potential of the Added Years. In *Our Aging Society.* Alan Pifer and Lydia Bronte, eds., 53–78. New York: W. W. Norton.

Ritzer, George. 1986. Crime. In *Social Problems.* New York: Random House.

Roach, Jack L. and Janet K. Roach. 1980. Turmoil in Command of Politics: Organizing the Poor. *Sociological Quarterly* 21:259–270.

Robertson, Ian. 1980. *Social Problems.* New York: Random House.

Robins, Eli. 1981. *The Final Months.* New York: Oxford University Press.

Rodgers, G. B. 1979. Income and Income Inequality as Determinants of Mortality. *Population Studies* 33:343–351.

Roebuck, Julian B. and Raymond G. Kessler. 1972. *The Etiology of Alcoholism.* Springfield, IL: Charles C Thomas.

Roethlisberger, Fritz J. and William J. Dickson. 1939. *Management and the Worker.* Cambridge, MA: Harvard University Press.

Rollins, Boyd C. and Harold Feldman. 1970. Marital Satisfaction Over the Family Life Cycle. *Journal of Marriage and the Family* 32:21.

Rose, David J. et al. 1984. Reducing the Problem of Global Warming. *Technology Review,* May/June:48–57.

Rose, Thomas, ed. 1969. *Violence in America: A Historical and Contemporary Reader.* New York: Random House.

Rosenberg, Morris. 1979. *Conceiving the Self.* New York: Basic Books.

Rosenberg, Morris. 1984. A Symbolic Interactionist View of Psychosis. *Journal of Health and Social Behavior* 25:289–302.

Rosenberg, Morris and R. G. Simmons. 1972. *Black and White Self-Esteem: The Urban School Child.* Washington, DC: American Sociological Association.

Rosenfield, Sarah. 1984. Race Differences in Involuntary Hospitalization: Psychiatric vs. Labeling Perspectives. *Journal of Health and Social Behavior* 25:14–23.

Rosengren, William R. 1980. *Sociology of Medicine: Diversity, Conflict, and Change.* New York: Harper & Row.

Rosenhan, David L. 1973. On Being Sane in Insane Places. *Science* 179:250–258.

Rosenman, R. H. et al. 1975. Coronary Heart Disease in the Western Collaborative Group Study. *Journal of the American Medical Association* 233:872–877.

Rosenman, R. H. and M. A. Chesney. 1980. The Relationship of Type A Behavior Pattern to Coronary Heart Disease. *Activitas Nervosa Superior* 22:1–45.

Rosenman, Ray H. and Margaret A. Chesney. 1982. Stress, Type A Behavior, and Coronary Disease. In *Handbook of Stress,* L. Goldberger and S. Breznitz, eds., 547–565.

Ross, Catherine E. and Joan Huber. 1985. Hardship and Depression. *Journal of Health and Social Behavior* 26:312–327.

Ross, Christopher O. 1987. Organizational Dimensions of Metropolitan Dominance: Prominence in the Network of Corporate Control. *American Sociological Review* 52:258–267.

Rossi, Alice S. 1984. Gender and Parenthood. *American Sociological Review* 49:1–18.

Rossi, Alice. 1986. Sex and Gender in the Aging Society. In *Our Aging Society.* Alan Pifer and Lydia Bronte, eds., 111–140. New York: W. W. Norton.

Rothman, David J. 1971. *The Discovery of the Asylum.* Boston: Little, Brown.

Rousseau, Jean J. 1968. *Social Contract.* Baltimore: Penguin.

Roy, Alec. 1986. Alcoholism and Suicide. In *Biology of Suicide,* R.W. Maris, ed., 16:244–273. New York: The Guilford Press.

Rozak, Theodore. 1979. *Person/Planet: The Creative Disintegration of Industrial Society.* Garden City, NJ: Doubleday Publishing.

Rubenstein, David. 1981. The Neighborhood Movement. *The Progressive,* March.

Rubin, Beth A. 1986. Class Struggle American Style: Unions, Strikes, and Wages. *American Sociological Review* 51:618–634.

Rubin, Lillian B. 1976. *Worlds of Pain.* New York: Basic Books.

Rubington, Earl and Martin S. Weinberg. 1981. *The Study of Social Problems: Five Perspectives.* New York: Oxford University Press.

Rufolo, Anthony M. 1978. Housing Decay: Cause or Symptom of Urban Decline? *Business Review,* March/April.

Rushing, William A. 1985. The Supply of Physicians and Expenditures for Health Services with Implications for the Coming Physician Surplus. *Journal of Health and Social Behavior* 26:297–311.

Russell, Diana. 1982. *Rape in Marriage.* New York: Macmillan.

Rutledge, Gary L. and Susan L. Trevathian. 1982. Pollution Abatement and Control Expenditure, 1972–1980. *Survey of Current Business,* February.

Rutter, Laurence. 1981. Strategies for the Essential Community: Local Government in the Year 2000. *The Futurist,* June.

Ryan, William. 1981. *Equality.* New York: Pantheon.

Sagan, Carl et al. 1985. Nuclear Winter: The World-Wide Consequences of Nuclear War. In *Social Problems 86/87.* Leroy W. Barnes, ed., 164–169. Guilford, CT: Dushkin.

Sahlins, Marshall. 1976. *The Use and Abuse of Biology.* Ann Arbor: University of Michigan Press.

Sampson, Anthony. 1973. *The Sovereign State of ITT.* Greenwich, CT: Fawcett Books.

Samuelson, Jane. 1981. The Paths to Alcoholism: The Roads to Recovery. *Chicago Magazine,* September.

Sandell, Roland. 1982. Atomic Electrical Power: Pros and Cons. *Collage,* October:80–85.

Santrock, John W. 1984. *Adolescence.* Dubuque, IA: Wm. C. Brown Publishers.

Sargent, Alice G. 1985. *Beyond Sex Roles.* St. Paul, MN: West.

Satir, Virginia. 1972. *Peoplemaking.* Palo Alto, CA: Science and Behavior Books, Inc.

Saunders, C. 1977. Dying They Live: St. Christopher's Hospice. In *New Meanings of Death.* H. Feifel, ed. New York: McGraw-Hill.

Schaefer, Richard T. 1979. *Racial and Ethnic Groups.* Boston: Little, Brown.

Scheff, Thomas J. 1964. The Societal Reaction to Deviance. *Social Problems* 11:401–413.

Scheff, Thomas J. 1966. *Being Mentally Ill: A Sociological Theory.* Chicago: Aldine Publishing.

Scheff, Thomas J. 1968. The Role of the Mentally Ill and the Dynamics of Mental Disorder. In *The Mental Patient.* S. P. Spitzer and N. Denzin, eds., 10. New York: McGraw-Hill.

Scheff, Thomas J. 1974. The Labelling Theory of Mental Illness. *American Sociological Review* 39:444–452.

Scheff, Thomas J., ed. 1975. *Labelling Madness.* Englewood Cliffs, NJ: Prentice-Hall.

Schnaiberg, Allen. 1980. *The Environment: From Surplus to Scarcity.* New York: Oxford University Press.

Schneider, Joseph W. 1985. Social Problems Theory: The Constructionist View. In *Annual Review of Sociology, Vol. II.* Ralph H. Turner, ed., 209–230. Palo Alto, CA: Annual Reviews Inc.

Schnurnberger, Lynn E. 1984. When To Butt In. *Parents,* December:169–178.

Schrag, Clarence. 1967. Elements of Theoretical Analysis in Sociology. In *Sociological Theory: Inquiries and Paradigms.* L. Gross, ed., 220–253. New York: Harper & Row.

Schuman, Howard et al. 1985. *Racial Attitudes in America.* Cambridge: Harvard University Press.

Schur, Edwin M. 1971. *Labeling Deviant Behavior: Its Sociological Implications.* New York: Harper & Row.

Schur, Edwin M. 1979. *Interpreting Deviance: A Sociological Introduction.* New York: Harper & Row.

Schwartz, Edward. 1979. Neighborhoodism: A Conflict in Values. *Social Policy,* March/April.

Schwartz, Morris S. and Charlotte Green Schwartz. 1964. *Social Approaches to Mental Patient Care.* New York: Columbia University Press.

Schwartz, Richard. 1985. In *Modern Criminology.* J. Hagan, ed., 282. New York: McGraw-Hill.

Sebald, Hans. 1984. *Adolescence: A Social Psychological Analysis.* Englewood Cliffs, NJ: Prentice-Hall.

Selltiz, Claire et al. 1976. *Research Methods in Social Relations.* New York: Holt, Rinehart & Winston.

Selye, Hans. 1956. *The Stress of Life.* New York: McGraw-Hill.

Selye, Hans. 1982. History and Present Status of the Stress Concept. In *Handbook of Stress.* L. Goldberger and S. Breznitz, eds., 7–17. New York: Free Press.

Servin, Manuel P., ed. 1974. *An Awakened Minority: The Mexican Americans.* Beverly Hills, CA: Glencoe Press.

Shail, J. 1985. *Size Distribution of Income.* Washington, DC: The World Bank.

Sheldon, William H. 1949. *Varieties of Delinquent Youth: An Introduction to Constitutional Psychiatry.* New York: Harper & Row.

Shepelak, Norma J. and Duane F. Alwin. 1986. Beliefs About Inequality and Perception of Distributive Justice. *American Sociological Review* 51:30–46.

Shneidman, Edwin. 1985. *Definition of Suicide.* New York: John Wiley & Sons.

Shoemaker, Donald J. 1984. *Theories of Delinquency.* New York: Oxford University Press.

Siegel, Jacob S. and Cynthia M. Taeuber. 1986. Demographic Dimensions of An Aging Population. In *Our Aging Society.* Alan Pifer and Lydia Bronte, eds., 79–110. New York: W. W. Norton.

Siegler, Miriam and Humphrey Osmond. 1979. The Sick Role Revisited. In *Health, Illness, and Medicine.* Gary L. Albrecht and Paul C. Higgins, eds., 146–166. Chicago: Rand McNally.

Silberman, Charles. 1978. *Criminal Violence, Criminal Justice.* New York: Random House.

Simmel, Georg. 1936 (original 1902–1903). The Metropolis and Mental Life. In *Second Year Course in the Study of Contemporary Society.* Translated by E. Shils, 221–238. Chicago: University of Chicago Press.

Simmel, Georg. 1908. The Number of Members as Determining the Sociological Form of the Group. *American Journal of Sociology* 7(1):1–46.

Simon, David R. 1981. The Political Economy of Crime. In *Political Economy: A Critique of American Society.* S. G. McNall, ed. Glenview, IL: Scott, Foresman.

Simon, Eric J. 1980. Opiate Receptors and Their Implications for Drug Addiction. In *Theories on Drug Abuse.* Dan J. Lettieri et al., eds., 303. Rockville, MD: National Institute on Drug Abuse.

Simon, Julian L. 1981. *The Ultimate Resource.* Princeton, NJ: Princeton University Press.

Simpson, George E. and J. Milton Yinger. 1985 (Fifth Edition). *Racial and Cultural Minorities: An Analysis of Prejudice and Discrimination.* New York: Plenum Press.

Skinner, B. F. 1953. *Science and Human Behavior.* New York: Macmillan.

Skinner, B. F. 1971. *Beyond Freedom and Dignity.* New York: Alfred A. Knopf.

Skolnick, Arlene. 1985. The Paradox of Perfection. In *Marriage and Family in a Changing Society.* J. M. Henslin, ed., 59–66. New York: Free Press.

Skolnick, Jerome H. and E. Currie. 1985. *Crisis in American Institutions.* Boston: Little, Brown.

Slocum, Kenneth G. 1973. The Dying Lake. In *Environmental Decay in Its Historical Context.* R. Detweiler, J. N. Sutherland, and M. S. Werthman, eds. Glenview, IL: Scott, Foresman.

Smith, A. Wade. 1985. Social Class and Racial Cleavages on Major Social Indicators. In *Research in Race and Ethnic Relations.* C. B. Marrett and C. Leggon, eds., 33–66. Greenwich, CT: JAI Press.

Smith, Adam. 1937 (original, 1776). *The Wealth of Nations.* New York: Random House.

Smith, Edward A., J. Richard Udry, and Naomi M. Morris. 1985. Pubertal Development and Friends: a Biosocial Explanation of Adolescent Sexual Behavior. *Journal of Health and Social Behavior* 26:183–191.

Snell, Bradford. 1985. American Ground Transport. In *Crisis in American Institutions.* J. H. Skolnick and E. Currie, eds., 319–342. Boston: Little, Brown.

Snyder, Solomon H. 1975. Biology. In *A Handbook for the Study of Suicide.* Seymour Perlin, ed., 113–130. New York: Oxford University Press.

Snyder, Solomon. 1980. *Biological Aspects of Mental Disorder.* New York: Oxford University Press.

Sobell, M. B. and L. C. Sobell. 1973. Alcoholics Treated by Individualized Behavior Therapy: One-Year Treatment Outcome. *Behavior Research and Therapy* 11:599–618.

Solaun, Mauricio and E. Velez. 1985. Racial Terminology and Discriminatory Integration in Latin America. In *Research in Race and Ethnic Relations.* C. B. Marrett and C. Leggon, eds., 139–160. Greenwich, CT: JAI Press.

Solomon, Jeanne and Dan Rather. 1980. The Kyshtym Disaster. Segment of "60 Minutes," November 9.

Sorensen, Glorian et al. 1985. Sex Differences in the Relationship between Work and Health: The Minnesota Heart Survey. *Journal of Health and Social Behavior* 26:379–394.

Sorokin, Pitirim. 1957 (original volumes, 1937–1941). *Social & Cultural Dynamics.* Boston: Porter Sargent.

Sourcebook of Criminal Justice Statistics. Washington, DC: U.S. Bureau of Justice Statistics.

South, Scott J. and Glenna Spitze. 1986. Determinants of Divorce over the Marital Lifecourse. *American Sociological Review* 51:583–589.

South, Scott J. et al. 1982. Social Structure and Intergroup Interaction: Men and Women in the Federal Bureaucracy. *American Sociological Review* 47:187–206.

Spaeth, Joe L. 1985. Job Power and Earnings. *American Sociological Review* 50:603–617.

Spector, Malcolm, and J. I. Kitsuse. 1977 (Reprinted, 1987). *Constructing Social Problems.* Menlo Park, CA: Benjamin/Cummings Publishing.

Spencer, Herbert. 1904. *Social Statics.* New York: Appleton-Century-Crofts.

Spitzer, Steven. 1975. Toward a Marxian Theory of Deviance. *Social Problems* 22:638–651.

Srole, Leo et al. 1975. *Mental Health in the Metropolis: the Midtown Manhattan Study* (Revised Edition). New York: Harper & Row.

Stahara, John M. 1987. Suburban Socioeconomic Status Change: A Comparison of Models, 1950–1980. *American Sociological Review* 52:268–277.

Stanfield, John H. 1985. Theoretical and Ideological Barriers to the Study of Race-Making. In *Research in Race and Ethnic Relations.* C. B. Marrett and C. Leggon, eds., 161–182. Greenwich, CT: JAI Press.

Starr, Paul. 1982. *The Social Transformation of American Medicine.* New York: Basic Books.

Statistical Abstract of the United States. 1985, 1986, 1987. Washington, DC: U.S. Bureau of the Census.

Stein, Peter J. 1985. The Voluntary Singles. In *Marriage and Family in a Changing Society.* J. M. Henslin, ed., 245–251. New York: Free Press.

Steiner, Claude. 1974. Radical Psychiatry. In *Is America Possible?* Henry Etzkowitz, ed., 191–195. St. Paul, MN: West Publishing.

Steinhardt, Peter. 1983. The Edge Gets Thinner. *Audobon,* November:94–126.

Sterling, Claire. 1981. *The Terror Network.* New York: Holt, Rinehardt & Winston.

Stern, Paul C. and Gerald T. Gardner. 1981. Psychological Research and the Energy Problem. *American Psychologist* 36:340–341.

Sterns, Linda B. and John R. Logan. 1986. The Racial Structuring of the Housing Market and Segregation in Suburban Areas. *Social Forces* 65:28–42.

Stobaugh, Robert and Daniel Yergin. 1982. *Energy Future.* New York: Vintage Books.

Stockman, David. 1985. Economic Crisis Ahead. *Fortune* September 2:68–71.

Stott, Dennis. 1982. *Delinquency.* New York: S. P. Medical & Scientific Books.

Stoyva, Johann. 1981. Learning Principles, Biofeedback, and Behavioral Medicine. In *Understanding Human Behavior in Health and Illness.* R. Simons and H. Pardes, eds., 552–562. Baltimore: Williams & Wilkins.

Straus, Murray A., Richard J. Gelles, and Suzanne K. Steinmetz. 1980. *Behind Closed Doors: Violence in the American Family.* New York: Doubleday Anchor.

Strauss, Robert. 1976. Alcoholism and Problem Drinking. In *Contemporary Social Problems.* R. Merton and R. Nisbet, eds., 193. New York: Harcourt Brace Jovanovich.

Strauss, Robert. 1984. The Need to Drink Too Much. *Journal of Drug Issues* 14(1):125–136.

Summer, William Graham. 1960 (original, 1906). *Folkways.* New York: Dover Publications.

Sussman, Marvin B., Donna Vanderwyst, and Gwendolyn K. Williams. 1979. Will You Still Need Me, Will You Still Feed Me, When I'm 64? In *The Age of Aging.* Abraham Monk, ed., 303–311. Buffalo, NY: Prometheus Books.

Sutherland, Edwin H. 1937. *The Professional Thief.* Chicago: University of Chicago Press.

Sutherland, Edwin H. 1949 (uncut version, 1983). *White-Collar Crime.* New York: Holt.

Sutherland, Edwin H. and Donald R. Cressey. 1978. *Criminology.* Philadelphia: Lippincott.

Szasz, Thomas S. 1961. *The Myth of Mental Illness.* New York: Harper & Row.

Szasz, Thomas S. 1970. *The Manufacture of Madness.* New York: Harper & Row.

Szasz, Thomas S. 1975. *Ceremonial Chemistry: The Ritual Persecution of Drugs, Addicts, and Pushers.* Garden City, NY: Doubleday/Anchor.

Szasz, Thomas S. 1978. Nobody Should Decide Who Goes to the Mental Hospital. *Coevolution Quarterly,* Summer:59–62.

Szasz, Thomas S. 1985. Suicide: What Is the Clinician's Responsibility? Unpublished speech presented at Harvard University, Department of Continuing Education. Cambridge, MA.

Taber, Clarence W. 1970. *Taber's Cyclopedic Medical Dictionary.* Philadelphia: F. A. Davis Co.

Taggart, Harriett T. and Kevin W. Smith. 1981. Redlining: An Assessment of the Evidence of Disinvestment in Metropolitan Boston. *Urban Affairs Quarterly* 17:99–107.

Tanne, Janice H. 1985. The Last Word on Avoiding AIDS. *New York* October 7:28–34.

Tanney, Bryan L. 1986. Electroconvulsive Therapy and Suicide. In *Biology of Suicide.* R. W. Maris, ed., 198–222. New York: The Guilford Press.

Tavris, Carol and Carole Offir. 1977. *The Longest War: Sex Differences in Perspective.* New York: Harcourt Brace Jovanovich.

Taylor, Patricia A. 1987. On Honors and the Reproduction of Inequality. *American Sociological Review* 52:143–154.

Taylor, Stuart, Jr. 1983. Strict Penalties for Criminals: Pendulum of Feeling Swings. *New York Times,* December 13.

Terkel, Studs. 1974. *Working.* New York: Pantheon.

Thibaut, John W. 1950. An Experimental Study of the Cohesiveness of Underprivileged Groups. *Human Relations* 3:251–278.

Thio, Alex. 1978. *Deviant Behavior.* Boston: Houghton Mifflin.

Thomas, William I. and Florian Znaniecki. 1918–1920. *The Polish Peasant in Europe and America, 5 Volumes.* Boston: Richard Badger.

Thomas, W. I. 1923. *The Unadjusted Girl.* Boston: Little, Brown.

Thompson, Maxine S. 1986. The Influence of Supportive Relations on the Psychological Well-Being of Teenage Mothers. *Social Forces* 64:1006–1024.

Thornton, Arland and Deborah Freedman. 1982. Changing Attitudes Toward Marriage and Single Life. *Family Planning Perspectives* 14.

Thurow, Lester C. 1980. How to Wreck the Economy. *New York Review* May 14:3–8.

Thurow, Lester C. 1980. *The Zero-Sum Society.* New York: Basic Books.

Tickameyer, Ann R. 1981. Wealth and Power: A Comparison of Men and Women in the Property Elite. *Social Forces* 60:463–481.

Tierney, John. 1986. Why Star Wars is Not Like the Manhattan Project. In *Social Problems 87/88.* L. W. Barnes, ed., 177–181. Guilford, CT: Dushkin.

Toffler, Alvin. 1970. *Future Shock.* New York: Random House.

Townsend, John M. 1976. Self-Concept and the Institutionalization of Mental Patients: An Overview and Critique. *Journal of Health and Social Behavior* 17:263–271.

Townsend, John M. 1978. *Cultural Conceptions and Mental Illness: A Comparison of Germany and America.* Chicago: University of Chicago Press.

Trafford, Abigail and Stanley Wellborn. 1986. Stark Fallout from Chernobyl. *U.S. News & World Report* May 12:18–21.

Trice, Harrison M. 1984. Alcoholism In America Revisited. *Journal of Drug Issues* 14(1):109–123.

Troyer, Ronald J. and Gerald E. Markle. 1984. Coffee Drinking: An Emerging Social Problem. *Social Problems* 31:403–416.

Tsuang, Ming T. and Randall Vandermey. 1980. *Genes and the Mind: Inheritance of Mental Illness.* New York: Oxford University Press.

Turner, Jonathan H. 1986. *The Structure of Sociological Theory.* Chicago, IL: Dorsey Press.

Turner, J. H. and C. E. Starnes. 1976. *Inequality: Privilege & Poverty in America.* Pacific Palisades, CA: Goodyear.

Twaddle, Andrew C. 1974. The Concept of Health Status. *Social Science and Medicine* 8:29.

Tylor, Edward B. 1871. *Primitive Culture.* London: J. Murray.

Unesco Courier. 1985. The World's Urban Explosion. March:24–29.

Uniform Crime Reports for the U.S. 1986. Washington, DC: U.S. Government Printing Office.

United Nations. 1986. *Demographic Yearbook, 1984.* New York: Publishing Service of the United Nations.

Unseem, Michael and Jerome Karabel. 1986. Pathways to Top Corporate Management. *American Sociological Review* 51:184–200.

Updike, John. 1960. *Rabbit Run.* New York: Alfred A. Knopf.

Updike, John. 1981. *Rabbit Is Rich.* New York: Alfred A. Knopf.

Urquhart, John. 1982. Canada to Propose to U.S. That Emissions of Acid Gases to be Cut 50 Percent in Next Decade. *The Wall Street Journal,* February 24.

U.S. Bureau of the Census. 1985. *Persons of Spanish Origin.* Current Population Reports, Series P–20, Population Characteristics #403. Washington, DC: U.S. Government Printing Office.

U.S. Bureau of the Census, *Characteristics of the Population, 1980, Volume I, Part I.* 1983. Washington, DC: U.S. Government Printing Office.

U.S. Department of Health and Human Services. 1985. *Health, United States, 1985.* Hyattsville, MD: National Center for Health Statistics.

U.S. Department of Health, Education, & Welfare. 1978. *President's Commission on Mental Health, Vol. II.* Washington, DC: U.S. Government Printing Office.

U.S. Department of Health, Education, and Welfare. 1978. *Third Special Report for the U.S. Congress on Alcohol and Health,* Washington, DC: U.S. Government Printing Office.

U.S. Monthly Vital Statistics Report. Hyattsville, MD: National Center for Health Statistics, U.S. Department of Health and Human Services.

U.S. National Institute of Mental Health, 1985. *Mental Health, United States, 1985.* Rockville, MD: U.S. Government Printing Office.

U.S. News & World Report. 1983. Soaring Hospital Costs. August 22:39.

Usdin, E. and D. Effron. 1972. *Psychotropic Drugs and Related Compounds.* Washington, DC: U.S. Government Printing Office.

Vaillant, George E. 1977. *Adaptations to Life.* Boston: Little, Brown.

van den Berghe, Pierre L. 1978. *Man in Society: a Biosocial View.* New York: Elsevier.

van den Haag, Ernest. 1975. *Punishing Criminals: Concerning an Old and Very Painful Question.* New York: Basic Books.

Veroff, Joseph, Richard A. Kulka, and Elizabeth Douvan. 1981. *Mental Health in America.* New York: Basic Books.

Vetter, Harold J. and Ira J. Silverman. 1986. Crime and Delinquency. In *Social Problems in American Society.* M. DeFleur, ed., 30–61. New York: Houghton Mifflin.

Wacquant, Loic. 1985. Heuristic Models in Marxian Theory. *Social Forces* 64:17–45.

Waddington, Conrad H. 1978. *The Man-Made Future.* New York: St. Martin's Press.

Wagenfeld, Morton O. and Stanley S. Robin. 1976. Boundary Busting in the Role of the Community Mental Health Worker. *Journal of Health and Social Behavior* 17:112–222.

Wagenzar, Alexander C. 1982. Public Policy Effects on Alcohol Consumption in Maine and New Hampshire: 1970–1980. *Contemporary Drug Problems* 11:3–20.

Waite, Linda J., Frances K. Goldscheider, and Christina Witsberger. 1986. Nonfamily Living and the Erosion of Traditional Family Orientations among Young Adults. *American Sociological Review* 51:541–554.

Waite, Linda J., Gus Haggstrom, and David E. Kanonse. 1986. The Effects of Parenthood on the Career Orientation and Job Characteristics of Young Adults. *Social Forces* 65:43–73.

Waldron, Ingrid. 1986. Why Do Women Live Longer Than Men? In *The Sociology of Health and Illness.* P. Conrad and R. Kern, eds., 34–44. New York: St. Martin's Press.

Walker, Samuel. 1985. *Sense and Nonsense About Crime.* Monterery, CA: Brooks/Cole Publishing.

Walklet, Donn C. 1979. The Problems and Pitfalls of Predictability. *Public Utilities Fortnightly,* August 2:11–14.

Wallace, Robert A. et al. 1981. *Biology: The Science of Life.* Glencoe, IL: Scott, Foresman.

Waller, W. W. and R. Hill. 1951. *The Family: A Dynamic Interpretation.* New York: Dryden Press.

Wallerstein, Judith S. and J. B. Kelly. 1985. Effects of Parental Divorce. In *Marriage and Family in a Changing Society.* J. M. Henslin, ed., 440–452. New York: Free Press.

Wallis, Claudia. 1985. Children Having Children. *Time,* December 9:78–90.

Walters, Robert and Martha Angle. 1979. Enterprise Zones Worth American Exploration. *Alton Telegraph,* September 29.

Walton, John. 1986. *Sociology and Critical Inquiry.* Chicago: Dorsey Press.

Wambaugh, Joseph. 1981. *The Glitter Dome.* New York: Bantam.

Wantz, Molly S. and John E. Gay. 1981. *The Aging Process: A Health Perspective.* Cambridge, MA: Winthrop Publishers.

Warner, W. Lloyd et al. 1949. *Social Class in America.* Chicago: Science Research.

Wayne, Edward A. 1986. Will the Young Support the Old? In *Our Aging Society.* Alan Pifer and Lydia Bronte, eds., 243–262. New York: W. W. Norton.

Weber, Max. 1925 (2d Edition). *Wirtschaft und Gesellschaft.* Tubingen: J. C. B. Mohr.

Weber, Max. 1947 (original, 1922). *The Theory of Social and Economic Organization.* Translated by A. M. Henderson and T. Parsons. New York: Oxford University Press.

Weinstein, Raymond M. 1979. Patient Attitudes toward Mental Hospitalization: A Review of Quantitative Research. *Journal of Health and Social Behavior* 20:237–258.

Weinstein, R. M. 1983. Labeling Theory and the Attitudes of Mental Patients: A Review. *Journal of Health and Social Behavior* 24:70–84.

Weir, David and Mark Shapiro. 1980. The Circle of Poison. *The Nation,* November 15:118–121.

Weir, David and Mark Shapiro. 1985. The Circle of Poison. In *Environment.* J. Allen, ed., 118–121. Guilford, CT: Dushkin.

Weiss, Robert. 1975. *Marital Separation.* New York: Basic Books.

Weiss, Robert S., Edwin Harwood, and David Riesman. 1976. The World of Work. In *Contemporary Social Problems.* R. K. Merton and R. Nisbet, eds., 605–637. New York: Harcourt Brace Jovanovich.

Weitz, Shirley. 1977. *Sex Roles: Biological, Psychological, and Social Foundations.* New York: Oxford University Press.

Weitzman, Lenore J., Deborah Eifler, Elizabeth Hokada, and Catherine Ross. 1972. Sex Role Socialization in Picture Books for Pre-School Children. *American Journal of Sociology* 77:1125–1150.

Werkmeister, W. H. 1959. Theory Construction and the Problem of Objectivity. In *Symposium on Sociological Theory.* Llewellyn Gross, ed., 483–508. Evanston, IL: Row, Peterson.

Westhoff, Charles F. and Elise F. Jones. 1979. The End of Catholic Fertility. *Demography* 16:20–217.

Weston, Louise C., ed. 1979. *Social Problems Courses: A Set of Syllabi and Related Materials.* Washington, DC: American Sociological Association.

Wethington, Elaine and Ronald C. Kessler. 1986. Perceived Support, Received Support, and Adjustment to Stressful Life Events. *Journal of Health and Social Behavior* 27:78–89.

Wheaton, Blair. 1983. Stress, Personal Coping Resources, and Psychiatric Symptoms: An Investigation of Interactive Models. *Journal of Health and Social Behavior* 24:208–229.

Wheeler, Stanton and M. Lewis Rothman. 1982. The Organization as Weapon in White-Collar Crime. *Michigan Law Review* 80:1403–1426.

Whyte, William F. 1943. *Street Corner Society.* Chicago: University of Chicago Press.

Williams, Robin M., Jr. 1951. *American Society: a Sociological Interpretation.* New York: Alfred A. Knopf.

Williams, Roger M. 1977. Facelift for Detroit. *Saturday Review,* May 14.

Williamson, John B. et al. 1982. *The Research Craft: An Introduction to Social Research Methods.* Boston: Little, Brown.

Willie, Charles V. and Susan L. Greenblatt. 1978. Four Classic Studies of Power Relationships in Black Families. *Journal of Marriage and the Family* (Nov.):691–693.

Wilsher, Peter and Rosemary Righter. 1975. *The Exploding Cities.* New York: Times Books.

Wilson, Edward O. 1975. *Sociobiology: The New Synthesis.* Cambridge, MA: Harvard University Press.

Wilson, James Q. 1983. *Thinking About Crime.* New York: Basic Books.

Wilson, John. 1983. *Social Theory.* Englewood Cliffs, NJ: Prentice-Hall.

Wilson, William J. 1978. *The Declining Significance of Race: Blacks and Changing American Institutions.* Chicago: University of Chicago Press.

Winder, David. 1984. The World's Shrinking Forests. *The Christian Science Monitor,* January 10.

Wirth, Louis. 1945. The Problem of Minority Groups. In *The Science of Man in the World of Crisis.* Ralph Linton, ed., 347–372. New York: Columbia University Press.

Witkin, Herman A. et al. 1976. Criminality in XYY and XXY Men. *Science.* 193:547–555.

Wittig, M. 1980. One Is Not Born a Woman. *Feminist Issues* 1:1103–1111.

Wittgenstein, Ludwig. 1953. *Philosophical Investigations.* New York: Macmillan.

Wolf, Charles. 1986 (original edition, 1983). Energy. In *Social Problems in American Society,* M. DeFleur, ed., 508–535. Boston: Houghton Mifflin.

Wolfe, Linda. 1981. *Women and Sex in the 80s: The Cosmo Report.* New York: Bantam.

Wolff, Charlotte. 1971. *Love Between Women.* New York: Harper & Row.

Wolfgang, Marvin. 1981. Testimony, U.S. Congress, Senate, Committee on the Judiciary. Hearings on *Violent Juvenile Crime.* Washington, DC: U.S. Government Printing Office.

Wrong, Dennis. 1979. *Power: Its Forms, Bases, and Uses.* New York: Harper & Row.

Wonnacutt, Paul and Ronald Wonnacutt. 1982. *Economics.* New York: McGraw-Hill.

Woodward, Bob. 1984. *Wired: The Short Life and Fast Times of John Belushi.* New York: Simon & Schuster.

Yahraes, H. 1979. Physical Violence in Families. In *Families Today.* E. Corfman, ed. Washington, DC: U.S. Government Printing Office.

Yergin, Daniel. 1982. The Agenda after Reagan: Energy. *New Republic,* March 31.

Yerkes, Robert M., ed. 1921. Psychological Examining in the U.S. Army. *Memoirs National Academy of Science* 15. Washington, DC: National Academy of Science.

Zangwill, Israel. 1909. *The Melting Pot: Drama in Four Acts.* New York: Macmillan.

Zawitz, Marianne W., ed. 1983. *Report to the Nation on Crime and Justice.* Rockville, MD: Bureau of Justice Statistics.

Zborowski, Mark. 1952. Cultural Components in Response to Pain. *Journal of Social Issues* 8:16–30.

Zeitlin, Maurice. 1978. Who Owns America? The Same Old Gang. *The Progressive* 42 (June):15.

Zelnick, M. and J. Kantner. 1980. First Pregnancy in Women 15–19. In *Adolescent Behavior and Society.* R. Muss, ed. New York: Random House.

Zimbardo, P. 1970. In *Nebraska Symposium on Motivation,* W. J. Arnold and D. Levine, eds. Lincoln: University of Nebraska Press.

Zinn, Maxine Baca. 1986. Sex Roles and Sexism. In *Social Problems.* D. Stanley Eitzen, ed., 236–285. Boston, MA: Allyn & Bacon.

Zitrin, A. et al. 1976. Crime and Violence among Mental Patients. *American Journal of Psychiatry* 133:142–149.

Zola, Irving K. 1979. Culture and Symptoms, An Analysis of Patients Presenting Complaints. In *Health, Illness, and Medicine.* Gary L. Albrecht and Paul C. Higgins, eds., 41–62. Chicago: Rand McNally.

Zopf, Paul E., Jr. 1984. *Population: An Introduction to Social Demography.* Palo Alto, CA: Mayfield Publishing.

Name Index

T

U

V

W

X–Y

Z

Subject Index

Q–R

S

T

U

V

About the Author

Ronald W. Maris received his Ph.D. in sociology from the University of Illinois where he was a National Science Foundation Fellow and received the George Huff Award for outstanding scholastic and athletic achievement. Maris did graduate work in philosophy at Harvard University and was a postdoctoral fellow and Associate Professor in psychiatry at the Johns Hopkins University School of Medicine. He has taught at Arizona State University, Dartmouth College, and the Johns Hopkins University. Maris is currently professor of sociology and professor of preventive medicine at the University of South Carolina. He directs the Center for the Study of Suicide and Life-Threatening Behavior.

Maris has been a World Health Organization Fellow in West Berlin, a Deputy Medical Examiner in Baltimore, and in 1980 was a Foundation's Fellow Fund Research Fellow in psychiatry at the University of Vienna School of Medicine. In 1986 Maris was Killam Distinguished Visiting Professor of Psychiatry at the Calgary Medical School in Alberta, Canada. He is past-president of the American Association of Suicidology.

He is currently editor of *Suicide and Life-Threatening Behavior,* the official journal of the American Association of Suicidology. Maris is the author or editor of six books and about fifty articles. In 1985 Maris received the Louis I. Dublin Award for his studies of suicide. He has received several federal and state research grants to investigate suicide, has lectured widely, appeared on regional and national television, and treated individual suicidal patients and their survivors.